D1558935

THE CONSTITUTION OF CANADA

An Introduction to its Development and Law

W.P.M. Kennedy

Introduction by Martin Friedland

OXFORD
UNIVERSITY PRESS

OXFORD
UNIVERSITY PRESS

Oxford University Press is a department of the University of Oxford.
It furthers the University's objective of excellence in research, scholarship,
and education by publishing worldwide. Oxford is a registered trade mark
of Oxford University Press in the UK and in certain other countries.

Published in Canada by
Oxford University Press
8 Sampson Mews, Suite 204,
Don Mills, Ontario M3C 0H5 Canada

www.oupcanada.com

Library and Archives Canada Cataloguing in Publication

Kennedy, W. P. M. (William Paul McClure), 1879-1963, author
The constitution of Canada / W.P.M. Kennedy.

Reprint. Originally published: London and Toronto, Oxford University Press, 1922.
Includes bibliographical references and index.
ISBN 978-0-19-900957-2 (pbk.)

1. Constitutional history—Canada. 2. Constitutional law—Canada.
I. Title.

JL15.K4 2014   342.7102'9   C2013-908533-5

Cover image: Picture of W.P.M. Kennedy probably taken in 1923, when he was 44,
now in the Friedland Papers in the University of Toronto Archives.

Printed and bound in the United States of America

1 2 3 4 — 16 15 14

THE ENIGMATIC W.P.M. KENNEDY
Martin Friedland[1]

I have a three-fold interest in W.P.M. Kennedy, the author of the ground-breaking, *The Constitution of Canada* published in 1922.[2] He was the first dean of law at the University of Toronto. In 1972, I became the school's fourth dean. As the founder of the law school, Kennedy holds an exalted position in the history of the faculty. Studying his career, I believed, would give us a better understanding of the origins·and the development of the faculty of law.

I am also interested in Kennedy because in 1983 my wife and I bought the Kennedy family cottage north of Huntsville, just west of Algonquin Park, where Kennedy and his wife spent almost four months each summer until shortly before he died in 1963. He had purchased the cottage on Beaver Lake in 1940 and each summer had his correspondence redirected to the post-office in the nearby Town of Kearney. He loved the cottage and is buried, along with his wife, in an Anglican cemetery in the neighboring town of Emsdale. The cottage came with a collection of his books and a trunk full of letters and documents which he had accumulated over the summers, but did not need to take back to the city. I subsequently donated the material relevant to Dean Kennedy, including the picture on the cover of this new edition, to the University of Toronto Archives.[3]

One of the most important events in the history of the University of Toronto Law School took place at that cottage. Kennedy, a non-lawyer, who had, it seems, never taken a formal course in any legal subject, started the undergraduate "honour law" program between the wars. Graduates of that program received a BA degree from the University but were given no credit by

---

1   Martin L. Friedland, CC, QC, LLD, FRSC, University Professor and James M. Tory professor of law emeritus, University of Toronto. I have benefitted from discussions with and comments from a number of constitutional scholars and others, in particular, Alan Cairns, Judith Friedland, Peter Hogg, Ian Kyer, Patrick Macklem, Patricia McMahon, Mayo Moran, Robert Prichard, Kent Roach, Sydney Robins, Carol Rogerson, Peter Russell, David Schneiderman, Robert Sharpe and participants at a faculty workshop on September 23, 2013. I was fortunate to have had the research assistance of an excellent summer research assistant, Stephen Aylward, who had just completed his law degree at the University of Toronto and had not yet left for Ottawa to clerk for Supreme Court Justice Thomas Cromwell. Harold Averill and his colleagues at the University of Toronto Archives and Sufei Xu and her colleagues at the Bora Laskin Law Library provided their usual expert assistance.

2   W.P.M. Kennedy, *The Constitution of Canada* (London: Oxford University Press, 1922). There was a second impression in 1931 and a second edition in 1938. The second edition reprinted the first edition and added four chapters relating to the years after 1922 as well as two appendices on current events, one on the Canadian New Deal cases and another on the abdication of Edward VIII.

3   Martin Friedland, *My Life in Crime and Other Academic Adventures* (University of Toronto Press, 2007), pp. 33–35.

the Law Society of Upper Canada, which operated Osgoode Hall Law School, the only professional law school in the province.[4] Cecil Augustus Wright— usually referred to as "Caesar" Wright—was a professor at Osgoode (later its dean) and was unhappy with the way legal education was being delivered there. He thought of it as a "trade school." In 1945, he and his good friend and fellow lawyer Sidney Smith, who had become the president of the University of Toronto, developed a plan[5] to transfer professional legal education from Osgoode Hall to the University of Toronto. One aspect of the plan was that Bora Laskin, who many years later would become the chief justice of Canada, would leave the University of Toronto, where he had been a student and later a professor, and join Osgoode Hall Law School. Then, at an appropriate time, Wright, Laskin, and others, such as John Willis, would leave Osgoode and start a professional law school at the University of Toronto, with Wright as the dean.[6] Wright wrote to Smith about coming to the University: "*I will go*—provided there is hope—and enough money to live on—and I am sure I can take Laskin and Willis—both of whom should be there."[7] How much Laskin knew about the plan is not clear.[8]

The scheme required Kennedy's blessing—or at least his acquiescence. Laskin was one of Kennedy's favourite colleagues. So one summer day in mid-July 1945, after Laskin had discussed the strategy with Caesar Wright at Wright's northern cottage, Wright and Laskin went to see Kennedy at his cottage near Kearney. Wright and Kennedy walked along a well-groomed waterside trail, with Laskin walking slightly behind. Kennedy could see some merit in the scheme as could President Smith, which, as events unfolded, did indeed, come to pass. Laskin went to Osgoode that year and in 1949 Wright, Willis, and Laskin left Osgoode and founded the so-called "modern law school" at the University of Toronto. The Law Society, however, did not give up its monopoly on legal education. Graduates of the University

---

4   Osgoode Hall Law School remained in downtown Toronto, run by the Law Society, until it was transferred to York University in the 1960s.
5   Claude Bissell, in his memoir, *Halfway up Parnassus* (University of Toronto Press, 1974), wrote that they "worked out a coup" (p. 99).
6   See Ian Kyer and Jerome Bickenbach, *The Fiercest Debate* (University of Toronto Press, 1987), p. 164 et seq.; Friedland, *My Life in Crime*, pp. 33–35; and Friedland, *The University of Toronto: A History* (University of Toronto Press, 2002), pp. 438–42.
7   Wright to Smith, July 12, 1945, cited in Kyer and Bickenbach, p. 168.
8   See Bora Laskin, "Cecil A. Wright: A Personal Memoir," *University of Toronto Law Journal* 33 (1983): 148 at 159. But see Philip Girard, *Bora Laskin: Bringing Law to Life* (University of Toronto Press, 2005), which assumes that Laskin was involved (pp. 152–54). Girard states that the argument that Wright and Laskin put to Kennedy on the lakeside walk was that "Laskin could act as a bridge between Osgoode and Toronto, between the benchers and the university authorities, with a view to establishing a professional university based law school" (p. 153).

of Toronto had to spend an extra year at Osgoode until 1957, when the U of T law school was recognized by the Law Society, and other law schools in Ontario were created.[9] Like Kennedy, I keep that path along the lakeshore of our cottage very well groomed, and may someday put up a plaque in honour of the event that took place there.

I was also very interested in Kennedy, who I never met, because, as the author of *The University of Toronto: A History*,[10] I discovered that Kennedy was one of the University's most distinguished, engaging, and enigmatic personalities. His book, *The Constitution of Canada*, is still well known to students of the Canadian constitution. In 1998, my colleague R.C.B. Risk published a brilliant article on Kennedy, appropriately entitled "The Many Minds of W.P.M. Kennedy,"[11] which I have, in part, drawn on for this introduction. Unfortunately, Kennedy destroyed all his personal papers in Toronto shortly before he died.[12] To write a full biography of him would be difficult, although not impossible.

The year 1922—the year *The Constitution of Canada*, was first published— is a particularly important date in the history of the University of Toronto. Canada had survived the Great War and had become a more confident nation. It had been included as a member of the League of Nations and continued as a significant partner in the British Commonwealth. This optimism was reflected at the University of Toronto. The opening paragraph of chapter 24 of my history of the University notes the significance of that year:

> In early 1922, two important events took place at the University of Toronto: the discovery of insulin and the creation of the School of Graduate Studies. The former established Toronto's international reputation, and some would argue that the combination of the two was the turning point in Toronto's becoming the leading university in Canada.[13]

Kennedy was part of that renaissance.

---

9   Friedland, *My Life in Crime*, p. 35.
10   Martin Friedland, *The University of Toronto*.
11   R.C.B. Risk, "The Many Minds of W.P.M. Kennedy" *University of Toronto Law Journal* (1998): 48, republished in a collection of essays, R.C.B. Risk (Blaine Baker and Jim Phillips, eds.), *A History of Canadian Legal Thought: Collected Essays* (University of Toronto Press, 2006), p. 300 et seq.
12   Risk, "The Many Minds," p. 354; Gilbert Kennedy (W.P.M.'s son) oral interview (interview by Maryla Waters 1983, Victoria University), p. 15.
13   Friedland, *U of T History*, p. 285.

KENNEDY'S BACKGROUND

There are many gaps in our knowledge of W.P.M. Kennedy's background and some of what we know is opaque.[14] He was born on January 8, 1879, in Shankill, a suburb of Dublin, Ireland, the eldest of 10 children.[15] According to an oral interview with his son Gilbert in 1983, Kennedy left home at the age of 14. "Dad was a bit reticent about his early life,"[16] Gilbert told the interviewer. Gilbert's wife Betty recently told me that as far as she knows, Kennedy "ran away from home."[17] W.P.M. Kennedy's father was a Presbyterian minister, whose family had come from Scotland and Kennedy was raised in that faith. Kennedy's father later left Ireland and spent his last 25 years as a minister in Scotland. It appears that Kennedy did not visit his father in the summer of 1926, his only trip back to the "old country."[18]

W.P.M. Kennedy attended Trinity College Dublin, graduating in 1900 with a gold medal in history and English literature along with several other awards, including a prize in English prose. His earlier education, according to entries he prepared for *The Canadian Who's Who*, consisted of "private tuition; Paris, Vienna & Berlin."[19] Why he went to school—if he did go to school—in those cities is unclear. He certainly spent time in Paris because one of the books left in his cottage library, *Cavalier Poets*,[20] was signed by him and dated "Paris Xmas 1904."

After graduating, he became a private tutor for a number of years and for about two years before coming to Canada in 1913 taught school at a Catholic boys' school in Ramsgate, England,[21] near Canterbury, and then at a boys' college in Cuba. He left the latter and returned to England because

---

14   See W.P.M. Kennedy file at the U of T Archives; Risk, "The Many Minds"; Gilbert Kennedy's 1983 oral history: conversation with Betty Kennedy (Gilbert's wife), July 8, 2013; discussion with Frere Kennedy, July 16, 2013; various *Who's Who* volumes, obituary by Alexander Brady in *Proceedings of the Royal Society of Canada*, 1964, p. 109.

15   I did an on-line search of the census and the birth and death records from England and Ireland for the relevant periods, but could not find W.P.M. Kennedy's name or any version of his given names (linking it with his approximate date of birth and occupation, etc.) in the records amongst the great number of William Kennedy's listed.

16   P. 8.

17   Telephone conversation with Betty Kennedy, July 8, 2013.

18   Conversation with Frere Kennedy, July 16, 2013.

19   See, e.g., the 1948 edition (Toronto, Trans-Canada Press).

20   Clarence M. Lindsay (Abbey Press, New York, 1901).

21   A "to-whom-it may concern" letter from the head prefect of studies at St. Augustine's College, Ramsgate, February 30, 1912 in the St. Francis Xavier College files, saying that Kennedy was "an excellent disciplinarian, a capable and successful teacher."

he could not bear the heat.[22] He was unable to find an academic position in England.

Even his name is uncertain. Everyone knows him as William Paul McLure Kennedy—hence he is usually referred to as W.P.M. Kennedy—but his Trinity College records show him as William Waugh McLure Kennedy.[23] His early books—before coming to Canada—dropped the name Waugh and had him as "W. M. Kennedy" on the title page.[24] His mother was a McClure, but where the name Waugh came from is not certain.[25] Kennedy started using W.P.M. as early as 1904, according to his signature in the previously mentioned book of poetry.

Kennedy's doctorate from Trinity College, a "Litt.D," which he received in 1919, is also not clear-cut. He gave the impression in his *Who's Who* entries that it was a research doctorate in the traditional sense, as the official history of the department of history and my own history of the University assumed,[26] but it was, in fact, a doctorate that was granted on application based on published work, similar to such degrees granted by Oxford and Cambridge.

Between 1902 and 1911, he spent considerable periods of time at a monastery in Mirfield England, near Leeds, home of the High Anglican Community of the Resurrection.[27] According to the Community's archivist, he lived there in 1903, and in 1906 to 1908, inclusive, and perhaps in 1904 and 1905.[28] It may be that Kennedy's objective was to continue with a life in the Community of the Resurrection, perhaps as a church scholar. The head of Mirfield was at the time Walter Howard Frere, later Bishop Frere, an important Anglican Church scholar, who, with Kennedy's help, published a three-volume work on Tudor church history in 1910.[29] Kennedy assisted with the first two volumes and was named as the

---

22   Similar letter from the prefect of studies at The English College, Marianas, Cuba, August 12, 1912 in the St. Francis Xavier College files, saying that Kennedy was "an excellent teacher" and "a thorough disciplinarian."
23   This fact was discovered by Trinity College Dublin archivist Ellen O'Flaherty: e-mails dated May 2013.
24   *Archbishop Parker* (London: Pitman, 1908), *The "Interpretations" of the Bishops* (London: Longmans, 1908). The title page of volume 2 of *Visitation Articles and Injunctions* states "With the assistance of William McClure Kennedy, M.A." (3 vols; Longmans, 1910).
25   It likely comes from his mother's side of the family. There is a privately published history of the McLure family on the internet which mentions a justice of the peace in the eighteenth century, William Waugh McLure, who lived in Lurgan, Ireland, the same town where Kennedy's father was a minister.
26   Robert Bothwell, *Laying the Foundation* (Department of History, University of Toronto, 1991), pp. 47–48: "Kennedy, hired in 1916, possessed the only genuine research degree in the department." See also, Friedland, *The University of Toronto*, p. 297.
27   See Alan Wilkinson, *The Community of the Resurrection: a Centenary History* (London: SCM Press, 1992).
28   E-mail from the Community of the Resurrection archivist Brother Steven Haws, May 13, 2013.
29   See B. Gordon-Taylor and N. Stebbing, eds., *Walter Frere, Scholar, Monk, Bishop* (Norwich: Canterbury Press, 2011).

co-author of the second volume, published in 1910.[30] Kennedy named one of his sons—the person who sold us the cottage—Walter Howard Frere and is known simply as Frere. Frere Kennedy was trained in law, but became an Anglican priest and later entered and headed an Anglican monastery in Bracebridge, Ontario, relatively close to the cottage he had inherited. The monastery, the Society of St. John the Evangelist, grew out of the same movement—the Oxford Movement—that had established the Community of the Resurrection in England.[31] At the time of writing, Frere is in a retirement home in Ottawa.[32] He has a picture of Bishop Frere in his room, with a signed note that it is to his godson, Frere. Unfortunately, the Bishop Frere papers in England contain no correspondence to or from W.P.M. Kennedy.[33]

Kennedy was a significant Tudor scholar, publishing several books in 1908, including *Archbishop Parker*,[34] a book on the first Archbishop of Canterbury elected under Elizabeth I. This was written under the direction of a major ecclesiastical scholar, W.H. Hutton of St. John's College, Oxford, and was part of a series of books edited by Hutton, *Makers of National History*. Again, it is likely that Kennedy spent time at Oxford working on the Archbishop Parker book, although there is no record of him as a student in the St. John's College or other college records or of obtaining an Oxford

---

30   *Visitation Articles and Injunctions of the Period of the Reformation, 1536–1575.* The three-volume set was published by Longmans in 1910 for the Alcuin Club. When they were originally published, Kennedy was thanked in the preface to volume 1, made a co-author of volume 2 ("With the assistance of"), and was not named in volume 3. Frere stated in volume 1: "Mr. W.M. Kennedy worked at the whole in the earlier stages of preparation, and was responsible for seeing the greater part of the earlier set of documents through the press; but when that volume was printed off he was unable to give further help." In 1917, Kennedy presented a three-volume set to the University of Toronto Library and all three volumes state on their title pages: "Edited, with Introduction and Notes, by W.H. Frere, M.A., and W.P.M. Kennedy, M.A.". The three volumes are otherwise the same as the volumes originally published, as can be seen from the three volumes in the Trinity College Library at the University of Toronto and two of the three volumes at the Pontifical Institute's library (now online). Kennedy must have had Longmans' and/or Walter Frere's permission to change the authorship because he later published a note in the English Historical Review, October 1926, stating that the three volumes were jointly authored (pp. 577–79). No doubt Kennedy felt justified in requesting the change because of his 1908 book on the documents, which probably led to the more ambitious project at Mirfield on which Kennedy was certainly a collaborator. In the list of his other books at the front of *The Constitution of Canada*, Kennedy simply states for all three: "With Dr. W.H. Frere."

31   See Martin L. Smith, "Benson, Richard Mieux, 1824–1915," *Dictionary of National Biography*.

32   I met with Frere—now over 90—for over two hours in Ottawa on July 16, 2013.

33   Letter from Lydia Dean, Borthwick Institute for Archives, University of York, England, June 13, 2013.

34   (London: Pitman, 1908). There is a draft of this book in the Fisher Library. He also published that same year, *The "Interpretations" of the Bishops and Their Influence on Elizabethan Episcopal Policy* (London: Longmans, 1908) and in the preface to that book he thanks Reverend E. Rhys Jones, S. Luke's Vicarage, "beneath whose hospitable roof this little book was largely written." Jones was in a church in Reigate, about midway between London and Brighton, and so we can conclude that Kennedy spent some time there.

degree.[35] Although Kennedy did not claim an Oxford degree in his publications, he apparently never corrected the annual University Calendar, which certainly gives one the impression that he had a master's degree from Oxford as well as one from Trinity College Dublin. Each year—from the 1916–17 Calendar[36] until his death in 1963, part of the entry for Kennedy would read "M.A., Dublin, Oxon."

The Parker book was well received. The *Guardian* reviewer wrote: "Exceedingly well conceived, clearly expressed, and compiled with great care."[37] Kennedy likely spent time in London because he thanks historian Frederick Pollard of London University in the preface to another book, *Parish Life under Queen Elizabeth*, published in England under the name W.P.M. Kennedy in 1914 after he came to Canada and based on research notes that he brought with him from England.[38]

In 1913, at age 34, Kennedy moved to Canada, taking up a position teaching modern history and English literature at St. Francis Xavier College, a Roman Catholic college in Nova Scotia.[39] Some years earlier, perhaps during his stay at the Mirfield monastery, Kennedy had turned to Catholicism.[40] His application to the Nova Scotia college was supported by his former teachers at Trinity College Dublin, including a form reference letter, dated 1901, by the then eminent Shakespearean scholar Edward Dowden[41] (who

---

35   E-mails from Sian Astill, Oxford University Archives, May 2013, and from Michael Riordon and Alastair Wright, St John's College, Oxford, May 2013. A subsequent request by me to double check their records resulted in the following note from Sian Astill, Oxford University Archives, dated June 26, 2013, who conducted research in all their registers, and concludes: "We can find no record, therefore, that Kennedy was a member of the University or obtained the degree of MA at Oxford."
      Oxford University permits graduates of Trinity College Dublin and Cambridge and other universities, who are at Oxford studying for a degree, to obtain an Oxford BA "by incorporation." The process, which changed over the years, is fully described under the heading "incorporation" on the Oxford University website. There is no record that Kennedy ever received an Oxford degree by incorporation: e-mail from Emma Harrold, Oxford University Archives, September 30, 2013. Perhaps the thought that Kennedy could have received the degree if he had become a student at Oxford justified, in his mind, claiming it. Becoming a student, however, required the payment of fees and it is clear that from the Mirfield records he had no money.

36   The 1915–16 calendar is missing from the U of T Archives. All other calendars for the relevant years were consulted.

37   The review was found in an advertisement on the back pages of a book by W.H. Hutton on Thomas à Becket in the series he edited, *Makers of National History*.

38   (London: Manresa Press, 1914). See the preface to the book and Risk, "The Many Minds," pp. 355–56.

39   He describes himself in the *Parish Life* book as "Professor of Modern History in the University of St. Francis Xavier's College."

40   A book on Tudor history by Kennedy, *Elizabethan Episcopal Administration: An Essay in Sociology and Politics*, published in 1924, was dedicated to Frere, "my greatest friend," and refers to "a friendship which, since my university days, has known neither deviation nor shadow caused by turning." This is no doubt a reference to Kennedy becoming a Catholic, while at or after he was at Mirfield.

41   The *Globe*, June 14, 1913. I am grateful to the archivist at St. Francis Xavier, Kathleen MacKenzie, for providing documents on Kennedy's time in Nova Scotia.

is mentioned—unfavourably—in James Joyce's *Ulysses*, perhaps because Dowden refused to give Joyce a good reference for a position).[42] Kennedy, it will be recalled, had received numerous prizes, including the Shakespeare Prize, while at Trinity. The two schools Kennedy had taught at before coming to Canada stressed that Kennedy was a good teacher and a strict disciplinarian.[43]

The following year, 1914, he was invited to join the faculty at St. Michael's College in the University of Toronto, where he taught English literature, a college subject, for the next eight years.[44] His son Gilbert believes his father first came to Toronto during the summer of 1914 because he would talk about canoeing during that summer near Hudson's Bay with a friend and when they emerged from the wilderness discovered that war had been declared.[45] Why he stayed at St. F.X. for only one year is also not clear. His friend, Father Edmund McCorkell, who taught with him at St. Michael's and later became the head of St. Michael's College, stated in an oral interview in 1974: "I don't know what happened down there ... but McNeil, the Archbishop [of Toronto, who earlier had been the rector at St Francis Xavier], who was influential down there ... got him to come up here and got Father Carr to take him on the staff."[46] The rector of St. F. X was happy to see him go, writing to a college benefactor the following year that Kennedy had "a loose screw in his mechanism."[47] The vice rector was equally uncomplimentary, telling a contact at Oxford who was helping to find Kennedy's replacement: "For Heaven's sake try and get us a decent sober man with a level head."[48] In the same letter the vice-rector writes: "I wish you would try and find out through the Jesuits who this W.M. Kennedy is ... I understand he was once a Jesuit novice. He says he studied History at Oxford for a time." The St. F.X. files do not contain a letter of application from Kennedy. In a glowing report of an interview in the student newspaper in October 1913[49]

---

42   See Helen Sword, *Ghostwriting Modernism* (Cornell University Press, 2002), pp. 60–63. References to Dowden in *Ulysses* can be found in Random House's 1961 Modern Library Edition, p. 204 and p. 214.

43   See earlier footnotes on the two schools.

44   I am grateful for the assistance of St. Michael's College archivist Constance Lewin.

45   Gilbert Kennedy interview, p. 9.

46   Edmund McCorkell oral interview conducted by Richard Alway, June 1974, p. 81.

47   Letter from Rector Hugh MacPherson to John E. Somers, May 18, 1914, also referred to in James D. Cameron, *For the People: A History of St Francis Xavier University* (McGill-Queen's, 1996), p. 458, footnote 95. I am grateful to Professor Cameron for his further assistance in my quest to understand Kennedy's year in Nova Scotia.

48   Letter from Vice-Rector Jimmy Tompkins to J.M.P Coady, May 19, 1914; and see also the later letter to Coady dated June 3, 1914: "If you should chance to be [in Dublin] look up his history. I have an idea that it is somewhat unsavory." I am grateful to Anne Marie MacNeil of the Beaton Archives in Nova Scotia for locating these documents.

49   *The Xaverian.*

("Mr. Kennedy has won nothing but golden opinions from his students"), Kennedy is reported to have said that he "studied history under ... the late Prof Stubbs, Oxford," presumably after graduating from Trinity College. If so, it could not have been for long because Stubbs became ill in November 1900 and died in April 1901.

It seems likely that Kennedy had not planned on leaving St. F.X., because a few months before he left, the vice-rector told a friend that Kennedy and another person were "hard at work on a 600 page History of the Catholic Church in Nova Scotia."[50]

One curious fact about Kennedy's stay in Nova Scotia is that the book he published in 1914, which was written at St F. X., is dedicated to "S.J.C." and the dedication is dated October 12, 1913. Gilbert Kennedy states that in 1968 he met a priest that had been in one of W.P.M. Kennedy's classes in 1913–14, who told him that S.J.C. was a fellow student, Sarah Josephine Cameron, one of the very few women in the class.[51] According to Frere Kennedy, Gilbert remembers the priest asking Gilbert whether his father had married Sarah Cameron. That is all we know, except that Sarah's uncle was Bishop Cameron, a former rector of the college. The year after Kennedy left, Ms. Cameron became an editor of the college paper and published three articles, all of which would have interested Kennedy, one on the British Empire, one on Byron, and one on "conversation."[52] There was obviously some sort of close relationship between the two or the dedication would not have been made, but whether it was more than an intellectual bonding or perhaps simply re-search assistance is not known. Ms. Cameron, who graduated in 1916 with a number of prizes, became a teacher in Saskatchewan, never married, and died in 1990.[53] Historian P.B. Waite, who does not mention Ms. Cameron, put it this way in his book on Larry Mackenzie, who later worked under Kennedy at the University of Toronto: "The little college in the little town could not contain Kennedy. He was too hot to handle; if the girls in the St. Bernard residence were not scandalized, the Roman Catholic authorities of the college were. He was unloaded onto St. Michael's College."[54]

Kennedy continued to publish in Tudor history. A book, published in 1916, *Studies in Tudor History*, simply says "St. Michael's College, Toronto

50   Letter from Vice Rector Tompkins to David Allison, March 29, 1914.
51   See the introductory pages of the Gilbert Kennedy interview, where the interviewer sets out the publications of W.P.M. Kennedy. There were only two other women in Sarah Cameron's year.
52   *The Xaverian.*
53   See the Antigonish *Casket*, April 11, 1990, p. 7.
54   *Lord of Point Grey* (University of British Columbia Press, 1987), p. 58.

University."[55] While at St. Michael's he took the first steps in setting up a library of mediaeval history,[56] which may have played a role in laying the groundwork for what later became the world famous Pontifical Institute for Mediaeval Studies. No doubt, Father Carr, the president of St. Michael's, who told University President Robert Falconer that he wanted to make St. Michael's "the greatest Catholic education centre in the world,"[57] was involved in these early steps.

In spite of leaving St. F.X. after only one year in curious circumstances, Kennedy took the unusual step in 1915 of asking the rector of St. F. X.—the person who wrote one of the previously mentioned letters—if the college would grant him an honorary doctorate. "I write to ask you if St. F.X. could see its way to confer on me *causa honoris* an LL.D. for my work on Tudor History." He adds that "His Grace the Archbishop will visit Washington in February and will propose me there for an honorary D. Lit."[58] The rector replied that he had discussed the matter with some of the faculty and believed that "a resolution in favor of granting you an LL.D. would not carry at a Faculty meeting."[59]

McCorkell, who had been ordained as a priest in 1916, came to St. Michael's the following year to teach some of Kennedy's English courses.[60] McCorkell states in his oral interview that Kennedy "really was a very effective teacher, very brilliant, and he was quite a tonic here, and gave the place [a lift] in the way of scholarship and general interest." McCorkell "liked him personally a lot and I think we all did." But he added: "It was hard to discover his true background. He boasted about so many things that [people] figured that he had to have lived a hundred years to do all the things that he said he did."[61] R.C.B. Risk's assessment is that Kennedy was "inclined to exaggerate."[62] That is certainly my conclusion as well. Still, like McCorkell, in spite of Kennedy's exaggeration and self-promotion, I believe that if I had known him, I would also have "liked him personally a lot."

A year after moving to Toronto, he married a Roman Catholic woman, Teresa Johnson, who had recently come from England to Canada and worked

55   (London: Constable, 1916).
56   Letter from Falconer to Kennedy, September 3, 1915.
57   Friedland, *University of Toronto*, p. 218; see Carr to Falconer, May 10, 1916.
58   Letter dated January 6, 1915.
59   Letter dated January 15, 1915. It is not known whether the archbishop took steps to try to get an LL.D. from, I assume, the Catholic University of America in Washington.
60   McCorkell interview, pp. 1, 76–82.
61   McCorkell, pp. 76–79.
62   Risk, "The Many Minds," p. 355, note 5. Risk goes on to say: "but his reputation is itself also an exaggeration."

for the English publishing firm of J.M. Dent, which had opened in Toronto in 1913.[63] They were married in St. Basil's church on the St. Michael's campus and lived in an apartment across from the College on the south side of Wellesley Street.[64] Two years later, June 1917, they had a child, Gilbert, while at their summer cottage in Muskoka.[65] Gilbert and his sister Beatrice, born a little over a year later, were baptized as Roman Catholics. The family's financial situation would have been difficult as Kennedy's wife was unable to continue working and Kennedy's pay was relatively modest—a total of $2,000 a year, worth under $40,000 today.[66]

That same year, 1917–18, in part to supplement his earnings, Kennedy started teaching courses in constitutional history as a lecturer in the department of history. Unlike English, which was a subject taught and paid for by the colleges, modern history—for historical reasons[67]—was a university subject taught by persons appointed and paid by the University. George Wrong, the chair of history, wanted to reclaim jurisdiction over constitutional history,[68] which was then being taught by Henry Lefroy in the department of political economy. Kennedy taught three history courses that year, one in Canadian and two in English constitutional history, and was paid $750 on top of his St. Michael's salary.[69]

As his correspondence with President Falconer shows, Kennedy was eager to obtain a permanent position in the history department. Kennedy had been complaining to Falconer about his lack of a secure position and having to teach nineteen hours a week to barely get by financially.[70] He was teaching English literature as a professor at St. Michael's College; modern history as a lecturer in the department of history; and English as a "substitute lecturer" in W.J. Alexander's English department at University College. His main interest was constitutional history, he told Falconer, stating that English "is a minor subject with me."[71] The appointment as an assistant professor in the history department did not go through at that time, however.

63   Roy MacSkimming, *The Perilous Trade* (McClelland and Stewart, 2003), p. 28.
64   McCorkell interview, pp. 77–78.
65   Gilbert Kennedy interview, pp. 1, 38.
66   St. Michael's archive, treasurer ledger cards.
67   Friedland, *University of Toronto*, pp. 108–109.
68   March 23, 1911 letter from George Wrong to Falconer. Bothwell, *Laying the Foundation*, pp. 57–58; Ian Drummond, *Political Economy at the University of Toronto* (Faculty of Arts and Science, 1983), pp. 36–37; Alan Bowker, "Truly Useful Men: Maurice Hutton, George Wrong, James Mavor and the University of Toronto," 1880–1927 (Ph. D. thesis, 1975), pp. 326–27.
69   Bothwell, *Laying the Foundation*, p. 58.
70   Undated letter from Kennedy to Falconer, probably 1917.
71   Ibid.

Other appointments and financial issues, it seems, prevented it.[72]

The following year, both Falconer and Wrong agreed that Kennedy should become an assistant professor in the history department. "Mr. Kennedy is doing excellent work," Wrong wrote to Falconer, "and I understand that he is to get the rank of Assistant Professor."[73] For the 1919–1920 academic year, he was finally appointed an assistant professor in the department, receiving $2,200 while also continuing to teach English at St. Michael's College, at $1,000 a year.

Kennedy's ties with St. Michael's were severed at the end of the 1921–22 academic year.[74] At some point before that he had ceased being a Roman Catholic. Father McCorkell stated that even when he was at St. Michael's his religion was not clear, and his son Gilbert states in his oral interview that his father was not a church-goer.[75] In a letter to President Falconer in March 1922, Kennedy stated: "I write to ask you to change my religious affiliations to 'Church of England' on the records of the President's Office."

George Wrong[76] and Kennedy had a serious falling out in 1920. "I think their quarrel was basically over this student that Kennedy married," McCorkell stated in his oral interview: "I don't know the whole story at all."[77] It is likely that no-one now living knows it. We do know that Kennedy's first wife, who had two very young children, died at age 26 in the Spanish influenza epidemic in April 1919. Fifty thousand Canadians died of the flu— often an agonizing death—and a disproportionate number of them were women in their twenties.[78] Teresa's death certificate shows that, as was common in the case of the Spanish flu, she died of pneumonia, having had influenza for only 24 hours.[79] Kennedy's two young children were also infected. A week after his wife's death, he wrote to the chair of political economy, James

---

72   Letter from Falconer to Kennedy, dated June 28, 1918: "Professor Hodder Williams has been made an Assistant Professor in the Department this year, and Professor Wrong thought it was well to defer any action with regard to yourself until later."

73   Letter from Wrong to Falconer, December 18, 1918. See also letter from Wrong to Falconer, May 4, 1919.

74   Treasurer ledger cards, St. Michael's archives.

75   McCorkell interview, p. 77; Gilbert Kennedy interview, p. 62.

76   George Wrong was an ordained Anglican priest, whose appointment as professor of history at the University of Toronto was the cause of the famous student strike of 1895: see chapter 15 of Friedland, *The University of Toronto*.

77   McCorkell interview, p. 80. Vincent Bladen was equally vague, stating in his memoirs, *Bladen on Bladen* (privately published, 1978): Kennedy "had … some sort of conflict with Wrong. MacIver bailed him out by appointing him as a Special Lecturer in Mediaeval Economics and in Federal Institutions" (p. 37).

78   See generally, Esyllt W. Jones, *Influenza 1918: Disease, Death, and Struggle in Winnipeg* (University of Toronto Press, 2007); and Heather MacDougall, "Toronto's Health Department in Action: Influenza in 1918 and SARS in 2003," in M. Fahrni and E.W. Jones, eds., *Epidemic Encounters* (University of British Columbia Press, 2012), p. 225 et seq.

79   Death records of April 13, 1919 at Ontario Archives. The physician was a Dr. W.F. Plewes, who appears to have been an obstetrician; he may have delivered their two children.

Mavor, thanking him for his sympathy and adding: "Yes—we are fighting night and day for the lives of my two kiddies, Gilbert and Beatrice. Poor things they are still in danger—and we can only face each hour like flint."[80]

There was no suggestion of any difficulty between Kennedy and Wrong during that difficult period. Wrong wrote to Falconer in early May after hearing about "the dreadful tragedy," and suggested to Falconer that, if possible, Kennedy receive an increase in his salary.[81] Falconer also arranged a gift or loan to assist Kennedy.[82] That summer—the Falconer papers show—Kennedy went with his two children and a nanny back to his cottage in Muskoka, during which time he was placed under a doctor's care. "Insomnia plays hard with me & arterial trouble is threatening," Kennedy wrote Falconer.[83] Later that month, Falconer was informed by Professor George Brett that Kennedy did not think he would be able to teach in the next academic year.[84]

George Brett, the distinguished chair of philosophy, had a cottage close to the one Kennedy then owned on Lake Muskoka and kept Falconer informed about Kennedy's progress. On top of his wife's death, there was a fire at Kennedy's uninsured cottage and, according to Brett, "some affair in England greatly upset him." Kennedy, Brett wrote, became "temporarily unhinged—not to say deranged."[85] (It is worth noting that Brett's field was psychology; he was soon to publish the final book in his famous trilogy, *A History of Psychology*.[86]) Brett thought that perhaps Kennedy should take a year's leave in England, with some pay, and leave his children with his mother-in-law. By the end of the summer, however, Kennedy had recovered, telling Falconer: "The doctor's report is very favourable and there is good improvement ... I have no wish personally to get leave of absence if it can possibly be avoided ... I am cheered up by the doctor's latest, as the whole future of the kiddies depends on my health."[87]

In June 1920, fourteen months after Teresa died, there was an announcement in the *Globe* that Professor Kennedy had "very quietly" married Pauline

---

80   Letter to Mavor April 19, 1919. Betty Kennedy, the late Gilbert Kennedy's wife, confirmed in a telephone conversation on July 8, 2013 that both Gilbert and Beatrice had continuing medical problems—Gilbert's spleen was removed when he was a teenager—likely because of the Spanish Flu.

81   Wrong to Falconer, Wrong folder in Falconer Papers, May 4, 1919.

82   Letters from Hodder Williams to Robert Falconer, April 20, 1919 and July 17, 1919. The cost was estimated at $1,000, but in the end was a little over half that, including funeral expenses: letters from Hodder Williams, the acting chair of history, dated April 20 and June 7, 1919. Wrong thought that Kennedy should repay the money in course of time: Hodder Williams to Falconer, July 17, 1919. Kennedy told Falconer that he considered it a debt: August 14, 1919.

83   Kennedy to Falconer, August 4, 1919.

84   Brett to Falconer, August 15, 1919.

85   Ibid.

86   George Brett, *A History of Psychology* (London: G. Allen, 1921).

87   Undated, but likely late August 1919.

Simpson, an Anglican, from Hamilton, Ontario.[88] The marriage—Kennedy was then age 40, Pauline 25—had taken place at St. Michael's Cathedral in Toronto on June 8th that year.[89] She had been one of Kennedy's students—in English literature at University College, according to Gilbert Kennedy, but perhaps also in modern history.[90] She was a University College undergraduate student from 1915 to 1919, and in her final year served as the head of the UC women's residence. She had been expected to graduate with a B.A. in 1919—indeed, her graduation picture had been placed in *Torontonensis* in anticipation that she would graduate—but she did not do so.[91] She continued at the University as a special student. Why she did not graduate is not clear. She and Kennedy later had two children, Frere, born in 1923, and a daughter, Shelagh, in 1926. Pauline Kennedy stayed home to look after her family, but later became prominent in many charities, the Anglican church, and various women's organizations. In 1939 she became the president of the Women's Canadian Club of Toronto and during the war was the chair of the Consumer Branch Committee of the Wartime Prices and Trade Board.[92]

Others in the department of history, including Wrong's son Hume (later a senior official in External Affairs), were hostile to Kennedy and at various times tried to block his advancement, in part because of what Hume Wrong referred to in a letter to his father several years later as the "cause célèbre," which most likely refers to the circumstances surrounding his relationship with Pauline Simpson.[93] Five years later, Lester B. (Mike) Pearson, then a lecturer in the history department, also married one of his students, but, according to his biographer, John English, Pearson's colleagues, and especially Wrong, were apparently unaware of the developing romance.[94] The relationship between George

---

88   The *Globe*, June 22, 1920, stating that the marriage took place on June 8. Understandably, Gilbert's oral interview places the marriage two years after his mother's death, that is, in 1921 (p. 39). No doubt that is what he had been told by his parents. Until he was a teenager, he says, he did not know that his real mother had died and that his father had remarried.

89   The marriage license was obtained on May 3, 1920 and solemnized at the Cathedral at 200 Church Street. According to Frere Kennedy, Pauline's father had died when she was young and her mother got along well with her new son-in-law.

90   Gilbert Kennedy interview, p. 39. University records indicate that she took a number of courses which Kennedy could have taught in her four years as an undergraduate and as an occasional student, including some English courses at University College, where she was a student.

91   University records file. Gilbert assumes she never received her degree: "She got as far as fourth year at the U of T and was then picked up!" (p. 41).

92   Pauline Kennedy clipping file at the U of T Archives.

93   Hume Wrong letter to his father George Wrong, February 8, 1826. There are many letters in the George Wrong fond in the U of T Archives from George Wrong to his wife Sofia because he travelled extensively, but he was in Toronto in 1920 and so there are no letters from him to his wife that year.

94   John English, *Shadow of Heaven*, volume 1 (Lester & Orpen Dennys, 1989): "The secret, as usual, was poorly kept, although Mike's colleagues apparently did not know. Not even Methodist self-righteousness could have excused Mike's serious dalliance with one of his students in the eyes of George Wrong. Fortunately, they were able to avoid his stern gaze" (p. 109).

Wrong and Pearson, according to English, continued to be good.[95] (Pearson also had a good rapport with Kennedy, who suggested he should apply to the department of external affairs and not stay in the academic world, where he would have to compete with the likes of Donald Creighton.[96]) So the exact circumstances behind Wrong's dislike of Kennedy are unclear. A few weeks after his wedding, Kennedy wrote to James Mavor from Nova Scotia stating that he was resigning from Toronto in June of the following year and asking him to support his application to Dalhousie University, where the chair of history was vacant, as well as his applications to the archives in Ottawa and Toronto. "I am quite downhearted," Kennedy wrote to Mavor, "but G.M. W[rong] has played a curious game to which there is neither Alpha nor Omega."[97]

Kennedy asked Falconer to intervene in the dispute with George Wrong, but in the fall of 1920 Kennedy wrote Falconer: "On reflection it will be far better not to mention any personal differences between me & Mr Wrong ... I don't want ... to wash dirty linen, and above all, I do not wish to complicate a situation which will, someday & somehow straighten itself."[98] It never did. On November 25, 1920, Wrong wrote to Falconer asking that "official notice ... be given to Prof. Kennedy that his appointment terminates at the close of the present academic year."[99]

The termination did not go through that year, but there was obviously no future for Kennedy in the history department. There are a number of letters in the Falconer papers showing Falconer writing on Kennedy's behalf in 1921 and 1922 to a number of colleges in England, including the recently established Royal Air Force College, supporting Kennedy's applications for a teaching position in English literature.[100] No offers were apparently forthcoming.

Political economy then came to the rescue. In 1922, at age 43, Kennedy transferred from the department of history to the department of political economy,[101] where Robert MacIver was the acting head and would the following year become the head of the department.[102] Kennedy would be a

---

95   E-mail from John English, June 12, 2013.

96   English, *Shadow of Heaven*, pp. 138–39.

97   Kennedy to Mavor, June 26, 1920. In a letter to Berriedale Keith in the Edinburgh archives, undated but very likely the summer of 1922, Kennedy states without elaboration: "I've got into a hole with a graduate student here."

98   Letter from Kennedy to Falconer, November 29, 1920.

99   Letter from George Wrong to Falconer, November 25, 1920.

100   Letter from Falconer to Royal Air Force College, March 22, 1921. There was also a letter to Armstrong College, now part of Newcastle University, April 19, 1922.

101   Drummond, *Political Economy*, p. 37.

102   Drummond, *Political Economy*, p. 53. Kennedy taught for both departments that year: Drummond, p. 37.

xviii   The Constitution of Canada

lecturer on federal institutions and his total salary from political economy would be $2000.[103] Kennedy, who continued to teach in the history department, was demoted by Wrong to "special lecturer."[104] As stated earlier, he no longer had an academic position at St. Michael's College. He had gone from professor to lecturer in a few short years.

Kennedy dedicated his 1922 *Constitution of Canada* book to MacIver and also stated in the preface: "To Professor R.M. MacIver, University of Toronto, I am under the greatest obligations, and in the dedication I attempt not merely to acknowledge these, but to record a friendship which lies deeper than a common interest in history would suggest."[105] Given that MacIver is not otherwise mentioned in the book, it seems likely that personal reasons lie behind the dedication. MacIver and Kennedy came to the University of Toronto about the same time. MacIver was a Scotsman and Kennedy's family had come from Scotland to Ireland. Both had cottages on Lake Muskoka, as it seems did many members of the faculty. They also had similar interests in the development of national states.[106] MacIver likely supported Kennedy in the so-called "cause célèbre" and assisted in his transition from history to political science. Many years later, MacIver, who went on to a distinguished career at Columbia University, wrote in his memoirs about "the somewhat erratic but distinguished W.P. M. Kennedy."[107]

The final and strongest intellectual debt is given by Kennedy to Professor A.H.F. Lefroy, who died in 1919. Kennedy writes in the preface:

> For three years before his death he and I worked through carefully the cases in constitutional law while preparing his *Short Treatise on Canadian Constitutional Law* for publication. We discussed their bearing and importance, and in determining the form of his work we mutually agreed on many phrases and generalizations. Almost naturally I have fallen back on these, and I acknowledge my obligations elsewhere. I cannot, however, let this book go to the press without a recognition of Professor Lefroy's insight into Canadian

---

103   Memo from Falconer to file, April 12, 1922.
104   Falconer to Kennedy, June 5, 1922. See also a letter dated January 8, 1923, in the George Wrong papers from George Wrong to his son Murray, then studying at Oxford, where George Wrong refers to Kennedy and then adds: "who is, I am thankful to say, nearly out now."
105   Preface, p. ix.
106   See R.M. MacIver, *The Modern State* (Oxford University Press, 1926), which cites Kennedy's *Constitution of Canada*, but does not mention Kennedy or, indeed, anyone in the preface.
107   Robert MacIver, *As a Tale that is Told* (University of Chicago Press, 1968), p. 89.

federalism, and of a friendship which was so courteously willing to guide me in a new and difficult field.[108]

Lefroy was a lawyer, who continued to practice law, and at the same time—since the turn of the century—was a professor in the department of political economy. He was Canada's leading constitutional scholar, having published his major work, *The Law of Legislative Power in Canada* in 1897.[109] He was more than 25 years older than Kennedy. R.C.B. Risk describes him as "the leading common-law scholar in Canada in the late 19th and early 20th centuries."[110] Kennedy and Lefroy had much in common. Lefroy was an Oxford graduate and his roots on his father's side were Irish. His cousin, Tom Lefroy, was the chief justice of Ireland from 1852 to 1869—today better known as Jane Austen's "only known love interest who ... shaped Jane's outlook on love and life"[111]—and Professor Lefroy kept a portrait of the chief justice in his law office on Church Street. He kept a picture in his University office of his maternal grandfather, John Beverley Robinson, the chief justice of Upper Canada (later Canada West) from 1829 to 1862.[112]

Kennedy worked closely with Lefroy for the three years before Lefroy's sudden death in 1919. As stated above, he actively assisted Lefroy in the publication of his 1918 text, *A Short Treatise on Canadian Constitutional Law*, for which Kennedy wrote the historical introduction. In 1918 Kennedy also published *Documents of the Canadian Constitution*, which was meant for student use and no doubt involved many discussions with Lefroy, although, surprisingly he does not thank Lefroy in the preface to that book. As far as I can tell, this was Kennedy's first involvement in the publication of a book with Oxford University Press, although he had published articles in Oxford

---

108   The statement "I acknowledge my obligations elsewhere" probably refers to a lengthy and flattering obituary in *The Varsity* in the Lefroy clippings file in the U of T Archives, published March 10, 1919, shortly after Lefroy's death , signed simply "K."

109   (Toronto: Toronto Law Book, 1897).

110   DNB online article by R.C.B. Risk on Lefroy, volume XIV (accessed July 2013). In his earlier article on Lefroy, "A.H.F. Lefroy: Common Law thought in Late Nineteenth-Century Canada," Risk had said that Lefroy was "one of the leading common law scholars in Canada in the late nineteenth and early twentieth centuries" (*University of Toronto Law Journal* 41 [1991]: 307). The words "one of" were omitted after Risk had finished his survey of legal thought in Canada. The Lefroy essay in the collection of Risk's essays, *A History of Canadian Legal Thought: Collected Essays* (University of Toronto Press, 2006), states "one of" (p. 66).

111   See Laura Boyle, "Who was the Real Tom Lefroy?," July 16, 2011, <www.janeausten.co.uk/who-was-the-real-tom-Lefroy/>. The "love affair" is the subject of the 2007 movie, "Becoming Jane." In one letter, dated January 16, 1796, Jane Austin writes: "At length the day is come on which I am to flirt my last with Tom Lefroy, and when you receive this it will be over. My tears flow as I write at the melancholy idea." See <www.pemberley.com/janeinfo/brablet1.html#letter1>.

112   Lefroy file clippings in U of T archives.

publications.[113] The 1922 text, *The Constitution of Canada*, built on the material collected together in the book of documents. He dedicated the 1918 book of documents to George Wrong "as a token of friendship and esteem" and stated in the preface that the dedication "feebly acknowledges a friendship which lies deeper than common work in a common subject would suggest." When a second edition of the book came out in 1930, the dedication was changed from Wrong to two students who had died prematurely.[114] The preface to the first edition was repeated but the sentence about Wrong was omitted.

There is a substantial file in the Oxford University Press archives concerning the second edition of *The Constitution of Canada* that came out in 1938, but relatively little on the first edition of 1922. The Oxford archivist explained that this was "due to the earlier publication being handled by our London office, which shed a great deal of material during war-time evacuation and later weeding of its files."[115] I have little doubt that it would have been an interesting and thick file. The very small file on the first edition in the Canadian branch contains the surprising fact that the contract executed by Kennedy in October 1918 was to produce a book jointly with U of T historian W. Stewart Wallace to be entitled *The Development of Canadian Government*.[116] Royalties were to be 20 percent after the first 2,500 copies. In October 1921, however, Wallace withdrew from any connection with the book.[117] Perhaps he felt he had his hands full, having just been appointed the assistant librarian at U of T, soon to be the head librarian, and had also taken on the editorship of the recently established *Canadian Historical Review*.[118] And perhaps Wallace's close working relationship with George Wrong played a role in his withdrawal.[119] Kennedy simply mentions in the preface to his 1922 book that "Mr. W.S. Wallace has given me, especially in the earlier chapters, the benefit of his knowledge of Canadian history."

THE CONSTITUTION OF CANADA AND BEYOND

Kennedy's 1922 book was a great achievement, and was particularly remarkable considering all the turmoil in his life in the years leading up to its publication

---

113   See, for example, "Fines under the Elizabethan Act of Uniformity," *English Historical Review* 33 (1918): 517.
114   Noted by Maryla Waters, who prepared a full list of Kennedy's publications as part of her oral interview with Gilbert Kennedy in April 1983.
115   E-mail from Dr. Martin Maw, Archivist, Oxford University Press, July 8, 2013.
116   Memorandum of Agreement dated October 28, 1918.
117   Letter from Wallace to Kennedy dated October 3, 1921.
118   William Stewart Wallace, *The Canadian Encyclopedia*, online edition. Maybe Wallace had his eye on another book, *A First Book of Canadian History*, which he published in 1928 and sold over half a million copies. See Friedland, *The University of Toronto*, p. 306.
119   Robert Blackburn, *Evolution of the Heart* (University of Toronto Library, 1989), p. 132.

and the new courses he was preparing in those years. It received many excellent reviews. These were collected in a one-page sheet by Wm. Tyrrell and Company, booksellers and engravers at 8 King Street West, Toronto, who were selling the book for $5.00 plus 20 cents for shipping. The advertisement started with an endorsement from Viscount Richard Haldane, a past and later future Lord Chancellor of England, who said it was "a remarkable volume" as well as a quote from a member and future chair of the University's board of governors, the Reverend Henry Cody, later the president of the University of Toronto, who said that the book was "a national service to Canada and the Empire." There then followed excerpts from 23 reviews. The book was favourably reviewed in the major English papers and journals. The *Times* called it "a work of great accuracy and conspicuous fairness"; the *Observer*, "alive, human, dramatic"; the *Law Quarterly Review*, "an admirable and most readable book"; and the *New Statesman*, "a book which will rank high in the literature of political science." Canadian reviews were equally positive. The *Canadian Historical Review* said that it was "a theme worthy of a Macaulay"; and *Saturday Night* said it was "brilliant ... a monumental work." In the United States, the *Christian Science Monitor* called it "masterly" while in the *New Republic* Harold Laski wrote, "To say that Dr. Kennedy has written a valuable book is to do him less than justice; he has written what is likely long to remain the standard introduction to the study of the Canadian constitution."[120] No doubt, Kennedy was particularly pleased with the review by an unattributed reviewer in the Toronto *Star Weekly*, which compared his book to the discovery of insulin. "The sun of insulin is in the ascendancy," the unnamed reviewer stated dramatically, "but even its world rays cannot obscure other university stars of the first magnitude. One of the brightest of these is W.P.M. Kennedy, associate professor of modern history. His latest work, 'The Constitution of Canada,' is said to be in its way quite as epoch making as insulin."[121]

The *Star Weekly* characterization may have been an exaggeration, but the book was indeed a major triumph and was responsible for establishing Kennedy's reputation as a major constitutional scholar. Political scientist Alan Cairns states that Kennedy was "the most influential constitutional analyst of the period from the early twenties to the middle forties."[122] Kennedy

---

120 "Canada's Constitution," *The New Republic*, July 4, 1923, p. 159. For an insightful article on Laski and Canada, see David Schneiderman, "Harold Laski, Viscount Haldane, and the Law of the Canadian Constitution in the Early Twentieth Century," *University of Toronto Law Journal* 48 (1998): 521.
121 *Star Weekly*, October 20, 1923.
122 Alan Cairns, "The Judicial Committee and its Critics," *Canadian Journal of Political Science* 4 (1971): 301 at 306. See also J.M.S. Careless' survey of Canadian historical publications in 1971 which refers to Kennedy's "still-classic" text. *Papers of the Bibliographical Society of Canada* 10 (1971): 73 at 75.

was obviously pleased with the reception of his book. He kept Falconer informed of his scholarly work, writing: "The *Constitution* goes well. I had charming letters about it from [constitutional law scholar] Berriedale Keith of Edinburgh & from [Rodolphe] Lemieux the speaker [of the Canadian House of Commons]. [Ernest] Lapointe quoted it in the house." Kennedy added a P.S. to the letter: "Arthur Meighen wrote me a nice letter about an article of mine on Canada and the Imperial Conference."[123]

Kennedy may have been a name-dropper, but I do not doubt that he actually corresponded with the persons whose names he was dropping. The prime ministers' papers in the National Archives, for example, show items relating to W.P.M. Kennedy in the papers of Robert Borden, William Lyon Mackenzie King, Arthur Meighen, and Richard Bennett.[124] There are letters concerning gifts by Kennedy of books and articles, invitations to visit the University to address students, discussions of various public policy matters, and other items. By far the most entries are in the William Lyon Mackenzie King fond,[125] where there are 28 items listed, including letters congratulating King on election victories (1926, 1930, and 1935). They indicate that Kennedy was a Liberal supporter. "A thousand congratulations," he wrote at midnight of election day September 14, 1926: "I could not do much publically, but you may have recognized some of my handiwork in speeches and the press." Kennedy seemed to have had a friendly although a peripheral relationship with King.[126] It is possible that King knew about and sympathized with Kennedy's troubles with George Wrong. King had had his own run-in with Wrong over twenty years earlier. It was the appointment of Wrong—University chancellor Sir Edward Blake's son-in-law—as the professor of history in 1894 that caused King to lead the famous student strike on the issue of nepotism at the University of Toronto in 1895.[127]

123 Letter dated August 24, 1923 from Kennedy to Falconer. The article which Meighen mentions was published in July 1921.
124 I pass on to the reader that one can go to the "Prime Ministers' Fonds" under the letter "P" in the A–Z Index on the Library and Archives Canada home page, where one can search online for correspondees. This is not possible for the Laurier and Louis St. Laurent papers. There are, of course, some letters in other files at Ottawa and in other archives that I have not discovered or examined. There are, for example, a number of letters in the Sir John Willison files in Ottawa, which are interesting—he was the Canadian correspondent for the *London Times*, but are not sufficiently important for the purpose of this introduction. I am grateful to Ottawa historian Richard Clippingdale for sending me copies of these letters.
125 I am grateful to Ottawa researcher Christopher Cook for retrieving these letters for me.
126 An electronic search does not, however, mention Kennedy in King's diaries. There are many entries for persons named Kennedy, but none that could be W.P.M. Kennedy.
127 See chapter 15 of Friedland, *The University of Toronto*, where a full chapter is devoted to the strike. It is interesting to read the correspondence between George Wrong and Murray Wrong in the Wrong papers (see, e.g., George Wrong to Murray May 30, 1921 and January 8, 1923) which shows George Wrong's interest in securing academic positions at the University of Toronto for George Wrong's children.

There are a number of letters in which Kennedy is openly asking to be appointed to a position, such as being a delegate to the Imperial Conference of 1926 and as Canadian representative to the League of Nations Hague Conference on the Codification of International Law. With respect to the latter, Kennedy states that he has "given [his] life to this work," and then adds that "it is very improbable that I would be able to go, but an invitation by the Prime Minister of Canada to his alma mater in this connection would be a most grateful compliment." On the face of it, the request looks odd. Kennedy had not given his life to international law. Indeed, he had never taught international law. Still, he had a legitimate claim to have been invited because the conference was on codification of conflict of nationality laws and Kennedy had recently completed a study for the government on nationality.[128] In a note by King on Kennedy's letter, King asks his aide to draft a reply noting that Kennedy seems to have a need for "recognition."[129] Once again we see a large measure of exaggeration and seeking recognition. Other requests from Kennedy include asking King to propose him for an honorary Harvard doctorate[130] and a request that he be awarded a British honour—"maybe a c.m.g. on King's b'day or sometime."[131] He added a note to the latter letter that "this is a very personal letter and I do ask you to destroy it when you've read it and w'd not like it to survive with your papers." The letter, of course, did end up in the King papers. King replied that Canada was not sending a list of honours for the King's birthday that year, but instructed his staff to make sure that "consideration" be given to Kennedys name in future years.[132]

The previously mentioned 1923 letter to Falconer shows that Kennedy had plans for follow-up volumes to his book on the constitution. Kennedy wrote: "I've been collecting material for the second vol. of my *Constitution*, on 'The Government of Canada' which the Oxford Press have ordered. It may be two and will take me a year or two."[133] As we now know, his career path suddenly changed. At the end of the 1922 academic year, he was no longer, as the book states, an "assistant professor of modern history in the University of Toronto." He was a special lecturer in the department of

---

128   *Report to the Honourable Secretary of State for Canada on Some Problems in the Law of Nationality* (Ottawa: King's Printer, 1930).

129   Letter to King, February 11, 1930.

130   Letter dated May 20, 1926 and letter dated April 23, 1948.

131   Letter dated April 23, 1948.

132   King to Kennedy, April 27, 1948 and J.W. Pickersgill to the Undersecretary of State, E.H. Coleman, May 1, 1948.

133   A similar plan was revealed by Kennedy to Berriedale Keith in a letter to Keith in the Edinburgh archives, dated December 13, 1923.

political science as well as in the department of history. The two further proposed volumes were never prepared.

The 1922 book was followed by a three-volume study published in 1924 on Tudor ecclesiastical history, *Elizabethan Episcopal Administration: an Essay in Sociology and Politics*,[134] that was dedicated to Bishop Frere, his former colleague at the Mirfield Monastery. Perhaps Kennedy was covering the possibility that he would have to return to English literature or church history. It was a continuation of the earlier three-volume work that he and Frere produced that had been published in 1910.

Kennedy's scholarly output in the early 1920s, including many scholarly articles, was staggering. By the end of the 1920s, he had published ten books.[135] *The Constitution of Canada*, it was reported by the *Star Weekly*, had sold 3,000 or 4,000 copies in less than six months.[136] He was also giving lectures to the Bankers Educational Association that paid more than the lectures he had also been giving to the Workers Education Association.[137] His financial position was becoming more secure. In 1925 he moved with his four children from his house, no longer standing, at 110 Quebec Avenue, just north of High Park, to a fine home, still standing, at 77 Spadina Road in what is known as "the Annex." The Kennedy family, his son Frere states, had a billiard table in the basement and W.P.M. was known as an expert player. Frere told me that he remembers George Wrong, who lived a block away on Walmer Road, nodding respectfully to his mother, Pauline, on his walk to the University.[138] Frere also told me that he was not aware of any conflict between his father and George Wrong.

Kennedy did not shy away from public issues. In 1924, for example, he gave a public address in Convocation Hall on the situation in Ireland.[139] As early as 1917, he had urged women in a letter to the *Varsity* to insist on securing the vote.[140] One issue that he was careful to avoid, however, was the very controversial and well-known Byng-King dispute in which Governor General Byng refused Prime Minister Mackenzie King's request for dissolution of the House in 1926, and instead called on Arthur Meighen to form a

---

134   *Elizabethan Episcopal Administration*, 3 vols (London: Mowbray, 1924).
135   Risk, "The Many Minds," p. 365.
136   *Toronto Star*, March 7, 1924, in Kennedy's university file.
137   He gave courses to the Bankers Educational Association in 1926–27 and 1927–28. Vincent Bladen, *Bladen on Bladen* states that many members of the department taught evening classes (pp. 32–33). Workers Educational Association lecturers got $200 for a course, but the Bankers Educational Association paid $400.
138   Frere thought that his parents married in 1922, the year before he was born.
139   See Risk, "The Many Minds," p. 363.
140   Kennedy file. Letter in the Varsity of February 8, 1917.

government. That summer Kennedy was in England—the only time he ever returned to Europe.[141] "I've been driven crazy over the constitutional issue here by the papers," he wrote to President Falconer that summer, and went on to state that he had issued the following release to the Associate Press: "Professor Kennedy has a stringent rule to grant no interviews or to write on any matters in party politics. He cannot see his way in the present case, to break this rule."[142]

A jurisdictional struggle once again took place between the departments of history and political economy. Each claimed that constitutional history came within its jurisdiction. In the mid-1920s, the department of history was declared the winner.[143] In October 1927, the chair of political economy, E.J. Urwick, wrote to Falconer: "I should ... make it clear that Constitutional History is not in question, as we fully understand that this subject belongs to the Department of Modern History."[144] But he also told Falconer that it is their understanding that the department of political economy includes "Political Institutions and Law."

Kennedy's main subject of interest was, of course, constitutional history. What was he going to do? One possibility, it seems, was to go to Ottawa to replace Arthur Doughty as the National Archivist. Doughty was rumoured to have been offered the post of chief archivist for the Hudson Bay Company.[145] Kennedy was close with Doughty and may well have had his support. Hume Wrong wrote to his father that they had to block Kennedy's appointment.[146] "His departure," Hume Wrong wrote in 1926, "would be good for the University, but mighty bad for the Archives." But in an added note, he wrote that he had just learned that Vincent Massey had said privately that Doughty may stay on; Doughty did remain, after receiving an "increased salary," arranged by Prime Minister Mackenzie King.[147]

---

141 Gilbert Kennedy interview, p. 14. He went to England with Alexander Brady.
142 Letter to Falconer, August 2, 1926. Kennedy had been staying in Cambridge with Professor John Rose, the editor of the *Cambridge History of the British Empire*, for which Kennedy was editing the volume on Canada. A clipping from the *Star*, July 15, 1926, states that Kennedy "was taken ill and on medical advice returned home to Toronto to undergo [an] operation."
143 Drummond, *Political Economy*, p. 37. See Falconer note to file of January 20, 1926; Falconer to Kennedy of June 14, 1926; Alan Bowker, "Truly Useful Men: Maurice Hutton, George Wrong, James Mavor and the University of Toronto," 1880–1927 (Ph. D. thesis, 1975), pp. 326–27.
144 Letter from Urwick to Falconer, October 26, 1927 in Falconer Papers.
145 E-mail from former national librarian and archivist Ian Wilson, May 2013. Kennedy had been an advisor to the Archives of Ontario, 1919–23, according to his 1955–57 *Who's Who* entry.
146 Letter from Hume Wrong to his father, George Wrong, February 8, 1926.
147 King's diary of April 26, 1926. An examination of King's diary that year shows that Doughty was closely involved with King's day-to-day activities and was valuable to King. He did not retire until 1935 and died the following year.

Kennedy had no choice but to craft a new life for himself in the department of political economy. It was to be law. Law was not a subject that history was interested in teaching and MacIver wanted to build up the law side of his department[148] in the same way that political economy was also developing commerce and finance and other programs.[149] Kennedy, who, as previously stated, had absolutely no legal training,[150] had been designated as "Special Lecturer on Federal Constitutions in the Sub-department of Law" in the department of political economy.[151] In 1926, he became the head of the law program in the department and given the title "Professor of Law and Political Institutions."[152] In late 1928, Kennedy proposed an honours BA course in law, which came into effect in the 1929–30 academic year.[153] New legally trained faculty were hired, such as Larry Mackenzie (later the president of the University of British Columbia) in international law,[154] Frederick Auld in Roman law, and Jacob Finkelman (the first Jew appointed as an academic at the University of Toronto)[155] in administrative law. In the 1929–30 University Calendar, the degree of LLB first appeared after Kennedy's name and was there every subsequent year as well as in various *Who's Who* volumes. I have not, however, found any evidence in Convocation or Senate records that Kennedy was ever awarded an LLB, even an honorary LLB. When Bora Laskin and Caesar Wright prepared a lengthy memorial to the Senate after Kennedy died, there is no mention of Kennedy's LLB.[156]

This new law program was in part the result of Kennedy's ambitions in political economy being blocked. According to political economist Harold

---

148   P.B. Waite, *Lord of Point Grey* (University of British Columbia Press, 1987), p. 58.
149   Drummond, *Political Economy*, chapter four, "The MacIver and Urwick Years."
150   See Alexander Brady, *Proceedings of the Royal Society of Canada, 1964*, and Risk, "The Many Minds."
151   This first appeared, however, in the 1922–23 Calendar. I have drawn on the calendars for much of this paragraph, but it is sometimes misleading because some events took place too late for entry into the calendar. As Risk discovered (p. 371, footnote 75 in "The Many Minds"), the various changes are not entirely clear. We are still waiting for a definitive history of the law school.
152   Falconer to Kennedy, June 14, 1926, too late for the 1926–27 calendar, but included in the 1927–28 calendar. The same letter shows that Kennedy would continue to teach in history in the 1926–27 academic year. See Risk, "The Many Minds," p. 371. There were two undergraduate degrees, a BA and an LLB, plus, starting in 1930, graduate degrees: see letter from Kennedy to Falconer January 31, 1930 and March 10, 1930; Kyer and Bickenbach, *The Fiercest Debate*, pp. 58 and 149. There were, however, very few LLBs granted prior to 1949, often only a couple each year, according to the records of Convocation.
153   See the 1929 calendar and letter from Kennedy to Falconer December 21, 1928. See also Risk, "The Many Minds," p. 371, citing various 1928 law school papers in the Archives.
154   See P.B. Waite, *Lord of Point Grey: Larry Mackenzie of U.B.C.* (University of British Columbia Press, 1987).
155   Friedland, *University of Toronto*, p. 235. It is interesting to note that Kennedy—atypical of the times—invited a number of important foreign Jewish judges and academics to visit the law school, such as Justices Frankfurter and Cardozo, and Professor Arthur Goodhart: letter from Kennedy to Falconer, November 13, 1930. There were no Jewish superior court judges in Ontario until Abraham Lieff was appointed by Prime Minister Lester Pearson in 1963.
156   Law files in the U of T Archives.

Innis, Kennedy had wanted to be the head of political economy. MacIver had left for Columbia University in 1927 and E.J. Urwick, who had retired from the University of London and had come to Toronto as a special lecturer in 1925–26, had been appointed the head of the department.[157] In a letter to President Falconer in 1929, Innis claimed that this was a disappointment to Kennedy, who, along with a number of others, had wanted the position and thought that Urwick was appointed for only one year. Innis explained the background to the troubles in political economy:

> The various strong contestants were anxious to improve their rela-
> tive positions against the appointment of Prof. Urwick's successor.
> The rumor that Prof. Urwick was appointed for only one year was
> largely responsible for the tremendous energy which Prof. Kennedy
> displayed last year. He spent his energies and of course ended in fail-
> ure except that he succeeded in gaining control of a substantial part
> of the course over which he exercises complete jurisdiction.[158]

Kennedy was anxious to continue to reshape the honours program to concentrate on law and to separate law from political economy. Physical separation occurred when political economy moved to McMaster Hall on Bloor Street in 1933 and law remained on St. George Street.[159] In 1937 law became a separate division in arts and science, not connected with political economy.[160] Kennedy continued his quest for independence and in 1941 the department of law became the School of Law, a separate division in the University, with Kennedy as chairman, and three years later—in 1944—the school became a faculty, with Kennedy as dean and professor of law.[161] The University Calendars and the division itself, however, continued to call the institution the School of Law. The law school was responsible for teaching students in the five-year LLB program, graduate students seeking LLM and D.Jur. degrees, and the many students taking individual law classes in the faculty of arts and science and in the professional faculties.[162] Finally,

---

157 Friedland, *University of Toronto*, p. 297.
158 Letter from Innis to Falconer, no date, but in the 1929 correspondence file. Innis also notes in that letter that he "was subjected to severe and prolonged attacks from Prof. Kennedy."
159 Friedland, *University of Toronto*, p. 297.
160 Letter from President Cody to Kennedy dated June 1, 1936, stating that the change would be made in 1937.
161 *U of T Monthly* 44 (1944): 172. The change may not have been as clear as intended because in 1955 Caesar Wright got the senate to confirm that the law school was not the School of Law, but the Faculty of Law. See also the undated nine-page memorandum from Kennedy to Sidney Smith in the mid 1940s contained in the law school papers in the U of T Archives.
162 See the undated memo from Kennedy to Smith.

in 1949—as we have seen—the school became a second-entry professional faculty of law, with Caesar Wright as dean. At that point, Kennedy retired at the age of 70.[163]

The extensive correspondence between Kennedy and Falconer over more than a quarter century are replete with references to Kennedy's health. In 1923, to give one example, he wrote at the end of the summer: "I was laid up for two or three weeks in bed with the old intestinal trouble, and now I'm limping after a bad strained ankle."[164] In 1930, to give another, he wrote: "I am ordered to ... lie down each afternoon for two hours ... every ounce of strength has got to be conserved, and some effort made to avoid a complete breakdown."[165] At this stage of his career, his scholarly production did not slow down, in part because he was able to publish a significant number of books with co-authors.[166]

Kennedy developed a strong law faculty, with an interest in interdisciplinary studies, not unlike the present faculty of law, but with only a handful of professors. There were both undergraduate and graduate students. Bora Laskin, a student in the school, later wrote that Kennedy "introduced us to the riches of American legal scholarship, to Holmes and Brandeis and Cardozo, to Pound and Frankfurter ... and to so many others."[167] Laskin and Wright wrote in a tribute to the University Senate after Kennedy died: "He sought to emphasize the jurisprudence rather than the technology of the legal system."[168] In 1935 Kennedy founded the *University of Toronto Law Journal*—the first scholarly legal journal in Canada and, arguably, the preeminent law journal in Canada from its inception.[169] The journal reflected Kennedy's view, expressed the previous year, that "we study law as a social science, a great creative process of social engineering."[170]

Throughout his career Kennedy was known as a stimulating and sparkling teacher. J.J. Robinette, one of Canada's greatest lawyers, who was taught by Kennedy in the 1920s, recalled that "Kennedy was one of those brilliant Irishmen who could dazzle you ... a performer as much as a teacher."[171]

---

163 Friedland, *University of Toronto*, p. 306. Risk, "The Many Minds," p. 370 et seq.
164 Kennedy to Falconer, August 24, 1923.
165 Kennedy to Falconer, January 31, 1930.
166 See *The Law of the Taxing Power in Canada*, with Dalton Wells (University of Toronto Press, 1931); *The Right to Trade*, with Jacob Finkelman (University of Toronto Press, 1933); *The Law and Custom of the South African Constitution*, with H.J. Schlosberg (Oxford University Press, 1935); *The Canadian Law of Trade Marks and Industrial Designs*, by Harold Fox, edited by Kennedy (University of Toronto Press, 1940).
167 Bora Laskin, "Cecil A. Wright: A Personal Memoir," *University of Toronto Law Journal* 33 (1983): 148 at 150.
168 Law files in the U of T Archives.
169 R.C.B. Risk, "Volume 1 of the Journal," *University of Toronto Law Journal* 37 (1987): 193.
170 W.P.M. Kennedy, "Law as a Social Science," *South African Law Times* (1934): 100.
171 Jack Batten, *Robinette: The Dean of Canadian Lawyers* (Toronto: Macmillan, 1984), p. 27.

Sydney Robins, who attended the Law School in the early 1940s and was the president of the Law Club in his final year, recently wrote to me about "Doc Kennedy," as the students called him:

> His lectures to the small classes then at the school were given in his office, a rather large room on the second floor at 45 St. George Street. Every lecture was indeed a performance. He would speak while sometimes standing, sometimes sitting, sometimes walking around the room, and sometimes lying down on his psychiatrist-style couch. His lectures went beyond the law. He spoke also of history, politics, current events and the many prominent people he claimed to know and who had, or so he told us, sought his advice. He was certainly one of the most charismatic lecturers I ever had—always interesting, often funny, the words flowed effortlessly.[172]

Kennedy's programs attracted some of the best students in the University. Apart from Robinette, there were G. Arthur Martin, thought by many to be Canada's greatest criminal lawyer, William Howland and Charles Dubin, both distinguished chief justices of Ontario, the previously mentioned Sydney Robins, later the treasurer of the Law Society and a member of the Ontario Court of Appeal, Moffat Hancock, who joined the faculty and later became a noted professor of law at Stanford University, Bora Laskin, later the chief justice of Canada, and many more.[173] Their future success was disproportionate to their relatively small number. Perhaps they were inspired by Kennedy's view that legal education should "create a body of citizens endowed with an insight into law as the basic social science, and capable of making those examinations into its workings as will redeem it from being a mere trade and technique and ... make it the finest of all instruments in the service of mankind."[174]

KENNEDY'S IDEAS ON THE CANADIAN CONSTITUTION

It is not surprising that Kennedy became interested in the constitution of Canada. His knowledge of church politics in the Tudor era gave him a good understanding of the various forces and interests that shape change in society.

---

172 E-mail from Sydney Robins to me, August 19, 2013. To accommodate the construction of a new engineering building, the building that housed law at 45 St. George Street was later torn down to permit the much larger Forestry Building next door to be put on rollers and moved to the site.

173 See Kyer and Bickenbach, *The Fiercest Debate*, p. 58.

174 Friedland, *University of Toronto*, p. 307.

His colleague, political scientist Alexander Brady, wrote a memorial tribute in the *Proceedings of the Royal Society of Canada*, 1964, stating that Kennedy's "earlier explorations in ecclesiastical law and institutions exhibited the special bent of his mind, which in Canada found in the constitution a new and fascinating theme."[175] But it was more than that, as R.C.B. Risk rightly observes. Kennedy saw similarities between England under the Tudors and the constitutional development of Canada. The dominant objective of the Tudors, Risk argues, "was to make England a unified nation, under the control of the state" and Kennedy's "story of Canada's nationhood paralleled the story of the emergence of the English nation state under the Tudors."[176]

Kennedy's book traces the development of Canada from the earliest days of the French explorers until the date of publication. The comprehensive scope of the book is evident from an examination of the twenty five chapter headings. All the important familiar events are discussed: the Royal Proclamation of 1763, the Constitution Act of 1791, Lord Durham's Report of 1840, the granting of responsible government in 1848, the British North America Act 1867, and later events up to and including 1922. The study, Kennedy states in the preface, is "an evolutionary account of the various movements and stages which have issued into the organized political life of Canada to-day."[177] "It is well worth, studying," Kennedy writes, "as a recent example of the process of nation-making."

> To understand this nation-building, it is necessary to keep the social background always in view, to show how, under the special conditions of a new land, the conjuncture of groups detached from older countries, particularly England and France, the insistent near influence of a great neighbouring country already ahead in economic development, and the later influx of more heterogeneous elements from many lands ... have worked in the end to a certain unity and a sure nationhood.[178]

"The aim," he states,[179]

> is to trace the stream of development. The mere retelling of a well-known story lies more or less outside its purpose. It is rather an

---

175 P. 109.
176 Risk, "The Many Minds," pp. 356 and 361.
177 P. vii.
178 Preface, p. vii.
179 P. 6.

attempt to find in the facts the complex characters and divers conditions out of which they grew; to seek the causes which gave energy and purpose to the constitutional evolution; to animate dead documents with something of the vital energy which called them into being.

Kennedy succeeds admirably in presenting this historical and, indeed, sociological view of the development of Canada. Unexpected events occur, but everything leads towards the present, with Canada as a nation within the British Empire, a body which Kennedy strongly supported. The book is written with engaging style, which is not surprising given that Kennedy had won the prize in English prose at Trinity College Dublin. Here is how he describes the setting for the historic Quebec Conference of 1864, which led to the "federation" of 1867. (It was a federation, Kennedy insists, not a confederation.[180]) "On October 10, 1864," he writes, "there assembled at Quebec one of the most epoch-making conferences in history." He continues:

It is impossible to reconstruct those pregnant days without emotion. Outside, the most ghastly civil war in history was desolating a kindred race, Sherman was on the move, leaving destruction and ruin in his wake. Inside, broken little provinces had toiled for a long colonial night and caught apparently nothing. Sectionalism was a recent sore. Party politics then as now were unstable. Jealousies, but recently shed, might easily be reassumed. Suspicion, publicly cast out, lay watching in the secret recesses of every heart. Every step forward meant a backward look to see how others viewed it ...[181]

In the preface, Kennedy states that the book has two aims. One of the aims of the book, as stated above, was to study Canada "as a recent example of the process of nation-making." A second aim was to use Canada "as a most significant illustration of that real and yet not absolute sovereignty which defies the older theories of government and thereby leads us to a truer conception of the state."[182]
Kennedy attacks the so-called Austinian doctrine of sovereignty, a now-discredited doctrine that had been developed by legal philosopher

---

180   Kennedy, chapter xxiii.
181   P. 301.
182   P. vii.

John Austin in the nineteenth century,[183] which conditions statehood on full and absolute sovereignty. "As the law of nations now stands," Kennedy writes, "Canada is not a sovereign state ... Canada's position in the League of Nations is due to its position in the empire."[184] It "cannot negotiate directly with a foreign country in the political or any other important sphere."[185] Canada had signed the Versailles Peace Treaty acting on the advice of the British Secretary of State for foreign affairs.

Canada's status, he argues, should be recognized by the law of nations. The future of the British Empire requires it. Such an approach de-emphasizes nationalism. Nationalism, he argued, causes wars. In 1921, Kennedy had written that nationalism is "almost uniformly related to a fatherland; and it is of such consuming force that men will gladly die to preserve it."[186] In historian Carl Berger's words, Kennedy's view was that "modern nationalism and the striving for absolute sovereignty was a retrogressive and dangerous force."[187]

Groupings of nations are better. "It is the insistence of the older doctrine of sovereignty," Kennedy states, "which is the great stumbling block in the way of the evolution of the greater unities which political exigencies ... require today."[188] "While the civilized world is groping for the solution of the problem [absolute sovereignty] thus created, the British Empire is at least [suggesting] the form which that solution must take."[189]

Kennedy continued with this important theme over the years. "Having cast down the Austinian idol," he stated in 1924, "let us grind it to powder."[190] And in a speech on Irish politics in Convocation Hall that same year he stated that "sovereignty is that pestilential legal fiction which has drenched this poor world in oceans of blood."[191] He did not comment further on the danger of nationalism in the second edition in 1938. The growing threat of war caused by nationalism spoke for itself.

---

183   See, generally, Brian Bix, "John Austin," *The Stanford Encyclopedia of Philosophy* (Spring 2013 Edition), Edward N. Zalta (ed.), <http://plato.stanford.edu/archives/spr2013/entries/austin-john/>.

184   Pp. 446 and 452.

185   P. 451.

186   "Nationalism and Self-Determination," *Canadian Historical Review* 6 (1921): 10. The paper is in part reproduced in Marlene Shore, *The Contested Past: Reading Canada's History* (University of Toronto Press, 2002), pp. 104–107.

187   Carl Berger, *The Writing of Canadian History* (Toronto: Oxford University Press, 1976), p. 40.

188   Pp. 455–56.

189   P. viii.

190   Risk, "The Many Minds," p. 362; "The Conception of the British Commonwealth," *Edinburgh Review* 227 (1924): 238.

191   Risk, "The Many Minds," pp. 363–64. This paper by Kennedy is in the Kennedy Papers in the Fisher Rare Book Library.

Over the years, his views on the division of powers, however, changed dramatically. There is a marked contrast between the first and second edition with respect to his view of the Privy Council and its interpretation of the division of powers. In the first edition he has few complaints about the Privy Council and is optimistic about how the court interpreted the distribution of power in the British North America Act. He states: "Room was thus left for constitutional progress and for the development of a theory of constitutional law related as far as possible to the social and political growth of the people."[192] The Privy Council decisions, even those favouring provincial rights, "have humanized the British North America Act. They have given it the elasticity of life."[193]

Kennedy accepted without criticism, for example, Lord Watson's provincial rights view, set out in a 1892 case (the *Maritime Bank* case) that "[t]he object of the Act was neither to weld the provinces into one, nor to subordinate provincial governments to a central authority, but to create a federal government in which they should all be represented, entrusted with the exclusive administration of affairs in which they had a common interest, each province retaining its independence and autonomy."[194] "Lord Watson's conception," Kennedy states, "has been acted on to such an extent that to abandon it would upset much of the structure of the constitution."[195]

There is no demand in the first edition to abolish appeals to the Privy Council, although he writes of "a future when Canada might reasonably hope normally to make its own supreme court supreme in reality."[196]

In November 1921, however, the Privy Council released its judgment in the *Board of Commerce* case, dealing with a federal Act of 1919 controlling prices.[197] In a judgment delivered by Viscount Haldane, the court held the legislation invalid, stating that under the "peace order and good government" clause the legislation would only be constitutional "under necessity in highly exceptional circumstances."[198] The decision was not published in the official law reports until 1922 and was probably still on board a ship heading for Canada when Kennedy completed the proofs of his book. As all students of constitutional law learn, this case led to the Snider case in 1925, where

---

192   P. 436.
193   P. 431.
194   *Liquidators of the Maritime Bank of Canada v. Receiver-General of New Brunswick* [1892] A.C. 437 at 441-2. See Peter Russell, *Constitutional Odyssey*, 3rd edn (University of Toronto Press, 2004), p. 43.
195   P. 411.
196   P. 398.
197   [1922] 1 A.C. 191, November 11, 1921.
198   P. 198.

Haldane limited the "peace, order, and good government" clause to "extra-ordinary peril to the national life of Canada, as a whole."[199]

In the second edition of *The Constitution of Canada*, Kennedy—now age 59—strongly criticizes these decisions.[200] The federal government, he argues, was meant to have the residuary power that would allow it to pass laws "of national importance."[201] This was John A. Macdonald's view and also the view of the colonial secretary, Lord Carnarvon. Carnarvon had stated: "The real object which we have in view is to give to the central government those high functions and almost sovereign powers by which general principles and uniformity of legislation may be secured in those questions that are of common import to all the provinces."[202]

Haldane had therefore limited the "peace, order, and good government" section, in Kennedy's words, to "cases arising out of some extraordinary national peril."[203] Thus, says Kennedy, "the residuum of powers would appear to have passed largely to the provinces under their exclusive authority over 'property and civil rights.'"[204] The court's interpretation has "divorced it from history and from the intention of those who in truth framed it, with the result that the centrifugal forces in Canadian national life have been strengthened."[205]

The problem was created, he states in the second edition, because the Privy Council interpreted the BNA Act as a statute and not as a constitution.[206] Legislative history was, according to the techniques of statutory interpretation used at the time, not relevant. There had been some hope of a different approach following Lord Sankey's decision in the well-known *Persons Case* released in 1929, which decided that women were "persons" and so could be senators.[207] This was the case where the "living tree doctrine"—now widely used to interpret the *Charter of Rights and Freedoms*—was first enunciated, but the Sankey court also held that it did not apply to

---

199   [1925] A.C. 396.
200   P. 488 et seq.
201   P. 490.
202   P. 489.
203   P. 491.
204   P. 492.
205   P. 489.
206   P. 488.
207   *Edwards v. Attorney General of Canada* [1930] A.C. 124. See Robert Sharpe and Patricia McMahon, *The Persons Case: The Origins and Legacy of the Fight for Legal Personhood* (University of Toronto Press, 2007). An interesting footnote appeared on p. 384 of the first edition of Kennedy's *The Constitution of Canada* that mentions a document dated three days after the date of Kennedy's preface: "An official opinion of the federal minister of justice has laid it down that no woman senators can be created without an amendment of the B.N.A. Act, 1867." Kennedy does not, however, comment further on the opinion which led to the *Persons Case* in 1930.

the division of powers.[208] Kennedy criticized that aspect of the decision[209] and in a later case[210] Sankey adopted the living tree approach to the entire BNA Act. But in the *New Deal* cases in 1937[211]—to which Kennedy devotes a scathing supplementary appendix in the second edition[212]—Lord Atkin for the Privy Council struck down federal legislation on working conditions, unemployment insurance, and the regulation of natural products marketing schemes because, in his view, they intruded into provincial legislative power.

I took constitutional law from Bora Laskin in 1956–57 and I can still hear him vigorously denounce the privy council decisions, just as Kennedy, his own teacher, did in his second edition. Like Kennedy in his later career, Laskin was a centralist. "For Laskin," his biographer, Philip Girard, states, "only the federal government had the resources, the vision, and the power to implement a modernist agenda for Canada."[213] Indeed, in one case in 1983, his colleague on the Supreme Court, Brian Dickson, referred to Laskin's view as "blind centralism."[214] Many other legal academics in the thirties, such as Frank Scott of McGill and Vincent McDonald of Dalhousie, also adopted Kennedy's centralist approach.[215]

This is not the place for a detailed discussion of the Privy Council's interpretation of the BNA Act. It is one of the most, if not *the* most, discussed and written-about issues in Canadian constitutional law. Not everyone agrees with Kennedy's approach. Political scientist Alan Cairns, to pick one respected commentator, states in a thoughtful and provocative essay in 1971, "The Judicial Committee and Its Critics": "The interpretation of the British North America Act by the Judicial Committee of the Privy Council is one of the most contentious aspects of the constitutional evolution of Canada."[216] For two thorough

---

208   See Sharpe and McMahon at 202–206.

209   "The Judicial Interpretation of the Canadian Constitution," *Canadian Bar Review* 8 (1930): 703 at 706–707. See also the second edition of *The Constitution of Canada*, p. 494.

210   *British Coal Corporation v. The King* [1935] A.C. 500.

211   *A.-G. Can. v. A.-G. Ont.* [1937] A.C. 326 (PC); *A.-G. Can. v. A.-G. Ont.* [1937] A.C. 355 (P.C.); *A.-G. B.C. v. A.-G. Can.* [1937] A.C. 368 (P.C.); *A.-G. B.C. v. A.-G. Can.* [1937] A.C. 377 (P.C.); *A.-G. B.C. v. A.-G. Can.* [1937] A.C. 391 (P.C.); *A.-G. Ont. v. A.-G. Can.* [1937] A.C. 405 (P.C.).

212   P. 545 et seq. On p. 552 Kennedy says he predicted the decisions.

213   See Philip Girard, *Bora Laskin: Bringing Law to Life* (University of Toronto Press, 2005), p. 217–18.

214   Friedland, *University of Toronto*, p. 469; *R. v. Wetmore Close* [1983] 2 S.C.R. 284.

215   See Alan Cairns, "The Privy Council and Its Critics," *Canadian Journal of Political Science* 4 (1971): 301; R.C.B. Risk "The Scholars and the Constitution," *Manitoba Law Journal* 23 (1996): 496, reprinted in *A History of Canadian Legal Thought* (University of Toronto Press, 2006), p. 233 et seq.; Eric Adams, "Canada's 'Newer Constitutional Law' and the Idea of Constitutional Rights," *McGill Law Journal* 51 (2006): 435; and Adams' 2009 University of Toronto S.J.D. thesis, now online: "The Idea of Constitutional Rights and the Transformation of Canadian Constitutional Law, 1930–1960." Their centralist views continued after the war: see R.C.B. Risk, "On the Road to Oz: Common Law Scholarship about Federalism after World War II," *University of Toronto Law Journal* 51 (2001): 143.

216   Cairns, "The Privy Council," p. 301.

discussions of the various debates, see John Saywell's book, *The Lawmakers: Judicial Power and the Shaping of Canadian Federalism*[217] and Peter Russell's *Constitutional Odyssey*.[218] Alan Cairns shows that contrary to the critics, there is much to be said for the approach taken by the Privy Council. He argues that its "great contribution, the injection of a decentralizing impulse into a constitutional structure too centralist for the diversity it had to contain, and the placating of Quebec which was a consequence, was a positive influence in the evolution of Canadian federalism." He cites Pierre Elliott Trudeau's statement in Trudeau's 1968 book, *Federalism and the French-Canadians*, that if the Privy Council had been a centralist court, "Quebec separatism might not be a threat today: it might be an accomplished fact."[219]

The first edition of Kennedy's text did not call for immediate constitutional change. Canada, he stated, is not in the mood for serious reform: "No-one can seriously doubt that at present Canada is not enamored of constitutional changes. Mr. Meighen avoided the issue at the general election of 1921, and his successful opponent [Mackenzie King] is inclined to follow the Laurier tradition."[220] Canada moved along the path to independence within the British Empire with the enactment of the Statute of Westminster in 1931.[221] Canada now had, Kennedy argued in the second edition, "undoubted legal powers to abolish or curtail" appeals to the Privy Council.[222] But there was still no amending formula. Amendments still had to come from legislation at Westminster.[223]

In his second edition, Kennedy urged Canada to take control over amendments to the BNA Act. "The truth is," he writes, "that we have outgrown the British North America Act. Canada is attempting today to carry on the highly complex life of a modern state under a constitution drawn up for a primitive community, scarcely emerging from pioneer agricultural conditions …." The country is "attempting to deal with a vast network of national complexities, with the dominion driven from field after field by judicial decisions."[224]

---

217 (University of Toronto Press, 2002).

218 *Constitutional Odyssey: Can Canadians Become a Sovereign People?*, 3rd edn (University of Toronto Press, 2004).

219 Cited in Cairns, p. 324 (footnote). See Pierre Elliott Trudeau, *Federalism and the French-Canadians* (Toronto: Macmillan, 1968), p. 198.

220 Pp. 453–54.

221 See the second edition, chapter 28, "Canada and the Statute of Westminster, 1931," p. 518.

222 P. 526.

223 P. 450, 2nd edn. See Russell, *Constitutional Odyssey*, pp. 56–57.

224 P. 529.

The rewriting of the constitution, he argues in the second edition, "must proceed from at least substantial provincial agreement."[225] He set out his own scheme[226]—a scheme which he had earlier presented to a House of Commons Committee on the BNA Act.[227] That committee issued a report in 1935 which led to the Rowell Sirois Commission on Dominion-Provincial Relations in 1937, that, in turn, reported in 1940,[228] and for which Kennedy provided research assistance.[229] Some things, he told the Commons Committee, the federal government could do alone; some would require unanimity, and some needed the support of two thirds of the provinces. This is not unlike the amending formula adopted in the Constitution Act 1982, except that Kennedy did not require that the two-thirds majority also constitute half the population of Canada.[230]

There are a number of important constitutional issues that Kennedy did not mention in either edition, which are front and centre today. He did not, for example, mention the possibility of a *Bill of Rights* or a *Charter of Rights and Freedoms*. Nor did he have much to say about Aboriginal issues. And there are relatively few discussions of the American constitution, except to point out that the BNA Act was a reaction to the "great source of weakness" in the American system, that is, the power of the states.[231]

Nor does he discuss any reform of the senate—speaking of today's "front and centre." The lack of senate reform was the only major criticism of Kennedy's first edition that Harold Laski made in his review, where Laski states: "Dr. Kennedy's program does not include any full discussion of what may be termed the dynamics of the Canadian constitution. It would be interesting to know whether the Dominion Senate is really necessary now; it has been, clearly enough, the outstanding institutional failure."[232]

There is also no mention in either edition of the possibility of a province unilaterally seceding from the federation. He would clearly have said it was not possible because he states that "Canada's severance from the empire could only take place by imperial and not by federal legislation."[233]

---

225 P. 528.
226 P. 532.
227 House of Commons Special Committee on the British North America Act, 1935.
228 Report of the Rowell-Sirois Commission on Dominion-Provincial Relations, 1940.
229 Risk, "The Many Minds," p. 385.
230 Section 52(3) of the Constitution Act 1982.
231 P. 5 of first edition, quoting John A. Macdonald.
232 *New Republic*, July 4, 1923, p. 159.
233 2nd edn, p. 449.

The publication of the second edition in 1938, which was declared out of print in 1942, is not the end of the story. There is considerable correspondence in the files of Oxford University Press about Kennedy trying to encourage the publication of a third edition. This started in 1951, but Oxford was not interested. But then in 1952 the distinguished Canadian historian George Stanley, then at Royal Military College, proposed that he and Kennedy's son Gilbert, a professor of law at the University of British Columbia, prepare a new edition of the book.[234] Stanley and Gilbert had been colleagues at UBC in the late 1940s. This had W.P.M. Kennedy's blessing. Stanley would do the parts up to Confederation and Gilbert would do those after it. The project had the backing of the important constitutional scholar Sir Kenneth Wheare of All Souls College, Oxford, who was also on the Oxford publication board. Wheare wrote, "It is a very good book ... there is a great need for a good historical book, and Kennedy's holds the field .... It is true that if it were proposed that Kennedy himself should bring it up to date one might be a little nervous ... but I understand that is not the proposal at all. I support the idea very strongly, and I hope the Delegates will take it without any more delay."[235]

A contract was eventually signed, giving the authors £500 pounds instead of royalties, and Stanley wrote in March 1955 that "everything now seems to be in order for us to proceed with the task of preparing the book for publication." But first Gilbert Kennedy had to complete his doctorate for Harvard University and then the following year he was appointed the Deputy Attorney General of British Columbia. By 1961, Oxford concluded that "Kennedy fils has dropped out."[236] W.P.M. Kennedy suggested that Alexander Brady of political economy or Bora Laskin of law could take Gilbert's place. Whether they were ever approached is not known.[237] Nothing further happened with the project. Stanley went on to design the Canadian flag and to become the Lieutenant Governor of New Brunswick. In 1969 he used the material he had prepared for the Kennedy book to publish through Ryerson Press, *A Short History of the Canadian Constitution*.[238]

---

234 Letter, dated March 14, 1952, from Stanley to Oxford University Press, Toronto.
235 Letter dated October 5, 1953 from Wheare to the Secretary of the Board, D.M. Davin.
236 Note in 1961 from Ivon Owen of Oxford Canada to Peter Sutcliffe of Oxford England. Coincidentally, Sutcliffe was my editor for the publication of my thesis, *Double Jeopardy*, by the Clarendon Press, Oxford, in 1969. Another example of the fact that it is a small world is that my research assistant, Steve Ayelward, mentioned in footnote 1 is now clerking for Tom Cromwell, who is George Stanley's son in law and may possibly be able to shed some light on the project. But for the purpose of an "introduction" one has to stop someplace.
237 Possible collaboration with Stanley is not mentioned in Philip Girard's biography of Laskin.
238 (Toronto: Ryerson Press, 1969).

In his preface, Stanley simply notes that a book on constitutional history "has been unavailable ever since W.P.M. Kennedy's *Constitution of Canada* went out of print." Perhaps it is just as well that Stanley published his own book. Stanley favoured the so-called "compact theory of confederation" rather than the "centralist theory" advocated by W.P.M. Kennedy.[239] "Doc Kennedy" might not have been happy with the result.

As previously stated, Kennedy retired as dean in 1949, at age 70. R.C.B Risk states: "After the late 1930s, Kennedy wrote little and after he retired in 1949 he lived quietly until his death in 1963."[240] He was given an honorary degree by the University of Toronto in 1953, having received an honorary degree from the University of Montreal in 1939. The *Globe and Mail* reported a retirement banquet in his honour in the Crystal ballroom of the King Edward Hotel, stating that when he stood to reply after the tributes in his honour, "it was with the wry wit, the undimmed enthusiasm, the youthful idealism that made him famous."[241]

In his book on Bora Laskin, Philip Girard notes that "Caesar Wright, when he ultimately succeeded Kennedy ... would do all he could to exclude Kennedy from the life of the law school and to erase and obscure his place in the collective memory of the institution."[242] Kennedy was almost forgotten until Risk wrote his important article on Kennedy. He died at age 84 on August 12, 1963 in the Toronto General Hospital. The funeral service was at St. Paul's Anglican Church on Bloor Street East, with cremation at St. James the Less Chapel. Donations were directed to the Canadian Cancer Society.[243] His wife Pauline, who moved from 77 Spadina to a later-demolished apartment building, now a University residence, at the south-east corner of St. George and Bloor streets, died at age 71 in 1966. Both are buried at St. Mark's cemetery in Emsdale, near the cottage on Beaver Lake. Their son Frere Kennedy intends to be interred there.

CONCLUSION

The story of Kennedy's career, the writing and possible republication of *The Constitution of Canada*, and the founding of the University of Toronto Law School, illustrate a theme that has run through much of my own writing, that is, the accidental nature of change and the need to understand change

---

239   P. 154.
240   Risk, "The Many Minds," p. 386.
241   *Globe and Mail*, March 18, 1949.
242   Girard, *Bora Laskin*, p. 154.
243   Article and obituary, *Globe and Mail*, August 13, 1963.

in the context of the personalities, politics, and social conditions. One can see this in the development of laws,[244] the outcome of specific cases,[245] and the growth of institutions.[246] Each depends—to some degree—on personalities, politics, and pressure groups, although the mix varies, of course, from situation to situation.

The same is true of constitutional change, as Kennedy showed in *The Constitution of Canada*. In 2017, Canada will be celebrating the 150th anniversary of the passage of the British North America Act 1867. Kennedy's book, published about one third of the way through the intervening years and the change in approach set out in the second edition provide important sign-posts in our understanding of that journey.

And W.P.M. Kennedy? After this further examination of his life and career, I still end up, as I started, by finding him distinguished, engaging, and enigmatic.

---

244 See, for example, the issues of law and morality, gun control and codification of the criminal law, described in chapters 4, 14, and 17, respectively, of my memoirs, *My Life in Crime*.

245 See *The Trials of Israel Lipski* (London: Macmillan, 1984); *The Case of Valentine Shortis* (University of Toronto Press, 1986) and *The Death of Old Man Rice* (New York University Press, 1994).

246 See my University of Toronto History and *A Place Apart: Judicial Independence and Accountability in Canada* (Ottawa: Canadian Judicial Council, 1995).

THE CONSTITUTION OF CANADA

CANADA

An Introduction to its Development and Law

BY

W. P. M. KENNEDY, M.A., Litt.D.

TRINITY COLLEGE, DUBLIN

ASSISTANT PROFESSOR OF MODERN HISTORY IN THE UNIVERSITY OF TORONTO

HUMPHREY MILFORD

OXFORD UNIVERSITY PRESS

LONDON   EDINBURGH   GLASGOW   COPENHAGEN
NEW YORK TORONTO MELBOURNE CAPE TOWN
BOMBAY   CALCUTTA   MADRAS   SHANGHAI

1922

PRINTED IN ENGLAND
AT THE OXFORD UNIVERSITY PRESS
BY FREDERICK HALL

TO

ROBERT MORRISON MACIVER

PREFACE

ANY historical work which attempts to traverse the whole period of a nation's life, even if it be that of a young nation like Canada, must be either an outline of events or a study of development. In this work I have essayed the latter of these, endeavouring to present to my readers neither a description nor an analysis of the political institutions of Canada, but rather an evolutionary account of the various movements and stages which have issued into the organized political life of the Canada of to-day. Canada as a political unity has a distinctive, to some it may seem an anomalous, character. It is well worth studying, both as a recent example of the process of nation-making and as a most significant illustration of that real and yet not absolute sovereignty which defies the older theories of government and thereby leads us to a truer conception of the state. I have sought to unite these two aspects in this work. To understand the former it is necessary to keep the social background always in view, to show how, under the special conditions of a new land, the conjuncture of groups detached from older countries, particularly England and France, the insistent near influence of a great neighbouring country already ahead in economic development, and the later influx of more heterogeneous elements from many lands, with all the meeting and clash of traditions which this implied, have worked in the end to a certain unity and a sure nationhood. To understand the latter it is necessary to observe how the evolution of Canadian government has constituted a decisive challenge to the absolute Austinian doctrine of sovereignty.

This doctrine the very fact of the British Empire, as it has grown into a unity of self-governing peoples, by itself may be said to refute, but nowhere is that refutation so convincing as in the case of the country which names itself a Dominion and yet never hesitates in its allegiance to the mother country and to the Imperial system of which it constitutes a part. Without doubt Canada is a nation, and beyond question Canada owns a sovereignty. The situation creates both new problems and new visions. It is part of the whole world situation which the War emphasized. Absolute sovereignty in the last resort proves to be an illusory but most perilous claim in face of the facts of interdependence. While the civilized world is groping for the solution of the problem thus created, the British Empire is at least adumbrating the form which that solution must take. Canada has a special significance in this development. I have sought to bring out something of that significance in this work, and, particularly in the concluding chapter, have suggested the bearing of the Canadian situation on the whole issue of the interpretation of sovereign power. At any rate the history of Canadian constitutional development must be regarded as one of great moment, being full of achievement which once seemed to lie completely outside the possibilities admitted by time-honoured political theory.

Without attempting to record on every occasion my obligations to historians whose work has passed into the common heritage of history, I have however made every effort both in the foot-notes and in the lists of authorities to acknowledge my sources. The former are more particularly meant for students who may wish to follow the history more closely. The latter are deliberately placed at the end of each chapter, and I have, with special purpose, repeated the full titles of books. Of course, an exhaustive bibliography was out of the question, and I have only attempted to provide a working one to which reference on specific subjects can easily be made.

Finally I should like to hope that this study in Canadian history will be received as at least objective in spirit. I am quite conscious that I may have made interpretations which are incomplete or even invalid, and that I may have over looked material which would alter or modify my conclusions. On the other hand, I have tried to follow the development with as great detachment as possible, and all that I can venture to hope is that I have made a contribution to Canadian history not quite unworthy of its romantic development, its social values, its political import, and of the genuine pleasure which it has given me since my residence in Canada.

It would be impossible for me to acknowledge in detail the generous help which I have received from many friends both in England and in Canada, and I can only ask them to accept this general acknowledgement of their kindness and interest. I owe, however, debts which require more definite payment. To Professor R. M. MacIver, University of Toronto, I am under the greatest obligations, and in the dedication I attempt not merely to acknowledge these, but to record a friendship which lies deeper than a common interest in history would suggest. To Dr. A. G. Doughty and Dr. Adam Shortt I owe a sincere debt. I take this opportunity to place on record my appreciation of the services which they have rendered to historical research through the Dominion Archives and the Historical Manuscript Commission of Canada. I should also like to add that Dr. Doughty has gone far beyond his official duties to help me, and that he has freely placed at my disposal on every occasion not only his own services but those of his assistants. Colonel Fraser, Archivist of Ontario, has given me the greatest assistance, and has directed me to material which has helped to fill in the picture. Professor G. M. Wrong, University of Toronto, has taken an active interest in the book as it was written, and if I have escaped gaucheries into which a writer who is not a Canadian might easily fall, I owe it to him. Mr. W. S. Wallace has given me, especially in the earlier chapters, the benefit of his knowledge of Canadian history. Mr. C. R. Fay, Christ's College, Cambridge, has kindly read my manuscript and has given me many important suggestions. My wife has seen the book through the press and has compiled the index. My last acknowledgement is to the late Professor A. H. F. Lefroy, University of Toronto. For three years before his death he and I worked through carefully the cases in constitutional law while preparing his *Short Treatise on Canadian Constitutional Law* for publication. We discussed their bearing and importance, and in determining the form of his work we mutually agreed on many phrases and generalizations. Almost naturally I have fallen back on these, and I acknowledge my obligations elsewhere. I cannot, however, let this book go to the press without a recognition of Professor Lefroy's insight into Canadian federalism, and of a friendship which was so courteously willing to guide me in a new and difficult field.

W. P. M. KENNEDY.

UNIVERSITY OF TORONTO,
    TORONTO.
        March 18, 1922.

CONTENTS

CONTENTS

CHAPTER I

INTRODUCTION

CANADIAN constitutional development begins in the ages of absolutism and grows down the centuries. We can trace the stream of evolution with comparative ease, and though it is a long journey back to the rock of paternalism which French pioneers struck in the pathless wilderness, yet even to-day in the full flood of liberty it is possible to discern in the mingled waters something of the far-off source. Circumstances now and then changed the direction of the current, and it is quite easy to point to these; but the changes of direction could not prevent the stream from reaching inevitably the ocean of constitutional life. The persistent onflow lends a romantic fascination to Canadian history. In the spheres of political and constitutional liberty, of religious toleration, and of local autonomy within an empire, its course can be followed from point to point. To-day, political thinkers are watching a newer problem arise inexorably out of those already solved—the formal reconciliation of full Canadian citizenship with full citizenship of the British commonwealth.

The government of New France was paternal absolutism. Only during the régime of Frontenac does a momentary gleam of what political philosophy would call liberty appear. Until the fall of Canada, centralized control, bureaucracy, and royal supervision characterized the administration. Nor is there any evidence that the Canadians during this period longed for any share either in central or in local government. Indeed they looked somewhat askance at the English experiments in the colonies to their south, where the constant bickerings, political and ecclesiastical, did not tend to impress an apathetic and simple people with any desire for popular control. The British conquest did not bring to the Canadians any miraculous political conversion, and the somewhat arbitrary rule which continued in Canada to 1791 was as logical for the 'new subjects' as that under the French crown. The change of flags merely substituted, as Burke said, George III for Louis XVI.

In 1791, when Canada received representative institutions such as already existed in Nova Scotia and New Brunswick, the gift was forced by the unforeseen advent of the American Loyalists; and while it conferred on French-Canadians a primary education in political freedom, it withheld the fully developed scheme of responsible government. As a matter of fact, the recognition of what appears nowadays to be the necessary corollary of representative government lay outside the range of contemporary political thought. When responsible government in the modern sense of the term came into practice in 1849, it was not before the colonial office and the imperial government had spent many a bad quarter of an hour over a tantalizing problem of sovereignty, and the Canadians had learned in the hard school of experience, in which rebellions played a part, something of the duties which are the spiritual values of legal forms or constitutional conventions. Indeed, in Canada legal form curtailed the growth of the constitutional convention of cabinet government. The fact that the Act of Union of 1840 gave to Canada East and to Canada West equal representation, irrespective of population, in the united legislature which that Act set up, robbed Lord Elgin's experiment in 1849 of the full and complete implication of self-government. With the coming of federation in 1867, Canada at last obtained the widest application of representative and responsible institutions.

In relation to the growth of religious liberty it is possible to trace a somewhat analogous development. It is true that a few Huguenots came to New France in the experimental stages of French colonial rule, yet as early as 1627 they were excluded by the charter granted in that year to the Company of New France, and this prohibition virtually banished protestants from the colony. Whether this injunction was due to religious intolerance or to the growing belief in the political principle *cuius regio eius religio* or to a blend of both is of little importance. The fact remains that New France after 1627 was developed as a Roman catholic colony with the ecclesiastical machinery of a province immediately subject to the Holy See. After the cession of Canada appearances seemed to point to a reaction in a protestant direction. For a short time it seemed possible that the ' new subjects ' would receive a bare religious toleration. It is not surprising then, considering the letter of the law in England at the time, that there was much searching of hearts over the ambiguous phrase in the peace of Paris of 1763 : 'The new Roman catholic subjects may profess the worship of their religion according to the rites of the Romish church, as far as the laws of Great Britain permit.' The Quebec Act of 1774 was, however, a distinct step forward. It is interesting to find the reactionary group, represented by North, opposing the leading liberals of the day, represented by Burke and Fox, in fathering and carrying through a British parliament in the eighteenth century an act which not only granted to Roman catholics the free exercise of their religion, but also gave powers to the Roman catholic church to collect the customary dues from its members by process of civil law as in the days of the French régime. Legalists, it is true, continued to play with the fact that the freedom was subject to the Elizabethan Act of Supremacy ; but the concession in respect of church dues practically repealed that enactment and endowed the Roman catholic church. On the other hand, it must not be forgotten that the church of England was the established church of the province, and that both before and after 1791 it enjoyed privileges such as no other organized religious body possessed. Its endowment in 1791 by means of the clergy land-reserves produced an agitation which culminated in the loss of its peculiarly privileged position. It may be said that religious toleration is one of the corner-stones of the Canadian constitution.

Since federation in 1867 there have been signs of further growth. Canada has assumed actual control of her military forces and written out into realities the constitutional powers given her in this sphere of national life. The governor-general is now appointed with the full goodwill of the Canadian government, and he can no longer carry out in Canada functions which in England belong only to the crown acting through responsible ministers. Shading across the thin dividing line between constitutional and economic life, the developments are no less remarkable. Indeed, in trade relations they are almost spectacular. During the French régime trade was kept firmly under the thumb of the minister at Paris. With the advent of British rule, Canada came under the economic system perpetuated by the navigation laws. Canadian trade was controlled entirely by the mother country. ' England holds her colonies for the sole purpose of extending her commerce ' was the trite summing up of Hugh Finlay, a Canadian deputy-postmaster of the period. After 1791 the barriers were gradually lowered. Canada was allowed bit by bit to trade with other countries, until the advent of the free-trade school in England brought colonial politics into touch with the principles of *laissez-faire* and finally led to the abolition of the last remnant of the navigation laws in 1849. Canada was not slow to take advantage of the new situation. In 1854 Lord Elgin negotiated a reciprocity treaty with the United States on behalf of Canada, and in 1859 a tariff barrier was actually erected against Great Britain which has continued to the present day. Within recent years Canadian trade autonomy has been conceded. The position of adviser has become one of negotiator. These examples serve to illustrate the beginnings of a wider freedom, until to-day it is recognized, on the one hand, that commercial treaties binding the empire as a whole are hardly possible without consent; and, on the other hand, that a trade treaty can be negotiated by Canada with the cognizance of the imperial government. It is true that grave difficulties have arisen which the Great War prevented from being discussed; but that an advance has been made of considerable importance no one can deny.

The growth of Canadian autonomy has been accompanied by the growth of national feeling. This development gives guarantees to the constitutional advances already made and also postulates future problems for solution. That such a development must come was clear to the fathers of federation. The American Civil War without and the tragic political differences within lent special emphasis to the question of Canadian unity in those pregnant autumn days in 1867, when, under the shadow of party deadlock in Canada and of the neighbouring tragedy of disintegration, political faith made a new venture into the unknown. Canada began with a lesson learned. She avoided, as John Macdonald said, 'the great source of weakness in the United States'—the centrifugal force of 'state rights'. But something more was implicit in the lessons learned from the first great experiment in federal government. They contained the germs of Canadian nationality, national sentiment, national feeling, national loyalty—a fatherland. The citizens of Canada are first of all Canadians and secondly citizens of a particular province. The ideal of national unity to which the constitutional experiment of 1867 gave weight is symbolized in the lines of connecting steel. New provinces have grown up within the federation and have unconsciously accepted a national outlook. Canadians have grasped the significance of Canada, and they went out into the great adventure of war to preserve the inheritance through which their maturity was attained.

To-day, Canada is a distinct national group. A federation, it is true, but with a genius for balancing centrifugal and centripetal forces. Canada possesses all the problems peculiar to a nation; but a nation within an empire. To the future belongs the giving of a constitutional form to this new experience in history. In that further development lies Canada's crown of constitutional self-consciousness.

The aim of this book is to trace the stream of development. The mere retelling of a well-known story lies more or less outside its purpose. It is rather an attempt to find in the facts the complex characters and divers conditions out of which they grew; to seek the causes which gave energy and purpose to the constitutional evolution; to animate dead documents with something of the vital energy which called them into being. It is an attempt to judge by historical standards the gradual expression of a people's political life in constitutional forms and to estimate them in the light of their constructive contribution to human history.

CHAPTER II

THE GOVERNMENT OF NEW FRANCE

WHEN, in the sixteenth and seventeenth centuries, colonial expansion began to interest the nations of northern Europe, the chartered company seemed a practical and economical method of exploitation and of government. The organization of these companies might differ in detail and their relations to the state might vary, but it is not surprising that many colonizing nations made use of them, considering that the state of European finance did not permit a further drain on the national exchequers. The romance of discovery might have remained a mere romance much longer, had not these colonizing states been prepared to incorporate private companies which would bear the risks of opening up new lands. Of course, the monarchs, in return for royal licences, insisted on a share in the gains where such accrued, but the scheme offered a ready solution to a new problem at the smallest cost to the nation, while at the same time it preserved the national authority. France naturally copied her neighbours, and in the French adventure in Canada there was nothing original except the variety of imitation. The earliest French schemes bore analogies to English companies. Later, the Company of New France and the Company of the West Indies were not unlike the chartered trading companies of Holland. It was only after experiment in this method of administration that New France passed under direct royal control, in imitation perhaps of Spain and Portugal.

Before 1627 the student of constitutional history gains little of value from the study of the various charters granted to private individuals and companies. Indeed, from Cartier's taking possession of Canada in 1534 till the advent of Richelieu

in French colonial affairs, the period is largely a blank owing to
the pressure of religious wars on the French government and
people. The emphasis, too, in these early charters obscured
constitutional issues. The powers of government which the
trading monopolies carried with them were wide and far reaching, but the primary interest was exploitation rather than
colonization and constitutional experiment. The concessions
granted in 1540–1 to Cartier's associate are typical.[1] As
the king's lieutenant-general he was given 'full authority and
power'. He could make laws, edicts, statutes, ordinances—
political and otherwise. He could 'create, constitute, establish,
dismiss and remove captains, justiciars, and generally all other
officers as shall seem good to him'; and, according to one
version,[2] he had powers to 'punish either by corporal death or
any other exemplary punishment'. Roberval's patent became
a model, and its influence can be traced in the charters granted to
the companies which down to 1627 carried on such government
as there was in Canada. It was only after the pacification of
France by the Edict of Nantes in 1598 that France resumed her
colonizing efforts. The crowding, however, of six trading and
administrative monopolies into less than thirty years left little
place for constructive government.[3] For the moment the
failure, both economic and constitutional, of these early companies need not be considered; but no analysis, however
minute, of the charters under which they were incorporated
would throw much light on experiments which were so short-
lived. The years are too full of insecurity, of inexperience of
war, and of mistrust. Their history is rather that of trading
posts than of real colonial beginnings.

[1] H. Harisse, *Notes pour servir à l'histoire . . . de la Nouvelle-France*,
pp. 243 ff. (Paris, 1872).

[2] In Harisse this passage is corrupt. See *Collection . . . de Documents relatifs
à l'histoire de la Nouvelle-France*, vol. i, pp. 30 ff. (Quebec, 1883).

[3] The company of Pont-Gravé & Chauvin, 1599; of De Chastes, 1602;
of De Monts, 1603; of Rouen, 1613; of De Caën, 1620; of Montmorency,
1622.

When, in 1624, Richelieu became ' Grand-master, chief and superintendent-general of the commerce and navigation of France ', and thus acquired a controlling influence in French colonial adventure, it was not long before his fertile brain was busy with plans transcending mere private enterprise. Already his romantic imagination had laid the dream-foundations of a French empire in the new world, and soon he was playing with the organization of a huge company which would gather up and control with imposing efficiency all the overseas ventures of France. Practical politics, however, won the day for less cumbersome machinery. Under his guidance several new companies were formed, and in 1627 the destinies of Canada were entrusted to the Company of New France, otherwise known as the Company of One Hundred Associates. The list of shareholders indicates the entrance of the big interests. The smaller traders of the earlier companies are replaced by merchant adventurers of the capital, by noblemen, by officials from the court and public departments with Richelieu at their head. A new era seemed to have dawned. With the provision that half of the twelve controlling members must reside in Paris, of capital adequate for favourable beginnings, of two royal ships each year, and of a large trading monopoly, the Company of New France might well look forward to carrying out its part of the bargain. Even though Huguenots were excluded, it need not have been difficult to bring out a few hundred settlers in 1628 and four thousand before 1643.[1]

The administrative scheme also gave promise of success. No longer was a lieutenant-governor to act as viceroy. New France became part of the feudal territory of the crown, from whom the new company held direct ' en toute propriété, justice et seigneurie '. The actual government was delegated to a governor, nominated by the company and appointed

[1] See the charter in *Édits, Ordonnances Royaux . . . concernant le Canada*, pp. 5 ff. (Quebec, 1854).

triennially by the king. This royal supervision shows the growing importance of colonial expansion ; but the scheme was at first experimental, and the governor was as powerful as the old lieutenant-governors and commandants had been. Indeed, he exercised almost unlimited sovereignty.[1] In 1647 an attempt was made under royal decree to curb his arbitary powers. A council was organized, consisting of the governor, the Jesuit superior in New France, and the governor of Montreal, to whom was granted authority previously exercised by the governor alone. The change, however, did not furnish sufficient guarantee against high-handed action, and in the following year the inhabitants succeeded in getting the council reorganized. To the governor, Jesuit superior (acting until a bishop should arrive), and retiring governor were added from two to three representatives elected conjointly by the other members of the council, and the syndics of Quebec, Montreal, and Three Rivers. This introduced a popular element into the council, since the syndics themselves owed their position to direct popular favour.

The dim light of political freedom did not last long. Owing to a combination of causes, remote and immediate, the whole scheme disappeared in 1663. Among the latter may be included the arrival of Laval as Vicar-apostolic in 1659 with the title Bishop of Petraea *in partibus infidelium*—a triumph for the Jesuits in their unedifying dispute with their new rivals, the Sulpicians. Almost immediately church and state entered into a contest for authority, and petty details of precedure cumber the history of these years. Out of rather small incidents in an age-long struggle, the governor's correspondence awoke the French monarch's interest in the possibilities of development, which was further stimulated by Laval's presence in France. The charter of the Company of New France was taken

---

[1] See, for example, the commission, June 6, 1645, to Montmagny granting him powers, as governor, ' de juger souverainement et en dernier ressort ', *Complément des Ordonnances et Jugements*, pp. 15 ff. (Quebec, 1856).

back into the king's hands and New France became a royal province. The conflict of powers in the colony coincided with Colbert's advent in 1661 as chief minister, and his influence in the councils of Louis XIV soon made itself felt. If his advice is not directly seen in the abolition of the Company of New France, it is certainly clear a year later in colonial affairs.

The new machinery of royal government had scarcely begun work, when Colbert undertook a plan which had been in his mind since the beginning of his régime. Although not officially in charge of colonial interests till 1669, he early conceived the idea of making a magnificent challenge by means of two aggressive corporations to gain for France the *suprématie mondiale* to which the chartered commercial companies of England and Holland already laid proud claim. He aimed to beat them at their own game with similar weapons, and accordingly New France was handed over in 1664 to the new Company of the West Indies and remained under its control until 1674. The company was modelled on the Dutch West India Company, and it began its work with almost sovereign powers, backed with large finances and personally supported by the king and Colbert. However, its influence on the government of Canada was practically unimportant, and for the purposes of this study the period of royal government may be dated from 1663.

Within less than a century eight chartered companies had administered the affairs of Canada. The first and most obvious impression which they make is that of their brief duration and the witness which it bears to failure. It may well be asked what causes lay behind. Perhaps the clearest is the lack of consistency in policy, and of stability in purpose. While the companies received amazing powers, the very width of the grants guaranteed royal influence. Monopolies and sovereign authority made demands on their funds for religion, for exploitation, for administration, for justice, for war, and not infrequently to buy

the royal ear or to close it against the jealous whispers of would-
be rivals.   But there were deeper reasons for failure.   In not
a single instance did any chartered company keep its part of the
bargain in bringing out the stipulated number of colonists on
which its monopoly was founded.   It may be true that the
Jesuits did not want colonists and that a voluntary supply was
cut off by the exclusion of the Huguenots.   On the other hand,
such a company as that of New France carried on an exceedingly
profitable trade, while concealing the real resources of the
country and discouraging serious settlers.[1]   The great developments of the period were in the religious sphere, but these
failed to convince Louis XIV and Colbert that the imperial
idea was being realized.   The need for a more stable policy
and for more serious colonizing effort became at last apparent, if
France intended to become a serious rival in the new world.
After one final and futile experiment with a chartered company,
France turned almost instinctively to its own provincial system,
and proceeded to apply to New France the traditional organization of a French province—an organization which lasted till
the fall of Canada a century later.

When allowance is made for lack of uniformity, it is broadly
true to say that the majority of French provinces were administered by a governor, an intendant, and a bishop, with a
parlement or a sovereign council.   As the centralized state
developed and gathered strength, the wide powers granted to
the provincial governors were curtailed.   Indeed, the office of
intendant originated in a desire to curb their influence and
authority.   So successful was the experiment, that the intendant
soon left to the governor merely the ceremonial trappings of
control.   The provincial bishops and their place in the plan

---

[1] Consult an estimate of settlers from 1608 to 1645 by M. Benjamin Sulte in
Transactions of Royal Society of Canada (2nd series, vol. xi, sect. ii), pp. 99 ff. ;
and from 1632 to 1666 in ' Report on the Ethnological Survey of Canada ' by the
same author (*British Association for the Advancement of Science, Report*, 1900,
pp. 470 ff.).

Discover it all in Wainfleet Village

Labour Day Weekend

FREE Shuttle Service on site

ATM on site

NO PETS allowed

Admission $6.00 / person. FREE Parking.
Children under 10 FREE.
Saturday Only: Seniors (65+) $5.00/ person

Hours: 10:00 a.m. to 5:00 p.m.

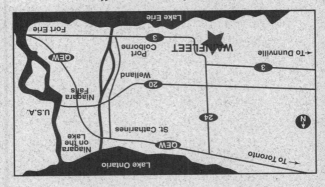

For Information call

905-899-9995

www.marshvilleheritagefestival.ca

Visit Wainfleet Village

Labour Day Weekend

Marshville Heritage Society Inc.
Presents

MARSHVILLE

Heritage Festival

Art and Craft Show and Sale

Featuring high quality handcrafted
merchandise by over 130 Juried
Artisans from Ontario.

An annual event sponsored & operated by
Marshville Heritage Society Inc.

represented the peculiar relationship between church and state in France. The *parlements* and sovereign councils acted in judicial capacities, and where the latter existed, they possessed spheres of authority which elsewhere belonged to the intendant alone. The divisions, however, which the tripartite nomenclature suggests were by no means mutually exclusive. The scheme was rather one of overlapping and of dove-tailing, in which no element should become too powerful and each should act in dependence on the others. It was a characteristic product of highly organized bureaucracy.

The transition from government by a chartered company to government as a royal province was easily accomplished in New France, as much of the machinery lay ready at hand. A governor and bishop were already in the colony and the council of 1648 could easily be reconstructed as a sovereign council. The new instrument of government—*Édit de Création du Conseil Souverain*—was issued in April 1663.[1] A sovereign council was created consisting of the governor, the bishop, five councillors, an attorney-general and secretary.[2] Any vestige of popular control disappeared, vacancies being filled by the governor and bishop jointly, and later by the king alone. The *Édit de Création* is silent about an intendant, though one was appointed in 1663. Talon, the first to hold the office in New France, did not arrive till 1665.

The workings of the system differed almost necessarily from that in France. Distance from the central authority and the unknown vastness of a new country combined, to the end, to militate against complete similarity. At first, with untamed Indians ready to wipe out the little colony and with the English to the south full of suspicions and ready to take offence, the governor gained much power owing to his military office. The bishop, too, began with experience in the country, and this fact

---

[1] *Édits, Ordonnances Royaux . . .* , vol. i, pp. 37 ff.
[2] The councillors were increased to seven in 1674 and to eleven in 1703.

gave him an initial influence which his missionary character confirmed. He was not bound down by the well-organized details of a complete diocesan life. Conflicting orders from France did not tend to simplify procedure or to encourage the development of similar provincial administration. Indeed, strong personalities alone made up later for the difficulties created in government through the lack of an intimate knowledge of colonial affairs by officials and ministers in France.

The governor was the king's personal representative and commander-in-chief of the forces of the crown within the province. Up to 1674 he was president of the sovereign council. Ousted by the intendant, with royal approval, his influence declined to that of a powerful councillor. On the other hand, governors like Frontenac and Beauharnois, relying not only on their military office but on those conditions which left room for the play of strong personality, could carry out high-handed actions, which, however, always incurred the risk of royal displeasure unless the circumstances could be used to prove the necessity of abnormal proceedings. The intendant was in the most real sense 'the royal man'—the personification of the king's authority. As a general rule, his influence was irresistible. Always in close personal communication with the minister, he passed, from being at first a spy on governor and bishop, to a position of the widest authority, to which his theoretical third place in colonial precedence made little difference. Up and down the province, his activities touched every phase of colonial life. At one time he is settling seigniorial disputes, at another giving judgement in some commercial or criminal case. And it was quick and ready justice. 'Everybody pleads his own cause', wrote La Hontan, ' our Themis is prompt, and she does not bristle with fees, costs and charges.' At another he is busy with public health, with roads and bridges, with Sunday observance, with offensive chimneys, with breaches of rules on the frozen streets of Quebec, or with new immigrants. On

almost every conceivable affair he issued regulations which as
a rule carried with them force and authority. In the finances
of the colony, in taxation, and expenditure he was practically
supreme. To help him in his multifarious work, he called in
local organization.[1] For the dispensation of justice the province was divided into three districts—Quebec, Montreal,
Three Rivers—in each of which was a court of first instance.
The administrative unit was the ecclesiastical parish, where the
intendant employed the captains of militia as his local representatives. They promulgated his edicts and judgements. It is
a singular testimony to the moral calibre of the thirteen men
who actually filled the office in New France that, with one or
two exceptions, they bore with honesty and clean dealing the
no light burden of colonial administration. In the routine
of government, with a strong governor or a strong intendant,
the bishop's public and official influence gradually declined, and
his attendance at the council became less and less regular.
But as bishop of Quebec he held no empty title. In 1703 he
obtained the right of having a deputy on the sovereign council,
and no affairs of importance passed without careful ecclesiastical
scrutiny. As often as not, where business interests were liable
to overshadow moral issues, his authority could read lessons to
the civil officials. Indeed, the colony always remained in many
respects a theocracy, in which the church's power, manifest
in episcopal office, never could have become merely spiritual.
Cartier's huge cross with the fleur-de-lis standing on the shores
of Gaspé was a symbol of New France.

The sovereign council had powers as a court of registration
and justice as well as in financial administration and legislation.
The latter power, as we have seen, passed largely to the intendant. Its change of name in 1674 from sovereign council to

[1] For an excellent survey of local administration see P.-G. Roy, ' Les
officiers d'état-major des gouvernements de Québec, Montréal, et Trois-
Rivières sous le régime français ' (*La Revue Canadienne*, 1917).

superior council bore witness to the gradual loss of much of its authority. To the end its judicial powers remained ; but even here much of its actual work passed to the king or to the intendant. When Canada fell the superior council possessed little of the authority which had been granted to it under the *Édit de Création.*

The note which runs strong through the whole royal organization is one of paternalism. For one moment, in 1672, Frontenac attempted a change, perhaps as part of his challenge to consolidate the civil power against the church. He called at Quebec an assembly of clergy, nobles, and the third estate—the States General of New France. The outcome was a severe official dispatch from Colbert : ' Your assembling of the inhabitants of the country to take the oath of fealty and your division of them into three orders or estates may have had a good effect for the moment ; but it is well that you should observe that you are always to follow in the government and administration of this country the forms in use here ; and, since our kings have long regarded it as for the good of their service not to call together the States General of the kingdom, in order perhaps to abolish insensibly that ancient institution, you on your part should very rarely, or to speak more correctly, never, give this corporate form to the inhabitants of the said country. You should even, as the colony grows stronger, suppress insensibly the office of syndic, who presents petitions in the name of the inhabitants ; for it is well that each should speak for himself and no one for all.' [1]

---

[1] ' L'assemblée et la division que vous avés faite de tous les habitants du pais en trois Ordres ou Etats pour leur faire prêter le serment de fidelité pouvoit produire un bon effet dans ce moment-là, mais il est bon que vous observiés que comme vous devés toujours suivre dans le gouvernement et la conduite de ce pais-là les formes qui se pratiquent ici, et que nos Rois ont estimé du bien de leur service depuis longtemps de ne point assembler les Etats Généraux de leur Roiaume pour peut-être anéantir insensiblement cette forme ancienne ; vous ne devés aussi donner que très rarement, et pour mieux dire jamais, cette forme au corps des habitans dudit pais, et il faudra

The dispatch throws an intimate light on the principles of government. After 1674 the king resumed much of the power originally granted. He made all the chief appointments, and his ministers were not above correspondence with the lesser colonial officials. He became a court for direct appeals. Even minor details, such as ordering to a convent an indiscreet colonial widow, came within his supervision and could command his attention. Regular reports reached him personally in which characters were pulled to pieces in terms of bitter rivalry, and by these the king regulated his frown or smile. The administration was meticulous in its royal supervision, and it was assuredly no ignorance of colonial dispatches that lost New France. An estimate, however, cannot be made before some consideration is given to the seigniorial system.

[AUTHORITIES.—The important documents are in : *Collection . . . de Documents . . . relatifs . . . à la Nouvelle-France* (4 vols., Quebec, 1883–5) ; *Édits, Ordonnances Royaux . . . concernant le Canada* (Quebec, 1854) ; *Complément des Ordonnances et Jugements* (Quebec, 1856) ; *Arrêts et Règlements du Conseil Supérieur de Québec, et Ordonnances et Jugements des Intendants du Canada* (Quebec, 1855) ; *Jugements et Délibérations du Conseil Souverain de la Nouvelle-France* (4 vols., Quebec, 1885–8) ; *Jugements et Délibérations du Conseil Supérieur de Québec* (2 vols., Quebec, 1889–91) ; *Correspondance Générale*, and the *Collection Moreau St. Méry* in the Canadian Archives ; *Ordonnances des Intendants* (4 vols., Archives de Québec, 1919) ; *Insinuations du Conseil Souverain* (Archives de Québec, 1921). The early trading charters are discussed in H. P. Biggar, *The Early Trading Companies of New France* (Toronto, 1901). The best general discussions of early colonial policy are in É. Salone, *La Colonisation de la Nouvelle-France* (Paris, 1906), and J. Chailley-Bert, *Les Compagnies de Colonisation sous l'ancien régime* (Paris, 1898). Special studies are M. Eastman, *Church and State in Early Canada* (Edinburgh, 1915) ; W. B. Munro, ' The Office of Intendant in New France ' (*American Historical Review*, October 1906) ; R. D. Cahall, *The Sovereign Council of New France* (Columbia University Studies, 1915) ; J.-Edmond Roy, *L'Ancien Barreau au Canada* (Montreal, 1897) ; G. Doutre and E. Lareau, *Le Droit Civil Canadien* (Montreal, 1872). Valuable information is contained in the Reports of Murray, Burton, and Gage (1762), printed in A. Shortt and A. G. Doughty,

même avec un peu de tems, et lorsque la Colonie sera encore plus forte qu'elle n'est, supprimer insensiblement le sindic qui présente des requestes au nom de tous les habitans, étant bon que chacun parle pour soi et que personne ne parle pour tous ': Colbert to Frontenac, June 13, 1673, *Collection Moreau St. Méry*, 1670–6, Série F, vol. 178, p. 208.

Documents relating to the Constitutional History of Canada, 1759–1791, pp. 47 ff. (Ottawa, 1918).   F. Parkman, *The Old Régime in Canada*, and A. Shortt and A. G. Doughty (editors), *Canada and its Provinces*, vols. i and ii, have been used throughout. The last work, in 23 volumes, is here generally acknowledged for the whole of this book, as well as L. J. Burpee and A. G. Doughty, *The Makers of Canada : Index and Dictionary of Canadian History* (Toronto, 1911).]

CHAPTER III

THE SEIGNIORIAL SYSTEM IN NEW FRANCE

Every charter which accompanied a trade monopoly included powers to create seigniories in New France, but with the early failures in colonization the creations were comparatively few. It was only after the colony had passed under royal control in 1663 that the seigniorial system became a reality. The main credit is due to the intendant Talon, whose vigorous immigration policy from 1665 to 1672 laid the foundations of an almost inconceivable advance, when the régime of the chartered companies is recalled. Such episodes as the disbanding of the Carignan-Salières regiment and the granting of seigniories to its officers helped the policy, to which the king and intendant devoted time, energy, and money. When Gédéon de Catalogne made his report in 1712 on the seigniories of Quebec, Three Rivers, and Montreal, he found that several million acres had been granted, of which, however, only fifty thousand were under cultivation.[1] Various tenures characterized the system. Analogous to free and common socage were those known as *en franc aleu noble* and *en franc aleu roturier*, the former carrying with it a patent of nobility. Corresponding to frankalmoign was that of *en franche aumône*, under which religious foundations obtained large grants. The most common tenures, however, were *en fief* or *en seigneurie, en arrière-fief*, and *en censive* or *en roture*.

The seignior held direct from the crown, *en fief* or *en seigneurie*, taking an oath of fealty or homage at the castle of St. Louis in Quebec. He bound himself to perform military service, to

---

[1] Printed in W. B. Munro, *Documents relating to the Seigniorial Tenure in Canada* (Toronto, 1908), and in the *Bulletin des Recherches Historiques*, 1915.

provide a map and census of his lands, to pay a relief [1] when the seigniory passed into other hands except by direct succession, and after 1711, to sub-infeudate his seigniory on pain of forfeiture [2]—an obligation peculiar to Canada and one which did much towards populating the seigniories. Grants *en arrière-fief* or in sub-seigniory were few in Canada, as the seignior preferred to grant his lands *en censive* or *en roture*. This tenure, which was invariably ignoble, governed the holdings of the censitaire or *habitant*. He was obliged to pay annually to his seignior *cens et rentes* : nominal money-payments or payments in kind or both, according to the terms of the grant. The *corvée* called him to work a stipulated number of days each year, but this he could commute for a money payment. He owed to his seignior *lods et ventes*, corresponding to the relief of seigniorial tenure and governed by the same rules, except that the amount was only a twelfth of the mutation price. In addition, he came under certain obligations governed by the *droit de banalité*, and the seignior could compel him to make use of the seigniorial grist-mill and bake-oven at a stipulated price. As a matter of fact, the seigniors were lax in providing mills, and the banality in connexion with ovens appears to have been exercised in only one instance.[3] As often as not it was the censitaires who appealed to the governor and council for the protection of their rights under the *droit de banalité*.

Judicial powers did not necessarily accompany every seigniorial grant. The *droit de justice*, while it appears usually to have been conferred, was an expressly given right. As a general rule, the seignior possessed high, low, and middle jurisdiction— *haute, moyenne et basse justice*—the extent of his jurisdiction

---

[1] The relief was also known as ' the quint ', as it amounted to one-fifth of the mutation price of the seigniory.

[2] *Édits, Ordonnances Royaux . . .* , pp. 324 ff. (Quebec, 1854).

[3] W. B. Munro, ' The " Droit de Banalité " during the French Régime in Canada,' *Annual Report of the American Historical Association*, 1899, vol. i, pp. 207 ff.

had no relation to the area of his seigniory. A grant of *haute justice* covered all criminal cases except against the person and property of the crown, and it included punishment by death or mutilation. In civil cases it was all-embracing. *Moyenne justice* included lesser criminal and civil cases, and *basse justice* covered all petty cases. Theoretically these rights were great, in practice they were hardly a severe burden. There is no recorded instance of the death penalty being imposed, and most of the seigniors were content to let the royal courts exercise all *haute justice*. The seigniorial courts usually confined their activities to disputes over land and titles and to the many local bickerings. Indeed, there was little encouragement for the seignior outside a desire for power to hold courts.

It is something of a surprise that a system which was honey-combed with decay in seventeenth-century France should be introduced into a new country and have continued there for more than two centuries. The seigniors of France had ceased to carry out their obligations. The court of an all-powerful sovereign was more attractive than provincial life, and too often the absentee landlord's only interest in his seigniory lay in the hard-wrung remittances from his bailiff. In Canada conditions allowed the revival of the system in its primitive freshness, and when we recollect the essence of feudalism, its introduction need cause little surprise. The military protection which it afforded was very useful to the little colony against Indians and English, while the simple social life provided opportunity for many of the best sides of seigniorialism to flourish. There the seignior lived in close touch with his people—their leader and protector in battle, their supporter and patron in peace. His privileges were not troublesome, and the general customs of life and work in New France were not corrupted by the class hatred of centuries. It is not too much to say that the introduction of the seigniorial system gave to New France its most enduring element. It was a source of strength for every colonizing

scheme. In some degree it took the place of municipal institutions, and it gave the colony a military organization much
superior to anything which the Thirteen Colonies possessed.

Autres temps, autres mœurs. With the fall of Canada and the
gradual elimination of paternalism the system finally became
an anachronism. Sentimental attachment alone can explain
its survival till 1854, when seigniorial tenures were converted
by the parliament of Canada into a general tenure *en franc aleu
roturier,* free from all feudal service.[1] From the constitutional
point of view the system thus disappeared from Canadian
history ; but relics of it linger, as many of the *habitants* did not
take advantage of the legislation of 1854 to compensate their
seignior by a lump sum, and the terms ' rentes constituées ' and
' seigniors ' can still be heard in the language of modern Quebec.

The system of French colonization was defective in theory
and practice. We are forced to make use of the threadbare
comparison between French and British methods, as it still
remains the best illustration. Both nations employed companies to advance their colonial enterprises, but the inherent
difficulty with those French companies which had any pretence
to reality was their dependence on the state. They thus lacked
the creative initiative of the British type, and they were too easily
made and unmade. Time, so necessary in colonization, waited
on political and royal caprice. Even when as a royal province
New France was most successful, it was an attempt to set up in
Canada the old régime. It derived its life from above. Its
vitality depended not on roots in the native soil, but on the
benevolence of a distant despotism. Everything was organized
on a system of perpetual political tutelage. Britain, on the
other hand, cared for nothing outside commerce, and soon the
unhampered colonists outstripped the motherland in political
thinking, in independence of outlook, and in the conception of
liberty. Thus, on the one side lie political apathy, indifference

---

[1] 18 Victoria, c. 3.

to citizenship—a paternal theocracy where everything was done *for* the colonists, not *by* them ; on the other, the keenest interest in the theory of government, ' a fierce democracy ', as it has been described, a belief in popular consent, a general political self-reliance, a wide flourishing through neglect. What New France gained as a unit was lost in lack of initiative, and what New England lost as a unit was recovered by those lasting qualities which lie behind and postulate development. The lack of initiative in New France killed its political unity for practical purposes, and Montcalm could tell a sorry enough tale of the closing scenes. New England's possession of initiative made up finally for the lack of unity and brought that unity as a certain development in the necessary hours of New England's history. Without disparaging the statesmanship of Chatham, the brilliant combination of Saunders and Wolfe, the more brilliant military achievements of Amherst, and the heroic defenders of the colony, the failure of New France lay deep in the nature of things, independent of the devious ways of diplomacy or of the caprice of the god of battles. The idyllic dream settlements along the St. Lawrence were not made of the stuff for endurance in a new continent, where the vigorous group-life of Anglo-Saxon pioneers was preparing lessons in political experiment destined to change the civilized world.

It may be asked, then, Why trouble to survey the constitutional history of New France ? Is it not wasted energy to study a system so lacking in permanence ? A moment's thought, however, will show that it is impossible to understand Canadian constitutional development without some such survey. The complete answer will appear running through the history ; but it may be well to note here that every important landmark in Canadian history bears marks of New France. Indeed, there are few other cases in the world's history where a conquered people have left, within such a short period, so many permanent impressions on the government set up by their conquerors. An isolated institution such as the shire-court may survive and prove of extraordinary importance in constitutional development ; but we no longer seek the origins of our greatest constitutional principles or institutions in Anglo-Saxon history. At every step in modern Canada we are forced inevitably back to that romantic failure which in reality triumphed on the Heights of Abraham.

[AUTHORITIES.—The most complete work on the seigniorial system has been done by Professor W. B. Munro in *The Seigniorial System in Canada : a Study in French Colonial Policy* (New York, 1907) ; *Documents relating to the Seigniorial Tenure in Canada* (Toronto, 1908) ; ' The Seigneurial System ' in *Canada and its Provinces*, vol. ii, pp. 531 ff., with an excellent bibliography in vol. xxiii, pp. 239 ff. The workings of the system can be followed in J.-Edmond Roy, *Histoire de la Seigneurie de Lauzon* (6 vols., Montreal, 1897–1907) ; M. Benjamin Sulte provides records and ordinances in ' Le Moulin Banal ' in his *Mélanges Historiques*, vol. v (Montreal, 1920).]

CHAPTER IV

THE 'RÉGIME MILITAIRE', 1759–64

FRENCH colonial possessions on the North American continent only gradually passed under the British flag [1] and the introduction of British institutions was equally gradual. It is best to postpone the constitutional history of those possessions, known in British history as the Maritime Provinces, as it fits in with the general discussion of representative and responsible government, and to continue the history under British rule of the settlements along the valley of the St. Lawrence. After the fall of Quebec in 1759, delay over the final peace made a period of military rule inevitable.[2] This period, known in Canadian history as the 'régime militaire', did not leave permanent marks on the development, but it is important that it should be considered for several reasons. Round this earliest point of contact between British officers and Canadian civilians has gathered an unfortunate tradition which needs examination. The actual history has become somewhat obscured and requires disentangling. Finally, within these years sprang up a friendship between the military chiefs and the French-Canadians which cannot be overlooked in the background of evolution.

In 1759 General Monckton, who had assumed command of the forces at Quebec, was granted leave on account of his

[1] Nova Scotia in 1713, Cape Breton in 1758, Citadel and district of Quebec in 1759, the remaining French possessions in 1760.

[2] Military rule lasted from September 18, 1759, to the establishment of civil government, August 10, 1764. The peace of Paris was signed February 10, 1763, but the introduction of civil government was delayed, because the terms of the peace allowed eighteen months to any Canadians who might wish to leave the country.

wounds, and he appointed the next senior brigadier, James Murray, military governor of Quebec, with Colonel Burton as lieutenant-governor, until the king's pleasure should be known.[1] As soon, however, as Montreal capitulated, General Amherst issued a ' placard ' appointing Colonel Burton governor of the administrative district of Three Rivers, and General Gage governor of the administrative district of Montreal.[2] The arrangements of Monckton and Amherst thus continued the three French divisions of government. Murray had already begun his work and made his plans for the district of Quebec, and he was not bound by Amherst's instructions to Burton and Gage. The date and source of his appointment produced in Quebec a type of military rule quite different from that in Three Rivers and Montreal.

While Murray was penned within the ramparts of Quebec in the months following Wolfe's victory, he appointed one of his officers, Colonel Young, to act as judge in civil and criminal cases within the city and its environs. A little later, on January 16, 1760, he extended the administrative machinery by appointing a seignior, Jacques Allier, civil and criminal judge ' for the well-being and profit of the inhabitants of the parish of Berthier and those lying beyond as far as Kamouraska inclusive '.[3] In the following October he issued an ordinance establishing a system of military courts.[4] For criminal and the more important civil cases, as well as for petitions and requests, the governor held a court every Tuesday. Here he might act summarily, or he might refer such cases as he thought fit to the ' military council ' or ' council of war ' which assembled

---

[1] Murray to Pitt, October 8, 1759 (A. and W. I., vol. lxxxviii) ; John Knox, *An Historical Journal of the Campaigns in North America for the years 1757–1760*, vol. ii, p. 241 (ed. A. G. Doughty, 3 vols., Toronto, 1914–16).

[2] Placard from his Excellency General Amherst, September 22, 1760, A. Shortt and A. G. Doughty, *Documents relating to the Constitutional History of Canada, 1759–1791*, pp. 40 ff. (Ottawa, 1918).

[3] *Ibid.*, p. 37.   [4] *Ibid.*, pp. 44 ff.

bi-weekly. All minor cases were left for trial ' to the com-
mandant of the troops in each locality ', subject to appeal
' to the military council if the case pertains thereto and there
is reason for it '. Within the district of Quebec the administration of justice thus passed into the hands of British officers.

In Three Rivers and Montreal other arrangements were
made. When Amherst organized these administrations, he
set up courts of first instance composed of French-Canadian
militia officers, who were as far as possible to settle amicably
all disputes and differences and to execute justice. Cases in
which an immediate decision was not possible were to go before
the officer commanding the troops in the district. Serious
cases and all appeals were to be dealt with by the governor.[1]
Amherst's instructions to Burton and Gage illustrate his plan
and show the spirit in which he acted : ' Take upon you the
administration of the whole, governing the same, until the
king's pleasure shall be known, according to the military laws,
if you should find it necessary ; but I should choose that the
inhabitants, whenever any differences arise between them,
were suffered to settle them among themselves agreeable to
their own laws and customs.' [2]

In October 1761 Gage reorganized the administration of his
government, dividing it into five districts with ' a chamber of
justice ' in each, composed of French-Canadian militia officers
presided over by a captain. The court sat fortnightly for civil
and criminal cases, and had powers to inflict corporal punish-
ments, to imprison, or to fine. The more serious cases, such as
felony or murder, were sent to trial before British courts
martial, which sat monthly for each group of two subdivisions.
All decisions were subject to the approval of the governor,
who might lessen or excuse the punishment, but might not

[1] *Ibid.*, pp. 40 ff.
[2] Amherst to Burton, Camp of Montreal, September 16, 1760. *Colonial
Office Records*, M. 216, pp. 250 ff. (Canadian Archives).

increase it.[1]   In the following year Haldimand, who had
succeeded Burton at Three Rivers, organized a similar scheme.
Conditions are well illustrated by the fact that a proclamation
suspended the ordinary administration of justice from August 7
to September 15, in order that those in charge might attend to
their duties on the farms.[2]

When an estimate is made of the ' régime militaire ', it is
possible to accept the statement of a modern French-Canadian
historian : ' the archives prove that the military régime,
instead of being capricious and harsh, was gentle and paternal.'[3]
We can afford to neglect the sweeping attacks on the period
and such statements as that the Canadians ' spurned the booted
and spurred legalists placed among them ', preferring to settle
their disputes before the priests.   The animosities of later years
have unfortunately coloured the history of this period.[4]   As
a matter of fact there was plenty of law ; Murray noted the
general ' litigious disposition ' of the people,[5] and Haldimand
complained that his captains of militia were worried by the
extraordinary love for litigation and by the incompetence of
Canadian lawyers.[6]

Leaving out of consideration the private manuscripts of the
period, we find from the official documents of the time that
the predominating administrative aim was conciliation through
equity in a mixed régime of martial and French civil law.
This spirit went so far that British officers used the French
language in speech and writing when they desired to communicate with this downtrodden people ![7]   Gage himself bore

[1] G. Doutre and E. Lareau, *Le Droit Civil Canadien*, pp. 503 ff. (Montreal,
1872).   [2] *Ibid.*, p. 533.
[3] J.-Edmond Roy, *L'Ancien Barreau au Canada*, p. 70 (Montreal, 1897).
[4] ' Les Canadiens repoussèrent les juges éperonnés ', &c., F. X. Garneau,
Histoire du Canada, vol. ii, pp. 372 ff. (Québec, 1852).
[5] Shortt and Doughty, *op. cit.*, p. 53.
[6] Haldimand to Amherst, June 22, 1762, *Haldimand Papers*, B. 1, 192
(Canadian Archives).
[7] See the documents quoted and commented on in M. B. Sulte, ' Le Régime

witness to the policy. It was with high satisfaction that he
reported that during his command he had made it his constant
care and attention to see that ' the Canadians should be treated
agreeable to his majesty's kind and humane intentions. No
invasion on their properties or insult on their persons have gone
unpunished. All reproaches on their subjection by the fate of
arms, revilings on their customs or country, and all reflections
on their religion have been discountenanced and forbid. No
distinction has been made betwixt the Briton and Canadian,
but equally regarded as subjects of the same prince. The
soldiers live peaceably with the inhabitants and they reciprocally
acquire an affection for each other.' [1] Murray recorded that
even those who were deceived by ' the many arrant falsehoods
and atrocious lies ' of interested persons were won over by the
' lenity, the impartial justice that has been administered '.
The general feeling between the soldiers and the inhabitants
was one of ' harmony unexampled at home '. When war and
famine had fallen hard on the people, British officers of every
rank subscribed largely for relief, and private soldiers ' threw
in their mite or gave a day's provisions or a day's pay in the
month '.[2] He flattered himself that no military government
was ever better conducted than his had been, and that he had
gained the affection and gratitude of the Canadians,[3] who
themselves acknowledged that Murray and his military council
administered to them ' all the justice that we could have
expected from the most enlightened jurists '.[4] The seigniors
declared their love for Murray as the ' father ' and ' protector '
of the people. They praised his charity, wise decisions, and

Militaire, 1760–1764' (*Proceedings and Transactions, Royal Society of Canada*,
2nd series, vol. xi, pp. xxvii ff.).
 [1] Gage to Amherst, March 20, 1762, Shortt and Doughty, *op. cit.*, pp. 91 ff.
 [2] Murray to Amherst, June 5, 1762, *ibid.*, p. 80.
 [3] *Letter Book of General Murray*, vol. i, January 26, 1764 (Canadian
Archives).
 [4] Shortt and Doughty, *op. cit.*, p. 227.

mildness of administration, resulting in a tranquillity which almost made them forget their mother country.[1]

If there existed material for trouble, it lay in two spheres, that of religion, where freedom was at issue, and that of finance, where bills of exchange created difficulties.[2] When the colony was invaded by the British, the church thundered against the heretics and schismatics. The fall of Montreal brought an official change, but the *curés* obeyed the letter and not the spirit of the episcopal orders. There was a general suspicion lest the freedom of religion granted at the capitulations would be changed.[3] Murray noted the importance of the problem, and Gage analysed the state of mind with astute criticism. A working arrangement with France over the thousands of bills of exchange which had been issued by the French officials to pay for the army, removed to a large extent one source of dissatisfaction ; but from the days of the ' régime militaire ' the fears with regard to religion never entirely disappeared. It is significant that when, in days to come, French-Canadian patriotism, strengthened by racial and political trouble within and revolutions without, sought concrete expression in propaganda, religion was not entirely forgotten, though guarded and guaranteed by Act of parliament.

The ' régime militaire ' need cause no regrets to the conquerors. It compared more than favourably with French rule in the Palatinate and along the banks of the Rhine and with the lot of the Acadians. For the conquered it brought a long-desired peace, an opportunity to resent attempts at seigniorial arrogance and ' to dispute the tithes with the *curés* '. Military rule, just and equitable, made little difference to a people who had no abstract idea of patriotism. The truth is that both in

[1] *Canadian Archives Report*, 1888, pp. 19 ff.

[2] Cf. Gage to Egremont, February 12, 1763, and Murray to Halifax, October 23, 1763, *State Papers*, Q. 1, pp. 64, 250 (Canadian Archives).

[3] Kennedy, *Documents of the Canadian Constitution, 1759–1915*, pp. 6, 10 (Oxford, 1918).

Canada and in France, on the eve of the peace of Paris, there were no regrets. Voltaire's plans with Choiseul and Mme de Pompadour to force the abandonment of the colony, and his luxurious celebration of the fact in his château at Ferney, reflected the general French attitude.[1] In Canada the *habitants* at the hour of their abandonment found in British officers kindly step-fathers ; and with looks hálf turned across the Atlantic and half turned to the kindly conquerors, they accepted a decision of the sword which was tempered with uniform consideration and humanity.

[AUTHORITIES.—The most important documents are in A. Shortt and A. G. Doughty, *Documents relating to the Constitutional History of Canada, 1759–1791* (Ottawa, 1918) ; in the *Haldimand Papers* and the *State Papers*, Q. 1–Q. 2 (Canadian Archives) ; in Doutre and Lareau, *Le Droit Civil Canadien* (Montréal, 1872). Interesting sidelights are found in the *Letter Books of General Murray* (Canadian Archives). The main authority for the period is *Règne Militaire en Canada . . . du 8 septembre 1760 au 10 août 1764* (Mémoire de la Société historique de Montréal, No. 5, Montréal, 1870). Miss J. N. McIlwraith's *Sir Frederick Haldimand* (Toronto, 1904) contains valuable material from the *Haldimand Papers*.]

[1] See a valuable note in F. X. Garneau, *Histoire du Canada*, vol. ii, app. i, pp. 719 ff. (cinquième edition, Paris, 1920).

CHAPTER V

THE ESTABLISHMENT OF CIVIL GOVERNMENT IN QUEBEC

THE far-flung Seven Years War at last reached an official end with the signing of the peace of Paris, February 10, 1763, and all the French possessions in North America, except the islands of St. Pierre and Miquelon, were ceded to Great Britain. During the negotiations Canada was weighed in the balance against Guadeloupe, so little were its possibilities understood.[1] To contemporary eyes it was ' a place fit only to send exiles to, as a punishment for their past ill-spent lives '.[2] Great Britain, however, felt the necessity of relieving the Thirteen Colonies from the French menace which had irritated them so long, and Canada passed to the British crown. Apart from this deciding issue, Canada was a mere detail in an unsolved problem in which predominated vast unsettled lands, Indian trade, and European settlements outside organized administration.

When the British government began to turn its attention ' to the establishment of civil government in the territories ceded by the treaty ', the efforts made to disentangle the various difficulties were neither clear nor definite. At first, care was mostly directed to the affairs of settlement and of the Indians, and a proclamation was planned dealing with these matters. Later, provisions were introduced into the pro-clamation creating and defining four distinct and separate governments—Quebec, East and West Florida, and the island of Grenada—but to each was granted an identically vague

[1] See an interesting discussion of contemporary opinion in W. L. Grant, ' Canada *versus* Guadeloupe : an Episode of the Seven Years War ' (*American Historical Review*, July 1912, pp. 735 ff.).

[2] *General Murray's Correspondence*, bundle viii (Canadian Archives).

system of law and administration, without the slightest attention being paid to differences in development, population, and political experience. The royal proclamation of October 7, 1763, gave Quebec its first civil government under British rule.[1] The ambiguous terms of the grant and the fact that they were due to an after-thought illustrate the initial casual interest in the administration of the province. In the following November, however, a commission[2] was issued appointing Murray 'captain-general and governor-in-chief in and over our province of Quebec in America', and this was amplified a month later by more detailed instructions.[3] Civil government was actually established on August 10, 1764.[4] Murray had thus three documents to guide him : the royal proclamation, his commission, and his instructions.

The proclamation, as far as the new province of Quebec was concerned, merely outlined an administration for the settled parts of New France.[5] The boundaries were such that the western country, with its trading posts extending to the prairies and to the Mississippi valley, was left under the control of the department of Indian affairs and outside the government of Quebec. Executive authority was placed in the hands of a governor and council. The former was instructed, ' so soon as the state and circumstances of the said colon[y] will admit thereof ', to call a popular assembly similar to those in the

[1] Kennedy, *op. cit.*, pp. 18 ff.
[2] Shortt and Doughty, *op. cit.*, pp. 173 ff.
[3] *Ibid.*, pp. 181 ff.
[4] See above, p. 24, note 2.
[5] ' The government of Quebec, bounded on the Labrador coast by the river St. John, and from thence by a line drawn from the head of that river through the lake St. John to the south end of the lake Nippissim ; from whence the said line, crossing the river St. Lawrence, and the lake Champlain, in 45 degrees of north latitude, passes along the high lands which divide the rivers that empty themselves into the said St. Lawrence from those which fall into the sea ; and also along the north coast of the Bay des Chaleurs, and the coast of the Gulf of St. Lawrence to Cape Rosières, and from thence crossing the mouth of the river St. Lawrence by the west end of the island of Anticosti, terminates at the aforesaid river of St. John.'

D

Thirteen Colonies. Power was given to the governor, council, and contemplated assembly to make laws, statutes, and ordinances. No provision, however, was made for legislation apart from ' the representatives of the people so to be summoned as aforesaid '. When it is remembered that one of the main reasons for introducing administrative clauses into such a miscellaneous document was ' to increase as much as possible the number of British and other new protestant settlers ',[1] the proclamation is exceedingly indefinite. The promise of an assembly is in itself remarkable, seeing that Murray had already assured the government that the country was not at all ripe for such an institution,[2] but apart from an assembly no hint of legislative power is given. The proclamation rested satisfied with the smug assurance, ' that until such assemblies can be called as aforesaid, all persons inhabiting in or resorting to our said colon[y] may confide in our royal protection for the enjoyment of the benefit of the laws of our realm of England '. The judicial system was to consist of civil and criminal courts governed by law and equity ' as near as may be agreeable to the laws of England ', with the right of appeal in civil cases to the privy council.

When the proclamation is submitted to criticism, it is clear that the interval between its earlier and final form had not provided any adequate conception of Canadian affairs. The documents of these months disclose neither insight nor knowledge. To cut off the western lands from the civil jurisdiction of the province merely helped to alienate the merchants of Montreal and Quebec, whose business in the western trade was Canada's strongest hold on economic prosperity. The conditions thus created remained unchanged until they were rectified in 1774 after pressure from the colonists. Nor did the

[1] Lords of Trade to Egremont, June 8, 1763, Shortt and Doughty, *op. cit.*, p. 142. Cf. same to Halifax, October 4, 1763, *ibid.*, p. 156.

[2] Murray to Egremont, June 7, 1762, *State Papers*, Q. 1, p. 23 (Canadian Archives).

provision for calling an assembly display any more enlightenment. To set up such an institution in a province overwhelmingly Roman catholic would have meant the passing of political
power into the hands of two or three hundred protestants who
alone could act as members according to the laws of England.
A racial and religious oligarchy must arise unless ' the state
and circumstances ' necessary for an assembly included the
arrival of a vast concourse of ' British and other protestant
settlers '. The regulations for the legal system bristle with
ambiguities. If they contemplated the disappearance of French
law, they were impracticable. A social upheaval, in which
the old seigniorial and contractual systems were destroyed,
alone could justify such a course. On the other hand, it would
have been a difficult problem to decide how nearly ' agreeable
to the laws of England ' a completely different civilization
could be brought without destruction.

On the negative side the proclamation was also weak. In
addition to the omission of a proviso fully explaining the
source of legislative power, nothing was said on the subject of
taxation. Presumably Great Britain had assumed the duties
in force in New France, but no plans were made for their
collection, and taxation remained on an unsatisfactory footing
for a decade.[1] With regard to religion there was a dangerous
silence, in view of the state of mind already noted as existing
under the ' régime militaire '. Nothing was done to define the
position of the Roman catholic church. The peace of Paris
begged the issue. It promised that the king's ' most precise
and effectual orders ' would guard his new subjects in the
profession of their religion. The gracious goodwill may have
been free from guile, but the royal ministers were careful to
add a saving clause, ' as far as the laws of Great Britain permit '.
It was a nice point to decide how far the recusancy laws of

[1] See Quebec Revenue Acts (14 Geo. III, c. 88, and 15 Geo. III, c. 40),
Kennedy, *op. cit.*, pp. 136 ff., 149.

England governed Canada. Finally, the whole proclamation
was called in question [1] by the argument that the king apart
from parliament could make no laws binding Quebec, and it
was not till 1774 that such doubts were quieted by Lord Mansfield in *Campbell* v. *Hall*.[2] That judgement not only decided
that a grant of legislative institutions such as that made by
the proclamation was irrevocable, but it established the proclamation as the legal constitution of Quebec until it was
repealed, as far as related to the province, by the Quebec Act
of 1774.[3] Vital as Lord Mansfield's decision is in the history
of colonial institutions, it came only after ten years of vigorous
controversy over the legality of the proclamation, and at a
moment when constitutional changes discounted its practical
importance.

The long commission and instructions given to Murray did
not entirely rectify these defects nor provide a clear scheme
of government. Both are full of regulations to govern the
future house of assembly and the future laws which it will pass.
The assembly, however, was far off—' impracticable for the
present '—and legislative authority was vested in the governor
with the advice of his council. The grant was not very comprehensive, as they could make no law which should ' any ways
tend to affect the life, limb or liberty of the subject, or to the
imposing any duties or taxes '. The governor acting on similar
advice could erect courts of justice, and could appoint judges
and justices of the peace with the goodwill of the majority of
his council. Nothing is said of the laws to be administered,
but English precedents were implied in the instruction that in
creating a judicial system consideration was to be given to
what had been done in the other colonies, especially in Nova
Scotia. In the public commission (which was published) no

---

[1] See Masères's memorandum as attorney-general of Quebec : Shortt and
Doughty, *op. cit.*, pp. 257 ff.

[2] Kennedy, *op. cit.*, pp. 79 ff.   [3] 14 Geo. III, c. 83, *ibid.*, pp. 132 ff.

attempt was made to clear up the religious ambiguity. The private instructions throw light on the difficulty and will be considered later in another connexion.

The criticism which has been made of the early scheme of government would be far from judicial, were it not for further considerations. The defects pointed out appear after the plan had been at work rather than at the moment of inception. On the surface, it must have seemed an easy enough thing to govern a people so far removed from any conception of free citizenship. The simplicity, however, was complicated by the fact that never before had Great Britain acquired half a continent, so to speak, in which another white race had made colonizing experiments. To govern a conquered white race was a problem of inexperience, and it was made all the more difficult because they must be ruled in close relationship to adjoining British colonists, alien in race and speech and religion, and without rivals in political thinking. There was plenty of room here for political, social, religious, or economic trouble. Were this survey complete, it would have presented an outlook difficult enough. Unfortunately there was also the ever-irritating and complex Indian problem, and to make matters more difficult still there were British settlers already in the province. It may be impossible to say that the documents were the product of studious care ; but ambiguities and defects might well be expected when all the contemporary circumstances are taken into consideration.

With goodwill and courage and with affection towards the Canadians, Murray began his task. On September 17, 1764, he set up a system of civil courts.[1] A court of king's bench was instituted, presided over by the chief justice, in which criminal cases and the more important civil cases were heard agreeable to English law and to the ordinances issued under the governor's authority. In this court all subjects were admitted as jurors

[1] Kennedy, *op. cit.*, pp. 37 ff.

without distinction. Murray explained that he thought it
' unjust to exclude the new Roman catholic subjects . . . as
such exclusion would constitute . . . two hundred protestants
perpetual judges of the lives and property of not only eighty
thousand of the new subjects, but likewise of all the military
in the province '. A court of common pleas was also set up
for the trial of lesser civil cases among French-Canadians only.
Once again Murray excused his deviation from his instructions.
A court for French-Canadians was necessary, and ' not to admit
of such a court, until they can be supposed to know something
of our laws and methods of procuring justice in our courts,
would be like sending a ship to sea without a compass : indeed
it would be more cruel, the ship might escape . . . but the poor
Canadians could never shun the attempts of designing men
and the voracity of hungry practitioners in the law. They
must be undone during the first months of their ignorance ;
if any escaped, their affections must be alienated and disgusted
with our government and laws.' [1] These arrangements were
doubtless the outcome of Murray's kindly disposition, which
unfortunately for Murray ended in his own undoing in Canada.
They illustrate, however, the indefiniteness and insecurity of
administrative provisions, which culminated in the constitutional recognition of conciliation as a policy in Canadian
development.

[AUTHORITIES.—The most important documents are in A. Shortt and
A. G. Doughty, *Documents relating to the Constitutional History of Canada,
1759–1791* (Ottawa, 1918) ; W. P. M. Kennedy, *Documents of the Canadian
Constitution, 1759–1915* (Oxford, 1918) ; the *State Papers*, Q. 1, Q. 2,
and the *Letter Books and Papers of General Murray* (Canadian Archives).
Light is thrown on the circumstances surrounding the royal proclamation
in C. W. Alvord, *Genesis of the Proclamation of 1763* (Michigan Historical
Society, 1908). The same author touches incidentally on the same subject in
The Mississippi Valley in British Politics (2 vols., Cleveland, 1917), which
also contains a long discussion, with a valuable bibliography, on the question
of the retention of Canada in 1763. The standard life of Murray, based on
a careful working of the available material, is R. H. Mahon, *Life of General
James Murray* (London, 1921).]

[1] *State Papers*, Q. 62, A. 2, p. 500 (Canadian Archives).

CHAPTER VI

THE CIVIL GOVERNMENT OF QUEBEC, 1764–74

As the new scheme of government took form, it is clear that at the beginning repression of the French-Canadians was part of the British policy. French law was apparently abolished by the royal proclamation. However strongly this may have been denied five years later by Hillsborough, president of the board of trade in 1763, there is no suggestion at the time that his interpretation was valid.[1] Quite apart from this denial, indications of a repressive policy are forthcoming. In relation to religion the evidence is clear. We have seen the guarded guarantee, repeated to Murray, of the peace of Paris. His commission and instructions throw light on the policy. The former [2] ordered him to accept as members of the future assembly only those who had subscribed to the statutory declaration against popery. In the latter [3] he was commanded to give all possible encouragement to the erection of protestant schools, to the maintenance of protestant ministers, and to the provision of protestant schoolmasters, ' to the end that the church of England may be established both in principles and practice, and that the said inhabitants may by degrees be induced to embrace the protestant religion and their children be brought up in the principles of it '. He was to see that the inhabitants ' conform with great exactness to the stipulations of the treaty ' in ' professing the worship of their religion '. The saving clause in the treaty rendered it ambiguous, and the governor's orders ' not to admit of any ecclesiastical jurisdiction of the see of Rome ', if carried out, must have meant the disappearance of the religious organiza-

---

[1] Hillsborough to Carleton, March 6, 1768, Kennedy, *op. cit.*, p. 57.
[2] Shortt and Doughty, *op. cit.*, p. 175.   [3] Kennedy, *op. cit.*, pp. 32 ff.

tion inherently necessary to the worship of the Roman catholic church. There was also a remarkable omission. When the French commander had asked, at the capitulation of Montreal, that the Canadians ' be obliged by the English government to pay their priests the tithes . . . they were used to pay under the government of his most Christian majesty ', he was told that the obligation would depend on the king of England's pleasure.[1] The tithe had been a source of clerical income since 1663 and had been regularly paid since 1667, under an order from the sovereign council.[2] During the ' régime militaire ' neglect had set in. Murray's instructions did nothing to conciliate the clergy in this connexion. The already existing suspicion with regard to religion was thus increased, and the good faith of the treaty was further questioned.

Did this evidence stand by itself it would be strong enough. It is supported by an official contemporary interpretation of the religious concession. Murray was informed, in the announcement of his appointment as governor, that the king suspected that the Canadians would use the liberty granted of professing their religion to hold on to the French connexion and to combine for the recovery of their country. The priests must be narrowly watched, and the slightest suspicion of interference by them in civil affairs must be punished by removal. The gift of the treaty was a mere toleration. When, during the peace negotiations, the French ministers proposed that after the grant of ' liberty of the Catholic religion ' the words *comme ci-devant* should be inserted, they did not abandon the demand until they were told that such words would be a deception and that the laws of Great Britain must prevail.[3] The idea may still survive

[1] Kennedy, *op. cit.*, p. 10.

[2] ' Un Épisode de l'histoire de la Dîme au Canada,' par M. l'abbé A. Gosselin (*Transactions of the Royal Society of Canada*, 2nd series, vol. ix, sect. i, pp. 45 ff.).

[3] Egremont to Murray, August 13, 1763, Shortt and Doughty, *op. cit.* pp. 168 ff.

that the phrase ' as far as the laws of Great Britain permit '
was merely a legal tag, like ' the laws of King Edward ' in the
early Norman charters ; but such valid contemporary comment
proves the unreality of the idea.

Opposition to the policy was at once apparent. Lord Mansfield wrote to Bute's successor, George Grenville, against the
whole tenor of the administrative proposals in the royal proclamation.[1] In Quebec the French-Canadians early petitioned
against the probable withdrawal of concessions,[2] and Murray
himself began a liberal rule with deviations from the letter of
his orders and with protests against repression. In asking for
religious privileges in Quebec, denied to Roman catholics at
home, he was specially emphatic, promising that ' perhaps the
bravest and the best race upon the globe ' would thus ' become
the most faithful and most useful set of men in this American
empire'.[3] He prayed that his retirement might be granted if ' the
popish laws must be exerted with rigour ' against the people whom
he loved and admired.[4] In the darkest days of his recall, he was
content to defend his conduct by saying that ' he could not be prevailed upon to persecute his majesty's Roman catholic subjects
in Canada ', though he thus ' displeased the little protestant
traders, who all—Quakers, Puritans, Anabaptists, Presby-
terians, Atheists, Infidels, and even Jews—joined in protesting
against any consideration being paid to the poor Canadians '.[5]
Murray's attitude in this period is not isolated. His successor,
Carleton, saw in the suppression of French law an unparalleled
severity, especially as he considered that Quebec, ' barring
catastrophe shocking to think of ', would always remain pre-

---

[1] Mansfield to Grenville, December 24, 1764, *Grenville Papers*, vol. ii, p. 476.
[2] Shortt and Doughty, *op. cit.*, p. 229.
[3] Murray to the Lords of Trade, October 29, 1764, *ibid.*, p. 231
[4] Murray to Lord Eglinton, October 27, 1764, *Letter Book of General Murray*
(Canadian Archives).
[5] Draft answers to the Articles of Complaint, n. d., *Murray Papers*, bundle
vii (Canadian Archives).

dominantly French.[1] His official dispatches are full of almost passionate pleading against a policy which abstract justice and local circumstances alike condemned.

The general fear and dissatisfaction resulted in a gradual mitigation of the letter of the law. Late in 1764, Murray was instructed that the royal proclamation should not be rigidly adhered to in taking away ' from the native inhabitants the benefit of their own laws and customs in cases where titles to land and modes of descent, alienation, and settlement are in question, nor to preclude them from that share in the administration of judicature which both in reason and justice they are entitled to, in common with the rest of our subjects '. Where life and liberties were concerned ' British laws and constitution ' must prevail.[2] Within a few years French-Canadian jurors and French-Canadian lawyers were given a legal status, and the old land-laws were confirmed. In ecclesiastical affairs concessions were finally winked at. At first, when the chapter of Quebec elected M. de Montgolfier bishop the British government did not recognize the election, and it was annulled at Rome, and for a long time no formal permission could be obtained for an appointment. Through influence in London, Murray gradually forced the issue.[3] Mgr. Briand was appointed bishop-designate, and after personal negotiations he was informed that the government would have no objection to his consecration and to his residence in Quebec, but would not recognize his title as bishop. Briand was quietly consecrated at Paris. He arrived at Quebec the day Murray sailed for England, and quickly assumed the full episcopal authority and style.[4]

In time the inherent difficulties of government might have

[1] Shortt and Doughty, *op. cit.*, pp. 284, 289.

[2] *Dartmouth MSS.*, M. 383, 50 (Canadian Archives).

[3] Cf. Cramahé to Murray, London, February 9, 1765, *Murray Papers* (Canadian Archives). Murray had opposed Montgolfier as a man ' too haughty and imperious ' : Doutre and Lareau, *op. cit.*, p. 541.

[4] See l'abbé A. Gosselin, *L'Église du Canada après la Conquête*, vol. i, 1760–75 (Quebec, 1916).

been surmounted, had it not been for the presence in the province of a few hundred British traders, on whom Murray lavished the wealth of a caustic pen. Grouping them with the adventurers who are the usual by-product of war and conquest, he characterized them as 'licentious fanatics', 'the most immoral collection of men I ever knew,' 'cruel, ignorant, rapacious fanatics', 'wild and mad'.[1] In more guarded language Carleton described them as, on the whole, fortune-hunters.[2] When all due allowances are made for the irritation which they caused to these two high-minded governors in a hard and trying situation, it is well to remember that there were among them men of honour and honesty who did not a little to lay the economic foundations of the province. In addition many of them had become settlers relying on the promise of British institutions and laws. When they saw the policy of conciliation taking form in actual administration, it was almost natural that they should proclaim that they had been grossly deceived. Among the best of them there was a strain of New England puritanism which carried with it no very happy memories either in tradition or experience of priest or prelate. Even had their political theory been somewhat modern, their religious affiliations would have prevented them from displaying any tolerant spirit. Almost at once they began to call for a house of assembly, and they soon became more persistent in their demands, as they watched with dismay sacrosanct British institutions and laws recede farther and farther from them down the full tide of concession and liberalism. For ten years they carried on an agitation that varied from sobriety and reason to tactlessness and folly, and included every line of attack. To follow its course in detail is here unnecessary,

[1] Murray to the Lords of Trade, October 29, 1764, Shortt and Doughty, *op. cit.*, p. 231 ; Murray to Burton, January 8, 1764 ; same to Eglinton, October 27, 1764 ; *The Letter Book of General Murray*; same to Shelburne, August 20, 1766, *Haldimand Papers*, B. 8, p. 1.

[2] Shortt and Doughty, *op. cit.*, p. 284.

but their demands in relation to the constitution must be noted.

Two months after the establishment of civil government the grand jury of Quebec made their presentment an occasion for attack, and as a climax they claimed that ' as the grand jury must be considered at present as the only body representative of the colony, they, as British subjects, have a right 'to be consulted before any ordinance that may affect the body that they represent be passed into a law '.[1]   Before long the merchants organized their opposition, and appointed an English barrister as their agent in London to safeguard their rights. This agent played no small part in Murray's recall. Charges of a personal nature were piled up. The governor was bitter in temper, rude in tongue, and flagrantly partial. His ' almost a total neglect of attendance upon the service of the church ' was not even counted to him as judicious righteousness. These personal attacks only witnessed to their hatred of the man whom they considered the fountain-head of unconstitutional government. As a fitting conclusion to them, they once more demanded representative institutions, ' there being a number more than sufficient of loyal and well-affected protestants, exclusive of military officers, to form a competent and respectable house of assembly ' ; and the French-Canadians might be allowed, if the king thought fit, to vote for these protestant assembly men.[2] Modern views may look on the latter suggestion as conceited condescension. Perhaps it was not made without great travail of soul and dour searching of heart.

Murray was recalled in 1766,[3] but his successor, Sir Guy Carleton, did not prove any more willing to find a *via media* for

[1] Presentment of the Grand Jury of Quebec, October 16, 1764, Shortt and Doughty, *op. cit.*, pp. 212 ff.

[2] *Ibid.*, pp. 232 ff.

[3] Murray was recalled to England April 1, 1766. On the 7th Carleton was appointed lieutenant-governor. He acted under Murray's official instructions till he was appointed governor-in-chief in 1768, when he received a new set for himself.

the minority.   When some of them submitted a rough draft for
a house of assembly and hoped that he would have no objection
to their having it signed by supporters, he told them that he had
many objections.   To assemblies in the abstract he might agree,
but he failed to see how a practical experiment could be made
in Quebec.   In writing to England, he maintained that the best
Canadians considered representative houses as the breeding-
place of refractory and insolent peoples, and that they did not
wish to gain the royal displeasure, as the southern colonies had
done through the misconduct of their legislatures.   Carleton's
mature opinion was that in a colony ' where all men appear
nearly on a level ', a popular assembly ' must give a strong bias
to republican principles '.[1]   The bluntness of the governor did
not silence the disaffected.   Petitions continued to rise in
ascending scale through the governor, the house of commons,
and secretary of state to the footsteps of the throne.   These,
however, do not afford much light on the situation.   Once
French-Canadians are claimed as being in favour of an assembly;[2]
and when the grant seemed finally denied, a request was made
that a legislative council should be appointed directly by the
king and rendered quite independent of the governor.[3]   Social
factors increased the discontent.   The government circle looked
down on the merchant class, not merely as traders but as
democrats.   The military also despised their so-called social
inferiors.[4]   When a merchant named Thomas Walker lost his
ear in a fracas distinguished ' by crêpe masks and blackened
features ', and the administration failed to bring his supposed
military assailants to justice, the hatred grew deeper, as
Walker's fellow tradesmen believed that the government had
taken the soldiers under the shelter of their authority.   The

[1] Carleton to Shelburne, January 20, 1768, Shortt and Doughty, *op. cit.*,
pp. 294 ff.
[2] *Ibid.*, p. 490.   [3] *Ibid.*, p. 520 ; and cf. p. 487.
[4] Murray to the Lords of Trade, March 3, 1764, *State Papers*, Q. 2, p. 377
(Canadian Archives).

economic, social, and military life of the province combined to give the political issues an ugly and dangerous appearance.

The attention of the British government was early drawn to the state of affairs ; and, with the origins of the Quebec Act of 1774 in view, it is necessary to summarize the considerations given to the constitutional problem during these years.   In 1765, in answer to a request for an opinion, the law officers of the crown reported that Roman catholics in Canada were not under the disabilities created by the penal laws.[1] A few months later the board of trade recommended a house of assembly elected by all the inhabitants, Roman catholic and protestant.[2] In the following year the law officers advised a mixed system of French and English law.[3] All these opinions, however, were English opinions, and the privy council decided to consult definitely the governor, chief justice, and attorney-general of Quebec.[4] The reports from Canada did not reach London till 1770.   Carleton left the work of drawing up a joint report to Francis Masères, the attorney-general, who drew up a long draft in which he examined the advantages and disadvantages of several methods of dealing with the legal system.[5] The draft was not at all acceptable to Carleton, who had already made up his mind. He sent in his own report recommending the laws of England with respect to criminal matters, and the revival of the whole body of French civil law which was in use before the conquest.[6] The chief justice and attorney-general thereupon sent independent reports in which they reported against Carleton and the whole French civil code, and advised a blend of English and French civil law.[7] Meanwhile, the board of trade had again reopened the matter and presented on July 10, 1769, another

[1] The Attorney-General and Solicitor-General to the Commissioners for Trade and Plantations, June 10, 1765, Shortt and Doughty, *op. cit.*, p. 236.

[2] Board of Trade to the King, September 2, 1765, *ibid.*, pp. 247 ff.

[3] Report of Attorney-General and Solicitor-General, April 14, 1766, *ibid.*, pp. 251 ff.

[4] *Ibid.*, pp. 285 ff.

[5] *Ibid.*, pp. 327 ff.

[6] *Ibid.*, pp. 369 ff.

[7] *Ibid.*, pp. 370 ff.

report far in advance of any previous opinion, in which they recommended the creation of a house of assembly with French-Canadian members for the rural constituencies.[1] This report was sent to Carleton under orders of the closest secrecy.

It might appear that the ground was now pretty well covered and that the time for action had come. It is hard, however, to believe that the ministry was serious in all its promises of a speedy *quietus* to the uncertainties and doubts and fears. The endless tangle was once again pulled to pieces by the solicitor-general, the attorney-general, and the advocate-general,[2] the two former leaning to Carleton, the latter to Masères, both of whom had returned to England and were making themselves felt. In Canada Cramahé carried on the government, where the British continued to agitate and added to their old methods ' American ideas in regard to taxation ', secretly urging that the British tyranny against the southern colonies could only be averted from Quebec by a house of assembly.[3] Memorials from the French-Canadians reached England early in 1774, which anticipated with too suspicious accuracy the final decisions of the Quebec Act—no assembly, a council, extended boundaries, French civil law. Masères claimed that these petitions actually became the foundations of the Act.[4] It may be that they were inspired from sources which Masères's Huguenot honesty least suspected.

Almost a veil of secrecy falls over the developments which culminated in the Quebec Act of 1774. It may never be possible to reconstruct the history as the new constitution passed through many drafts to its final shape. Carleton undoubtedly stands behind the scenes, which assume a strange interest when we remember that the Act was born amid the rumbling thunders of the coming American revolution. The

[1] *Ibid.*, pp. 377 ff.   [2] *Ibid.*, pp. 424 ff.
[3] Cramahé to Dartmouth, July 15, 1774, *ibid.*, pp. 503 ff.
[4] *Ibid.*, p. 504, note 2.

first great colonial empire, grown to manhood, was shaking its strong locks and stretching its fierce limbs to put to test newer principles, at a moment when the youngest child of empire— weary with political, religious, and racial struggle—was waiting in almost hushed melancholy the fiat of its foster-mother. Tears and hopes centred round Carleton. His dispatches during these years have not been studied here, as they fit more naturally into a discussion of the origins of the Act ; but he was at once the most loved and the most hated man, the hero and the villain of the piece.

In attempting to form a critical estimate of this period, the most striking point is the constitutional uncertainty. The governor did not know his powers ; the merchants did not know if they had been deceived ; the *noblesse* did not know their rights ; the Roman catholic church did not know its status ; the *habitants* were encircled in a gloom of apathetic doubt. As for the judicial system, it was an almost inexplicable tangle. To determine at any given moment the exact body of laws in force would have tantalized the most penetrating jurist. Even the organization of the council was in debate. In the actual affairs of everyday life there was no efficiency. There were many honourable and blameless officials, but there were also many ill trained in law and affairs and ignorant of French. They added greed and cunning to their incompetency. Anxious hours were spent over institutions when men were needed. The early local justices appointed after 1764 proved so tyrannical and useless that Carleton tried to curtail their powers.[1] A system of fees prevailed which encouraged litigation and discounted equity. So chaotic was the state of affairs that the French-Canadians looked back with regret to the ' excess of kindness ' during the ' régime militaire '.[2]

The self-evident desire of Great Britain to treat the province as one of the colonies was also a source of weakness. The

[1] Shortt and Doughty, *op. cit.*, pp. 401 ff.   [2] *Ibid.*, p. 507.

very liberties so dear to eighteenth-century Englishmen, and promised with such lavish profusion, were strangely unsuited to a Roman catholic people, heirs to the apathy born of paternalism and still children in political development. To recast the people of New France was too great a task ; to make them potential co-heirs with their British fellow citizens to institutions, laws, and systems which they did not understand was to court confusion ; to attempt assimilation was to accentuate differences. The royal proclamation, though practically futile, hung over the heads of the French-Canadians, a political sword of Damocles. To the British in the colony it represented a broken treaty, a scrap of paper, an ideal to strive for, a promise to be fulfilled. Even the good intentions of men like Murray and Carleton only paved the *via dolorosa* to a constitutional calvary. When at last courage was stiffened by other circumstances, it was little wonder that the Quebec Act was grimly entitled ' An Act for making more effectual provision for the government of the Province of Quebec in North America '.

[AUTHORITIES.—The important documents are in A. Shortt and A. G. Doughty, *Documents relating to the Constitutional History of Canada, 1759–1791* (Ottawa, 1918) ; W. P. M. Kennedy, *Documents of the Canadian Constitution, 1759–1915* (Oxford, 1918) ; Egerton and Grant, *Canadian Constitutional Development* (Toronto, 1907) ; *The State Papers*, Q. 2–Q. 10 (Canadian Archives) ; *The Letter Books of General Murray*, and *The Murray Papers* (Canadian Archives) ; *The Dartmouth Papers* (Canadian Archives). The publications of Masères are important, especially *A Collection of Several Commissions . . . relating to the state of the Province of Quebec* (London, 1772) ; *An Account of the Proceedings . . . to obtain a House of Assembly* (London, 1775) ; *Additional Papers concerning the Province of Quebec* (London, 1776). W. S. Wallace, *The Masères Letters* (Toronto, 1919), contains valuable material T. Chapais, ' Notre Question religieuse en 1764 ' in *Le Parler Français* December 1917, pp. 145 ff., is suggestive and valuable.]

E

CHAPTER VII

THE QUEBEC ACT, 1774

THE serious consideration of a new constitution for Quebec appears to have been begun during the closing months of 1773. Voluminous as the early reports were which have just been considered, prolific as the promises had been since 1766 that the government of the province would soon be settled, there is reason to believe that the mass of material was not critically digested till within a few months of the introduction of the Quebec Act. It was not entirely irresponsible opposition which made Townshend twit Lord North on a delay that had issued in anarchy and confusion.[1] However, when the subject was actually taken up, there was plenty of legal opinion, and much correspondence and consultation between the ministry, Carleton, Masères, Chief Justice Hey, and William Knox, under-secretary of state for the colonies, a man of considerable experience in English and American affairs. The bill passed through many hands and appeared in many forms before it was introduced on May 2, 1774, in the house of lords.[2] Only a few members of either house thought it worth their while to remain in London to take part in or to listen to the discussions, and the bill received the royal assent on June 22. During its progress through the house of commons important debates took place which will be considered later in connexion with the origin of the Act. For the moment it is only necessary to remark that Carleton's ideas largely prevailed in the new instrument of government.

[1] J. Wright, *Cavendish's Debates . . . on the Bill for making more effectual provision for the Government of the Province of Quebec* (London, 1839), pp. i ff. These debates are partially in Kennedy, *op. cit.*, pp. 86 ff., and in Egerton and Grant, *op. cit.*, pp. 23 ff.

[2] See the various drafts in Shortt and Doughty, *op. cit.*, pp. 535 ff.

If the Quebec Act of 1774 [1] is considered merely in its enactments and apart from everything else, generosity is written large over it. The Act might almost be summed up in the words of Burke : ' with regard to state policy . . . the preservation of their old prejudices, their old customs by the bill, turns the balance in favour of France. The only difference is, they will have George the third for Louis the sixteenth.' [2] The proclamation of 1763 as far as it applied to Quebec was revoked. A house of assembly was deemed inexpedient, and a nominated council was set up to assist the governor in legislation and in administration. A modified oath rendered it possible for Roman catholics to be admitted. The whole body of French civil law was revived. The Roman catholic church was given a legal status by the provision that tithes could be collected from its members by due process. This provision and the new oath seriously modified the Elizabethan Act of supremacy which guarded the religious grant. The regulations for taxation supplementary to the Act were embodied in a statute of the following year and only imposed duties analogous to those under the French régime. [3] Explicit conciliation may not have been intended, but the duties were less obnoxious to the French-Canadian than to the British element, who had already begun to disseminate ideas in the matter of taxation similar to those which had gained force in the Thirteen Colonies, and were threatening disintegration. [4] Under the proclamation of 1763 there was evidently an intention of creating a government for the trading country of the west, which, as a matter of fact, remained for ten years without any formal administration. Labrador, Anticosti, and the Magdalen Islands had been included under the government of Newfoundland. The fishing and fur-trading interests in Quebec protested against this arrangement, and economically

[1] Kennedy, *op. cit.*, pp. 132 ff. (14 Geo. III, c. 83).
[2] Cavendish, *op. cit.*, p. 289.
[3] Kennedy, *op. cit.*, pp. 136 ff. (14 Geo. III, c. 88).
[4] See above, p. 47.

much might be said in favour of a reconstruction of the boundaries. In spite of opposition from the secretary of state for the colonies, the Quebec Act reannexed Labrador to the province, and extended the boundaries to include not only modern Ontario but the limitless country indefinitely bounded by the Ohio and Mississippi rivers and by the territories of the Hudson's Bay Company.[1] There is concession here, for the intention, as will appear later, was to preserve the western hinterland as a vast French and Indian reserve to the exclusion of other settlers.

The machinery of government set up by the Quebec Act and amplified by instructions to the governor [2] was practically that

---

[1] ' All the territories, islands, and countries in North America, belonging to the crown of Great Britain, bounded on the south by a line from the Bay of Chaleurs, along the Highlands which divide the rivers that empty themselves into the river St. Lawrence, from those which fall into the sea, to a point in forty-five degrees of north latitude on the eastern bank of the river Connecticut, keeping the same latitude directly west through the Lake Champlain, until in the same latitude it meets the river St. Lawrence ; from thence up the eastern bank of the said river to the Lake Ontario ; thence through the Lake Ontario and the river commonly called Niagara ; and thence along by the eastern and south eastern bank of Lake Erie, following the said bank until the same shall be intersected by the northern boundary granted by the charter of the province of Pennsylvania, in case the same shall be so intersected ; and from thence along the said northern and western boundaries of the said province until the said western boundary shall strike the Ohio : But in case the said bank of the said lake shall not be found to be so intersected, then following the said bank until it shall arrive at that point of the said bank which shall be nearest to the north-western angle of the said province of Pennsylvania, and thence, by a right line, to the said north-western angle of the said province ; and thence along the western boundary of the said province, until it strike the river Ohio ; and along the bank of the said river westward to the banks of the river Mississippi and northward to the southern boundary of the territory granted to the Merchants Adventurers of England trading to Hudson's Bay ; and also all such territories, islands, and countries which have, since the tenth of February 1763 been made part of the government of Newfoundland—be . . . annexed to and made part and parcel of the province of Quebec as created and established by the . . . Royal Proclamation of the 7th October 1763.' For an interesting discussion of the western boundaries, see D. Mills, *A Report on the Boundaries of Ontario,* pp. 1 ff. (Toronto, 1873).

[2] Shortt and Doughty, *op. cit.*, pp. 594 ff.

of 1763. An assembly was shelved with no promises for the future. The council was increased from twelve members to not more than twenty-three and not less than seventeen, a new oath widening the choice of members. The only organic change was made in differentiating the executive and legislative functions of the council. Carleton was instructed ' that any five of the said council shall constitute a board of council for transacting all business in which their advice and consent may be requisite, acts of legislation only excepted '. He interpreted this order as justifying him in creating a kind of inner circle or ' privy council ' as he called it, to whom he entrusted all administrative work to the exclusion of the other members.[1] The chief justice, Peter Livius, challenged the arrangement and protested that the instruction was permissive, and that every member had a right to a summons whenever the council sat. A snub and dismissal were the governor's answer to the strict legalist.[2] Livius appealed to the British government, which decided in 1779 in his favour.[3] The decision forced the hand of Carleton's successor, Haldimand, who had continued the practice. In spite of the fact that he had been ordered to desist,[4] he raised the question ' whether every measure of government ought to be exposed and laid open to the mixture of people which compose our council '.[5] His purity of intention did not prevent him from receiving a severe rebuke and further peremptory orders.[6] The executive or privy council disappeared from history. In fact the distinction between the executive and legislative functions of the council remained, for while only five members were necessary for executive business, the presence of half the members was necessary for legislation. The legislative powers,

[1] *Ibid.*, p. 702.

[2] For the history and documents of this and other disputes see William Smith, ' The Struggle over the Laws of Canada, 1763–1783 ' (*Canadian Historical Review*, vol. i, pp. 167 ff.).

[3] Shortt and Doughty, *op. cit.*, pp. 698 ff.   [4] *Ibid.*, pp. 704 ff.

[5] Haldimand to Germain, September 14, 1779, *State Papers*, Q. 16. 2, p. 591 (Canadian Archives).   [6] Shortt and Doughty, *op. cit.*, p. 724.

however, were not wide. It could issue no ordinance touching religion, and could inflict no greater punishment than fine or imprisonment for three months. In taxation its authority was limited to levying taxes for public roads or buildings—' gathering stones from one place, and piling them up in another ', as the southern colonists described the ' insulting ' limitation.[1]

The provisions relating to the law need careful attention. British criminal law and French civil law were imposed on the province—Carleton's suggestion of 1769 [2]—the latter being substantially the *Coutume de Paris*, modified by the edicts and amendments of the governors and intendants of New France and amplified by French legal authorities.[3] Its provisions governed not merely land tenure, marriage, inheritance, and dower, but trade and commerce. Thus the prosperous business interests of the colony, largely in British hands, passed under a French code. The Act provided that ' in all matters of controversy, relative to property and civil rights, resort shall be had to the laws of Canada . . . and all causes that shall be hereafter instituted . . . shall, with respect to such property and rights, be determined agreeably to the said laws and customs of Canada, until they shall be varied or altered by any ordinances that shall, from time to time, be passed by the governor . . . by and with the advice and consent of the legislative council '. The criminal law of England was to govern criminal cases, until amended by the governor and council. Lord North in defending the civil and criminal codes said that they were merely a general basis,[4] and that the local machinery of government could change them to suit the province ; and Carleton, in his examination at the bar of the house, stated that he considered there

---

[1] Kennedy, *op. cit.*, p. 141.   [2] See above, p. 46.

[3] The *Coutume de Paris* was the French civil law codified in 1510. It had been introduced by royal *arrêt* into New France in 1664. See W. B. Munro, ' The Custom of Paris in the New World ' (*Sonderabdruck aus Juristische Festgabe des Auslandes zu Josef Kohler's 60. Geburtstag*, pp. 132 ff.). Stuttgart : F. Enke.

[4] Cavendish, *op. cit.*, p. 11.

would be no objections by the French-Canadians to alterations in respect to trade and commerce, provided the changes were explained.[1] In Carleton's instructions there is a distinct and more explicit continuation of the enactment and of North's comment on it. The governor and council were asked to consider whether ' the laws of England may not be, if not altogether, at least in part the rule for the decision in all cases of personal actions grounded upon debts, promises, contracts and agreements whether of a mercantile or other nature ; and also of wrongs proper to be compensated in damages ; and more especially where our natural-born subjects of Great Britain, Ireland, or our other Plantations residing at Quebec, or who may resort thither, or have credits or property within the same, may happen to be either plaintiff or defendant in any civil suit of such a nature '. The instructions went farther. The writ of *habeas corpus*, so vigorously contended for and so vigorously opposed at the passing of the Quebec Act, was recommended for adoption to the legislature of the province.[2]

It is obvious that there was created a loophole for the British in the colony. That there was not substantial legislation on their behalf is true, but the debates and royal instructions are not obscure and prove that the general principle laid down in the constitution was capable of modification on the spot. The scheme was this : an assembly could not be granted ; English criminal law was a good foundation ; French civil law was just, considering the local conditions ; changes could be made by the governor and council of the province— the system was not rigid. So clear was the purpose that Carleton was ordered to communicate to his council at once such of his instructions as required their advice and consent.[3]

Carleton's course is confusing. He did not immediately publish the full Act, but merely inserted in the *Gazette* an abstract which left the impression, so dear to popular histories,

---

[1] *Ibid.*, pp. 106 ff.   [2] Kennedy, *op. cit.*, p. 152.   [3] *Ibid.*, p. 150.

that the laws were English criminal law and French civil law, with no elasticity or avenue for change. He busied himself in reporting to England the gratitude of the ' new subjects ' and the suspicious proceedings of the traders.[1] The colonial secretary assured him of the king's goodwill to the disaffected, who would doubtless be reconciled when they heard and understood the complete plan.[2] When at length he published the full Act, he made no effort to explain its implications. When military exigencies allowed the council to meet for the first time in August 1775, he did not disclose a line of his instructions as ordered. The council was also left in blissful ignorance of the fact that the governor had in his possession a draft ordinance which had been approved by the British government. This would have satisfied the merchants and would have aroused no popular disapproval, as it permitted facts to be decided by juries, or if both parties preferred by the judges.[3] When the American revolution again allowed a council to be called in 1777, juries were ruled out, and the English law of evidence allowed. Livius broke another lance with the governor over the concealed instructions, but Carleton remained obdurate, for he knew that he had his council well in hand. The whole question was reopened under Haldimand, who was reprimanded by the British government for following Carleton's proceedings and ordered to communicate the necessary instructions, which he did in August 1781. The date is significant. The policy was too late. The army of Cornwallis was marching to its fate at York-town, with the old English tune of the surrender, ' The world turned upside down ', already haunting the October air. The importance of the episode may not appear at the moment, but when it is linked up later with a consideration of the Quebec Act as a whole, it will assume a distinct place in the historical interpretation.

---

[1] Shortt and Doughty, *op. cit.*, pp. 586 ff.   [2] *Ibid.*, pp. 585 ff.
[3] *Ibid.*, pp. 637 ff.

The provisions granted in the Act to the Roman catholic church are remarkable, when the legal disabilities in England are recalled. Although the church of England became the official church of the colony under very direct governmental control, the Roman catholic church was placed on an almost equal footing. The freedom of worship promised by the peace of Paris was once more granted. The condition attached was no longer vague, for the saving clause guarding the king's ecclesiastical supremacy disappeared in the legalizing of the clerical rights and dues, and in an oath which modified the Elizabethan model. It is true that the royal instructions to Carleton ordered that the Roman catholic bishop and priests should exercise their offices only under licence from the governor, and that he should remember that only toleration was granted and not ' the powers and privileges of an established church '. All appeals to the Vatican were prohibited, but this regulation was neglected from the beginning. There was no religious hatred for many a day to come, and Roman catholics and protestants shared the parish churches for their respective services. With this background it is now possible to discuss the origins and wisdom of the Act.

Looking at the history superficially, it would seem that there had been much anxiety over the government of Canada from the earliest days following the peace of Paris down to the Quebec Act itself. The state papers and dispatches are many, the official reports on conditions and possibilities are numerous. The question appears to have been considered from varied angles by varied minds. *A priori* there were reasons for a new constitution. The old one had been a dead letter, and had never been carried out. It was a bone of contention, a legal stumbling-block, a fly in the administrative ointment. It thus seems possible to say that the Quebec Act was a reasoned culmination to a series of carefully matured discussions, and that it represented a generous working foundation for a very much

needed new government. The debates largely bear out this
conception. Lord North emphasized again and again that the
scheme was the only one possible under the circumstances. The
attorney-general execrated the idea of imposing on the conquered the complete institutions of the conquerors, as such an
act would involve misery and slavery. The happiness of the
Canadians was at stake. Barbarity and tyranny alone could
descend to the theft of customs, religion, and laws. It certainly
looks like a remarkable miracle to find men traditionally tory
and reactionary handing out to a conquered people, of a race
historically hostile to Great Britain and of a religion condemned
by bell, book, and candle in scores of British statutes, such
a charter of liberties at the close of the eighteenth century. It
may be granted that the Act was generous, even miraculous.
The student of history, however, must ask if the generosity was
logical and spontaneous, if the suspension of the laws of party
politics arose from an overwhelming conviction that Canadian
conditions were such that the government bill appeared the
only solution. The Quebec Act requires more than an emotional
surrender even to a political miracle. There are other points
of view which must be considered in attempting a balanced
judgement.

We know that the reports were practically pigeon-holed for
years and were only considered in relation to practical politics
late in 1773. We know when the Act assumed its final form,
almost every legal and expert opinion was rejected, and
Carleton's ideas were almost completely incorporated. It is
necessary to trace the causes behind these facts. Carleton
undoubtedly, with Murray and Cramahé, was always well disposed to the French-Canadians. He, with his brother governors
and administrators, looked on their conquest as a mere accident
in a wider and more complicated issue than colonial jealousies.
Through no fault of their own they were treated as pawns on the
chessboard of European diplomacy. Carleton, however, was

a practical soldier, and he had no training in political thinking. There is no need to discount his soldierly and gentlemanly kindness to the conquered, in making a study of his relations to the problem of government which was forced upon him. He was too matter of fact in action to be misled wilfully by sentiment. All along he appears to have had definite opinions on the Canadian situation, which time and experience developed along their initial lines. As early as 1767 he had begun to relate Canada to the world, and to see the strategical position which the province would hold should the southern colonists prove recalcitrant.[1] The defences of the country and the guarding of communications with New York assumed serious proportions in his mind, and already he heard thousands of troops march at the beginning of a colonial war. While Carleton had his mind fixed on what appeared to him the only vital issue as far as Quebec was concerned, he was informed that the cabinet was seeking light on a new parliamentary constitution for the province, especially in connexion with the blending of laws to satisfy all the inhabitants.[2] His official report has been considered and was probably tied up in red tape with its fellows. His correspondence, however, was not overlooked. Here we find that official report amplified and explained. To a mind full of a military situation the cabinet brought a political problem, and in all the dispatches that follow, that problem is seen through the eyes of a soldier, who anticipated a war in which he and the province over which he presided would play perhaps a decisive part.

Believing that the request for light was firmly based on the idea of retaining Canada, he proceeded to show how he would guard that wish. Canada must be fortified, and the military establishment placed on a war footing. He attached much importance to the possibility of a French-Canadian army; at any

[1] Carleton to Gage, February 15, 1767, Shortt and Doughty, *op. cit.*, p. 280.
[2] Shelburne to Carleton, June 20, 1767, *ibid.*, p. 281.

rate the *noblesse* must be held, owing to their influence over the common people. The British element were unstable and fluctuating, and the province would remain predominantly French. If proper preparations were not made for war, a French alliance against England might make British rule precarious.[1] A little later, he again wrote home what is confessedly a continuation of his previous dispatch.[2] He blamed the entire constitutional scheme of 1763, and he outlined a political background for his military policy. There was no consideration ' of all the inhabitants ' in it. The old scheme was an unparalleled severity by a conqueror, and the only just way out of the disgrace was to repeal every regulation and to restore ' Canadian laws almost entire '. A month later he harped back to his two previous dispatches.[3] If the military proposals were carried out, he believed he could hold the province ; but the interests of Great Britain would only be half advanced ' unless the Canadians are inspired with a cordial attachment and zeal for the king's government ', and this attachment would come through concessions. Regiments of Canadian foot would materially help. Offices and councillorships must be opened to the French-Canadians, who, however, did not desire assemblies and their factious offspring. The dispatches were not unread. The secretary of state for the colonies informed Carleton that the king approved of ' his every sentiment '—military plans, French law, and administrative places for the Canadians—and desired him ' to prevail upon them to suffer patiently those delays which are unavoidable ' in making changes at such a distance.[4] A summary of the French laws accompanied Carleton's next communication,[5] and his ideas began to gain wider

[1] Carleton to Shelburne, November 25, 1767, Shortt and Doughty, *op. cit.*, pp. 282 ff.

[2] Same to same, December 24, 1767, *ibid.*, pp. 288 ff.

[3] Same to same, January 20, 1768, *ibid.*, pp. 294 ff.

[4] Hillsborough to Carleton, March 6, 1768, *ibid.*, pp. 297 ff.

[5] Carleton to Shelburne, April 12, 1768, *ibid.*, pp. 299 ff.

adherence. He was promised that in the drawing up of a new constitution toleration for the Roman catholic church would be given serious attention; meanwhile the ' new subjects ' must receive from the governor the necessary protection in the exercise of their religion.[1] Nor need he worry over the future; parliament had passed a resolution ' to preserve inviolate the supreme authority of the legislature of Great Britain over all parts of the British Empire '.[2] On his side, Carleton felt sure that the Canadians would not intrigue with France. Fears, however, troubled him.[3] France might throw in her lot with the colonies ' in their independent notions ', and the fate of America might be determined in Canada. Many of the seigniors desired to serve in the army. In the past ' we have done nothing to gain one man in the province '. The Canadians must be attached by being admitted to offices of trust. Once again approval followed. The necessity of giving the Canadians reasonable share in the new government would not be overlooked; faction and prejudice, however, might hinder their employment in military service.[4] Almost at once Carleton proposed the immediate inclusion of some twelve Canadian seigniors in the council; but so anxious had he become over the situation that he desired leave of absence to discuss the whole matter personally with the government.[5] A year and a half elapsed before he was able to leave Canada, and the correspondence continued in the old strain. Carleton urged conciliation and fortifications; the ministry promised concessions and approval [6] and desired him to remain in Canada

[1] Hillsborough to Carleton, October 12, 1768, *ibid.*, pp. 325 ff.

[2] Same to same, November 15, 1768, *State Papers*, Q. 5. 2, p. 839 (Canadian Archives).

[3] Carleton to Hillsborough, November 20, 1768, Shortt and Doughty, *op. cit.*, pp. 326 ff.

[4] Hillsborough to Carleton, January 4, 1769, *State Papers*, Q. 6, p. 3 (Canadian Archives).

[5] Carleton to Hillsborough, March 15, 1769, *ibid.*, p. 34.

[6] Same to same, May 9, 1769, *ibid.*, p. 63 ; Hillsborough to Carleton, May 13, 1769, *ibid.*, p. 12.

until the privy council had matured some plan.[1] When leave
was at length granted, he was assured that nothing would be
done until the Canadian point of view had been considered with
his presence and assistance.[2] Carleton was in England over
three years before real purpose of action was manifested by the
government, and it may well be asked why the ministry at
length took the matter up in earnest late in 1773. It is not
unreasonable to suppose that Carleton, who all along had built
up a political structure for Canada on a military foundation,
was driving home to them the significance of the Virginia
Resolves, Townshend's ' preamble ', the Boston Massacre and
Tea Party, and the Committees of Correspondence. He had
become obsessed with ' the colonial disturbances ', and the
development in political thinking which his civil experience
had brought to him was coloured by them.

It is impossible then to isolate the Quebec Act, unless the
history of the North American continent from 1766 to 1774 is
to be considered as consisting of water-tight compartments.
Carleton's dispatches, his policy, and its manifest influence on the
Act were all part of a larger problem. Nor do they stand
isolated. The complete motives behind the extension of the
boundaries are obscure ; but, in addition to economic pressure
from Quebec, American affairs figure in them beyond a doubt.
In the draft stages, Hillsborough objected to any legislation
on the boundaries as tending to make the westward country
Roman catholic and French, and objectionable to the British.[3]
During the debates the challenge was frequently thrown out
and as strongly denied that the object was to encircle the
Thirteen Colonies.[4] William Knox, the under-secretary for the
colonies, maintained that the object was to preserve ' the whole
of the derelict country . . . under the jurisdiction of Quebec . . .

[1] Hillsborough to Carleton, July 15, 1769, *State Papers*, Q. 6, p. 67.
[2] Same to same, December 1, 1769, *ibid.*, p. 127.
[3] Shortt and Doughty, *op. cit.*, pp. 551 ff.
[4] See, for example, Cavendish, *op. cit.*, pp. 17, 26, 42, 58, 73, 189, 196, 242.

with the avowed purpose of excluding all further settlement therein '.[1] It is possible to say, with Barré, that there was in the boundaries ' something that squints and looks dangerous to the inhabitants of the other colonies ', and to share Burke's fears of ' a line of circumvallation ' and the establishment of a ' siege of arbitrary power '.[2]

The evidence for the relation of the Quebec Act to the American revolution can be further strengthened. Lord North declared that the Act was brought in because ' His Majesty's message recommended parliament to take up the subject '. When the king's message of March 7, 1774, is examined, we find that he called upon the house of commons ' to enable him effectually to take such measures as might be most likely to put an immediate stop to the present disorders in North America, and also to take into their most serious consideration what regulations and permanent provisions might be necessary to be established for better securing the just dependence of the colonies on the crown and parliament of Great Britain '. The prime minister deliberately associated the Quebec Act with the four other ' intolerable acts ' passed against ' the present disorders '. The invitation which the first Continental Congress sent to the inhabitants of Quebec can be laughed at with its appeal to forget differences of religion and to join the cause of liberty against the new inquisition.[3] War propaganda makes poor historical material ; but it is impossible lightly to dismiss the reference to the Quebec Act in the ' Address to the People of Great Britain ' from the same congress. William Knox

[1] William Knox, *The Justice and Policy of the late Act of Parliament for making more effectual provision for the Government of Quebec asserted and proved, and the Conduct of the Administration respecting that Province stated and vindicated*, p. 20 (London, 1774) (Canadian Archives).

[2] See an interesting pamphlet by Thomas Bernard, *An Appeal to the Public ; Stating and considering the Objections to the Quebec Act*, pp. 51 ff. (London, 1774) (Canadian Archives). Bernard is very explicit in his view of the motives governing the boundaries.

[3] Kennedy, *op. cit.*, pp. 139 ff.

loyally supported the government as long as he was in office, and wrote, as we have seen, a defence of the Act ; but he secretly agreed with Carleton that the new constitution was a necessary piece of legislation owing to the coming storm. In later life, however, when passions were hushed, he opened the door to the secret chamber of British policy.[1] To Chatham, who had expressed a fear in the house of lords that the bill would ' finally lose the hearts of all his majesty's American subjects ',[2] a pamphlet was addressed by a writer well acquainted with the government's policy, in which honesty is more evident than party shrewdness. The policy was stated boldly : ' But there is another consideration which makes the affection of the Canadians still more desirable—I should be afraid to mention it if your lordship had not proclaimed it already—it is the present state of Boston. Should, my lord, (which God avert) a fatal necessity arise (as your lordship has has [sic] been too apt both to prognosticate and to advise) to coerce America, do you wish, in that melancholy event, to combine the heart of the Canadian with the heart of the Bostonian ? Was Canada now in the possession of France, and should the Bostonian resolve upon rebellion, there can be no doubt whither he would look for support and for encouragement. But the loss of that hope may happily dispose him to better thoughts.' [3]

The purpose of the Act thus takes on another aspect than that of generosity and goodwill, largely though these un-doubtedly figured in it. North and his advisers make it plain

[1] William Knox, *Extra Official State Papers, addressed to the Right Hon. Lord Rawdon*, &c. (London, 1789) (Canadian Archives). Knox's pamphlet throws important light on colonial policy in general and on the boundaries in particular (see pp. 43 ff.).

[2] *Chatham Correspondence*, vol. iv, pp. 351 ff.

[3] *A Letter from Thomas Lord Lyttelton to William Pitt, Earl of Chatham, on the Quebec Bill*, p. 19 (New York, reprinted 1774). This pamphlet was attributed to Lord Lyttelton by the colonists. It was published at first anonymously in London. Its real author appears to be Sir William Meredith, a privy councillor, who was fully acquainted with the imperial policy.

that the colonists were not quite undeceived in including it among the oppressive acts, and Knox discloses the whole spirit of the scheme. Canada was to be a military base, held quiet by an endowed church, a vast hinterland, a satisfied *noblesse*, a recognized priesthood, French civil law, and a disciplined and obedient population. The policy of Governor Carleton became the policy of the British cabinet. We can now understand why Carleton hid his instructions during the crucial days in Canada. He intended that no concessions should be made to the British, for fear especially of offending the seigniors on whom his reliance was placed.

The debates on the Act do not ring entirely true. Of the motives, origin, and objects of the bill, the ministry had no adequate explanations. Every single report on the state of Quebec by the experts and law officers was refused to the house of commons, and on two occasions specific votes for them were negatived.[1] That the government intended to make Canada a French province is the one thing clear. The motive, however, has been misinterpreted. In the light of the evidence available it is at present reasonable to conclude that the main idea seems to have been the continuation under another crown of the old French threat against the southern colonies. The loopholes in the Act in favour of the British settlers do not cut across this policy. It was possible to say that the best had been done in a complicated issue, that the vast majority had been considered; but if the future changed the conditions, there was an escape for the minority. It was quite the correct thing for the king to assent to the Act as 'founded on the clearest principles of justice and humanity'. But Carleton knew that in all probability he would return to Canada as civil governor and would control the situation. He had no disposition to disclose or to attempt concessions to the British. Even when he was most suspicious, most afraid, most contemptuous of their

[1] See Cavendish, *op. cit.*, pp. 94 ff.

attitude, he did not do his plain duty and carry out his plain orders. The conditions changed quickly, and the ministry intended that in those changed conditions the permissive clauses of the Act should be fully known. They were glad to catch at the straws of support when Carleton's instructions were issued in January 1775. Carleton did not move. An elementary political insight would have shown him that it would have been at least good policy, and would have immensely strengthened his own hand, had he let the British element know that there was a legal opening at least for hope. He would thus have minimized their reasons for becoming spies and traitors. Carleton preferred to be governed by his *idée fixe* : if the French-Canadians are with us, who can be against us ? A seignior and a priest in the hand are at present worth a few contemptible British traders in the bush. There is no necessity to deny the generosity of the measure. It is generous actually and potentially. The motives are in question. And no motives other than ulterior will serve entirely to explain why a government headed by Lord North and the servants of a ' patriot king ' handed out ' justice and humanity ' to the French-Canadians, and laws ' founded on the sentiments and inclinations of those who are to be governed by them ',[1] while at the same time and in the same parliament they were goading their own flesh and blood into the shambles of civil war.

The wisdom of the policy embodied in the Quebec Act can be studied from immediate and remote points of view. Its relation to the American revolution is evident and will become clearer. The Act did not pass unchallenged in England. Chatham thundered against it with eloquent pathos. Burke and Fox, the most advanced liberals of their day, could not rid their minds of the idea that the whole thing was policy ; they felt that it had not been discussed on its merits, and that there lay behind unexplained reasons. The merchants enlisted the

[1] Lord Lyttelton (?), *op. cit.*, p. 12.

services of Masères, who amplified the petitions from Quebec with numerous pamphlets. The corporation of the city of London petitioned the king against the breach of political faith and the endowment of Roman catholicism. They laid their protest before him personally on his way to assent to the measure.[1] In 1775 a motion was made in the house of lords to repeal the Act, and its defence fell on Lord Lyttelton, a member of the government, who employed the words of the most enlightened liberalism, while at the same time he congratulated the country that already the policy was bearing fruit. In spite of the ' non-importation agreement ', in spite of ' the factious resolutions of the assemblies, notwithstanding the inflexible enmity of the congress, the Canadians have opened a way for the English trader . . . these, my lords, are the consequences you have derived from this Canada bill '.[2]

A priori the Act appeared unwise. In reversing the policy of 1763, it was a distinct breach of faith. Many had come to the province relying on the promises given in the royal proclamation. Their hopes were disappointed, and it is hardly surprising to find that not a few of them cursed British perfidy and joined the rebels' cause. In addition, it is doubtful if the Act carried with it the goodwill of the Canadians as a whole. To the clergy, seigniors, and lawyers it was a *carta libertatum*—a grant of privileges—but to the *habitants* it was not so entirely acceptable. During the ten years of chaos before the passing of the Act they had become more independent, and not unfrequently the old ecclesiastical and feudal dues and rights remained unpaid. The idea of their being reimposed did not carry with it universal approval. Carleton soon found out that a process of disentegration had set in, of which his military mind had taken no account. When the seigniors and clergy called on the people to arm against the rebels and traitors of the south, there

[1] *Annual Register* (1774), pp. 129] ff., 232].

[2] *The Speech of Lord Lyttelton on a Motion made in the House of Lords for a Repeal of the Canada Bill, May 17, 1775*, p. 4 (London, 1775) (Canadian Archives).

was little response.   There are few more pathetic things in Canadian history than Carleton's dispatches during this period. Before long he was convinced that neither *noblesse* nor priest-hood could rally the *habitants* in defence of their country. Southern propaganda flourished in the rich soil of ignorance and suspicion.   He feared to assemble any great multitude, as few were disposed to take up arms for the king.   Every means failed to bring the people to a sense of their duty and only a mere handful marched against the enemy.   Gentry and clergy alike failed ' to retain their infatuated countrymen '.   They were ' a wretched people blind to honour '.   Many of them openly joined the invaders, and their adherence was measured by the strongest side.   Over and over again Carleton lamented his disappointment and the ignorance, fear, credulity, and per-verseness of the *habitants*.   The Act failed in that those most conciliated by it were unable, for reasons of which Carleton took no heed, to rally the Canadians to arms—' the most ungrateful race under the sun '.[1]

The Act failed in intimidating the southern colonies.   The day had passed when a French colony on their north would stay their hands.   The political ferment was already at its height, and the colonists whom French intrigue in land and trade and Indian affairs had failed to unite were now ready to draw a single sword in self-defence.   Acts of parliament were consolidating their ranks, and the Quebec Act instead of being a deterrent became a violent irritant to their purpose.

The Act laid on Quebec the old seigniorial and ecclesiastical system and buttressed up institutions which were already losing hold on the *habitants*.   It is also claimed that the presence of a solid French-Canadian group in modern Canada with all its attendant political difficulties can be traced to the folly of the Act.   Many political thinkers, quite apart from racial and

[1] Carleton's dispatches, from June 7, 1775, to September 28, 1776, which throw light on the history, are in *State Papers*, Q. 11 and Q. 12 (Canadian Archives).

religious prejudices, believe that a less complete recognition of French-Canadianism in 1774 would have been acceptable to the French-Canadians and would have eliminated such problems as are evident to-day in relation to race, creed, and education. They point to Louisiana, where no difficulties have arisen out of a failure to grant privileges. But it is futile to discuss the wisdom of the Act from the might-have-beens of history.

On the other hand, the Act saved the province, if we contemplate a situation in which priest and seignior had combined to rally the people against Great Britain—a situation made all the more dubious when France joined in alliance with the colonies. The United States might not have tolerated the perpetuation of French customs in the union, but the idea of Vergennes to make Canada an autonomous province under French suzerainty was not outside practical politics. The general indifference of the French-Canadians saved the situation, and even Lafayette failed to move them from their apathetic mentality. The decisive factor was the loyalty of the clergy and seigniors. Carleton indeed built better than he knew. The loyalty of the French-Canadian church and upper classes was secured and proved a powerful influence against disintegration. Not only in the American revolution, but in the French revolution, the Napoleonic wars, in 1812, and in the rebellions of 1837, the church and upper classes in Quebec set their faces like flint against organized treason and dismembering sedition.

It was a blessing for Canada that the Quebec Act settled the status of the Roman catholic church and removed it for generations out of that *damnosa haereditas*—religious politics. Had its position been left in the air without a statute behind it, the coming of the United Empire loyalists might have added another war of religion to the tragedies of history. As it was, the transition to a new constitution was infinitely less complicated. It is fair to state, however, that in the width of the concessions and in the comprehensiveness of the guarantees, little place was left for give and take, and there was thus

eliminated much of the sweet reasonableness of compromise.
To hold on and not to move, to fear further claims and to be
on guard, are a large price to pay. Quebec has brought essential
and vital and characteristic gifts to the life of Canada, and they
can be traced to the influence of the Roman catholic church
satisfied in 1774. In so far as Quebec is to-day a strong centrifugal force it can be traced to 1774. One thing is certain, the
Quebec Act strengthened the imperial tie, and we may too
lightly exaggerate the defects and too lightly appreciate the
virtues.

Quot homines, tot sententiae. In that subtle tantalizing world
of human motive and human endeavour it is seldom possible
to reconstruct history, had circumstances been different. There
is nothing easier than to say this might have been, that might
have happened, when dealing with the inconstant play of the
human will—but these are the *métier* of idlers and of dreamers.
All that can be hoped for, in dealing with such a question as
the Quebec Act, is to set down naught in malice, and to attempt
to avoid the advocate in trying to be the judge.

[AUTHORITIES.—Most of the documents are in A. Shortt and A. G. Doughty,
Documents relating to the Constitutional History of Canada, 1759–1791 (Ottawa,
1918) ; Egerton and Grant, *Canadian Constitutional Development* (Toronto,
1907) ; Kennedy, *Documents of the Canadian Constitution, 1759–1915* (Oxford,
1918) ; *State Papers*, Q. 11 and Q. 12 (Canadian Archives). The debates are
in Cavendish, *Debates on . . . the Bill . . . for the Government of the Province
of Quebec* (London, 1839). The pamphlet literature is of great importance. William Knox's *Justice and Policy of the late Act of Parliament*, &c.
(London, 1774), should be read in connexion with his *Extra Official State Papers*
(London, 1789) ; Lyttelton's (?) *Letter to William Pitt, Earl of Chatham* (New
York, 1774) and *Speech on a motion . . . for Repeal of the Canada Bill* (London
1775) throw light on the policy of the ministry. V. Coffin, *The Province of
Quebec and the Early American Revolution* (Wisconsin, 1896), is useful, but
narrow in outlook and lacking in wide historical background. (See an
important review by Adam Shortt in *Review of Historical Publications relating
to Canada*, vol. i, pp. 68 ff.) Justin H. Smith, *Our Struggle for the Fourteenth
Colony : Canada and the American Revolution* (2 vols., New York, 1907),
contains a mass of material. Abbé Lionel Groulx, *Vers l'émancipation* (Montreal, 1921), has an interesting chapter on the Quebec Act. A. G. Bradley,
Lord Dorchester (Toronto, 1907), is a useful introduction to the period, but
lacks documentation and authorities.]

CHAPTER VIII

THE COMING OF REPRESENTATIVE GOVERNMENT

IF the American revolution was influenced by the Quebec Act the revolution in its turn influenced Canada. Canada lost the territories south and west of the great lakes which had been included in the province. Arbitrary government was accentuated during the war. The progress of hostilities and the peace of 1783 brought into Canada a crowd of loyalists, who created a new situation with their just claims on a home under the British crown. Their advanced political thought, their experience in popular institutions, and their objections to arbitrary government not a whit removed from those of the triumphant colonists were bound to upset such equilibrium, in political, social and religious life, as existed in Canada. The American revolution made a new constitutional development inevitable.

When the revolutionary war was over, the boundaries remained to some extent unsettled and Great Britain held the western trading posts till 1794, hoping that the United States would in some way compensate the loyalists. The new boundary was defined in a long and detailed clause of the treaty,[1] but imperfect maps led to a series of boundary disputes which are best considered here. The north-west angle of Nova Scotia was exceedingly hard to find or to define, and a line due west from the Lake of the Woods to the Mississippi did not at all come near that river. It was only in 1818 that a line was agreed on, and the 49th parallel of north latitude became the boundary line west of the Lake of the Woods, while that between Maine and New Brunswick was not settled till the

[1] Kennedy, *op. cit.*, pp. 167 ff.

Ashburton Treaty of 1842.[1] The American 'wedge' thus created was a feature against federation in 1867.

Owing to the progress and issues of the war, the Quebec Act was almost a dead letter, and students are thus robbed of an opportunity to watch an interesting constitutional experiment completely at work. The political institutions of Canada did not pass unscathed through the ordeal. Carleton, who had returned to Canada in 1774, began with a clean slate, as the Quebec Act swept away all ordinances relating to civil government and the administration of justice before May 1, 1775. The revolutionary war made him more than ever careful. He organized in April 1775 a temporary court of common pleas,[2] but he had no intention of being either rash or communicative. He withheld his instructions and concealed concessions,[3] lest the seigniors should be alienated in a difficult situation which rendered the proclamation of martial law necessary.[4] His hands were full not merely with the war situation in Canada but with dispatches from home. The possibilities of French-Canadian assistance, as a return for the grant of the old laws and customs, now loomed up. Carleton's former estimates of the situation were recalled, and he was asked to furnish at first three thousand and later six thousand Canadian troops.[5] When at length disappointment, invasion, and intrigue allowed a resumption of civil government, Carleton was as far from concessions as ever.

Civil jurisdiction was organized, July 23, 1776, in the district of Quebec,[6] and in the following August a court of

---

[1] For a discussion (with detailed references) of the various boundary problems, see W. Houston, *Documents illustrative of the Canadian Constitution*, app. A, B (Toronto, 1891).

[2] *Quebec Gazette*, April 27, 1775.   [3] See above, pp. 55 ff.

[4] Masères, *Additional Papers concerning the Province of Quebec* (London 1776), p. 170 (Proclamation of June 9, 1775).

[5] Dartmouth to Carleton, July 1, 1775, *State Papers*, Q. 11, p. 152 ; same to same, July 24, 1775, *ibid.*, p. 182.

[6] Shortt and Doughty, *op. cit.*, pp. 674 ff.

appeal was set up consisting of the governor and council.[1] Early in 1777 the civil and criminal courts were reorganized and their proceedings regulated.[2] These ordinances reproduced essentially the system at work between 1770 and the Quebec Act ; but civil cases were withdrawn from the king's bench, where theoretically English law prevailed, and the optional use of juries to decide facts was discontinued, provision, however, being made to hear evidence according to English law. Carleton maintained that juries would spoil his regulations, and a motion in their favour was voted down.[3] Captains of militia were revived as coroners and peace officers throughout the parishes. The governor and council acquired a judicial power which, added to their executive and legislative functions, recalled the authority of the old sovereign council. The very name of jury was ruled out and French-Canadians resumed local administrative functions. The French note was distinct throughout. American conditions reacting on the province raised a storm which was long and bitter. Carleton's estimate of his plans is noteworthy : ' these ordinances have been framed upon the principle of securing the dependence of this province upon Great Britain, of suppressing that spirit of licentiousness and independence that has pervaded all the British colonies upon this continent, and was making, through the endeavours of a turbulent faction here, a most amazing progress in this country.' [4]

The storm began early with petitions from the traders, and gathered strength at the period when Haldimand was brought to book for disobedience to official orders.[5] In the reprimand, the privy council referred the whole subject of the administration of justice to the governor and council, and asked for a report. The administration became divided on definite racial lines.

[1] *Ibid.*, pp. 672 ff. [2] *Ibid.*, pp. 679 ff.
[3] *Minutes of the Legislative Council*, D, p. 13.
[4] Carleton to Germain, May 9, 1777, Shortt and Doughty, *op. cit.*, p. 676.
[5] See above, pp. 53, 56.

Haldimand inherited Carleton's outlook and training. He had no experience as a civil governor and conditions made him suspicious and nervous. He feared changes and he supported the narrowest terms of the laws and ordinances. Carrying the majority of his council with him he crushed every movement in favour of English commercial law and the writ of *habeas corpus*. Professing an entire indifference to the form of government, he considered the rigid interpretation of the Quebec Act as ideally adapted for Canada.[1] When the war was over and the peace signed, the party in the council opposed to arbitrary rule grew stronger. Led by two imperial officials, Lieutenant-Governor Hamilton and Hugh Finlay, the deputy postmaster-general, they succeeded in forcing Haldimand to grant the substance of *habeas corpus*. After Haldimand's departure, the new policy enjoyed a brief temporary triumph. In 1785 an ordinance was passed granting the right of trial by jury in civil cases and in personal actions for damages.[2] There, however, the encroachment on the scheme of the Quebec Act stopped. Hamilton, the lieutenant-governor, was dismissed from office, and a successor was found in Brigadier-General Hope, one of Haldimand's right-hand men, on whose zeal and discretion the king relied to put down party spirit.[3] At once there was a reversion to the old policy.[4] It might thus appear that the American revolution was about to leave an unfortunate legacy to Canada of arbitrary and bureaucratic government, but it produced in reality a change which might not otherwise have taken place until modern times. With the coming of the loyalists new forces began to work. At first small and inarticulate and only used to support older positions, they at length

[1] Haldimand to North, October 24, 1783, Shortt and Doughty, *op. cit.*, p. 737.   [2] *Ibid.*, pp. 780 ff.

[3] Sydney to Hope, August 20, 1785, *State Papers*, Q. 25, p. 35 (Canadian Archives).

[4] Hope to Sydney, November 2, 1785, Shortt and Doughty, *op. cit.* pp. 793 ff.

became strong enough to produce developments whose form lasted for half a century and whose principles remained permanent in the constitution.

When Carleton returned to Quebec late in 1786 as Baron Dorchester, he faced a situation in which the old internal difficulties had become more complicated and those outside more serious. France was standing on the threshold of a movement destined to rock the foundations of the civilized world. In the United States, one of the great new political parties was full of hatred for Great Britain and of resentment against its opponents because Quebec had not been added to the triumphant colonies. In Quebec itself every old sore lay open. In addition, a newer Canada was being carved out of the virgin forest by those who had passed through dark waters to new homes in a French province. Petitions and movements for change had continued intermittently from 1774, but after the conclusion of the war a new series began, more concrete and more emphatic. The financial situation of the province had become precarious and once more the prospect of a house of assembly loomed up. Naturally the French-Canadians protested, but the scheme took form. All the older points of vantage were maintained, but there were notes of peace. The proposals included ' new ' as well as ' old subjects ', and a recognition that the concessions to the Roman catholic church were permanent. On the other hand, the repeal of the Quebec Act was demanded.[1] There was also an important new addition to the statement of claims. The coming of the loyalists was emphasized and the fact that the régime of a French feudal province was hardly likely to command their adherence or sympathy. On their side the French-Canadians recognized the essence of the Quebec Act, when they protested that their only desire was to continue as before the conquest.[2] Before

---

[1] Petition of November 24, 1784, *ibid.*, pp. 742 ff.
[2] *Ibid.*, p. 766.

long the loyalists began to plead their own cause and petitioned
for a separate government distinct from the province of Quebec.[1]
In the legislative council, their position added force to the old
faction fights which broke out once more over proposals to
give the loyalists some independent petty jurisdictions, and
' to render the British constitution desirable as well as venerable '. For the moment everything was held up with the
announcement that nothing would be done until Carleton had
come to the province once more and had reported on the new
conditions.[2]

A pathetic interest gathers round this period of Carleton's
rule in Canada. A quiet process of change had been taking
place in his mind. He saw even before he arrived the necessity
of removing voluntarily every burden which might render the
constitutional position of the inhabitants of Canada inferior
to that of the United States and lead to changes of allegiance.[3]
Perhaps no one better could have been selected, and he showed
wisdom when he made his acceptance of the appointment
conditional on the help of William Smith as chief justice, who
had had wide legal and judicial experience in New York.
Quite apart from the altered circumstances, the first thing that
must have struck the new Baron Dorchester was the fact that
his pet constitution, so carefully guarded by Haldimand and
Hope, had proved a failure. The council was no longer tractable.
He succeeded, however, in getting committees appointed to
inquire into the state of the province.[4] The records of the
investigation leave the impression that, with the best of goodwill, no one could either have succeeded in carrying out the
principles of law and equity or have failed to escape charges
of injustice and favouritism.[5] It gradually dawned on

---

[1] Petition, April 11, 1785, Shortt and Doughty, *op. cit.*, pp. 773 ff.
[2] Sydney to Hope, April 6, 1786, *ibid.*, pp. 805 ff.
[3] Memorandum of February 20, 1786, *State Papers*, Q. 26. 1, p. 53.
[4] Dorchester to Sydney, June 13, 1787, Shortt and Doughty, *op. cit.*,
pp. 865 ff.   [5] *Ibid.*, pp. 874 ff.

Dorchester that the régime under the Quebec Act was over. For the moment he was not sure of his mind. He could only advise that the system of land tenure be changed, reserving in every township five thousand acres as crown lands.[1] In the cabinet a plan had begun to crystallize. At the close of 1787 it was hinted to Dorchester that the province might be divided, and his opinion was asked.[2] The path was made no easier when private members of the house of commons began to urge action and to introduce bills. It was an extraordinary picture. After thirty years of British rule nothing was stable, no one secure. Faction, race, privileges, and counter privileges trip over one another in the records against a sad enough background of hardship, and often of actual struggles for existence. Where material conditions were better, passion was always prepared to break out, and the pens of ready writers never seemed to dry as attack and defence continued their petitions to the governor or to the crown.

Dorchester had scarcely created and organized new districts,[3] when Adam Lymburner appeared before the house of commons on behalf of those who desired a house of assembly. In a singularly calm manner he advanced reasonable arguments in favour of representative institutions and English commercial law.[4] The debate which followed was insincere, partisan, and ill-informed; but Pitt took the situation in hand and promised official action during next session, while Dorchester once more was urged to reconsider a problem which must long ago have become a perfect nightmare to him. The division of the province seems to have been the cabinet's most constant plan, and to the idea the governor's attention was specially drawn.[5]

[1] Dorchester to Sydney, June 13, 1787, *ibid.*, pp. 946 ff.
[2] Sydney to Dorchester, September 20, 1787, *ibid.*, pp. 863 ff.
[3] *Ibid.*, pp. 953 ff. and 963 ff.
[4] The ' Paper read at the Bar of the House of Commons by Mr. Lymburner ', *State Papers*, Q. 62–A. 1, pp. 1 ff. (Canadian Archives).
[5] Sydney to Dorchester, September 3, 1788, Shortt and Doughty, *op. cit.*, pp. 954 ff.

In reply Dorchester opposed division : ' A division of the province, I am of an opinion, is by no means advisable at present, either for the interests of the new or the ancient districts, nor do I see an immediate call for other regulations than such as are involved in the subject of the general jurisprudence of the country. Indeed, it appears to me that the western settlements are as yet unprepared for any organization superior to that of a county. This has lately been given to them. . . . But though I hold a division of the province at present inexpedient, yet I am of opinion that no time should be lost in appointing a person of fidelity and ability, in the confidence of the loyalists, to superintend and lead them, and to bring their concerns with dispatch to the knowledge of government under the title of lieutenant-governor of the four western districts above named. Should a division of the province notwithstanding be determined by the wisdom of his majesty's councils, I see no reason why the inhabitants of those western districts should not have an assembly.' [1]

In October 1789 the British government had made up its mind, and William Grenville forwarded to Dorchester the earliest draft of the new constitution, providing for the division of the province with an executive council and assembly in each division and ' an hereditary legislative council, distinguished by some mark of honour '.[2] The covering dispatches throw light on the conception. The aim was to assimilate the constitution to that of Great Britain, while at the same time to grant concessions as favours before they were extorted by necessity. The creation of a titled colonial aristocracy was destined to give the Upper House ' a greater degree of

[1] Dorchester to Sydney, November 8, 1788, Shortt and Doughty, *op. cit.*, pp. 958 ff.
[2] William Knox seems to have been the first to suggest a special colonial aristocracy. On the eve of the American revolution he drew up a memorandum for the cabinet in which he referred to the plan : ' My second object was to amend the colonial constitutions by creating an aristocratic estate in them.' *Extra Official State Papers*, p. 30.

weight and consequence than was possessed by the councils in the old colonial governments, and to establish in the provinces a body of men having that motive of attachment to the existing form of government which arises from the possession of personal or hereditary distinction '. The distinct racial groupings in the upper and lower divisions of the province suggested ' separate legislatures, rather than that these two bodies of people should be blended together in the first formation of the new constitution '. ' The state of France is such as gives us little to fear from that quarter in the present moment. The opportunity is therefore most favourable for the adoption of such measures as may tend to consolidate our strength and increase our resources, so as to enable ourselves to meet any efforts that the most favourable event in the present troubles can ever enable her to make.' [1] Once again, as in 1774, external policy helps to govern the situation. The lesson from the revolutionary war was to make the British constitution a reality in Canada, and the French-Canadians must be considered and consolidated in order to cut off any disadvantages in case of war with France.

Dorchester replied enclosing a draft drawn up in co-operation with Chief Justice Smith. There was no discussion of the wisdom of the policy. A few details called for attention. The boundary must be made vague owing to outstanding difficulties with the United States. Honours and titles would ill suit conditions and were better omitted. A wider vision breaks momentarily across the history. Dorchester began to think of a united British North America and enclosed the plan of an embryo federal system drawn up by the chief justice.[2] Dorchester's draft did not arrive in time to allow for the introduction of legislation in the session of 1790 ; but in the following

---

[1] Grenville to Dorchester (two dispatches), October 20, 1789, Shortt and Doughty, *op. cit.*, pp. 969 ff. and 987 ff.

[2] Dorchester to Grenville, February 8, 1790, *ibid.*, pp. 1002 ff.

session the king's message [1] drew attention to the policy, and
early in March 1791 William Pitt introduced the bill in the
house of commons, in a short speech which outlined the royal
purpose.   During the progress of the bill Lymburner was
heard against any division of the province and several unimportant changes were made.   On May 18 the bill passed
through the house of commons and was assented to on June 19,
1791.

British North America thus acquired representative institutions in all its governments.   For a period, Nova Scotia had
been administered by a governor or lieutenant-governor with
the aid of a council, which acted in an executive and legislative
capacity.   Attention, however, was called to the fact that the
governor's instructions contemplated an assembly.   Governor
Lawrence put off summoning it, pleading the scattered population, but more than likely being influenced by the coming
shadow of the Seven Years War.   Finally, the imperial government informed him that, as the settlers had been promised an
assembly, it must be called.   This peremptory command was
founded on the fact that the law officers of the crown had
given an opinion that legislative power in the province was
probably exercised in an illegal manner apart from an elected
chamber.   As a consequence, the first popularly elected
parliament ever summoned in what is now British North
America met at Halifax, October 7, 1758.[2]   Prince Edward
Island, which had been placed under the government of Nova
Scotia in 1763, was created a separate colony in 1769 under
a lieutenant-governor and council acting as executive and
legislature.   For similar reasons to those which affected Nova
Scotia an assembly was organized and met in 1773.   In 1784,
owing to the influx of United Empire loyalists, New Brunswick

[1] 'State Papers,' February 25, 1795, *Annual Register for 1791* (London,
1795), p. 124*.
[2] *Selections from the Public Documents relating to Nova Scotia* (Halifax,
1869).

was carved out of Nova Scotia and created a province with a council acting in the time-honoured dual capacity, and an assembly.[1]

The Constitutional Act of 1791 [2] needs careful analysis. The Act did not divide Quebec, but assumed that such a division would take place. Various suggestions had been made to get over diplomatic friction with the United States, but as these proved futile the boundaries were left for a subsequent order in council. The Quebec Act was repealed, in so far as it related to the appointment and powers of the council, and legislative authority was vested in the governor or lieutenant-governor acting with the advice and consent of the legislative council and assembly in each of the two new provinces. The legislative council, consisting of at least seven members in Upper Canada and fifteen in Lower Canada, was to consist of persons summoned under the great seal of the province. Additional members could be added by royal direction. All members were to be over twenty-one years of age and natural-born or naturalized British subjects. Membership was for life, and permission was given (though it was never exercised) to create a provincial nobility whose members could demand a writ of summons to the legislative council. The governor appointed and could remove the speaker of the council.

The king was to authorize the governor to call the house of assembly and to divide the provinces by proclamation into electoral districts. The minimum number of members was sixteen in Upper Canada and fifty in Lower Canada. The franchise was wide. The right to vote in rural districts was based on a forty shilling freehold or its equivalent in any other tenure, while in towns it was granted to those who possessed a residence valued at five pounds or rented at ten pounds and had resided at least one year in the province. Members

---

[1] Canada, *Sessional Papers*, 1883, No. 70.

[2] Kennedy, *op. cit.*, pp. 207 ff. (31 Geo. III, c. 31).

of the provincial council and all clergymen were ineligible for
seats in the assembly. There was no property qualification for
membership. The provincial parliament was to be summoned
once in every twelve months, and was not to continue longer
than four years ; but the governor could dissolve it at any time.
When a bill had passed both houses, the governor could assent
to it, reject it, or reserve it for the king's pleasure. Even a bill
to which his assent had been given might be disallowed by the
British government any time inside two years. The governor
and executive council were constituted as a court of appeal,
with the right of appeal from them to the privy council.

The question of religion was dealt with in careful detail.
The guarantees of the Quebec Act to the church of Rome were
confirmed, and previous instructions relating to tithes from
protestants for the support of protestant clergy were continued.
A new provision, however, for the latter was added. The
governor was authorized ' to make from and out of the lands
of the crown within such provinces such allotment and appropriation of lands for the support and maintenance of a protestant clergy within the same as may bear a due proportion
to the amount of such lands within the same as have at any
time been granted by or under the authority of his majesty '.
The proportion was fixed as ' equal in value to the seventh part
of the lands so granted '. All rents arising from these ' clergy
reserves ' were to be devoted exclusively to the support of
a protestant clergy. At the same time provision was made for
royal authorization to the governor and executive council to
erect parsonages or rectories ' according to the establishment
of the church of England ', and to endow them with such
sections of the clergy reserves as the council should deem
expedient. Presentation to such parsonages was a royal gift,
but spiritual jurisdiction over them was placed in the hands
of the bishop of Nova Scotia. The parsons were ' to have all
rights, profits, and emoluments, . . . as fully and amply . . .

as the incumbent of a parsonage or rectory in England '. An elaborate enactment covered local legislation, repealing and modifying these and former provisions touching religion. Such legislation was not unconstitutional ; but the king could not assent until it had lain before both the British houses of parliament for thirty days ; and his assent must be withheld if either house within that time addressed his majesty to withhold his assent. In any case, no such legislation could be made fully valid unless the provincial parliament, in the same session as it had passed such legislation, addressed the governor or lieutenant-governor describing the Act and asking that it should be transmitted to England for such consideration as that outlined. The royal supremacy, as asserted in the Quebec Act, remained unrepealed ; but the forms of the oaths in the bill recognized religious equality.

The new constitution also dealt with trade and commerce and land tenure. All lands in the new province were henceforth to be granted in free and common socage, and grants made in feudal tenure in this new province before 1791 could be changed on petition into grants in socage tenure. In Lower Canada the settler could obtain grants in socage tenure if he desired to do so, but subject to such alterations in its nature and consequence as the legislature of the province with the king's consent might determine. A section covered the commercial relations between the provinces and Great Britain. It recited an Act [1] passed during the revolutionary war, in which the parliament of Great Britain declared that it would pass no Act imposing duty, tax, or assessment for the purpose of raising a revenue in any colony, excepting only such duties as might be expedient for the regulation of commerce. It was considered ' necessary for the general benefit of the British Empire ' that this power should be retained, and as a consequence nothing in the Constitutional Act could be construed to prevent the

[1] Kennedy, *op. cit.*, pp. 165 ff. (18 Geo. III, c. 12).

king from regulating navigation and commerce between Upper and Lower Canada or between either and Great Britain, or any other colony or foreign state, or to give the local parliaments power to vary, repeal, or obstruct such regulations. The net product, however, of such duties was to be applied to the use of the respective provinces.

On August 24, 1791, an order in council divided the province of Quebec into Upper and Lower Canada,[1] and instructed the secretary of state to prepare a warrant authorizing the governor of the province to fix a date for the commencement of the Act within the provinces not later than December 31, 1791. On November 18 Alured Clarke issued a proclamation bringing the Act into effect on December 26, 1791.[2] In September 1791 Dorchester's commission and instructions were issued as governor-in-chief of Upper and Lower Canada, and Alured Clarke and John Graves Simcoe were appointed lieutenant-governors of Lower and Upper Canada respectively.[3] On May 7, 1792, Clarke divided Lower Canada into twenty-seven electoral districts returning fifty members to the house of assembly, and in the following July Simcoe divided Upper Canada into nineteen counties which were to elect sixteen members.[4]

When we turn to consider the debates [5] on the Constitutional Act certain principles governing the new consitution appear. The division of the province was intended to put an end to the competition between the French-Canadians and the British.

---

[1] A. G. Doughty and D. A. McArthur, *Documents relating to the Constitutional History of Canada, 1791–1818*, pp. 3 ff. (Ottawa, 1914).

[2] *Ibid.*, pp. 55 ff. Clarke was appointed lieutenant-governor of Quebec March 19, 1790, and began his duties in the following October. When Dorchester left for England in August 1791, Clarke administered the government of Lower Canada until Dorchester's return in September 1793.

[3] *Ibid.*, pp. 5 ff., 54 ff.   [4] *Ibid.*, pp. 72 ff.

[5] See the *Annual Register* for 1791 ; *History and Proceedings of the Lords and Commons* (' Parliamentary Debates ') (London, 1791) ; Robert Gourlay, *Statistical Account of Upper Canada*, vol. ii (London, 1822).

The idea was distinctly stated by Pitt : the creation of two separate colonies which should be left to work out their own destinies. The guiding force, however, was the reproduction as far as possible in each province of the eighteenth-century British constitution, with a local aristocracy and an established church. This reproduction was to act as a kind of charm. It was to prevent the repetition of the first great colonial tragedy ; and Pitt actually believed that Lower Canada, seeing the beneficent workings of this venerable constitution in the neighbouring province, would sigh for the gift and embrace the whole system from conviction. He dropped no hint in public, as Grenville had done in private, of possible trouble and war with France and of the necessity to conciliate French Canada, but he declared that the division aimed at satisfying both races in order finally to unite them. The future unity was to come, because the French-Canadians, initially satisfied by being separated from the British, would actually become dissatisfied because of the separation. They would finally sink race, religion, and traditions and rush to accept the British constitution out of sheer jealousy, lest Upper Canada should enjoy a monopoly in such a life-giving, wonder-working scheme. Division would suit the ' jarring interests ' and ' opposing views ' of the present ; but the very example of the ' image and transcript of the British constitution ' would compel union. It would be a leaven to leaven the whole lump. The shadow of Abbé Sieyès must have fallen over Pitt during the debate, for it is seldom that a constitution was formed on such principles. Pitt feared racial strife ; but he was prepared to use provincial jealousies in order to produce union. Nature was against his benevolent purpose. The discord lay deep in the heart of Lower Canada, and while that rankled Lower Canada would look with no longing to Upper Canada to heal constitutional trouble. The British in Lower Canada had opposed the division of the province. They had spoken in clear-cut terms through

Adam Lymburner at the bar of the house of commons. It is
no judgement based on experience that would criticize Pitt.
To Dorchester information had been given that the danger in
Europe necessitated the consolidation of every available
interest in the Empire. Grenville made it clear that concession
to the French-Canadians was an international necessity. They
were to be kept quiet from possible French influences in case of
a European war, by having their nationality recognized and
buttressed in a province where numerical superiority would
guarantee their predominating influence. That is one point
of view. In due course, having fulfilled this function in international policy, this nationalism was to dissolve and fade out
of a convinced and voluntary desire to possess in its entirety
the whole administrative scheme of an alien race. Such sublime
faith, like all sublime faiths, can only be ascribed to ignorance
—ignorance of Canada, of history, of nationality. While Burke
was giving way to frenzied temper and Fox was wiping eyes
tear-stained over a broken friendship, Pitt was inaugurating
a constitutional experiment in Canada which could never
produce the results which he intended. Constitutions are not
supernatural. They flourish and are successful where they
reflect social development, and where the friction in the political
machine is reduced to the lowest point. Pitt's Constitutional
Act was charged with friction, and in time Upper Canada
found the eighteenth-century British constitution an excuse
for radicalism, and Lower Canada used it to increase rather
than to diminish separatist tendencies.

The period in Canadian history which follows is almost the
inevitable working out of failure. This failure is due not merely
to the short-sightedness of Pitt's general principles, but to the
functioning of institutions under the Constitutional Act. Each
province must be considered separately. Upper Canada will
provide illustrations differing from Lower Canada, and separate
treatment will bring to light varied points of view in the inter-

action of similar institutions and different social and economic and racial conditions. It will then be possible to study the failure of representative government under broad generalizations derived from the history of each province, to which Nova Scotia, New Brunswick, and Prince Edward Island will add their experiences.

[AUTHORITIES.—The documents are in A. Shortt and A. G. Doughty, *Documents relating to the Constitutional History of Canada, 1759–1791* (Ottawa, 1918) ; A. G. Doughty and D. A. McArthur, *Documents relating to the Constitutional History of Canada, 1791–1818* (Ottawa, 1914) ; Kennedy, *Documents of the Canadian Constitution, 1759–1915* (Oxford, 1918) ; Egerton and Grant, *Canadian Constitutional Development* (Toronto, 1907). The debates are in *Parliamentary Debates, 1791,* and complete in R. Gourlay, *Statistical Account of Upper Canada,* vol. ii (London, 1822). The state papers are in *State Papers,* Q. 10–Q. 57. 2 (Canadian Archives). The pamphlet literature of importance includes Masères, *Additional Papers concerning the Province of Quebec* (London, 1776) ; *State of the Present Form of Government of the Province of Quebec, &c.* (London, 1789) ; *Observations on a Pamphlet :* ' *State of the Present Form,*' &c., by a citizen of Quebec (London, 1790) ; *Thoughts on the Canada Bill* (London, 1791).]

CHAPTER IX

REPRESENTATIVE GOVERNMENT IN
LOWER CANADA, 1792–1838

LORD DORCHESTER sailed for England on August 18, 1791, and the duty of inaugurating the new constitution in Lower Canada fell to Major-General Alured Clarke, a soldier inexperienced in civil government. His first delicate problem was the division of the province into electoral districts and the regulation of representation. Except for a foolish nomenclature which introduced the names of English counties into a French colony, Clarke's plan was as successful as could be expected. Four members each were assigned to Montreal and Quebec, two to Three Rivers, one to William Henry, two to each of the twenty-one counties, except Orleans, Bedford, and Gaspé, which were each given one. For the moment the arrangement was equitable, but before long it failed to satisfy the growing cities and the Eastern Townships. The provincial or imperial legislature could amend the proclamation. The latter was unwilling to interfere and the former had little desire to organize a redistribution which would give greater representation to the British, and thus strengthen the hands of the executive in the assembly. When at length redistribution took place, the number of counties was increased, but the divisions in the cities and towns remained the same. The first provincial election took place in June 1792, and parliament met for business on December 17, with thirty-four French and sixteen British representatives. Historians are almost agreed in considering this first assembly the strongest during the period, including as it did some of the best men in the province.

It is a strange picture. The vast majority of the electors had no conception of the political machine which they were called on to create. Largely illiterate and uneducated, they could not have understood the scheme even had the seigniors been willing to give them more enlightenment upon it than that it contained a menace of taxation. The gift, if such it was, came unasked and unsought, and, if reports were true from the lost colonies, with no very creditable past. The grant itself is almost *doctrinaire*. An apathetic, conservative, docile, and non-political people were entrusted with a constitution implying knowledge and insight. No attempt had been made to instruct them in its ordinary workings, much less in those delicate, intangible conventions and indeterminate traditions which gave it force and vitality. The French-Canadians received the skeleton of an alien system in the hope that they would inevitably clothe it with profound respect, and, having done so, would seek union with Upper Canada. With them were associated British settlers who could not imagine why they had been given such strange political bed-fellows.

Unconsciously in the first assembly race clannishness appeared, to remain the fundamental problem of Lower Canadian history during the period. Jean Antoine Panet was elected speaker after a division on practically racial lines. His brother had the insight to see that the speaker ought to be bilingual and should address the governor in English as the general language of the empire.[1] The British members seized on the latter idea, but failed to convince the assembly. It early became a standing rule that the speaker should read a motion in English and French if he could do so ; if not, he should read it in the language most familiar to him, and the reading in the other language should be done by his clerk or deputy. There was a further difficulty over the language of enactment.[2] A motion to make English the legal language was

[1] *Quebec Gazette*, December 20, 1792.
[2] See an important study Thomas Chapais, ' Les débuts du Régime parle-

lost, even though supported by the plea of imperial unity and by the suggestion that a subordinate legislature could not change the language of law. A decision was finally reached in which the assembly did not insist on French as the language of enactment, but agreed that bills respecting the criminal laws of England and the protestant clergy should be introduced in English, and those relating to the laws and usages of the province in French.[1] Clarke was thus saved the necessity of disagreement,[2] and the British government offered no objections to the use of both languages, but insisted on English as the language of law.[3]

The first parliament was prorogued, after passing some miscellaneous bills and drawing up rules of procedure, in a speech announcing war with France. Clarke noticed the general line of division. The French-Canadians were practically solid and controlled the house. The quorum was fixed so that no session could be held without a French-Canadian majority. Goodwill and patience had allayed much of the jealousy, but there was a distinct racial cleavage.[4] On the other hand, an impression was abroad that organized efforts were being made to mould the assembly and council to the wishes of the English party.[5]

When Dorchester returned there was little opportunity for constitutional issues. The judicial system was carefully and elaborately organized under a judicature act, which remained the basis of the system in Lower Canada till the union.[6] Strained relations with the United States and French propaganda in Canada occupied the attention of the executive and called for abnormal measures. But Dorchester had little

---

mentaire : La question de langue ' (*Le Canada Français*, Sept.–Oct. 1918, pp. 11 ff., 95 ff.).

[1] Doughty and McArthur, *op. cit.*, p. 105.

[2] Attorney-General Monk to Nepean, May 8, 1793, *State Papers*, Q. 66, p. 283 (Canadian Archives).

[3] Dundas to Dorchester, October 2, 1793, *ibid.*, Q. 65, p. 319.

[4] Clarke to Dundas, July 3, 1793, *ibid.*, Q. 63–2, p. 307.

[5] Monk to Nepean, January 3, 1793, *ibid.*, Q. 66, p. 261.

[6] Doughty and McArthur, *op. cit.*, pp. 125 ff.

sympathy with the new constitution. Doubtless he was getting old and irritable, and probably more conservative. At any rate he complained bitterly of the growing weakness of government owing to the division of the province. Whatever motives —political, military, or personal—may have lain behind his dispute with Lieutenant-Governor Simcoe, he was unable to rid his mind of the fatal policy of the Constitutional Act, with its ' dividing and subdividing ', its ' independent governments ' instead of unity and consolidation.[1] It was well that he did not remain in Canada to witness deeper failure, and that in his last speech he could congratulate the legislature on ' unanimity, loyalty, and disinterestedness manifested by this first provincial parliament, which have never been surpassed in any of his majesty's provincial dominions '.

There were undercurrents, however, which cannot be overlooked. French agents were planning an invasion of Canada, relying on the anti-British party in the United States. A new assembly, elected in September 1796, was mostly French-Canadian, and many of its members were suspect in the situation.[2] Indeed Prescott, Dorchester's successor, feared to call it together on account of its complexion and the spirit of insubordination.[3] When the storm clouds cleared, a new situation arose which disclosed a looseness in the constitutional structure. In attempting to reform glaring abuses in connexion with land grants, Prescott found that the executive on which he relied were the worst offenders. The actual dispute and its details are immaterial, but the lieutenant-governor, chief justice, and executive were soon at loggerheads. The growing consciousness of French-Canadian unity found comfort in the unedifying dispute among the British. The colonial office could only point with sorrow to the fatal effect of the jarring interests on executive

[1] Dorchester to Portland, February 20, 1795, *ibid.*, pp. 183 ff.
[2] Prescott to Portland, September 3, 1796, *State Papers*, Q. 77, p. 209.
[3] Same to same, October 28, 1796, *ibid.*, Q. 78, p. 14.

authority and appeal to Prescott's ' good sense, integrity, and zeal ' to regain control.[1] The rupture became a local scandal, and the chief justice attempted to form a party in the assembly in actual hostility to the governor.[2] Other disintegrating forces were at work. The Anglican bishop was urging greater consideration for his communion, and could not reconcile himself to the position granted to the Roman catholic church.[3] Rumours were abroad that the royal supremacy might be brought into operation. The chief executive lost influence and power when the government passed to non-military administrators. When military authority lay in the hands of an officer in Upper Canada, the French-Canadians began to look down on their own governor.

There was thus plenty of disorganization, jealousy, and fear abroad, when Robert Shore Milnes succeeded Prescott, and it was unfortunate that these should be accentuated in a racial issue under the régime of a well-disposed but rather futile civil governor. Milnes, however, wrote a dispatch which is of great value in throwing light on Lower Canada at the beginning of the nineteenth century. He noticed with fear the increase of popular power. The lessening of seigniorial authority, the independence of the Roman catholic church and priesthood, the disembodying of the militia, and the endless discussions in a popular house of assembly had all combined to destroy aristocratic influence. More protestant settlers were needed, and the Roman catholic bishop must be induced to exercise his authority under government control by offering him an increased renumeration. Meanwhile it was a source of congratulation that the executive did not depend on the assembly for supplies, as nothing could be more fatal for authority than placing a colonial government under the financial thumb of

---

[1] Portland to Prescott, October 11, 1798, *State Papers*, Q. 80–2, p. 435.
[2] Prescott to Portland, February 4, 1799, *ibid.*, Q. 82, p. 126.
[3] Bishop Mountain of Quebec to same, April 15, 1799, *ibid.*, Q. 83, p. 332. Cf. same to Camden, October 24, 1804, *ibid.*, Q. 96, p. 171.

a popular institution.[1]   The British government shared Milnes's fears.   They were prepared to do anything to improve the situation, and to allow the bishop almost any increase in order to bring the local clergy under the crown's undoubted power of issuing licences to them.   An annual militia training lay in the executive's own hands, but the home authorities would encourage protestant settlers to offset the popular influence of the French-Canadians.[2]   Before the new bulwarks of aristocracy could be erected, the executive government witnessed a popular episode of permanent and far-reaching importance.

A bill had been passed providing for the erection of common gaols in Quebec and Montreal and throwing the expense exclusively on the business and trading interests.   The merchants petitioned against it, the assembly replied with counter petitions, and the bill was not disallowed.[3]   The matter might have rested there, had not the merchants of Montreal met in festive protest at Dillon's Tavern.   The toasts included ' the legislative council friendly to constitutional taxation ' ; ' our representatives who proposed a proper mode of taxation ' ; ' may our representatives be divested of local prejudices ' ; ' prosperity to agriculture and commerce, may they aid each other by sharing a due proportion of advantages and burdens '.   These toasts were drunk, while the band played ' Rule, Britannia ', ' The Roast Beef of Old England ', ' The Conquering Hero ', and ' Britons, strike home '. The *Montreal Gazette* was accused by the house of assembly of a ' false, scandalous and malicious libel ' in publishing an account of the jovial opposition.   The *Quebec Mercury* entered the fray and widened the challenge beyond a mere question of privilege or of freedom of the press : ' this province is already too French for a British colony.   Whether we are at war or in peace, it is essential that we should strive by all means to oppose

---

[1] Milnes to Portland, November 1, 1800, Kennedy, *op. cit.*, pp. 238 ff.

[2] Portland to Milnes, January 6, 1801, *ibid.*, pp. 244 ff.

[3] Cf. Milnes to Camden, April 12, 1805, *State Papers*, Q. 97, p. 59, and Dunn to Castlereagh, April 6, 1806, *ibid.*, Q. 100, p. 62.

the growth of the French and of their influence.' Within a few months the leaders of the French party established a newspaper to protect the interests of their race. In November 1806 the first number of *Le Canadien* appeared with the significant motto, ' Notre langue, nos institutions, et nos lois '. The controlling staff were Panet, the speaker of the house of assembly, and Pierre Stanislas Bédard, an influential member. The tone of the paper was outspoken, incisive, and blunt. There were no denunciations of England, but the local executive came in for many a broadside of direct attack in which an intimate knowledge of the older classical writers on the British constitution did good service. External circumstances gave the paper an historical importance. The necessity of combining the civil and military organization in the hands of the governor was more urgent than ever, and in October 1807 Sir James Henry Craig arrived at Quebec. He had spent most of his life on active service, and almost instinctively he began by carrying into the civil government of the province a military autocracy and discipline, which were all the more rigid owing to his state of health.

Craig found the actual framework of parties in existence. The merchants had begun to combine with the officials and the executive and legislative councils. This was the strongest group, because of their influence over actual administration. Opposed to them were the French-Canadians, who controlled the assembly, led by doctors, lawyers, and journalists. The episode of ' the gaols' Act ' had helped to weld this group into something like a political party. It derived its real strength, however, from the fact that it represented the vast majority of the population and was bound together by the more subtle forces of race, language, and religion, intensified by suspicions of attack. It was Craig's misfortune to take into his confidence such extremists as Herman W. Ryland, his secretary, and Jonathan Sewell, the chief justice, who were both active in repressive policies. Ryland aimed to assimilate ' the colony in its religion, laws, and manners with the parent state ';[1] while Sewell declared that ' the province must be converted into an English colony, or it will ultimately be lost '.[2]

The French-Canadian party—for such they can now be called —at once became aggressive. The exclusion of the judges from the house of assembly was a good enough platform, and certainly it irritated Craig. Prorogations brought little consolation, and when he dismissed five French-Canadians including Panet and Bédard from their militia commissions, he only consolidated the opposition. Nor did elections bring relief. Dissolution gave him opportunities to pour scorn on the assembly for ' its frivolous contests ' and ' its abuse of its functions ',[3] but the opposing forces only appeared all the stronger, and in their strength he saw an ultimate goal of the subordination of the executive to the assembly, who ' either believe or affect to believe that there exists a ministry here, and that in imitation of the constitution of Britain that ministry is responsible to them for the conduct of government '.[4] The British cabinet doubted the wisdom of Craig's methods and advised him at any rate to moderate his language and to control his tongue.[5]

A new assembly proved that Craig had misjudged the influence of the executive in electioneering, and that he had made a grave error in policy. The French-Canadians came back stronger and more solid than ever and with a very definite method of attack. Craig's more temperate speech in a glowing setting of British victories was met with a resolution that his previous addresses had been censures on the house and were dangerous attacks on the liberties of the subject.[6] The resolution

[1] Kennedy, op. cit., p. 248.   [2] Ibid., p. 268.
[3] House of Assembly, Journals, 1809, p. 302. Cf. Doughty and McArthur op. cit., pp. 360 ff.
[4] Craig to Castlereagh, August 5, 1808, Kennedy, op. cit., p. 250.
[5] Castlereagh to Craig, September 7, 1809, ibid., pp. 254 ff.
[6] Doughty and McArthur, op. cit., pp. 365 ff.

might have been overlooked, but a more constructive policy followed. There were three sources of revenue in Lower Canada —firstly, the casual and territorial revenues of the crown ; secondly, proceeds from duties and licences under the Quebec Revenue Act of 1774 ; thirdly, amounts voted by the local legislature. The first two were at the disposal of the crown. In February 1810 the assembly passed a resolution agreeing to vote the necessary sums for the civil expenses of the government of the province, and prepared an address to the king and British houses of parliament stating their unwillingness that the crown revenues should be used to defray provincial expenses. The move was obvious. The assembly were learning the power of the purse. Craig pointed out technical mistakes in procedure, but he agreed to forward the address to the king. Bédard challenged the governor's interpretation of constitutional custom, and the house proceeded to exclude the judges by resolution and to appoint an agent in London. The governor was shrewd enough to see the implication of every move, especially that the appointment of an agent aimed to hurt the local executive and that the assumption of provincial expenditure would make the assembly 'complete masters of the country'. He dissolved the house.[1] In March Craig carried the war farther into the enemy's camp. The ' seeds of pernicious principles among the ignorant ' had been sown too long by ' the democratic party ', and he determined ' to take decisive steps to quell the dissatisfaction '. He suppressed *Le Canadien*, and arrested the printers and three of the proprietors, including Bédard, ' on the charge of treasonable practices '.[2]

Craig's policy met with little success. He found church and race too powerful and the passion which he would have crushed was only intensified by his methods. He had no solution, but wavered between suspending the constitution and

[1] For the whole history see Doughty and McArthur, pp. 366–78.
[2] Craig to Liverpool, March 24, 1810, *State Papers*, Q. 112, p. 55.

uniting the provinces.[1] Finally he sent Ryland to London, where for almost two years he tried in vain to induce the government to curb the powers of the Roman catholic church. Liverpool's government had its hands too full to reopen the Canadian question, and could only advise repeated doses of prorogation for such recalcitrant assemblies, while at the same time emphatically denying any possibility of bringing the executive under the control of the legislature. The 'nature of a colony' excluded any such arrangement.[2]

It is possible to excuse Craig's methods. He had great limitations, both natural and accidental. It was his misfortune not to understand local conditions. He looked for gentlemen and seigniors in the assembly, and he lamented that he could have nothing in common with 'shopkeepers', 'common habitants', 'the most ignorant of labouring farmers', 'black-smiths', 'millers', 'even the advocate and notaries', 'not one person coming under the description of a Canadian gentleman'. His outlook made him despair of the future of a colony in which such social pariahs had a share in government.[3] On the other hand, he had a difficult duty to perform, and he did it with soldierly brusqueness and honesty. Napoleon was still un-defeated, French agents were active in Canada, the Roman catholic church in the province was not unfavourable to France since the Concordat, and feelings in the United States were none too friendly. No excuse can be offered for Ryland. It is a penetrating commentary on colonial affairs that a man like him should have acquired such influence. His failure was more fatal than success. He complicated the whole constitutional issue, for he brought into it religious hatred. There grew up in relation to his activities a state of mind which lent to political disputes the emotional strength of suppressed suspicion. It is

---

[1] Craig to Liverpool, May 1, 1810, Kennedy, *op. cit.*, pp. 256 ff.
[2] Liverpool to Craig, September 12, 1810, *ibid.*, pp. 276 ff.
[3] Craig to Liverpool, May 1, 1810, *ibid.*, pp. 258, 264.

H

a sad acknowledgement of failure that Craig should bid farewell
to Canada confessing that among the French-Canadians the pre-
vailing sentiments were mistrust, jealousy, envy, hatred : ' the
line of distinction is completely drawn ; friendship and cordiality
are not to be found, even common intercourse scarcely exists.' [1]

Much of this history may appear petty and unimportant and
least of all constitutional. Craig's régime—' the reign of
terror '—is vital in the development, in which race, language,
finance and social life mingle with constitutional history. It
will be possible to move more quickly over the policy and work
of his successors, to curtail as it were the central acts of the
tragedy ; but his government cannot be minimized. During
it the organization took place of most of those forces which
wrecked the constitution of 1791. French-Canadian nationalism realized itself, and on that realization was begun a
structure which gave Lower Canada a particularly irritating
constitutional problem. Perhaps the greatest misfortune of
Craig's rule was that no one in England seemed to notice how
successful it had been in disclosing the failure of the machinery
of government The attitude towards the constitution of 1791
continued to be one of a profound aspect, which excluded the
contemplation of change. Governor after governor was sent out
to tighten or to loosen the administrative screw as the personnel
of the colonial office fluctuated ; but no one thought that the
failure lay in the screw. Meanwhile French-Canadians increased
their solidarity. Their programme may not have been constructive, clear or logical ; but this at least can be said for it,
it was just as valid as that which emanated from the colonial
office, from whose well-intentioned ignorance, in the final
analysis, the most loyal men in both provinces devoutly prayed
to be delivered.

Extremes had failed. The blustering rigour of the soldier had
created a grave enough situation. The local oligarchy, the

---

[1] Kennedy, *op. cit.*, p. 256.

' bureaucrats ' or ' château clique ', stood face to face with
a practically solid French-Canadian opposition. Without much
apparent grasp of the situation or of the manner in which
a change of policy would be interpreted, an era of conciliation
was begun by Craig's successor, Sir George Prevost. The change
doubtless produced good results during the war of 1812, but
constitutionally it was liable to misinterpretation. When the
militia officers whom Craig had cashiered were restored, and
when Bédard was made a judge, there was a danger that conciliation might be mistaken for surrender, and moderation
be interpreted as weakness. The motive behind these dealings
seems in fact to have been the necessity during a war period for
internal harmony and goodwill. There was no change of heart.
Prevost deliberately set himself to cultivate the French-
Canadians, as he found conciliation the only method by which
' he could hope to carry his measures '.[1] His success was
a personal one, and in debates none the less passionate the
assembly distinguished between him and his ' evil-disposed
advisers '.[2] There was growing up also a constitutional consciousness, which found actual expression during his government.
In petitions against Prevost's recall the French-Canadians'
point of view was clearly expressed. It was a source of complaint
that offices were filled by British, that the house of assembly was
regarded as a foreign body, and that the only communication
between the representatives of the people and the government
was by means of ' conseillers et gens en place de la minorité, qui
étant rivaux de la majorité sont peu propres à la bien repré-
senter '. Disloyalty had become a pet term in the mouths of
the governing class, and the province was split into factional
fragments. The governors who were advised by British
officials gradually came to believe that the French-Canadians
were ' mauvais sujets toujours opposés à leur gouvernement et

[1] Prevost to Bathurst, September 4, 1814, *State Papers*, Q. 128–1, p. 208.
[2] Same to same, March 18, 1814, *ibid.*, Q. 127, p. 264.

aux Anglais '. On the other hand, if a governor showed the
least favour to the French-Canadians the ' gens en place ' were
consumed with jealousy and hatred. As a remedy an interesting suggestion was made : ' La Chambre d'Assemblée offre un
moyen d'en obtenir d'une manière régulière, sans que ce soit
sur les recommandations de ceux du parti anglais. Si le
Gouvernement avait le pouvoir d'appeler au conseil les princi-
paux membres de la majorité de la Chambre d'Assemblée, il
aurait par là un moyen d'entendre les deux partis, et de n'être
point obligé de ne connaître l'un que par les informations reçues
de l'autre, il ne serait plus privé des connaissances et des
conseils qu'il pourrait tirer des anciens habitans du pays, et
nécessité de n'écouter que ceux qui viennent du parti opposé,
qui n'est pas celui où il y a le plus de connaissance du pays, ni
le plus d'intérêts conformes à ceux du pays.' [1]

Sir John Coape Sherbrooke continued a policy of tactful
humouring. He succeeded in pacifying the assembly over their
supposed right of impeachment. He enlisted on his side the
conciliating power of the Roman catholic bishop,[2] to whom he
gave a seat on the executive council,[3] and he recommended that
the speaker of the house of assembly should also be appointed
to that body in order to establish confidence in the government.[4]
It was due to him that the British cabinet decided to permit the
legislature to vote the expenses of the province apart from the
territorial revenue of the crown and the duties under imperial
Acts. Sherbrooke laid a financial statement before the assembly
in 1818 with an estimate of expenditure and pointed out how
far it fell short of monies at the disposal of the crown. After
long debate the house voted the estimated deficit. The triumph,
however, was personal, and even then it was partial. The

[1] Kennedy, *op. cit.*, pp. 282 ff.
[2] Sherbrooke to Bathurst, February 1, 1817, *State Papers*, Q. 143, p. 126.
[3] Same to same, January 1, 1817, *ibid.*, p. 1 ; same to same, February 5,
1818, *ibid.*, Q. 148–1, p. 117.
[4] Same to same, April 21, 1817, *ibid.*, Q. 143, p. 392.

assembly voted supplies only for a year, and with a perversity which soon became incarnate in Louis Joseph Papineau, their speaker, they failed to recognize the obvious triumph which they had won and refused to meet the British government half-way by making permanent provision for administration in a civil list. Sherbrooke's successor, the duke of Richmond, faced another financial crisis. With the personal element absent, the assembly took the entire estimates into consideration and examined charges against the crown revenue as minutely as those against provincial income. They treated the financial proposals as though they had control of them by constitutional law. They reduced salaries at will and censured officials by omitting their remunerations. Naturally the legislative council promptly refused to pass such arbitrary estimates. Apparently a civil list was out of the question, but it might have been possible to have tided over difficulties by annual grants. The assembly, however, claimed two things : to control the whole machinery of government by recasting at pleasure the estimates made by the executive, and to do so by treating the legislative council as non-existent. In addition, the majority had found in Papineau a fitting leader for exploiting the doctrinaire theories of the new liberalism. Where Bédard would have yielded to legalism and accepted a constitutional triumph, Papineau was stubborn and virtually demanded that the constitution should be at once abandoned. What Bédard lacked in visionary enthusiasm, Papineau supplied a hundred-fold. Bédard objected to the governor's patronizing speech to the assembly ' at the close of a session as at the last judgement the good were separated from the bad and each received the sentence he deserved ' ; but he saw that there might be ' no greater tyrant in the world than an assembly ', and that it was of ' the first importance that it should understand its constitutional rights '.[1]

[1] Bédard to J. Neilson, May 1 and June 20, 1819, *Neilson MSS.* (Canadian Archives).

The coming storm broke over the head of Lord Dalhousie, who acted as governor for over eight years. He was instructed to secure ' the permanent assignment of a fixed annual revenue to meet the charge of such a civil list as the province requires for its proper administration '.[1] When he met the legislature in December 1820, he presented a statement of the costs of government and he asked the assembly to provide sufficiently and permanently for them. The assembly missed the careful hands of Prevost and Sherbrooke. The estimates, remodelled and changed, were voted for a year, and the crown revenues were included as under provincial control. The council rejected the bill and censured the assembly, but the executive was left financially helpless. A year later Dalhousie explained with infinite patience that permanent provision was merely asked for permanent expenditure and that the general expenditure could be covered by a yearly vote. A motion for a civil list was overwhelmingly defeated. The assembly aired their views in an address to the king, proceeded to appoint a member of the house of commons as provincial agent in London, and threatened not to renew certain expiring revenue acts. The latter course would have further thwarted the executive, and in addition would have hurt Upper Canada, which depended for financial assistance on a share of customs' duties at Lower Canadian ports.[2] To grant the claims of the assembly meant that the constitution would be upset at the bidding of one colonial house. The assembly might become supreme in Lower Canada and hold up the entire government or render it dependent on imperial funds dubiously applied. In addition, Upper Canada, already irritable under the injustices of the financial arrangements between the two provinces, would be materially injured by constitutional issues which did not concern it. It was obvious that

[1] Bathurst to Dalhousie, September 11, 1820, *Colonial Office Papers*, G. 11 (Canadian Archives).

[2] Dalhousie to Bathurst, January 25 and June 10, 1822, *State Papers* Q. 161, pp. 50, 218.

conciliation must give place to some method of government more productive of administrative efficiency in the one province and of justice towards the other.

In June 1822 the under secretary for the colonies introduced a bill into the house of commons which embodied a change of policy. The two provinces were to be united under one legislature, each division having sixty members in a new assembly independent of population. A high property franchise was proposed which would have disfranchised most of the *habitants*. After fifteen years, French was to disappear as a parliamentary language and the Roman catholic church was to be brought under the Act of supremacy as previously suggested by Craig and Ryland.[1] The measure was postponed until Canadian opinion had been sounded, but its financial clauses were passed as the Canada Trade Act,[2] by which the legislature of Lower Canada was restrained from legislating about the customs' duties in such a way as to hurt the upper province.

Quite apart from the fact that the British parliament interfered with the taxing powers of the local assembly, the Act was such a bare-faced attack on the French-Canadian party that Papineau and John Neilson had no difficulty in organizing opposition. Politically the measure meant subordination if not absorption, ecclesiastically it alienated the priesthood, and seigniors and *habitants* alike were scared at clauses which threatened the traditional land system. In Upper Canada opinion was divided. Dr. Strachan and Beverley Robinson led a strong opposition, and the only consistent backing came from the Eastern Townships.[3] Papineau and Neilson easily convinced the British cabinet of the folly of the measure, and meanwhile the house of assembly watched events in comparative quiet. No sooner was the bill withdrawn, than it presented

[1] Kennedy, *op. cit.*, pp. 307 ff.   [2] 3 Geo. IV, c. 119.
[3] See the petitions for and against the union of the provinces in Kennedy, *op. cit.*, pp. 318 ff.

another scene. The immediate danger was over, but Papineau now possessed a political party, and with indecent violence he attacked Dalhousie as the living embodiment of the anglicizing policy. He led the assembly into another financial *impasse* by proposals which included the reduction of the governor's salary. Dalhousie could only close the session in despair, and point out how unconstitutional claims were not only hurting the province but handing on the seeds of certain destruction to each succeeding parliament.[1] During Dalhousie's absence in England the lieutenant-governor, Sir Francis Burton, acting in ignorance of instructions, and anxious to nullify such a gloomy view, presented the estimates as a whole and made no distinction between permanent and local revenues. He pointed out the estimated deficit and asked for a vote. The assembly examined the entire revenue, made considerable reductions in the appropriations, and voted what they considered adequate for a year. Burton reported a quiet session and thought that financial difficulties could now be settled between the two houses.[2] The assembly interpreted their ' quietest session for twenty-five years ' as one in which they had established constitutional control over the purse. Burton was severely censured.[3] When Dalhousie returned to the old method of distinguishing charges against the permanent revenue from charges against the casual revenue, he was met with challenging resolutions by the assembly : ' to the legislature alone appertains the right of distributing all monies levied in the colonies.'[4] He prorogued parliament in a speech of dignified regret, and in one memorable sentence he concisely summed up the constitutional issue : ' I have seen . . . in this session a positive assumption of executive authority instead of that of legislative, which last is alone your share in the constitution of the state.'[5] The electors refused to

---

[1] Kennedy, *op. cit.*, pp. 338 ff.
[2] Burton to Bathurst, March 24, 1825, *State Papers*, Q. 171, p. 12.
[3] Bathurst to Burton, June 4, 1825, Kennedy, *op. cit.*, pp. 339 ff.
[4] *Ibid.*, pp. 340 ff.   [5] *Ibid.*, pp. 341 ff.

accept the challenge of Dalhousie's speech, and Papineau swept the country. During the campaign he lavished such personal abuse on the governor that Dalhousie refused to accept him as a speaker.

The dreary petitions and counter petitions chased one another across the ocean to the colonial office. Dalhousie was finally removed to India, and a committee of the house of commons was appointed to consider the civil government of Canada.[1] The report confirmed the Canadians of French extraction in the enjoyment of their religion, laws, and privileges. It recommended a redistribution bill ' on a compound basis of territory and population '. While acknowledging the crown's right over certain revenues, the opinion was given .' that the real interests of the province would be best promoted by placing the receipt and expenditure of the whole public revenue under the superintendence and control of the house of assembly '. The governor, members of the executive council, and judges should be rendered independent of annual votes, and all revenues except territorial and hereditary should be handed over to the representative body. The legislative councils should be improved by withdrawing from them such a numerous group of office-holders. The entire reform was pronounced possible under ' an impartial, conciliatory, and constitutional system of government ', in which the legislative assembly and the executive government would be placed ' on a right footing '. The report was never debated and the ' system ' and the ' footing ' remained an unsolved mystery.

An attempt was made to conciliate. The secretary for the colonies pointed out that while the imperial statutes were unrepealed, the revenues under them could not be surrendered ; but that after the salaries had been paid to the governor and

[1] The report is in *British Parliamentary Papers*, 1828, vii. 569. The evidence is of exceptional value. The most important constitutional sections are in Kennedy, *op. cit.*, pp. 345 ff.

judges, the balance would not be appropriated until the assembly had been given an opportunity of discussing the best means of using it in the interests of the province. The financial concerns of Lower Canada would be settled by legislation. Shortly after this conciliatory dispatch, he introduced a bill, which was not passed, to hand over the revenue collected under the Quebec Revenue Act in return for a civil list. The result was ominous. The assembly replied in a series of resolutions claiming an inherent and constitutional right to control the whole public revenue, and repudiating the jurisdiction of the imperial parliament in the matter. A permanent settlement with the consent of the assembly alone would produce a civil list.[1] The report was received as ' an imperishable monument of justice and profound wisdom ', but there was no disposition to work towards it. The Eastern Townships, however, at long last received eight representatives under a new distribution bill.

When Lord Aylmer took over the government, he was instructed to continue the policy of conciliation and to neglect the implied *impasse* of the resolutions. He offered to hand over the provincial revenues, except from casual and territorial funds, in return for a civil list. The assembly was now on a very high horse. The civil list was refused. The debates contained newer and more extreme notes, such as a proposal to abolish the legislative council, to refuse all subsidies, and to repeal the constitution of 1791. Finally an address of grievances was drawn up, which Aylmer received with the implied sarcasm, ' Is this all ? ' Meanwhile the imperial government were busy on further concessions. They were willing to make the judges independent and to exclude them from the executive and legislative councils, excepting the chief justice, in return for permanent salaries. Practically a complete surrender was made to all the assembly's demands. In 1831 a law was passed handing over unconditionally the crown revenues under the Quebec Revenue Act.[2]

---

[1] Kennedy, *op. cit.*, pp. 351 ff.

[2] *Ibid.*, pp. 356 ff. (1 & 2 William IV, c. 23)

The spirit of the assembly remained the same. The imperial authorities asked for a bill securing the independence of the judges, guaranteeing their salaries, and providing a small civil list for the governor and a few officials. A bill was passed making the judges independent, but on an annual salary, and the civil list was rejected. The imperial government curtly disallowed the bill, and informed the assembly that the civil list outside the judicial salaries would be met from other sources. Papineau was leading his followers to a dizzy height of fatuity. When a few French-Canadians were killed by soldiers in an election riot at Montreal he cried out in the assembly, ' Craig only imprisoned his victims, Aylmer slaughters them '. Public meetings on racial lines fanned the political flames and folly added another triumph to the cause, when during an outbreak of cholera Aylmer was accused of having ' enticed the sick emigrants into the country in order to decimate the ranks of the French-Canadians '. Debates on countless wrongs transformed the assembly into a dangerous institution. The king was petitioned to allow the summoning of a ' general assembly ' of the people analogous to those in the United States, and to make the legislative council elective.[1] On its side, the legislative council opposed these suggestions and set out a justification for its existence that through it alone could the British element in the province receive security. Any changes in the constitution such as those suggested by the assembly would only result in civil war between the provinces and would ' drench the country with blood '.[2] Aylmer transmitted replies. The threat of war was severely rebuked. An elective legislative council was ' inconsistent with the very existence of monarchical institutions ', and if changes must come in the constitution they might be of a nature little likely to appeal to the popular party.[3]

The assembly girded its loins for one supreme effort, and on February 17, 1834, Elzéar Bédard, Pierre Bédard's son, intro-

---

[1] *Ibid.*, pp. 358 ff.   [2] *Ibid.*, pp. 362 ff.   [3] *Ibid.*, pp. 364 ff.

duced the famous Ninety-Two Resolutions,[1] commonly assigned to the pen of Auguste Norbert Morin, who afterwards held ministerial office. These resolutions. represented the extreme of constitutional demands in a framework of doctrinaire theory and implied revolution. They were the Grand Remonstrance, the Declaration of Right of the party which Papineau now completely controlled, and were described, probably by John Neilson : ' eleven stood true ; six contained both truth and falsehood ; sixteen stood wholly false ; seventeen stood doubtful ; twelve were ridiculous ; seven were repetitions ; fourteen consisted only of abuse ; four were false and seditious ; and five were good or indifferent.' [1]

The description may stand. The framework, however, discounted real grievances. The home government did not care to be told that toryism was dead in America, which prospered under widespread republicanism, and that the United States flourished under free institutions, whereas British North America stagnated under autocracy. Nor was there ordinary common sense in reminding Great Britain of the American revolution, or in suggesting that if grievances were not redressed only two alternatives remained for the province—either ' of submitting to an ignominious bondage or of severing those ties endangered which unite [it] to the mother country '. Insistence on ' conventions of the people ' and on an elective second chamber did not gain much support with a British cabinet from being linked up with examples from ' our neighbours ', who understood ' the manners and social state of the inhabitants of this continent '. The solemn impeachment of ' his excellency Matthew, Lord Aylmer of Balrath . . . for his illegal, unjust and unconstitutional administration of the government ', in addition to its impudence, was too much like cabinet government in the hands of a colonial assembly, even though it was ' the grand inquest of the province '.

[1] Kennedy, *op. cit.*, pp. 366 ff.
[2] Aylmer to Stanley, May 1, 1834, *State Papers*, Q. 216–2, p. 283.

On the other hand, they were attacks on genuine evils. The legislative council was the creature of the executive council and it had become 'inevitably the servile tool of the authority which creates, composes, and decomposes it'. The judges were not above suspicion ; pluralities among officials were common ; the expenditure of public money without popular consent was at least dangerous and volcanic. There was unfortunately little constructive suggestion, outside that of the application of the elective principle to the legislative council. There was not a hint of responsible government unless it was implied in Aylmer's impeachment and in vague phrase 'the vicious composition and the irresponsibility of the executive council'. Perhaps the most interesting results of the Resolutions were undreamed of by their authors. They proclaimed the parting of the ways. The saner men, such as John Neilson, Augustin Cuvillier, F. A. Quesnel, and Andrew Stuart, broke away from Papineau's leadership. Even Elzéar Bédard found a place for repentance. The church stiffened its back against the sentiments of democracy, revolution, and republicanism. The deserters, if such they were, did not turn tory and reactionary. They lent weight to societies for constitutional reform. It would be far from judicial to represent the '*patriotes*' as the only reformers. The 'constitutionalists' saw much that demanded change. The judicature and the irresponsible land-granting department needed revision. The accumulation of offices in the hands of the families and friends of legislative councillors was held up for reprehension. The executive council was inefficient and had feeble claims on the confidence of the community. The colonial office was incapable of handling the affairs of the colony.[1] The last complaint at this period became common, and it was unfortunately made clearer at the moment when Stanley, afterwards earl of Derby, allowed himself to propose a select committee of the house of commons to inquire into conditions

[1] Kennedy, *op. cit.*, pp. 388 ff.

in Lower Canada. This committee could offer no better advice
than an expression of its duty to withhold any opinion on the
points in dispute, and of its persuasion ' that the practical
measures for the future administration of Lower Canada may
best be left to the mature consideration of the government
responsible for their adoption and execution '.[1]

The ascent from folly to tragedy now began. Papineau
gained strength at the elections of 1835, and supplies were cut
off. Expenses were met by borrowings from the military
chest, a move which the assembly described as ' destroying the
wholesome and constitutional influence which the people ought
to have through their representatives over every branch of the
executive government '. The constitution was apparently
paralysed. The imperial government recalled Aylmer and
sent out a royal commission, consisting of the earl of Gosford
as governor—a good-natured and innocuous Irishman,—Sir
George Gipps, an eighteenth-century whig, and Sir Charles Grey,
a retired Indian judge, a typical tory and the reputed nominee
of William IV. This commission was supposed to handle with
constructive insight demands covering a complete surrender of
all public revenue, an elective second chamber, a reorganized
executive, and the abandonment of the system of chartered
companies in settlement as the advance guards of a subtle
process of anglicization.

The colonial secretary, Lord Glenelg, issued Gosford's
instructions.[2] The inexperienced Irishman was impressed in
high sounding terms with the nobility and pregnant purpose of
his mission, and was told to report his ' matured sentiments ' on
provincial affairs. He was above all to bear in mind that he was
sent on a ' mission of peace and conciliation '. The instructions
were a strange compound of giving with one hand and taking
away with another. To the hoary demand for control of all the

---

[1] The report is in *British Parliamentary Papers*, 1834, vol. xviii, p. 449.
[2] Kennedy, *op. cit.*, pp. 399.

revenue and the equally old refusal of a civil list, there was no solution offered. The crown was prepared to hand over all sources of income for an adequate civil list, for the management of the waste lands, and for pensions for retired officials. The constitution of 1791 was relied on. To debate salaries annually would establish the recognition of a principle that offices and officials were open to revision by the assembly. On the other hand, the king actually thought an elective legislative council might be considered, ' because his majesty [was] not prepared to deny that a statute which has been in effective operation for something less than forty-three years [might] not be capable of improvement '. Every schoolboy knows that William IV objected on ' sound constitutional principle to the adoption of the elective principle in the constitution of the legislative councils of the colonies '. Indeed, the concession made to the idea of constitutional change was virtually withdrawn in succeeding sections of the instructions.

Gosford thus began with a willing spirit, but the flesh was weak. His first assembly dragged on a dreary session until Papineau learned from Marshall Bidwell of Upper Canada that Gosford had not given the real substance of his instructions in his opening speech. This seemed to differ from the verbatim extracts quoted from the commissioners' instructions by Sir Francis Bond Head to the legislature of Upper Canada. At once the old noise of battle broke out. The legislative council refused to accept a supply bill different from that proposed by the government, and the legislature was prorogued, leaving the government without legal revenue for the fourth year to carry on the administration. Prorogation did not take place, however, until the assembly once more placed on record its demand for an elective legislative council. In dealing with the executive council it comes as near as the French-Canadian party ever came to responsible government : ' on the subject of the executive council we abstain from entering on any details because we hold this question to be closely connected in practice with the other more important subjects of colonial policy. We shall confine ourselves in saying that the full and entire recognition of the rights of this house and of the people by those whom your majesty may be pleased to call to your councils, and their constitutional responsibility based on the practice of the United Kingdom, will be essential motives for confidence in your majesty's government.'[1]

Under the shadow of inevitable failure the commissioners presented six reports.[2] The most important recommendations were that the imperial Act of 1831 be repealed,[3] and that no responsibility of the executive council to the legislature be recognized. The British cabinet were unwilling to repeal the statute. Gosford laid all his instructions before the legislature which he summoned on September 22, 1836. There was no progress. 'Colonial degradation' and 'metropolitan ascendancy' were the notes; but there was a clear-cut resolution which must be quoted at length, as it is at once the most constructive constitutional statement in the tantalizing history : ' The principal object of those reforms is :—To render the executive council of this province directly responsible to the representatives of the people, in conformity with the principles and practice of the British constitution as they obtain in the United Kingdom ; to extend the principle of election to the legislative council, which branch of the provincial legislature has hitherto proved, by reason of its independence of the people, and of its imperfect and vicious constitution, insufficient to perform the functions for which it was originally designed ; to place under the constitutional and salutary control of this house the whole of the revenues levied in this province from whatever source arising ; to abolish pluralities or the cumula-

---

[1] Kennedy, *op. cit.*, pp. 421 ff.
[2] Reports are in *British Parliamentary Papers*, 1837, vol. xxiv, p. 50.
[3] See above, p. 106.

tion in one person of several or incompatible offices ; to procure the repeal of certain statutes passed by the imperial parliament in which the people of this province are not and cannot be represented, which Acts are an infringement of the rights and privileges of the legislature of this colony and are injurious to the interests of the people thereof ; to obtain over the internal affairs of this province and over the management and settlement of the wild lands thereof (for the advantage and benefit of all classes of his majesty's subjects therein without distinction) that wholesome and necessary control which springs from the principles of the constitution itself, and of right belongs to the legislature and more particularly to this house as the representatives of the people ; which reforms are specially calculated to promote the happiness of his majesty's subjects in this province, to draw more close the ties which attach the colony to the British empire, and can in no way prejudice or injure the interests of any of the sister provinces.' [1]

The British government was at its wits' end. Lower Canada received special mention in the king's message to parliament in January 1837, and on March 6 Lord John Russell introduced ten resolutions [2] which were passed in the face of some keen radical opposition. They empowered the governor-general to use monies in the hands of the receiver-general to pay arrears of salaries. They refused an elective legislative council, the introduction of executive responsibility, and the cancellation of the North American Land Company's charter. They promised legislation on land tenure in conformity with a suitable local Act, and complete control of revenue in return for permanent judicial salaries and a civil list. They authorized the Canadian legislatures to adjust trade disputes between the two provinces. Steps were taken to give the resolutions the force of law by legislation. Gosford was instructed meanwhile to call the legislature of Lower Canada and to give it, as it were, a last

---

[1] Kennedy, *op. cit.*, p. 426.   [2] *Ibid.*, pp. 434 ff.

chance. The king's death and the accession of Queen Victoria stayed legislation, and the government of Lower Canada was temporarily provided for by a vote of credit.

In the province the ten resolutions fanned the embers of nationalism into a glowing heat. They were denounced as ' violations of the social contract ' and as ' foul stains '. On all sides meetings of protest were held and the ' cap of liberty ' was set up in scenes of flamboyant enthusiasm. ' Papineau et le système électif ', ' Papineau et l'indépendance ', ' A bas le despotisme ' were the shouts and devices of new revolutionaries. Gosford's legislature of August 1837 was merely a more respectable edition of what was going on outside its walls. It was pure waste of time to submit to it the ten resolutions, and to hold them aloft as a veiled threat was pure folly.[1] The reply was ominous. ' It is our duty ', said the assembly, ' to tell the mother country that if she carries the spirit of these resolutions into effect in the government of British America, and of this province in particular, her supremacy therein will no longer depend upon the feelings of affection, of duty, and of mutual interest which would best secure it, but on physical and material force.'[2] On August 26 Gosford prorogued the legislature, and, as events turned out, the legislature of Lower Canada never reassembled. A few days later he informed the colonial secretary that it might be necessary to suspend the constitution.[3]

In November the first shots were fired in a tragedy of civil war, and the first lives were sacrificed in Canada for a political ideal. The church saved the situation, and Bishop Lartigue of Montreal in a noble pastoral rallied the rank and file of the clergy and people to the cause of peace.[4] It is impossible to

[1] Kennedy, op. cit., pp. 436 ff.

[2] Ibid., pp. 438 ff. The ten resolutions did not pass unchallenged in Upper Canada and the legislative council of that province submitted them to severe criticism : Journals of Legislative Council, February 13, 1838.

[3] Gosford to Glenelg, September 2, 1837, State Papers, Q. 238–1–2, p. 71.

[4] Same to same, October 30, 1837, ibid., p. 403.

reconstruct those pathetic and ephemeral scenes of foolhardy devotion amid the first snows of a Canadian winter without something of pity for idealists deserted by their leaders and something of shame for conditions that made civil war possible. To rebel was unreasonable ; but failure covers a multitude of sins. On January 16, 1838, Lord John Russell introduced a bill which after amendment and recasting was passed on February 10 as ' An Act to make temporary provision for the government of Lower Canada '.[1] The constitution of 1791 was suspended from the date of the proclamation of the Act to November 1, 1840. The crown was given power to constitute a special council, by authorizing the governor to summon special councillors. The laws passed by this council were limited in operation to November 1, 1842, ' unless continued by competent authority '. The council could impose no new taxes and could make no constitutional changes. The governor alone could introduce a law, and five councillors must be present to give it legal force. The Act was the creation of a dictatorship which, Lord John Russell announced, was to be conferred on Lord Durham. Meanwhile the Act was sent to Sir John Colborne, and he was instructed to summon a special council for temporary needs, leaving Durham free to form his own. Colborne's council consisted of twenty-one members, of whom eleven were French-Canadians. On April 18 the council met and was prorogued on May 5, 1838.

[AUTHORITIES.—The documentary material is in A. G. Doughty and D. A. McArthur, *Documents relating to the Constitutional History of Canada, 1791–1818* (Ottawa, 1914) ; Egerton and Grant, *Canadian Constitutional Development* (Toronto, 1907); Kennedy, *Documents of the Canadian Constitution, 1759–1915* (Oxford, 1918) ; the *State Papers*, Q. 60–Q. 241 (Canadian Archives) ; the *Neilson MSS.* (Canadian Archives) ; R. Christie, *A History of the Late Province of Lower Canada* (6 vols., Montreal, 1866) ; the *Minutes of the Legislative Council of Lower Canada*; *Journals of the House of Assembly of Lower Canada*. Lord Durham, *Report on the Affairs of British North America* (ed. Sir Charles Lucas, 3 vols., Oxford, 1912), is an essential book for the

[1] Kennedy, *op. cit.*, pp. 445 ff. (1 & 2 Victoria, c. 9).

period, and Sir Charles Lucas's introduction is invaluable. N. E. Dionne, 'Pierre Bédard et ses Fils' (*Galerie Historique*, i, Quebec, 1909), and 'Les Trois Comédies du " Statu Quo " 1834' (*Galerie Historique*, ii, Quebec, 1909) are useful. The preface to the latter is of the greatest value in connexion with the split in 1834. Dr. Dionne also prints the ' Ninety-two Resolutions ' with a very valuable commentary. E. Cruikshank, 'The Administration of Sir James Craig; A Chapter in Canadian History' (*Transactions of the Royal Society of Canada*, 3rd series, vol. ii, sect. ii, pp. 61 ff.), is based on contemporary material. F. X. Garneau, *Histoire du Canada* (cinquième edition, Paris, 1913–20), gives the history from the French-Canadian point of view. A good general introduction with a short bibliography is A. D. DeCelles, *The ' Patriotes ' of '37* (Toronto, 1915). The period from 1791 to 1812 is fully discussed in Thomas Chapais, *Cours d'histoire du Canada* (vol. ii, Montreal, 1921). The *British Parliamentary Papers* contain much valuable material, among which may be noted specially—*The Report of the Select Committee on the State of the Civil Government of Canada* (1828, vii. 569) ; *Fourth Report of the Standing Committee of Grievances on Lord Aylmer's Conduct as Governor* (1836, xxxix. 570) ; *Report of Commissioners on the Grievances complained of in Lower Canada* (1837, xxiv. 50) ; *Evidence before Select Committee on Lower Canada in 1834* (1837, vii. 96) ; and *Report* of same (1834, xviii. 449).]

CHAPTER X

REPRESENTATIVE GOVERNMENT IN UPPER CANADA, 1792–1838

THE constitution of 1791 could hardly have found a more ideal foster-father than Lieutenant-Colonel John Graves Simcoe, first lieutenant-governor of Upper Canada. He was a soldier, an aristocrat, a strong believer in the established church and in that due gradation of social life so dear to his class. To him the British constitution was only less sacred than the bible, and it was almost with reverence that he undertook the work of organizing the government of the new province. On September 17, 1792, he opened the first legislature at Newark. The scene has passed into the romance of Canadian history. All available pomp of circumstance was pressed into service, and in a clearing in the Canadian woods an attempt was made to reproduce with solemn seriousness and due decorum the glory of Westminster. The one regret in Simcoe's eyes was that so many members of the house of assembly were ' one-table men ' —dined in common with their servants—and did not belong to what he considered the best class in the province.

The scene, however, is more than a romance. It is an index to Upper Canadian life. Founded on an aversion to republicanism and on loyalty to monarchical principles, Simcoe laid very permanent foundations for Upper Canada. The governor was to be a real viceroy, the legislative council a western house of lords, the legislative assembly a gracious cog in the political machine. The Anglican church was to shed the kindly influence of its decent and established moderation in balancing society and in eliminating such zealots as the Methodists, ' a set of ignorant enthusiasts, whose preaching [was] calculated to perplex the understanding, to corrupt the morals, to relax the nerves of industry and to dissolve the bands of society'. The toleration given to the Roman catholic church was due to Simcoe's recognition that its priests were ' interested in a connexion with the authority of thrones, and who therefore never lose sight of the principle to preserve and propagate arbitrary power '.[1]

The province was at once organized along British lines. English civil law and trial by jury were introduced and the foundations of local representative government were laid.[2] Local taxation was regulated. Arrangements were made to pay members of the house of assembly and to define their qualifications. A judicial system was set up and a criminal law thoroughly established.[3] Simcoe, however, would have reproduced the entire English system. He incorporated towns on the British model and he created county lieutenants.[4] Even the home government was persuaded to give a doubtful sanction to his schemes.[5] His ruling passion was to stem the tide of ' democratic subversion . . . to establish the form as well as the spirit of the British constitution by modelling all the minutest branches of the executive government after a similar system, and by aiming as far as possible to turn the views of his majesty's subjects from any attention to the various modes and customs of the several provinces from which they emigrated to the contemplation of Great Britain itself as the sole and primary object of general and particular imitation '.[6] He was little pleased when Portland pointed out how colonial circumstances might be detrimental to such slavish adherence to British models and precedents, and especially how it might weaken

---

[1] La Rochefoucault-Liancourt, *Travels in Canada, 1795*, pp. 47 ff. (edited W. R. Riddell, Ontario Archives, Toronto, 1917).

[2] Kennedy, *op. cit.*, pp. 227 ff.

[3] Doughty and McArthur, *op. cit.*, pp. 91, 146, 158, 194, 246.

[4] Simcoe to Portland, December 21, 1794, *ibid.*, pp. 196 ff.

[5] Portland to Simcoe, May 20, 1795, *ibid.*, pp. 204 ff.

[6] Simcoe to Portland, January 22, 1795, *ibid.*, pp. 200 ff.

the hands of the governor himself. Simcoe disputed the implied censure and his political faith survived the shock of dispatches. He informed the cabinet that his zeal was necessary to check ' the elective principle ' on the continent, and that he rejoiced in an ideal legislative council which saved him refusing many bills from a ' tenacious and untractable ' house of assembly.[1] There may have been personal pique when he resented what he considered Dorchester's interference in the affairs of the province, but his devotion to the constitution undoubtedly was the moving force in his protests.

Outside the actual machinery of government it is necessary to reconstruct something of the social background against which this ' British senator soldier ' administered no ' mutilated constitution ', but one that was ' the very image and transcript of that of Great Britain, by which she has long established and secured to her subjects as much freedom and happiness as is possible to be enjoyed under the subordination necessary to civilized society '.[2] First were the military, who took their cue from the lieutenant-governor and out-heroded Herod in being British. Then came the original United Empire loyalists, who had earliest shaken off the republican dust from their feet, and soon created a rustic aristocracy with almost complete control of the councils. Then there were the regular immigrants from the United States, whose devotion to republicanism was not superior to a love for good Canadian farm-lands. This group was looked down on by the true loyalist, who had come out of Egypt with clean heart and unsoiled hands. Lastly, there was a growing population of British settlers, who were in turn despised as foreigners and emigrants by those who now claimed a monopoly in the British name.

With Simcoe at the head of affairs, Upper Canada inevitably

[1] Same to same, October 30, 1795, *ibid.*, pp. 206 ff.
[2] Simcoe to legislature, October 15, 1792, *Journals of Legislative Assembly of Upper Canada*, p. 18 (Ontario Archives, Toronto, 1909).

began its life with some sort of a governing class, and it was not many years before a local oligarchy or clique, known to history as ' the family compact ', practically controlled the situation. No one seriously doubts their general ability and their general good intentions, qualities which as a rule lay behind their power. But too frequently their caprice, interest, arrogance, and folly stand out in the history in such a way as to make it impossible for criticism to bow the head silently before the shrine of loyalty. It is the impact of this group on the stern pioneer reality of a new world that created the constitutional issues in Upper Canada. It widened its borders by including noble and baseborn, Anglican and Methodist, the good, the bad, the indifferent ; and by a process now lost to minute investigation it gained executive control. It lined the frontier, while dubious settlers were located deeper in the forest. York, Newark, and Kingston reflected its life. Peter Russell, the administrator till the arrival of General Hunter as lieutenant-governor, began to build up its fortunes or at least its property qualifications in huge land grants. Secure behind an Alien Act passed in 1804, which gave the government power to arrest and deport those of suspected loyalty who had not resided six months in the province, Upper Canada might look forward to the reproduction in America of the British constitution and the British class-system. The crown lands were ready for decent speculation, and land never tainted the hands as trade did. The clergy reserves were the symbol in every township of that combination of church and state so eminently respectable and revered.

Unfortunately for the dawn of another England, a group of reformers early entered the scenes of ordered peace.[1] In

[1] The documents connected with these early reformers are printed *in extenso* in *Report of the Canadian Archives*, 1892, pp. 33 ff. (Ottawa, 1893). There are several letters from C. B. Wyatt over his case in *Baldwin MSS*. [A], E. 6–7, pks. 17–24 (Ontario Archives). See also W. R. Riddell, ' Mr. Justice Thorpe ' (*Canadian Law Times*, November 1920, pp. 907 ff.).

February 1805 William Weekes, an Irish barrister, was elected to the house of assembly. Almost immediately he introduced a motion ' that it is expedient for this house to enter into the consideration of the disquietude which prevails in the province by reason of the administration of public offices '.[1] He could only rally four votes to his side. A year later he returned to the attack. The government had passed on Hunter's death into the hands of Alexander Grant, ' pitchforked into power by a clique '. Weekes found the executive insecure, and succeeded in having a committee appointed, with power to call witnesses, to consider the state of the province.[2] It reported against the arbitrary methods in land granting, against the wretched roads throughout the country, and the lack of general education.[3] The resolutions were not momentous, but Weekes continued his unwelcome interest in affairs. He took up the cause of ' Metho-dists, Quakers, Mennonists, and Tunkers '.[4] He was largely responsible for the discovery that a considerable sum of money had been paid out of the provincial treasury without the authority of parliament or a vote of the assembly. A committee of the house reported that its rights and privileges had been violated, and Weekes drew up the address to the administrator lamenting the departure from ' constituted authority and fiscal establishment ' as painful to a free people and their representa-tives, and expressing a hope that he would ' more than sympa-thize in so extraordinary an occurrence '. Grant replied that he regretted the dissatisfaction, and could only plead custom as the executive's excuse. He promised, however, an ' immediate investigation '.[5] His reply was referred, on Weekes's motion, to a committee of the whole house, which reported having passed

[1] *Journals of the House of Assembly of Upper Canada* (March 1, 1805), p. 48 (Ontario Archives, Toronto, 1911).
[2] *Ibid.* (February 10, 1806), p. 64.
[3] *Ibid.* (February 12, 1806), pp. 67 ff.   [4] *Ibid.*, pp. 72 ff.
[5] *Ibid.* (February 28, March 1, 1806), pp. 101 ff., 107. See also Doughty and McArthur, *op. cit.*, pp. 318 ff.

a resolution ; but the assembly, on the speaker's vote, refused to receive a report.[1] The legislature was prorogued the same day and the matter dropped. In writing to the British government, however, Grant took an opportunity to regret the 'intemperate address ', and laid it at the door of those who endeavoured ' to perplex, if not to distress the administration ', by influencing members ' sequestered from the world ' and without ' the benefit of a liberal education '. When the lieutenant-governor, Francis Gore, came to the province in August 1806, he returned the money in dispute to the provincial treasury. The assembly expressed its ' full satisfaction ' and the house passed a resolution relinquishing its claim to the appropriation.[2] In the minority of two against the resolution appeared the name of Robert Thorpe, of whom Gore, in announcing the resolution to the colonial office, said ' he has uniformly opposed every measure that could promote the peace or strengthen the hands of this government '.

Robert Thorpe was another Irishman who was appointed judge of the king's bench for Upper Canada in July 1805, after an unfortunate three years in Prince Edward Island. His attitude towards public affairs can be estimated by the fact that within five months he thought himself competent to write to the home government a report on the province : ' I find that Governor Hunter has nearly ruined this province ; his whole system was rapaciousness, to accumulate money by grants of land was all he thought of . . . unjust and arbitrary, he dissatisfied the people and oppressed the officers of government. He had a few Scotch instruments about him . . . that he made subservient to his purpose, and by every other individual he and his tools were execrated. Nothing has been done for the colony. No roads ; bad water communication ; no post ; no

---

[1] *Journals of the House of Assembly of Upper Canada* (March 3, 1806), pp. 113 ff. (Ontario Archives, Toronto, 1911).
[2] *Ibid.*, pp. 122, 125, 174–5.

religion ; no morals ; no education ; no trade ; no agriculture ; no industry attended to.' Thorpe felt that his special care should be directed towards conciliating the people, and he tried to lead the assembly, though as yet not a member of it, in the direction of popular rights against ' extortion and oppression '. His correspondence at this time leaves the impression that he considered it his duty to take care of the province. ' I will labour to keep everything quiet at least till the governor comes.' His method was extraordinary. He made ' the courts of justice the theatres for political harangues ' and his charges to juries occasions for his quieting labours. He received addresses from them in which he was recognized as a channel for the communication of grievances. ' I shall lay before the governor everything you desire, . . . may [he be] Promethean heat and animate the province from the centre to the extremity.' The new lieutenant-governor, Francis Gore, arrived while Thorpe was on circuit. He had thus an opportunity to hear of Thorpe's strange doings from the executive council, and was not at all friendly when he interviewed him for the first time.

Thorpe was destined for further notoriety. William Weekes, while engaged in a case before Thorpe at Niagara assizes, took occasion to deliver a kind of political speech in which he described General Hunter as a ' gothic barbarian whom the providence of God had removed from this world for his tyranny and iniquity '. Thorpe sat ' with the greatest composure to hear this abuse '. One of the council in the case ' warmly reprobated such language ' and as a consequence received a challenge from Weekes, who fell mortally wounded in a subsequent duel. Public rumour claimed that Thorpe was not only a party to the speech, but instigated the unfortunate tragedy, after passing a night with Weekes at a public tavern. At any rate, Weekes's death created a vacancy in the house of assembly and Thorpe was asked to contest the seat, an invitation which he at once accepted. Gore tried to dissuade him, by pointing

out ' the impropriety of a judge becoming a candidate for a seat
in a popular assembly ', but Thorpe replied that his office was
no constitutional disqualification, and the assembly later supported him in a resolution of the house.[1] He went to the
opening of the poll ' invoking the shade of his departed friend
as looking down from heaven with pleasure on their exertions
in the cause of liberty '. Every effort was made to elect a strong
government candidate. Thorpe maintained that the lieutenant-
governor, with his ' Scotch pedlars ' and ' shopkeeper aristocracy ', used ' every species of undue influence, bribery, coercion,
and oppression . . . and himself demeaned by trying to seduce
both high and low '. Gore replied by accusing Thorpe of
marching to victory under an Irish rebel flag, and amid unblush-
ing references to the American revolution and to Charles I.

Thorpe's return was an occasion for repression. Gore attacked
the freedom of the press, and closed the columns of the *Upper
Canada Gazette* by order, when Thorpe sought to answer a
challenge from his late opponent which had appeared in that
journal. In addition, the lieutenant-governor attacked and
dismissed some officials who had supported Thorpe, notably the
surveyor-general, C. B. Wyatt, and the sheriff of the home
district, Joseph Willcocks. It is doubtless true that both these
men were out of sympathy with the government, and equally
true that as officials they might have been less prominent in
a political fray. Wyatt was too loose-tongued in his hope that
after Thorpe's election ' the government would go to the devil ' ;
but Gore went out of his way to invent or to create charges of
incompetency and fraud against him, which Wyatt, who left for
England, finally disproved.[2] Against Willcocks the record of
a convivial evening at the house of John Mills Jackson was
alone brought as evidence. ' Push the bottle about ' was the
standing command, and before long Willcocks was damning

---

[1] *Journals of the House of Assembly of Upper Canada* (February 9, 10,
1806), pp. 127 ff., 135.　　　　　[2] *Annual Register*, vol. lviii, p. 294.

the governor and government and the 'Scotch faction', while Jackson urged him on as having been treated by Gore as 'a damned rascal'. Later on Jackson had the question of Canadian government brought up in the house of commons, but the pamphlet [1] which he published on the political state of Upper Canada was too strong for the house of assembly, which passed a unanimous resolution describing it as a libel full of 'unexampled insolence and contumely'.[2] Jackson's propaganda was intended to help the parliamentary debate in London,[3] and the censure may have been due to Gore's efforts to provide Castlereagh with counter-material.[4] At any rate, Gore was under suspicion during the period. Willcocks, who had founded a newspaper, charged his fellow members with being in the pay of the government, and implied that he had information. At Gore's instigation apparently prosecution for libel was dropped. Willcocks, however, threw discretion to the winds and was imprisoned by order of the speaker till the end of the session.[5] During 1812 he obstructed the war policy of the government, and finally was killed fighting on the American side at the siege of Fort Erie.

It is somewhat difficult to form an estimate of this group who later were looked back on as the pioneers of reform. Weekes, Thorpe, Wyatt, and Willcocks were Irishmen, and it may be that jealousy of the 'Scotch pedlars' entered into the history. Willcocks is the easiest judged. His zeal was of a disloyal nature. He was undoubtedly tinged with republicanism six months before he became a member of the legislative assembly,

---

[1] *A View of the Political Situation of the Province of Upper Canada in North America*, &c. (London, 1809).

[2] *Journals*, &c. (March 10, 1810), p. 369. Cf., however, pp. 370 and 375. Four members, including Willcocks, who entered the assembly on January 1808, opposed the drafting and engrossing of an address to Gore containing the resolution.

[3] Jackson to Willcocks, July 19, 1809, *State Papers*, Q. 313–2, p. 460.

[4] Gore to Castlereagh, March 11, 1810, *ibid.*, Q. 313–1, p. 245.

[5] *Journals*, &c. (February 18, 20, March 16, 1808), pp. 225, 228, 274.

when he was writing to New York expressing his admiration
for the government of the United States and his enmity against
the British institutions of Upper Canada.[1] Thorpe was fundamentally a blatant demagogue, with a fatal command of words
and a conceited and tactless personality. Wyatt and Jackson
were a better type, and their opposition was embittered by
what they considered rather high-handed methods. Gore
possibly inspired the opposition to the group in the assembly,
which then, as in the future, was easily moved by the very
appearance of sedition and responded to any skilful suggestion
of disloyalty. There can be little doubt that Gore's advisers
used the fact that most of the reformers were officials against
them. Even his attorney-general, William Firth, entered the
fray and joined the faction in London demanding his recall.
Firth had a caustic pen and could enlarge on the ' tyranny of
Mr. Gore and his abandoned iniquitous council ' and pour
contempt on government circles at York, ' that more than
Sodom and Gomorrah of the Western World '.[2] On the other
hand, it must be noted that these men gained the support of
some of the sanest citizens of the province, and they cannot
lightly be dismissed as mere flotsam and jetsam of political
agitation. They were foolish, tactless, impetuous, and filled with
a sense of their own importance ; and it was a serious error in
tactics to oppose the executive, while receiving government
pay. Their enthusiasm, however, was genuine, and it was
directed to the service of humbler men outside the charmed
official circles. Their history is the first chapter in the rebellion.
They were the political fathers of more dangerous democrats.
The ' Scotch pedlars ' became the ultra-loyalists of later days,
and Gore set an example of electioneering which other lieutenant-
governors followed in after years.

[1] Willcocks to J. and D. Cozens, July 24, 1807, *State Papers*, Q. 313-2,
p. 328.
[2] Firth to W. W. Baldwin, February 13, 1812, *Baldwin MSS.* [A], E. 6-7,
pk. 20 (Ontario Archives).

The war of 1812 marked a real turning-point in Upper Canadian history. First of all it divided the sheep from the goats—the loyalists who saved the province from the later immigrants from the United States. It lies outside this history to attempt an adequate consideration of this point, but both before and during the war the government kept careful vigilance. ' Itinerant fanatics enthusiastic in political and religious matters ' had come in from the United States, ' were cordially received, and thus disseminated their noxious principles.' [1] Brock early noted the number of aliens in the province. *Habeas Corpus* was suspended and martial law proclaimed. The latter measure caused trouble in the house of assembly, which passed a resolution declaring it ' arbitrary and unconstitutional '.[2] The war, however, increased the power of the original United Empire loyalists and their descendants. They and theirs had played the most prominent and most efficient part in it. It had been an imperial war, but such success as had been gained in it was Canadian. It was just the occasion for men of robust convictions and perhaps robuster prejudices. Democrats, itinerant orators, and even good settlers of a later date were insecure in a crisis. As a result, the loyalists after the peace were more loyal and more anti-democratic than ever. Their magnificent devotion intensified their self-confidence and self-esteem. They built up an administrative oligarchy no longer founded merely on the past but on present loyalty. Secondly, there grew out of the war other social dangers which were to react on the constitutional history. There was delay in settling the pay of the militia and much dissatisfaction over the small land grants for military service.[3] Many of the rank and file were thus thrown into opposition to the government. American soldiers took back accounts of the splendid lands of Upper

---

[1] Drummond to Bathurst, April 30, 1814, *State Papers*, Q. 318–1, p. 81.
[2] Doughty and McArthur, *op. cit.*, pp. 435 ff.
[3] Gore to Bathurst, October 17, 1815, *State Papers*, Q. 319, p. 117.

Canada, and soon thousands came to conquer with the axe
what they had failed to conquer with the sword. At first it
was a 'general rush', as Gore described it. Later 'land
speculators undertook to settle the province with citizens of the
United States'. The assembly joined in the business and
refused to tax vacant lands. Gore felt the danger and prorogued
the legislature. 'If early attention', he wrote, 'is not paid to
compose the spirit arising by the machinations of land speculators in this province, the king's government will be exposed
in all future time to purchase tranquillity by the disagreeable
measure of stifling sedition by rewards, and thus encouraging
the growth of the evil.'[1] Before long American schoolmasters
were abroad in the country districts who used books ' tinctured
with the principles of their government and constitution and
holding up their own worthies as perfect patterns of every moral
excellence, whilst our public and private characters are represented in the most odious and disgusting light '.[2] In addition,
the fall of Napoleon brought a crowd of emigrants, many of
whom were British radicals and disciples of Cobbett. The new
settlers of all classes were largely sectarians with little sympathy
for the church of England.

The loyalist oligarchy had gained in personnel. John
Strachan, a converted Presbyterian schoolmaster, had become
rector of York. In 1815 he was appointed to the executive
council, and in 1817 he became a member of the legislative
council. Strachan was a fierce fighter, with all the zeal of
a convert. His personality was so strong that he soon exercised
a powerful influence over the government. Unfortunately he
proved a stormy petrel for Upper Canada. He developed into
a kind of Anglican Hildebrand. In 1816 his pupil, John
Beverley Robinson, became solicitor-general, and later attorney-
general. Robinson was a man of narrow views ; but brilliant

---

[1] Gore to Bathurst, April 7, 1817, *State Papers*, Q. 322, 1-2, p. 129.
[2] McDonnell to Bathurst, January 16, 1817, *ibid.*, Q. 323, p. 177.

natural gifts and high moral character redeemed him from devious ways. These two were supported by Chief Justice Powell, Henry John Boulton, the solicitor-general, and a group of others, if less known to history, yet none the less self-important. An examination of the civil list of Upper Canada for 1818 discloses the fact that the entire legislative and executive councils were composed of members of the ' family compact ', and that all the members of the executive council were also members of the legislative council. The same group also controlled the high court, the law offices, and the militia and surveyor-general's departments.

As for the sentiments and affiliations of the house of assembly it is somewhat hard to decide. Their refusal to tax waste lands was not due to any desire to thwart the governing class, but to a rather human weakness which looked for a share in the spoils. On the other hand, their ' rights and privileges ' were carefully guarded. They carried on an elaborate dispute with the legislative council over supplies, and asserted that the latter could assent to or reject money bills, but could not amend them. Borrowing the phraseology of 1678, they maintained that they possessed in this matter ' the constitutional and immemorial rights of the commons of Great Britain '. The attitude of the council filled the assembly with ' emotions of the highest interest ', for it was ' in [its] essence pregnant with principles subversive of the exercise of the functions of the representative body of the people '. Intercourse between the two houses was broken off. A petition was drawn up affirming the legality of the proceedings and deploring as a national and constitutional evil that legislative and executive functions were vested in the same persons. Samuel Smith, who carried on the government between Gore's departure and the arrival of Sir Peregrine Maitland, closed the session with ' its business unfinished '.[1]

---

[1] *Journals of the House of Assembly of Upper Canada* (March 12, 19, 21, 23, 24, 26, 27, 30, April 1, 1818), pp. 521 ff. (Ontario Archives, 1912). Cf. Doughty

A widely distributed pamphlet defended the assembly and sustained them in ' the proud privilege of the people, to keep in their hands the exclusive right to hold the purse-strings '. It deplored the administrator's closing speech : ' but why should we wonder ? For, as the fickle goddess turns round the wheel, sometimes a statesman or a warrior is at the head of affairs ; and at another a fool, a glutton, or a fly-catcher ; for Rome had her Trajans and her Domitians ; and in this province, too, we have not been wanting in variety.' [1]

Such is the human background. The physical is no less interesting. Surveying had been going on from the first, but with the rush of settlers and the boom in land jobbing it acquired an acceleration in inverse ratio to its accuracy. Before long men were looking for their boundaries and their limits. This state of affairs naturally caused anxiety to the older inhabitants, who began to doubt their surveys. In addition, the constitution of 1791 had imposed on the country physical barriers against wise colonization. In each township there were huge reserves of land set aside for the protestant clergy and for the crown. These, of course, remained undeveloped. With the increase in land speculation, lands were withdrawn from settlers who would gladly have cleared them, and were held idle as the market fluctuated. There was thus created a forest barrier between many a colonist's hut and that of his neighbour. Communications were deplorable and the growth of population was retarded. Whole stretches of country were without roads and bridges, schools and churches.[2] The constitution sanctioned economic conditions of a serious nature. Real settlers, anxious for the development of the province, were isolated by vast areas of waste lands. Social life was handicapped. Pioneer conditions

and McArthur, *op. cit.*, pp. 540 ff., and Smith to Bathurst, April 6, 1818, *State Papers*, Q. 324–1, p. 51.

[1] *Jones Papers*, [A], E. 36. 1 (2), May 1818 (n. p.) (Ontario Archives).

[2] For the method adopted in land granting, see Durham, *Report*, App. A (ed. Lucas, vol. iii, pp. 1 ff.).

were made harder, and the civilizing effects of community spirit in religion, education, amusement, and everyday intercourse were curtailed. The political aspect of the clergy reserves will appear later.

Among the crowd of new emigrants who came into such a world was Robert Gourlay, a Scotch radical whose most serious defect was lack of social discretion.[1] He was a man of university education and of good family, and had been a member of a commission appointed to inquire into the causes and effects of pauperism in Great Britain. He believed that emigration was the cure for the disease, while at the same time it would help to develop and to populate the colonies. On his arrival in Upper Canada in 1817 he set up as a land agent, and almost instinctively began to formulate plans for organized colonization. Naturally desiring to make his schemes as effective as possible, he issued a list of thirty-one questions to the townships of the province, asking for information which he considered necessary to a serious immigration policy. The sting lay in the last question : ' What in your opinion retards the improvement of your township in particular, or the province in general, and what would most contribute to the same ? '[2] The general impression left by the answers is that crown and clergy reserves, lack of capital, few settlers, and above all an ill-organized land system had combined to hurt the country. No unprejudiced critic could doubt that the facts were so. Unfortunately for Gourlay criticism was the leading deadly sin in Upper Canada. His innocent inquiry took on a political aspect and he found himself a dangerous suspect on the part of the ' family compact ' clique. His association with Barnabas Bidwell, an immigrant from Massachusetts, was also against him. The ruling class had an ingrained hatred of Americans, and they dreaded the signs,

[1] The best account of Gourlay is by W. R. Riddell in *Ontario Historical Society : Papers and Records*, vol. xiv (Toronto, 1916). The author vindicates Chief Justice Powell, who banished Gourlay.

[2] Gourlay to Torrens, February 7, 1818, *State Papers*, Q. 150–1, pp. 24, 39.

which were not wanting, that the house of assembly might not be disposed to discriminate against them. Shortly after his arrival Gourlay was counted as a dangerous supporter of the radical element in the assembly, and his proceedings were reported to England as ' inflammatory amongst an ignorant population, from the want of truth, reason, and decorum '.[1] His chief opponent was Strachan ; and the ' busy malice of the parson of Little York ' found sedition in some of the phrases which Gourlay used in various addresses to the resident land-owners.

Gourlay's offence, however, reached a point too dangerous for the ' family compact ' when he issued a call to these proprietors to attend a convention where grievances in general might be discussed and petitions forwarded to England. In due course delegates selected from the various townships met at York. They were a body of entirely respectable men, who had done real work in clearing and settling the province. Resolutions were passed and an address drawn up condemning the entire land-granting system and its evil influence on colonization, and calling on the British parliament to issue a commission of inquiry into the government and affairs of Upper Canada. By this time Gourlay had been unwittingly transformed from an immigration theorist in general into an Upper Canadian ' reformer ' in particular. The township meetings were enthusi-astic over his ' leadership and genius ', and even private correspondence bears witness to the place which he had assumed in popular imagination : ' Times are amazingly dull at Little York. No such thing as cash to be seen. We expect our governor, Mr. Gourlay, from below, soon. He is doing all he can to put our land-granting gentry and big men through their facings, and all I can say for him is good speed his plough.'[2]

---

[1] Smith to Bathurst, February 23, 1818, *State Papers*, Q. 324–1, p. 21.
[2] *Canniff MSS.*, Case 15 (1818). (Lennox and Addington Historical Society, vol. ix, Napanee, 1917.)

Even the governor-general, Sir John Sherbrooke, reported to England ' the troubled state of things in the upper province '. He forwarded a pamphlet with an account of some of Gourlay's meetings. Only bad health kept him from going to Upper Canada to check the insubordinate spirits.[1] The agitation had taken on a political aspect. Smith, the administrator, had withstood pressure which members of the executive, especially Strachan, had brought to bear on him to prosecute Gourlay. Indeed, Gourlay claimed that Smith and the chief justice had approved his questionnaire. The convention, however, brought matters to a head, and finally Smith agreed that Gourlay should be prosecuted for libel against the administration.

At this point Sir Peregrine Maitland arrived as lieutenant-governor. His military qualities and personal charm emphasized rather than discounted his toryism, and he had little sympathy with ' a man named Gourlay, half Cobbett, half Hunt, who has been perplexing the province '.[2] No jury, however, would convict. Maitland and his advisers began a devious course. Relying on the legislature's well-known jealousy of its privileges, he included in his first speech a reference to the situation : ' you will, I doubt not, feel a just indignation at the attempts which have been made to excite discontent and to organize sedition. Should it appear to you that a convention of delegates cannot exist without danger to the constitution, in framing a law of prevention your dispassionate wisdom will be careful that it shall not unwarily trespass on that sacred right of the subject to such a redress of his grievances by petition.'[3] A series of resolutions was passed which affirmed, while guarding the right of petition, ' that the commons house

---

[1] Sherbrooke to Goulburn, June 8, 1818, *State Papers*, Q. 148–2, p. 411.

[2] Maitland to Bathurst, August 19, 1818, *ibid.*, Q. 324–1, p. 129.

[3] *Journals of the House of Assembly of Upper Canada* (October 12, 1818), p. 3 (Ontario Archives, 1913). Maitland deplored the fact that the executive were not sufficiently alive to the dangers, and he claimed that he himself urged the resolutions and subsequent Act : *State Papers*, Q. 325–1, p. 233.

of assembly are the only constitutional representatives of the people of this province '. Gourlay's convention at York, ' for the purpose of deliberating upon matters of public concern,' was pronounced ' highly derogatory and repugnant to the spirit of the constitution of this province ' and tending ' greatly to disturb the public tranquillity '. His supporters were treated to some sound advice on the folly of good citizens endangering the security and the good name of Upper Canada both in the United States and in England by ' lending their countenance to measures so disgraceful '.[1] A statute was passed constituting such meetings unlawful assemblies and making those in any way connected with them guilty of high misdemeanour.[2] Gourlay attacked the bill in the public press. His article was promptly pronounced a gross libel by the assembly [3] and the editor was severely punished. Proceedings were taken against Gourlay under the old alien Act of 1804. An ignorant and uneducated member of the assembly, Isaac Swayzie, actually swore against common knowledge that Gourlay had not resided in the province for the statutory six months, and that he was a seditious character. It was little wonder, when ordered to leave the province within ten days, that Gourlay ignored the verdict. He was arrested and imprisoned. He established the falsity of the charges against himself on a writ of *habeas corpus* before the chief justice, who, however, refused bail on a technicality. For months he lay in Niagara jail, and when finally he was tried he was no longer capable of self-control. He was condemned on a mere quibble—that he had not left the country when ordered—and sentenced to death without benefit of clergy unless he departed from Upper Canada within twenty-four hours. Gourlay lived to be an old man. His sufferings were pronounced illegal and unconstitutional by the Canadian

[1] *Journals, &c.* (October 22, 1818), p. 16.

[2] November 27, 1818, Doughty and McArthur, *op. cit.*, p. 554. This Act was repealed two years later.

[3] *Journals, &c.* (July 5, 1819), p. 173.

parliament in 1842. Finally he returned to Canada and was granted an annual pension which he refused to accept. Those who had been indiscreet enough to attend his convention suffered. If they had claims to lands, they could not enter into possession of them until they had confessed their sins to the lieutenant-governor, and asked pardon for their indiscretion and the obliteration of the stigma on their characters. So grave was the offence that such cases were referred to England.[1] Maitland actually told the legislature that he did not consider himself justified in granting lands to the veterans of the late war who had been foolish enough to support Gourlay. The councils approved of his action, but he only carried the assembly by the casting vote of the speaker.[2]

Gourlay's history, taken by itself, proves that he was foolish and impulsive, and that he lost excellent opportunities for constructive reform by flying too much in the face of unfavourable conditions and by allowing his pen to conquer his sanity. His character does not enter into the question. An unbiased examination of his authentic words and acts up to his departure from the province does not disclose anything which might not pass as justifiable in the ordinary give and take of public life. There is a certain ruggedness and an offensive vulgarity in his writings which can be put down to the conditions of the time ; but no effort was made to examine his charges or to refute them with evidence. Gourlay's deadly sin was that he even ventured to suggest that the governing class were not doing their very best for the province. The deadly sin of the 'family compact' was that it made criticism sedition and calendered in the criminal code any opposition with disloyalty. The spirit of the Elizabethan council animated the executive of Upper Canada.

With the ' crazy democrat ' out of the country, Maitland and

---

[1] Cf. a petition from Ensign Hicock in these terms to Maitland, October 16, 1822, *State Papers*, Q. 331, pp. 230 ff.

[2] *Journals, &c.* (June 7, 9, 1819), pp. 99, 101.

the governing clique affected to feel secure. The cry of ' disloyalty ' had apparently done its work. They singularly
misjudged the situation. The province was full of men who
stood by ' reform ' principles, and the assembly was far from
being a servile tool. The only insight which the executive seems
to have possessed was in realizing that Upper Canadians were
easily moved by the suggestion of treason. On the other hand,
when men who had fought to defend Upper Canada against the
United States were deprived of their land grants for venturing
to attend a meeting which confirmed the opinions of the greater
part of the province, trouble was inevitable. In so far as
Gourlay might be seditious his teachings would command
popular opposition ; but when the ' family compact ' condemned them without distinction or discrimination, public
opinion soon began to question the whole Gourlay episode. It
stands then as a necessary prelude to the history of reform in
Upper Canada. Gourlay made a challenge, and before long
tory and reformer were clear-cut designations in politics. The
reforming zeal of Gourlay and his friends had attacked the land
system as the most evident cause of distress and stagnation.
Failing redress from the governing class, and finding that all
complaints were brushed aside as sedition, men came into the
political arena to demand reform not merely in social and
economic affairs, but in the constitution and in the political
machinery which sanctioned injustice and inequality.

Almost at once the forces began to organize. The most
obvious point of attack was the house of assembly, and in 1821
a strong United Empire loyalist constituency, Lennox and
Addington, returned Barnabas Bidwell, Gourlay's friend, at
a by-election. In the assembly, the tory group challenged his
election and questioned his past. By a majority of one he was
expelled from the assembly.[1] The election of his son, Marshall

---

[1] *Journals* (January 4, 1822), pp. 149 ff. (Ontario Archives, 1915). Cf. Maitland to Bathurst, April 15, 1822, *State Papers*, Q. 331, p. 90. There is an account

Spring Bidwell, was voided by the assembly because he was an alien, but in 1824 the same constituency chose him as its member, and he was allowed to hold his seat.[1] The ' Bidwell affair ', as it was called, emphasized the discontent over the alien question, which had become serious for several reasons. In 1820 the province had been redivided into counties and population had been made the basis of representation. Under this Act thirty-eight members were returned to the assembly. When the Bidwells were challenged, the whole question of citizenship was opened up. In addition, in 1824 a ruling had been handed down by the chief justice of England that those who had remained in the United States after 1783 could not retain or transmit British citizenship, and that they could not inherit real estate within the empire. The opinion came as a bombshell into Upper Canada, for it meant that a large percentage of the population were not British citizens, and that their titles to land were invalid. So grave was the situation that Maitland received a dispatch directing him that it was advisable to sanction local legislation conferring ' civil rights and privileges of British subjects upon such citizens of the United States as being heretofore settled in Canada are declared by the judgement of the courts of law in England and by the opinion of the law officers to be aliens ; and of including in the same enactment the disbanded officers and soldiers of foreign corps which were in the British service, and such foreigners resident in Canada, who are in truth aliens, though they have hitherto enjoyed without question the rights of British subjects '.[2] The legislative council passed a bill along the lines of this dispatch, but it was strongly opposed in the assembly on the

by an eyewitness of Bidwell's dramatic defence of himself before the legislature in a letter from William Macaulay to John Macaulay, December 31, 1821, *Macaulay Papers*, [A], E. 45–6, iii. 3 (Ontario Archives).

[1] *Journals, &c.*, pp. 216–17, 306, 313–14, 441–4.

[2] Bathurst to Maitland, July 22, 1825, *Colonial Office Records*, Q. 371–A, p. 43.

ground that it did not grant complete naturalization. The
assembly and many of the people regarded the proposals as some
kind of cunning attack. Maitland was apparently acting
according to instructions, but suspicion was abroad and a bitter
controversy followed in which the executive lost ground.
Finally, in 1828 an Act was passed acceptable to the vast
majority. British birth was conferred on those who had
received crown grants, who had held public offices, who had
taken the oath of allegiance, and on all who had resided in the
province since 1820. All others resident on March 1, 1828, were
to be admitted to the rights and privileges of citizenship after
seven years and on taking a prescribed oath. The imperial
parliament extended to all persons naturalized by the legislature
of Upper Canada the right to become eligible for seats in
the legislative council and in the assembly, as well as that of
voting for members of the latter. The dispute was not settled,
however, before an opinion had grown up that the local government intended to deal in an arbitrary way with American
settlers.

During the Maitland régime, the status of the church of
England fell across the political life of the province and accentuated the constitutional situation. The Simcoe theory that
the church of England was the established church of Canada
had never been abandoned. There were thus religious disabilities under which the non-episcopal protestant churches laboured.
Their ministers could not solemnize marriages. The assembly
passed a bill in 1824 removing this grievance and ' authorizing
ministers of the Society of Methodists to solemnize marriage '.
The legislative council rejected the bill. This was the beginning
of a fatal policy. Religion was thrown into the political arena,
and the Methodists, a growing communion in the province, were
given a political grievance. Even when the disability was
substantially rectified in 1829, nonconformist clergy were
required to take out a certificate from the court of quarter

sessions in their district, while clergymen of the church of England solemnized marriages *ex officio*.[1]

Under the Constitutional Act of 1791 large reserves of land for ' the protestant clergy ' had been sanctioned. In 1823 the discontent in connexion with this question, passed from the social into the political sphere. Resolutions and an address were carried in the house of assembly in that year claiming a share in the clergy reserves for the church of Scotland as an established church.[2] The election of 1825 brought in a strong group of reformers which included Marshall Bidwell, Peter Perry, John Rolph, and John Matthews, as well as William Morris, who had taken a prominent part in connexion with the resolutions in favour of the church of Scotland. With Bidwell an outstanding figure, opposition was organized against the government. An address was drawn up protesting against any increase in the clergy reserves and praying that the present reserves should not be confined to the church of England, but should be shared in by all christian denominations.[3] Maitland informed the assembly that no increase was intended. Undeterred, the assembly protested that ' protestant clergy ' did not mean clergy of the church of England exclusively, and suggested the sale of the lands for the support of education and of religion in general. Strachan entered the fray with ' an ecclesiastical chart of Upper Canada ' in favour of an Anglican ' majority ' in the province.[4] Egerton Ryerson replied on behalf of the Methodists, and the house of assembly challenged the implied position of the church of England both in an address and in a report from

[1] See a fully documented study by W. R. Riddell, ' The Law of Marriage in Upper Canada ' (*Canadian Historical Review*, vol. ii, pp. 226 ff.).

[2] *Journals, &c.*, pp. 560 ff., 606 ff.

[3] Maitland to Bathurst, March 7, 1826, *State Papers*, Q. 340–1, p. 33. The assembly had become alarmed over transactions, in which the ' clergy reserves ' figured, between John Galt and the British government. See R. K. Gordon, *John Galt*, pp. 45 ff. (University of Toronto Studies, 1920).

[4] Strachan to Wilmot Horton, May 16, 1827, *State Papers*, Q. 345–2, p. 342.

a special committee of the house on Strachan's chart.[1] The
dispute was laid before the select committee on the civil government of Canada in 1828.[2] In its report special attention was
drawn to the political difficulties created in Upper Canada by the
position granted to the church of England by the subservience
of the legislative council. Nothing, however, was done, and
' the most mischievous practical cause of dissension ',[3] as
Durham called ' the clergy reserves ', remained to form, as we
shall see, a motive for rebellion. The reserves and the money
coming in from them were finally secularized in 1854 by a
Canadian Act, which facetiously recited the desirability of
' removing all semblance of connexion between church and
state '.

The religious question thus became the main key to the
political situation in Upper Canada. The governing clique,
however, were not content to let the issues crystallize. They
pursued a pin-prick policy. John Matthews had his pension as
a half-pay officer stopped, and he was ordered to return to
England, because he was present at a performance given by
a company of American actors, under the patronage of the
assembly. The evening was old-world in its conviviality, and the
audience momentarily forgot the ' family compact ', when
' Yankee Doodle ' was rendered with ' hats off '. The *Colonial
Advocate* of William Lyon Mackenzie had been transferred from
Queenston to York in November 1824. In the following summer
the printing press was wrecked by a group of young bloods. Of
course the authorities had no part in the attack, and of course
it was a youthful revenge for much abuse ; but the reform
party interpreted it as a premeditated action inspired by the
older heads. It brought a strange vengeance, for the damages
awarded to Mackenzie and collected among the ' family com-

[1] Maitland to Huskisson, May 12, 1828, *State Papers*, Q. 347, p. 16 ; George
Ryerson to Hay, June 7, 1828, *ibid.*, Q. 350-2, p. 341.
[2] See Kennedy, *op. cit.*, p. 346.   [3] *Report*, ii. 179 (ed. Lucas).

pact ' reconstructed not merely his press and paper, but his fortunes. Other instances of foolish policies—some wilful, some perverse, some accidental, but all arrogant—might easily be drawn from the history of Maitland's régime. Their force was cumulative, though they contributed only indirectly to the main issues. They were witnesses to a state of mind in government circles rather than permanent influences. Maitland was recalled in August 1828, but he did not leave Canada before the province had given a judgement on his rule. In the elections which were held previous to his departure, the ' family compact ' in all its ramifications was the predominating issue. Everything was called into service—clergy reserves, the marriage legislation, Strachan's chart, freedom of the press. Echoes were even heard of Gourlay's convention and of the persecution of those who had attended it. The government had no episode ready of sufficient notoriety to be given a disloyal tinge, and the reformers gained a respectable majority which included William Lyon Mackenzie, Jesse Ketchum, Marshall Bidwell, John Rolph, and Peter Perry. Robert Baldwin in 1829 was elected to fill the seat vacated by John Beverley Robinson on his appointment as chief justice. When Maitland left, the state of affairs was by no means hopeless ; but he handed over a delicate enough situation to his successor Sir John Colborne, who was perhaps as good a man as any available. Although a soldier and an outstanding figure at Waterloo and a tory of the old school, Colborne possessed a kindly personality and a sympathetic character. Behind his professional rigidity and his somewhat self-conscious devotion to the dignity of his office, he had more insight into civil problems than any of his predecessors. He would have succeeded under more favourable conditions. His sympathies were chilled by the cold exclusiveness of the oligarchy and his insight warped by his being compelled to take advice from those who professed to have the only adequate grasp of local affairs.

The British government desired to do something along the

lines suggested by the report of 1828, and Colborne's instructions represented the intent and extent of that purpose.[1] For
the present there was no necessity to open up the question of
revenue control, and as a matter of fact if trouble arose the
government could easily be maintained. On the ' clergy
reserves ' full information was asked, and a promise was given
that any proposals concerning education, especially such as
might deal with the ' exclusive connexion ' of the University
with the church of England, would receive very careful consideration. There were doubts about making the judges
independent ; but the legislative council would be rendered
less subservient by discontinuing the appointment of officials
to it. Before Colborne had time to orientate himself the
assembly opened an attack. The address to the lieutenant-
governor was based on the idea that the elected of the people
ought to be the advisers of the crown, and he was warned of the
fatal consequences which would follow a continuance of the
traditional policy. Wounded feelings, injured interests, and
popular discontent would be the price paid for power. The
complete control of finance and the right of appropriation were,
unfortunately for the future, vain cries in the constitutional
night, for the executive could afford to neglect threats in this
connexion. Colborne, with no insight as yet into political and
social conditions, was unable to give any adequate reply.
A dry platitude that it was easier to find troubles than to efface
them did not help.

A short residence, however, soon convinced him where the
sources of trouble lay. Of the seventeen members of council,
not more than fifteen ever attended, and of these, six belonged
to the executive council, and four held offices under the government. ' Composed as the legislative council is at present, the
province has the right to complain of the great influence of the

---

[1] Murray to Colborne, September 29, 1828, *Colonial Office Records*, Q. 372,
[A], pp. 53 ff. (Canadian Archives).

executive council in it.'[1] He hoped to make the second chamber more independent. In the religious-political world his observation was equally keen. He found that Strachan's political course had destroyed his clerical influence, and the dissenters, in seeking to protect their communions against him, had become political bodies. The lieutenant-governor was forced to confess that he could not blind himself so far as not to be convinced that the political part which Strachan had taken in Upper Canada had destroyed his value as a clergyman, had injured the episcopal church, and had done harm to real religion.[2] If there was going to be a militant established church with a champion in the councils in Upper Canada, Colborne at once saw that the province would have to be governed in opposition to the wishes of the vast majority of the people.

Colborne was more or less helpless. When the assembly in 1830 asked him to dismiss his advisers, as they had lost the confidence of the country, he could only return a curt thanks for the address. His keeping silence even from good words must have seemed to justify itself, for the reformers lost the next election. It is impossible to decide the reasons for the change. At any rate two may be suggested. Colborne had nothing of Gore's pettiness and of Maitland's subserviency, and Anglo-Saxon common sense grasped the fact that he was just and honourable. In addition, a reform assembly was helpless against the legislative council. The average voter, who had plumped for a new heaven and a new earth, did not grasp the constitutional difficulties. Ceaseless speeches, manifold committees, democratic addresses, spent themselves in vain against the serried phalanxes of privilege, and the voters who had looked for reforming bread and received doctrinaire stone must have been a little disappointed. The campaign is otherwise interesting. Mackenzie issued a platform which included the

[1] Colborne to Murray, February 16, 1829, *State Papers*, Q. 351–1, p. 29.

[2] Colborne to Hay, March 31, 1829 ; same to Bishop of Quebec, February 13, 1829, *ibid.*, pp. 86, 106.

independence of the judges, reform of the legislative council, religious equality, and ' an executive government responsible for its conduct '. The appeal was clear-cut and the rejection is inexplicable except for the reasons suggested. At the same time, it is worth while to remember that as long as Beverley Robinson led the government party in the assembly there was a certain amount of dignity. His was talented arbitrariness. When Henry John Boulton, Robinson's successor, and Christopher Hagerman led the tory forces, tactful autocracy gave place to domineering aggressiveness and they drove the iron into the soul of a people. As events proved it was fortunate for Upper Canada that the election turned out as it did. To this assembly fell the lot of dealing with the financial proposals under the imperial Act of 1831.[1] Early in the session a permanent civil list was granted, and thus one source of irritation was removed.

Had Hagerman and Boulton been content to let Mackenzie, Perry, and their like blow off steam in the absence of more moderate reformers from the house, and to accept with something of Robinson's political wisdom the civil list which lifted the lieutenant-governor, the judges, and themselves as solicitor-general and attorney-general out of the turmoil of an annual vote, there might have been no rebellion. Mackenzie was taken too seriously. His opposition to the civil list was based on the comprehensive principle of being always against the government. When it was passed, he flooded the dykes of administration with an ocean of abusive rhetoric. Real reform—and there was much of it in his speeches and writings—was discounted by excess and lack of discrimination. The *Colonial Advocate* enjoyed a perfect surfeit of vilification. The executive was compared with the arbitrary, iron despotism of the czar, and the constituencies which returned government supporters were impaled on the finest points of scurrilous ridicule. The ' sycophant ' assembly and the ' mean and mercenary ' executive at

---

[1] See above, p. 106, note 2.

last lost patience. The house declared the editorials breaches of privilege, and Mackenzie was expelled as Boulton's ' reptile ' and Hagerman's ' spaniel dog '. Constitutionally and legally right, politically and diplomatically wrong, the assembly made the reforming editor a popular hero. Little York was outraged, and, with a growing self-importance, the inhabitants asked the lieutenant-governor to dissolve the house. Colborne was not so foolish. York, however, returned their maltreated member at the by-election. Necessarily he was admitted to the house, but only to meet a new charge of libel. Once again he was expelled, and, foolishly and illegally, he was declared incapable of holding a seat. Once again his constituents sent him back. As the house was not sitting when the election took place, Mackenzie prepared to seek redress in London and set sail on May 1, 1832. In England he interviewed Lord Goderich, the colonial secretary, and created a mixed but not entirely ineffective impression. Meanwhile Boulton and Hagerman advised the legislature, which opened on October 31, that Mackenzie had no right to sit. The government carried the assembly and a new writ was ordered. In his absence Mackenzie was returned unopposed.

The assembly was in no mood for discriminating thought. Lord Goderich had sent a dispatch written with care and judgement, in which, however, grievances were recognized.[1] He instructed the lieutenant-governor to publish the dispatch. Colborne hesitated to do so before prorogation and thought that caution should be used ' in dealing with a demagogue formidable from perseverance and cunning '.[2] Finally he decided to transmit the dispatch to the legislature. The old impatience of criticism once more was in evidence. No attention was paid to the censures on Mackenzie and his methods. Goderich had actually received a man expelled from the

---

[1] Goderich to Colborne, November 8, 1832, *State Papers*, G. 69.
[2] Colborne to Hay, January 16, 1833, *State Papers*, Q. 377-1, p. 183.

assembly, and given him audience as though he were an agent for reporting grievances and oppression.[1] Boulton and Hager-man led the attack on the colonial secretary and Mackenzie was expelled for the fourth time. The home government was growing weary of high-handed proceedings in which legality had now no place. Warnings had been in vain, and Goderich acted after his patience had been exhausted. He informed Colborne that he was surprised that Boulton and Hagerman should hold office and disregard the wishes of the cabinet. He also pointed out, while wishing to interfere in no arbitrary way, that a member of either house who held office at the pleasure of the crown and at the same time could not approve of the policy of the ministry in power must be prepared to choose between his seat and his official situation.[2] Boulton and Hagerman were promptly dismissed. Boulton managed to get a judicial appointment in Newfoundland, from which he was also removed, and he returned to Canada as a supporter of responsible government. Hagerman wheedled Goderich's successor, Lord Stanley, into restoring him to office. The lieutenant-governor did not escape censure. The tory party were now outraged beyond measure. Loyalty gave place to rebellious sentiments and threats, and the government papers reflected the resentment. It is well to keep in view this state of mind. The ' family compact ' group were just as ready to prove recalcitrant as any other group in the province, if their peculiar privileges and their still more peculiar feelings were touched. Mackenzie pricked ' the loyalty-bubble '. The government party were unwilling to accept defeat or censure. Mackenzie was again expelled after a scene of indecorum and passion. For the moment, his ambitions were satisfied when he became first mayor of York on its incorporation as the city of Toronto. Unfortunately for his cause and for the cause of reform, he rashly published a letter

---

[1] Colborne to Goderich, February 16, 1833, *State Papers*, Q. 377–1, p. 218.
[2] Goderich to Colborne, March 6, 1833, p. 93, Series G. 70, p. 43.

from Joseph Hume, the radical politician who had helped him with Lord Goderich, in which Hume anticipated a crisis in Canada ' which [would] terminate in independence and freedom from the baneful domination of the mother country and the tyrannical conduct of a small and despicable faction in the colony '.[1] Mackenzie's indiscretion hurt the reforming party at the elections held in October 1834. Indeed the publication of Hume's letter corresponds in a degree to the issuing of the Ninety-two Resolutions in Lower Canada. Constitutional reformers were alarmed and did not feel secure concerning the future. Ryerson and the Methodists began to separate from what might be considered the Papineau platform.[2] As it was, the reformers were in the majority in the new assembly. But the Baldwins, Jesse Ketchum, and Rolph had refused to stand, and the party were thus split over Mackenzie's policy. Mackenzie succeeded in having a select committee of the assembly appointed to inquire into grievances. He was elected chairman and all the members were his close followers. The report which this committee brought forward was never formally approved by the assembly, but it may be considered as representing the opinions of the Mackenzie group of reformers.

The *Seventh Report of Grievances* covered most issues in Upper Canadian politics. Patronage, salaries, the church of England, the land department—all were subject to severe criticism. It cannot be denied that there were grievances, but no concessions were made to conditions, and any good results were overlooked. The ' family compact ' were nothing if not competent, and while crumbs fell from the rich man's table, there was no real organized public peculation under their régime. The interest of the report lies largely in its discussion of constitutional questions. The committee felt that the machinery of government

[1] *Colonial Advocate*, May 22, 1834.

[2] See an address from the Wesleyan conference condemning Hume's letter which Colborne forwarded to Stanley, July 1, 1834, *State Papers*, Q. 382–2, p. 449.

was behind the grievances. They were justified in complaining that little respect was paid, even in subordinate matters, to the wishes of the assembly. On the other hand, there is no clear suggestion for reform. Under the influence of Lower Canada an elective second chamber was asked for, but there is no hint of the recommendation of cabinet government. The executive council was to be rendered responsible to public opinion, but the method was vague. The committee noticed that some witnesses suggested ministerial responsibility, and the terms approach the idea of cabinet control; but there is nothing in the report which can be interpreted as an acceptance of this suggestion. The report was at once printed and copies were sent to Lord Glenelg, now colonial secretary, and to the members of the imperial parliament. The cabinet was alarmed. Colborne was censured for having misjudged the situation and for withholding full information from the imperial government. He defended himself as best he could. He regretted the attention paid to Mackenzie and his party, who, he was convinced, could not be attached to the government by concessions.[1] He recalled his suggestion of 1832, of filling up the country as speedily as possible with staunch British settlers, as such a policy would eliminate all anxiety about the Canadas and would counteract factions.[2] The cabinet was convinced that a new policy must be begun, and Colborne was recalled to make room for Sir Francis Bond Head, who was sworn in at Toronto on January 25, 1836. Colborne left the next day to assume command of the military forces in British North America.

Colborne did not leave before he carried out an act which was singularly inopportune. He established and endowed out of the clergy reserves forty-four rectories for the church of England. The history is rather confusing. In 1831 the British government

---

[1] Colborne to Glenelg, September 16, November 9, December 2, 1835, *State Papers*, Q. 387–1, p. 98 ; Q. 387–2, pp. 279, 349, 410.
[2] Colborne to Hay, September 21, 1832, *ibid.*, Q. 374–4, p. 887.

decided to abandon the idea of endowment, as the system had proved not only financially futile, but had ' a direct tendency to render odious to the inhabitants ' the ministers of religion.[1] A bill was prepared for the provincial legislature repealing the clauses of the Constitutional Act dealing with the clergy reserves and transforming them into crown lands.[2] The bill was actually introduced by the attorney-general, but it disappeared in Colborne's prorogation of the legislature. In February 1832 Colborne suggested the use of monies from the clergy reserve funds to build rectories or churches. In the following April Goderich concurred in this view. In November 1832 Goderich stated that the imperial government had abstained from endowing literary or other corporations until he should obtain advice from the representatives of the Canadian people. In 1834 and in 1835 the assembly passed bills for the sale of the clergy reserves and for the application of the monies received to education, but the legislative council blocked the scheme. In January 1836, on the eve of his departure, the executive council recommended to Colborne the creation of fifty-seven rectories and patents were issued for forty-four. Colborne and the executive council could plead implicit approval ; but the whole thing was carried through without the immediate know-ledge of the imperial government. At any rate, while Colborne had the law on his side, there can be little doubt that the action was impolitic and frictional. The idea of creating rectories and endowing them was at least as old as Maitland's time ; but the fact that there had been varieties of opinion even in imperial circles made Colborne's last official act take on the appearance of a challenge. The province began to view the church of England as a subtle schemer taking advantage of a situation before conciliation could become an active policy.

Head's appointment provides an opening for criticism of the

[1] Goderich to Colborne, November 21, 1831, Series G. 68, p. 251.
[2] Colborne to Goderich, February 3, 1832, *State Papers*, Q. 374–1, p. 177.

colonial office. Unknown in any capacity save as a poor law
commissioner, no one was more surprised than Head himself
when he was roused from his bed to receive the king's messenger
offering him the lieutenant-governorship of Upper Canada.[1]
He had the common sense to decline the offer, but Glenelg was
insistent, and there began in January 1836 a régime almost
tragical in its fatuity. Its only redeeming feature is the comic
figure of the lieutenant-governor, who within a few weeks
developed to his own satisfaction theories of colonial government childish in their folly. Head ostensibly came to Canada
to carry out concessions in answer to the report on grievances.
It was little wonder then that he was received in Toronto as
a popular hero and as ' a tried reformer '.[2] The length to which
Lord Glenelg was prepared to go can be seen from his instructions
issued to Head.[3] Patronage could not be abandoned entirely,
as every person in office must be held subordinate to the head
of the government. Whatever patronage was unnecessary in
preserving that principle might be given up. A general retrench-
ment in expenditure was recommended in so far as compatible
with efficiency. The cabinet refused to interfere in relation to
the dispute over the clergy reserves, which was a local matter
and not of such vital importance as to demand imperial legislation. With regard to responsible government, Glenelg was
a strict constructionist. He held that there was plenty of
responsibility. The lieutenant-governor was accountable to
king and parliament—' a responsibility which was second to
none,' and the assembly could bring it into active operation at
any time by address or petition. Every public officer must hold
his position at the pleasure of the crown, and he must be

[1] There is a tradition that the appointment was made in error and was
intended for Sir Edmund Head. Cf. Hincks, *Reminiscences of his Public Life*,
pp. 14 ff. (Montreal, 1884).

[2] He was actually recommended as such to Mackenzie by Hume: Hume to
Mackenzie, December 5, 1835, *Robinson Papers*, [A], E. 22–3, ii. 10 (1)
(Ontario Archives). See F. B. Head, *A Narrative*, pp. 32 ff. (London, 1839).

[3] Glenelg to Head, December 5, 1835, Kennedy, *op. cit.*, pp. 412 ff.

removed if he opposed the lieutenant-governor's policy. These principles, according to Glenelg, constituted an 'effective system of responsibility '.

Before long Head grasped the implications of the scheme. He was viceroy, responsible to no one in Canada. Downing Street had given him an excellent system and one free from ambiguities. Almost at once he took a violent dislike to Mackenzie and Bidwell, but in his rôle as ' tried reformer ' some public act was necessary, and he called to the executive council Robert Baldwin and John Rolph. Head's theoretical popularity now became actual. He was hailed as the father of responsible government, and there can be no doubt that Baldwin and the reformers believed that Head had inaugurated a new constitutional régime. ' The appointment of executive councillors ', wrote Bidwell, ' gives us great satisfaction. It was with our full approbation, and I may say at our request, that these gentlemen accepted office. They have our entire confidence and go in without the least sacrifice of principle.' [1] Appearances had been deceptive. Head had no idea of being guided by an executive council. He went his own way, and when he asked advice he rejected it as lightly as he had requested it. On March 4 the entire executive council protested, and asserted that they were held responsible in public opinion for measures which had never received their approval. Head replied in the strict letter of his instructions : ' The lieutenant-governor maintains that the responsibility to the people (who are already represented in the house of assembly) which the council assume is unconstitutional ; that it is the duty of the council to serve *him*, not *them* ; and if on so vital a principle they persist in a contrary opinion, he foresees embarrassments of a most serious nature—for as power and responsibility must, in common justice, be inseparably connected with each other, it is evident

[1] M. S. Bidwell to A. N. Buell, February 26, 1836, *Jones Papers*, [A], E. 36, 2 (5) (Ontario Archives).

to the lieutenant-governor, that if the council were once to be permitted to assume the *latter*, they would immediately as their right demand the *former*.' On March 12 the executive council resigned in a body, and Head lost no time in forming a new council of four, which was immediately met with a resolution in the assembly maintaining the principle of ' a responsible executive council to advise the lieutenant-governor on the affairs of the province '. Ten days later the assembly passed a vote of no confidence in the new council. Head talked louder and less guardedly than ever, and the assembly finally refused supplies. In the issue the lieutenant-governor harangued the house for over an hour and finally dissolved it. Writs were issued for an election in June.

Head entered the fray with Francis Gore's experiment behind him. He became a political leader with all the patronage of the province at his disposal. He entered it, too, at issue with the colonial office. Glenelg would not grant his request to obtain the repeal of the revenue Act of 1831, and sent him a dispatch, which had already been forwarded to New Brunswick, instructing him to introduce into the executive council men having the confidence of the people. Head ran the elections on his own plans: he made a personal appeal and placed the choice between himself and the reformers. The old bogy of disloyalty was brought out of the campaign cupboards. The tories rallied round it as in the days of Maitland. Their opponents organized to obtain an elective legislative council, an executive responsible to public opinion, the surrender and control of all provincial revenue and the elimination of the imperial cabinet from the internal affairs of the colony. Head swept the country, and the reformers were virtually wiped out. The disloyalty cry undoubtedly worked wonders in the mouth of a lieutenant-governor, and personal influence—and perhaps more—turned many votes. But the controlling force in the election was the Methodists under the direction of Egerton Ryerson. Ryerson feared the future, and there must have been a strong sense of impending danger when he led his followers into the tory and Anglican camp.[1]

The lieutenant-governor now lost all sense of proportion. He informed Glenelg that, after a single-handed combat in the severest moral issue in colonial history, he had ' saved the Canadas '. Glenelg could not withhold congratulations, but he pointed out that mere ' transient results or temporary triumphs ' were not looked for by the government. After a tour of the province, Head summoned the legislature. The outstanding difficulties remained. It is true that the erection of rectories was ratified, but the clergy reserves could not be settled, as the Methodists wavered between a religious or an educational application of the funds. Supplies, however, were granted in profusion, and large votes were made for improvements in spite of a huge debt and of a grave financial situation among the banks of the United States. The promised ' economic reform ' which had figured so largely in the election campaign did not make its appearance, and before long Head's triumph had lost whatever significance it may have had. The colonial office grew tired of his conceit, especially as he had broken away from the theory of government which he so gladly accepted from his instructions. He dismissed officials on suspicion and refused to restore them when ordered by the cabinet. He also declared his unwillingness to promote Bidwell to the next vacant judge-ship at the bidding of the colonial office. Glenelg could only fall back on his theory of responsibility and recall the almost independent lieutenant-governor.

Before the recall reached Toronto, armed rebellion had broken out, and it was due in no small measure to Head's foolish self-confidence in denuding the province of troops. The details of the rebellion lie outside this history, but when the

[1] Ryerson, *Story of my Life*, ch. xviii ff. (edited J. G. Hodgins, Toronto, 1883).

mingled blood of Upper Canadian and Lower Canadian was
drained to a common earth, Canadians gained the first constitutional step towards political liberty. On the surface the ' family
compact ' had triumphed ; but the rebellion was symptomatic.
Small in itself, it was enough to convince the imperial cabinet
that the constitution was worn out. When a British province
took up arms against the administration it was high time to
seek the fundamental causes. The Canadian rebellions brought
Lord Durham to Canada. Sir Francis Head, however, did not
pass out of Canadian history without memorials for which
students may be grateful. His legislative council and his
' bread and butter ' assembly [1] drew up reports on the state of
the provinces, which are in many respects remarkable documents.[2] Naturally the theories of the old colonial system colour
the criticism, and there is much praise for Head and ' loyal
men '. On the other hand, there is insight and restraint. The
summary of Lower Canadian history is of the greatest value,
and imperial policy in that province is subjected to an examination which cannot be overlooked. Both reports attacked
severely the colonial office for its imperfect knowledge of
colonial affairs, for its want of stability and firmness, and for its
absence of constructive continuity. Indeed, the dissatisfaction
was so strong that a board of empire was suggested which
should have Canadian members. There was a dawning vision
of a united British North America expressing itself in representation of all the American colonies in the imperial parliament.
However hard history has been forced to deal with the political
faith and the administrative practice of the tory group in

[1] 'If you choose to dispute with me and to live on bad terms with the
mother country, you will —to use a homely phrase—only quarrel with your
bread and butter': Head to the electors of the District of Newcastle.

[2] *Journals of the Legislative Council*, February 13, 1838 ; *Journals of the
Assembly,* Appendix, 1837–8, pp. 257 ff. The latter is partially printed in
Kennedy, *op. cit.,* pp. 448 ff. Both reports were published in pamphlet form
in 1838.

Upper Canada, it is impossible to question the intellectual vigour of writings such as these, and the uncanny skill with which they distributed praise and blame.

[AUTHORITIES.—*The Journals of the Legislative Council and Legislative Assembly* ; A. G. Doughty and D. A. McArthur, *Documents of the Constitutional History of Canada, 1791–1818* (Ottawa, 1914) ; Egerton and Grant, *Canadian Constitutional Development* (Toronto, 1907) ; Kennedy, *Documents of the Canadian Constitution, 1759–1915* (Oxford, 1918) ; *The State Papers*, Q. 278–Q. 358, Q. 374–Q. 395 (Canadian Archives) ; *Series of Origina Dispatches, Upper Canada*, G. 53–G. 107 (Canadian Archives) ; *Canadian Archives Report*, 1891, ' Note E : Marriage Law in Upper Canada ' ; 1892, ' Note D : Political State of Upper Canada, 1806–7 ' ; 1896, ' Note C : Roman Catholic Church in Upper Canada ' ; 1897, ' Note A : Proposed Union, 1822 ' ; 1898, ' Note C : Naturalization Question ' ; 1899, ' Note A : The Clergy Reserves '. The best general introduction is W. Stewart Wallace, *The Family Compact* (Toronto, 1915) : this book is founded on careful and thorough research and has a useful bibliography. Charles Lindsey, *The Life and Times of William Lyon Mackenzie* (2 vols., Toronto, 1862), is the official biography based on private papers. C. W. Robinson, *Life of Sir John Beverley Robinson* (Edinburgh and London, 1904), is valuable but is formal and uninspiring. All Gourlay's publications are valuable, especially the *Banished Briton and Neptunian* (Boston, 1843) and *Statistical Account of Upper Canada* (2 vols., London, 1822), which contains many documents. A. N. Bethune, *Memoir of the Right Rev. John Strachan* (Toronto, 1870), is useful but inadequate. *The Seventh Report from the Select Committee of the House of Assembly of Upper Canada on Grievances* (Toronto, 1835), Sir Francis Bond Head, *A Narrative* (London, 1839), and Glenelg's *Dispatches* (London, 1839) are essentials, as well as Mackenzie's *Colonial Advocate* and the New York *Albion*. In the last can be found the contemporary ' family compact ' point of view.]

CHAPTER XI

THE FAILURE OF REPRESENTATIVE GOVERNMENT IN THE CANADAS

LORD JOHN RUSSELL's ten resolutions did more than lay down principles of colonial government and precipitate rebellions. In Lower Canada they transformed a sentiment into a dangerous hushed melancholy, and in Upper Canada they intensified an aspiration. For the failure of representative government had distinct characteristics in each province, and the different effects of the resolutions on the psychology of Lower Canadians and of Upper Canadians were due to definite causes. Common causes there were, and these will appear later, but the failure can best be considered by beginning with the different backgrounds.

From the fall of Canada Great Britain treated the French-Canadians as a distinct group. In the earlier years the treatment was more or less tentative. It lacked definiteness and insight and never assumed the clearness of a concrete political purpose. There was a good deal of floating sentiment, of kindliness, and of generosity which carried French-Canadians across the rough places in British law and the more difficult rough places in British traditions. The beginnings of the colonial troubles, as we have seen, transformed all this. They lifted the whole position out of the realms of emotion into those of practical conceptions. With the Quebec Act the French-Canadian race was given a statutory charter of privileges, and the distinct group life of a distinct nationalism was recognized by law within the empire. The application of this charter to the actual life of the province fell to the hands of Carleton and Haldimand, who, for reasons which have already been discussed, interpreted it in the strictest sense and made the grant far stronger by hiding the spirit of the Act. The British in the province were treated almost as non-existent, and at any rate they were persistently snubbed. In due course the French-Canadian rank and file, who had been at first suspicious of the Danaän gift, came to look on the Quebec Act as the visible sign and symbol of their group life, and there grew round it a race emotion which gathered strength with the years. When colonial difficulties again forced a change, no attempt was made to break up this life or to divert this emotion. A British constitution was given to a French people in the fond hope that the alchemy of such generosity would be magical, and that in the laboratory of constitutional experience they would forsake language, laws, religion, and race itself. No account was taken of the peculiar persistence of racial differences, and in the final analysis the French-Canadians bent the constitution to racial ends.

When the shadow of Craig's régime fell across the popular life of Lower Canada, opposition did not express itself fundamentally in political terms, nor did it use political weapons. ' Notre langue, nos institutions et nos lois ' seemed on the surface a political trinity, and by the shallow-thinking administration both in the province and in England it was interpreted as an expression of political ends which would be guarded at all costs. As a matter of fact the challenge was one of race, and the triple watchword only stood for things French-Canadian in so far as they were living racial forces. The popular assembly in Lower Canada never in reality took on a political or constitutional aspect. It was an arena for French-Canadianism, an organized expression of race consciousness, a guardian of a people within the gates of an alien system.[1] Its theatrical

[1] ' The cause of the assembly became the cause of the entire race. The principles that it affirmed, the rights that it insisted upon, the whole race affirmed and insisted upon with an emotion that was at the same time enthusiasm and anger. These principles and these rights were in fact synonymous

and persistent vigils were made all the more intense because a few British members represented another race in a French province. They were considered outposts of an anglicizing policy unfortunately entrenched in the lieutenant-governor and the executive and legislative councils. It is impossible to work through any considerable portion of the vast historical papers of the period, or to attempt to view the history with contemporary eyes, without being forced to the conclusion that racial antipathies governed the issues. Behind the quietness which conciliation produced and the aggressiveness which more arbitrary methods intensified, there lay an energizing life deriving its vitality from the most subtle, most tantalizing, and most disintegrating force in history. The clash was inevitable under a constitution which was not framed for such a situation.

But a racial clash must express itself in actual concrete actions. It will seldom be satisfied with art, literature, music, or more peaceful spheres than the world of affairs. From the house of assembly there came almost naturally the ever-widening challenges. This was an assembly of French-Canadians elected by French-Canadians. Its business was to make it an effective instrument for French-Canadians. As a consequence, it made all the difference in the world what laws were passed and who interpreted those laws ; what taxes were levied and how they were appropriated. The Lower Canadian house of assembly attacked every one of these problems. It is in reality to miss the essential when these attacks are judged solely from the point of view of constitutional law. Here was the very core of a chapter in political theory. There were fundamental contradictions in being allowed a say in passing laws without controlling the judges who interpreted them ; in being allowed to vote taxes without deciding the items of appropriation ; in being a constitutional part of the government without an

with the preservation of the French race' : Laurier, quoted in O. D. Skelton, *Life and Letters of Sir Wilfrid Laurier*, vol. i, pp. 68 ff. (Oxford, 1921).

effective voice in the administration.   The French-Canadian
house of assembly never saw these difficulties politically isolated
or politically correlated.   They attacked one and all, but
always when they felt that their race and nationality were in
danger.   Law the French-Canadian must obey ; taxes the
French-Canadian must pay ; judges the French-Canadian must
face ; administration the French-Canadian must experience ;
and the challenge given in turn to each was a challenge fundamentally inspired by racial homogeneity and kept alive by
those fears, suspicions, arguments, and aggressions which are
the peculiar weapons of nationalism when fettered and unfree
in a servile state.

This view of the situation can easily be illustrated.   The
assembly at one period in its history became enamoured of
impeachment.   It seemed a logical deduction from a constitution so persistently emphasized as British, and an admirable
method of getting even with the protagonists of anti-French
proceedings.   When the legislative council blocked the plan,
there could only be one result.   The legislative council must
be made French-Canadian by the introduction of the elective
principle.   If the council threw out bills passed by the French-
Canadian assembly, it was high time that the legislative
aspirations of a people should be rescued from ineffectiveness.
If the governor and executive spent funds drawn from
French-Canadian sources, no specious epithet such as ' crown
lands and territorial revenues ' should render them outside
French-Canadian control.   The demand for an elective legislative council was perfectly logical.   The clamour to control
all revenue was perfectly natural.   Once nationalism had been
recognized, once it had been given an organized voice, it was
absurd to expect the French-Canadians to sit down under
a British governor, under a council largely British, and to see
their racial feelings outraged by judges who were crown
servants, their laws discarded by foreigners, and monies derived

from their fatherland disbursed by aliens. The demand for an agent in London was equally logical. If communications must be carried on between Lower Canada and the imperial parliament, it was only right that the channel of communication should be French-Canadian or the direct choice of French-Canadians. The desire to exclude the judges was not inspired by any wholesome political theory of rendering them independent. They represented a British system, they were too close to a British executive, they were too likely to be pliable in the hands which created them. A French-Canadian assembly desired no contact with them. The refusal of a civil list yields to the same explanation. It must have seemed absurd to the assembly to be asked to provide permanent pay for an anti-French oligarchy. The fundamental defect of nationalism, its impatience of limitations, ran riot in Lower Canada. The French-Canadians had no conceptions of constitutional reform. Race became a blinding passion, and demanded a sphere of limitless expression. The solitary voices raised in adumbrations of responsible government were those of Neilson and his group. Papineau was swept off his feet by racial emotions, which took in actual issues a political and constitutional aspect. The fundamental race consciousness expressed itself in institutional terms, for in the institutions set up by the Constitutional Act of 1791 French-Canadians professed to find an active scheme for the suppression of their race.

It may be asked then, why did French Canada not rise as a man in 1837. There are several answers. The rebellion was premature and Papineau's sentiments ran to seed in ineffectual organization. Fortunately, too, the theatrical rodomontade of emotional preparation had stirred the military to something like effective preparedness. The church, however, was the deciding factor. The Roman catholic clergy found it necessary to apply the brakes to the racial machine. There was an obvious probability that the racial troubles might take on a popular political colour, and the church had not had a very happy experience in history with popular movements. The appeal, too, to the institutions of the United States and the foolish hope that aid would come from the hills of republicanism stiffened the back of the hierarchy. It may be said that the Quebec Act saved the situation in 1837–8, and—it may be said also to have created it.

In Upper Canada the failure of the constitution was due to political causes. The popular movement in that province was never racial, although there had been moments when the ' family compact ' gave to the term ' Yankee ' an ethnological significance. A Yankee was fundamentally a different person from an Upper Canadian loyalist. The history of reform in Upper Canada is that of an appeal against constitutional rigidity. Simcoe's ideal had become stereotyped in institutional stagnation. There was a recognized privileged class in the executive and legislative councils—a group had cornered the administration. The church of England held the position of an established and privileged communion. As a consequence it perpetuated disabilities for which there was no excuse in a new country, it outraged the religious sentiments of the majority of the population, and its endowments cut across the economic and educational life of the province. A privileged social class, a privileged administrative group, and a privileged church had entrenched themselves behind the constitution. The reformers aimed to see if they could not be forced to move without destroying the constitution. The constructive reformers of Upper Canada never dabbled in conventions, complete popular institutions, or direct political control. They desired to remove the constitution from the position of being a rigid shelter for privilege and to work it in such an elastic way as to give freedom and political liberty to all. They practically arrived at a theory of responsible government. They demanded reform for its own sake, for political ends. The problem in

M

Lower Canada was how to lower every barrier for the advantage of race consciousness. The problem in Upper Canada was how to divide political authority so that 'the advice of the house of assembly' might be an efficient fact as well as a constitutional theory. The reformers felt that they had, at least in embryo, a political principle which would preserve the framework of the constitution, while giving it the elasticity of life and the vitality of freedom. To this principle they held fast. The rebellion in Upper Canada never had a chance of success. Mackenzie and his group fell under the influence of Papineau, and, misinterpreting as political the motives of Lower Canadian aggression, they borrowed his theories and rushed to arms without the shadow of the actual or potential support which Papineau had behind him. In addition the people of Upper Canada had no desire to help Lower Canada in arms when they had suffered at the hands of Lower Canada in peace. The constitution of 1791 had left Upper Canadian revenue at the mercy of the Lower Canadian legislature. No effort at a working basis had in reality been successful, and there was in Upper Canada a resentment against the lower province which was too strong to allow any widespread revolt which might be interpreted as a sympathetic rebellion.

The outward expression of race seeking to destroy alien institutions and the outward expression of reform seeking to galvanize the same institutions into life afford an opportunity to consider in common certain functional weaknesses in the constitution of 1791. The crown exercised a very real power in the Canadas. The royal supremacy in religion was recognized in Upper Canada to the detriment of the non-episcopal churches and the growth of constitutional liberty. There was a moment in Lower Canada when its practical exercise was demanded and when religious animosities were in danger of being added to the racial struggle. The theory of crown lands and crown territorial revenue was a common source of friction. First of all, they created economical disadvantages. Through them privilege could be buttressed, immigration controlled, and settlers judiciously placed. They also created enormous strategical advantages in administration. The governor always had at his disposal crown revenues which included funds provided by the home government for the military chest. Thus the crown in Canada could at any time work the machinery of government. The history is full of painful illustrations of the crown's independence of grants and of its carrying on the administration of the provinces without monies voted by the legislatures. This was one of the broad issues. The protagonists of the popular houses in this connexion were often factious and recalcitrant demagogues, but behind their wearisome protests and the endless reiteration of their claims there lies a fact of experience in modern government, that there can be little hope of political stability as long as the executive is financially independent.

In addition, there was in the constitution no definition of the legislative sphere peculiar to the imperial and provincial parliaments. Issues in themselves strictly affecting the provincial life and yet of vital importance to the entire scheme were reserved for the consideration of the British cabinet. Among these was the power to amend the provincial constitutions. To any one only superficially acquainted with the system, it must be clear that there were bound to be clashes between the various constituent parts of the administrative machinery which only constitutional amendments could remove. At first the Lower Canadian assembly, for reasons which have been pointed out, tried petitions for change, but when Great Britain failed to provide remedies which apparently lay with the imperial government to provide, the assembly passed from one point to another until it claimed the power itself of changing the constitution, a position which erected another barrier between the crown and the popular house.

But perhaps the most serious cause of failure in the functioning of the constitution was the fact that the crown had no constitutional responsibility to the houses of assembly, and yet there could be no legislation without them. The question was how to link up the chief executive authority with the elected chambers. As a matter of fact no adequate answer to that question was found within these years. A financially irresponsible executive was also constitutionally independent, and the houses of assembly in seeking vaguely and for different reasons to cure a disease which they had not in reality diagnosed frequently overstepped their spheres, with the result that they were dissolved time after time. Constitutionally the governors had as much right to dissolve them as the king had to dissolve the imperial parliament, but in the latter case the king would act on the advice of responsible ministers in a spirit of nebulous, if royal neutrality. In the Canadas, when the governors resorted to this extreme, they were driven to act in the capacity of political party leaders. As a consequence another element was added to the growing forces of discontent with the executive, while the houses of assembly became more and more aggressive in asserting what they conceived to be their rights. In Lower Canada a considerable proportion of the executive council were members of the legislative council; in Upper Canada the entire executive council belonged to the legislative council. The situation was made all the more complicated by this state of affairs. The executive and legislative councils were used by the crown as bulwarks against the popular assemblies, and appointments to them were as a rule confined to those who could be relied on to support the administration. The whole system was vitiated by possessing an executive authority which did not need to rely on public opinion.

Two consequences of a serious nature followed. In Upper Canada control passed almost automatically into the hands of a governing clique. Only the good sense of the people held back popular fury, and the rebellion was merely a shadow cast by its flamboyant leader. In Lower Canada events passed from point to point of pathetic folly. It was a fatal move to suggest the union of the two provinces in 1822. When the British cabinet attempted a constitutional change which apparently lay with the imperial government alone, it was embodied in a bill which intensified the racial cause of the French-Canadians. It was equally fatal for Lower Canada to pass through the storm and stress of struggle under leadership which was not only too often undisciplined, but was inspired by racial, not political motives. On the other hand, there was in reality no remedy at hand, and if foolhardy rebellions in both provinces closed the constitutional experiment under the Constitutional Act of 1791, Great Britain had nothing to replace it, just as Oliver Cromwell had no working system ready at the close of the civil war. As we read the history to-day, it is easy to see the points in which the whole scheme was weak, but no one in 1838 had worked out the problem. The sovereignty of the crown seemed an insurmountable obstacle to colonial responsible government. To conceive of a governor responsible to a local executive dependent on a majority in a house of assembly seemed to mean the disintegration of the empire. No one could grasp a constructive *via media* which would reconcile local autonomy with imperial solidarity.

Lord Durham's words sum up the situation : ' representative government coupled with an irresponsible executive ... constant collision between the branches of the government ; the same abuse of the powers of the representative bodies, owing to the anomaly of their position, aided by the want of good municipal institutions, and the same constant interference of the imperial administration in matters which should be left wholly to the provincial governments.'[1] Indeed Durham's last sentence hints at an irritating procedure which turned the lieutenant-

[1] *Lord Durham's Report*, vol. ii, p. 194 (ed. Lucas, Oxford, 1912).

governors into intendants. The state papers and dispatches of the period illustrate conditions of meticulous supervision, which must have been pregnant sources of resentment. It is wearisome reading to turn page after page of requests for direction about the smallest details of provincial life. The crown in the Canadas was too weak as well as too strong. The representatives of the sovereign never felt secure in matters of no vital importance, and to constitutional issues was added the painful patience of delays in everyday pedestrian affairs. It seemed as though the whole life of the province, from high and difficult political concerns down to humble dealings, was centred at Westminster, and that the lieutenant-governors were merely agents to direct the activities of an outlying imperial machine.

The period closes almost in darkness with the *non possumus* of Russell's resolutions, the tragedy of rebellions, and the suspension of the constitution of Lower Canada. In darkness, but not in entire failure. These years, thick with error, brought with them an invaluable quota of experience. The hushed racial melancholy of Lower Canada and the stifled political aspiration of Upper Canada bore witness to the fact that race could not be crushed or satisfied in its active life by inadequate constitutional recognition, and that a political people could not for ever sit down quietly under the domination of privilege. The persistence of Upper Canada's aspiration is the significant note in the history, and in that persistence lay, as events turned out, happiness for Lower Canada.

CHAPTER XII

LORD DURHAM AND THE AFFAIRS OF BRITISH NORTH AMERICA

LORD DURHAM arrived in Canada on May 29, 1838. He came with exceedingly wide powers which can be studied in detail in the various commissions, instructions, and dispatches which he received from the cabinet. They can be summed up in the words of Lord Glenelg. He was given ' a general super-intendence over all British North America ', and he was to consider any proposals which he might think ' conducive to the permanent establishment of an improved system of govern-ment in her majesty's North American possessions '.[1] He also came with a preconceived idea of the future government. Before he left England he had drawn up the outline of a federal plan, believing that under a monarchy such a federation would gradually change into a complete legislative union of all the provinces.[2]

On his arrival he disclosed the purpose of his mission in a proclamation to the people : ' The honest and conscientious advocates of reform and of the amelioration of defective institutions will receive from me, without distinction of party, race, or politics, that assistance and encouragement which their patriotism has a right to command from all who desire to strengthen and consolidate the connexion between the parent state and these important colonies ; but the disturbers of the public peace, the violators of the law, the enemies of the crown and of the British empire will find in me an uncom-promising opponent. . . . I invite from you the most free and

[1] Glenelg to Durham, January 20, April 21, 1838, *Report*, vol. iii, pp. 305 ff. (ed. Lucas, Oxford, 1912).

[2] Charles Buller, ' Sketch of Lord Durham's Mission to Canada', *ibid.*, pp. 336 ff. The idea may have been suggested by Glenelg ; see *ibid.*, p. 309.

unreserved communications. I beg you to consider me as a friend and arbitrator, ready at all times to listen to your wishes, complaints, and grievances, and fully determined to act with the strictest impartiality. If you on your side will abjure all party and sectarian animosities and unite with me in the blessed work of peace and harmony, I feel assured that I can lay the foundations of such a system of government as will protect the rights and interests of all classes, allay all dissensions, and permanently establish under Divine Providence that wealth, greatness, and prosperity of which such inexhaustible elements are to be found in these fertile countries.' [1] The proclamation proclaimed him a liberal imperialist. His goodwill was immediately evident. He dissolved the old council and appointed a new one, which, with the exception of Dominick Daly, the provincial secretary, consisted of members of his staff. His desire to be surrounded with unbiased advisers met with universal approval.

With all its defects Durham's *Report* on the affairs of British North America remains the greatest state paper in colonial history. The minutest criticism has been applied to it since the time of its appearance. Much of this criticism is valid. The 'family compact', for example, subjected it to searching examination, and a committee of the legislative council of Upper Canada produced a report in which forceful restraint is combined with a logic which from many points of view can never be denied.[2] The sections on Upper Canada are decidedly weak. Politically there is fairness, socially and economically there are exaggerations and distorted views. The part dealing

---

[1] In English and French, enclosed in dispatch to Glenelg, May 31, 1838, *State Papers*, Q. 246–1, p. 45.

[2] Kennedy, *op. cit.*, pp. 470 ff. The legislative assembly also made a report to which a reply was issued by Francis Hincks, editor of the *Toronto Examiner*, whose paper had made a strong plea for ' responsible government ' during Durham's residence in Canada. His pamphlet is entitled *A brief Review of the Report of the House of Assembly of Upper Canada on Lord Durham's Report* (Toronto, 1839).

with Lower Canada can only be described as brilliant, and the situation there is diagnosed with the greatest insight, which is made all the more remarkable by the occasional slips in fact and errors in interpretation. In his efforts to grasp the problems which called for solution Durham gave himself up to five months of ceaseless activity. His resignation cut him off from perfecting his summary in detail, and had he remained longer it is reasonable to expect that he would have learned more of Upper Canada. He felt, however, that the most pressing issue was that of French-Canadianism, and on it he expended the greater part of his tireless energy. Of the Maritime Provinces he said little. The blow from England fell on him at the moment when he was in the middle of a conference with eastern delegates, and his *Report* was finished leaving the history a mere sketch, with no comprehensive grasp of the difficulties which the interview brought to light. Contact, however, with the Maritime Provinces brought him into touch with Sir John Harvey of New Brunswick, Sir Colin Campbell and William Young of Nova Scotia, Sir Charles Fitzroy of Prince Edward Island, and others, from whom he learned something of conditions and before whom he laid his plan of British North American federation. The attitude of each eastern province was different for different reasons.

In the Maritime Provinces there had been much social, political, religious, and economic progress. In the course of time constitutional friction appeared similar to that in the Canadas. The issues, however, were held well in hand, and there was never any public clamour of a disloyal nature. In Nova Scotia and New Brunswick the executive council and the legislative council consisted of the same persons. In 1830, when Lord Goderich was dealing with questions raised by the parliamentary report of 1828 on the Canadas, he wrote to the lieutenant-governors of both provinces suggesting the advisability of making the councils more independent by appointing to them a greater number of members who were not government officials and by excluding the puisne judges. Two years later he sent a dispatch to Sir Archibald Campbell, lieutenant-governor of New Brunswick, proposing that in future the executive council and the legislative council should not consist of the same members and that the former should be small and include ' one or two influential members of each branch of the legislature'. He also recommended that the legislative council should be increased, and that membership of it should not of necessity carry with it membership of the executive council. Campbell agreed with these suggestions, pointing out that the previous state of affairs constituted an anomaly which ought never to have existed. By a royal commission dated November 20, 1832, New Brunswick was given two distinct councils, one entirely executive and one entirely legislative.

In 1836 a deputation from New Brunswick visited England headed by the reform leader Lemuel Wilmot. They suggested reforms in the personnel of the councils, but they made no demands for responsible government or for an elective second chamber. Their main object was to secure from the colonial office general concessions such as had been offered in the Canadas by Gosford and Head. They asked for the control of the crown revenues in return for a civil list and for a reform in the crown lands' department. These requests were at once granted, and arrangements were agreed on for carrying them out. Unfortunately Campbell feared that the concessions were too extreme, and he carried on an undignified dispute with the house of assembly, dissolving it on a side issue. An election brought him no relief, and finally he resigned. His successor was Sir John Harvey, whom Durham met in Canada, and the reforms agreed on in England were carried out without serious trouble. New Brunswick would have been the gainer from federation. The Maine boundary was still in dispute, and in case of war with the United States New Brunswick would have been the earliest point of attack. Harvey, however, knew that the province had just passed through a political crisis in which reactionary and reform forces had been engaged in a bitter quarrel, and he was not anxious to introduce new proposals before the recent changes had passed out of an atmosphere of local political controversy.

In Nova Scotia the strong English element centred round Halifax stiffened the forces of conservatism, and it was not till 1837 that the councils were separated. When the legislature opened in that year Joseph Howe proposed a series of reform resolutions, demanding among other things that the council should no longer hold their seats for life and ' treat with contempt or indifference the wishes of the people '. Howe made a fighting speech in which he repudiated any separatist or republican tendencies, but claimed the fullness of self-government. The council threatened to refuse the supply bill, and Howe withdrew the resolutions after he had secured a majority in their favour in the assembly. The tactics were admirable. The supply bill was saved, and Howe embodied the resolutions, which had fulfilled their purpose as a test of opinion, in an address to the king. The address asked for the control of the casual and territorial revenues, and an elective legislative council. Failing the latter the assembly desired that the executive and legislative councils should be separated, and that provision should be made in both for a just representation of all the great interests of the province. They also asked that the executive council should include ' some members of the popular branch', and that thus the province might secure ' responsibility to the commons '. Glenelg replied granting the concessions which had been made in the other provinces, but he expressed a doubt as to the possible success of separating the councils.[1] For the moment he avoided reference to the

---

[1] Glenelg to Campbell, April 30, 1837, *Sessional Papers, Canada* (1883), No. 70, pp. 17 ff.

demand for responsibility. He was pleased that the resolutions
had been withdrawn. A few months later, in connexion with
the request for popular control of the executive, he wrote : ' Her
majesty's government must oppose a respectful but at the
same time a firm declaration that it is inconsistent with a due
advertence to the essential distinctions between a metropolitan
and a colonial government and is therefore inadvisable.' [1]
The executive and legislative councils were formally separated
by Durham's commission and instructions as governor-in-chief
of Nova Scotia.[2]

In Nova Scotia the issue of responsible government was thus
already before the people, and there was no desire to complicate
the situation by the discussion of the wider question of federation. William Young called Durham's attention to the situation.
Nova Scotia was happy in ' impartial administration of justice,
in perfect freedom of conscience, in the unfettered exercise of
industry, and in the absence of oppression in every form '.
There was, however, discontent over lands, fisheries, and
customs, and because of the fact that official salaries, not under
control of the legislature, were too large for the means of the
colony. Two chief causes of friction overshadowed all others.
The councils were unfavourable to all reform, and contained
too many members belonging to the church of England;
the house of assembly had no effective control.[3] Nova Scotia
had joined hands with the Canadas.

In Prince Edward Island there was no constitutional difficulty.
In 1834 the assembly asked for an executive council distinct
from the legislative council. This was refused. When Sir
Charles Fitzroy was going out as lieutenant-governor in 1837
Glenelg asked him to examine the composition of the councils.
As a result the assembly in the following year renewed their

[1] Glenelg to Campbell, July 6, 1837, *Colonial Office Papers.*
[2] Instructions to Durham, February 6, 1838, *Sessional Papers, op. cit.*, p. 39.
[3] William Young to Durham, September 20, 1838, *Report*, vol. iii, pp. 12 ff.

request, and supported it by pointing to the changes just made in Nova Scotia. Fitzroy lent his weight to the petition, which was granted in due course.[1] The real grievances in Prince Edward Island were economic and arose from absentee owner- ship of most of the land. This had become an ever-growing cause of complaint, and Fitzroy felt that he could not encourage Durham in promoting comprehensive schemes of government with the social situation so grave in the island.

Durham's idea of a federation, gradually changing to a closer union, had to be abandoned. He found that those who were closest in touch with sentiment in the Maritime Provinces were not encouraging from their personal knowledge of the political situations. In addition means of communication were so inadequate as to rule the plan out of immediate practical politics, and he saw no prospect of at once improving them in such a way as to warrant an appeal to the legislatures of the Maritime Provinces on a union of any kind—a course which he considered essential. The greatest influence, however, in caus- ing him to suggest other changes was Lower Canada. Before he had come into close contact with the French-Canadians he had believed that they were fighting a liberal battle against the forces of reactionary constitutionalism. His enthusiasm underwent a gradual decline, for he could only see stagnant apathy and ignorant indifference in political questions. He had believed, too, that the British were nothing but an oligarchy holding on to power. He found that he was confusing the rank and file with their narrow visionless leaders, and he began to dread that any wholesale neglect of British opinions might hurt imperial unity and might even throw Upper Canada into the hands of the United States. When he had finally made up his mind definitely on the constitutional changes which he would

[1] The dispatches are in *Correspondence with Colonial Office, Prince Edward Island*, Series G, 275–6 (Canadian Archives). For the constitution of the Legislative and Executive Councils in the Maritime Provinces see *British Parliamentary Papers*, 1839, vol. xxxiv.

recommend, he thought that they must be fully applied before any scheme embracing British North America was brought forward. He decided to advise the reuniting of the two Canadas under responsible government. Reunion, as he found things, was a necessary preliminary training towards any greater constitutional synthesis, and it was emphatically essential for the future of French Canada. Indeed his suggestion was chiefly influenced by the latter consideration.

Durham's proposal for the Canadas was not merely a legislative union. It was a fusion. The French-Canadians were to be absorbed, amalgamated, absolutely united. He had decided on principles in colonial government. Responsible government was the foundation. His study of the situation did not shake him in his theory, but it caused him to propose changes in the conditions without which he believed his theory would not work. The first change was to deprive Lower Canada of its political institutions by merging them into common institutions for the whole of Canada. He had no doubt that the root of the trouble in Lower Canada was racial.[1] This led to a second change. Race must be swamped in the reunion by assuring a British majority. 'The fatal feud of origin, which is the cause of the most extensive mischief, would be aggravated at the present moment by any change which should give the majority more power than they have hitherto possessed. A plan by which it is proposed to assure the tranquil government of Lower Canada must include in itself the means of putting an end to the agitation of national disputes in the legislature, by settling at once and for ever the national character of the province. I entertain no doubts as to the national character which must be given to Lower Canada; it must be that of the British empire.'[2] Lower Canada was to be slowly but surely anglicized, and nationalism was to be crushed out. 'I repeat that the alteration of the character of the province

---

[1] *Report*, vol. ii, pp. 63, 72.   [2] *Ibid.*, p. 288.

ought to be immediately entered on, and firmly though cautiously followed up : that in any plan which may be adopted for the future management of Lower Canada the first object ought to be that of making it an English province, and that, with this end in view, the ascendancy should never again be placed in any hands but those of an English population.'[1] His aim was no sham union, no mere merging of the houses of assembly, nothing of a federal nature. Everything French-Canadian, except religion, everything which ' la nation canadienne ' stood for, was to be entirely crushed. Durham believed his policy was a beneficial one. He had no sympathy with a race consciousness which seemed to him a detriment to advance. French-Canadians were to be saved by compulsion from ' some idle and narrow notion of a petty and visionary nationality '.[2] Common institutions, common purposes, common economic interests—all British when the drastic processes were over—would enable French-Canadians to enjoy a common British North American nationality, towards the final creation of which out of all the provinces French Canada would contribute a lost racial individuality.

To the fused Canadas, to the Maritime Provinces, and to the future united British North America—an ideal which Durham never abandoned—he recommended the grant of responsible self-government. Durham left no doubts as to his meaning. ' The wisdom of adopting the true principle of representative government and facilitating the management of public affairs by entrusting it to persons who have the confidence of the representative body has never been recognized in the government of the North American colonies. All the offices of government were independent of the assembly.'[3] He meant cabinet government in the British constitutional sense ; government by an executive responsible to the majority. ' I know not how it is possible to secure . . . harmony in any other way than

[1] *Ibid.*, p. 296.   [2] *Ibid.*, p. 265 ; cf. p. 324.   [3] *Ibid.*, p. 77.

by administering the government on those principles which have been found perfectly efficacious in Great Britain. I would not impair a single prerogative of the crown; on the contrary I believe that the interests of these colonies require the pro-. tection of prerogatives which have not hitherto been exercised. But the crown must on the other hand submit to the necessary consequences of representative institutions; and if it has to carry on the government in unison with a representative body, it must consent to carry it on by means of those in whom that representative body has confidence '.[1] The Canadas were to be reunited immediately by imperial legislation, but such legislation ' should contain provisions by which any or all of the other North American colonies may, on the application of the legislature, be, with the consent of the two Canadas or their united legislature, admitted into the union on such terms as may be agreed on between them '.[2] The immediate change and the hoped-for future were both to be made real by entrusting administration to such men as could command a majority in the elected houses. In addition, Durham, who was no doctrinaire theorist, recommended the establishment of thorough municipal government. He saw there the practical political training-ground of his race, and he believed that such a system in all the provinces would not only strengthen the workings of responsible institutions but would deprive the legislatures of occasions to sin.[3] He advised imperial legislation for the purpose in imme-diate connexion with that for the reunion of the Canadas,[4] and he included municipal organization as an ' essential part of any durable and complete ' wider union.[5]

In recommending responsible cabinet government, Durham knew that he confronted an issue which had already caused much searching of hearts in England. As far back as 1810 Liverpool had denied the possibility of a colonial executive

---

[1] *Report*, vol. ii, p. 278.   [2] *Ibid.*, p. 323.   [3] *Ibid.*, p. 287.
             [4] *Ibid.*, p. 324.   [5] *Ibid.*, p. 322.

being responsible to the local legislature.[1] Glenelg had formulated a theory of responsibility on which Head wrecked himself in Upper Canada, and he had stated that colonial self-government and imperial sovereignty were irreconcilable.[2] The ten resolutions in 1837 refused the grant as ' unadvisable ', and Lord John Russell in proposing them said that he considered the demand that the executive council should be responsible in the same way as a British cabinet was a ' proposition . . . entirely incompatible with the relations between the mother country and the colony. . . . That part of the constitution which requires that the ministers of the crown shall be responsible to parliament and shall be removable if they do not obtain the confidence of parliament is a condition which exists in an imperial legislature and in an imperial legislature only. It is a condition which cannot be carried into effect in a colony—it is a condition which can only exist in one place, namely the seat of the empire '. He repeated the same ideas during the debates in the following January on the suspension of the constitution of Lower Canada. The objections took the form of a political dilemma : if the colonial executive is responsible to the colonial legislature, it cannot be responsible to the British parliament ; but the colony is part of the empire, therefore its executive can be responsible to the imperial legislature alone, through a governor responsible to the imperial cabinet.

With these objections in his mind Durham attempted to get out of the difficulty by a division between colonial and imperial subjects : ' I know that it has been urged that the principles which are productive of harmony and good government in the mother country are by no means applicable to a colonial dependency. It is said that it is necessary that the administration of a colony should be carried on by persons nominated without any reference to the wishes of its people ; that they

[1] Liverpool to Craig, September 12, 1810, Kennedy, *op. cit.*, p. 278.
[2] Glenelg to Head, December 5, 1835, *ibid.*, p. 419 ; same to Campbell, July 6, 1837, *Colonial Office Papers*.

N

have to carry into effect the policy, not of that people but of
the authorities at home, and that a colony which should name
all its own administrative functionaries would in fact cease to
be dependent. I admit that the system which I propose would
in fact place the internal government of the colony in the
hands of the colonists themselves, and that we should thus
leave to them the execution of the laws, of which we have long
entrusted the making solely to them. Perfectly aware of the
value of our colonial possessions and strongly impressed with
the necessity of maintaining our connexion with them, I know
not in what respect it can be desirable that we should interfere
with their internal legislation in matters which do not affect
their relations with the mother country. The matters which
so concern us are very few. The constitution of the form of
government—the regulation of foreign relations, and of trade
with the mother country, the other British colonies, and
foreign nations—and the disposal of the public lands, are the
only points on which the mother country requires a control.
This control is now sufficiently secured by the authority of the
imperial legislature, by the protection which the colony derives
from us against foreign enemies, by the beneficial terms which
our laws secure to its trade, and by its share of the reciprocal
benefits which would be conferred by a wise system of colonization.   A perfect subordination on the part of the colony on
these points is secured by the advantages which it finds in the
continuance of its connexion with the empire. It certainly
is not strengthened, but greatly weakened, by a vexatious
interference on the part of the home government with the
enactment of laws for regulating the internal concerns of the
colony, or in the selection of persons entrusted with their execution.'[1] Durham's attempt to draw a clear-cut distinction between
colonial and imperial concerns takes no account of overlapping,
and as it stands his division would have left the colonies only
something like municipal powers. It is, however, to his credit that

[1] *Report*, vol. ii, pp. 280 ff.

he saw the way out of the dilemma, and that he anticipated the solution of history in pointing to the dual rôle of the governor.

Distinct as was the line which Durham drew, it did not storm the barriers of opposition. Doubtless nothing would have convinced ' the die-hards ', whose political logic was too strong for their common sense. But men like Lord John Russell gave anxious hours to what they conceived a hopeless dilemma and could not see the appearance of a solution. It is an entirely unjust view which pictures England holding back in miserly clutch the golden gift of responsible government, and Canada stretching out ineffectual hands in the glory of new-found political wisdom. The political thought of the day was still anchored fast to the Austinian theory of sovereignty. Yet in spite of that, there were many in England who were hard at work on the problem and would have granted Canada responsible government had they been able to reconcile it with imperial sovereignty. When Durham's *Report* had been laid on the table of the house of commons, and when resolutions were under consideration in June 1839 for the reunion of the Canadas, Russell again spoke on the subject. Durham had not convinced him. He still adhered to his position of two years previously : ' it does not appear to me that you can subject the executive council of Canada to the responsibility which is fairly demanded of the ministers of the executive power in this country. . . . The governor of Canada [acts] not in that high and unassailable position in which the sovereign of this country is placed. He is a governor receiving instructions from the crown on the responsibility of a secretary of state. Here then at once is an obvious and complete difference between the executive of this country and the executive of a colony.'[1] On the other hand, it was well that Russell took over colonial affairs from the feeble Lord Normanby in September 1839. He returned again and again, as we shall see, to wrestle with the dilemma, and finally his dispatches began the

[1] Kennedy, *op. cit.*, pp. 478 ff.

transition to responsible government. In addition, students
of colonial history and students of political thought can hardly
regret the speech just quoted. In answer to it Joseph Howe
of Nova Scotia wrote four letters which are not unworthy to
stand by Durham's *Report*.[1] They occupy a distinct place in
political literature for their insight into the old colonial system,
for their cogency of argument and their powerful logic, combined with the badinage of a native humour.

Howe began by a series of questions : Was responsible
government withheld from a suspicion of disloyalty ? Colonial
loyalty would bear examination. Was Lord Durham's remedy
for the situation and discontent dangerous ? There were no
dangers. Did dependence in an empire imply constitutional
inferiority ? If so, why should a minority rule ? Would
a majority be more ' disloyal ' under their own government
than under the continual irritation of an executive pleasing
only to a small minority ? Was the queen in danger because
the citizens of London governed themselves ? Would the
lord mayor declare war on France ? Would Canada do it ?
He then proceeded to examine carefully Russell's objections
to responsible government. The governors could be made
responsible to the assembly as the ministers of the crown in
England without any invasion of the crown's sovereignty.
If they received unconstitutional advice, what then ? Might
not this occur in England ? Suppose a typical governor made
mayor of Liverpool, with all the present bag and baggage of
dispatches, instructions, and all the present method of government as known in the North American provinces, ' he must
be an angel of light indeed if he does not throw the good city
of Liverpool into confusion '. What would be the answer to
such a result ? The ' mayor ' could blame some one else—
could throw the responsibility on the ' colonial office '. ' No
form of government could well be devised more ridiculous.'
The ' mayor's ' officials—the executive—would be much more

[1] Kennedy, *op. cit.*, pp. 480 ff.

irresponsible. Howe followed Durham's division of jurisdictions. The questions involved were those of local, not
imperial concern. No governor could constitutionally allow
interference in foreign affairs, and a declaration of war would
only be the act of madmen. If there were difficulties in connexion with trade or commerce, irresponsible government had
failed to solve them. Russell might ask what is proposed.
Howe replied that foreign affairs, control of the naval and
military forces, colonial trade with Great Britain, and that
general supervision analogous to that over an incorporate
town would be left to the imperial parliament. The colonial
secretary's duties must become those of mere oversight. The
governors, who on their arrival were like ignorant ' overgrown
schoolboys ', must in future find themselves surrounded by
' schoolmasters ' who had the confidence of the colony which
they were supposed to govern wisely, and not by those who
only represented themselves, or a minority, or the whims of
their excellencies' predecessors. The governors would then ' do
no wrong in any matter of which the colonial legislature had
the right to judge '. Under responsible government Papineau
and Mackenzie might never have existed as rebels; perhaps
they might have developed into constructive statesmen.

[AUTHORITIES.—The standard edition of Durham's *Report* is Sir Charles
Lucas, *Lord Durham's Report* (3 vols., Oxford, 1912). The notes and intro-
duction are invaluable. A careful analysis of Durham's work in Canada and
of his conclusions is in F. Bradshaw, *Self-government in Canada* (London, n.d.).
The most important of his dispatches are in Egerton and Grant, *Canadian
Constitutional Development* (Toronto, 1907), and Kennedy, *Documents of the
Canadian Constitution, 1759–1915* (Oxford, 1918) ; see also *British Parlia-
mentary Papers*, 1839, vol. xxxii. The *State Papers* are in Canadian Archives,
Series G, vols. xxxviii–xli ; Series Q. 246. 1–Q. 247. For the Maritime
Provinces, the *State Papers* are in the Canadian Archives and are in process
of reconstruction. J. A. Chisholm, *The Speeches and Public Letters of Joseph
Howe* (2 vols., Halifax, 1909), is essential. G. M. Grant, *Joseph Howe* (Halifax,
1904), and W. L. Grant, *The Tribune of Nova Scotia : A Chronicle of Joseph
Howe* (Toronto, 1915), are valuable, and the latter is very suggestive and
written with great insight. J. Hannay, *Wilmot and Tilley* (Toronto, 1907), is
useful. Valuable documentary material is in *Canada Sessional Papers*, 1883,
No. 70 ; *House of Commons Papers, Nova Scotia*, &c., August 1839, No. 579.]

CHAPTER XIII

LORD SYDENHAM'S COLONIAL SYSTEM

LORD DURHAM's insistence on the reunion of the Canadas produced an immediate effect. The British government decided to carry out his suggestion at once and a bill was introduced in June 1839 for that purpose. Opposition was strong, however, in Upper Canada, and the house of assembly, while approving of the plan, laid down conditions which the imperial parliament could not accept.[1] The measure was therefore postponed until the new governor-general, Charles Poulett Thomson, afterwards Baron Sydenham of Sydenham and Toronto, had gone to Canada and made a full report on the provinces. Thomson was a civilian who had had a wide financial and business experience, and he brought to his work a nervous energy and a tenacity of purpose which surprised men who were intimately acquainted with him. A liberal in politics, he had the entire confidence of Lord John Russell, and the combination in colonial administration tided Canada over one of the most difficult periods in its history and, as the issues proved, laid permanent foundations for constitutional development. Thomson landed at Quebec on October 19, 1839, and at once began his work, which may be considered as two-fold. First it was his duty to gain Canadian adherence to the imperial proposal, and secondly he was to deal with a constitutional principle which would inevitably crop up—the problem of ' responsible government '.

His instructions covering these main duties and lesser subjects

---

[1] Cf. Kennedy, *op. cit.*, p. 531, and see G. Poulett Scrope, *Memoir of the Life of the Right Honourable Charles, Lord Sydenham, with a Narrative of his Administration in Canada*, p. 152 (second ed., London, 1844).

were contained in three dispatches from Lord John Russell.[1]
He was to promote ' a legislative union of the two provinces
—a just regard to the claims of either province in adjusting
the terms of that union—the maintenance of the three estates
of the provincial legislature—the settlement of a permanent
civil list for securing the independence of the judges, and to the
executive government that freedom of action which is necessary
for the public good—and the establishment of a system of local
government by representative bodies freely elected in the various
cities and rural districts '.   In order to carry the assembly of
Upper Canada he was, if necessary, to dissolve it and appeal to
the good sense of the inhabitants.   On the subject of responsible
government Russell's instructions disclose the fact that he had
continued to grapple with the problem.   He felt that such
a constitutional principle could not be reduced to the form of
a positive enactment, but he counselled a course which was
a distinct advance :   ' The importance of maintaining the
utmost possible harmony between the policy of the legislature
and of the executive government admits of no question, and it
will of course be your anxious endeavour to call to your councils
and to employ in the public service those persons who, by their
position and character, have obtained the general confidence and
esteem of the inhabitants of the province.'   On the other hand,
he could not see the way clear towards the establishment of
full cabinet government : ' if we seek to apply such a practice
to a colony we shall at once find ourselves at fault.   The power
for which a minister is responsible in England is not his own
power, but the power of the crown, of which he is for the time
the organ.   It is obvious that the executive councillor of a colony
is in a situation totally different.   The governor under whom he
serves received his orders from the crown of England.   But
can the colonial council be the advisers of the crown of

[1] Russell to Thomson, September 7, October 14, 16, 1839, Kennedy, *op. cit.*,
pp. 516 ff.

England ? Evidently not, for the crown has other advisers for the same functions and with superior authority. It may happen, therefore, that the governor receives at one and the same time instructions from the queen and advice from his executive council totally at variance with each other. If he is to obey his instructions from England, the parallel of constitutional responsibility entirely fails ; if, on the other hand, he is to follow the advice of his council, he is no longer a subordinate officer, but an independent sovereign.' Russell's principle was to be one of mutual harmony between executive and legislature, depending neither on an enactment nor on a convention, but on good sense and ' a wise moderation '. To encourage the idea he instructed Thomson to make it generally known that in future good behaviour would not be considered a guarantee that an office which was held during pleasure would be held during life : ' Not only will such officers be called to retire from the public service as often as any sufficient motives of public policy may suggest the expediency of that measure, but . . . a change in the person of the governor will be considered as a sufficient reason for any alterations which his successor may deem it expedient to make in the list of public functionaries, subject of course to the future confirmation of the sovereign.' Thomson was in thorough agreement with the policies outlined, and at once began to put them to the test.

On November 11 he summoned at Montreal the special council which had acted under Sir John Colborne. His shrewdness was immediately apparent. He did not intend to make any changes nor to call a council of which he chose the members. His object was to escape the imputation of creating a body specially selected because of their favouring the project of union.[1] Nor did he intend to tolerate disorganized proceedings as under Colborne—' his council ran riot '. He laid the project of union before the body, gave them his ' opinion strongly ', and carried

[1] Thomson to Russell, November 18, 1839, Kennedy, *op. cit.*, p. 525.

his proposals.[1] The council accepted the union in six resolutions, which included agreement with the request for a civil list and for the blending of the public debts of the provinces. They urged at the same time the reprovision of constitutional government as quickly as possible.[2] Thomson believed that the majority of the province, British and French, were behind him, arbitrary though the methods were which the law allowed him to use under the temporary Acts for the administration of Lower Canada. In his heart, however, he was convinced that such methods were ideal for the province : ' If it were possible the best thing for Lower Canada would be a despotism for ten years more, for in truth the people are not yet fit for the higher class of self-government—scarcely indeed at present for any description of it '.[3] Before long, too, he changed his mind about the approval which he thought he had behind him. In Lower Canada he found ' no such thing as a political opinion. No man looks to a practical measure of improvement. Talk to any one upon education, or public works, or better laws, let him be English or French, you might as well talk Greek to him. Not a man cares for a single practical measure—the only end, one would suppose, of a better form of government. They have only one feeling, a hatred of race. The French hate the English and the English hate the French, and every question resolves itself into that and that alone.'[4] The council might accept the union, but in the final analysis their resolutions were imposed on them by the arbitrary will of the governor. They reflected, broadly speaking, only that will. Thomson's greatest failure lay in thinking that the race feeling which he so vividly described would lie down quietly under a form of government which provided it with anything like freedom. If it was true, as he professed to believe, that the great mass of the people held

---

[1] Same to a friend, November 20, December 8, 1839, *ibid.*, p. 528.
[2] *Ibid.*, pp. 527 ff.   [3] See note 1.
[4] Thomson to a friend, March 13, 1840, Scrope, *op. cit.*, p. 168.

an opinion 'in favour of the union measure', then it was equally true, as he failed to see, that their favour was influenced by racial motives.

In Upper Canada there was no chance of gaining the consent of the legislature by high-handed methods. When Thomson met it early in December 1839, he disclosed the political skill in which he gradually became a past master. His first address to the house of assembly was exceedingly well planned. He laid stress on the financial state of the province—the stagnation in public and private affairs, the heavy provincial debt. A larger revenue was needed, not merely to cancel the past but to secure the future. Lower Canada had always been a financial stumbling-block to Upper Canada. Lower Canada held the key to more revenue, and without Lower Canadian co-operation navigation and the development of natural resources must remain futile. The imperial government were glad that the house of assembly had previously agreed to the principle of union, and it only remained for the governor-general to ask them to moderate their conditions and to accept others which would hasten those changes towards improvement which Upper Canada so much needed and desired. Thomson outlined the imperial terms : equal representation of each province in the united legislature, a sufficient civil list, the placing as a charge on the United Province a fair proportion of the existing public debt of Upper Canada which had been contracted on works of a general nature.[1]

The address was masterly, and it worked like magic on a house of assembly of which Thomson has left a lively picture : ' The assembly is such a house—split into half a dozen parties. The government having *none*—and *no one man* to depend on. Think of a house in which half the members hold places, yet in which the government does not command a single vote ; in which the place-men generally vote against the executive, and

[1] Kennedy, *op. cit.*, pp. 529 ff.

where there is no one to defend the government when attacked or to state the opinions or views of the governor. How with a popular assembly government is to be conducted under such circumstances is a riddle to me.' [1] Thomson's address was the first move in solving the riddle. ' The wise moderation ' which was Russell's elixir of political life was brought into action in the appeal to the hard common sense of the province. The gate to prosperity was closed and the key to it was legislative union. More skilful still was the publication in the *Upper Canada Gazette* of the dispatch relating to the tenure of public offices. It was unaccompanied by any explanatory note. The new rule was self-evident—no one would be continued as a public official unless he was of service to the governor and to the province. The strategy was astounding. Thomson had already begun his method of government. The session was scarcely three weeks old when he carried his proposals with substantial majorities in both the legislative council and in the house of assembly.[2] In informing Russell of his success, his dispatches were almost exuberant. He had neglected the ' family compact ' and the office-holders, and he had made his appeal to the reformers and moderate conservatives.[3] The union was carried, but not ' without trouble and a prodigious deal of management, in which my house of commons tactics stood me in good stead, for I wanted above all things to avoid a dissolution. My ministers vote against me. So I govern through the opposition, who are truly " her majesty's ".' [4]

---

[1] *Ibid.*, p. 529.   [2] *Ibid.*, pp. 532 ff.

[3] Thomson to Russell, December 24, 1839, Scrope, *op. cit.*, pp. 154 ff.

[4] Thomson to a friend, December 31, 1839, *ibid.*, p. 156. In an interview with Sir George Arthur, the lieutenant-governor of Upper Canada, November 24, 1839, on the question of gaining Upper Canadian support for the union, Thomson left the clear impression that his object was to secure ten or twelve years of good government, and that by that time ' ministers hoped to find a convenient opportunity of dropping the connexion ', since the Canadas would have developed ' the groundwork of an independent state separate from the neighbouring republic ' : Memo. of confidential interview

A week before he had gained the assent of the assembly, the question of ' responsible government ' was raised, and Thomson was asked for any dispatches which he might have received on the subject.   His tactful answer gained him support.   He lightly brushed aside his inability to communicate the dispatches to the house, but he informed them that he had been commanded to administer the government ' in accordance with the well-understood wishes and interests of the people, and to pay to their feelings, as expressed through their representatives, the deference that is justly due to them '.[1]   This was generally interpreted to mean that at least the old colonial system was dead.   Indeed Robert Baldwin stated to the electors of Toronto before the union his ' conviction that the great principle of responsible government as we have always claimed it . . . is effectually conceded '.[2]   Thomson, however, had arrived at a method of administration which was peculiarly his own. His aim was to destroy that idea of ' responsible government ' which at this time Baldwin thought had been conceded.   He was a minister, not a sovereign, and his executive council could not be responsible to the assembly, for he was not in a position uniformly to accept their advice : ' I cannot get rid of my responsibility to the home government, I will place no responsibility on the council ; they are *a council* for the governor to consult, but no more.' [3]   He determined to lead the people of these colonies ' from fruitless and idle disputes upon theoretical points of government '.[4]   He aimed to avoid belonging to one party or to the other, and ' to take the moderate men from both sides, reject the ' extremes, and govern as [he thought]

between G. G. and Sir George Arthur in *Macaulay Papers* [A], E. 45 a, 6 (15) (Ontario Archives).

[1] Kennedy, *op. cit.*, p. 536.

[2] Baldwin to the electors of Toronto, January 16, 1841, *Baldwin Papers* [A], E. 6–7, 29 (17) (Ontario Archives).

[3] Thomson to a friend, December 12, 1839, Kennedy, *op. cit.*, p. 532.

[4] Same to citizens of Halifax, July 1840, Scrope, *op. cit.*, p. 179.

right and not as they fancy '. ' I can make a middle reforming party, I feel sure,' he wrote in the utmost confidence.[1]   Thomson was as much a party leader as any preceding governors, but he created his party.   He chose the best men of all shades of moderate opinion.   He would ' devolve the responsibility of his acts on no man ', for he believed such a course would endanger the empire ; but he was always ready to listen to all opinions and ' to seek the advice of those who may be considered to represent the well-understood wishes of the people '.[2]

Thomson at once proceeded to put his system to further test. He had formulated a theory of responsibility.   The problem now was to see if the latter would work in another relation where the imperial wishes were not so clearly defined.   He took a moment when his popularity was at its height to ' try his hand at the clergy reserves '.[3]   In the church lands he saw perhaps the most disintegrating force in the social background of Upper Canada.   They had stirred up religious bitterness, broken up the economic life of the province, and reacted detrimentally on the administration.   He hoped to get some satisfactory arrangement through the legislature before the united parliament opened.   To remove such a source of discontent seemed more than wise, for there were enough difficulties ahead along the new path of constitutional progress.   With the clergy reserves unsettled, he felt that no constitution, however new and however constitutionally accepted, would make for either advance or content.   In addition, Thomson, like Durham, was a strong imperialist.   He diagnosed with concern a certain unrest, an impatience with England's colonial policy, a state of mind not explicitly disloyal, but certainly not sympathetic towards the dealings with the Canadas.   There was a danger, if the union did not get away to a good start, that all this might be fatally accentuated.   He therefore determined to see if Upper Canada itself could not settle the clergy reserves question.   He risked

[1] *Ibid.*, p. 164.   [2] *Ibid.*, p. 259.   [3] *Ibid.*, p. 155.

his previous success, and he stood to gain nothing with the
British government if he accomplished his purpose. Indeed he
might irretrievably damage his reputation. On the other hand,
there never had been such a favourable moment to take a risk
for the benefit of the province.

Thomson was personally opposed to a solution which would
turn over the clergy reserves to education, and the legislative
council had all along rejected such a proposal. He could not
bring himself to sanction the transference to any other object
of lands granted for a religious purpose, and he believed any bill
to that effect would be disallowed by the imperial cabinet.
There were two extreme opinions in the province. The vast
majority of the people favoured a settlement for education.
Strachan and his group held fast by the belief that they were
'the protestant clergy' of the Constitutional Act. Thomson
prepared a bill which went through the legislature as a compromise. The clergy reserves were to be distributed among the
various religious bodies in proportion to their membership. The
bill was suspended until it had lain before the British parliament and received special approval from the crown according
to the terms of the Constitutional Act.[1] Meanwhile Thomson
was triumphant. In spite of Strachan's bitter opposition he
felt that he had removed 'the great overwhelming grievance,
the root of all the troubles of the province, the cause of the
rebellion—the never-failing watchword at the hustings—the
perpetual source of discord, strife, and hatred . . . it is worth
ten unions'.[2] Unfortunately legal opinion decided that the
provincial legislature could not deal with the matter and his
bill was disallowed. An imperial Act was passed along the same
lines, but Strachan had been busy and the church of England
received a share out of all proportion to its numerical importance.
Thomson was naturally offended. The new arrangement would
only aggravate the evil. However, there were compensations.

[1] See above, p. 83.   [2] Scrope, *op. cit.*, pp. 160 ff.

No new reserves could be created, lands sold in the past were divided between the church of England and the church of Scotland, and the monies derived from sales in the future would be divided in a general way among all the religious bodies on a basis of membership. Thomson's fears were for the moment groundless, and his personal popularity quieted a people of whom the vast majority felt that the imperial legislation had done another injustice to Canada. He closed the last legislature of Upper Canada with just pride. ' On your return to your different districts ', he said, ' I earnestly hope that it will be your endeavour to promote that spirit of harmony and conciliation which has so much distinguished your proceedings here. Let past differences be forgotten—let irritating suspicions be removed. I rejoice to find that already tranquillity and hopeful confidence in the future prevail throughout the province. Let it be your task to cherish and promote these feelings ; it will be mine cordially to co-operate with you, and by administering the government in obedience to the commands of the queen, with justice and impartiality to all, to promote her anxious wish that her Canadian subjects, loyal to their sovereign and attached to British institutions, may, through the blessing of Divine Providence, become a happy, an united, and a prosperous people.' His personal letters were full of the closing scenes : ' I have prorogued my parliament . . . never was such unanimity. When the speaker read [the speech] to the commons, after the prorogation, they gave me three cheers, in which even the ultras united. In fact, as the matter now stands, the province is in a state of peace and harmony which three months ago I thought was utterly hopeless.' [1] There certainly had not been such a scene since Simcoe opened the first legislature.

Thomson's success had been phenomenal, but his strong-willed vitality would not allow him to rest. He saw the constitutional break-down of the past outlined against a background

[1] *Ibid.*, p. 164.

of everyday life. His dealings with the clergy reserves illustrate
his hold on the situation. He was not content with a theoretical
reform of the functioning of institutions. He realized that
institutions were not miraculous, and that they were only vital
when they worked for a people and expressed a social consciousness. He desired then to create as many favourable
conditions as possible for the union not only in the Canadas but
in British North America. Friction in the other provinces
would react on the Canadas, and he feared any neighbouring
constitutional struggle until they had been given a chance to
secure their footing. The history of the year immediately preceding the union may not be one of intense importance, but
it is a real illustration of the governor's purposeful grasp of the
intimate relationship between social life and institutional life,
of his conception of colonial government as a whole, and of his
personal administrative system.

In Lower Canada there was chaos. ' There is positively no
machinery of government,' he wrote; ' everything is to be done
by the governor and his secretary. There are no heads of
departments at all, or none whom one can depend on, or even
get at ; for most of them are still at Quebec, and it is difficult
to move them up [to Montreal] because there are no public
buildings. The wise system hitherto adopted has been to
stick two men into some office whenever a vacancy occurred—
one Frenchman and one Britisher ! Thus we have joint crown
surveyors, joint sheriffs, &c., each opposing the other in everything he attempts. Can you conceive a system better calculated
to countenance the distinction of race ? . . . The hand of the
government is utterly unknown and unfelt at present out of
Montreal and Quebec, and not the slightest means exist of
knowing what is passing in the rural districts.' [1] Before such
a state of affairs Thomson almost lost heart, as he knew that
many of the needed reforms would require parliamentary

[1] Scrope, *op. cit.*, pp. 168 ff.

legislation. He proceeded to gather up, as it were, as many loose ends as he could. The French-Canadians were a fact, and he approached their ostensible leader, Louis Hippolyte La Fontaine, and offered him the office of solicitor-general of Lower Canada, at the same time fully acquainting him with his political ideas and methods. There was diplomacy. La Fontaine was a violent opponent of the union, and Thomson hoped to detach him from the opposition and to secure his abilities for the future province. La Fontaine refused. This was Thomson's first rebuff; but in reality it was a triumph, for he had made a public confession of desiring to work with the French-Canadians. However, he was far from cheerful: 'As for the French, nothing but time will do anything for them. They hate British rule—British connexions—improvements of all kinds, whether in their laws or in their roads; so they will sulk, and will try, that is, their leaders, to do all the mischief they can.'[1] In the special council his power was practically supreme, and he prepared and carried through ordinances of much importance. He heard with dismay that Russell had not included municipal clauses in the Act of Union.[2] 'No man in his senses', he wrote, 'would think for a moment of the union without its being accompanied by some sort of local government, in which the people may control their own officers and the executive at the same time obtain some influence in the country districts. Without a breakwater of this kind between the central government and the people, government with an assembly is impossible in Lower Canada, and most difficult in Upper Canada.'[3] He organized a municipal system for the lower province which still remains the foundation of local government in modern Quebec. His motive was not single. He knew when he proposed a similar system for Upper Canada

[1] Ibid., *op. cit.*, p. 191.
[2] Thomson to Russell, September 16, 1840, Kennedy, *op. cit.*, pp. 551 ff., and Russell to Thomson, October 25, 1840, *ibid.*, pp. 554 ff.
[3] Thomson to a friend (1840 ?), *ibid.*, p. 555. Cf. Durham, *Report*, ii, p. 287.

that the fact that Lower Canada already possessed local government would be a strong force in his favour. Lastly, he passed an ordinance for the establishment of registry offices. Perhaps nothing had ·been so detrimental to development in Lower Canada as the extraordinary laxness of mortgage regulations and the want of facilities for finding out the incumbrances on a piece of land. Settlement had been retarded, the unsuspecting had been deluded and even the wary taken in. The legislature had tried in vain to improve matters, and Thomson was determined not to leave the subject any longer open. He drove through ' a registry bill—the " asses' bridge " of the province for the last twenty years—which [met] with nearly universal assent from both French and English '.[1] Broadly speaking, however, the French-Canadians remained suspicious and had little sympathy with Thomson's activities. They hung back from his advances under the threatening shadows of Durham's *Report*, and he laboured under no delusions. He summed up their state of mind to Russell: ' The French-Canadians have forgotten nothing and learnt nothing by the rebellion and the suspension of the constitution, and are more unfit for representative government than they were in 1791 . . . actuated by the old spirit of the assembly and without any principle except that of inveterate hostility to British rule and British connexion.'[2] The union would begin with a hostile French Canada.

In Upper Canada there was little that could be done in the way of actual measures, but Thomson secured the province by two methods. Firstly, he let it be known that he was preparing new plans relating to immigration, the simplification of the land system, the advance of public works, and the floating of a huge loan to be arranged by the imperial parliament. His knowledge of human nature told him that, quite apart from urgency in these

[1] Thomson to a friend, November 23, 1840, Scrope, *op. cit.*, p. 198.
[2] Same to Russell, February 26, 1841, *State Papers*, G. 391, pp. 168 ff.

matters, he was making an appeal which would touch a practical
spot in the hearts of Upper Canadians. Secondly, he toured
the province practically as a party leader. This tour is perhaps
the key to his system. It was the triumphant progress of
benevolent despotism, which depends for its stability on
popular support. He took every opportunity to receive
addresses, and in reply to explain the magnificent future which
lay before the country if sanity, good feeling, and unity were
allowed to prevail. His own words best sum up his success :
' *All* parties uniting in addresses at every place, full of confidence
in my government, and of a determination to forget their
former disputes. Escorts of two and three hundred farmers on
horseback at every place from township to township, with all
the etceteras of guns, music, and flags. What is of more
importance, my candidates everywhere taken for the ensuing
elections ; in short, such unanimity and confidence I never saw,
and it augurs well for the future. Even the Toronto people,
who have been spending the last six weeks in squabbling, were
led, I suppose by the feeling shown in the rest of the province,
into giving me a splendid reception and took in good part a
lecture I read them, telling them that they had better follow the
good example of peace and renewed harmony which had been
set them elsewhere, instead of making a piece of work about
what they did not understand. The fact is that the truth of my
original notion of the people and of this country is now confirmed. The *mass* only wanted the vigorous interference of
a well-intentioned government, strong enough to control both
the extreme parties, and to proclaim wholesome truths, and
act for the benefit of the country at large, in defiance of ultras
on either side.' [1]   It is impossible not to recall the political
activities of Francis Gore and Sir Francis Bond Head, when
they placed themselves at the head of actual local parties.
Thomson did not discard their methods, but he knew a better

---

[1] Thomson to a friend, September 18, 1840, Scrope, *op. cit.*, p. 190.

way. He created a party on whose platform the governor-general—representative of the crown and responsible to the imperial cabinet—and Charles Edward Poulett Thomson, Upper Canadian reformer, could meet. Meanwhile theories of government took care of themselves, and the constituencies accepted his candidates.

Echoes of a 'mighty storm in a very small ocean '[1] reached him from Nova Scotia. Lord John Russell's dispatch on the tenure of public offices produced different results in the Maritime Provinces. In New Brunswick Sir John Harvey announced his intention of following it implicitly, and there was thus eliminated any acute transition to responsible government. In Nova Scotia, however, Sir Colin Campbell made no effort to reform an executive council in which the assembly had practically no confidence. Joseph Howe forced the issue and carried a resolution in the assembly which declared that ' the executive council, as at present constituted, does not enjoy the confidence of the commons '. He convinced James Boyle Uniacke, the government leader in the assembly and the future first reform premier in Nova Scotia. The lieutenant-governor did not move in spite of Uniacke's desertion, and answered the resolutions in vague and non-committal terms. Howe carried further resolutions and asked Campbell to carry on the government according to the wishes of the people. No advance was possible, because Campbell would not or could not see the force of Russell's formula. He affected to believe that agreement with the address would bring about a fundamental constitutional change which Russell could not have intended. Howe fell back on an implication from Glenelg's theory of responsibility.[2] If the governor had a real responsibility ' to his majesty and to parliament ', and if they were ready ' to devote a patient and laborious attention ' to any representations which might be

[1] Thomson to Russell, July 27, 1840, Scrope, *op. cit.*, p. 180.
[2] Kennedy, *op. cit.*, p. 419.

addressed to them from the colonies, had the time not come for such complaints in Nova Scotia ? He carried an address to the queen which contained a famous petition : ' that your majesty will join with this house in obviating the necessity for such appeals—that you will repress these absurd attempts to govern provinces by the aid and for the exclusive benefit of minorities, this assembly confidently believes ; and in asking your majesty to remove Sir Colin Campbell and send to Nova Scotia a governor who will not only represent the crown, but carry out its policy with firmness and good faith, the representatives of Nova Scotia perform a faithful duty to their sovereign and to their constituents, but recommend the only remedy which they fear can now be applied to establish harmony between the executive and legislature of this province.' The boldness of the demand was astonishing, and a public agitation arose in which Howe fanned the agitation for popular government into a white heat.   The imperial government entrusted the settlement to Thomson, as Nova Scotia came within the scope of his commission, and left him full discretion to deal with the issues.   On his arrival at Halifax, he instinctively grasped the situation and within a fortnight his recommendations were on their way to England.   The executive council must be reformed to include ' only the leading official servants of the government and a few of the most influential members of either house—but especially those of the house of assembly '.   All members of the executive council who were not members of either house must be removed, and the law officers of the crown and other public servants should when necessary become members of the assembly as well as of the executive council.   The legislative council must be opened to representation from the popular party.   Thomson formed a high opinion of the province and praised its adherence to constitutionalism.   Campbell was removed to make room for Lord Falkland, who attempted to apply to Nova Scotia Thomson's system.[1]

[1] Scrope, *op. cit.*, pp. 175 ff.

Meanwhile the Act [1] for the reunion of the Canadas had passed the imperial parliament and Thomson had been raised to the peerage in recognition of his services. He must henceforth appear in the history as Baron Sydenham of Sydenham and Toronto. It is hardly necessary to analyse the Act in detail. The two provinces were to be formed, by proclamation, into one province of Canada within fifteen months after the passing of the Act. The general scheme of government was little changed. There was erected one legislative council, members of which held office for life on good behaviour, and one house of assembly, the members of which were to consist of an equal number from each old province and must possess property worth at least £500. Provision was made for altering ' the apportionment of the number of representatives '. The speaker of the council was to be nominated by the governor, and of the assembly to be elected by its members. The status of the church of England, of the Roman catholic church, of waste lands, and of religious toleration was clearly defined. Arrangements were made for a consolidated fund out of which the expenses of the judiciary, government, and pensions might be paid. The rest of the revenue was placed at the disposal of the united legislature, which assumed the debts of the two old provinces. Appropriation and taxation must originate with the governor, and were then open to discussion in the house of assembly. The laws in force in either division were to continue until repealed or amended. All written and printed documents relating to the council and assembly and all proceedings of either house were to be in English. Translation of documents and papers into French was allowed. Lord John Russell explained that this section only dealt with English as the language of ' original record '. There was nothing in the Act against French as the language of debate, and it was used as such from the time of the first united parliament.[2]

[1] Kennedy, *op. cit.*, pp. 536 ff. (3 & 4 Victoria, c. 35).
[2] The first speaker was a French-Canadian. Rules were adopted for

A proclamation brought the union into force on February 10, 1841, and in April the first elections were held, with the result that there were six groups varying in numbers from a ' family compact ' party of seven to a ' government ' party of twenty-four. The ' French party ' was computed at twenty and that of the ' Moderate Reformers ' at the same figure.[1] The nomenclature, however, is purely arbitrary and there was no severe group adhesion. ' A ministerial crisis ',[2] as Sydenham described it, occurred on the eve of the opening of the legislature.[3] Sydenham appointed a ' ministry ' which he intended as a coalition of the English parties, and included W. H. Draper, a conservative, as attorney-general for Canada West, and Robert Baldwin the reformer as solicitor-general for Canada West. The French were to be neglected. Baldwin was careful to explain that he had not come in by means of any coalition with the attorney-general or with any one else. He believed that in accepting public office at all he gave a public pledge that the government of the country would be carried on according to the principles of ' responsible government ' which he had ever held, and he accepted office with that idea under the governor-general. When chosen for ministerial office in United Canada, he informed Sydenham that he had only confidence in three of his colleagues. The results of the elections gave to the ultra-reformers of Canada West only five seats, and Baldwin saw a solid and well-organized French group returned. Before parliament met private negotiations were carried on between the two parties, and Baldwin was recognized as leader of a United Reform party, which represented the opinions of the majority

procedure in the assembly. No. 29 provided for the translation of papers, &c., and No. 38 provided for the reading of a motion in both French and English : *Standing Rules and Regulations of the Legislative Assembly of Canada* (Kingston, 1841).

[1] Scrope, *op. cit.*, p. 217.

[2] *Ibid.*, p. 233.

[3] The history of the Baldwin episode is told in the fullest detail in J. L. Morison, *British Supremacy and Canadian Self-government, 1839–54*, pp. 109 ff. (Glasgow, 1919).

of the electors and could control the house. Acting logically Baldwin desired to bring the executive council into harmony with the United Reformers, and he pointed out to Sydenham that four councillors could not be considered as sympathetic. It was tantamount to a request that the governor should remove them, and it was the challenge of a thorough and consistent believer in cabinet government to Sydenham's half-way house. Baldwin could not accept a principle which would allow the governor to neglect party affiliations, however indistinct, by choosing ministers at will from any or all the political groups. The United Reformers were in the majority, and the logic of British precedent to which Baldwin uniformly adhered demanded, firstly, that the council should reflect entirely their opinions, and secondly that French-Canadians should be admitted to it. There was nothing for Sydenham to do, if his whole administrative methods were to escape destruction, except to deny the logic of Baldwin's position. To cabinet government he was a convinced opponent, and Baldwin disappeared from office under a rebuke of unambiguous severity, while echoes of the crisis reached England in dispatches full of contemptuous wrath.

To describe adequately Sydenham's legislature would need a graphic pen. Behind everything was the irrepressible governor, as autocratic as any of his predecessors, but convinced that his means justified his ends. He has left a vivid picture of the opening days : ' I have got the large majority of the house ready to support me upon any question that can arise, and, what is better, thoroughly convinced that their constituents, so far as the whole of Upper Canada and the British part of Lower Canada are concerned, will never forgive them if they do not. Whoever follows me now may, with management, keep everything quiet and rule with comfort. . . . We have discussed all the great topics—the union, responsible government, the parliamentary conditions of the Union Act, confidence in the administration—every subject on which excitement might have been raised, and the agitators have entirely and signally failed. Except the rump of the old house of assembly of Lower Canada and two or three ultra-radicals who have gone over with my solicitor-general, whom I have got rid of, every member is cordially with me and my government.'[1]   He soon found that every move had to be carefully watched. All day and far into the night he worked not merely with papers and projects but with men and minds. No prime minister, no party whip could have been more active, more open to interviews, more adaptable to circumstances, more free in personal intercourse. Bored to death with ceremonial and bowing and the 'misery of always being on parade', he worked like a party-leader obsessed with a platform, and like a reformer obsessed with a mission. In the game which he played the members of the legislature were mere pawns on the board, mere pieces to hoodwink the theorists. He did not believe that the old hospital at Kingston where his parliament met was the home of Canadian healing. He looked out beyond its walls to the average citizen who wanted peace, content, and above all a slower process of change. His majority was the heart and soul of common-sense citizens. Doubtless he had no intention of being forced to dissolve, and he bent his energies to obtain parliamentary majorities with the zeal of an old lobbyist. He was not afraid to rely on the veto of the legislative council. But he knew his goal, the extent of his purpose, and the tremendous necessity of carrying on. He kept his legislature busy on measures which would make him more powerful than ever throughout the country. The foundations of common school education were laid. A board of works was established in the hope that private members might refrain from jobbing the public funds. The customs laws were revised in the direction of commercial enterprise and increased revenue. He outlined a scheme of public works on which the new loan guaranteed by the imperial cabinet might be most efficiently spent. He

[1] Scrope, *op. cit.*, p. 233.

succeeded in getting a measure of local government through against a combination of conservatives and radicals. The former opposed it because it brought a further measure of self-government into the province, the latter because the district wardens were appointed by the crown.[1] In legislation for banking he failed. The private banks were too strong, and he had to abandon his scheme for a national bank with a monopoly in the issuing of notes. It is worth while drawing attention to the practical nature of his bills. Sydenham was a business man using a legislature for business ends. He was putting goods that were in demand on the provincial market, and he was convinced that if the personnel of his establishment failed him, there were more than enough men in Canada who would break the strike.

With all his skill he could not ward off a discussion which he considered dangerous on those ' theoretical points of government '. Towards the end of the session Baldwin moved for copies of Lord John Russell's dispatches on responsible government, and these were laid on the table by Samuel Bealey Harrison. On September 3 Baldwin moved six resolutions which were seconded by a French-Canadian member: ' (1) That the most important as well as the most undoubted of the political rights of the people of this province is that of having a provincial parliament for the protection of their liberties, for the exercise of their constitutional influence over the executive departments of their government, and for legislation upon all matters which do not, on the grounds of absolute necessity, constitutionally belong to the jurisdiction of the imperial parliament as the paramount authority of the empire. (2) That the head of the provincial executive government of the province, being within the limits of his government the representative of the sovereign, is not constitutionally responsible to any other than the authorities of the empire. (3) That the representative of the

---

[1] Sydenham to his brother, August 28, 1841, Kennedy, *op. cit.*, p. 563.

sovereign for the proper conduct and efficient disposal of the public business is necessarily obliged to make use of the advice and assistance of subordinate officers in the administration of his government. (4) That in order to preserve that harmony between the different branches of the provincial parliament which is essential to the happy conduct of public affairs, the principal of such subordinate officers, advisers of the representative of the sovereign and constituting as such the provincial administration under him as the head of the provincial government, ought always to be men possessed of the public confidence, whose opinions and policy harmonizing with those of the representatives of the people would afford a guarantee that the well-understood wishes and interests of the people, which our gracious sovereign has declared shall be the rule of the provincial government,[1] will at all times be faithfully represented to the head of that government and through him to the sovereign and imperial parliament. (5) That as it is practically always optional with such advisers to continue in or to retire from office at pleasure, this house has the constitutional right of holding such advisers politically responsible for every act of the provincial government of a local character, sanctioned by such government while such advisers continue in office. (6) That for the like reason this house has the constitutional right of holding such advisers in like manner responsible for using, while they continue in office, their best exertions to procure from the imperial authorities the exercise of their right of dealing with such matters affecting the interests of the province as constitutionally belong to those authorities in the manner most consistent with the well-understood wishes and interests of the people of this province.' [2]

Baldwin's resolutions were founded on two ideas. Firstly, on the distinction made by Durham and Howe between executive authority over imperial and over colonial concerns—a distinc-

[1] See above, p. 188.   [2] Kennedy, *op. cit.*, p. 564.

tion which Russell had taught Sydenham was invalid: secondly, on cabinet responsibility in colonial affairs—a convention which Sydenham could not accept because of Russell's instructions. To allow the resolutions to pass would be granting permission to a colonial assembly to revoke imperial dispatches already on the table of the house, and would be conceding that the method of government which the governor had followed was not that implied in those dispatches. Sydenham therefore drew up or inspired four amendments, which were moved by Harrison : [1] '(1) That the most important as well as the most undoubted of the political rights of the people of this province is that of having a provincial parliament for the protection of their liberties, for the exercise of a constitutional influence over the executive departments of their government, and for legislation upon all matters of internal government. (2) That the head of the executive government of the province, being within the limits of his government the representative of the sovereign, is responsible to the imperial authority alone ; but that, nevertheless, the management of our local affairs can only be conducted by him, by and with the assistance, counsel, and information of subordinate officers in the province. (3) That in order to preserve between the different branches of the provincial parliament that harmony which is essential to the peace, welfare, and good government of the province, the chief advisers of the representative of the sovereign, constituting a provincial administration under him, ought to be men possessed of the confidence of the representatives of the people, thus affording a guarantee that the well-understood wishes and interests of the people, which our gracious sovereign has declared shall be the rule of the provincial government, will, on all occasions, be faithfully represented and advocated. (4) That the people of the province have, moreover, a right to expect from such provincial administration the exertion of their best endeavours

[1] Scrope, *op. cit.*, pp. 236, 259.

that the imperial authority within its constitutional limits shall
be exercised in the manner most consistent with their well-
understood wishes and interests.'[1] These amendments, which
were adopted, represent the furthest point to which Sydenham
felt that he could go. In less than three weeks his hands fell
from the helm of state. He died at Kingston September 19,
1841.

Sydenham's system of government is easy to state. He was
governor and prime minister in one. He could never be
responsible to a local cabinet as long as he was an imperial
officer, but he could so follow and guide local opinion that it
would not clash with his duties and would produce such general
satisfaction as would eliminate constitutional theories. His
great solvent was work in a practical direction. He kept
his legislature so busy on beneficial measures that they had
neither the time nor the energy to persist in worrying him with
abstract questions. He recognized a local responsibility which
none of his predecessors would concede. It was not cabinet
responsibility, but it was one of common sense. An intelligent
people do not want wilfully to wreck their state. Sydenham
deliberately catered to that fundamental human fact, and he did
it in such a way that the electors believed he was carrying out
their wishes. In the house of assembly he gradually gained the
support of moderate practical men. He may have doctored
the electoral divisions to gain support. He may have planned
further doctoring. The fact remains he succeeded, and he must
be judged by his success. He began when the Canadas were
without form and void, and he carried out a work of creation.
It is extremely probable that if he had conceded Baldwin's
demands in the summer of 1841, there would have been another
political *débâcle*. He refused French Canada. It was perhaps
providential that he did so. Had French-Canadians come in
in 1841, there would have been no lessons learned. La Fontaine

[1] Kennedy, *op. cit.*, pp. 564–5.

would have led a group of doctrinaire demagogues, who had not acquired any grip on constitutional reform. Canada East needed Sydenham's silent rebuke. In addition, the Canadas had no constitutional organization. Parliamentary procedure was more like that in a rustic debating society than in a responsible legislature. There was no system, no method, no administrative insight, no civil service. The union was all very well, but sixty-two sections of even an imperial act never yet saved a province. Sydenham's great work was the recognition that neither con-stitutional theory nor constitutional fact works automatically. The rigidity of the eighteenth-century constitution on the one hand and the elasticity of cabinet government on the other could not produce content in the Canadas. What the people of the Canadas needed was organized concrete direction rather than constitutional space. Sydenham gave them what they needed. For the theory—he was the queen's servant, the council must be his servants. Behind the theory, the elemental human fact that all government is based on consent. He succeeded in combining the autocratic and the popular. In fact he would have repudiated the former epithet. He was the father of his people, the shepherd of his flock, and circumstances made for his success.

It is impossible, however, to leave Sydenham's work without more searching criticism. He took terrific risks: what if he had failed? Perhaps the nearest answer to that question will be found in the Campbell-Howe episode. Sydenham approved the address for Campbell's recall, and he would have been prepared perhaps to leave the Canadas by a similar method. That, of course, might work where there was obvious unwilling-ness to carry out imperial orders. But had Sydenham failed to carry the assembly with him, had they said that in spite of goodwill, practical measures, business administration, they wanted to be masters in their own colonial house, there is no evidence that he had any answer to a situation which might easily have arisen. There is evidence, however, that he was overdoing his paternalism, and that the sheep were getting to know the paddock. It is extremely doubtful if he could have held his parliament together for another session. Indeed, the French were kind to him, and the volcano of racial hate was quiet enough and certainly quieter than it might have been. He did a necessary work, by nature transitory. That is rather a pathetic summary, but it is in truth praise. Sydenham came with a definite mission—to establish organization, political methods, and administrative machinery; to point out that government can gain popular approval without losing self-respect, and that respect for authority is the foundation of citizenship. Sydenham fulfilled his mission. It was a typically Anglo-Saxon mission. No high flights, no great dramatic moments, no pomp and circumstance of glory, no magnificent fame. He stepped off the stage, his work done, his method in reality dying with him.

On the other hand, when his successor, Sir Charles Bagot, looked-back after a few months' interval on Sydenham's régime, he probed to the very depths and found failure. Bagot's estimate is all the more important in forming a judicial opinion because it is that of a man whose correspondence discloses honesty, wisdom, and balance, and because it was made at a moment when it was possible to fix some of the conditions which are so elusive, and whose loss renders historical criticism weak and insecure. Writing to Lord Stanley a confidential dispatch, Bagot said : ' I have given a general sketch of Lord Sydenham's policy—were I further to lift the thin veil of success which covers it, much of deformity would be found underneath. Towards the French-Canadians his conduct was very unwise. He made enemies of them unnecessarily at a time when he should have propitiated them and diminished their objections to the union. He treated those who approached him with slight and rudeness, and thus he converted a proud and courageous people, which even their detractors acknowledge them to be, into personal and irreconcilable enemies. He despised their talents and denied their official capacity for office. In this respect he was mainly right ; but there was the lesser reason for fearing their power when held in check and for endeavouring further to weaken it by measures which will not stand the test of justice. Such, for instance, was the cutting off the suburbs from the electoral districts of Quebec and Montreal. His alleged reason was to give a commercial representation to these two towns ; [1] his real reason, well known to his council, was to secure the exclusion of the French from the representation and the acquisition of four supporters to his government. The first point he gained, but not the latter, as out of the four members, three opposed him. Another measure, open to the same objection, was the choice of the *chefs-lieux* for the district courts. These he selected in the French counties without any regard to the wants and conveniences of the French population, but rather in opposition to them. In one case he chose a small and decayed village, in a most inaccessible part of the country, but in the neighbourhood of a population of 2,000 English, instead of the former chief town, five or six times the size of the other, in the most convenient position, and in the centre of a population of 20,000 French-Canadians. Can it be wondered then that this party opposed the union and all Lord Sydenham's measures with their utmost force—that they rejected his overtures and endeavoured to overthrow his government ? The mode in which several of the elections were carried in both provinces, but especially in Lower Canada, weakened his position with the honest and uncompromising reformers in the upper province and gave even Sir Allan MacNab a pretext for opposing him. With regard to the position of the government during the past session, nothing could be more precarious or difficult. It was only by dint of the greatest energy, and, I must add, the unscrupulous personal interference

[1] Sydenham's reasons were fully laid down in a dispatch to Russell, February 26, 1841, *State Papers*, G. 391, pp. 168 ff.

of Lord Sydenham, combined with practices that I would not use and your lordship would not recommend, in addition to the promise of the loan and the bribe of the public works, that Lord Sydenham managed to get through the session. Afterwards came the day of reckoning. The means and appliances being exhausted, the power that wielded them being broken (alas! how rudely), up sprung a crowd of malcontents. Those who were before opposed to the government took courage; those who were overawed by Lord Sydenham's boldness or firmness shook off their unwilling fealty; all who had, or fancied they had, to complain of disappointed hopes or broken pledges joined in the defection. . . . Lord Sydenham was in fact the sole government—he decided everything and did it himself—sometimes consulting his council, but generally following his own opinion, and seldom bringing them together and consulting them collectively. To effect this required all the energy, activity, and habits of business which he individually possessed, together with his extraordinary boldness and unscrupulosity in dealing with individuals.' [1]

Sydenham's accomplishment must inevitably be judged in the light of the situation which Sir Charles Bagot found when he undertook office and in his estimate of those of Sydenham's actions which created that situation.

[AUTHORITIES.—The documents are in Egerton and Grant, *Canadian Constitutional Development* (Toronto, 1907); Kennedy, *Documents of the Canadian Constitution, 1759–1915* (Oxford, 1918); G. P. Scrope, *Memoir of the Life of the Right Hon. Charles, Lord Sydenham* (London, 1844); *Correspondence relative to the Affairs of Canada, 1840–1*; *Correspondence relative to the Reunion of Upper and Lower Canada, 1840*; *Journals of the Special Council of Lower Canada*; *Journals of the House of Assembly, Upper Canada*; *Journals of the House of Assembly, Canada*; *State Papers*, Series G, vols. cviii–cx (Canadian Archives). Adam Shortt, *Lord Sydenham* (Toronto, 1908), is the standard life, written with a thorough knowledge of the material. The most brilliant study of Sydenham's government is in J. L. Morison, *British Supremacy and Canadian Self-government, 1839–54*, pp. 70 ff. (Glasgow, 1919) (cf. the same author in *Queen's Quarterly*, July–September 1910).]

[1] Bagot to Stanley, September 26, 1842, *Bagot Correspondence*, M. 163, p. 211 (Canadian Archives).

P

CHAPTER XIV

THE TESTING OF SYDENHAM'S SYSTEM

SIR CHARLES BAGOT and his successor Sir Charles (afterwards Lord) Metcalfe are usually studied in contrasts. There is much to encourage this point of view. Bagot was an old-world, cultured tory, a Georgian figure. When he came to take part in affairs, he drifted almost naturally into diplomacy, and he might have drifted into practical obscurity had not he been sent to Canada, where in one crowded year he achieved a permanent place in the history of the empire. He was the intimate friend of Thomas Grenville, who sent him congratulations on his appointment and the ' cordial regrets of an old man losing one of his most intimate friends ' ;[1] of Lord Clarendon, who promised him fame in Canada and interested Lord John Russell on his behalf ;[2] of Sir George Murray, who knew the Canadas and recommended to him ' the French-Canadians as the most anti-Yankee and also the most monarchical portion of the province ' ;[3] and of the Marquis Wellesley, who foretold his advantageous colonial policy.[4] His dispatches form perhaps the most human set of documents in Canadian history. They are full of playfulness and wit, they are enlivened with *jeux d'esprit*, and they display the charm of a letter-writer who belonged to a period and to a social circle when even diplomatic correspondence was a literary art. The perfect man of the world moves through them, allowing the glimmer of a charming personality to peep out here and there. They display a growing

[1] Grenville to Bagot, August 9, 1841, *Bagot Correspondence*, M. 158, p. 33 (Canadian Archives).
[2] Clarendon to Bagot, September 15, October 9, 1841, *ibid.*, pp. 41, 170.
[3] Murray to Bagot, October 7, 1841, *ibid.*, p. 144.
[4] Wellesley to Bagot, October 9, 1841, *ibid.*, p. 174.

confidence, a gradually developing grasp of a situation, an increasing logical conviction, and a continuous sincerity of purpose which lend them almost the vitality and romantic interest of a novel, with a group of character studies worked up to a central and dramatic situation which gradually recedes before Bagot's lonely vigil with death. Were he to be estimated from these dispatches alone, he would appear as the self-restrained, even-tempered associate of Canning, with plenty of adaptability and possessing a reserve of determined courage, which he held in check until he had explored with tact every loophole of an easier way, and affairs demanded boldness rather than the risk of a compromise. With all his delicate touch, with all his cultured ease, Bagot was no weak figurehead. He had once been candid to a czar of Russia, and he had once taught the prince of Orange and the court of the Netherlands lessons in the manners of diplomacy.

Sir Charles Metcalfe was an Anglo-Indian who had spent his life in the east and had administered the government of Jamaica. He described himself as against the corn laws and religious intolerance, and in favour of vote by ballot, extension of the suffrage, improvement of the poor law, and equality of civil rights, but ' totally disqualified to be a demagogue '.[1] He was trained from his youth up in the devious ways of devious governments and he had had experience with a popular assembly. He had unbounded love for the empire, for British institutions, and for law. He was a man of the highest virtue and the greatest public spirit. He was one of the most successful governors of his day, who had devoted himself to the service of the crown in creating and working out administrative systems. He lacked, however, Bagot's elasticity of mind, and that calm confidence in necessary change which comes from

---

[1] Metcalfe to R. D. Mangles, January 13, 1843, J. W. Kaye, *Life and Correspondence of Charles, Lord Metcalfe*, vol. ii, pp. 454 ff. (2 vols., London, 1854).

varied contact with keen and studious minds. His dispatches
stand in violent contrast with those of his predecessor. They
are ponderous and stately, severely honest and wilfully wooden.
For Metcalfe could not dream, if he would, of letting fancy or
wit slip into an affair of state, or of allowing a human glow to
touch the stern dignity of the queen's representative. There
is no glad love for duty, no graceful yielding. They toe a line.
They follow a course. They stand four-square. Metcalfe did
not know the meaning of taking risks. The queen and empire
made demands. They were his superiors, and it was not for
him to temper the wind of commands to any shorn Canadian
lamb. If he were as liberal as he professed to be, his liberalism
was nullified by a rigidity of mind which had been cultivated
and perfected in the unchanging east. He was a public servant
who carried out the letter of his orders in unquestioning obedience. The régime of Bagot and of Metcalfe in Canada naturally
reflected these different personalities.

On the other hand, it is possible to drive the contrast too
far, for both contributed by different ways to the solution of
a political problem. Both were sent to govern Canada in the
terms of Lord John Russell's dispatches. Their faces were
directed to the future. They were to maintain the union, to
hold themselves free from any party connexions, and to govern
the country according to the well-understood wishes and
interests of the people. Bagot began his administration in all
seriousness and practically in detachment—his suspicions of
Baldwin and the colonial office's warning against the French
he held in reserve. The union he would maintain, party he
would abjure; the third command presented difficulties. He saw
only one conclusion, government by an executive which was
trusted by the majority in the assembly. Metcalfe too would
maintain the union and abjure party; the third command was
not difficult, for the colonial office would inform him at any
time who ' the people ' were. He soon learned that they were

not the majority, and he acted accordingly. In refusing, however, to accept the majority, and in following the colonial office's definition, he finally endangered the union which he had sworn to maintain, and became a party-leader, which he had declared was anathema to him.

Bagot and Metcalfe can, from this point of view, be studied together. Both started from the Russell-Sydenham pact of 1839. Bagot saw that in order to interpret his government in terms of the union and of the governor's disinterested impartiality, he must accept the logic of the Harrison-Sydenham resolutions of 1841 and follow it in order to save the new constitution and the administrator's new rôle. He could not find the wishes of the people either in space or in a vague general will. He could not seek them in the 'family compact' rump or in the colonial office. He could not turn back the clock. He could not divert the stream of development. He found the answer to the 'responsible government cry' in the affirmative of responsible government itself. Metcalfe started from the same points and found a similar answer by negative means. Trained in India, he was a man under authority. If the British government said that the clock must go back, that the stream must flow another way, Metcalfe bowed the head. To the colonial office all things were possible and even expedient, and he was prepared at all costs not merely to obey orders, but to obey any method of carrying them out. Bagot saw things in terms of an honest mind working with elastic adaptability and the power of balancing choices which the spirit of his instructions would bear. Metcalfe's mind was equally honest, but working in terms of an experience where the succession of time did not count, and where the diverting of streams was a regular occurrence. If the colonial office said, 'This is the way, walk in it', he did so. They had used 'union' and 'party' and 'people'; it was their duty to define and he would follow. In the issue, he proved Bagot's conclusions. By accepting the colonial office's definition of ' people ' he nearly wrecked the union, and by heading the ' people ' he became in spite of himself a party-leader. His experience met that of Bagot in the practical matter-of-fact mind with which Lord Elgin finally solved the question.

Bagot's instructions were issued by Lord Stanley on October 8, 1841.[1] Stanley was nothing if not brilliant, but his brilliancy was often of such a nature as to obscure any other light on a subject. He was a moderate conservative, who could not believe that there were real parties in Canada—nothing but parish politics and disloyal factions. If any one was to have power he preferred that it should be the old reactionary group headed by Sir Allan Napier MacNab. He did not want political power to pass into the hands of any one section in the province, and he impressed this wish on Bagot. But as difficulties gathered and he found that comprehension did not work, he pointed out to the governor a line of action : ' A stream you will have to pull against, do not doubt it ; but having done your best to neutralize opposition by the nature of your measures, if the stream be still against you, bend your back to your oar like a man, and, above all, take none into your crew who will not bend their backs too, and who, instead of pulling with you, will either be cutting (*sic*) crabs or backing water when they are most wanted for " hard all ". . . . MacNab is to dine with me on Thursday. . . . I think he is well disposed and reasonable. . . . but, although I am far from wishing to re-establish the old " family compact " of Upper Canada, if you come into difficulties that is the class of men to fall back upon, rather than the ultra-liberal party ; at least, unless I am much mistaken they are both the soundest and carry with them the greatest individual and moral influence '.[2]

Stanley, however, was forced to recognize Sydenham's

---

[1] *Bagot Correspondence*, G. iii, p. 46.
[2] Stanley to Bagot, May 17, 1842, *ibid.*, M. 165, p. 60.

work—indeed he recognized it to such an extent as to use at times his words and ideas—and his instructions were drawn up in the light of ' a great experiment actually in progress '. The momentous nature of his work was pointed out to Bagot, and he was promised by express command of the queen every assistance from the imperial cabinet, and ' the most favourable construction ' on any course which his judgement directed him to pursue. The general policy was outlined in the following terms : ' You cannot too early and too distinctly give it to be understood that you enter the province with the determination to know no distinction of national origin or religious creed ; to consult in your legislative capacity, and so far as may be consistent with your duty to your sovereign and your respon- sibility to her constitutional advisers, the wishes of the mass of the community ; and, in your executive capacity, to adminis- ter the laws firmly, moderately, and impartially. You will invite to aid you in your labours for the welfare of the province all classes of the inhabitants ; you will consider it your bounden duty to be accessible to the representations and prepared to listen to the complaints or the statements of the views of all ; and the only passports to your favour will be loyalty to the queen, attachment to British connexion, and an efficient and faithful discharge of public duty.'   This policy was avowedly that of Lord Sydenham. So strongly was Stanley impressed with the necessity of following it out that he borrowed words used by Sydenham at Halifax in 1840 :[1] ' It must be your policy to withdraw the legislature and the population generally from the discussion of abstract and theoretical questions, by which the government of Canada in former times has been too often and too seriously embarrassed, to the calm and dispassionate consideration of practical measures.' Bagot was to attempt to carry the assembly with him by continuing the benevolent paternalism of his predecessor, and ' responsible

[1] Scrope, *op. cit.*, p. 179.

government ' was to be shelved as a dangerous theory by an appeal to material interests.

Bagot was not long in the province before he found out that, excellent as his instructions were in spirit, there were serious difficulties before him.   Sydenham had as it were trained a team which were going out to test themselves, and it was of the utmost importance if they could be taught to play to the whistle.   The trainer had done his work, but he had not tested his men.   Bagot realized, after a few weeks in consultation with his executive council, that Sydenham could never have hoped to control the assembly in a new session.   Draper and Harrison informed him that they did not expect that the government would win on a vote of confidence.   The Sydenham experiment was on the verge of failure.   The moderate men were powerless against an ' unnatural alliance ' between the ' family compact ' and the French.   The exclusion of the French-Canadians at once impressed Bagot as a political volcano. ' The narrowness of the foundations ' on which the government was based constituted a grave error in tactics, and had resulted in the most unlikely political combinations to defeat or to obstruct the administration.[1]   In actual life it had produced chaos.   Acting under the direction of John Neilson, ' the bitterest opponent of the union ', the local government of the lower province was at a standstill.   The French-Canadians refused to put in motion the municipal machinery and assumed an attitude of ' passive resistance ', intending to hurt the central authority through a break-down in local affairs.[2]   Bagot anticipated that a discussion of the civil list would take place in the assembly; and he had little hope of carrying out the imperial instructions.[3]   He found that Sydenham had entered into a personal quarrel with the French-Canadians as a race,

[1] Bagot to Stanley, February 23, 1842, *Bagot Correspondence*, M. 162, p. 153.
[2] Same to same, March 10, 1842, *ibid.*, M. 162, p. 176.
[3] Same to same, March 16, 26, 1842, *ibid.*, M. 162, p. 23 a ; M. 160, p. 107.

and that, in spite of hopes to the contrary, he inherited it.[1] They stood aloof in sulky antipathy.

Bagot tried hard to arrive at any course of action which was free from misinterpretation. 'I have discovered', he wrote, 'that the pomps and circumstances attendant upon the great station of top-sawyer in these woods scarcely compensates for the constant effort to keep oneself upright and steady on the log.'[2] He decided against an immediate summoning of the legislature. His executive warned him that he had not 'sufficient materials to occupy their time and attention through the sessions', and that thus the assembly would be left 'to create business for themselves by the discussion of abstract and inconvenient questions, such as non-confidence in ministers', which they might 'possibly carry at this particular moment'. He considered that the legislative council needed widening, and that the judicial system of Lower Canada must be placed on a more secure footing.[3] After long correspondence with the colonial office, in which Stanley canvassed the names suggested from every angle of loyalty and safeness, Bagot succeeded in appointing several French-Canadians to the higher judicial places. In his efforts to make his councils more comprehensive, he included Francis Hincks, a reformer and a financier of first-class ability. He failed to secure a strong member of the 'family compact' in J. S. Cartwright. Cartwright saw the necessity even of giving weight to the French-Canadians, but he refused to sit on any executive which included such a pronounced liberal as Hincks.[4] Bagot, however, continued to hope that he could treat his advent as a new starting-place, 'a new chapter in the history', by 'doing away with all the old party divisions'. In spite of Stanley's warning that his blendings of

---

[1] Bagot to Stanley, June 12, 1842, *ibid.*, M. 160, p. 255.
[2] Same to same, March 27, 1842, *ibid.*, M. 165, p. 36 a.
[3] Same to same, January 24 (?), 1842, *ibid.*, M. 160, p. 16.
[4] Cartwright to Bagot, May 16, 1842, *ibid.*, M. 158, p. 310 ; cf. N. F. Davin, *The Irishman in Canada*, pp. 478 ff. (Toronto, 1877).

' white ' toryism and ' black ' radicalism might not produce
' a good grey ', he considered that the effort might be justified,
even if it succeeded merely in taking away grounds of complaint.[1] It was soon evident that these methods had failed to
win over the French-Canadians or to break the solidity of their
opposition. Every French-Canadian who accepted an appointment of any nature became immediately ' le vendu ', and
' le vendu ' he remained. He immediately lost his influence
over his compatriots. An individual was gained, not a race.[2]
The problem had passed beyond Sydenham's formula, and
Bagot began to seek the intimate advice of Draper, a moderate
conservative, and Harrison, a moderate reformer. With the
advice which he received from them the plot thickened to its
dramatic *dénouement*, and the dispatches from July to September 1842 became pregnant with momentous movements.

A dispassionate view of the situation disclosed to Bagot the
fact that the government would go down to almost certain
defeat without the French-Canadian vote, which undoubtedly
possessed the political power. The executive was opposed to
the representatives of the people and could command no
confidence. The Sydenham-Harrison resolutions left no course
open to them but to resign. The governor-general could then
adopt one of two courses. He could dissolve the assembly and
appeal to the people, with the certainty of having the vote of
no confidence carried by the electorate. He could send for
Baldwin and La Fontaine. Harrison advised the latter course
immediately. It was the only wise solution.[3] Draper was
equally certain that the government must be reconstructed
and that ' public business could only be carried on through the
French party '. A single appointment would avail nothing,
the trial must be made of appealing to the leaders : ' One thing

[1] Bagot to Stanley, June 12, 1842, *Bagot Correspondence*, M. 160, p. 225.
[2] Same to same, July 10, 1842, *ibid.*, M. 160, p. 325.
[3] Harrison to Bagot, July 11, 1842, *ibid.*, M. 158, p. 412.

I do not doubt at all, and that is that with the present house of assembly you cannot get on without the French, while it is necessary for me at the same time to declare frankly that I cannot sit at the council board with Mr. Baldwin. My resignation will be immediate on my becoming aware of his appointment.'[1] Bagot hesitated. For nearly a fortnight he worked at the situation. He knew defeat for the government was practically inevitable. He had ' no fear of admitting the French as a party into a share of the government ' as far as regards any hostility to the union. He believed their admission ' to a share in the government, to which, after all, they were, theoretically at least, justly entitled ', would result in lifting their theories and discontents out of discussion. Baldwin was the crux. Bagot was prepared to take ' any hazards rather than see him again introduced into the council '. He had betrayed Sydenham and his inclusion would dissolve the ministry as then constituted. To make the plunge would call forth united opposition in England, would give the lie to Durham's advice on the French-Canadian problem, and would provide an immediate censure of Sydenham's régime. No illusions, however, remained : ' the moment has come when this question must be determined one way or the other, and this government be carried on either in professed exclusion and defiance of the Canadians of French origin, or by their admission to such a share in it as they may be contented to receive, and the mother country may deem it safe and reasonable to give them. . . . It is impossible to disguise from oneself that the French members of the assembly possess the power of the country, and whoever directs that power by the most efficient means of controlling it is in a situation to govern the province most effectually.' Bagot had not, he confessed, the political

---

[1] Draper to Bagot, July 16, 1842, *ibid.*, M. 158, p. 442 ; Draper to Egerton Ryerson, September 16, 1842, *Hodgins Papers*, [A], I. D. 11. 2 (Ontario Archives).

courage to decide, and he asked for a ' simple " yea " or " nay "'
from the imperial cabinet.[1]   A small majority might possibly
be secured, and he proposed to follow Sydenham's methods and
open the session with a speech suggesting popular measures,
perhaps an amnesty.[2]

In England, Stanley was under no wise guidance in Canadian
affairs.   MacNab was telling him ' that the loyal party in
Canada . . . felt that an unprincipled departure from the
conservative policy had placed the country in the most imminent
peril '.   They had been ' insulted, degraded, many of them
ruined ' from the encouragement given by the administration to
men ' whose whole career had been unmitigated hostility to
the crown, government, and institutions '.   The associates of
rebels ' sat at the governor's table ', and ' the " compact party ",
which took arms to suppress the rebellion ', had been disappointed in their loyal hopes.[3]   The news from Canada did
not thus fall on very well-prepared ground, and Bagot's
dispatches drove the colonial office into frenzied panic.   Stanley
sent them at once to Sir Robert Peel, and informed him that if
Bagot could not command a majority ' the union was a failure
and the Canadas were gone '.   He hoped the governor would
multiply ' vendus ' and disintegrate the French party, rather
than dream of attempting to govern with traitors.[4]   Peel
pleaded lack of intimate knowledge, but on general principles
he advised to accept defeat and not to dissolve the legislature.
Bagot could nurse the good sense and justice of the province,
if the French party in case of extremes were called to power
but wished to dictate terms.   He appealed to the skill of
George III and of Louis-Philippe in managing legislatures, and
pointed out how ' firmness, moderation, and dignified long-
suffering ' would help the perplexed and sorely tried governor

[1] Bagot to Stanley, July 28, 1842, *Bagot Correspondence*, M. 161, p. 22.
[2] Same to same, August 25, 1842, *ibid.*, M. 163, p. 36.
[3] MacNab to Stanley, August 2, 1842, *ibid.*, M. 165, p. 125.
[4] Stanley to Peel, August 27, 1842, *ibid.*, M. 165, p. 143.

in 'combating a majority in a popular assembly '.[1]   Peel's lack of knowledge was self-evident.   Stanley went over the lists of the assembly with Murdoch, whom Bagot had inherited from Sydenham as civil secretary, and he thought he could just see a majority.   Eight or ten seemed to be 'waiters on Providence or rather on patronage '.   The deduction ought to be self-evident.   To call in the French could only be a last, final resort, and ought not to be done ' until it is manifest to this country, and manifest to the conservatives and supporters of British influence in Canada generally, that you cannot carry on the government without the French party, and that you can carry it on through and by them.   Do not mistake me. When I say the French party, I mean that party conducted by its present leaders and headed by men more or less implicated in the late rebellion.   You may ultimately be *forced* to take these men ; but do not take them till the world shall see that you are so forced, and my hope and belief is that the necessity will never arise.'   Multiply ' vendus '.   It may not conciliate the party, it may ruin the men, but ' the example will be found catching '.   The amnesty would be ' a difficult card to play '.[2]

Stanley's dispatch was not received till September 21. Meanwhile Bagot summoned the legislature on the 8th, and delivered a practical speech in which he alluded to the better relations with the United States under the recently concluded Ashburton treaty and to the possibility of a reform of the Canadian tariffs.[3]   He had decided to meet the legislature with his composite council.   The challenge to his courage was not long in coming.   On the first day John Neilson, ' that lover of all mischief for its own sake ',[4] moved for copies of any imperial dispatches relating to ' an indemnity and general pardon '.

---

[1] Peel to Stanley, August 28, 1842, *ibid.*, M. 165, p. 146 ; cf. C. S. Parker, *Sir Robert Peel from his private Papers*, vol. i, pp. 379 ff. (London, 1899).

[2] Stanley to Bagot, September 1, 1842, *Bagot Correspondence*, M. 165, p. 151.

[3] Bagot to Stanley, September 10, 1842, *ibid.*, M. 163, p. 52.

[4] Same to same, March 26, 1842, *ibid.*, M. 160, p. 105.

Early in the afternoon of the 13th, Bagot wrote to Stanley
hoping that he could shelve the question by an expression of
goodwill.[1]   Before nightfall, the circumstances necessary for
justification before the world had arisen, a working majority
could not be secured.   The day closed in dramatic episodes.
Bagot communicated with La Fontaine and made him large
offers, which he hesitated to accept.   The governor hesitated
to advance.   In the tense crisis, the executive council sent
a unanimous communication stating that unless negotiations
with the French-Canadians were successful the government
could not be carried on, and that in accordance with the Sydenham-Harrison resolutions they must resign.[2]   Bagot at once sat
down and wrote, with the advice of his executive, to La Fontaine offering him four seats in the cabinet and the clerkship
of the council.   La Fontaine was asked to become attorney-
general for Lower Canada with a seat in the executive council.
His suggestions were invited in filling the office of solicitor-
general for the same province.   A French-Canadian was to
become commissioner for crown lands with a seat in the council,
and the post of confidential clerk was to be offered to a French-
Canadian.   Baldwin's name inevitably entered into the communications, and Bagot expressed his willingness to avail
himself of his services.   The surrender meant Draper's resignation and the necessity of getting rid of Charles Richard Ogden,
the attorney-general, and John Davidson, the crown-lands'
commissioner.   Bagot felt compelled to lay down a condition
that the two last should be provided with pensions.[3]   Meanwhile the 'high conservative party', headed by the 'intriguing,
slippery, unprincipled man', MacNab, 'had made overtures
to the French-Canadians and the extreme opponents of the
government and were prepared to combine with them in order

[1] Bagot to Stanley, September 13, 1842, *Bagot Correspondence*, M. 161, p. 88.
[2] Same to same, September 13, 1842 (at night), *ibid.*, M. 161, p. 97.
[3] Bagot to La Fontaine, September 13, 1842, *ibid.*, M. 161, p. 109.

to overthrow the executive council, heedless of the incon-
sistency of such a course '.   La Fontaine still held out, and
a vote of ' direct expression of want of confidence was moved '.
Bagot decided on a bold move.   He authorized Draper to read
to the house his written proposals to La Fontaine : ' The effect
was instantaneous.   The negotiation was renewed the next
morning, the point at issue was compromised, and the arrangement completed.' [1]   The pensions were to be left an open
question, and in addition to previous offers Baldwin was to
come in as one of the law officers for Upper Canada, sacrificing
the present holder of the office.   Accordingly, Ogden, Davidson,
and Sherwood were firmly but courteously removed.   Bagot's
letters to them practically amounted to peremptory commands,
and the thin veneer of praise and regret could not hide the hard
bargain which had been driven.[2]

A motion confirming the new executive in the confidence of
the assembly was carried with only five dissentients.   Bagot
summed up the result in one of his most brilliant and analytical
dispatches : ' I have united the voice of seven-eighths of the
house of assembly in present support of the government. . . .
I have met the wishes of a large majority of the population of
Upper Canada and of the British inhabitants of Lower Canada.
I have removed the main ground of discontent and distrust
among the French-Canadian population.   I have satisfied them
that the union is capable of being administered for their
happiness and advantage and have consequently disarmed
their opposition to it.   I have excited among them the strongest
feeling of gratitude to the provincial government, and if my
policy be approved by H.M.'s government, I shall have removed
their chief cause of hostility to British institutions, and have
added another security for their devotion to the British crown

[1] Bagot to La Fontaine, September 16, 1842, *ibid.*, M. 158, p. 595 ; La
Fontaine to Bagot, September 16, 1842, *ibid.*, M. 158, p. 593.

[2] Bagot to Sherwood, September 16, 17, 1842 ; same to Ogden, September
19, 1842, *ibid.*, M. 161, pp. 103 116, 125.

. . . The present crisis has offered the occasion; I have seized it.'
In calm and dignified reserve he was prepared to receive
blame at home from the partisans of ' the exclusive system ',
perhaps from the cabinet. To the latter he trusted himself.
He realized the gravity of his action. The welfare of the
province was the issue, and he could only ask for ' prompt
sanction and firm support', which were essential to the successful
working of his policy.[1] If approval were possible, he asked
for it in full measure, as it would ' cast the veil of oblivion
over past disaffection, and remove the brand of rebels from
those to whom the Act of Union has given all the powers of
representative government '.[2] ' I found the union was not
completed. Sydenham had effected the *fiançailles*—the marriage, as he very well knew, must be the work of his successor.
Every circumstance appeared to me to combine in suggesting
that the moment was favourable for performing that ceremony.
Accident forced upon me the necessity of immediate decision,
and upon my own responsibility I have decided. If I have
judged wrong . . . let me urge upon you the expediency of
immediately disavowing it by my public recall. . . . I can say
no more. I must, and I am prepared to, stand or fall by the
statement of all that has occurred . . . if to fall, to fall without
remonstrance or complaint, and with unfeigned deference to
those who in such matters must have more knowledge than
I can be supposed to have.'[3] The government was reconstructed on September 26th, with La Fontaine as attorney-
general and Thomas Cushing Aylwin as solicitor-general for
Canada East, and Baldwin as attorney-general and John
E. Small as solicitor-general for Canada West. Within a few
days it was in working order and La Fontaine was writing in
French to the governor pointing out that John J. Girouard

---

[1] Bagot to Stanley, September 26, 1842, *Bagot Correspondence*, M. 163, p. 57.
[2] Same to same, September 26, 1842 (confidential dispatch), *ibid.*,
M. 163, p. 211.
[3] Same to same, September 26, 1842 (private letter), *ibid.*, M. 161, p. 131.

could not accept office as crown-lands' commissioner, and suggesting to him the name of his personal and political friend, Auguste Norbert Morin. Bagot replied in French accepting the suggestion.[1]

In Canada a storm broke over Bagot's head. He had ' handed the British over to the vindictive disposition of the French mob '. He was ' a governor without any opinion of his own, ready to veer about at every breath of opposition '. ' A radical ministry cannot last long. Loyal men must begin to combine and act : they need not despair : they have God on their side and a fair cause, over which no treachery can finally triumph. . . . It is impossible to approach these subjects without feelings which defy expression.'[2] The papers which had not such an insight into the workings of the divine mind were less dignified. ' According to the " family compact " journals ', wrote Bagot, ' I am a " radical ", a " puppet ", an " old woman ", an " apostate ", and a renegade descendant of old Colonel Bagot who fell at Naseby fighting for his king.'[3] From Lower Canada came the vital insight : ' The great principle of responsibility is formally and solemnly recognized by the representative of the crown, and sealed with the approbation of the assembly. From this period dates a revolution effected without blood or slaughter ; but none the less glorious.' It was the beginning of a genuine preservation of the ' connexion between this country and the mother country . . . not a union of parchment, but a union of hearts and of free born men '.[4]

In England, Stanley continued to hope for the best and promised the imperial support in case of defeat.[5] When the

[1] La Fontaine to Bagot, September 27 ; Bagot to La Fontaine, October 1, 1842, *ibid.*, M. 158, pp. 618, 633.
[2] *Church Extra*, September 17, 1842, *Robinson MSS.* [A], E. 24, 23 (22) (Ontario Archives).
[3] Bagot to Stanley, October 28, 1842, *Bagot Correspondence*, M. 161, p. 164.
[4] Baldwin's defence of his position in the House of Assembly, *Kingston Chronicle and Gazette*, September 17, 1842.
[5] Stanley to Bagot, October 8, 1842, *Bagot Correspondence*, M. 165, p. 177.

blow fell he was startled and surprised. He had hoped that
the French would never be recognized as a party, and he
deplored the circumstances so opposed to the wishes of the
cabinet.[1] The advice of the executive in Canada to bring in
La Fontaine was ' injudicious, and in giving it they went
beyond the proper limits of their functions '. They could
resign, but to suggest their successors was unconstitutional.
Bagot's procedure was open to grave objections, and to enter
into correspondence on terms was impolitic. But Stanley had
to face facts. He saw a government working smoothly with
the governor and house of assembly and he was forced to write :
' Her majesty's government are prepared to acquiesce in the
line of policy which you have taken and to advise the queen to
sanction and confirm it. It will be my duty, acting on her
majesty's behalf, to give to your administration a cordial
support and to the measures which it may bring forward the
most favourable consideration. . . . I have to express the hope
that its formation may have the effect of extinguishing party
and national animosities, and of directing the minds of all men
in Canada, of whatever origin, to the advancement of the
prosperity of their native or adopted country. I cannot but
entertain the sanguine hope and belief that, as her majesty
cheerfully assents in the composition of your executive council
to that which appears to be the general wish of the colony,
in compliance with those constitutional principles on which the
Act of Union was framed, her subjects of all denominations will
look upon that Act as at once the protection and the limit of
their rights, and recognize in a strict adherence to its conditions the best security for a due adjustment of the prerogative
of the sovereign and the liberties of the people.'[2] This quotation will help to dispel some of the illusions. Whatever the
future, the imperial government in its official dispatches gave

[1] Stanley to Bagot, October 16, 1842, *Bagot Correspondence*, M. 165, p. 180.
[2] Same to same, November 2, 1842, *ibid.*, G. 115, p. 127.

to Bagot's experiment full approval after a special meeting of the cabinet. What Stanley most feared was not a situation in Canada, but a situation in England hurtful to his party. Bagot could only be defended, and the government in England with him, on the lines that suspected rebels had compelled their own selection. On the necessity of the case alone would the governor receive public defence. He was promised that it would be cordial and in earnest, but the general policy was outlined in unmistakable terms. Impressions in Canada might matter, but ' impressions at home ' and the ' possible effect on other countries ' were serious and vital considerations. To recall Bagot would only make a checkmate certain for his successor in trying, as *ex hypothesi* he must, to retrace the steps which had been taken. ' *We do not disapprove your policy,* we are prepared to support it, and defend you for having pursued it. Only we must rest your defence on the impossibility of your carrying on the government without having recourse to the men whom you have called to your councils. . . . The present seems to me a favourable time for impressing on your government, as a body, the propriety and the necessity of adopting the Act of Union as a whole, and of declaring their intention to stand by its provisions, including the civil list and every other debatable question—to take it in short as a *fait accompli,* which in the main has secured to them good government and the power of self-government.' [1] Self-government they assumed it to be, and Bagot confessed that it was virtually responsible government.[2]

The concluding months were full of pain and hope. Bagot suffered from a long illness, heroically endured, but at last he was forced to resign. Sir Charles Metcalfe was selected to succeed as the man ' quite prepared to follow out the lines which Bagot had traced and to give full effect to his policy '.[3]

[1] Stanley to Bagot, November 3, 1842, *ibid.,* M. 165, p. 186.
[2] Bagot to Stanley, October 28, 1842, *ibid.,* M. 161, p. 164.
[3] Stanley to Bagot, February 3, 1843, *ibid.,* M. 165, p. 216.

When Bagot heard the news he was delighted. 'So far as I am concerned', he wrote, 'nothing could be so satisfactory to me as the appointment of Sir Theos. Metcalfe; often have I lain upon my bed considering whom I should most desire to have as my successor and to play out my hand here, and Metcalfe has invariably presented himself to me.'[1] Almost Bagot's last words were, 'I have found no reason to regret my course . . . the general tranquillity of the *country throughout* is beyond what I could have ventured to anticipate. My belief is that this state of things will continue, and more especially under the idea and management of such a man as Sir C. Metcalfe, who is, from all that I know and can learn of him, the *unicus homo* for the post.'[2] It was well for Bagot that he did not live to see the fateful destiny which lay before his successor. At any rate, had he lived he would have had the satisfaction of knowing that Metcalfe's policy was his own best justification.

The closing scene fitfully concludes the life of one of the greatest colonial statesmen. 'The sympathy expressed towards him in all the province is very strong : among the Lower Canadians it has exhibited itself in a mode that never before greeted a governor of this province—in masses and public prayers.'[3] His last letter was a message to his executive council : 'My reputation is in your hands. I know that you will all protect it—I am too exhausted to say more.'[4] La Fontaine and Baldwin proved worthy executors. In the destiny of the young nation, at whose birth-pangs Bagot stood, they guarded his reputation not merely in private but in the

---

[1] Bagot to Stanley, February 23, 1843, *Bagot Correspondence*, M. 171, p. 295.
[2] Same to same, March 26, 1843, *ibid.*, M. 161, p. 318.
[3] Rawson (Bagot's civil secretary) to Arthur Blackwood (of the colonial office), December 27, 1842, C.O. 42, vol. 495. For a less pleasing side of the picture see, *inter alia*, Richardson, *Eight Years in Canada, embracing a Review of the Administration of . . . Sir Charles Bagot . . .* (Montreal, 1847).
[4] Bagot to Aylwin, March 29, 1843, *Bagot Correspondence*, M. 161, p. 325.

fierce light of publicity, and gave to responsible government its
final security within the empire.

[AUTHORITIES.—The chief authority for Bagot's government is contained
in the *Bagot Papers and Correspondence* (Canadian Archives), which has been
used throughout.   The contemporary newspapers are invaluable, especially
the *Montreal Gazette*, the *Montreal Transcript*, the *New York Albion*, the
Toronto Herald, the *Kingston Chronicle and Gazette*.   *Baldwin's Correspondence*
(the Reference Library, Toronto) begins to be of importance.   F. Hincks,
The Political History of Canada between 1840 and 1855 (Montreal, 1877), and
Reminiscences of his Public Life (Montreal, 1884) are of first-rate importance.
J. L. Morison, *British Supremacy and Canadian Self-government, 1839–54*
(Glasgow, 1919), contains an excellent study of Bagot's régime.   Consult also
the same author's *Sir Charles Bagot : An Incident in Canadian Parliamentary
History* (Bulletins, History and Economics, No. 4.   Kingston, 1912).]

CHAPTER XV

SELF-GOVERNING OR CROWN COLONY

It is impossible to read Sir Charles Metcalfe's life or to study his dispatches without regretting that he came to Canada. It is true that in making the last attempt by a representative of the crown actually to govern, he proved the impossibility of doing so, but he hurt a magnificent reputation in the service of the empire. He stands among the foremost men in history in disinterested duty and in noble conceptions of responsibility. The 'Metcalfe crisis' owed its origin to these virtues. He believed that the royal prerogative was in danger, and rather than betray a definite trust committed to him by his sovereign, he almost precipitated another rebellion which might have lost the Canadas to the empire to which the devotion of a lifetime had been given. He had no desire to govern contrary to public opinion, or to act the petty tyrant or the arbitrary autocrat. He was willing to go as far as possible with Bagot's experiment. He regretted it and expressed his regret in clear-cut terms. If driven to its full logic, he could see only separation and independence ahead. He created a dilemma for himself—how to work responsible government in such a way as to secure governing powers of a real nature to the governor. There came a point in actual affairs when a choice was forced upon him, and he made it deliberately and honestly because he believed that he could not surrender what he considered the patronage of the crown. He refused to accept the full implications of responsible government. He would not grant that there was a 'cabinet' or a 'ministry' in Canada, and he endured untold physical and mental suffering in sheer devotion to his duty as he saw it, in order to hand over to his successor a colony to which he had taught a lesson on behalf of the crown's rights. The issue was for him a moral one, and never for a moment did he deviate from the path of his duty. It is well that a consideration of his government in Canada should be prefaced with a tribute to his character. In the most trying moments, when the noise of battle was deafening, when uncontrolled forces of invective were let loose in a rugged, ill-trained, uncultured, and uncouth province, he never once forgot that the position which he filled demanded gentlemanly dignity. In the fierceness of the most bitter election in Canadian history, and one in which he felt called on to take part, he did not descend for a moment to the levels of vulgar abuse. There is not a malignant word in his dispatches, not a sharp innuendo in all his recorded writings. His political experience never hardened his kindly generous heart. It was an excellent object lesson, both for tactless friends and for unbridled foes, to come into contact with a man who never allowed his official life to warp the private social amenities. In the darkest days, when even his terrible disease aroused hopes for his quick removal either by death or by resignation, he bore himself with calm courtesy and continued his wide and generous charity. His kindness was boundless and his goodwill knew neither friend nor foe. In the cold analysis of history, the man is liable to be obscured. For Metcalfe reasserted the claim that the governor had the power to govern, and could exercise it if he wished; that executive government depended not on public sanction, but on his private favour. The claim was such a challenge to constitutional evolution that it has overshadowed all that was best in Metcalfe, leaving little place for that necessary consideration of circumstances which alone gives to historical judgements any validity.

His rigidity of mind has already been pointed out, as well as his unsuitability in a government such as the Canadas. But he had another defect for his new position which at once appeared. His conception of the empire made him incapable of seeing things in their true character, and his devotion to the imperial idea was so much like that of an uncritical lover that it obscured his judgement and numbed his sense of political values. He was the greatest United Empire loyalist in Canadian history. His loyalty, however, drove him to think of unity in terms of uniformity and obscured differences and developments in the constitutional parts. He had scarcely been a week in the province before he was deploring the fact that he had not the same material to work on that he had in Jamaica,[1] and when he contemplated the executive council and the house of assembly bequeathed to him by Bagot, he compared his task to that of a governor in India with a Mohammedan council and a Mohammedan popular chamber. He had no intention of submitting in a challenge : ' I cannot . . . surrender the queen's government into the hands of rebels and . . . become myself their ignominious tool. I know not what the end will be. The only thing certain is that I cannot yield.' [2]

Within a month, he had apparently weighed the Canadian situation in a balance with which he was most familiar, but which unfortunately was perhaps the most dangerous possible for the Canadas—that of loyalty to the mother country. To Metcalfe this meant the loyalty of childhood, and to the tory group it meant social status, privilege, places, and patronage. He deplored that the ' republicans ' were in power and that he was ' condemned . . . to carry on the government to the utter exclusion of those on whom the mother country might confidently rely in the hour of need '. He saw no remedy ' without setting at defiance the operation of responsible administration which has been introduced into this colony '.[3]

[1] Metcalfe to his sister, April 9, 1843, J. W. Kaye, *Life and Correspondence of Charles, Lord Metcalfe*, vol. ii, p. 471 (2 vols., London, 1854).

[2] Metcalfe to Colonel Stokes, *ibid.*, p. 528.

[3] Metcalfe to Stanley, April 25, 1843, J. W. Kaye, *Selections from the Papers of Lord Metcalfe*, pp. 407 ff. (London, 1855).

If Metcalfe had not fallen already into the hands of the 'family compact', it is only possible to conclude that Stanley had biased his outlook, which is strangely like that of the colonial secretary's dispatches to Bagot. In trying to analyse public opinion, he was forced to believe that in the coercion of his predecessor party government had been set up. Bagot completed Sydenham's work : ' the events were regarded by all parties in the country as establishing in full force the system of responsible government, of which the practical execution had been before incomplete.' As a result ' the tone of the public voice regarding responsible government has been greatly exalted. The council are now spoken of by themselves and others generally as " the ministers ", " the administration ", " the cabinet ", " the government ", and so forth. Their pretensions are according to this new nomenclature. They regard themselves as a responsible ministry and expect that the policy and conduct of the governor shall be subservient to their views and party purposes.' [1] Durham might theorize at leisure ; Sydenham might risk an idea which for the greater part of his administration had no existence and was only coming into operation when he died ; Bagot might be forced into a position which he did not live to dispute: ' now comes the tug-of-war '.[2] The governor saw that a struggle was inevitable and he formulated at once his policy : ' the general purpose which I purpose to pursue towards the council is to treat them with the confidence and cordiality due to the station which they occupy ; to consult them not only whenever the law or established usage requires that process, but also whenever the importance of the occasion recommends it, and whenever I conceive that the public service will be benefited by their aid and advice.' He was prepared to treat his executive with more than constitutional confidence, but at the

[1] Metcalfe to Stanley, April 24, 1843; Kaye, *Life*, vol. ii, p. 477.
[2] Same to same, May 12, 1843, *ibid.*, p. 479.

same time he was prepared to be on his guard ' against their encroachments '. He anticipated ' a difference with them in their claim that the government shall be administered in subservience to their party views. They expect that the patronage shall be bestowed exclusively on members of their party.' [1]   The storm soon began to gather, and the one vital question which kept ringing in Metcalfe's head was what was to become of the governor-general.[2]   It is well to give in his own words his summary of conditions before the storm of encroachments finally broke.

' I learn ', he informed Stanley, ' that my attempts to conciliate all parties are criminal in the eyes of the council. . . . I am required to give myself up entirely to the council, to submit absolutely to their dictation, to have no judgement of my own, to bestow the patronage of the government exclusively on their partisans, to proscribe their opponents, and to make some public and unequivocal declaration of my adhesion to those conditions—including the complete nullification of her majesty's government. . . . Failing of submission to these stipulations I am threatened with the resignation of Mr. La Fontaine for one, and both he and I are fully aware of the serious consequences likely to follow the execution of that menace, from the blindness with which the French-Canadian party follow their leader. . . . I need hardly say, that although I see the necessity for caution, I have no intention of tearing up her majesty's commission by submitting to the prescribed conditions. . . . The sole question is, to describe it without disguise, whether the governor shall be solely and completely a tool in the hands of the council, or whether he shall have any exercise of his own judgement in the administration of the government. Such a question has not come forward as a matter of discussion, but there is no doubt that the leader

[1] Metcalfe to Stanley, April 24, 1843, Kaye. *Life*, vol. ii, p. 492.
[2] *Ibid.*, p. 476.

of the French party speaks the sentiments of others of his council besides himself. . . . As I cannot possibly adopt them, I must be prepared for the consequence of a rupture with the council, or at least the most influential portion of it. . . . I must expect it, for I cannot consent to be the tool of a party and to proscribe all those who defended their party in the hour of need against foreign invasion and internal rebellion. I am an advocate for entire forgetfulness of past offences against the state ; but it is provoking to find that those who claim amnesty for rebels and brigands, with whom to a certain extent they sympathized, are inveterate in their hostility to those who were faithful to their sovereign and country. . . . Government by a majority is the explanation of responsible government given by the leader in this movement, and government without a majority must be admitted to be ultimately impracticable.   But the present question—and the one which is coming on for trial in my administration—is not whether the governor shall so conduct his government as to meet the wants and wishes of the people and obtain their suffrages by promoting their welfare and happiness, nor whether he shall be responsible for his measures to the people through their representatives, but whether he shall or shall not have a voice in his own council ; whether he shall be at liberty to treat all her majesty's subjects with equal justice, or be a reluctant and passive tool in the hands of a party for the purpose of proscribing their opponents, those opponents being the portion of the community most attached to British connexion, and the governor required to proscribe them being a British governor.   The tendency of this movement is to throw off the government of the mother country in internal affairs entirely, but to be maintained and supported at her expense, and to have all the advantages of connexion as long as it may suit the majority of the people of Canada to endure it.   This is a very intelligible and very convenient policy for a Canadian aiming at independence, but the part the representative of the mother country is required to perform in it is by no means fascinating.'[1]

It might be possible to dismiss this dispatch by saying that Metcalfe wrote it, but that MacNab conceived it, and unfortunately it has been so dismissed.   On the other hand, there is a background of circumstances which will not permit such a cursory judgement.   On his arrival in the province, Metcalfe was deluged with addresses which disclosed the existence of severe extremes.   He was invited to resist the anti-British faction and to show himself a constitutional governor by dismissing his council ; or, he was solemnly but conscientiously enjoined to hold fast to La Fontaine and Baldwin lest worse things should come upon him.   He believed before long that ' the violence of party spirit ' was so great that civil war was not improbable.   His duty lay in quelling the spirit.   He saw the council preparing an issue on the question of patronage. He believed honestly, and perhaps with truth, that they intended to use it for party ends.   As all appointments were made in his name, he refused to become the unwilling patron of party, especially as it meant that ' the loyal portion of the people ' would not receive a share from ' a rebel government '. In addition, the handing over of all patronage to the executive council would rob him of what he considered the best available means at his disposal for crushing the threatening factions. ' I wish ', he wrote ' to make the patronage of the government conducive to the conciliation of all parties, by bringing into the public service the men of greatest merit and efficiency without any party distinction.   My powers of usefulness . . . will be paralysed by my being forced in any degree to act as the supporter of a party.'[2]   He aimed to govern through an executive government whose support would rest on the votes

[1] Metcalfe to Stanley, May 12, 1843 Kaye, *Life*, vol. ii, pp. 493 ff.
[2] Same to same, April 24, 1843, *ibid.*, p. 493.

of those whom his measures had made happy and contented; and he intended to distribute the patronage of the province in such a way that the recalcitrant citizens would keep quiet hoping for their turn. Pending the time when he had an executive and an assembly elected on the platform of ' the governor and happiness ', Metcalfe did not see that he was making himself a party-leader against the majority of the province. Patronage was a royal prerogative. It could best be used in conjunction with popular wishes, but it must never be surrendered exclusively to party control, even though that control reflected the overwhelming wishes of the people.

Metcalfe determined to get the issues clear, and an interview between his civil secretary, Captain Higginson, and La Fontaine towards the close of May 1843 was undoubtedly a *ballon d'essai*. The immediate question was that of an appointment to the vacant office of provincial aide-de-camp, and was in itself of little importance or bearing. The significance lies in the fact that La Fontaine drew up an account of the interview, which is of the utmost importance in the light of future events. Higginson politely protested that he was acting in a private capacity—and he was doubtless formally correct—when he requested an opportunity to discuss the name of a certain officer and the general constitutional situation. He asked La Fontaine to explain what he meant by responsible government and its implications. La Fontaine informed him that it included the responsibility of the executive to the legislature for all acts of government, and that when the legislature withdrew its confidence the executive would resign. That he and his colleagues had taken office relying on the Sydenham-Harrison resolutions. The discussion then turned to the question of consultation or non-consultation among the cabinet in the exercise of patronage. La Fontaine pointed out that appointments to all offices were part of the responsibility owed by the entire executive to the legislature, and consultation was thus necessary; but the governor could accept or reject the nominations of his council, ' his excellency not being bound, and it not being possible to bind him, to follow that advice, but, on the contrary, having a right to reject it; but in this latter case, if the members of the council did not choose to assume the responsibility of the act that the governor wished to perform contrary to their advice, they had the means of relieving themselves from it by exercising their power of resigning.' Higginson challenged this interpretation of the Sydenham-Harrison pact. He refused to accept the principle of united executive responsibility. He believed that each member of the administration ought to be responsible for the acts of his department alone, and that he ought as a consequence to have the liberty of voting with or against his colleagues whenever he judged fit; that thus an administration composed of the principal members of each party might exist advantageously for all parties, and would furnish the governor the means of better understanding the views and opinions of each party, and would not fail, under the auspices of the governor, to lead to the reconciliation of all. La Fontaine replied that if that was Metcalfe's idea of responsible government, the sooner he let the council understand it the better, in order to avoid future complications. He repudiated the interpretation of the resolutions.[1] Metcalfe was thus well on the way to a serious crisis. His executive had one conception of government and he another, both derived from a formula to which the crown had assented. It was little wonder that, with disagreement in his councils and with ' the wars of the ins and the outs ' raging outside, he felt the burden of toiling on in the ' slough of despond ', and found ' the whole concern rotten at the core '.[2]

[1] La Fontaine's account of the interview is in Hincks's *Reminiscences of his Public Life*, pp. 93 ff. (Montreal, 1884).

[2] Metcalfe to a friend, July 15 ; to his sister, August 27, 1843, Kaye, *Life* vol. ii, pp. 500, 505.

'Hope I have none, not even of escape.' With these words
in his mouth, he heroically attacked the entire problem *ab
initio*, and in two long dispatches he summed up the Canadian
system of government and his own position.[1]   He had no difficulty in concluding that Sydenham would never have accepted
La Fontaine's claims.   His position was that a vote of want
of confidence in the assembly would be unconstitutional, but
the assembly could constitutionally petition for the governor's
recall.   The Sydenham rule was, 'The governor is the responsible
government, his subordinate officers are responsible to him not
to the legislative assembly, he is responsible to the ministers
of the crown and liable to appeals from the colony against his
proceedings ; it being at the same time incumbent on him to
consult local feelings and not to persist in employing individuals
justly obnoxious to the community'.   Sydenham, however,
made the provincial theory of responsible government inevitable,
and he could never have hoped to withstand it had he lived.
Metcalfe doubted if Durham meant to advise cabinet government in the colonies, and thus to render the governor a cipher,
but Sydenham had created such beginnings that Bagot could
be coerced into accepting a council no longer chosen by himself
but by the assembly for him.   There was thus a cabinet, and
thus there were parties, which he hated.   The issues were,
however, deeper : ' it becomes a question whether party
government can be avoided.   The experiment of responsible
government in this colony hitherto would indicate that it
cannot.   It seems to me inevitable in free and independent
states where responsible government exists ; . . . but there is
a wide difference between an independent state and a colony.
In an independent state all parties must generally desire the
welfare of the state.   In a colony subordinate to an imperial
government, it may happen that the predominant party is

---

[1] Metcalfe to Stanley, August 5, October 9, 1843, Kaye, *Papers*, pp. 411 ff.,
435 ff.

hostile in its feelings to the mother country, or has ulterior views inconsistent with her interests.' He found his ' extreme and possible case ' so far applicable to Canada that the well affected and loyal had no political power. The prospects for change from ' democratic and party government ' were few, but unless they came the governor must remain a mere ' tool in the hands of a party '. If only the power were in ' the hands of a party thoroughly attached to British interests and connexions, there would be a ground of mutual cordiality and confidence which would render real co-operation more probable, concessions more easy, and even submission more tolerable '. For the present he could only bear with his council, and hope for a better day.

Metcalfe's imperialism had by this time taken a definite form. The introduction of the cabinet system he viewed with the confident dismay that it would lead to independence. He mistrusted it in a colony. As a consequence he had no patience with the party system, especially as it had lifted into power ' reformers, republicans, and French '. There was much truth in the descriptions which he drew—' reformers ', ' republicans ', ' rebels ', ' tories and family compact men ', ' the hostile virulence of orangemen and repealers '—a chaos of watchwords and shibboleths in an atmosphere of undisciplined invective. The difficulty was that Metcalfe could not kill the parties—he recognized that himself—and in hating them as signs of reform, perhaps of separation, he slowly but surely drifted into the arms of the high and dry tories, who had sounded the loyal note so loud and so long that it had become pleasant in Metcalfe's willing ear. He could not believe that loyalty could be otherwise than guileless, and he was quite broken-hearted to report that ' the whole colony must at times be regarded as a party opposed to her majesty's government '. He could not be indifferent to parties : ' this indifference is scarcely possible to a governor having any spark of British feeling, when almost all who have British feelings are arrayed on one side, and all who have anti-British feelings on the other '.[1] The real difficulty lay in the fact that Metcalfe did not see that a Canadian feeling was growing up. In his eyes all citizens of the empire were British or anti-British. His duty clearly lay with the former. As a consequence he became the leader of a party in the colony in spite of all his theoretical protestations. His party was anti-Canadian. A new synthesis of empire was beginning under his eyes, and he could not grasp a Canadian party representing the vast majority of the people and protesting, through Baldwin, its loyalty to the mother country. Metcalfe believed that loyalty was the peculiar property of the ' British " family compact " party ', and it seemed to him that there must be something ' rotten ', to use his own word, in a protested loyalty which did not include in its ranks the tried men of British feelings.

In doubt and fear Metcalfe opened the legislature in September. A certain amount of business was got through, notably a resolution in favour of Montreal as the seat of government, a statute to prevent judges and public officials from sitting in the assembly, and a complete reform of the judicial system of Lower Canada. Two measures, however, created the fiercest controversy. A bill was passed, commonly known as ' the secret societies' bill ', which constituted all secret societies, except the freemasons, illegal, and declared that their members should be held incapable of holding official appointments or of serving on juries. The measure was introduced with Metcalfe's knowledge and approval, but he reserved it, when passed by an overwhelming majority, for the sanction of the imperial authorities, which was finally refused. The opposition considered that the bill was specially aimed at the orange order and was class legislation of a particularly autocratic type; but Baldwin and La Fontaine replied that it was straining the

[1] Metcalfe to Stanley, May 13, 1845, Kaye, *Papers*, pp. 449 ff.

R

constitution in reserving the Act. The second measure was Baldwin's attempt to secularize higher education by transferring the lands granted to King's College to a new state institution—the University of Toronto. Strachan consolidated the ranks of the church of England, and outdid himself in violence. The bill proposed, according to this champion, ' to place all forms of error on an equality with truth, by patronizing equally within the same institution an unlimited number of sects whose doctrines are absolutely irreconcilable : a principle in its nature atheistical and so monstrous in its consequences that, if successfully carried out, it would lead . . . to greater corruption than anything adopted during the madness of the French revolution . . . a fatal departure from all that is good without a parallel in the history of the world '.[1] The church papers described Baldwin's proposals as disclosing ' the true atheistical character of the popular dogma of responsible government '.[2] Religious feelings were aroused to extremes and the bill was making stormy progress, when Metcalfe came face to face with the *impasse* which he most dreaded.

Towards the close of November the government heard that a conservative had been appointed to a minor office without their approval. Baldwin and La Fontaine interviewed Metcalfe privately, and opened up the question of patronage at the executive council. The governor-general refused to accept their demands, and on November 26 the entire government resigned, with the exception of Dominick Daly. It is difficult to arrive at the motives which lay behind this drastic action. Apparently La Fontaine and Baldwin drove the Sydenham-Harrison resolutions to their logical conclusion and included all patronage supported by provincial funds as part of the responsibility of the ministry in power. They complained that

---

[1] See the petition which he presented, November 6, 1843, *Journals of the Legislative Assembly of Canada*.
[2] *The Church* (Toronto), November 17, 1843.

the differences between the executive and the governor were not theoretical but actual, as appointments had been made against their advice, and proposals for appointments had been laid before him when the opportunity for advice had passed. They resented the reservation of ' the secret societies' bill ' after Metcalfe had given his consent to its introduction as a government measure. They felt that they were in an anomalous position, being responsible for all acts of the executive to the legislature, and not being consulted on all acts by the governor. There was apparently a sphere in which the governor could control provincial appointments, and he maintained that the council need not defend or support in parliament his actions within that sphere.

Metcalfe disputed the explanations of the ministers. He declared that the statement, which has just been considered, was too full and that the issue was not on a theory of responsible government, but merely on the question of the governor-general's complete surrender to the council of his control over all appointments. He refused to accept any position of subordination which would convert patronage into party channels, ' degrade the character of his office, . . . violate his duty, and surrender the prerogative of the crown '.[1] Other interpretations of the episode were forthcoming at the time. Hincks maintained that the whole thing was part of a plan, which originated with the colonial office, to wreck Bagot's work.[2] Edward Gibbon Wakefield saw in it a party move, as the government was already tottering and needed to rally public opinion in its favour.[3] Although Metcalfe lent some support

[1] The statement of La Fontaine and Baldwin and Metcalfe's reply are in *The Addresses presented to His Excellency the Rt. Hon. Sir Charles T. Metcalfe on the Occasion of the Resignation of his late Advisers* (Toronto, 1844).

[2] Dent, *Canada since the Union of 1841*, vol. i, pp. 272 ff. ; cf. Hincks, *The Political History of Canada between 1840 and 1855* (Montreal, 1877).

[3] *A Letter on the Ministerial Crisis* (Kingston, 1843) ; *A View of Sir Charles Metcalfe's Government in Canada* (London, 1844).

244 SELF-GOVERNING OR CROWN COLONY

to Wakefield's statement by referring to it in a dispatch, there
is no doubt that his view of the situation had no basis in fact.[1]
As for the suggestion put forward by Hincks, it can be dismissed as an insult to a man of Metcalfe's honour. Egerton
Ryerson entered the contest with puerile conceptions of constitutional law, and defended Metcalfe by an interpretation
of British practice, which was lashed to pieces in Sullivan's
merciless satire.[2] The latter resolved the question into its
simplest terms : if Metcalfe was right, then Canada should
not have representative institutions at all, and the Sydenham-
Harrison resolutions to which the colonial office had assented
were meaningless. The executive claimed to be a cabinet
representing a party and, as such, to have full control over the
patronage of the province. Metcalfe claimed the right, not
merely in theory—which was conceded—but in fact, to make
appointments apart from the executive, as part of the prerogative rights of the crown. The executive defended their position
as part and parcel of their conditions on taking up office.
It was unfortunate that the challenge should have been over
patronage, as the conservatives and Metcalfe were able to raise
a kind of ethical cry over bought votes and tarnished power.
But Baldwin and La Fontaine knew well enough that the same
patronage would be claimed by their opponents if in office, the
only difference being that Metcalfe and MacNab would call it
the just reward for British loyalty.

Metcalfe now cast himself on the country to seek a new
council, and following cabinet conventions, to get ready for
a new election. Daly remained and was joined by Benjamin
Viger, who deserted his compatriots after having suffered in
their cause.[3] Later W. H. Draper was secured and the three
formed a provisional government. A war of pamphlets and

---

[1] Metcalfe to Stanley, December 26, 1843, Kaye, *Papers*, pp. 422 ff.
[2] Egerton Ryerson, *Sir Charles Metcalfe defended* (Toronto, 1844) ; R. B.
Sullivan (' Legion '), *Letters on Responsible Government* (Toronto, 1844).
[3] See Viger's defence in *La Crise ministérielle* (Kingston, 1844).

newspapers, addresses and counter-addresses, broke out which knew nothing of civilized conventions. The ' Canada crisis ' was debated in the imperial parliament, and Stanley served up the Sydenham-Russell correspondence of 1839 as if it were an original contribution. He also sat in judgement dividing Canadians into loyal sheep and rebel goats. The student of party politics can only regret that no one in the house of commons then knew that he had absolutely forbidden Bagot to appoint Viger to the legislative council, because he had been a traitor, whom he was now defending as a member of Metcalfe's provisional government.[1] When Metcalfe finally got together an executive council and faced the electors in November 1844, the air was charged with electricity. Bitterness passed all bounds. Virulence passed for truth, invective took the place of logic. Every conceivable weapon was pressed into service. Metcalfe himself made it clear that he considered loyalty and the British connexion were at stake, and in a reply to an address from the district of Gore he practically issued an election manifesto. He refused to surrender himself or the patronage of the crown to any executive however supported. To do so would be ' incompatible with the existence of a British colony '. He was ' responsible to the crown and the parliament and the people of the mother country ' for every act which he performed.[2] ' He felt ', says his biographer, ' that he was fighting for his sovereign against a rebellious people.' His sincerity must remain his only defence. On the eve of the election he firmly believed that there were only two issues : British connexion and supremacy or a form of government inconsistent with either.[3] The elections thus took on the

---

[1] ' It is impossible to overlook the fact that Viger was in truth one of the most active partisans of the late disturbances . . . imprisoned on a charge of treason . . . conspicuous by his refusal to give bail for future peaceable conduct. . . . I cannot consent to confer a mark of distinction on one who was foremost in the ranks of disaffection': Stanley to Bagot, April 1, 1842, *Bagot Correspondence*, G. 113, p. 4.

[2] Kaye, *Life*, vol. ii, pp. 533 ff.   [3] *Ibid.*, pp. 562 ff.

aspect of a grim struggle between loyalists and traitors, and the numerous and fatal riots which accompanied them were viewed as contests between the forces of the crown and rebels. The tory group rallied their supporters to a man, the Eastern Townships stood solid, Ryerson had directed the Methodists, and many a doubter finally followed the cry of loyalty rather than the dictates of his convictions. In the issue the governor's party—for such it undoubtedly was—was returned with a small majority, which by three votes gave MacNab the speakership.

The long contest ended at least in a paper victory, and Metcalfe had the satisfaction of knowing that the imperial government and even the leading men of the liberal opposition, including Lord John Russell, were on his side, while the queen conferred on him a peerage in cordial approbation of the ability and fidelity with which he had carried out the important trust confided to him.[1] He had done the work which the cabinet had sent him to do. He had deviated neither to the right hand nor to the left, and he had kept the faith. It is well that the student of these bitter days can recall the figure of a dying man, almost sightless with cancer, holding fast to his post, in order to preserve the unity of the empire which he considered was absolutely incompatible with colonial responsible government. The iron, however, entered into his soul before he retired from office. His new council exercised little influence and commanded little support. In the noise of battle a small majority had been secured, but when the tumult had died away men began to find that the war-cries were ill suited to the days of peace, and that loyalty was a poor substitute for efficient administration. For Metcalfe personally the last months in Canada were a sad revelation. The single-minded governor had become a partisan, the peace which he hoped to favour was almost outraged by civil war, and the races which were

[1] Kaye, *Life*, vol. ii, pp. 582 ff.

beginning to work together stood in bitter opposition as in the days of Craig and Aylmer. On the other hand, Metcalfe put the entire colonial office theory into practice. He had no conceivable use for Sydenham's ill-working paternalism or for Bagot's logical concessions. He was the ideal man for Stanley's instructions, and he proved to the imperial cabinet that it was one thing to put in practice their theory and quite another thing to make it work. Government by imperial selection had proved just as futile as government by a ' compact ' or a ' clique '. The decay which had set in went on apace. Draper attempted to arrest it by trying to induce La Fontaine to join forces with the conservatives of Upper Canada.[1] He thought to obtain a working majority in each division of the province. The negotiations fell through and the decay continued until Draper was glad to resign. His successors—the so-called Sherwood-Daly ministry—could not avert the inevitable, and Elgin, with the country behind him, dissolved ' the loyal assembly ' on December 6, 1847. Perhaps the most interesting by-product of Metcalfe's government was a prophecy by Baldwin that any attempt to carry on the administration by a ' double majority ' would ' perpetuate distinctions, initiate animosities, sever the bonds of political sympathy, and sap the foundations of political morality '.[2]

[AUTHORITIES.—*The State Papers* are in Series G. 117–22, 183, 460 (Canadian Archives). *Baldwin's Correspondence* is in the Reference Library, Toronto J. W. Kaye, *Life and Correspondence of Charles, Lord Metcalfe* (2 vols., London, 1854), *and Selections from the Papers of Lord Metcalfe* (London, 1855), contain many letters and dispatches. F. Hincks, *Political History* (Montreal, 1877), and *Reminiscences* (Montreal, 1844), are of great importance. J. C. Dent, *The Last Forty Years, or Canada since the Union of 1841* (2 vols., Toronto, 1881), is valuable and owes much to Hincks. The pamphlet literature is extensive and throws contemporary light on the history. It includes

[1] *Correspondence between the Hon. W. H. Draper and the Hon. R. E. Caron ; and between the Hon. R. E. Caron and the Hons. L. H. La Fontaine and A. N. Morin* (Montreal, 1846 ?).

[2] Baldwin to La Fontaine, 1845–6 (?), *Baldwin Papers* (Toronto Reference Library).

Ryerson, *Sir Charles Metcalfe defended against the attacks of his late Councillors* (Toronto, 1844) ; R. B. Sullivan, *Letters on Responsible Government* (Toronto, 1844) ; D. B. Viger, *La Crise ministérielle* (Kingston, 1844) ; F. Hincks, *The Ministerial Crisis* (Kingston, 1844) ; *Correspondence between Hon. W. H. Draper and the Hon. R. E. Caron, and between Hon. R. E. Caron and the Hons. L. H. La Fontaine and A. N. Morin* (Montreal, 1846) ; *Addresses presented to . . . Sir Charles Metcalfe . . . on the occasion of the Resignation of his late Advisers* (Toronto, 1844) ; *The ' Crise ' Metcalfe and the La Fontaine-Baldwin Cabinet defended* (Quebec, 1844). Stephen Leacock, *Baldwin, La Fontaine, Hincks* (Toronto, 1907), is valuable especially for its use of contemporary journals. J. L. Morison, *British Supremacy and Canadian Self-government, 1839–54* (Glasgow, 1919), discusses with great insight Metcalfe's failure and its significance.]

CHAPTER XVI

THE NEW COLONIAL POLICY

METCALFE'S successor, Lord Cathcart, only remained in office until the Oregon boundary dispute was settled. Queen Victoria had suggested Lord Elgin's name to Stanley before the fall of the tory government.[1] The new whig ministry at once returned to the idea of a civil governor, and neglecting party divisions they appointed Elgin to work out with Earl Grey, the colonial secretary, adequate and stable administrative principles in Canada. Elgin had carried out some successful social reforms in Jamaica, but his experience was of little importance compared with the fact that he belonged to the group of liberal-minded conservatives associated in history with the person and policy of Sir Robert Peel. He thus brought with him into the visionless mazes of Canada's storm-tossed political life the traditions of calm and discriminating liberalism, of wise insight, of dispassionate objectivity, and of a freedom from doctrinaire theory which were the most permanent contributions of the Peelites to English history. In addition, he had married Lord Durham's daughter, and his advent linked up Canadian development with a name which symbolized for the vast majority of Canadians a new colonial policy. During the seven years of his régime unparalleled and almost unhoped-for advances were made. The older tantalizing problems in local politics were settled. The race question was placed on a newer footing and foundations were laid upon which a nobler synthesis of empire has been built.

Before considering the problems which Elgin faced, it is well to sketch in bold outline the background of British opinion

[1] *Letters*, vol. ii, p. 55.

and to seek some justification for it. There is no general and comprehensive formula. Perhaps the best explanation of the toryism of the tories and the whiggism of the whigs in colonial affairs can be found in the still unchallenged Austinian theory of sovereignty. The most judicial and unprejudiced political thinkers could not conceive of a divided authority or of a multiplicity of cabinets giving the crown responsible advice. Other influences were at work. To the tory group, freedom was the father of independence. Had it been possible to see beyond a theory of doubtful validity, self-government meant to them separation. The only lesson which they could derive from the American revolution was that popular control ended in disloyalty, disruption, and rebellion. They aimed in colonial policy to avoid the outbreak of another political epidemic by large doses of preventive medicine, and they uniformly classed ' reformers and liberals ' as dangerous germ-carriers. The whig group accepted Austin, but they gradually acquired a greater belief in liberty and a wider mistrust of over government. When it came to a point of reconciling sovereignty with liberalism, they did not find a dilemma. With little conception of empire, they believed that colonial destiny pointed to the creation in a not very remote future of new states. In this belief they did not stand alone. When an apparent logic of facts penetrated the tory mind with the choice of either self-government or independence, not a few were prepared to accept the latter rather than resist the former with force.

It was a fortunate coincidence that Elgin should come to Canada at a moment when perhaps liberal-imperialism was best represented by the colonial secretary. Earl Grey had his dark moments. At times the lamp of faith burned dim. It is, however, his unique virtue that he was the only colonial secretary up to this time who had any faith at all. He brought to his work a trained, practical mind. He saw not merely the past outlined in a failure which was almost uniformly misinterpreted, and the present beset with the dangers of a very ugly dilemma. But also he saw the future in terms of neither constitutions nor laws nor theories but in those of higher values. He was a statesman for the simple reason that he was prepared to take risks, and that he refused in the final analysis to make it an article of faith that a liberal colonial policy meant the inevitable tory end or the high whig destiny. His statesmanlike faith is all the more remarkable for two reasons. He was willing to trust the untrained, untamed, uncouth colonials to work out their own future. He found a *via media* between the *non possumus* of the tory and the *laisser faire* of the whig in a conception of empire which is largely that of to-day. To illustrate these two points will require long quotations, but their importance in the history of the world is more than adequate justification.

In repudiating the custom of giving directions in all details of colonial policy, Grey began a new era by laying down general principles which conceded the recommendations of Durham and the demands of Howe. In a dispatch to Sir John Harvey, lieutenant-governor of Nova Scotia, he wrote : ' The object with which I recommend to you this course is that of making it apparent that any transfer which may take place of political power from the hands of one party in the province to those of another is the result not of an act of yours but of the wishes of the people themselves, as shown by the difficulty experienced by the retiring party in carrying on the government of the province according to the forms of the constitution. To this I attach great importance ; I have therefore to instruct you to abstain from changing your executive council until it shall become per-fectly clear that they are unable, with such fair support from yourself as they have a right to expect, to carry on the govern-ment of the province satisfactorily and command the confidence of the legislature. Of whatsoever party your council may be composed it will be your duty to act strictly upon the principle you have yourself laid down . . . that namely " of not identifying yourself with any one party " ; but instead of this, " making yourself both a mediator and moderator between the influential of all parties ".   In giving therefore all fair and proper support to your council for the time being, you will carefully avoid any acts which can possibly be supposed to imply the slightest personal objection to their opponents, and also refuse to assent to any measures which may be proposed to you by your council which may appear to you to involve an improper exercise of the authority of the crown for party rather than for public objects. In exercising, however, this power of refusing to sanction measures which may be submitted to you by your council, you must recollect that this power of opposing a check upon extreme measures proposed by the party for the time in the government depends entirely for its efficacy upon its being used sparingly and with the greatest possible discretion.   A refusal to accept advice tendered to you by your council is a legitimate ground for its members to tender to you their resignation, a course they would doubtless adopt should they feel that the subject on which a difference had arisen between you and themselves was one upon which public opinion would be in their favour.   Should it prove to be so, concession to their views must, sooner or later, become inevitable, since it cannot be too distinctly acknowledged that it is neither possible nor desirable to carry on the government of any of the British provinces in North America in opposition to the opinion of the inhabitants.'[1]   This dispatch became Elgin's talisman in Canada, and Grey never deviated from it.   He was willing that the crown in Canada and elsewhere should accept a ministry on that ' system of parliamentary government which has long prevailed in the mother country '.[2]

The concession followed the broad lines of distinction which Durham and Howe had drawn between local and imperial

[1] Grey to Harvey, November 3, 1846, Kennedy, *op. cit.*, pp. 570 ff.
[2] Same to same, March 31, 1847, *ibid.*, pp. 573 ff.

concerns. The general power of veto laid down in the Act of Union had been modified, and the governor had been given full power to assent to any laws ' which properly belonged to the internal government of the province and which did not involve what was dishonourable and unjust '.[1] Grey, however, was inclined to believe that even in local affairs there might arise occasions when the imperial cabinet was bound to interfere. His faith wavered, for example, before the idea of a Canadian tariff. The new gospel of free trade was in full tide, and Grey debated whether Canada ought to be allowed to reject the glad tidings.[2] Another temporary ingredient in his imperialism was a trust in the necessity of the ' moderating influence ' of the home government on the excesses of colonial factions.[3] Under Elgin's influence and reacting to Elgin's experience, he gradually passed to a stronger belief based on higher conceptions. Economic advantages, the prestige of empire, the glamour of power finally took on another colour. His imperialism found a moral justification, and he saw in free countries under the crown ' a powerful instrument under Providence of maintaining peace and order in many extensive regions of the earth and thereby assisting in diffusing among millions of the human race the blessings of christianity and civilization '.[4]

At the close of January 1847 Elgin arrived in Canada. He found a ministry dragging on an anaemic existence, a house of assembly which did not command popular support, the French-Canadians in a state of dangerous gloom, and the imperial relationship dubious and insecure. There was plenty of noise in the clash of parties, but he could see nothing either essential or logical in their differences. The most dangerous issue was the actual principle of government, and with it was bound up the imperial

[1] Gladstone to Cathcart, February 3, 1846, *State Papers*, G. 123.
[2] Grey to Elgin, October 25, 1847, *Elgin-Grey Correspondence*.
[3] Same to same, March 22, 1848, *ibid*.
[4] Earl Grey, *The Colonial Policy of Lord John Russell*, vol. i, pp. 13 ff. (2 vols., London, 1853).

connexion in respect to the governor-general's place in the scheme. Face to face with these interwoven problems, Elgin had definite convictions. An imperialist in the best sense of the word, he realized that Canada would be bound to the empire, if bound at all, by his acceptance of positions which would accord with Canadian wishes. ' My course ', he wrote, ' is I think clear and plain. It may be somewhat difficult to follow occasionally, but I feel no doubt as to the direction in which it lies. I give to my ministers all constitutional support, frankly and without reserve, and the benefit of the best advice that I can afford them in their difficulties. . . . I have never concealed from them that I intended to do nothing which may prevent me from working cordially with their opponents if they are forced upon me.' [1] He said to them, ' While you continue my advisers you shall enjoy my unreserved confidence ; and *en revanche* you shall be responsible for all acts of government '.[2] This position conceded responsible government. Of course Elgin saw his dual position in relation to the imperial and local legislatures. He felt that a middle course of ' moral influence ' would emerge, but for the present he had no intention of falling ' on the one side into the *néant* of mock sovereignty, or on the other into the dirt and confusion of local factions '. His practical mind saved him from endless anxieties. He did not stop to discuss difficulties or to worry over the nicely calculated less or more of imperial or local affairs. He faced issues as they arose, without entangling himself in theories about the consequences of his decisions.

The reconstructed ministry gained no strength. Overtures to individual French-Canadians proved as useless as before, and at the close of 1847 Elgin dissolved the legislature. The new principle was clear. If the ministry were sustained they would acquire a very necessary vitality. If they were defeated they

---

[1] Elgin to Grey, July 13, 1847, Kennedy, *op. cit.*, pp. 577 ff.
[2] Same to Cumming Bruce, September 1852, *ibid.*, pp. 589 ff.

had no claim to office. Robert Baldwin's election address is of interest : ' We shall have no more representatives of the sovereign making the doctrines of the Charleses and the Jameses the standard by which to govern British subjects in the nineteenth century . . . henceforth their viceregal governments will be distinguished by adherence to the constitutional principles acknowledged by all parties in England . . . principles which will relieve her majesty's representative from the invidious position of the head of a party and will render him . . . a living spirit, and the connecting link which binds this great colony to the parent state in affectionate and prosperous union.' [1] The election went adversely for the ministry and they were heavily defeated on a vote of no confidence. Elgin at once sent for La Fontaine and Baldwin, the opposition leaders, who formed the first real cabinet in Canada. Earl Grey emphasized the change. The executive might bring in wise or foolish measures and the vital interests of the country might suffer, but he saw no middle course between accepting the verdict of the electorate and resorting to imperial coercion, which was out of the question.[2] Responsible government was solved by the gift itself, and the governor passing unsullied through the election approached his new sphere of ' moral influence '. The full grant came none too soon. It was a dangerous period in history, but with popular government established the province escaped influences which might have been retrograde or tragic. Elgin remained long enough in Canada to show that cabinet government had few of the terrors which its opponents feared. He gave full support to his executive independent of, and often against, his personal feelings and convictions. He taught the Canadians

---

[1] Baldwin to the electors of York, December 8, 1847, *Baldwin Papers*, [A], E. 6–7, 29 (15) (Ontario Archives). Elgin used the same terms in defining, at the close of his régime, the position of the governor—' the link which connects the mother country and the colony ': Elgin to Sir George Grey, December 18, 1854, Kennedy, *op. cit.*, p. 591.

[2] Grey to Elgin, February 22, 1848, *Elgin-Grey Correspondence*.

the true meaning of the constitutional convention. La Fontaine and Baldwin, ' the rebel and disloyal leaders ', found in the governor an undisguised willingness to support them to the full constitutional limit. When their party passed from power, he turned to his bitterest personal opponent, Sir Allan MacNab, and accepted a ministry formed by him with equally full constitutional recognition.

The establishment of responsible government decided a principle, and in doing so certain corollaries followed. The office of governor-general took on a new aspect. The governor was lifted ' above the strife of parties ' and ceased to be a machine for registering ' rescripts from Downing Street '. His influence became ' wholly moral—an influence of suasion, sympathy, and moderation which [softened] the temper, while it [elevated] the aims of local politics '. Elgin found his position transfigured and transformed. Instead of being an object of suspicion to reformers and the peculiar private preserve of ' loyalists ' with all the undignified consequences of such a place, he acquired a remarkable influence. His opinion was respected, his advice sought. He became a source of imperial faith which had suffered so tragically through the obscurity of past definitions.[1] The most remarkable answer to Metcalfe's passionate cry of ' What is to become of the governor ? ' is Elgin's : ' In Jamaica there was no responsible government, but I had not half the power I have [in Canada] with my constitutional and changing cabinet.' [2]

In addition, the French-Canadian problem was placed in a just setting out of which national salvation arose in the future. Elgin gave the lie direct to Durham's policy of denationalization. He recognized the futility of attempting to suppress race, and he saw that such attempts only succeeded in giving it renewed

[1] Elgin to Cumming Bruce, September 1852, Kennedy, *op. cit.*, pp. 589 ff.
[2] Theodore Walrond, *Letters and Journals of James, Eighth Earl of Elgin*, p. 125 (London, 1872).

vigour. No repression would anglicize the French; it might succeed in driving them into the arms of the United States. ' Let them feel, on the other hand, that their religion, their habits, their prepossessions, their prejudices if you will, are more considered and respected here than in other portions of this vast continent: who will venture to say that the last hand which waves the British flag on American ground may not be that of a French-Canadian ? ' [1] At the opening of the legislature he announced that the imperial parliament had placed French on a level with English as an official language, and for the first time the governor read his speech in both languages. He never lost sight of the dangers of nationalism, and he was fully aware of the special and peculiar problem of French-Canadian race solidarity. In attempting to overcome it, he abandoned the useless methods of trying to detach influential men and to incorporate them in a ' loyal ' cabinet. He reverted to Bagot's policy. He aimed to nullify as much as possible the consciousness of distinct origins in a general scheme of constitutional development. In linking La Fontaine with Baldwin he recognized the political unity of Canada, and he established a principle which for better or worse held the field till federation. He learned too that disintegrating radicalism was least likely to flourish in French Canada. He foresaw, if he did not actually initiate, that Anglo-French political combination which was later to emerge as the constructive force of liberal-conservatism and to give John A. Macdonald his strongest hold on ministerial power. Above all he gave French Canada justice. The rebellion losses bill [2] will serve not only to illustrate this point, but to throw contemporary light on the new-born principle of government, the new position of the governor-general, and the relationship between the colony and the mother country.

The story of the bill is too well known to need retelling at any

[1] Elgin to Grey, May 4, 1848, *ibid.*, p. 54.   [2] 12 Victoria, c. 58.

S

length. Previous governments had undertaken to provide compensation for destruction during the rebellions. Much money had already been expended in Canada West, and Metcalfe's parliament had planned a scheme to include both divisions of the province. Commissioners had been appointed to examine claims and to sift rebels from non-rebels. The matter then did not originate under Elgin and the reform ministry. There were several cross-currents. If the measure were withheld La Fontaine and Baldwin would not continue in office. Elgin knew that they had the electors behind them and that he could not grant responsible government with one hand and take it away with the other. In addition, he believed that a measure of justice was due to French Canada. Doubtless there was a danger that public money might go to some who had been in arms, although the fact was beyond proof. He feared that civil war, if not an international complication with the United States, might arise if the recrudescence of the ' loyalty cry ' were allowed to control the situation. Responsible government, the place of the French-Canadians, the impartiality of the government, and the general good faith of the imperial cabinet were on their trial. In due course the bill passed with a majority in each division of the province. Fierce opposition arose in the tory ranks and Elgin was petitioned either to refuse assent or to reserve the bill. The issues before him were clear-cut. His ministers were responsible ministers. The measure was a Canadian measure. He refused what appeared to him the weak course of throwing the complicated burden on the home government. He determined to bear it himself, and he assented to the bill.[1]

Scenes of disgraceful licence followed. Elgin was almost killed. The parliament house was looted and burned, and for a time mob law prevailed. Elgin remained perfectly calm, refused to allow the military to handle the situation, and left

[1] Elgin to Grey, March 14, 1849, *Elgin-Grey Correspondence.*

self-government to work out its own solution. In one of his most penetrating dispatches he analysed the mentality of the ' loyal ' rioters. For his position he made neither defence nor excuse. He made it perfectly clear that a minority had had their feelings hurt, and that the turmoil was only due to a peculiar type of loyalty which claimed a right to regulate by violence what could not be gained by constitutional means. In the hands of others this was rebellion, with them it was accounted righteousness.[1] The bill was the *reductio ad absurdum* of ' family compact ' claims. Every possible constitutional force was on Elgin's side, and tory loyalty was proved to be only the older monopoly of privilege in a newer setting. As privilege receded down the democratic tide, loyalty and imperialism were not so conspicuous. When the annexation movement was at its height not a few of the ' loyalists ' longed for the flesh-pots of Egypt and joined with extremists in promoting a movement opposition to which had been the strongest force in their political *raison d'être*. This aspect of the episode needs little comment, but the measure had a most important influence. Responsible government was vindicated. French Canada was convinced of the sincerity of the concession, and the ' reds ' never acquired any lasting influence. The ' family compact ' was dissolved in political death, and John A. Macdonald was already beginning to see in the future a combination of parties in which race and privilege were to surrender their places to constitutional nationalism. In the house of commons the whole affair was canvassed. Russell and Grey defended Elgin and acknowledged the right of Canada to legislate on the matter. The majority of the Peelites voted with the government. The tories reproduced the ' loyalist ' cry of ' compensating rebels ' and ' French domination '. Gladstone pleaded that, as virtual rebels might receive public funds, the Act be either disallowed or an amendment passed in Canada to provide for clearer definitions. He appeared

---

[1] Elgin to Grey, April 30, 1849, Kennedy, *op. cit.*, pp. 579 ff.

to believe that the measure was beyond colonial legislative competency. The debates led to a letter from Hincks, then in London, in the columns of *The Times*, which deserves a distinct place in Canadian history.[1] He' poured scorn on the trite meaningless phrases, the party shibboleths which passed for arguments. He claimed a share for the Canadian government and their supporters in the loyalty which British and Canadian tories seemed to consider their peculiar monopoly. He pointed out that imperial criticism would need to rely on facts and on judicial estimates of colonial feeling, otherwise it was ' very unsafe for parties at a distance of three thousand miles to interfere in Canadian affairs '. The letter was a polite but firm request to England to mind its own business.

Another delicate situation arose out of inconsiderate and inconsistent imperial actions.[2] The Canadian Corn Act of 1843 had given Canadian wheat and flour preference in the British market. Large quantities of American wheat were imported to Canada, which gained preferential treatment when sold as Canadian flour. Canadians had invested much capital in making provision for handling the extensive trade. Like a bolt from the blue, with no thought of the consequences in component parts of the empire, the imperial government annulled colonial preference and lowered the walls of protection. As a consequence, bankruptcy swept over Canadian business life and economic gloom settled down on the country. Property became utterly worthless and the public credit of the province ceased to exist. Elgin confessed that he did not know how the Canadians kept their heads. Peaceful annexation, however, was openly advocated, and with the political crisis over the rebellion losses bill it gained wide support.[3] Elgin blamed the unskilled policy which

---

[1] *The Times*, June 20, 1849.   [2] Walrond, *op. cit.*, p. 60.

[3] The annexation manifesto and Elgin's dispatches connected with it are in Egerton and Grant, *op. cit.*, pp. 336 ff.   Consult C. D. Allin and G. M. Jones, *Annexation, Preferential Trade, and Reciprocity : An Outline of the Canadian Annexation Movement of 1849–50* (Toronto, 1911), and C. D. Allin, ' The British

adopted free trade in 1846 and retained the navigation acts till 1849. He dealt summarily with manifestoes, and officials who had signed them were removed from office. But there was no doubt that a serious mistrust of Great Britain was widespread. He finally rallied the commercial classes by negotiating a reciprocity treaty with the United States and by convincing the imperial government of its necessity. Even then his difficulties did not disappear. When he was doing his utmost to bind Canada to the empire and to drive in double harness a colonial and an imperial cabinet, the prime minister of England was addressing the house of commons on the empire and began to anticipate a day when responsible government would have prepared the colonies for decent but inevitable independence. Elgin took up the challenge, which almost moved Baldwin to tears. ' You must renounce the habit ', he wrote to Grey, ' of telling the colonies that the " colonial " is a provisional existence ; you must allow them to believe that, without severing the bonds which unite them to Great Britain, they may attain the degree of perfection and of social and political development to which organized communities of freemen have a right to aspire. . . . Is not the question at issue a most momentous one ? What is it indeed but this : Is the queen of England to be the sovereign of an empire, growing, expanding, strengthening itself from age to age, striking its roots deep into fresh earth and drawing new supplies of vitality from virgin soils ? Or is she to be, for all essential purposes of might and power, monarch of Great Britain and Ireland merely—her place and that of her line in the world's history determined by the productiveness of 12,000 square miles of a coal formation, which is being rapidly exhausted, and the duration of the social and political organization over which she presides dependent on the annual expatriation, with a view to its eventual alienation, of the surplus swarms of her born

North American League, 1849 ' (*Ontario Historical Society, Papers and Records,* vol. xiii, Toronto, 1915).

subjects ? ' ¹ ' I have been possessed (I use the word advisedly,
for I fear that most persons in England still consider it a case of
possession) with the idea that it is possible to maintain on this
soil of North America and in the face of republican America,
British connexion and British institutions, if you give the latter
freely and trustingly.   Faith, when it is sincere, is always
catching ; and I have imparted this faith more or less thoroughly
to all Canadian statesmen with whom I have been in official
relationship since 1848 and to all intelligent Englishmen with
whom I have come in contact since 1850.' ²

Before considering the new colonial policy in the Maritime
Provinces, it is necessary to take a closer view of some other
aspects of Canadian life, in order to understand the reorienta-
tion of parties which took place before Elgin left Canada.   The
La Fontaine-Baldwin ministry was baffled by two questions.
The clergy reserves, in spite of Sydenham's legislation, remained
a bone of contention and the demand for their secularization
gained strength.   On the one hand, Bishop Strachan was com-
passing heaven and earth to maintain a privileged place for his
communion ; on the other, George Brown was leading an attack
on the *status quo* in the *Globe*, which was in reality the first
blast of a new radicalism.   The ministry was divided.   La
Fontaine favoured Baldwin against secularization, and they
seem to have had Elgin's support ; but the executive contained
many who were opposed to their leaders.   The moderation of
the government came in for increased criticism both in the
legislature and outside.   Secondly, seigniorial tenure had become
an anachronism as the alienation fines were a heavy burden
with land a commercial commodity.   La Fontaine felt that he
could not handle the matter, and this lent further weakness to
the party in power.   A new political alinement, slow but sure,
was also going on in the province.   The liberal party in Canada

¹ Elgin to Grey, March 23, 1850, Kennedy, *op. cit.*, pp. 583 ff.
² Elgin to Cumming Bruce, September 1852, *ibid.*, pp. 589 ff.

West was breaking into moderate reformers and radicals or ' clear grits '. When George Brown finally brought his fiery personality to the service of the latter and linked up extreme anti-papal views with extreme reform it was clear that party changes lay near at hand. In Canada East a similar but less-pronounced cleavage was visible. A ' rouge ' group arose, who were virtually republicans. Never numerically strong, they possessed fine debating powers and often brilliant gifts, which, however, failed to move the French-Canadians, whose liberalism, now that their place in the sun had been secured, took on its natural conservative colour. Finally La Fontaine and Baldwin felt that their work had been accomplished, and in October 1851 ' the great administration ' closed. Hincks and Morin reconstructed the ministry with two ' clear grits ', Malcolm Cameron and John Rolph. Like most similar movements, the scheme failed in its object. The ' clear grits ' refused to rally to the support of the government. The government was sustained in the elections at the close of the year and by practical legislation they staved off defeat. A ' Canadian Reform Bill ' was passed which increased the representation of each division of the province to sixty-five and made provision for a redistribution of constituencies. An address was carried praying for freedom to reconstruct the legislative council on an elective basis, which was finally embodied in an imperial Act.[1] The legislative council, however, rejected a bill on seigniorial tenure.

There were soon signs of disintegration. Hincks became involved in financial transactions which brought public discredit to the ministry, and he was no more prepared to deal with the clergy reserves than his predecessors, although he had reformed the cabinet with that as an issue. The fall of Lord John Russell and the advent of the Derby ministry provided an excuse for delay. When the Aberdeen ministry promised enabling legislation he was as little ready as before. A sudden

[1] Kennedy, *op. cit.*, pp. 592 ff. (17 & 18 Victoria, c. 118).

appeal to the country in June 1854 did not strengthen his hands. The ' clear grits ' and the tories combined and the government resigned in September. Parties, however, were not reconstructed on any logical basis. The extreme liberals hoped that radicals from both Canada East and Canada West would coalesce and by drawing moderate reformers command political power. A new hand was at the helm in the person of John A. Macdonald. The tories and moderate men of Canada West joined against the radicals, and it was not difficult to effect an alliance with the French-Canadian ministerialists. Thus there came into being, in the MacNab-Morin ministry of September 1854, the liberal-conservative party of Canadian history. In the following January the ministry was reconstructed. Morin was elevated to the bench and his place taken by E. P. Taché. In 1856 the reformers of Canada West grew tired of MacNab. Macdonald was behind the revolt, and in May 1856 the Taché-Macdonald ministry was formed. In the following year Taché retired and power passed into the hands of Macdonald and Cartier, both of whom had now become dominant figures. Liberal-conservatism was strong in its leaders and in the borrowed programme of reform. The opposition had for the moment no vital planks in its platform and extensive legislative achievement gave the ministry power. The clergy reserves and the seigniorial tenure were finally settled. The legislative council was made elective. The reciprocity treaty was ratified. The establishment of a militia system bore witness to a growing consciousness of self-governing capacity. On the other hand, the settlement of outstanding questions robbed party politics of definite dividing lines. The problem which now faced the Canadas was that of making responsible government efficient and workable. When the big accomplishments were over, difficulties loomed up which became potent forces for change, and combining with other issues over which Canada had no control postulated a newer and wider development.

While Elgin was carrying out reform in the Canadas advances were taking place in the Maritime Provinces. In Nova Scotia Lord Falkland took office on Sir Colin Campbell's removal, and hopes were entertained that Howe would succeed in getting his principles accepted under a lieutenant-governor who was not only a whig, but was sent to take the place of a man whose resignation had been virtually forced on the imperial cabinet. Falkland, however, did not prove the promised deliverer. He had nothing to offer but a weak imitation of the Sydenham-Metcalfe policy. Howe had accepted a place in the executive council, but his presence there only emphasized the fact that a ' ministry of all the talents ' were hopelessly divided. A general election failed to decide whether tories or reformers should govern. The election resulted in an almost even balancing of parties, and the representatives of neither resigned from the executive. The appointment of a pronounced anti-reformer to the council forced Howe's hand and he resigned with his colleagues. The contest practically resolved itself into a personal one between Falkland and ' the tribune of Nova Scotia '. Howe brought to it an unrivalled satiric pen and a tongue which knew how to combine effectively political arguments with rugged native humour. He had behind him the general support of the people, who watched with interested enthusiasm the progress of a struggle which drove Falkland from office in 1846. To his successor, Sir John Harvey, Grey laid down those principles of colonial government to which reference has already been made. At first he tried to arrange a coalition ministry, but the liberals refused to take office. He then forwarded to Grey memoranda prepared by the council in which a request was made for further light on methods of administration and a defence was set up of Metcalfe's system.[1] Grey amplified in his reply his general adherence to the principle of responsible government. He

[1] Harvey to Grey, February 2, 1847, *Parliamentary Papers*, H. C. 621 (1848), p. 15.

emphasized the necessity for the executive government possessing the support of the house of assembly, and he drew a distinction between public offices similar to that existing in the United Kingdom. He advised that those of attorney-general, solicitor-general, provincial secretary, and possibly two others should be political, but that others should be governed by the British rules of permanent tenure.[1] When the dispatch was laid before the legislature, the assembly which had been elected in August 1847 defeated the ministry, which resigned with the exception of the provincial secretary. The opposition, relying on Grey's enumeration, refused to take office and the secretary was finally removed by the exercise of the prerogative of the crown. The reform ministry were not prepared to allow the provincial treasurer to hold his appointment, and insisted on his removal without compensation to make room for a division of his duties under a receiver-general and a financial secretary. Sir John Harvey attempted in an unofficial way to induce the ministry to reconsider their proposals. When he failed, he gave the executive his full support and Grey defended him against an attack in the house of commons.[2] The coming of responsible government in Nova Scotia thus coincided with its advent in the Canadas. The struggle had not been so bitter, and there were no tragic regrets, no fatal extremes. In his most impetuous moments Howe never deviated from constitutional methods. It is impossible to find in the records of the Nova Scotian reformers a disloyal expression or a separatist innuendo, although they had their share of opprobrious epithets from their tory and official opponents. When Elgin was passing through dark waters because he was brave enough to be consistent, and when disgruntled toryism was joining hands in the Canadas with revolutionary extremists, Howe lent the weight of his brilliant pen to the cause which he had so ably served.

---

[1] Grey to Harvey, March 31, 1847, Kennedy, *op. cit.* pp. 573 ff.
[2] *Parliamentary Papers*, H. C. 621 (1848), pp. 33 ff.

Liberal though he was, he possessed that great asset of constructive moderation, backed by a grasp of political thought, to which no colonial statesman has made more important contributions.

In New Brunswick reform did not move public opinion as quickly as elsewhere. During the régime of Sir John Harvey, Russell's dispatch [1] on the tenure of offices was accepted as the virtual concession of responsible government. When Russell laid down that the holders of the chief administrative offices should be removed whenever any ' sufficient motive of public policy demanded it ', Harvey saw that opposition to these in the assembly would afford sufficient guarantee that the conditions had been fulfilled. The elections of 1842 saw the defeat of the liberal party. It took a flagrant act of favouritism to educate the electorate. Harvey's successor, Sir William Colebrooke, evidently thought that he had the power, apart from local advice, to appoint any one whom he liked to office. Acting on principles similar to those enunciated by Metcalfe in Canada he proceeded in 1845 to fill the vacant office of provincial secretary, and worse still he gave the appointment to his own son-in-law. This was more than even a conservative executive could stand, and those who had opposed responsible government in 1842 now resigned as a protest against the lieutenant-governor's action. The colonial office refused to sanction the appointment, but the episode served to break up the typical ministry and to arouse interest in the general issue. The reform leaders who had temporarily followed the Sydenham scheme informed Colebrooke that they also must oppose his methods, which were too violent. The conservatives maintained that he had no right to appoint some one entirely unknown to the country ; the liberals, that he had no right to appoint any one, known or unknown. The reformers won the elections of 1848, and when the dispatches on responsible government were laid

[1] See above, p. 196.

on the table the assembly formally approved by resolution of the principle.[1]

In Prince Edward Island the demand for responsible government arose out of a quarrel between the lieutenant-governor, Sir H. V. Huntley, and the speaker of the assembly over a proposal to increase the former's salary. From this episode public opinion rallied to the idea that the assembly should control all local expenditure. The opinion was also gaining ground that a responsible executive might prove capable of settling the peculiar land problems of the colony. In 1847 an address was forwarded from the assembly to the imperial cabinet, asking that an executive of four chosen from the popular party should constitute a responsible government.[2] The colonial office replied that the colony was in a position to pay official salaries, excluding that of the lieutenant-governor, but that the small and scattered population was against the complete system of government asked for in the address. The assembly replied expressing its willingness to assume the financial burden if responsible government were granted, all the revenues and crown lands surrendered, and all claims to quit-rents abandoned. The colonial secretary conceded every request except the first. An election resulted in the strengthening of the reformers and a vote of want of confidence was carried on the motion of George Coles, the reform leader. To bring the matter to a head the assembly refused to vote supplies and was prorogued by the lieutenant-governor, Sir Donald Campbell, who censured them for their ' premeditated neglect of their legislative functions '. When they reassembled in 1851, Sir Alexander Bannerman laid before them a dispatch in which he was instructed to concede the full demands of the reformers. Thus within the same decade of the nineteenth century the representative institutions of British North America were made ready for further constitutional development by the grant of responsible government.

[1] *Parliamentary Papers*, H. C. 621 (1848), p. 40.
[2] *Ibid.* (1847), 566.

[AUTHORITIES.—The documents are in the *Elgin-Grey Correspondence* (Canadian Archives) ; Egerton and Grant, *Canadian Constitutional Development* (Toronto, 1907) ; Kennedy, *Documents of the Canadian Constitution, 1759–1915* (Oxford, 1918) ; T. Walrond, *Letters and Journals of James, Eighth Earl of Elgin* (London, 1872) ; *State Papers*, G., vols. 126–47, 281–5, 461–2 ; J. H. Chisholm, *The Speeches and Public Letters of Joseph Howe* (2 vols., Halifax, 1909). Of biographies, the most useful are J. W. Longley, *Joseph Howe* (Toronto, 1904) ; G. M. Grant, *Joseph Howe* (Toronto, 1904) ; J. Hannay, *Wilmot and Tilley* (Toronto, 1907) ; J. G. Bourinot, *Lord Elgin* (Toronto, 1903) ; G. M. Wrong, *The Earl of Elgin* (London, 1905). Joseph Pope, *Sir John Macdonald* (2 vols., Ottawa, 1894), and O. D. Skelton, *The Life and Times of Sir A. T. Galt* (Toronto, 1920), contain much valuable material. Lord Grey, *The Colonial Policy of Lord John Russell's Administration* (2 vols., London, 1852), is important for imperial policy. F. Hincks, *The Political History of Canada between 1840 and 1855* (Montreal, 1877), is essential. J. L. Morison, *British Supremacy and Canadian Self-government, 1839–54* (Glasgow, 1919), contains the only adequate study of the Elgin-Grey correspondence (cf. the same author, 'Lord Elgin in Canada', *Scottish Historical Review*, October 1912, pp. 1 ff.). For the clergy reserves question, H. E. Egerton, *Selected Speeches of Sir William Molesworth* (London, 1903), and C. Lindsey, *The History and Present Position of the Clergy Reserves* (Toronto, 1851), should be consulted.]

CHAPTER XVII

THE FAILURE OF RESPONSIBLE GOVERNMENT IN THE CANADAS

RESPONSIBLE government settled some problems and inevitably created others. Political energy was diverted from constitutional discussions which had broken up the life of the province for generations, and almost every group recognized that for good or ill the principle of government had passed for ever out of the realms of debate. The great step had been taken, and there was no possibility of retracing it without irretrievable or tragic disaster. As a consequence the old tory party could not in future hope to rally the province to their support as the sole guardians of loyalty and the unique repositories for privilege and patronage. Nor could they hope that their influence would continue to resolve in their favour any doubts which might arise at the colonial office. With the close of Lord Elgin's administration the governor-general passes more and more into the position which Baldwin and Elgin saw must be his under the new system. The nearest approach to independence was in 1858, when Sir Edmund Head would not grant George Brown's request for a dissolution, and in 1862, when Lord Monck passed over the more influential M. H. Foley and sent for John Sandfield Macdonald to form a ministry. Head's action was interpreted as a party trick engineered by John A. Macdonald; but he acted in a strictly constitutional way, nor yet did he lower the dignity of his office. Monck's action was also constitutional, and was inspired by motives which are beyond dispute. In the actual administration the change was soon apparent. The executive council had become a cabinet and the conventions of cabinet government were early brought into play. The governor's presence at meetings became as anomalous as the king's in

England. The royal instructions made his presence normally necessary and cast doubts on executive acts carried out in council when he was absent. In 1858 the law officers of the crown could offer no concessions other than that during the physical incapacity of the governor ' measures might be taken by the council with his subsequent concurrence '.[1] Head outlined the custom which was growing up in Canada. He supported it by stating that the Canadian law officers did not think that his attendance was necessary to give legal effect to executive actions, and he added the expression of a personal belief that with the grant of responsible government it was ' most inexpedient as a general rule that the governor should be present during the discussion in council of particular measures. He is at liberty at all times to go into council and discuss any measures which he or the council thinks require it, but his presence as a regular and indispensable rule would check all freedom of debate and embarrass himself as well as his advisers '.[2] Responsible government meant that active leadership would pass from British to Canadian hands. The prime minister of Canada became the important figure, and the governor-general gradually assumed a place analogous to that of the monarch in Great Britain. The dispatches to the colonial office took on a formal and business-like monotony compared with those before 1854. The constitutional powers of the governor-general gradually declined and his real influence became moral and personal.

Indeed, during this period there is early evidence of what was recognized during the Great War as a new and distinct triumph for dominion autonomy. Canadian ministers went on frequent missions to London and discussed Canadian affairs directly, and not through the governor, with the imperial government. The equality of empire cabinets was already on the horizon of constitutional progress. Perhaps the most illuminative

---

[1] Labouchere to Head, January 25, 1858.
[2] Head to Labouchere, March 4, 1858.

utterances on the dissolution of the older relationship between
the crown and the province were uttered by George Brown during
the crisis over the choice of a provincial capital, to which as
many cities and towns laid claim as sought the honour of being
considered Homer's birthplace. The weakness of party government resulted in the leaving of the decision to the queen. In
reality this meant that Sir Edmund Head would be consulted.
To oppose her supposed choice was branded as disloyalty.
Brown repudiated the charge, and with a clear grasp of the
position now fully conceded declared, 'Do you think her
majesty cares a straw where the seat of government of Canada
is fixed ? People prate about our insulting the crown because
we speak out what nine-tenths of the whole people think ; but
do you ever hear from such people anything about insulting
the people ? If ever an insult was given to a people, it was
when the legislature and government of Canada declared that
the Canadian people were unable to settle for themselves where
their seat of government ought to be, and that they must go
to a colonial minister three thousand miles off, who never had
his foot on Canadian soil, to settle it for them under back-
stairs advice. I voted against that reference ; I used every
influence to prevent so ungracious a task being thrown on the
imperial government ; I urged that they should not act upon
the reference. . . . The first thing in my consideration was the
interests of the whole people of Canada and not servility to
Mr. Labouchere or any other colonial minister. I yield to no
man for a single moment in loyalty to the crown of England
and in humble respect and admiration of her majesty. But
what has this purely Canadian question to do with loyalty ? It
is a most dangerous and ungracious thing to couple the name
of her majesty with an affair so entirely local and one as to
which the sectional feelings of the people are so excited.'[1]

[1] Alexander Mackenzie, *The Life and Speeches of the Hon. George Brown*,
p. 272 (Toronto, 1882).

Responsible government created problems. No effort had been made to settle its contents. It was fortunate that this was so. An attempt to classify imperial and colonial concerns would only have proved a source of friction, and, worse still, would have tended to curtail elasticity, to narrow readjustments by rigidity, and to rule out the reasonableness of give and take through which advance and development come. In relation to tariff and defence it is possible to see two issues. Firstly, provincial self-consciousness began to claim a wider sphere for responsible government and the challenge shaded off into a further challenge to the formal ties of empire. For a considerable time Canada accepted the position that the imperial government should regulate the tariffs of the empire. A fine distinction had been attempted between seaborne commerce and inland commerce with the United States; but, broadly speaking, the imperial regulation of foreign trade was recognized, and Hincks in 1849 had laid it down that the imperial connexion would have no meaning if Great Britain were shut out of the colony's markets. Parallel with the growth in government there developed colonial business instincts and self-confidence. The business men looked for economic expansion through a protective tariff, and the Canadian government were not unwilling to help them as the province was badly in need of increased revenue. In 1859 Alexander Galt, the finance minister, increased the duties on manufactured articles, and thus incidentally affected certain British concerns. Those of Sheffield appealed to the Duke of Newcastle, the secretary of state for the colonies. Their language was hardly tactful : ' It cannot be regarded as less than indecent and a reproach, that while for fifteen years the government, the greatest statesmen, and the press of this country have been not only advocating but practising the principles of free trade, the government of one of her most important colonies should have been advocating monopoly and protection. . . . We conceive that her majesty's

T

government has a right to demand that what revenue is needed shall be raised in some other way than that which is opposed to the acknowledged commercial policy of the imperial government and destructive of the interests of those manufacturing towns of Great Britain which trade with Canada.' Newcastle was hardly less tactless. In forwarding the memorial to Head and expressing his opinion that ' probably ' he would advise that the royal assent be given to the authenticated act of the legislature, he digressed to discuss the dangers of protection, the virtues of free trade, and to lecture the provincial government.[1]

Galt drew up a report which was forwarded, with the approval of the Canadian executive, to the colonial office. We are not here concerned with the economic aspects of Galt's reply, but the constitutional statement is of great importance. Galt pointed out his surprise that the representations of a provincial town in England should have had such weight as to produce what amounted to a censure on almost three millions of people. The deliberate acts of the Canadian legislature should not have been condemned merely in answer to a memorial ' professedly actuated by selfish motives '. Elementary courtesy demanded not only that the legislature should have been given an opportunity to explain its policy, but that such representations should not be allowed to produce such effects. Since the possibility of disallowance had arisen Galt felt it was ' the duty of the provincial government distinctly to state what they consider to be the position and rights of the Canadian legislature '. These he outlined in unambiguous terms : ' Respect to the imperial government must always dictate the desire to satisfy them that the policy of this country is neither hastily nor unwisely formed ; and that due regard is had to the interests of the mother country as well as of the province. But the government of Canada, acting for its legislature and people,

---

[1] *Parliamentary Papers*, H. C. 400 (1864), pp. 7 ff.

cannot, through those feelings of deference which they owe to the imperial authorities, in any manner waive or diminish the right of the people of Canada to decide for themselves both as to the mode and extent to which taxation shall be imposed. The provincial ministry are at all times ready to afford explanations in regard to the acts of the legislature to which they are party ; but, subject to their duty and allegiance to her majesty, their responsibility in all general questions of policy must be to the provincial parliament, by whose confidence they administer the affairs of the country ; and in the imposition of taxation it is so plainly necessary that the administration and the people should be in accord, that the former cannot admit responsibility or acquire approval beyond that of the local legislature. Self-government would be utterly annihilated if the views of the imperial government were to be preferred to those of the people of Canada. It is therefore the duty of the present government distinctly to affirm the right of the Canadian legislature to adjust the taxation of the people in the way they deem best, even if it should unfortunately happen to meet the disapproval of the imperial ministry. Her majesty cannot be advised to disallow such acts, unless her advisers are prepared to assume the administration of the affairs of the colony irrespective of the views of its inhabitants. The imperial government are not responsible for the debts and engagements of Canada. They do not maintain its judicial, educational, or civil service. They contribute nothing to the internal government of the country, and the provincial legislature acting through a ministry directly responsible to it has to make provision for all these wants. They must necessarily claim and exercise the widest latitude as to the nature and extent of the burdens to be placed upon the industry of the people. The provincial government believes that his grace must share their own convictions on this important subject ; but, as serious evil would have resulted had his grace taken a different course, it is wiser to prevent future complication by distinctly stating the position that must be maintained by every Canadian administration.'[1]

John A. Macdonald defended the position taken up by the Canadian executive. He could not surrender the right of self-taxation as the Canadian people desired. ' The ministers of Canada dependent on her people ' would have failed in their duty had they not protested against an interference, explicit or implied, by the colonial office. Newcastle at least ' owned up ' that he was wrong.[2] Further correspondence took place on the economic issues, but Galt's memorandum closed the era of attempted control. From that time the legal and constitutional right has been conceded that Canada can regulate its economic policy without any fear of such remonstrances as those addressed by Newcastle to the Canadian government.

With trade autonomy conceded and with the outbreak of the American civil war, the question of Canadian defence came into prominence. The old idea that the imperial government should provide practical defence in return for trade advantages lost its logic with Galt's tariff, and there soon arose in England a demand against supporting British troops in Canada now that preference over other nations had disappeared. A gradual reduction began of imperial regiments in Canada, and the question of defence automatically forced itself on the Canadian government. A good deal was done, but in an inefficient manner, and the financial difficulties of 1859 produced further economy. With the antagonizing of the North in the Civil War and the apparent British sympathy with the South a storm gathered. The *Trent* affair increased the dangers. The newspapers of the United States indulged in an orgie of yellow journalism. If Canada were not immediately attacked, the northern army would annex it later in the hour of their triumph. Fortunately

[1] *Canada Sessional Papers* (1860), No. 38, pp. 4 ff. ; *Parliamentary Papers*, H. C. 400 (1864), pp. 11 ff. ; partially in Egerton and Grant, *op. cit.*, pp. 349 ff.

[2] Galt to John A. Macdonald, December 14, 1859, Pope, *Correspondence of Sir John Macdonald*, p. 7 (Oxford, 1921).

Lincoln and Lord Lyons, the British ambassador at Washington, kept their heads. There was just a danger, however, that the people on each side of the international line might sweep their governments off their feet in one of those outbursts of group emotionalism so characteristic of the North American continent. Preparations of some sort appeared necessary. The government prepared a militia bill after a commission had examined the difficulties of a peculiar and explosive situation. The house of assembly rejected the proposals and the government was defeated.

The motives for the rejection need not be discussed here. Monck was inclined to think that the measure was merely the occasion of an inevitable defeat and that the administration had already lost the confidence of the assembly.[1] In imperial relations, however, the history is of great interest. There broke out in England a panic of abuse at Canadian blindness and infatuation. The tired Northern armies would turn with joy to the rich provinces, and Great Britain could not bear the expenses of defence. Instead of rejecting the bill, Canada should have risen to a man and protested against its miserable and insufficient provisions. This attitude of mind was deeply resented in Canada. Sober criticism pointed out that if there was a war, the responsibility would lie at the door of British diplomacy, and that while Canada would bear her part of the burden, it could not be expected to assume the entire weight in a quarrel originating in a foreign policy in which Canada was a negligible quantity. The Canadian government embodied this defence in a careful and moderate memorandum.[2] The motives behind this do not concern the issue. The great point was that Canada in receiving responsible government had reached a place where Canadians, not British, were going to

[1] Monck to Newcastle, July 28, 1863.
[2] *Canada Sessional Papers* (1863), No. 15 ; cf. *Journals of the Legislative Assembly of Canada* (1865), pp. 9 ff.

decide the policy. The documents of the episode disclose no wilful plan to dislocate the defence of the empire. The public opinion of Great Britain was guilty of an interpretation due to ignorance and panic. All that had happened was that Canadians were untying another legal and formal knot in the bands of empire. Responsible government had brought the right to tax as the people liked, and it had brought the right to provide defence as the people liked. Canada resented the general outcry in the mother country because it seemed too much like an unofficial attempt to dictate a policy to the province. As a matter of fact, the ' militia crisis ' helped in another way. When the everyday pedestrian workings of responsible government are considered and their defects disclosed, constructive minds will be seen at work on the Canadian problem as a whole, and in it national defence became an important and cumulative force.

The distinction between self-government and responsible government should at this point be made perfectly clear. While self-government connoted the domestic control by Canada over its own affairs, responsible government implied a particular set of institutions through which the legislative power and executive authority were brought into relation to the will of the people. In the British constitutional development this meant cabinet and party government. The significance of the distinction lies in the fact that at this juncture in Canadian history the general advance in self-government was vitiated by a general stagnation in the process of responsible government. With the settlement of the larger questions, and with the formation of the liberal-conservative party, there was little place left for distinct platforms. The opposition offered by the ' clear grits ' and the ' rouges ' was such that it could not command a working support of the province. The former were too radical for their day, and the anti-papal views of Brown were such that the party could not hope to draw any aid from Lower Canada. The

' rouges ' were mistrusted throughout the country. Party government, then, degenerated in a recurrence of dissolutions and elections which settled nothing. There were, too, fundamental difficulties in the constitution, which loomed up with the disappearance of the more important issues. French Canada had been recognized by the Quebec Act and by the Constitutional Act as a distinct race group. The hoped-for blending of the two peoples had never taken place. The events of 1837–8, the Durham Report, the Sydenham experiment, the reaction against Bagot's system, the recognition of a dual ministry under La Fontaine and Baldwin, all combined to emphasize the fact that two distinct races were living together in one province and that each was prepared to guard its privileges. Bagot and Elgin tried to divert the race consciousness of the French-Canadians into political channels, but both were forced to recognize political groupings based on nationality, and every ministry from 1849 on was constructed on the foundations of representation from Canada East and from Canada West, with practically a prime minister from each division. As a consequence there grew up a kind of unwritten convention that a government should have a majority in east and west. At times the cabinet resigned if defeated in one division, at times it clung to office. In addition, Canada West was becoming a difficult bed-fellow. The older race hatred was dying out and Brown's extreme religious propaganda only harmed himself; but he voiced a perfectly valid constitutional objection to the Act of Union when he pointed out that the identical representation of each division of the province was unjust to Canada West, which had now passed Canada East in population. His statement of the case was often fierce and tactless, but ' representation by population ' was bound to gain supporters from its obvious logic and justice. On the other hand, Canada East now looked on the once hated Act of Union in the light of a treaty, a charter, a fundamental document. The fact that the attack on the Act came from Brown only served to consolidate the French-Canadians and to bring once more to the front those irritating features of racialism which are so disintegrating when challenged. Political parties practically became divided on sectional lines. A fortuitous combination of irreconcilable groups could defeat a ministry, which often returned to power, leaving the matter on which it was originally defeated an open question.

The situation might be summed up as fundamentally and incidentally impossible. First, an attempt was made to govern by a unitary system two distinct communities. A common legislature was called on not merely to act in matters where some general public opinion might be expected, but in details suitable to different races. Secondly, this attempt was made under a constitution which was politically unjust to the increasing economic development and population of Canada West. Thirdly, the stability which race, religion, language, traditions, and customs gave to Canada East irritated its neighbour; and, fourthly, any attempts to change the constitution were incidental forces which intensified the fundamental difficulties. In other words, when the inherent defects in the machinery were pointed out, such opposition was raised as made the hope of change far off and problematical. It is not surprising, then, that with fundamental weaknesses, grave incidental differences, and no great political party issues, government was reduced to an absurdity. Within ten years ten ministries held office. In three years four ministries were defeated and two general elections had provided no working majorities. The issue reduced itself to the very simple question of how it would be possible to carry on the government of the country. To follow in detail the history of these years would throw little light on the deadlock and the break-down of party government, but it is necessary to consider the various expedients brought forward, for out of them the solution finally came.

At times hopes were turned to an irresponsible executive and a written constitution such as those of the United States. The civil war served to kill ideas round which there had been much political grouping. 'Representation by population' appeared as early as 1850, and it was originally part of the tory programme. The liberal-conservative combination naturally succeeded in handing over the plank to the radicals, who divided the legislature on it year after year with increasing support from Canada West. John A. Macdonald opposed it on conservative and party principles, but the final decision lay with French Canada, and Cartier never deviated an iota from the letter of the Act. Brown's position, roughly stated, was that Canada West was ruled by French-Canadian votes, and that that was unjust. The weakness of his solution lay in the fact that, had representation by population been conceded, Canada East would have been ruled by Canada West. The vicious principle recurred—two peoples in a unitary system. John Sandfield Macdonald attempted to solve the problem by a definite adherence to the 'double majority' principle, which aimed at a working plan that no legislation should be passed affecting one division of the province which was not supported by a majority of members from that division. The idea was to develop further the bastard federal union, to which the ministries since 1841 bore actual witness. With different representation in the cabinet, hyphenated premiership, separate legal systems, and annual legislation applying only to one division, it seemed reasonable to J. S. Macdonald that the 'double majority' should be recognized and tried. Once in his career John A. Macdonald proposed that formal but extra-constitutional recognition should be given to the principle; but there was enough common sense left to prevent this motion being carried. The impossibility of dividing local issues and of the attempt to apply a federal method under a unitary system saved Canada from another ghastly experiment. J. S. Macdonald, however, formed a ministry ostensibly to make the attempt, and there is a certain grim humour in the circumstances which convinced this rather dour politician of his folly. His ministry only carried its separate school bill for Canada West by the votes of Canada East.

Tinkering with the constitution produced no results. When the steadier heads began to look objectively at the political situation, they saw that there were two sets of problems—those of a local and those of a general nature; that there were two races, French and British. No conceivable adjustment of the existing machinery would satisfy the conditions. Across the international line, a constitution was being tested which at any rate professed to be based on a formula suitable to Canadian conditions. The idea of federation came once more to the front. The growth and fruition of that idea at last brought political healing.

[AUTHORITIES.—The standard biographies are practically sources—Joseph Pope, *Memoirs of the Right Honourable Sir John A. Macdonald* (2 vols., Ottawa, 1894); John Boyd, *Sir George Étienne Cartier* (Toronto, 1914); Alexander Mackenzie, *The Life and Speeches of the Hon. George Brown* (Toronto, 1882); O. D. Skelton, *The Life and Times of Sir Alexander Tilloch Galt* (Oxford, 1920). The pamphlet literature is full of contemporary criticism : Dunbar Ross, *The Seat of Government of Canada . . . also the Composition and Functions of the Legislative Council and the ' Double Majority ' Question* (Quebec, 1856); Joseph Cauchon (?), *Étude sur l'Union projetée des Provinces Britanniques de l'Amérique du Nord* (Quebec, 1858); Isaac Buchanan, *Letters illustrative of the Present Position of Politics in Canada* (Hamilton, 1859); A. T. Galt, *Canada 1849 to 1859* (Quebec, 2nd ed., 1860), are four of the most important. *The Mirror of Parliament*, the *Journals of the Legislative Assembly of Canada*, and the files of the Toronto *Globe* are essentials. J. C. Dent, *The Last Forty Years, Canada since the Union of 1841*, vol. ii (Toronto, n. d.), contains a good outline.]

CHAPTER XVIII

THE GROWTH OF THE FEDERATION IDEA

THE history of Canada contains many well-known suggestions for some form of union among the British North American colonies, but the co-operating circumstances which would have given them reality never took place, and they passed into the realms of unrealized and premature hopes. Deadlock and the failure of party government brought once more to the front the possibility of federation. It would be a mistake, however, to assign the final accomplishment to them alone, as Goldwin Smith has done. We have already seen forces working and conditions existing which made it impossible for the Canadas to live together under a legislative union. These made cabinet government exceedingly difficult, but they would inevitably have nullified any kind of free government. In a single state such as the Canadas it would have remained impossible so to balance the fundamental centripetal and centrifugal forces as to produce a reasonably effective administration. The break-down of the machinery was merely the occasion which turned men's minds to the basic problems and made them realize the inherent sources of failure. In groping after stability and expansion many obstacles loomed up. Communications were primitive. The people of the Canadas knew little of one another and much less of the Maritime Provinces. There were social backgrounds peculiar to the different colonies round which local sentiment had gathered. There were institutions and laws, customs and traditions, to which each province had become attached. In addition, neither Great Britain nor British North America had decided what path colonial empire was to travel. A few statesmen had glimpses of a greater empire more solidly

united than ever before ; but the vast majority seemed to have
lost faith and were prepared for dissolution. For many years
there can only be heard a few voices crying in the political
wilderness.   These utterances were generally received as
academic and impracticable, and they rallied no forces to
a movement.   Even when J. W. Johnstone and Joseph Howe
of Nova Scotia presented suggestions for federation to the
imperial government there was little inclination to work out
a scheme which was generally considered theoretical and at the
best visionary. The greatest enthusiast would thus have found
himself face to face with geographical, economic, and social
obstacles, and, worse still, with political indifference. This last
was the most serious, for it implied lack of faith and of all those
intangible conditions which make for progress. It is remarkable
that out of the stagnation in the Canadas should arise a prophet
who, before federation seemed within the bounds of possibility,
gave to British North American politics a Pisgah view of the
promised land.

In the session of 1858 the various suggestions which were
outlined at the conclusion of the last chapter were aired and
discussed.   Alexander Tilloch Galt brought forward resolutions of far-reaching import.   The ' irreconcilable difficulties '
demanded a federal union of Canada East and Canada West,
which should be widened and strengthened by the inclusion of
the North-western and Hudson's Bay territories and the Maritime Provinces. Such a union would be ' calculated to promote
their several and united interests by preserving to each province
the uncontrolled management of its peculiar institutions and
of those internal affairs respecting which differences of opinion
might arise with other members of the confederation, while it
will increase that identity of feeling which pervades the possessions of the British crown in North America ; and by the
adoption of a uniform policy for the development of the vast
and varied resources of these immense territories will greatly

add to their national power and consideration '.[1] Galt emphasized his plan as the real solution for Canadian difficulties. But
he widened the outlook by pointing out the inspiration which
his suggestion would afford to ' national strength and national
prestige '.   Galt, too, borrowed shafts from George Brown's
quiver.   Brown had become the enthusiastic preacher of the
annexation of the North-west lands.   Galt declared that
Canada ' should assume the responsibility of occupying that
great empire . . . such a thing had never occurred to any people
as to have the offer of half a continent . . . the door should be
opened to the young men of Canada to go into that country,
otherwise the Americans would go there first . . . half a continent
is ours if we do not keep on quarrelling about petty matters
and lose sight of what interests us most '.   The debates disclose
pathetic narrowness.   None of the prominent leaders, not even
Brown, spoke during this discussion.   Some thought the proposals interesting.   Some desired federation as a step to independence, some opposed it on the same grounds.   The lack of
transportation was a barrier which might be surmounted, but
that lay years ahead.   Ignorance of the other colonies and lack
of trade with them seemed to negative a larger union, and
if it were accomplished Canadian money would only go to
develop local works in the eastern provinces.   The colonies
needed no defence other than that provided by Great Britain.
Possibly a federal union of the Canadas might be engineered.
One member alone supported Galt whole-heartedly in his larger
conception.   The defeat of the ministry on questions arising in
connexion with the capital prevented the resolutions from being
put to the vote, but it is hardly possible to think that they
would have been accepted.   The short-lived Brown-Dorion
ministry accomplished one thing.   The governor-general decided
to pass over the well-known leaders and to ask Galt to form
a cabinet.   A combination of circumstances convinced Galt

[1] O. D. Skelton, *op. cit.*, pp. 219 ff.

that he could hardly hope to succeed, and he advised Sir Edmund Head to send for Cartier, and Galt entered the new government on condition that federation as he had outlined it should be made a government measure. It is doubtful how far Cartier and Macdonald were prepared to go. They saw, however, a way out of the problem created by the dispute over the capital. That issue could be shelved pending a consideration of a federal union, which was accordingly promised in the ministerial programme. If nothing else happened, the process of education was carried a stage farther. It was a singular triumph to have linked up the French-Canadian leader with the wider project. An immediate result followed. Cartier accompanied Galt and John Ross, the president of the council, on a mission to England.

On their arrival they presented a memorial, drawn up by Galt, to Sir Edward Bulwer Lytton, secretary of state for the colonies in Derby's conservative government.[1] Federation was urged not only as a cure for the distresses in Canada, but as a great constructive scheme. The Canadian ministers professed to feel that the time had arrived for a general constitutional discussion. The British North American colonies were like isolated and weak foreign states, a condition which was ' considered to be neither promotive of the physical prosperity of all, nor of that moral union which ought to be preserved in the presence of the powerful confederation of the United States '. The imperial government was requested to authorize a meeting of delegates from all the colonies and from the two divisions of Canada to consider a federal union and to discuss the principles on which it could be based. The memorialists firmly believed that the larger synthesis would create a great and strong country ' valuable in time of peace, and powerful in the event of war—for ever removing the fear that these colonies may ultimately serve to swell the power of another nation '. The memorial was covered with a confidential letter which outlined

[1] O. D. Skelton, *op. cit.*, pp. 239 ff.

the framework of government.[1] The federal government was to consist of a governor-general, a senate elected on a territorial basis of representation, and an assembly elected on the basis of population, with a responsible executive. It should have control over customs, excise, and trade, the postal services, the militia, banking, currency, weights and measures, national public works, public lands and debts, criminal justice, unincorporated and Indian territories. For the moment it was left undecided whether these enumerated subjects should exhaust the federal power, or whether it should be further widened by the inclusion of other matters not specifically entrusted to the provincial legislatures. Suggestions were made for a federal court of appeal, for the allocation of the revenue from public lands to the province in which they were situated, and for financial support to each province from federal sources. Emphasis was specially laid on the fact that the new constitution would not be derived from the people, but from an imperial Act, and that the local legislatures would be granted nothing of sovereign power. Defects could thus be easily remedied, the forces of disunion weakened, and the provinces bound to the federal authority. The whole scheme aimed at creating a stronger union than that of the United States with ' so much of the federation principle as would join all the benefits of local government and legislation upon questions of provincial interest '. This letter was drafted by Galt, and, taken with his resolutions of 1858, is a singular anticipation of the future.

Events in London seemed to point to success. The Canadian ministers lent support to a delegation from the Maritime Provinces who had come to urge a demand for imperial support to an intercolonial railway. Galt used the occasion to strengthen his constitutional proposals. He pointed out how clearly federation and transportation were bound together. Three million British subjects were isolated in the interior of America

1 *Ibid.*, pp. 242 ff.

during the winter. Cut off from Great Britain and from the eastern colonies, except through a jealous foreign country, they were forced to depend on supplies from the United States. If the latter repealed its bonding laws, the whole commerce of the province would be dislocated. Trade, not policy, was the only safeguard against such an eventuality. Galt did not promise that Canada would use the railway if shorter and cheaper routes were available ; but if war or political changes came, it would be an outlet and a security. Under any circumstances, it would assist federation ' to build up a nation worthy of England from her North American possessions '. The delegates got nothing more than courtesy. Financial assistance for the railway was definitely refused for the very good reason that there were more urgent claims at home.[1] The constitutional suggestions inspired no enthusiasm. Galt attempted to supply it by actually outlining a dispatch for Lytton to send to the governor-general. There was, however, too much indifference, if not actual hostility. Lytton avoided action through the lame excuse that Canada alone had made official overtures, and that it would be an act of discourtesy to propose a meeting of delegates until the other provinces had definitely assented to the federal principle. He forwarded dispatches to the other provinces outlining the actual state of the question. Nothing resulted from communications of such a cold and uninspiring nature.

Even in Canada the ministerial support weakened. With the larger scheme shelved, the cabinet bent its energies to get rid of the thorny problem of the provincial capital. The ratification of Ottawa as the seat of government gave them immense relief, and there was no consuming desire to open up difficult projects. Galt was forced to admit that they had little hope of success apart from strong support in the imperial cabinet. Although the Canadian ministry had adopted the idea as a ministerial measure, they did not feel called upon to resign. Brown saw

[1] Lytton to Head, December 24, 1858, *State Papers*, G. 158.

behind the failure a definite lack of ministerial interest and sincerity. Cartier, however, carried a motion in the executive council that a full account of the proceedings and copies of the dispatches should be sent to the other provinces.[1] Publicists gave the federation idea a wider public. J. C. Taché foretold the constitutional and economic strength of the future dominion;[2] Alexander Morris looked ahead to a new nation ' with free institutions, with high civilization and entire freedom of speech and thought, and with its face to the south and its back to the north, with its right and left resting on the Atlantic and the Pacific, and with the telegraph and the iron-road connecting the two oceans ' ;[3] while D'Arcy McGee began to see visions of a British-American nationality.[4]

The great reform convention held at Toronto in 1859 rejected the general scheme as too remote for present Canadian difficulties and adopted a proposal for a kind of federal government for Canada. This proposal was brought before the legislature in 1860, only to be defeated.[5] John A. Macdonald, however, gave an unequivocal support to a confederation of all the provinces. His mind was definitely fixed on a conception of the union which he never abandoned. The provinces were to be subordinate. He aimed to see ' a powerful central government, a powerful central legislature, and a powerful decentralized system of minor legislatures for local purposes '. His hope was framed in glowing words : ' We were standing on the very threshold of nations, and when admitted we should occupy no unimportant position among the nations of the world. Long might we remain connected with Great Britain. He hoped for ages, for ever,

---

[1] *Journals of the Legislative Council, Canada* (1858).

[2] J. C. Taché, *Des Provinces de l'Amérique du Nord et d'une Union fédérale* (Quebec, 1858).

[3] Alexander Morris, *The Hudson's Bay and Pacific Territories : a Lecture,* pp. 56 ff. (Montreal, 1859).

[4] D'Arcy McGee in the *British American Magazine,* August 1863, pp. 337 ff.

[5] *The Mirror of Parliament,* No. 41, pp. 2 ff. ; and cf. Alexander Mackenzie, *op. cit.,* pp. 71 ff.

Canada might remain united with the mother country. But we were fast ceasing to be a dependency, and assuming the position of an ally of Great Britain. England would be the centre, surrounded and sustained by an alliance, not only with Canada, but Australia and all her other possessions, and there would thus be formed an immense confederation of free men, the greatest confederacy of civilized and intelligent men that ever had an existence on the face of the globe.' Thomas D'Arcy McGee began at the same time to give to the federation idea in the legislature the support of his brilliant tongue and his warm imagination. He looked forward to a day ' when we should be known not as Upper or Lower Canadians, Nova Scotians, or New Brunswickians, but as members of a nation designated as the Six United Provinces '.[1]

Influences other than parliamentary and personal were at work. In both Canada and the United States there was taking place a change of opinion in respect to tariffs. Horace Greeley had aroused public opinion in favour of high protection. When war came this opinion gained strength owing to the absence from congress of free-traders from the Southern States. Indeed, the tariff of 1860 was passed when they had withdrawn on the eve of war. The civil war itself helped to confirm the changes, as the new expenditures demanded recourse to every available source of revenue. In Canada governments were looking for money to cover the improvident speed in public works, and the tax-payers had already begun to think of protection as a remedy for their financial ills. The fate of Elgin's reciprocity treaty was thus already in the balance some years before it actually expired after due notice from the United States. The interest, however, in connexion with federation lies in the fact that new markets might shortly be needed, and that Canadian financiers and economists began to link up economic with political unity and to think of the strength which would be afforded to material

[1] *Mirror of Parliament*, No. 38, p. 3.

development and to the powers of negotiation if the British North American colonies could present a common policy. This influence towards union may appear small, but John A. Macdonald noticed it as an important cumulative force.[1]

The civil war, however, provided a more subtle assistance to the political movement in the colonies. At first they shared with Great Britain a public opinion in favour of the North. This changed with almost lightning suddenness. British aristocratic and middle class sympathy turned to the South after the first failures of the Northern forces. The upper classes saw in the war a struggle between materialistic and arrogant democracy and refined conservatism. They welcomed the evidence that the latter could maintain traditional superiority in arms. Business men lost their heads in panic over the possibility of a cotton market curtailed by the victory of the high-tariff North. The government proclaimed a strict neutrality, but in doing so they appeared to recognize the Southern Confederacy as a belligerent nation. The majority of the newspapers grew Southern in their sympathies and patronizing in their comments. The anti-British sentiment, pent up since the revolutionary war, broke out with vehemence in the Northern States. Its most serious aspect was seen in the idea, to which Seward, Lincoln's secretary of state, lent weight, of promoting a war against a foreign state in the hope of nullifying the separatist tendencies of the South.[2] In Canada this was interpreted as a veiled threat, and public opinion turned against the North in sufficient strength to be remarkable. Some of the Northern papers were not slow to notice the change, putting it down to servile colonial imitation of the mother country, and holding out annexation as the just punishment. The *Trent* affair fell like a spark into this charged atmosphere. Palmerston and

---

[1] *Parliamentary Debates on the Subject of the Confederation of the British North American Provinces*, p. 32 (Quebec, 1865); Kennedy, *op. cit.*, p. 604.

[2] Lord Charnwood, *Abraham Lincoln*, p. 211 (New York, 1917).

Earl Russell prepared for war. Northern emotionalism was ready to take up the challenge. In the British colonies the dread shadow fell across peoples who had no part in the diplomacy out of which the crisis had arisen. They saw their provinces the theatre of tragic events, their lands invaded by hostile armies, their citizens called to service in an imperial issue. Resolution there was and plenty of it, but it struggled with the knowledge that there was little defence ready and that there was no political machinery available to give to the unconnected provinces the efficiency so necessary for actual warfare and the emotional and unifying solidarity which was a condition of possible success. It was well that Lincoln, Seward, Lord Lyons, and the queen were not swept off their feet by Palmerston's arrogance, Russell's impetuosity, and the jingoes of both countries. The crisis passed, but it left behind bitter memories. It brought home, however, to an increasing number of British Americans their isolation and weakness. In Canada there was not sufficient force in politics to rise superior to party, and the militia bill was defeated. That episode need not be considered a reflection of public opinion, as succeeding governments did their utmost to cut their defence coat according to the financial cloth. The remarkable thing is that the events did not lend enough weight to the federation movement to give it an irresistible impetus. Canada prepared to try once again to make the badly assembled political engine work. Defeats, elections, ministries, followed one another with as traditional consistency as though no foreign foe had recently thundered at the unguarded gate.

In the Maritime Provinces and in Great Britain federation gained ground. The former felt more than ever their geographical and political insecurity. Nova Scotia once again declared for a maritime or general union, and the colonial secretary informed the lieutenant-governor that the imperial government was prepared to give any proposals favourable consideration.

Galt, who was in England at the time, reviewed recent events in Canada. In his public utterances there he once more emphasized the beneficial results of colonial union and drove home his arguments from the war scare. He realized that the rejection of the militia bill had produced a strong sentiment in England in favour of separation; but he advocated federation as an immediate policy, which, whether separation came at once or in the future, would enable the colonies 'to stand alone and resist further aggression'. British public opinion had grown tired of an empire which was prepared to cut off the mother country from colonial markets, and apparently ready to refuse aid to imperial foreign policy against the mighty. This strong separatist sentiment welcomed federation as a preliminary necessity to enable the mother country to get rid of the colonies and at the same time to render them sufficiently secure from becoming the prey of the United States. To the small but constructive group who had formed a new conception of empire, federation appeared more than ever desirable as the first step towards creating a new state within the imperial ties. Thus, from two different angles, British opinion united to lend support to colonial union.

The result might only have ended in a federation of the Maritime Provinces had not the Canadian constitutional stage-coach become so deeply embedded in political ruts, now beyond all repair, that its further progress was out of the question. No single group could move the chariot; and if all had been willing to push, the road ahead was just as bad. At this moment George Brown, who had done not a little to make political travelling impossible, bent his energies to a constructive policy. In 1864 he moved for a select committee of the legislature to consider a federal union on the basis of Galt's memorandum of 1858.[1] Just as the Taché-Macdonald ministry were getting ready for the rut, the committee reported on June 14 that there

---

[1] See above, p. 284.

was sufficient unanimity to warrant them suggesting further consideration of the idea at the next session.[1]   John A. Macdonald voted against the report for reasons which are not now clear. His opposition made little difference, if it was inspired by political motives, as the ministry was defeated on the same evening as the report was presented. While the lobbies were busy with the crisis and members were preparing once more to go through the farce of an election, Brown suggested to some friends of the defeated cabinet that advantage should be taken of the situation to settle for ever the constitutional difficulties between Canada East and Canada West, and he assured them that he was prepared to ' co-operate with the existing or any other administration that would deal with the question promptly and firmly, with a view to its final settlement '. It was evident that the dawn might break, and John Henry Pope and Alexander Morris, with Brown's permission, communicated this conversation to John A. Macdonald and to Galt.

The situation was delicate. Macdonald and Brown had been bitter political opponents for years, and their private life had known nothing of personal intercourse. The past was carried into the present. They met ' standing in the centre of the assembly room ', so anxious was each to avoid the appearance of evil. Macdonald addressed his political and personal enemy and asked him if he had any objections to meet Galt and himself for a discussion. Brown replied laconically, ' Certainly not '. The Rubicon was crossed. On Friday, June 17, 1864, the three met at the St. Louis Hotel. Brown justified his course by the extreme urgency of the crisis and declared that only the hope of finally destroying the sectional differences could justify such a meeting. Macdonald and Galt accepted ' that footing ', and stated that they represented the cabinet in asking Brown to assume office with them. Brown felt that such a union would be ' highly objectionable ' and that ' the public mind would be

Alexander Mackenzie, *op. cit.* pp. 85 ff.

shocked '. Macdonald insisted on the necessity of Brown's presence in the ministry which proposed a federal union of all the British American colonies as the solution of the sectional difficulties. Brown momentarily rejected the remedy as it had not been sufficiently considered, and harped back to representation by population in the Canadas. Macdonald and Galt pointed out the impossibility of accepting such a proposal, as no government could hope to carry it, and suggested a compromise ' in the adoption either of the federal principle for all British North American provinces, as the larger question, or for Canada alone, with provisions for the admission of the Maritime Provinces and the North-western Territories '. Brown stood out for the lesser federation first, and the conference adjourned, but agreed to report progress to the legislature, as hopes were not wanting of an ultimate understanding.

Galt, however, was unwilling that matters should be left in such an unsettled state, and the same evening he saw Brown alone and arranged an interview for the following morning, at which Taché and Cartier should be present. Macdonald, Galt, Brown, and Cartier (Taché was out of town) met the next day, and the following memorandum was drawn up for submission to Brown's supporters after approval by the governor-general and cabinet, and after Brown had interviewed the governor-general in private : ' " The government are prepared to state that, immediately after the prorogation, they will address themselves, in the most earnest manner, to the negotiation for a confederation of all the British North American provinces. That, failing a successful issue to such negotiations, they are prepared to pledge themselves to legislation during the next session of parliament for the purpose of remedying existing difficulties by introducing the federal principle for Canada alone, coupled with such provisions as will permit the Maritime Provinces and the North-western Territory to be hereafter incorporated into the Canadian system. That for the purpose of carrying on the negotiations and settling the details of the promised legislation, a royal commission shall be issued, composed of three members of the government and three members of the opposition, of whom Mr. Brown shall be one ; and the government pledge themselves to give all the influence of the administration to secure to the said commission the means of advancing the great object in view. That, subject to the house permitting the government to carry through the public business, no dissolution of parliament shall take place, but the administration will again meet the present house." Shortly after 6 p.m. the parties met at the same place, when Mr. Brown stated that, without communicating the contents of the confidential paper entrusted to him, he had seen a sufficient number of his friends to warrant him in expressing the belief that the bulk of his friends would, as a compromise, accept a measure for the federative union of Canada, with provision for the future admission of the Maritime colonies and the North-west Territory. To this it was replied that the administration could not consent to waive the larger question ; but, after considerable discussion, an amendment to the original proposal was agreed to in the following terms, subject to the approval on Monday of the cabinet and of his excellency : " The government are prepared to pledge themselves to bring in a measure next session for the purpose of removing existing difficulties by introducing the federal principle into Canada, coupled with such provisions as will permit the Maritime Provinces and the North-west Territory to be incorporated into the same system of government. And the government will seek, by sending representatives to the lower provinces and to England, to secure the assent of those interests which are beyond the control of our own legislation to such a measure as may enable all British North America to be united under a general legislature based upon the federal principle." '

Difficulties next arose over the number of seats in the cabinet

which the administration were prepared to yield. Brown asked
for half, with the recent division in the assembly in his mind.
Macdonald and his friends said this was impossible, but promised
to consult their colleagues. Brown desired four offices for his
supporters and wished himself to remain out. Macdonald
promised to consult with him as to the conservative personnel
of the Cabinet. It was a hard-fought fight. There would be
only three liberals in a cabinet of twelve. Taché's work was
finished, and Macdonald would be the real prime minister. The
presidency of the council which Brown was offered was a place
of little influence or importance. The big public to whom the
Globe was only second to the bible lay outside ready to miscon-
strue, ready to condemn. Broken friendships lay ahead. The
radical party would look hopelessly to the future, feeling that they
had been betrayed. Brown made perhaps the greatest constructive decision in Canadian history, certainly in his career. He had
seen the vision. He turned his back on the past. With no
coward's bent head, but with forward look and with squared
shoulders, he went out from his Ur of the Chaldees with faith,
and knowing not whither he went.

[AUTHORITIES.—*State Papers*, [A], Series G. 292, 296, 298, 465 (Canadian
Archives); *Journals of the Legislative Council and Assembly of Canada*.
O. D. Skelton, *Life and Times of Sir A. T. Galt* (Oxford, 1920); J. Pope,
Memorials of the Right Honourable Sir John A. Macdonald, vol. i (Ottawa,
1894); Alexander Mackenzie, *The Life and Speeches of George Brown* (Toronto,
1882), contain much valuable material. The pamphlet literature of importance
includes J. Cauchon (?), *Étude sur l'Union projetée des Provinces Britanniques
de l'Amérique du Nord* (Quebec, 1858); Alexander Morris, *Nova Britannia : or
British North America, its Extent and Future* (Montreal, 1858); *The Hudson's
Bay and Pacific Territories* (Montreal, 1859); A. T. Galt, *Canada, 1849–59*
(Quebec, 1860); C. B. Adderley, *Letter to Rt. Hon. Benjamin Disraeli on the
Present Relations of England with the Colonies* (London, 1861); T. D. McGee,
'Plea for British American Nationality' (*The British American Magazine*,
August 1863). C. D. Allin, *The Genesis of the Confederation of Canada*
(Kingston, 1912), discusses the influence of the British American League in
the federation movement.]

CHAPTER XIX

THE COMING OF FEDERATION

MACDONALD and Brown came together none too soon. The Maritime Provinces had seen the wider colonial synthesis grow more hopeless as the Canadas continued to cling to party warfare. Nova Scotia was specially irritated by the apparent lack of constitutional purpose and of constructive energy in relation to transportation, and determined to urge a union among the Maritime Provinces, which, if worked out, would restore in some respects the original historical union which had existed before New Brunswick and Prince Edward Island had been erected into separate governments. Before Brown took the great step forward, Charles Tupper, relying on the dispatch from the colonial office to which reference has been made,[1] moved a resolution in the assembly of Nova Scotia for a legislative maritime union to be worked out by delegates sitting in conference at Charlottetown. Tupper did not abandon hope of a British North America, which he had frequently urged in public, but he felt that the smaller union which he now proposed might give occasion to Canada to waken up from its apparent apathy. At any rate, internal and external events within recent years pointed to the necessity for local consolidation. There had been no dangerous and arresting difficulties in government, but separation disclosed weaknesses in the negotiating of policies with the imperial cabinet and in meeting the innuendoes of American politicians. Personal reasons, wholly praiseworthy and constructive, entered into the proposals. Many began to look for a wider sphere of political activity than that afforded by a sparsely populated province. Tupper succeeded in con-

[1] See above, p. 292.

vincing Nova Scotia, New Brunswick, and Prince Edward Island of the necessity for action, and a conference was called to meet at Charlottetown on September 1, 1864. In Canada the event was considered propitious, and at the request of his cabinet Lord Monck entered into communication with the lieutenant-governors of the Maritime Provinces and asked if a Canadian delegation might join the conference and lay before it the plans on which the coalition ministry had been formed in Canada. Permission was only too gladly given, and in due course eight Canadian ministers, including Macdonald, Brown, Cartier, and Galt, joined the conference.

The details of what took place are apparently lost, if ever they were committed to writing. But it is possible to piece together enough of the history to give the Charlottetown conference its due place in the developments. The Maritime delegates were unwilling that their own scheme should be discussed first, lest such a discussion should prejudice wider plans. Accordingly the Canadians were asked to open the general debate. While professing to favour the union of the Maritime Provinces as a step in a greater union, they were not unwilling to disclose their ideas and the consultations which had taken place in their cabinet since its formation. Galt dealt with the financial aspects of a general union. Brown outlined the organization, scope, and work of a federal legislature. Macdonald sketched the general framework of government. It would thus seem that many vital questions were opened up. The delegates from the Maritime Provinces then proceeded to the separate consideration of the proposals to which their respective legislatures had agreed. It was at once apparent that the local union could not hope for immediate success. New Brunswick was doubtful. Prince Edward Island refused to surrender its local government. Nova Scotia alone was prepared to support whole-heartedly the plan out of which the conference had arisen. Federation seemed to satisfy the conditions. The desire for strength,

influence, and width would be satisfied with a central government, and local sentiment would not be outraged by the destruction of local institutions.   On adjourning to Halifax,
Macdonald was able to announce that the delegates were one in
believing that a general federal union could be formed.   Arrangements were made for delegates from all the colonies to assemble
at Quebec during the following month to consider, and if possible
to work out, a plan to the possibilities of which the Charlottetown conference had agreed.   There were, however, vague
indications of danger.   Joseph Howe was unable, owing to his
official duties as imperial commissioner for fisheries, to go to
Charlottetown.   He professed to give support to anything that
might be agreed on.[1]   When the Quebec conference had concluded its sittings he found on his return from Newfoundland
that the actual foundations had been laid without him.   His
influence in his native province was so great that his absence
from the negotiations might and did prove highly detrimental.
In addition, Arthur Hamilton Gordon, lieutenant-governor of
New Brunswick, and Sir Richard Graves MacDonnell, lieutenant-
governor of Nova Scotia, were not at all sympathetic.   From
these three sources future difficulties arose.

On October 10, 1864, there assembled at Quebec one of the
most epoch-making conferences in history.   It was an assembly
of almost all the greatest British North Americans in public
life—Taché, the aged French-Canadian premier ; Cartier, who
bore the olive branch of union to his countrymen ; Galt, whose
genius saved the proposal from wreck on the dangerous shoals of
financial difficulties; Macdonald and Brown, who had shed party
for the higher vision ; Tupper and Tilley and others of less note,
but of no less necessity at the moment.   The Quebec conference
saw the death with the autumn of 1864 of the visionless past,
and by its constructive work it took a place among the great

---

[1] See Tupper to Howe, August 16, 1864, and Howe to Tupper, August 16,
1864, J. W. Longley, *Joseph Howe*, pp. 176 ff. (Toronto, 1904).

ventures of political faith. It is impossible to reconstruct those pregnant days without emotion. Outside, the most ghastly civil war in history was desolating a kindred race, and Sherman was on the move, leaving destruction and ruin in his wake. Inside, broken little provinces had toiled for a long colonial night and caught apparently nothing. Sectionalism was a recent sore. Party politics then as now were unstable. Jealousies, but recently shed, might easily be reassumed. Suspicion, publicly cast out, lay watching in the secret recesses of every heart. Every step forward meant a backward look to see how others viewed it. Upper Canada and Lower Canada composed a kind of armed neutrality. The Maritime Provinces were on guard lest they should sell their birthright for a mess of Canadian pottage. Historical darkness lies almost impenetrable over the scene. No official record has survived. Only a few notes kept by Lieut.-Col. Hewitt Bernard, the executive secretary, and A. A. Macdonald, a delegate from Prince Edward Island, have come down to us. At times the issue was ambiguous, at times doubtful, at times hopeless. Men's hearts almost failed them because of fears. It is only possible to imagine the heated discussions, the clash of interests, the balancings of hope and despair, when behind closed doors strong men tried to crush down passion with the hands of creative faith. Joy came at length in the morning. In less than eighteen days seventy-two resolutions were agreed on, which practically became the British North America Act of 1867, and the Quebec conference gave not only a constitution to the colonies but an example and an inspiration to states yet unborn within the empire. Canadian unity may not have behind it as prelude the military achievements of ' the embattled farmers ' which gave to the world its first great federal system, nor the dramatic and brilliant faith which launched the union of South Africa. It has, however, a singular romance. There was, too, a stroke of genius in selecting Quebec as the place for the momentous conference. Where

Montcalm and Wolfe fell as foes, Frenchman and Anglo-Saxon achieved a greater and more subtle victory.

The available details need consideration. Taché, the Canadian prime minister, was elected chairman. Each division of the Canadas and each province had one vote. After a motion had been put to the vote, the representatives from any province could retire and discuss it among themselves privately. The conference allowed free discussion and sat as in committee of the whole. When resolutions had been passed in this committee, they were open to reconsideration and were carried as though the legislature were sitting with the speaker in the chair. Early in the proceedings J. A. Macdonald proposed and Tilley seconded a motion, which was carried unanimously, in which the principle of a federal union of British North America was accepted, provided it could be worked out ' on principles just to the several provinces '. Macdonald emphasized the difficulties in Canada, the isolation of all the colonies, and the general benefit resulting from union. He laid special stress on the necessity of avoiding the weaknesses which the civil war had disclosed in the constitution of the United States. There must be no reservation to the provinces of all powers not given to the federal government. A strong central government must be aimed at, to which all powers not specially conferred on the provinces should belong. The monarchical principle must be preserved and strengthened by an upper and lower house. In the former the federal plan would be preserved by giving provincial equality ' to three divisions—Upper Canada, Lower Canada, and the Maritime Provinces '. He expressed himself as open-minded on the method of appointing the senators, but for the moment he favoured nomination by the crown. Having committed the conference to general principles, it was possible to examine details.

The Canadian delegates were requested to prepare a series of resolutions based on the general expression of opinion at

Charlottetown. These were drawn up, and after introduction by Macdonald were debated *seriatim*. The problems need not be examined closely, but there are several outstanding discussions which require special treatment. Firstly, Macdonald never for a moment abandoned his consistent support of a strong central government. When one of the delegates from New Brunswick pointed out that the proposal to specify the powers of the local legislature tended to create a legislative union, Macdonald accepted the challenge and insisted that any imitation of the United States in this connexion would end in disaster. Macdonald's wishes prevailed. Not only were federal and provincial powers enumerated, with an undefined residuum of powers left to the former, but the federal government was given power to appoint and to dismiss for due cause the provincial lieutenant-governors, and to disallow provincial Acts. The conference gave the scheme a strongly centralized bias. Indeed Brown would have been willing to have had a kind of local municipal administration which could not deal with political matters, and a local executive modelled on the American plan. The conference was evidently in general favour of making the federal government as powerful as possible and of controlling the provinces through federal safeguards. We shall consider in another chapter how this has worked out, but for the present it is only necessary to record the outline of the federal and provincial constitutions.

The financial terms and the scheme of representation in the central legislature gave rise to graver problems. Prince Edward Island had agreed to representation by population at Charlottetown, but when it found that it would only be given five members, with the adoption of sixty-five as a fixed number for Canada East, the delegates from the Island strongly objected. They also thought the financial proposals inadequate, and their dissatisfaction anticipated the future. None of the other provinces objected to the suggested scheme of making Canada East the pivotal province for representation, but the financial issues were exceedingly difficult. The Maritime Provinces had no municipal organization by which taxation for local works could be raised. They carried on all kinds of public activities through revenue raised by the central executive alone. For a period it seemed that no *modus vivendi* could be arrived at. Finally a proposal was carried that ' the finance ministers of the several provinces should meet, discuss the matter among themselves, and see if they could not agree upon something '. As a result, a scheme of provincial subsidies was accepted, based on a fixed grant ' per head of the population as established by the census of 1861 '. The arrangement proved neither final as such, nor did it in the immediate issue resolve the doubts of the Maritime Provinces.

The organization of the senate was another issue almost equally destructive of agreement. There was the difficulty about the political complexion of the first senate. Brown feared that the liberals might not be given just treatment, and was only quieted when it was decided that the senators should be fairly representative of both parties. There does not seem to have been much division of opinion over the method of appointment. Macdonald and Brown were strongly against the elective principle. Brown's two liberal colleagues, Oliver Mowat and William McDougall, were in favour of it, but it was rejected by the conference without leaving any bitterness. There was a great deal of discussion over the division of membership. The Maritime Provinces were early considered a unit from this point of view, with Prince Edward Island dissenting, but they protested against making population the deciding factor in the number of members to be nominated. They pointed out that the only safeguard which the small provinces would possess was in the senate. Several divisions took place, and the final resolution was carried against the vote of Prince Edward Island.

When agreement on the seventy-two resolutions was finally

reached, proposals were carried that the provincial governments should submit them to their legislatures at the next session. They were to be considered as a whole, rejected or accepted as a basic agreement. On the other hand, there is no record that the delegates desired them to be looked on as a kind of fundamental document. They constituted rather a working treaty, and the object was to prevent the necessity of further conferences. There was no evidence then, nor has any since emerged, which would warrant the conclusion that the Quebec conference thought that it had drawn up a sacrosanct instrument of government. The point is perhaps small, but it has had not unimportant bearings on constitutional interpretation.

With the close of the conference the scene shifts to the provincial legislatures, whose concurrence was necessary, and to England, which must provide enabling legislation. Brown went almost immediately to London to report progress and to see how the land lay. He wrote that the scheme had given ' prodigious satisfaction '.[1] Lord Monck forwarded the resolutions to the colonial office, and a dispatch of December 3 congratulated the conference on its results and expressed great satisfaction with the scheme. Minor objections were raised. The imperial cabinet did not approve of vesting the power of pardon in the provincial lieutenant-governors. There was also a fear lest with a senate nominated for life and with fixed numbers, it might prove difficult to restore harmony between the houses in the event of some serious difference arising without some special provision in the constitution.

The Canadian parliament opened on January 19, 1865, and on February 3 Macdonald introduced the seventy-two resolutions. His speech on the occasion was one of the ablest that he ever delivered. In singularly dispassionate terms he traced the past history, weighing carefully the remote and immediate

---

[1] Brown to Macdonald, December 22, 1864, Pope, *Memoirs of Sir John A. Macdonald,* vol. i, pp. 273 ff. (Ottawa, 1894).

causes which lay behind the federation idea, and linking them
up with the imperial and foreign affairs which amplified and
accentuated it. He gave the interpretation of the federal
principle as he thought it applicable to British North America,
stated frankly his preference for a legislative union, and pointed
out how modifications had been accepted to make the central
government strong and far-reaching. The constitution of the
senate was defended as a following suitable to local conditions
of British institutions. According to Macdonald the senate
was intended to guard provincial rights. As for representation
in the commons, he explained that Quebec was made the pivotal
province because its population was most constant. The speech
was tactful in the extreme and Macdonald had evidently
weighed every word. Galt dealt with the financial proposals in
careful detail, and moved from point to point with confident assurance. It remained for Cartier and for Brown to
strike deeper notes. The former saw in the scene before him the
creation of a ' new nationality '. His mind went back over the
weak, broken provincial existence, and looked forward to a
state in which differences of race, language, and religion would
lose their disintegrating power before the sweep of a higher
conception. He saw the French-Canadianism of his own province, the Anglo-Saxonism of the other provinces, take on
a new colour—Canadianism. It is a remarkable fact that the
first glimpse of this inner consequence should have come from
a man who once had been in arms on a racial issue. Most
interesting, because most human, was Brown's more sober
enthusiasm. Perhaps his speech on this occasion discloses him
at his best. For the moment, lifted beyond the bitterness of
past years, with their harvest of venom, invective, and passion,
Brown turned to the French-Canadian members and said : ' The
scene presented by this chamber at this moment, I venture to
affirm, has few parallels in history. One hundred years have
passed away since these provinces became by conquest part

of the British empire.   I speak in no boastful spirit—I desire
not for a moment to excite a painful thought—what was then
the fortune of war of the brave French nation might have been
ours on that well-fought field.   I recall those olden times merely
to mark the fact that here sit to-day the descendants of the
victors and the vanquished in the fight of 1759, with all the
differences of language, religion, civil law, and social habit nearly
as distinctly marked as they were a century ago.   Here we sit
to-day seeking amicably to find a remedy for constitutional
evils and injustice complained of—by the vanquished ?   No,
sir, but complained of by the conquerors ! Here sit the representatives of the British population claiming justice—only justice ;
and here sit representatives of the French population discussing
in the French tongue whether we shall have it.   One hundred
years have passed away since the conquest of Quebec, but here
sit the children of the victor and the vanquished, all avowing
hearty attachment to the British crown—all earnestly deliberating how we shall best extend the blessings of British institutions,
how a great people may be established on this continent in
close and hearty connexion with Great Britain.'   It is interesting
to note that Brown's trust in federation as a link of empire ran
through the debates strongly, if not unanimously, and served
a purpose in educating British public opinion.

All, however, was not plain sailing.   The resolutions came in
for searching criticism by astute and capable minds.   Dorion,
Dunkin, Holton, and John Sandfield Macdonald were opponents
which any measure might fear.   Nor was all the criticism purely
political and purely futile.   Not a little was inspired by insight.
The financial terms, so bitterly attacked, soon proved unacceptable.   Dunkin's anticipation of difficulties in cabinet making
has cost many a Canadian premier sleepless nights.   Nor did
the ' ambiguities ' which he hunted up and down the resolutions
prove mere imaginings.   The courts have had more than their
share of Canadian constitutional cases.   Perhaps the most

serious point of attack lay in the challenge that a virtual treaty
had been made by those to whom no such commission had been
entrusted and that the terms of federation had not been submitted to the people. The point led to much discussion then and
since. The cabinet defended itself by stating that the matter
had been under discussion at least since 1858, and that many
by-elections in 1864 had returned candidates in favour of the
scheme. No public meetings were widely organized against it,
and no adverse petitions were presented. The government felt
justified in assuming that the resolutions ' in principle met with
the approbation of the country, and it would be obviously
absurd to submit the complicated details of such a measure to
the people '.[1] The legislative council and the assembly passed
the resolutions by large majorities.[2]

In the midst of phenomenal success news, ominous and dis-
turbing, came from the Maritime Provinces. The government
of New Brunswick determined to appeal to the people before
opening a discussion in the legislature. At the elections, they
suffered defeat. Macdonald believed that they deserved it.
' The course of the New Brunswick government ', he wrote,
' in dissolving their parliament and appealing to the people
was unstatesmanlike and unsuccessful, as it deserved to be.
Mr. Tilley should have called his parliament together, and,
in accordance with the agreement of the conference at Quebec,
submitted the scheme. Whatever might have been the result
in the legislature, the subject would have been fairly discussed
and its merits understood, and if he had been defeated, he then
had an appeal to the people. As it was, the scheme was submitted without its being understood or appreciated and the
inevitable consequences followed '.[3] Only six supporters of
federation were returned from forty-one constituencies. The

[1] J. A. Macdonald to John Beattie, February 3, 1865, Pope, *Correspondence
of Sir John Macdonald*, p. 21 (Oxford, 1921).

[2] The speeches here referred to are in *Confederation Debates* (Quebec, 1865).

[3] Macdonald to J. H. Gray, March 24, 1865, Pope, *op. cit.*, p. 23.

effect on Nova Scotia was disastrous, and unfortunately it helped to accentuate a hostile state of mind there which continued to exist for a generation. There was already an undercurrent of suspicious dread abroad when Howe returned from Newfoundland to find the Quebec resolutions and Tilley's defeat subjects of animated discussion. It is unnecessary either to blame or to defend Howe's actions. He believed that Nova Scotia had been duped into an injurious scheme, and firm in that conviction he entered the lists as champion of the province. Tupper, however, was wise enough not to follow Tilley's example. He left the wider federation an open issue, and a motion was adopted in favour of the old plan for a legislative union of the Maritime Provinces. He defended his action in an astute letter to Macdonald. He had robbed the opposition of a resolution which they would have brought in, had the Quebec plan been introduced, and he had gained time not only for his own province to calm down but for Tilley to begin again.[1] The imperial government removed Lieutenant-Governor MacDonnell to Hong-Kong, and Gordon of New Brunswick visited England, where apparently he received instructions to give the movement help instead of opposition. In Prince Edward Island the legislature was practically unanimous in rejecting the larger federation, and the house of assembly memorialized the crown that the colony should not be joined to Canada or to any province.

The disappointment in Canada was widespread. The Canadian government feared that the opposition might gain weight if action were not immediately taken. Parliament was hurriedly prorogued, and Macdonald, Cartier, Brown, and Galt left for England to discuss the speedy accomplishment of the British North America federation, the defences of Canada,

[1] Tupper to Macdonald, April 9, 1865, *ibid.*, pp. 25 ff. ; Tupper to Sir R. G. MacDonnell, May 10, 1865, Pope, *Memoirs of Sir John A. Macdonald*, vol. i, pp. 358 ff.

reciprocity with the United States, the settlement of the North-west Territory and of Hudson's Bay Company's claims, and generally the critical state of affairs.[1] The imperial government assured them that every legitimate means would be used to procure the assent of the Maritime Provinces, that the promised guarantee for a loan towards an intercolonial railway still held good, that adequate care would be made for defence, for securing the North-west Territories, and for the renewal of the reciprocity treaty.[2] Early in July, Macdonald returned to Canada, and within a few weeks he was forced to face a political problem occasioned by the death of Taché. Monck immediately asked him to form a government, and in accepting the task he had Cartier's full support. Brown refused to serve under either Macdonald or Cartier, and a compromise was reached by which Sir Narcisse Belleau became prime minister. The session closed in the middle of September after having passed an important Act, which amplified and consolidated the Lower Canadian civil code. It was evident, however, that all was not well. Brown was working uneasily with a cabinet which Macdonald virtually controlled. He ostensibly resigned because he doubted the government's methods in connexion with the reciprocity treaty, but there can be little doubt that Brown felt his own position clearly.[3] His two liberal colleagues, assisted by Fergusson Blair, who took Brown's place, honourably continued to carry out the coalition pact, but it was unfortunate that the liberal leader should have felt the necessity of withdrawing from the ministry at such an ambiguous moment.

With the Maritime Provinces apparently hostile and with Brown no longer an active colleague, the outlook was sufficiently gloomy to inspire fear and to necessitate delay. In addition, economic negotiations with the United States and possible

[1] See the memorandum in Pope, *Memoirs of Sir John A. Macdonald*, vol. i, pp. 279 ff.

[2] *Journals of the Legislative Assembly, Canada*, Second Session, 1865, pp. 8 ff.

[3] For Brown, see Pope, *Memoirs of Sir J. Macdonald*, App. IX and XI.

Fenian invasions were matters of urgent importance. In New Brunswick necessity assisted at the birth of hope. A. J. Smith's ministry had apparently no strong feelings against federation, although they had stepped into power largely on an anti-union agitation, and in other respects they were not united in policy. The colonial office tactfully but firmly urged federation on the province and used the Fenian scare to point to the defenceless state of the New Brunswick frontier. Public opinion began to veer and showed itself at by-elections. When the legislature opened, the lieutenant-governor's speech showed that he had changed his own position. Later he explained that the cabinet had privately agreed to his statements. The legislative council passed an address thanking him for his speech and asking him to obtain an imperial Act of union. Gordon unconstitutionally accepted the address without the intervention of his ministers and expressed his satisfaction at the sentiments which it contained. The ministry resigned as a matter of course. Smith might have put up a good fight had he kept his head and not allowed his tongue to get the better of his discretion.[1] A new ministry was formed and the legislature dissolved. At the elections the cause of federation swept the province, and the house of assembly at the close of June 1866 passed by an overwhelming majority a resolution authorizing the appointment of delegates to arrange ' with the imperial government for the union of British North America upon such terms as will secure the just rights and interests of New Brunswick, accompanied with provision for the immediate construction of the intercolonial railway '.[2] In Nova Scotia, Tupper was watching events with careful persistency. When changes were taking place in New Brunswick, the time for action came. William Miller, who had opposed the Quebec resolutions, made

---

[1] For a careful account of the incident see Tilley to Macdonald, April 14, 1866, *ibid.*, pp. 296 ff.

[2] Pope, *Confederation Documents*, p. 95 (Toronto, 1895).

a speech in the middle of the cabinet crisis in New Brunswick, asking that the resolutions be considered as non-existent and that authority be given for delegates to consult with the imperial cabinet on a just and fair scheme of general union. Tupper saw his chance and put Miller's ideas in the form of a motion. The debate which followed was one of the most bitter in British American history, but Tupper's motion was finally carried by a substantial majority.[1]

Meanwhile in Canada Macdonald was waiting the turn of the tide, and the governor-general urged haste when Macdonald saw the need for tactics.[2] He refused to ask for the opening of parliament before the matter had taken on a different aspect in the Maritime Provinces. When it met he objected to any attempt to rush him off his feet. A delegation from Nova Scotia came to Ottawa to urge an immediate journey to England. Macdonald saw that there was vital work to be done before he could leave Canada. A change of ministry in England turned Monck into an advocate of delay, and the Maritime delegation went to London, where they spent four fruitless months. The Canadian parliament carried resolutions providing for the legislatures and governments of Upper and Lower Canada;[3] but Galt retired from the ministry owing to disagreement over the cabinet's educational policy for Lower Canada. Macdonald's long explanation of the events before the Canadian ministers sailed for England on November 7, 1866, discloses a masterly tactician at work. He did not want any delays in London. Monck must be there to guide the final arrangements, and it would have been fatal had discussions begun after the imperial parliament had risen. Macdonald felt that as New Brunswick and Nova Scotia had not accepted the Quebec resolutions there

---

[1] Pope, *Confederation Documents*, p. 95 ; *Journals of the Assembly, Nova Scotia*, 1866, p. 70.

[2] For the history and correspondence, see Pope, *Memoirs of Sir John A. Macdonald*, vol. i, pp. 299 ff., 374 ff.

[3] Pope, *Confederation Documents*, pp. 89 ff.

would necessarily arise new consultations, and he did not want any of them to ' reverberate through the British provinces ' until the bill, finally settled just before the meeting of the British parliament, should be carried *per saltum*. On December 4 the delegates from Canada, Nova Scotia, and New Brunswick assembled in conference at the Westminster Palace Hotel in London in order to frame resolutions upon which an imperial Act might be built.

The conference was organized along the lines similar to those which had prevailed at Quebec, and on Christmas eve sixty-nine resolutions were agreed on, based on those of the Quebec conference, and forwarded to the colonial secretary. None of the debates were acrimonious. The delegates pledged themselves to a federal scheme in order to strengthen the imperial tie. There were signs of difficulties over the senate. It was feared that it might block legislation. Suggestions were made that the period of service should be limited and that appointment should be vested in the local legislatures. Some delegates dreaded the creation of an oligarchical second chamber, and proposed that the crown should be given power to appoint additional members in case of emergency. This fitted in with an earlier idea from the colonial office and was finally embodied in the imperial Act. Galt watched with anxious care the regulations connected with education. He was not satisfied with the resolution at Quebec which, in assigning education to the provinces, guarded the rights and privileges which the protestant and Roman catholic minorities in the Canadas might possess at federation. Lower Canadian protestants feared the future and wished to fence round and extend their school system. The Canadian government accordingly introduced a measure which aimed not only to confirm the rights of the minority in Lower Canada, but to set up a separate administrative machinery and to provide separate authority in secondary as well as in primary education. Suddenly a bill was brought in

claiming similar privileges for the Roman catholic minority in
Canada West. Opposition at once gathered. It was argued
that the separate school law of 1863 had been thoroughly
debated and had been accepted as a final measure for Canada
West. So grave was the situation that Macdonald decided not
to proceed with the legislation on behalf of Lower Canadian
protestants.[1] Galt felt bound in honour as their champion to
resign, but he did not blame Macdonald's course and willingly
accompanied the delegation to London, where he drew up the
resolution on education which finally became section ninety-
three of the British North America Act. The subsidies to the
provinces were increased. Provisions were made for the future
inclusion of Prince Edward Island and Newfoundland, as these
provinces had definitely withdrawn for the present from co-
operation. The pardoning power of the lieutenant-governor
was limited. The resolution in favour of the intercolonial
railway was made more binding, and it was laid down that its
construction was ' essential to the consolidation of the union
of British North America and to the assent thereto of Nova
Scotia and New Brunswick '.

When the conference resumed after the holidays Lord Monck,
the governor-general, and Lord Carnarvon, the colonial secretary,
attended its meetings accompanied by Sir Frederic Rogers,
afterwards Lord Blachford, the permanent under-secretary.
Attempts were at once begun to draft a bill. With the final
resolutions before them, at least six drafts were drawn up.[2]
The seventh and last printed in imperial form was dated for
revision February 9, 1867, and was the outcome of consultation
between the imperial representatives and the members of the
conference. Perhaps the most interesting fact about these
drafts is that at first the name of the new federation was left
to the decision of the queen. Later it appeared as ' the kingdom

[1] Skelton, *op. cit.*, pp. 402 ff. ; Hodgins, *Documentary History of Education
in Upper Canada*, vol. xix, p. 211.
[2] Pope, *Memoirs of Sir J. Macdonald*, pp. 123 ff.

of Canada ', and in the final draft as ' one dominion under the name of Canada '. Macdonald was ' the ruling genius ' with power in ' management and adroitness '.[1] There can be little doubt with his strong bias in favour of a legislative union that he desired to form an auxiliary kingdom out of the colonies, and he deplored in later life the lack of insight which rejected the title.[2] He fought hard for its retention, but it was withdrawn at the instance of Lord Stanley, the minister for foreign affairs, who feared that it ' would wound the sensibilities of the Yankees '. It was appropriate that the name of Canada should be chosen in preference to the fantastic titles suggested by the press, but history does not relate from what source or for what reasons the word ' dominion ' was added.[3]

No serious opposition met the bill in the imperial parliament. Lord Carnarvon in the lords ventured to see in the Act the creation of a great state, the crown of free institutions, which perhaps one day would overshadow the mother country. The bill passed practically as presented, and it can thus be considered the product of Canadian statesmanship. Indeed, no one seems to have cared much about it, and certainly there was no enthusiasm. Macdonald compared its progress to that of ' a private bill uniting two or three English parishes '.[4] Galt deplored deeply the state of public opinion. He felt that

[1] G. E. Marindin, *Letters of Frederic, Lord Blachford*, pp. 301 ff. (London, 1896).

[2] Macdonald to Lord Knutsford, July 18, 1889, Pope, *Correspondence of Sir John Macdonald*, pp. 449 ff.

[3] Many suggestions have been offered and need not be considered. It is possible, however, that the title ' dominion ' had a colonial origin. In the fifth, or so-called ' third ', draft of the bill—which was drawn up by the colonial delegates—the title was ' one united dominion under the name of the kingdom of Canada '. When the delegates and the imperial representatives came together to draw up or to agree on the final draft, Stanley's objections were doubtless mentioned. Some one sitting at the table may have drawn his pen through the words ' united ' and ' of the kingdom '—J. A. Macdonald perhaps—and the final title ' one dominion under the name of Canada ' automatically emerged.

[4] Pope, *Correspondence of Sir J. Macdonald*, p. 451.

England was possessed ' with a servile fear of the United States ' and would prefer to abandon Canada rather than defend it against that country. Sentiment in favour of connexion had become very weak.[1] Sir Frederic Rogers merely looked on federation as a decent preparation for divorce, and Bright and Gladstone thought that the cession of Canada to the United States would not be too great a price for peace. It is true that the dominion of Canada which was created by proclamation on July 1, 1867, consisted of only four provinces, but a little vision might have seen that the clauses in the British North America Act allowing territorial extension were at least pregnant with magnificent possibilities. Be that as it may, the fact remains that Canada was born in a period of mid-victorian gloom.

With Galt depressed, Cartier blind to what was passing around him, the statesmen of the Maritime Provinces disappointed with the imperial attitude, it is not surprising that there was not much rejoicing in the dominion. Macdonald felt that his first duty was to the present, especially as Lord Monck, the new governor-general of Canada, had asked him to form the first federal ministry, and that was task enough, since the request made it clear that the duties of premier would fall on his single shoulders and that the old dual control had gone for ever.[2] There were obvious difficulties. Macdonald desired to continue the liberal-conservative coalition, but his very desire might embarrass his choice. In addition, Brown felt that the federation pact had done its work, and that he was now free to reorganize his party and to invite back into it those who had temporarily suspended their allegiance. At a great liberal

[1] Galt to his wife, January 14, 1867, Skelton, *op. cit.*, pp. 410 ff.

[2] ' I desire to express my strong opinion that, in future, it shall be distinctly understood that the position of first minister shall be held by *one* person, who shall be responsible to the governor-general for the appointment of the other ministers, and that the system of dual first ministers, which has hitherto prevailed, shall be put an end to ': Monck to Macdonald, May 24, 1867, Pope, *Correspondence of Sir J. Macdonald*, p. 46.

convention held at Toronto on the eve of the first Dominion Day he rallied his followers. He declared that only the interests of his country could justify ' the degradation ' of his having joined the coalition, and that it was the happiest day of his life when he got out of it. Howland and McDougall, the liberals who had remained with Macdonald, addressed the convention by invitation. The former pointed out that the liberalism of the dominion would be adequately represented in the new administration ; while the latter, remembering doubtless Brown's championship of the territories and of an ocean-bounded British North America, emphasized the fact that federation was as yet only half accomplished, and that a strong party with this in view ought to combine in perfecting the work begun under Brown's auspices. It was clear that the old divisions were in some respects to disappear even though Brown would be in opposition.

Other difficulties, which Dunkin had foreseen, at once presented themselves.[1] There were many interests which would claim representation in the cabinet, and in recognizing these Macdonald created a precedent, which will be dealt with later, destined to become gradually almost a constitutional convention.[2] Firstly, Ontario, Quebec, and the Maritime Provinces would require territorial recognition. Secondly, the French-Canadians never doubted the special claims of their race. Thirdly, the Irish Roman catholics looked on themselves as strong enough to deserve a cabinet minister. Fourthly, the English minority in Quebec felt that they had peculiar claims for similar representation. Thus, the federal idea and creed and race were early to the front in the completion of a federal cabinet. The partial shedding of the older political affiliations also complicated Macdonald's choice. The French-Canadians were early promised three portfolios in a cabinet of thirteen. Galt came in to satisfy the English of Quebec. Ontario was given five members

[1] *Confederation Debates* (Quebec, 1865), p. 497.   [2] See below, pp. 381, 413-14.

and Nova Scotia and New Brunswick received two each. When
the cabinet was finally announced, the absence of the names of
Tupper and D'Arcy McGee disclosed Macdonald's difficulties.
Cartier insisted on three French-Canadians. If McGee, who sat
as an Irish Roman catholic for a Quebec constituency, had
been admitted, the Quebec representatives with Galt would
have numbered five. Howland and McDougall, knowing the
old liberal watchwords, claimed that Ontario should have one
more member than Quebec. Had Macdonald desired to satisfy
these claims and to stick to Galt and McGee, it would have
meant that Ontario and Quebec would have eleven members, and
that, if the other provinces were proportionately represented,
the cabinet would have been larger than he desired. The
outlook seemed so difficult that Macdonald almost lost heart
and determined to advise Lord Monck to send for Brown.
Tupper, in this dilemma, at once came forward and placed his
office at Macdonald's disposal. McGee, with his generous
enthusiasm, followed Tupper, and Edward Kenny came in as
an Irish Roman catholic and the second representative from
Nova Scotia.[1]

The first general elections for the dominion were held in
August and September. In Ontario, Quebec, and New Brunswick the government was overwhelmingly supported and Brown
lost his seat in South Ontario. In Nova Scotia there was
another tale to tell. Tupper alone of nineteen government
candidates was returned. There was a certain amount of consolation in the fact that he defeated William Annand, Howe's
right-hand man, and afterwards the chief promoter of repeal in
the province; but Macdonald feared that 'that pestilent fellow
Howe' might give some trouble in England, and he at once
bent his energies to frustrate him. A bill for the intercolonial
railway was at once put through parliament as an immediate
evidence of the government's intentions not only to carry out

[1] Pope, *Memoirs of Sir John A. Macdonald*, vol. i, pp. 329 ff.

the letter of the British North America Act, but of its desire to give Nova Scotia as little cause for complaint as possible. The province, however, seemed bent on a separatist course. The provincial elections were a sweeping defeat for federation. The legislature passed an address in favour of a repeal of the union, and a delegation headed by Howe was sent to London to lay the address before the crown and to explain the sentiments and feelings which lay behind it. The dominion government sent Tupper to London to oppose the Nova Scotians. His presence, from that point of view, was hardly necessary. The imperial cabinet had no intentions, as far as they were concerned, of allowing Nova Scotia to destroy a plan so long in progress and so recently matured. On the other hand, Tupper had an interview with Howe, in which he pointed out that if he insisted in antagonizing the imperial and dominion governments he would hurt not only himself and his party but the province to which he was devoted. Defeated in England, Howe returned in a doubtful state of mind. In a conversation with Tilley he left the impression that concessions might be arranged. Tilley reported to Macdonald that a convention of anti-federalists was shortly to assemble in Halifax and that Howe thought that a visit from Macdonald would do good. This invitation was supported by Tupper, who followed the prime minister from Ottawa to Toronto to press it home. Accordingly Macdonald, Cartier, McDougall, and John Sandfield Macdonald at once proceeded to Halifax.

Howe was sobering. He found that the anti-union movement was getting out of hand, that there was a possibility that the law might be resisted, and that the idea of annexation to the United States might gain ground. Macdonald informed him that Canada had no objections to consider ' better terms ', and that Nova Scotia would be perfectly justified in agitating for changes, but that the principles of the Act were inviolate. He invited Howe to join the ministry to strengthen constitutional reform if his province desired it, and at any rate to prevent it being hurt through lack of due support at Ottawa. Howe hesitated. The emotions of the people were at the moment too much out of hand to allow such a course. Finally Macdonald and Cartier addressed the convention, where they practically repeated their advice to Howe. The immediate result was a resolution against extremes and a pledge to use constitutional means for repeal, and a promise that the local legislature would carry on the provincial business. Macdonald distinguished between the members of the assembly and those of the house of commons. The former were evidently extremists, and some of the local cabinet were at least disloyal in words, but the latter did not seem entirely wedded to repeal and would ' come round by degrees '. Macdonald did not let the grass grow under his feet. He carried on for four months a long correspondence with Howe, retold him the hurt which Nova Scotia must suffer, and drove home the dangers which lay in the growing disaffection. The Canadian finance minister opened up the plan for ' better terms '. Finally these were agreed to, and Joseph Howe entered the dominion ministry on January 30, 1869, as president of the council.

[AUTHORITIES.—The main sources are : John Boyd, *Sir George Étienne Cartier* (Toronto, 1914) ; Joseph Pope, *Confederation Documents* (Toronto, 1895) ; *Memoirs of Sir John A. Macdonald* (2 vols., Ottawa, 1894) ; *Correspondence of Sir John Macdonald* (Oxford, 1921) ; O. D. Skelton, *Life and Times of Sir A. T. Galt* (Oxford, 1921) ; Alexander Mackenzie, *Life and Speeches of the Hon. George Brown* (Toronto, 1882) ; *Parliamentary Debates on the Subject of the Confederation of the British North American Provinces* (Quebec, 1865) ; A. G. Doughty, ' Notes on the Quebec Conference, 1864 ' (*Canadian Historical Review*, March 1920) ; J. H. Chisholm, *The Speeches and Public Letters of Joseph Howe* (2 vols., Halifax, 1909). Among the pamphlet literature the following are most important : A. T. Galt, *Speech on the Proposed Union of the British North American Provinces delivered at Sherbrooke, C.E.* (Montreal, 1864) ; T. D'Arcy McGee, *Two Speeches on the Union of the Provinces* (Quebec, 1865) ; Joseph Howe, *Confederation considered in relation to the Interests of the Empire* (London, 1866) ; Charles Tupper, *A Letter to the Rt. Hon. the Earl of Carnarvon* (London, 1866) ; William Annand, *A Letter to the Rt. Hon. the Earl of Carnarvon* (London, 1866) ; E. G. Penny,

The Proposed British North American Confederation : Why it should not be imposed on the Colonies by Imperial Legislation (Montreal, 1867) ; *Proceedings of the Reform Convention at Toronto, June 1867* (Toronto, 1867). The files of the Toronto and Halifax newspapers, especially the *Globe* and the *Chronicle,* are useful. J. H. Gray, *Confederation : the Political and Parliamentary History of Canada from 1864 to 1871* (Toronto, 1872), Sir Charles Tupper, *Recollections of Sixty Years in Canada* (London, 1914), Sir Richard Cartwright, *Memories of Confederation* (Ottawa, The Canadian Club, 1906), *Reminiscences* (Toronto, 1912), do not add materially to the history, but they supply many personal touches and afford interesting sidelights. The best general introduction is A. H. U. Colquhoun, *The Fathers of Confederation* (Toronto, 1916). Dr. Colquhoun's little book is based on a thorough knowledge of the material and is written with judicial insight. L. J. Burpee, ' Joseph Howe and the Anti-Confederation League ' (*Transactions of the Royal Society of Canada*, 3rd series, vol. x, sect. ii, pp. 409 ff.), contains valuable material. T. C. Blegen, ' A Plan for the Union of British North America and the United States, 1866 (*Mississippi Valley Historical Review*, March 1918, pp. 470 ff.), discusses a bill introduced into the house of representatives for the union of British North America and the United States, and incidentally throws light on some of the forces at work during the completion of Canadian federation. The British Parliamentary Papers include : *Correspondence respecting the proposed Union of the British North American Provinces, December 1864–January 1867* (London, 1867) ; *Letter opposing Confederation addressed to Lord Carnarvon . . . by Howe, Annand, and McDonald, with an Appendix of Documents* (London, 1867) ; *Representations of Nova Scotia against inclusion in the Dominion* (London, 1867–8). Consult also *Correspondence and Negotiations connected with the Affairs of Nova Scotia* (Ottawa, 1869).]

CHAPTER XX

THE DOMINION OF CANADA

THE federation of 1867, great though it was in actual accomplishment, was greater in its possibilities. The original dominion comprised only four provinces, but the faith which hoped for a Canada extending from ocean to ocean did not die. In the constitution itself it found expression in a clause which contemplated the inclusion of Newfoundland, Prince Edward Island, Rupert's Land, and the North-western Territory. Canadian statesmen for many years were inspired by this magnificent prospect, which runs through the federation debates, and they believed that the consolidation of British North America was a first charge on their political abilities. Such a future, if realized, meant that there would inevitably grow up the national consciousness of a distinct group which would either gradually seek independence as a sovereign state in international law, or would create within the empire changes in colonial status and in the imperial relationship. There remain to be considered, firstly, the territorial expansion of Canada ; secondly, with that accomplished and with the imperial tie still binding, the extension of Canadian autonomy to which the former gave force and the latter provided delicate problems ; and thirdly, the constitutional place which Canada at present holds under the British crown.

Beyond the stories told by a few adventurers and traders, New France for generations knew little of the great western lands. For years a few posts were all that bore witness to the dreams of Cartier, Champlain, and La Salle, who looked for a north-west passage to the Indies and saw in imagination a western highway to the riches of the east. It was only during the last decades of the French régime that Pierre de la Vérendrye and his sons discovered and explored much of the central prairies. Their chain of posts aimed not only at trade, but at confining the English to the districts round Hudson's Bay so that the north-west might be added to the dominions of Louis XV. With the necessity of guarding the original and settled territory from Indian attacks which might come at any moment, and from the more subtle and less concrete aggression of British diplomacy, the vision gradually faded, until New France became a small oasis of civilized life in a vast undeveloped northern continent. Half a century later Alexander Mackenzie crossed the mountains to the Pacific, and on the cliffs of the western ocean he inscribed the date July 22, 1793, and took possession in the name of Canada. For years the importance of these voyages remained unappreciated, and the rival traders of the Hudson's Bay Company, the North-west Company, and the X. Y. Company were the only white men inhabiting the regions. In 1801 Mackenzie published an account of his voyages which gave Lord Selkirk the idea of settling on the fertile prairies a group of distressed Scottish crofters. He obtained a large grant from the Hudson's Bay Company which included the valleys of the Assiniboine and Red River. The district was named Assiniboia, and a settlement was begun in 1811. The jealousies of the North-west Company practically wrecked the colony, which dragged out a stagnant existence, supplemented by French-Canadians, half-breeds, and a few Americans.

The jealousies of the various companies were finally laid to rest in 1821, but not before the rivalry had driven their traders farther and farther west until they reached the ocean. Until the Washington Treaty of 1846, which settled the frontier, they alone were in possession, and their presence there probably served to preserve for the empire the future colony of British Columbia. Canada had thus a sufficient historical connexion with the west to make it seem a rightful heritage round which, as we have seen, emotion and policy had begun to gather. When a select committee of the imperial parliament was appointed in 1857 to consider the monopoly claimed by the Hudson's Bay Company, the legislative assembly of Canada boldly claimed the Pacific ocean as its just and rightful boundary. Two years later a group of Canadians founded a newspaper at Fort Garry for the purpose of attacking the company's claims and of carrying on a propaganda in favour of the annexation of the North-west to Canada. The British government were willing to further the idea, at least in connexion with the districts on the Red River and the Saskatchewan, but they laid down as conditions of occupation that Canada should open up communications and provide for local administration. If practical Canadian interest was not forthcoming the committee suggested the creation of some kind of authority, possibly that of a crown colony. Nothing came of either plan, but enthusiasts such as George Brown and Alexander Morris never ceased to point out the path to a clear-purposed goal. On the eve of federation, John A. Macdonald began to grasp the situation. ' If Canada ', he wrote, ' is to remain a country separate from the United States, it is of great importance to her that they (the United States) should not get behind us by right or by force, and intercept the route to the Pacific.' He looked, however, on the acquisition of the west merely as a necessity in establishing a future highway to the Pacific, and he feared the possession of too much unoccupied lands lest ' the youth and strength of the country ' should be drained.[1]

No sooner had the federation got under way than Macdonald's conception expanded. He began to see wider possibilities than those implied in a barren passage for steel rails. Early in the first parliament of the dominion he arranged for a debate on

[1] Macdonald to E. W. Watkin, March 27, 1865, Pope, *Memoirs of Sir John A. Macdonald*, vol. ii, p. 43.

'the Hudson's Bay question'.[1] In December 1867 William McDougall introduced a series of resolutions, on which an address was founded praying the crown to unite with Canada Rupert's Land and the North-western Territory. Macdonald sought 'a broad country for the expansion of our adventurous youth'. The demand for annexation, he declared, was not only sentimental but practical. The country could only remain British by being included in the federation scheme, and Canada needed it to round off its territory and as an 'outlet for its adolescent population'. Before anything could be done it was necessary to arrive at some plan by which the rights of the Hudson's Bay Company over Rupert's Land might be acquired. The imperial law officers were convinced that these rights were beyond dispute, and until they were transferred to Canada the latter had no desire to possess the North-western Territory, separated as it would be from the dominion by lands in the possession of the Company. The colonial office also pointed out that an imperial Act was necessary to legalize any arrangement between the company and Canada for the transfer of Rupert's Land. An imperial Act was passed in July 1868 by which the crown was empowered to accept the surrender of 'all rights of government and proprietary rights and all other privileges, franchises, powers, and authorities', and to declare Rupert's Land by order in council a part of the dominion of Canada ; and the parliament of Canada was given authority 'to make, ordain, and establish within the land and territory so admitted, all such laws, institutions, and ordinances, and to constitute such courts and offices as might be necessary for the peace, order, and good government of her majesty's subjects and others therein'.[2]

In the following October Cartier and McDougall were sent

[1] Macdonald to Charles Bischoff, October 17, 1867, *ibid*, p. 3 *n*.
[2] 31 & 32 Victoria, c. 105 (Rupert's Land Act, 1868). The commercial and trading rights in Rupert's Land and elsewhere were preserved to the company.

to England to hasten negotiations. Cartier urged Lord Granville, the colonial secretary—' pussy Granville ' of ' bland, soft manners '—to help in completing ' the whole work of confederation '. Granville acted with great tact. He kept the Canadians in one room and ' the H. B. people in another ' until he arranged a settlement.[1] For the sum of £300,000 the company surrendered their interests to the crown, with the reservation of one-twentieth of the fertile belt ' bounded on the south by the United States boundary, on the west by the Rocky Mountains, on the north by the northern branch of the Saskatchewan River, on the east by Lake Winnipeg, the Lake of the Woods and the waters connecting them '. In addition to this reservation the company also received forty-five thousand acres adjacent to each trading post. The Canadian parliament by address accepted on June 1, 1869, the arrangements arrived at by Cartier and McDougall, and the crown was asked to unite Rupert's Land to Canada on the terms therein set forth and also to unite the North-western Territory on the terms of the previous address.[2] An understanding was reached for the formal transfer on December 1, 1869. In anticipation, the dominion parliament passed on June 22, 1869, ' an Act for the temporary government of Rupert's Land and the North-western Territory when united with Canada '. This Act was a preliminary step in taking over the districts from the local authorities. The name ' North-west Territories ' was given to the entire country, and provision was made for the appointment of a lieutenant-governor who should administer justice and establish laws, institutions, and ordinances subject to their ratification by parliament. He was to be guided by instructions issued from time to time under order in council, and was to be assisted in administration by a council. Until further provisions

[1] Cartier to Macdonald, February and March 6, 1869, Pope, *Correspondence of Sir John Macdonald*, p. 91.
[2] *House of Commons Journals* (1869), pp. 169 ff.

were made, existing regulations were to remain in force and public officials were to continue in office. Under this Act McDougall was appointed lieutenant-governor, and he left on September 28 to take up his duties.

It is hardly necessary to retell the story of the Red River rebellion except in so far as it affected the territorial organization. The half-breeds of the district were led to believe that the transfer of the country might place in jeopardy their claims to lands, and this discontent was further increased when the French Roman catholics began to fear that their linguistic and religious rights or privileges were in danger. A Canadian surveying party in the summer of 1869 did not attempt to dispel these ominous suspicions or to act with discretion and tact. The settlement determined to resist, and a provisional government was set up under Louis Riel. Circumstances combined to create difficulties. The company had given the government no indication of the state of mind which existed. Their governor, McTavish, was seriously ill, and—more unfortunate still—the Roman catholic bishop, Taché, was absent in Rome. McDougall did not move with either caution or insight. His initial instructions ordered him to proceed to Fort Garry, and, ' on hearing of the transfer of the country to Canada ', to make ' all preliminary arrangements for the organization of the government '.[1] When he reported the opposition, he was ordered to act with the greatest care, as he was in reality in a foreign country still under the government of the company. Macdonald advised him to ascertain who were the two leading half-breeds and to include them in his council. When McDougall wrote of being sworn in and of undertaking the government as soon as official notice reached him of the transfer, Macdonald again warned him against such a course unless he saw the way clear to its effective performance. That he would be obeyed was only an assumption, and if his authority

[1] Pope, *Memoirs of Sir John A. Macdonald*, vol. ii, p. 52.

was rejected the dominion would be rendered ridiculous to the settlers and to the people of the United States, and an excuse would be given to the inhabitants to form, *ex necessitate*, a government of their own.

In cable communication with the colonial office, the Canadian cabinet absolutely declined to accept the transfer while the district remained in such a distracted and rebellious state. A special minute of council was drawn up on December 16, 1869, which placed on record the matured judgement of the executive. A hasty assumption of rule by Canada would probably end in bloodshed, and thus the future sentiment and attitude of the people would be prejudiced. The Indians and the restless Americans would be irresistibly tempted to join the insurgents. The transfer must be delayed to prevent war. Even were the purchase money paid, it would be unstatesmanlike to end the only constituted authority in the country and forcibly to replace it by another. The dispatches to McDougall may have been delayed, but he assumed that the transfer had taken place, and neglecting his initial instructions he issued a proclamation on December 1, and attempted to assume the administration by a *coup de main*. Macdonald's fears were realized. The lieutenant-governor's position at Pembina became precarious. He was forced to retreat to St. Paul. Canada was humiliated, and the hopes and pretensions of the insurgents increased.[1] Worse still, the work of a special mission which hoped to arrive at Christmas was rendered hopeless from the start. Riel set up a dictatorship, imprisoned the mission, and was responsible for a cruel and cold-blooded murder. Finally it became necessary to take serious action, and a force of imperial regulars and Canadians advanced on Fort Garry, which was reached in August 1870. Riel and his followers fled before a shot was fired.

On May 2, 1870, Macdonald introduced a bill into the Cana-

---

[1] Macdonald to Rose, December 31, 1869, Pope, *Memoirs of Sir John A. Macdonald,* vol. ii, pp. 59 ff.

dian parliament constituting the old district of Assiniboia a new province of the dominion under the name of Manitoba.[1] This Act, which was confirmed by an imperial Act granting general power to the dominion to create new provinces and to legislate for the territories,[2] established Manitoba on lines analogous to the other provinces, but included special provisions in connexion with education, and for quieting existing titles.[3] The name North-west Territories was given to the portion of Rupert's Land and the North-western Territory not included in Manitoba; and the Act of June 1869, which, as has been pointed out, was passed for the whole territory, was re-enacted temporarily for the new and limited North-west Territories, with the proviso that the lieutenant-governor of Manitoba should also become lieutenant-governor of the North-west Territories. On May 3 orders were issued for paying over the purchase money to the Hudson's Bay Company. On May 20 A. G. Archibald was appointed first lieutenant-governor of Manitoba. On June 23, under the authority of the ' Rupert's Land Act ',[4] an imperial order in council was issued which formally transferred Rupert's Lands and the North-western Territories to Canada and gave the dominion full power to legislate for their welfare and good government. In addressing the late council of Assiniboia, the new lieutenant-governor outlined the future : ' Now that the province has been incorporated with the dominion it will partake of the prosperity of the older communities. Politically joined to the other provinces, new routes of communication will soon be opened up. The telegraph system, extended to this place as it shortly will be, will give you hourly communication with Canada and Europe. The highway and the telegraph will

---

[1] Kennedy, *op. cit.*, pp. 689 ff. (33 Victoria, c. 3).

[2] *Ibid.*, p. 694, The British North America Act, 1871 (34 & 35 Victoria, c. 28).

[3] For the education disputes in Manitoba see Willison, *Sir Wilfrid Laurier and the Liberal Party*, vol. ii, pp. 201 ff. (Toronto, 1903) ; Skelton, *Life and Letters of Sir Wilfrid Laurier*, vol. i, pp. 439 ff. ; vol. ii, pp. 13 ff.

[4] See above, p. 325.

remove the isolation in which you have been hitherto kept by the boundless prairies of the south and the impassable swamps and lakes of the east, and make you part and parcel of the living and moving world.'[1]

The government of the North-west Territories was provisional, and they achieved separate political existence under a dominion Act of April 8, 1875, which substituted election for nomination in the selection of part of the council. When David Laird was appointed lieutenant-governor on October 7, 1876, a new era began which saw the foundation of educational and municipal systems, the suppression of a half-breed rebellion, and the establishment of a judiciary. In 1886 representation in the dominion parliament was conceded. In 1888 an elected legislative assembly took the place of the legislative council. The judges were allowed to sit in it as expert but non-voting members. In 1897 the executive was made responsible. In the following years a quasi-provincial constitution took form with a lieutenant-governor, an executive appointed from an assembly of thirty-one members elected on manhood suffrage, and authority to legislate on many local matters. In 1905 two new provinces, Alberta and Saskatchewan, were created, without, however, the control of their crown lands.[2]

With the creation of these two provinces there remain the Yukon and portions of the North-west Territories. The commissioner of the North-west Territories is assisted by a council not exceeding four in number appointed by the dominion government. The powers of the commissioner in council to make ordinances are defined under dominion legislation of 1906.[3] The laws of Canada, unless otherwise specified, are applicable to the Territories, but the governor-general in

---

[1] Archibald to late council of Assiniboia, Fort Garry, September 6, 1870, E. H. Oliver, *The Canadian North-west : its Early Development and Legislative Records*, vol. i, p. 623 (2 vols., Ottawa, 1914).

[2] Kennedy, *op. cit.*, pp. 700 ff.

[3] Revised Statutes of Canada, 1906, c. 62.

council possesses special power in relation to intoxicants, arms and ammunition, and judicial affairs, and may apply acts not otherwise in force. In 1898 the Yukon was created a separate Territory by Act of parliament, and till 1908 government was vested in a commissioner and a legislative council partly elected and partly nominated by the governor-general under his privy seal.[1] In the latter year a council was organized consisting of ten members—two from each of five electoral districts—elected on a manhood suffrage basis.[2] Every council continues for three years unless previously dissolved by the commissioner, and must assemble at least once every year. The commissioner constitutes the executive government and is under instructions from the governor in council or the minister of the interior. The commissioner in council can legislate on subjects defined by dominion legislation, and on education.[3] Every ordinance, however, dealing with education must provide that the majority of taxpayers in any district may create such schools and levy such school taxes as they think expedient, and that the minority may establish separate schools and assign their school rates to them alone. Responsible government does not exist, but since 1908 the commissioner is expected to carry out as far as possible the wishes of the legislative council. The Yukon has returned a member to the dominion parliament since 1902.[4] The regulations governing the laws of Canada in relation to the North-west Territories are applicable to the Yukon.

When the Oregon boundary dispute between Great Britain and the United States was settled in 1846, there remained in the possession of the former Vancouver Island and the territory afterwards known as British Columbia. In 1849 Vancouver Island was granted to the Hudson's Bay Company for ten years

[1] 61 Victoria, c. 6, amended by 62 & 63 Victoria, c. 11.
[2] 7 & 8 Edward VII, c. 76.
[3] Revised Statutes of Canada, 1906, c. 63 ; Yukon Ordinance, No. 27, 1902.
[4] 2 Edward VII, c. 37.

upon terms which implied colonization. A governor was appointed to administer the colony with a nominated council of not more than seven members, but powers were granted to him to call an assembly. When the new governor, Richard Blanshard, arrived from England, he found that the company was supreme, and after remaining a few months he retired in disgust. James Douglas, the chief factor, took his place, and with a servant of the company in control there was no advance in settlement, as the company did not want to encourage colonization at the expense of their own rich fur trade. Provision had been made for the revocation of the grant if at the end of five years successful settlement had not been carried out. A petition in 1853 from the few hundred white men on the island for the enforcement of this provision was overruled owing to the company's influence in London, but Douglas was instructed to call an assembly. The Island was divided into four electoral districts returning seven members. The franchise was fixed at ownership of twenty acres and the qualifications for membership were based on the possession of fairly high freehold property. The first legislature met in August 1856, with a legislative council of three and a house of assembly, both composed of officials and servants of the company.

The mainland remained practically a hunting preserve leased to the same company, until, with the discovery of gold on the Fraser River in 1856, a stream of immigration began, and it became necessary to erect some sort of local administration. In 1858 Douglas severed his connexion with the company, and in November of that year he was appointed lieutenant-governor. Under the name of British Columbia the continental territories west of the Rockies began political life as a crown colony.[1] The colonial secretary instructed the governor to seek the goodwill and confidence of the immigrants, to show no preference to British settlers at the expense of Americans or other foreigners,

[1] 21 & 22 Victoria, c. 99.

and to remember that the colony was destined at the earliest convenient moment for a house of assembly. As soon as there was a permanent population, however small, free institutions must be set up. Governor Douglas justified the confidence which was placed in him, and his rule was characterized by wisdom and impartiality. With the influx of English settlers it was inevitable that the demand for popular government should arise, and it was unfortunate that Douglas could not unite Vancouver Island and British Columbia. He acted as executive head of both colonies, and he supported the colonial office in favour of the union with the gradual extension to the united colony of representative institutions such as existed in Vancouver Island. Local jealousies hindered the project. The Island was in favour of free trade with a view of developing its capital, Victoria, as a free port. As a consequence revenue was derived from direct taxation. On the mainland direct taxation was out of the question. The miners were strongly opposed to it, and the only hope of revenue adequate for the development of the colony's vast natural wealth lay in import duties. In addition, there were sentimental difficulties. Vancouver Island was prospering out of the mining activities of the mainland, and Victoria was rapidly growing in commercial prosperity. The fact that the governor resided there furnished additional irritation. Difficulties, too, presented themselves owing to the agitation in British Columbia for a house of assembly. The Indians still formed a large majority of the population. The white population was scattered and fluctuating. Mining was as yet the chief occupation, and was carried on largely by foreign immigrants who never intended to settle. There were few landowners or business men, and these lived far apart from one another and from the seat of government at New Westminster. The choice thus lay between creating an assembly controlled by a small group who could attend it or by a fluctuating population without any serious interest in the colony beyond a hope for immediate gain. A system of imperfect representation was contemplated and the plan for union abandoned. Hardly, however, had the decision been arrived at, when both colonies began to look on union with favour. Early in 1865 the assembly of Vancouver Island placed on record a desire for unconditional union. Frederick Seymour, who had succeeded Douglas as governor of British Columbia, led an opposition ;[1] but as the gold fever subsided there was a general development of opinion that future prosperity lay in a combination of interests on the Pacific coasts, and in 1866 an imperial Act united the two colonies with a single chamber partly elective.[2] This step led to further progress.

The assembly in Vancouver Island had been abolished. Public sentiment in the Island combined with that on the mainland, and an agitation began not merely for representative but for responsible government. In March 1867 the legislative council, although it had a majority of nominated members, passed a resolution in favour of federation, and asked the governor to take measures for the admission ' on fair and equitable terms ' of British Columbia into the dominion. Seymour did not favour the idea, and pointed out difficulties, some of which were valid at the time. Adequate communication with Canada was practically non-existent, and the transfer of the Hudson's Bay Company's lands east of the Rockies had not yet taken place. The governor's diffidence, however, did not damp public enthusiasm. The colonists were quick to grasp the possibilities of progress, both political and material, which inclusion in the dominion implied. In January 1868 a public meeting at Victoria urgently declared in favour of union, and a memorial was forwarded to the Canadian govern-

[1] F. W. Howay, 'The Attitude of Governor Seymour towards Confederation' (*Trans. Royal Society of Canada*, 3rd series, vol. xiv, sect. ii, pp. 31 ff.).
[2] 29 & 30 Victoria, c. 67.

ment which claimed that there was general support behind the movement. Terms of admission acceptable to the colony were outlined, and included the assumption by Canada of the public debt of the province, a fixed annual subsidy, provincial responsible government, and adequate representation in the parliament of the dominion. The construction of a wagon-road from Lake Superior to the head of navigation on the Fraser River within a period of two years after the union was laid down as an essential condition. As the Canadian government received no official communication from the colony they forwarded the memorial to England. Two difficulties stood in the way. The imperial government were unwilling to act until the negotiations between Canada and the Hudson's Bay Company had been completed, and Seymour remained obstinate. Meanwhile, agitation continued in the colony and a convention of delegates met at Yale in which the project was urged and terms discussed. Seymour's death took place a few weeks after Cartier and McDougall had completed arrangements in London with the Hudson's Bay Company. Anthony Musgrave, governor of Newfoundland, was appointed his successor on Macdonald's recommendation.[1] Musgrave was a strong believer in British North American federation, and his faith was strengthened by a dispatch from Lord Granville which endorsed federation in unambiguous language and left only the terms open for discussion.[2] The whole project was debated in the legislature of British Columbia in 1870 and resolutions were carried in its favour. Delegates were sent to Ottawa to arrange terms. An agreement was arrived at in July, and included a promise to begin within two years and to complete within ten years a railway to the Pacific. The terms were approved by the colony at a general election, and ratified by the legislature in the following January. On July 20, 1871, the union came into

[1] Pope, *op. cit.*, vol. ii, p. 144.
[2] Granville to Musgrave, August 14, 1869, *Colonial Office Papers*, G. 350.

force, and responsible government was at once introduced in accordance with the express terms agreed on between British Columbia and the government of Canada.[1]

Prince Edward Island and Newfoundland still remained without the fold. The latter definitely refused in 1869 to come in, and only once since that date has it shown any desire to reopen negotiations. Macdonald continued to hope for a change of heart, but the ' ancient colony ' has preferred to work out its own destiny. In Prince Edward Island anti-federation sentiment developed quickly and with great force. The legislature viewed the idea as ' disastrous to the rights and interests of the people ' and declared that Canada could offer no terms which would be acceptable. As a consequence there was no representative of the Island at the Westminster Palace Hotel conference. The premier, James C. Pope, happened to be in London at that time, and although he had voted in the legislature against federation, proposals were made to him that in addition to the general terms agreed on at the Quebec conference, the dominion was prepared to allow the Island $800,000 to extinguish the proprietary rights of the absentee landlords which had hung round the neck of the province for generations. Pope was impressed by the offer, but before it could be laid before the legislature his government suffered defeat. In 1869 Canada made further proposals, but they were again rejected. In 1872 the Island found it difficult to raise the capital necessary for internal development, and the financial needs came to the notice of the banking house of Morton, Rose & Company in London, of which Sir John Rose, a Montreal barrister who had lost silk for signing the annexation manifesto in 1849, was a member. His financial abilities attracted attention in England, and finally resulted in brilliant success in London. Never losing interest in Canada, he kept up correspondence with John A.

[1] See Report of the Canadian cabinet, April 19, 1890 (*House of Commons Papers*, 194, pp. 11 ff.).

Macdonald, in the course of which he informed him of the situation in Prince Edward Island. Macdonald was cautious. He refused to allow Canada to open negotiations, but he asked Lord Dufferin to inform the lieutenant-governor that the terms of 1869 were still available. The governor telegraphed asking if the debt of the railway would be taken into consideration. The dominion government replied that it was a proper subject for discussion and that any proposals with regard to it would be carefully considered. A few months later, delegates came to Ottawa to arrange a basis of union, and on July 1, 1873, Prince Edward Island joined the Canadian federation.

It lies outside this history to consider the work done by the railway builders of Canada, but amid the hard facts which gave the political dream realization their work is the most romantic. Political and financial circumstances combined to delay the day when Halifax and Vancouver were linked up by steam. When, however, the eastern and western branches of the Canadian Pacific Railway were at last connected and the last spike driven home in November 1885 by Donald Smith, afterwards Lord Strathcona, political faith was made visible across the continent and the lines of steel became symbolical bonds of Canadian national unity. Without the hope and courage of the railway builders and the political vision which refused to be dimmed, the full territorial heritage of the dominion would have remained, as John A. Macdonald said, ' a geographical expression '.[1]

[AUTHORITIES.—For the earlier period the material is in *Report from the Committee appointed to inquire into the State and Condition of the Countries adjoining to Hudson's Bay* (London, 1749); *Report from the Select Committee on Hudson's Bay Company* (London, 1837); *Parliamentary Papers* (1819), ' Red River Settlement '; *Canadian Archives Report* (1897), Note D; *The David Thompson Papers* (Ontario Archives). Very valuable are : Elliott Coues, *New Light on the Earlier History of the Great North-west* (3 vols., New York, 1897); J. B. Tyrrell, *David Thompson's Narrative of his Explorations in*

[1] Macdonald to Northcote, May 1, 1878, Pope, *Correspondence of Sir John Macdonald*, p. 239.

Western America, 1784–1812 (Toronto, 1916) ; Chester Martin, *Lord Selkirk's Work in Canada* (Oxford, 1916) ; L. A. Prud'homme, 'Pierre Gaultier de Varennes, Sieur de la Vérendrye' (*Trans. Royal Soc. of Canada*, 2nd series, vol. xi, sect. i, pp. 9 ff.) ; G. Dugas, *L'Ouest Canadien, sa Découverte par le Sieur de la Vérendrye* (Montreal, 1896 ; also in English, Montreal, 1905) ; A. Mackenzie, *Voyages from Montreal through the Continent of North America, 1789 and 1793* (London, 1801 ; reprint ed. by W. L. Grant, 2 vols., Toronto, 1911). For the later periods consult *Colonial Office Papers*, series G, 335–59, 360–5 (Canadian Archives) ; *Report from the Select Committee on Hudson's Bay Company* (London, 1857) ; *Hudson's Bay Papers* (London, 1859) ; *Copy or Extract of Correspondence . . . relating to the Surrender of Rupert's Land, &c.* (London, 1869) ; E. H. Oliver, *The Canadian North-west : Its Early Development and Legislative Records* (2 vols., Ottawa, 1914) ; E. O. S. Scholefield, *Report of the Provincial Archives Department of British Columbia* (Victoria, 1914), *Minutes of the Council of Vancouver Island . . . August 30, 1851, to February 6, 1861* (Victoria, 1918), *Minutes of the House of Assembly, Vancouver Island, August 12, 1856, to September 25, 1858* (Victoria, 1918), *House of Assembly, Correspondence Book, August 12, 1856, to July 6, 1859* (Victoria, 1918) ; N. F. Black, *A History of Saskatchewan and the Old North-west* (Regina, 1913) ; E. O. S. Scholefield and F. W. Howay, *British Columbia from the Earliest Times to the Present* (2 vols., Vancouver, 1914) ; J. N. E. Brown, 'The Evolution of Law and Government in the Yukon Territory' (*University of Toronto Studies : History and Economics*, vol. ii, 1907). There is no adequate history of the Hudson's Bay Co. : consult Willson, *The Great Company* (London, 1889) ; Bryce, *The Remarkable History of the Hudson's Bay Co.* (London, 1900) ; *Mackenzie, Selkirk and Simpson* (Toronto, 1910) ; Coats and Gosnell, *Sir James Douglas* (Toronto, 1910).]

CHAPTER XXI

THE DEVELOPMENT OF CANADIAN AUTONOMY

(i) *From Federation to 1914*

THE development of Canadian autonomy falls naturally into two periods. The first, extending from 1867 to 1914, saw the evolution of full self-government and of authority in commercial matters. It is characterized by growing assurance, slowly developing self-confidence, and that widening interest in economic affairs which belongs to the life of a young nation rich in material possibilities. The second period, from the beginning of the Great War to the present time, is the period of national manhood suddenly matured by the unparalleled events. During it constitutional advances were made which have revolutionized the relationship of Canada to the empire. In dramatic growth and in spectacular achievement these years are the most momentous in Canadian constitutional history.

After the territorial ' rounding off ' of the dominion there began to grow up a national emotion.[1] At first this was scattered and unorganized, but in 1870 a group of young men, known as ' the Canada First party ', began to lend it a greater influence and a wider life. Of these, W. A. Foster, a Toronto barrister, was the most brilliant. In a lecture entitled *Canada First ; or, Our New Nationality,* published in 1871, he called on Canadians to strengthen the foundations of their identity and to render the different races homogeneous by the development of an all-Canadian national feeling. For a year or two the party resisted the allurements of politics, but at length it expanded into the Canadian National Association with definite

[1] For a full discussion see ' The Growth of Canadian National Feeling ', by W. S. Wallace (*Canadian Historical Review,* June 1920).

political aims. These included a voice in treaties affecting Canada, the imposition of revenue duties for the fullest encouragement of native industry, and a militia system under Canadian officers. Hopes sprang high when Edward Blake, in his famous speech delivered at Aurora on October 3, 1874, adopted and amplified the platform.[1] Blake urged the cultivation of a Canadian national spirit as a preparation for the fullness of citizenship by ' four millions of Britons who are not free '. Fortunately for the future, Blake soon resumed friendly relations with the liberal party, and the emotion of Canadian nationalism was thus saved from ambiguous affiliations. Both the great historic parties have contributed to its development in sentiment as well as in fact. Indeed, it was insight that led Macdonald to call his protectionist system ' the national policy ', for he meant it to be the economic counterpart of national emotion. Laurier's defeat on the reciprocity issue in 1911 was in a large measure due to the fact that Canadians believed that such a system would impair national life. On the other hand, ' the Canada First ' movement must not be lightly overlooked. It came at an opportune moment in Canadian history to provide, as it were, an emotional impetus towards nationhood.

When Edward Blake became minister of justice in the year following his speech, he must have been convinced that his words were hardly a platform exaggeration, for the dominion was still heavily shackled even in domestic affairs. Legislation was still liable to disallowance. The governor-general was specially instructed to reserve certain classes of bills, and he possessed the right of pardon, a prerogative which the crown in England no longer enjoyed. There was no Canadian control over British immigration. The position of defence was still doubtful with the presence of imperial soldiers, and with an imperial officer in command of Canadian forces. There was no

[1] For a reprint of the speech, see *Canadian Historical Review*, September 1921.

supreme court at Ottawa. Needless to say Canada had little or no voice in international affairs. Under both conservative and liberal administrations extension of Canadian autonomy was achieved, but it was fortunate that the initial steps were made by Blake, as he gave to Canadian nationalism sobriety of judgement, wide scholarship, and legal insight, which were invaluable in the early days of advance.

As minister of justice Blake piloted through parliament the measure which set up the supreme court of Canada. The bill included a clause closing appeals to the judicial committee of the privy council. The government were compelled to withdraw this clause as the imperial cabinet pointed out that the royal assent would be withheld.[1] The court, however, has been a remarkable success. It has received many appeals from the provincial courts which otherwise would have gone to Westminster. It has helped to develop constitutional law and it has lent dignity and confidence to the Canadian judiciary. In the executive sphere Blakes's accomplishment was more remarkable.[2] From the time of federation, Canadian self-government was severely limited by the commissions and instructions issued by the imperial cabinet to the governors-general. They were ordered to refuse assent to any bill for divorce; for grants to themselves; for making paper or other currency legal tender; for imposing differential duties; for interference with the naval or military forces of the crown in the dominion, with treaty obligations, with the royal prerogative, with the property of British subjects not resident in Canada, or with the trade and shipping of the United Kingdom; for re-enacting any measure which had been disallowed or to which assent had been previously refused. In the case of an offender condemned to death they were commanded to with-

---

[1] Cf. *Nineteenth Century*, July 1879, p. 173. See Judicial Committee Act, 1844 (7 & 8 Victoria, c. 69), which places the right of appeal on a statutory basis.
[2] See *Canada Sessional Papers*, 1877, No. 13 ; 1879, No. 181.

hold or to extend pardon or reprieve according to their own deliberate judgement whether the Canadian ministers concurred therein or not. The case of Ambroise Lépine, a prisoner sentenced to death for his part in the Red River rebellion, brought to the front the entire question of the governor-general's power. In 1875 Lord Dufferin, acting on his instructions, commuted Lépine's sentence to two years' imprisonment with permanent deprivation of political rights. It is true that Dufferin consulted his ministers, but he was careful to explain in an official communication to Blake that he was justified in acting ' according to his independent judgement and on his own personal responsibility '.[1] The case raised in an acute form the subject of the responsibility of the Canadian cabinet for the governor's official acts. Blake visited England, with the result that the imperial government recast the commission and instructions. The enumeration of subjects on which legislation must be reserved was discontinued and the prerogative of pardon must only be exercised on ministerial advice.[2]

During the discussions, Blake submitted to the colonial secretary a memorandum which occupies an important place in the history of Canadian constitutional development. He argued that the governor-general's position should be that of a constitutional monarch, that he should be allowed no personal discretion where the power of pardon was concerned, and that he should be given freedom to assent to all Canadian Acts, leaving the imperial cabinet to disallow them if necessary. The government of Canada must be made responsible for all Canadian affairs which did not involve imperial interests. Blake considered that the latter eventuality would seldom occur ; but it could be dealt with when it arose, and no formal record should diminish the sphere of Canadian self-government. He added : 'The existing forms in the case of Canada have

---

[1] *Canadian Gazette, Extra*, June 19, 1875 ; *Canada Sessional Papers*, 1875, No. 11. [2] Kennedy, *op. cit.*, pp. 696 ff.

been felt for some time to be capable of amendment, for reasons which require that special consideration should be given to her position and which render unsuitable for her the forms which may be eminently suited for some of the colonies. Canada is not merely a colony or a province : she is a dominion composed of an aggregate of seven large provinces federally united under an imperial charter, which expressly recites that her constitution is to be similar in principle to that of the United Kingdom. Nay, more; besides the powers with which she is invested over a large part of the affairs of the inhabitants of the several provinces, she enjoys absolute powers of legislation and administration over the people and territories of the North-west, out of which she has already created one province, and is empowered to create others, with representative institutions. These circumstances, together with the vastness of her area, the numbers of her population, the character of the representative institutions and of the responsible government which as citizens of the various provinces and of Canada her people have so long enjoyed, all point to the propriety of dealing with the question in hand in a manner very different from that which might be fitly adopted with reference to a single and comparatively small and young colony. Besides the general spread of the principles of constitutional freedom, there has been in reference to the colonies a recognized difference between their circumstances, resulting in the application to those in a less advanced condition of a lesser measure of self-government, while others are said to be invested with " the fullest freedom of political government " ; and it may be fairly stated that there is no dependency of the British crown which is entitled to so full an application of the principles of constitutional freedom as the dominion of Canada.' Since Blake's time there has been no friction with reference to either ministerial responsibility, assenting to bills, or granting pardons. This fact in itself amply justifies the changes which he brought about, but the political setting in which Blake framed his position is perhaps of greater importance. Blake was a lifelong advocate of fuller Canadian autonomy, and it is significant that he found himself in later life unable to co-operate with the liberal party when he feared that its economic policy in relation to the United States would tend to complicate and to endanger Canada's political future.[1]

It was, however, in matters of trade and commerce that the greatest advances were made before 1914. From the establishment of responsible government there was always a tendency to work with Canada in these spheres, which is illustrated by Elgin's reciprocity treaty of 1854 and by Macdonald's work at Washington in 1871, when the question of Canadian fisheries and territorial waters was discussed. On the other hand, it was only when the trade depression of the late seventies forced Canada to seek wider markets for her exports, that the actual problem of commercial treaties came to the front. With the fall of the liberal ministry in 1878, Macdonald sent Galt to England for the purpose of discussing, for the benefit of Canadian trade, tariff agreements with foreign states. Galt made arrangements with the imperial government that in such proposals to France and Spain, the British representatives there should carry on the formal negotiations, ' the settlement of the details of the arrangement being dealt with by Sir Alexander Galt '. This method of procedure conceded Galt's position as the real negotiator, while at the same time it was a clear indication that assent to a Canadian bill imposing differential duties was no longer liable to be withheld. Political changes in France and Spain and the cross-currents of European diplomacy rendered Galt's mission unsuccessful, but beginnings had been made which pointed at least to a new economic group. Four months later, Macdonald, Tupper, Tilley, and Galt discussed in London

---

[1] See Willison, *op. cit.*, vol. ii, pp. 172 ff. ; Skelton, *op. cit.*, vol. i, pp. 419 ff. ; and cf. Tupper, *Recollections of Sixty Years*, pp. 304 ff.

with the British government the railway situation in Canada. Difficulties in this connexion led to the proposal for the appointment of a permanent Canadian representative in England. A memorandum was drawn up and presented to the British cabinet in August 1879 in which the proposal was justified. Canadian development required more constant and more intimate communication between the two governments than that afforded by formal and official dispatches through the governor-general. Canada was ' no longer an ordinary possession of the crown ', and it was evident that many questions would arise demanding personal discussion. It would be a serious inconvenience for Canadian ministers to go constantly to London, and as direct trade negotiations with foreign powers had already been recognized, it seemed reasonable that there should be a permanent representative in England, whom the crown should ' accredit to the foreign court, by association for the special object with the resident minister or other imperial negotiator '. With this end in view, the government of Canada proposed to appoint a Canadian minister to a ' quasi-diplomatic position at the court of St. James '. The memorandum received none too favourable consideration. The colonial secretary threw doubts on the suggested diplomatic character of the office, and also pointed out that the imperial foreign secretary alone could decide on the exact functions which its holder might exercise in foreign affairs.

A dignified answer was returned by the Canadian cabinet. It was pointed out that Canada as a portion of the empire could not carry on strictly diplomatic missions, but the Canadian government had as much right to advise the crown as the imperial government had. Indeed such powers had been conferred on Canada that the imperial government had little claim to give advice on them, and ' in considering many questions of the highest importance, such as the commercial and fiscal policy of the dominion as affecting the United Kingdom, the promotion of imperial interests in the administration and settlement of the interior of the continent, and on many other subjects, indeed on all matters of internal concern, the imperial government and parliament have so far transferred to Canada an independent control that their discussion and settlement have become subjects for mutual consent and concert, and thereby have, it is thought, assumed a quasi-diplomatic character as between her majesty's government representing the United Kingdom *per se* and the dominion, without in any manner derogating from their general authority as rulers of the entire empire '.   This minute of council hinted, it is true, at preferential tariffs within the empire, but the constitutional implication has been rather ignored.   Canada was seeking the right in the economic sphere to expand her group life.[1]   Finally the British government agreed to the appointment of a ' High Commissioner of Canada in London '.   In April 1880 Macdonald laid the correspondence on the table and moved the appointment of Galt, who reached England during the same month, and remained there till 1883.   Perhaps there is only one outstanding fact in connexion with Galt's tenure of office.   In a speech at Greenock he declared that Canada would not remain satisfied with its present position, and that the empire had completely outgrown its political organization.   He turned his back on his own old defence of independence and looked to a federation of all the self-governing British states.   The suggestion is of no more and of no less importance than those of a similar nature, but the speech was a remarkable declaration of the growing consciousness of Canadian nationhood.[2]

[1] For the memorandum, minute of council, and correspondence, see *Canada Sessional Papers*, 1880, No. 105, and compare Macdonald to Galt, February 26, 1882, and to Lord Stanley, August 15, 1890, Pope, *Correspondence of Sir John Macdonald*, pp. 285, 471.

[2] A. T. Galt, *The Relations of the Colonies to the Empire : Present and Future*. Macdonald advised Galt to use discretion in his public utterances lest he might complicate the Canadian government on account of the position which he held : ' The Canadian High Commissioner is now acknowledged to be an ambassador,

Tupper, who succeeded Galt, was recognized by the imperial government not merely as adviser but as actual negotiator in commercial treaties, and in 1893 he signed such a treaty with France.   These concessions implied others.   It soon became evident that it would not be possible for Great Britain to make in future general commercial treaties which would bind Canada, and the plan was soon adopted of including a clause which gave Canada the right to adhere or to refuse to adhere to such treaties.   This in turn raised the further question whether Canada should be bound by old treaties in the framing of which there had been neither consultation with Canada nor agents acting for Canada.   This problem took on further difficulties when Canada began to think of arranging a scheme of pre-ferential trade with the mother country.   It was found that a treaty of 1862 with Belgium and of 1865 with the North German Confederation precluded such preference without the inclusion of these two countries and of course of all countries with most-favoured-nation clauses in their treaties.   In 1894 the matter was discussed at a conference at Ottawa.[1]   Imperial preference was ruled out of practical politics by the British government, who, however, laid down in the following year certain general regulations covering separate commercial treaties with foreign states in the matter of dominion trade. The treaty must be between the imperial government, not the dominion, and the foreign power, since the imperial government would be held responsible for keeping the terms of the treaty. To grant Canada the power of independent negotiation would concede its sovereignty in international law and would amount to the admission that Canada had ceased to be a part of the empire, a result desired neither by Great Britain nor the dominion.   Negotiations must be conducted by the imperial

and as such it is his duty to be *persona grata* to the government to which he is accredited': Macdonald to Galt, February 21, 1883, Pope, *op. cit.*, p. 298.
   [1] *Parliamentary Papers*, Cd. 7553.

representative at the foreign court aided by a Canadian representative as a second plenipotentiary or as a subordinate. Any treaty which they might conclude would be signed by the plenipotentiaries only after its terms had been approved by the imperial and Canadian governments. It would ultimately be ratified by the crown on the advice of the British government if the Canadian government so desired ; or, in the event of legislation being requisite to make its terms effective, if the Canadian legislature so desired. Conditions of negotiations were laid down : concessions made to any foreign power must be made to any other foreign power having by existing treaties most-favoured-nation rights in Canada ; any concessions so made must be extended without compensation to all British possessions ; no concession must be accepted from a foreign government which would be prejudicial to other parts of the empire.[1]   These principles were once again laid down by Sir Edward Grey in 1907. He informed the imperial representatives in Paris and Rome that Canada desired to begin negotiations with the French and Italian governments in order to promote closer commercial relations. He outlined the conditions of 1895, but stated that he did not think it necessary in this case to adhere to the strict letter of those regulations, which aimed rather to prevent the dominion from beginning negotiations unknown to and independent of the imperial government than to curtail its activities when there was mutual confidence. The selection of the negotiator was chiefly a matter of convenience, and in this case the Canadian prime minister and minister of finance were obviously most suited to carry out arrangements, and they would doubtless inform the imperial representative from time to time of the progress of the negotiations. The latter, in the event of a successful issue, would sign the agreement jointly with the Canadian negotiator, to whom full powers would be granted for the

[1] *Parliamentary Papers*, Cd. 7824.

special purpose.[1] Of course, all treaties made under these instructions of 1895 and 1907 have been subject to the fullest imperial consideration before being finally concluded. Canada, on several occasions, has made informal trade arrangements through the consular representatives of foreign states, but these have not been considered as treaties, and have, therefore, not been ratified by the imperial government. The arrangements, however, were carried into effect by orders in council, and an opportunity was thus given through the governor-general for imperial objections.

The Canadian feeling in favour of a British preference emphasized the desire that all old treaties which curtailed the freedom of Canadian action should be abrogated. After discussions at the colonial conference in 1897, the British government arranged the termination of the treaties with Belgium and Germany to which reference has been made.[2] In 1899 the principle was begun that, in concluding new commercial treaties, Canada should be given the right of separate withdrawal as well as of separate adherence. Finally, the position has been established, through the conclusion of a long series of treaties between Great Britain and powers with whom most-favoured-nation treaties existed, that the crown on giving a year's notice can withdraw with respect to Canada or any self-governing dominion, without hurting the validity of the treaty in relation to other parts of the empire. Thus Canada is now able to make commercial arrangements with a foreign state without being under the compulsion of extending similar treatment to other powers under rights established by existing treaties.

In the matter of commercial treaties the development has reached this position. Canada is not bound by any trade treaty to which its consent has not been given. Canada will

[1] *Parliamentary Papers*, H. C. (1910), 129.
[2] *Parliamentary Papers*, Cd. 8596.

be consulted by the imperial government when a general commercial treaty is under consideration in order that special concessions, if desired by Canada, may be secured. If Canada wishes to establish closer commercial relations with a foreign state, the imperial government will appoint Canadian plenipotentiaries to carry on negotiations, and they will sign jointly with an imperial representative any treaty which may arise out of the discussions. The interests of the empire at large must not be sacrificed and Canada must extend to the empire all concessions granted to a foreign power. The treaty must be ratified by the crown on the advice of the imperial ministry acting on the request of Canada.

Closely allied to economic matters are international conferences on miscellaneous questions of general concern—such as protection of fur seals or the opium traffic. To these the dominions and even their constituent provinces have sent representatives, but where an international agreement was aimed at as the outcome of such a conference it was formerly the custom for the dominions to have no representatives or merely to help in advising the imperial delegates. Changes gradually took place which culminated in 1912, when the four great dominions sent delegates to the Radio-telegraphic conference, who acted with full powers, under the great seal of the United Kingdom, as plenipotentiaries for their respective states. The custom then established has been continued at other international conferences held since that date. The fundamental change lies in the fact that Canadian plenipotentiaries, for example, are no longer merely included among the British group, which must cast their vote as a unit. As arrangements now are, Canada has plenipotentiaries of its own acting independent of those from Great Britain, and may accordingly differ in opinion from the imperial view. The position is an international recognition of a constitutional anomaly, for the British crown may express several divergent decisions. On the other hand, it must not be forgotten that the Canadian plenipotentiaries receive their fullness of authority at the hands of the imperial executive, and that the final ratification rests with the crown acting on the advice of imperial ministers. The anomaly can thus be overcome although circumstances will hardly arise to create the necessity. Its existence, however, bears excellent witness to new difficulties created by the growing nationhood of the dominions.

During this period there have been no remarkable developments in the sphere covered by strict political treaties. As international law stands Canada cannot make an independent political agreement. It is clearly recognized that the crown must act on the imperial cabinet's advice in making a political treaty for the simple reason that international responsibility lies with Great Britain. On the other hand, no political treaty as such can change the law of Great Britain or of Canada. If Canada is concerned, the duty of making the treaty effective lies with Canada, acting as a rule through the Canadian parliament. Within the limitations imposed by international law there has been growth. Since Elgin's time a working principle has been recognized that Canada would be consulted where Canadian questions were involved. In 1886 this principle was given a fuller meaning, when the imperial government repudiated a theory laid down by the United States that Canada, as a non-sovereign state, could not deal with any matter involving treaty rights.[1] This position received additional sanction in 1910, when the international Hague tribunal provided for legislation by the Canadian parliament in the matter of the fishery dispute with the United States.[2] The right of the imperial government to hold the place of ultimate interpreter of a political treaty has never been disputed by Canada, but

---

[1] *Parliamentary Papers*, Cd. 4937 ; cf. Tupper, *op. cit.*, p. 177, and Borden, *Canadian Constitutional Studies*, p. 76.

[2] *Parliamentary Papers*, Cd. 5396.

in 1908, when an arbitration treaty was concluded with the United States, Great Britain expressly reserved the right to obtain Canadian concurrence before accepting an agreement for submitting a matter to arbitration in which Canada was concerned. Canada thus secured the right of refusing a treaty where Canada was concerned. The problem of ultimate interpretation is simplified, for as a rule Canada will not be involved in a political treaty without a previous record of its willingness to be bound by it. It is clear that, within the empire at least, Canadian autonomy in political treaties has already reached almost complete fullness.

At the imperial conference of 1911, the question of general international agreements of a quasi-political nature was discussed.[1] Matters of vital importance to the self-governing dominions had been dealt with in the Declaration of London which arose out of the Hague conference of 1907. Australia formally protested against the failure to consult the dominions. The imperial government defended themselves by stating that the dominions had never been previously represented at the Hague, and indeed had expressed no wish for such representation. The imperial conference agreed that the dominions should be consulted when instructions were issued to British delegates at future conventions, and that, when agreements were reached which might affect the dominions, they would not be signed without previous consideration by the dominions. In other international agreements where time and circumstances permitted and the dominions were concerned, a similar procedure would normally follow. The Australian prime minister made a suggestion, which was not pressed, that the dominions should enter into direct communications with the foreign office, but Sir Wilfrid Laurier made it clear that Canada did not wish to establish as a rule of procedure the principle of consultation on all international affairs. He maintained that

[1] *Parliamentary Papers,* Cd. 5745.

such general consultation would imply that Canada had undertaken responsibilities which he believed she was not prepared to carry out. An immediate result followed from the discussions. The delegates were invited to attend a meeting of the committee of imperial defence, when the foreign secretary explained the general scheme of British foreign policy and its relations to the defences of the empire. The political situation in Europe was at the moment extremely threatening, and the dominions approved, as far as they could apart from their legislatures, of the renewal of the Anglo-Japanese alliance. It was also arranged that members of the cabinets of the dominions should be invited to all the future meetings when naval and military matters affecting them were under discussion, and that a defence committee should be organized in each dominion. Reference to these arrangements naturally brings up the growth of Canadian control in defence. It is possible to outline shortly the development up to 1911 ; but from that date the consideration involves foreign affairs in such a way that it is impossible to study either subject in isolation.

The grant of responsible government implied that the imperial parliament would throw the onus of maintaining internal peace on the self-governing colonies, and in 1862 the imperial house of commons resolved that, while all parts of the empire must receive imperial aid against possible attack arising out of imperial policy, the colonies with responsible governments should bear the expenses of their own internal defence and ought to assist in external defence.[1] The application of this resolution to Canada was slow, even after federation.[2] The dominion had been given exclusive control over ' militia, military and naval service, and defence '.[3] The first Canadian cabinet contained a minister of militia and defence ; but Canada

[1] *Hansard*, ser. 3, vol. clxv, pp. 1032 ff.

[2] For Macdonald's opinion on the policy see Macdonald to Carnarvon, April 14, 1870, Pope, *op. cit.*, p. 133.

[3] British North America Act, 1867, sect. 91.

only gradually assumed authority. Imperial money was freely spent on fortifications and an imperial force was available under an imperial officer during the Red River rebellion of 1870.   When the more serious North-west rebellion broke out in 1885 Canadian forces under Canadian officers coped success-fully with the situation. The imperial government, however, continued to garrison Halifax and Esquimalt owing to their strategic importance. The repeated disasters to British arms during the Boer war caused Canada to offer to maintain garrisons at Canadian expense, and imperial troops were finally withdrawn.[1]   At the conclusion of that war a new naval policy reduced the importance of these ports, and in 1910 arrangements were concluded to hand over to Canada the admiralty property, with the proviso that docking and coaling facilities should be provided for the imperial navy and that the naval dockyards should be kept in a state of adequate repair.[2] With the departure of imperial forces, the rule that an imperial officer should be in command of the Canadian militia became more absurd. Indeed, it had never worked out satisfactorily. The appointment lay with the governor-general in council, but many of these imperial officers were indiscreet and not at all anxious to recognize that they were under the Canadian ministry. Canadian opinion began to call for the ' appointment of a Canadian officer without reference to the horse guards or war office '. The dominion government moved slowly, but insisted that the method of appointment should not be formal and that consultation and an exchange of views should take place with the imperial cabinet.[3] The arrangement was unsatisfactory, and ended in 1904 in the dismissal of Lord Dundonald by the Canadian

[1] *Parliamentary Papers*, Cd. 2565.

[2] See Naval Establishments in British Possessions Act, 1909, and Orders in Council, October 23, 1910, and May 4, 1911.

[3] Macdonald to Lorne, to Knutsford, to Connaught, August 18, 20, 1890, Pope, *op. cit.*, pp. 473 ff.

government for indiscretion.[1] A new plan was established by an imperial Act, and the practice by which the commanding officer of the Canadian militia was always an imperial officer was discontinued.[2] The right of course remains for the imperial government to station troops and to recruit for the imperial army in Canada, and the imperial Army Act cannot be over-ridden by Canadian legislature. On the other hand, the imperial government has no control of any kind over Canadian troops raised for home defence, and there is no agreement between the two governments binding Canada to send troops overseas.[3] Any aid given outside Canadian territory to the empire depends entirely on the will of the Canadian legislature for the time being. Canadian soldiers serve overseas volun-tarily ; or, if organized, under an *ad hoc* Canadian law. In the control of this supreme obligation of citizenship, Canadian autonomy is complete.

In the matter of naval defence little has been done, as the imperial navy rendered adequate protection. The European situation became, however, so complicated in 1909 that, out of consultations, Canada offered to create a naval force to operate on the Atlantic and the Pacific and reaffirmed its obligations in connexion with the dockyards at Halifax and Esquimalt. An Act was passed in 1910 regulating the force and providing for a building programme.[4] The principle was laid down that the fleet should be under the absolute control of the dominion, but provision was made that in cases of emergency and under proper authority the ships and men should be at the disposal of the crown for general service in the royal navy. The debates

[1] *House of Commons Debates* (1904), pp. 4580 ff. For an admirable account of the Dundonald episode, see Skelton, *op. cit.*, vol. ii, pp. 196 ff.

[2] 4 Edward VII, c. 23.

[3] See an interesting proposal, however, made by Macdonald in 1885 : ' The reciprocal aid to be given by the colonies and England should be made a matter of treaty, deliberately entered into and settled on a permanent basis' : Macdonald to Tupper, March 12, 1885, Pope, *op. cit.*, p. 338 ; cf. *ibid.*, p. 468.

[4] 1 & 2 George V, c. 43.

on this Act are of great interest.[1]   Opinions were expressed that the dominion was doing too little, that it was setting up a claim to remain neutral when Great Britain was at war, that steps were being taken to involve Canada in foreign wars in which it had no interests.   Laurier's position was clearly stated.   Whether Canada liked it or not, Canada was necessarily in a state of war when Great Britain was at war.   Canada could not afford to be indifferent to this fact and must be prepared to do its share in defending itself.   But the prime minister was careful to state that Canadian forces would not be placed automatically at the disposal of Great Britain, and that Canada did not surrender the right of deciding whether it would take part in a war or give no aid.   Mr. Borden, the leader of the opposition, directed his criticism mainly against the government's refusal to co-operate in all British wars and against the decision to create a Canadian fleet rather than to offer an immediate monetary contribution to the imperial building programme.

The fall of the Laurier government in 1911 found the Canadian plans unadvanced, and the conservatives did not desire to forward them.   Mr. Borden visited England, and on December 5, 1912, he laid on the table of the house an admiralty memorandum prepared at his request.[2]   He emphasized the position which he had taken in parliament the previous year and outlined a vote for building ships of the first strength to be placed at the disposal of the admiralty, but capable of retransference to the dominion if a future decision should create a Canadian navy.   The senate rejected the proposals on a strict party vote.   Meanwhile a step of great importance was taken at the instance of the Canadian prime minister.   On December 10, 1912, the colonial secretary embodied in a dispatch the principles agreed on in 1911 by the imperial defence

[1] *House of Commons Debates* (1909–10), pp. 1732 ff.
[2] *Parliamentary Papers*, Cd. 6513.

committee and afterwards provisionally confirmed by Mr. Borden. Among these was the suggestion that a Canadian cabinet minister should attend meetings of the committee, and that a committee of defence should be organized by the Canadian government. Mr. Borden saw no difficulties in a Canadian minister residing some months of the year in London, but he expressed a desire that such a minister should receive in confidence full and complete information relating to foreign affairs and should have free access to all British ministers with this end in view. The imperial government agreed to the suggestion, but pointed out that the committee was an advisory, not an executive body, and that ultimate responsibility remained with the imperial cabinet.[1] As a matter of fact, Mr. Borden merely arranged for the working in a developed form of previous proposals, and on his part the colonial secretary explained that the natural and laudable desire of the Canadian government did not involve the difficult problems of an empire constitution or of taxation. Mr. Borden, in referring to the matter in the Canadian house of commons, saw in the arrangement only a provisional plan, but he struck a new note. The admiralty memorandum, it is true, laid stress on the fact that the imperial government were prepared in the future as in the past to supply the resources necessary for imperial defence, and that there was no desire to influence Canadian public opinion or to interfere in any way with the Canadian parliament in making a decision on a matter which was exclusively within its jurisdiction. Mr. Borden, however, saw in the whole discussions, in the proposals relating to the imperial defence committee, and in the naval situation in Europe an important implication. Great Britain was willing that the burden of the defence of the empire should be shared. In this connexion Mr. Borden declared, ' When Great Britain

[1] *Parliamentary Papers*, Cd. 6560 ; cf. Viscount Esher, *The Committee of Imperial Defence : Its Functions and Potentialities* (London, 1912).

no longer assumes sole responsibility for defence upon the high seas, she can no longer undertake to assume sole responsibility for or sole control of foreign policy, which is closely, vitally, constantly associated with defence in which the dominions participate '. Mr. Borden saw clearly that participation in defence would bring with it, inevitably and as an outcome of Canadian public opinion—when that participation was arranged and confirmed by the Canadian parliament—the demand for a voice in the councils of the empire touching the momentous issues of peace and war and in the control of foreign policy out of which they arose. Developments were slow even in connexion with the immediate proposals. It was not till after Lord Strathcona's death in 1914 that Sir George Perley, a Canadian cabinet minister, was appointed to perform the duties of high commissioner, while carrying out those of resident minister in London. The appointment, belated though it was, was evidence that the Canadian government was prepared to link up Canada with the defence of the empire through the presence of a responsible minister in England.

The developments which have been considered afford ample illustration of the workings of the principle of consultation, but no record would be at all adequate without a reference at least to the various conferences which have been held regularly since 1887, at first under the title of colonial conferences. A vast amount of work has been accomplished and, as has appeared, many advances of a distinct nature have been the outcome. Of course, the share in empire responsibility has been nominal, but Canada received an insight into international problems and its national consciousness developed to such an extent that any proposals for a more real partnership were abandoned. Indeed, the conferences themselves provided an opportunity for a very definite attitude. In April 1905 the colonial secretary proposed to change the name to that of imperial councils, and that a permanent imperial commission should be created with offices in London for the civil affairs of the empire. The Canadian government issued a reply stating that they considered that the name, if changed at all, should be changed by the conferences, and they proposed that of ' imperial conference ', which was accepted by the colonial conference of 1907. The suggestion was accompanied with a reasoned explanation : ' they entertain with some doubt the proposal to change the name of the colonial conference to that of the imperial council, which they apprehend would be interpreted as marking a step distinctly in advance of the position hitherto attained in the discussions of the relations between the mother country and the colonies. As the committee [i.e. the Canadian cabinet] understand the phrase, a conference is a more or less unconventional gathering for informal discussion of public questions, continued, it may be, from time to time, as circumstances external to itself may render expedient, but possessing no faculty or power of binding action. The assembly of colonial ministers which met in 1887, 1897, and 1902 appears to the committee to fulfil these conditions. The term council, on the other hand, indicates, in the view of your excellency's ministers, a more formal assemblage, possessing an advisory and deliberative character, and in conjunction with the word " imperial " suggesting a permanent institution which, endowed with a continuous life, might eventually come to be regarded as an encroachment upon the full measure of autonomous legislative and administrative power now enjoyed by all the self-governing colonies '. The proposal for a commission was also criticized, because the Canadian government could not ' wholly divest themselves of the idea that such a commission might conceivably interfere with the working of responsible government '.[1]

[1] *Parliamentary Papers*, Cd. 1785. The conference of 1907, in addition to accepting Canada's suggested title, arranged the constitution for future conferences. An important advance was made when the conference agreed, after strong insistence by Canada and Australia, that future conferences

We stand perhaps too near these years to form a clear historical estimate of their constitutional importance, but this minute of the Canadian cabinet affords perhaps the best insight into the progress or lack of progress. The most constant and powerful motive during these years was that Canadian autonomy should not be damaged. As far as it is at present possible to make any judgement, that influence seems to have been sufficiently strong to merit the statement that it was the outcome of Canadian public opinion. It is impossible to study the processes through which actual advances came without being convinced that they took place in those spheres where Canada thought her autonomy was not endangered but rather advanced. They have thus been consolidated and become part of Canadian constitutional consciousness. On the other hand, it would seem that certainly up to 1912 no Canadian statesman. was prepared to bring forward large and new proposals in relation to defence and foreign affairs. When reasons are sought there can be little doubt that this attitude was guided by an insight into and a correct reading of Canadian public opinion. There was abroad a sufficiently strong belief to allow a generalization that Canadians feared an excess even of consultation in these matters because it might imply some surrender of self-government ; while any proposals towards an empire constitution through which control might be regularized were looked askance on as the inevitable pooling of a certain amount of Canadian autonomy. Doubtless it is quite possible to recall much evidence on the other side, and not a few Canadians have expressed opinions in favour of giving constitutional effect in defence and foreign policy to Canada's national status ; but such evidence must not be exaggerated. Just because of its exceptional nature it has received, like most

should be ' between his majesty's government and the governments of the self-governing dominions beyond the seas ' and not between the colonial office and the dominions.

exceptional matters, a larger amount of public notice than the general pedestrian opinions which, being ordinary, command no notoriety. Statesmen like Sir Robert Borden and Mr. Doherty have spoken during this period of a necessary co-operation in foreign affairs, but always in connexion with defence. Up to 1914, however, little that was effective was done to arrive at a policy of defence for the empire, and it is difficult to estimate how much influence these statesmen exercised in these matters. The fact seems clear that the one outstanding emphasis has been on complete self-government and on the refusal to become committed to a legal, constitutional, organized policy for the empire which would bind Canada as a consenting party in an imperial responsible executive. Many motives have been suggested to explain this state of mind—selfishness, lack of international consciousness, national youth, and so on. The political thinker need not necessarily concern himself with these—all or none of which may have been at work, but he cannot be blind to the wisdom which refuses to make constitutional advances until public opinion is ready for them. There has been no dispute during the period that territorially Canada was at war when Great Britain was at war, but what has been avoided with deliberate purpose was the acceptance of principles implying aid in war, among which was a voice in foreign policy. The delay in sending Sir George Perley to London is in itself significant. In spite of the advance made in the proposals and arrangements of 1912, Canada does not seem to have been in any hurry to rush into wider fields, and these only consultative. The outbreak of the Great War undoubtedly destroyed the normal opportunity of watching at work the constitutional ideas of Sir Robert Borden's ministry, differing as they did from those of his predecessor, and it must as a consequence remain problematical to decide how far they carried with them Canadian public opinion.

(ii) *1914 to the Present Time*

When the British government declared war against Germany on August 4, 1914, the declaration brought to the front the exact relationship between Canada and Great Britain. Hostilities were begun on the sole responsibility of the imperial government. Canada had no voice in a situation in which it had a vital interest. It is true that there was little time before the fatal event to carry on consultations, and that Canada had little opportunity to weigh the tragic import, but the very suddenness of the crisis served to bring into greater relief the vagueness of the constitutional ties. Not only was Great Britain solely responsible for the declaration of war, but the decision of the imperial government involved Canada automatically. The legal consequences were clear before the world. Canada was at war with Germany, and, by subsequent imperial declarations, with all the German allies. Canadian citizens became the legal enemies of those nations against whom the imperial government began hostilities, and Canadian territory was legally liable to invasion or to attack. Of course, the outbreak of the war did not create these conditions ; but the immensity of the struggle revealed in an unprecedented way to Canadians the implications of their place in the empire. It was well that the issues were as clear as they were at the beginning, otherwise the consequences of such a gigantic struggle to a country in the full tide of national development might have endangered imperial unity.

The declaration of war doubtless laid stress on Canada's legal limitations, but it also emphasized the autonomy which Canada had achieved. In every detail the imperial government acted with a scrupulous regard for Canada's status. Though the necessity was pressing and the situation unparalleled, no demand was made for men or money. Not even the slightest influence was brought to bear by the imperial government which might have impaired Canadian authority or wounded

Canadian sentiment. Neither imperial legislation nor the exercise of the prerogative infringed Canadian autonomy. Where legislation was necessary it was left open to Canada to accept or to reject it, and when the war prerogative was brought into operation, care was taken that it should cover only powers clearly and essentially belonging to the crown and that Canada should be left free in other matters to deal with war conditions. Imperial proclamations dealing, for example, with high treason and its by-products were merely due and legal notice to citizens of the empire as a whole. British ships registered in Canada were excluded from the operations of the imperial Shipping Acts.[1] Canadians temporarily resident in Great Britain were explicitly exempted from the military service imposed on certain classes of residents in Great Britain by imperial legislation. When the imperial parliament saw fit to strengthen the law against aliens and against trading with the enemy, no attempt was made to bind Canada. Even the Naturalization Act of 1918, touching as it did such a fundamental matter as allegiance to the crown, was not applied to Canada. In addition, the constitutional rights and conventions arrived at before 1914 were strictly observed. The imperial government had no connexion of any kind with the raising of Canadian troops, and Canadian military and naval activities remained entirely and exclusively in the hands of the Canadian government and legislature. The imperial government never once thought of exercising its perfectly legal right of recruiting men in Canada. It would be possible to illustrate from many other angles the meticulous care exercised by the imperial authorities in order to preserve fully Canadian autonomy.

Perhaps this emphasis was responsible for a certain executive aloofness between the government of Canada and the imperial

---

[1] Difficulties arose, however, over the claim made by the imperial government to requisition ships owned and registered in Canada. This claim was controverted by the Canadian cabinet, January 30, 1917 : Borden, *op. cit.*, pp. 121 ff.

government in the early years of the war. Indeed Canada did not appear interested in the suggestions for an imperial conference which were abroad in 1915, and was content with a promise that when the time came the imperial government would consult most fully the Canadian prime minister and discuss possible terms of peace. On the other hand, Sir George Perley's presence in London at the outbreak of the war afforded opportunities for consultation. The imperial government carried out loyally the arrangements of 1912 and entered into the fullest communications with him, as they also did with Sir Robert Borden when he visited England in the summer of 1915, going even so far as to invite him to be present at meetings of the British cabinet. Perhaps, however, at this period the nearest approach to concerted action was taken by the economic conference at Paris in June 1916, when Sir George Foster represented Canada. Although ministers from all the dominions visited England there was no effective partnership within the empire. Sir Robert Borden slowly began to grasp the political situation. He laid stress in England on the status of the dominions, and pointed out that their participation in the war must lead to participation in foreign policy. He thus assisted in developing an opinion that there had been lack of vision in not bringing together at once the statesmen of the empire. Doubtless the tremendous burden of local problems weighed heavy in these early years, and the overwhelming pressure of the ordeal left little room for reconstructions. There can, however, be little doubt that the desire on the part of the imperial government to respect Canadian autonomy was carried to too great a length if it helped to hold back proposals from the imperial government for real co-coperation. When the opportunity at length came there was abroad a general feeling that the step should have been taken early in the war.

When a new government was formed in the United Kingdom in December 1916, plans were at once forthcoming for develop-

ment, owing to the urgent necessity of the situation created by
the war. With Mr. Lloyd George as prime minister, an idea
grew up that a large cumbersome cabinet was an inefficient
body in the crisis. As a consequence a war cabinet was created.
Whatever its success or failure, its creation marked an important epoch in the problem of empire. For the moment an
imperial conference of the traditional type was ruled out of
practical politics, and on December 14 Canada was' invited to
send representatives to London for the purpose of consultation.
The invitation explained the nature and novelty of the meeting.
The imperial government asked the Canadian prime minister
' to attend a special and continuous series of meetings of the
war cabinet, in order to consider urgent questions affecting
the prosecution of the war, the possible conditions on which,
in agreement with our allies, we could consent to its termination,
and the problems which will then immediately arise. For the
purpose of these meetings your prime minister will be a member
of the war cabinet.' Canada was represented at all sessions
of the war cabinet, and thus took part in consultations on
foreign policy and on defence. A resolution was passed expressing a hope that at the conclusion of hostilities the imperial
cabinet ' should consist of the prime minister of the United
Kingdom and such of his colleagues as deal specially with
imperial affairs and of the prime minister of each of the dominions or some specially accredited alternate, possessed of equal
authority '. On May 17, 1917, Mr. Lloyd George explained
the principles governing the war cabinet in the house of commons. The purpose aimed at was ' that the responsible heads
of the governments of the empire, with those ministers who are
specially entrusted with the conduct of imperial policy, should
meet together at regular intervals to confer about foreign
policy and matters connected therewith and come to decisions
with regard to them which, subject to the control of their own
parliaments, they will then severally execute. By this means.

they will be able to obtain full information about all aspects of imperial affairs, and to determine by consultation together the policy of the empire in its most vital aspects, without infringing in any degree the autonomy which its parts at present enjoy. To what constitutional developments this may lead we do not attempt to settle. The whole question for perfecting the mechanism for " continuous consultation " about imperial and foreign affairs between the " autonomous nations of an imperial commonwealth " will be reserved for the consideration of that special conference which will be summoned as soon as possible after the war to readjust the constitutional relations of the empire '.[1]   Sir Robert Borden emphasized the changed status in various speeches.[2]   The prime minister of England was in the war cabinet only *primus inter pares*, and each nation preserved in full its autonomy, its self-government, and its ministerial responsibility. Prior to the organization, he declared, Canada lacked full national status, because the imperial government was the main factor in the foreign policy of the empire. With the creation of the war cabinet inferiority of status had disappeared, as the dominions had been admitted into equality of consultation. He described the war cabinet as ' a cabinet of governments ' in which the Canadian prime minister was responsible to his own parliament and to his own people, without which no conclusions arrived at could be carried out.

When the war cabinet of the United Kingdom was thus expanded, it was believed that an imperial conference would be unnecessary, but circumstances altered the situation and as a matter of fact imperial conferences were held in 1917 and in 1918. In these, general problems and questions of minor importance compared with those to which the war cabinet gave

[1] *War Cabinet: Report for 1917. Parliamentary Papers*, Cd. 9005.
[2] See specially his speeches to the Empire Parliamentary Association, April 3, 1917, and June 21, 1918.

its attention were discussed. The only organic change from the constitution of the imperial conferences lay in the fact that the secretary of state for the colonies and not Mr. Lloyd George presided over the imperial conferences. In the conference of 1917 the following important resolutions on the constitution of the empire were passed on the motion of Sir Robert Borden : ' The imperial war conference are of opinion that the readjustment of the constitutional arrangements of the component parts of the empire is too important and intricate a subject to be dealt with during the war, and that it should form the subject of a special imperial conference to be summoned as soon as possible after the cessation of hostilities. They deem it their duty, however, to place on record their view that any such readjustment, while thoroughly preserving all existing powers of self-government and complete control of domestic affairs, should be based upon a full recognition of the dominions as autonomous nations of an imperial commonwealth and of India as an important portion of the same, should recognize the rights of the dominions and of India to an adequate voice in foreign policy and in foreign relations, and should provide effective arrangements for continuous consultation in all important matters of common imperial concern, and for such necessary concerted action, founded on consultation, as the several governments may determine '. Sir Robert Borden was emphatic that future changes must be based on these foundations and must fully recognize the rights of the dominions to a voice in foreign policy and foreign relations. He pointed out that the willing acceptance of these principles by Great Britain was in itself an immense stride in advance. Equally significant for Canada was the statement of General Smuts that the resolutions negatived the federal solution to the constitutional problems of the empire.[1]

The war conference of 1918 did not disclose in its published

---

[1] *Parliamentary Papers*, Cd. 8566.

proceedings any further resolutions of a constitutional nature, but a lengthy discussion took place on the channel of communication between the dominions and the imperial government. The former felt that their new status rendered communications through the colonial office undesirable. The colonial secretary admitted that the older methods could not remain indefinitely in use, but he pointed out that there would be a certain amount of impracticability in expecting the imperial prime minister to carry the additional burden contemplated by the change and that the office of the governor-general should not be forgotten. Finally the matter under discussion was referred to the imperial war cabinet, on a resolution from the conference that development was necessary and that the war cabinet should consider the creation of suitable machinery.[1] As a result the war cabinet arrived at the following arrangement : ' The prime ministers of the dominions, as members of the imperial war cabinet, have the right of direct communication with the prime minister of the United Kingdom and vice versa. Such communication should be confined to questions of cabinet importance. The prime ministers themselves are the judges of such questions. Telegraphic communications between the prime ministers should, as a rule, be conducted through the colonial office machinery, but this will not exclude the adoption of more direct means of communication in exceptional circumstances. In order to secure continuity in the work of the imperial war cabinet and a permanent means of consultation during the war on the more important questions of common interest, the prime minister of each dominion has the right to nominate a cabinet minister either as a resident or visitor in London to represent him at meetings of the imperial war cabinet, to be held regularly between the plenary sessions.' [2]

---

[1] *Parliamentary Papers*, Cd. 9177.
[2] *War Cabinet : Report for 1918*, Cmd. 325.

It is necessary at this point to examine the developments with great care as there has been a tendency to lend them at least an emotional exaggeration. Firstly, the use of the term ' cabinet ' to describe the meetings of empire ministers has led to the belief that the war cabinet was an executive body for the empire. This belief is unwarranted. The war cabinet had no prime minister—only a president—and his colleagues were not his own selection, but were chosen by the cabinets of the dominions. Collective responsibility did not exist. Each member was directly responsible to his own parliament. Decisions arrived at remained mere decisions until concurred in by each dominion cabinet and approved of by each dominion parliament. If a dominion prime minister failed to obtain such concurrence or approval he did not suffer the penalty of being excluded. More important still, if the British members failed to carry the goodwill of the dominion members on any matters, they could have their wishes carried out, provided no new legislation was necessary, through the ordinary channels of the British departments of state. Indeed, where agreement was reached, and where the dominion ministers obtained the necessary authority from their states to make these agreements actual, the ultimate and legal responsibility lay with the imperial cabinet. The imperial war cabinet differed in degree and not in kind from the imperial conferences. The former dealt with the vital and overwhelming problems of an unparalleled tragedy, the latter with problems commonplace in comparison. Since the peace, the position has become clearer, and Canada has made no effort to take advantage of the technical resolution of 1918. Doubtless this was natural with a special constitutional conference ahead. The imperial conference of 1921, however, shelved such a conference by a resolution stating that no advantages could be gained from it. Mr. Lloyd George dissociated the imperial government from a current belief that the imperial government were dissatisfied with the constitution of the empire and were in favour of revolutionary changes. He expressed himself satisfied with the progress achieved through full and free consultation between the prime ministers. He welcomed the idea of a Canadian minister at Washington. He emphasized that the dominions had been ' accepted fully into the comity of nations by the whole world', and that they were 'equal partners in the dignities and the responsibilities of the British commonwealth ', with ' liberty as its binding principle . . . based not on force but on goodwill and a common understanding '. Mr. Meighen, then prime minister of Canada, got no nearer any concrete proposals, and the conference closed with a significant address to the king pointing out its ' unanimous conviction that the most essential of the links that bind our widely spread peoples is the crown '.[1]

Before leaving the subject of Canadian autonomy it is necessary to consider shortly Canada's relation to the peace conference and to the league of nations. The imperial government early in the war had assured the dominions that they would be consulted on the terms of peace. When it came to the actual peace conference there were discussions over the method of representation. It seemed natural and reasonable that the British empire should be represented by a single delegation on which Canadian ministers might serve, but which would act as a unit. On the other hand, the methods already referred to in connexion with the Radio-telegraphic conference appeared more suitable to the new conditions, especially as Canada pressed for separate representation. An agreement was reached that the dominions should be secured a place equal to that of the smaller powers and that their solidarity with the United Kingdom should be maintained. In order that international effect should be given to this agreement, the supreme war council altered their original plans in order to admit the dominions separately. The British empire, the

[1] *Parliamentary Papers*, Cmd. 1474.

United States, France, Italy, and Japan were assigned five delegates, the lesser powers were grouped into classes having three, two, and one representative for each state within each class, and Canada was assigned two delegates. Each delegation had the right to set up a panel from which the delegates present on any occasion might be chosen, and Canadian delegates might be included by this panel system in the representation of the British empire. Canada thus enjoyed double representation, and thus full opportunity was given for the expression of Canadian views, while it stood before the world as an autonomous member of the British empire, which for the first time appeared under that name at a peace conference, and presented its proposals and decisions for the first time after consultation with the dominions and India. When practical considerations necessitated the handing over of actual decisions to the council of four, Canadian interests could be secured only by pressure on Mr. Lloyd George. There was doubtless a certain amount of irritation owing to this decision. On the other hand, even France and Italy felt that there was something anomalous in the presence of dominion delegates at the conference, and a rule was made that the dominions should not possess a vote apart from the British empire, if formal voting were necessary in any matter. Constitutionally the rule is of interest, although practically it was of little importance as the council of four controlled the situation. The mode adopted of signing the treaty was as follows. In the treaty with Germany the contracting parties were the British empire and the Allied and Associated powers.[1] Canada did not appear as a distinct sovereign state, for that would have been tantamount to a declaration that the empire had been dissolved, but Sir George Foster and Mr. Doherty were included among 'the representatives of his Majesty the King of the United Kingdom of Great Britain and Ireland and of the British Dominions

[1] *Parliamentary Papers*, Cmd. 153.

beyond the Seas, Emperor of India ', and they signed the treaty as representing the king for the dominion of Canada. This method was followed in the other treaties except that of June 28, 1919, when the king, subject to the United States undertaking a similar obligation, agreed to support France against unprovoked German agression.[1] British delegates alone signed this treaty, and while its terms implied that it bound the empire, it was expressly laid down that it imposed no obligations on the dominions until ratified by the dominion parliament concerned.

After the signature of the treaty, the imperial government desired that it should be ratified without submission to the parliaments of the empire. Sir Robert Borden emphatically protested by telegram to a course which would have lowered Canada's status and placed it in an inferior position to that of the United Kingdom. As a consequence, the Canadian parliament approved the treaty by motion in favour of ratification, and the ratification of the British empire was not deposited by the foreign secretary until similar motions had been passed by the parliaments of the other dominions. On the other hand, it is important to notice that in all the proceedings the empire's unity was guarded. The Canadian plenipotentiaries were nominated and authorized to act for Canada by the Canadian government, but the full and formal powers to sign were received from the king acting on the advice of the imperial foreign secretary, on whose advice also was signified the ratification of the crown for the whole empire.

The covenant of the league of nations is perhaps the most remarkable recognition of Canada's constitutional development.[2] Canada is included as an original member of the league in its own right, possessing a vote in the assembly of the league and the right to be represented there by not more

---

[1] *Parliamentary Papers*, Cmd. 221.
[2] *Canadian Sessional Papers*, No. 41 h (1919).

than three delegates, in the same manner as the British empire.[1] The latter *eo nomine* is also entitled as one of the principal allied and associated powers to permanent membership of the council of the league and to have one representative at its meetings. The assembly is, however, entitled to select from time to time four other members of the league who should vote in the council. On the suggestion of Sir Robert Borden an express and special declaration was signed by Mr. Lloyd George, President Wilson, and M. Clemenceau which made it clear that a representative of a self-governing dominion could be selected and named as a member of the council. In other respects the interpretation of the covenant of the league is somewhat difficult. The peace conference recognized the empire as a unit; but the covenant appears to say that the dominions guarantee the territorial integrity and political independence of one another and of the British empire and India, and that if one of them resorted to war in disregard of covenanted obligations it would be considered as having committed an act of war against the other members of the league, which would then be under obligations to apply to it commercial, if not military and naval pressure. A strict construction might create a situation when the imperial unity of the peace conference would be broken and a dominion bound to assume an attitude of active hostility to the United Kingdom and vice versa. It is, however, possible to get out of the dilemma by falling back on the proviso that ' nothing in this covenant shall be deemed to affect the validity of international engagements . . . for securing the maintenance of peace ', and it is open to contend that the measures of constraint contemplated are applicable only to sovereign states of ' existing political

---

[1] The covenant of the league recognizes that each member has ' nationals ' of its own. As a consequence ' Canadian nationals ' were defined by a federal Act in 1921 (11 & 12 George V, c. 4). The status of ' Canadian nationals ' as British subjects is not touched. Certain British subjects are merely declared to have a status as ' Canadian nationals '.

independence '. The ambiguities are unfortunate ; but the creation of a league at a moment when the British empire was undergoing constitutional changes did not make for clearness of expression or for rigidly legal or correct terms.

On the other hand, the entire conception of treaty and league was not received in Canada without disapproval. The liberal opposition raised strong objections and disclosed quite a different conception of the empire from that taken by the Canadian delegates at the peace conference.[1] They claimed that all that had been done was purely formal and meaningless. Canada was not and could not be a state under the British North America Act, and to seek representation in the matter of treaties and foreign affairs was not only undesirable but unnecessary. Canada could act if occasions arose when Canada was specially affected or concerned. The covenant of the league also came in for severe attacks. It imposed on Canada obligations to enter European disputes, to maintain armed forces to carry out its covenanted duties, even to enter war against the mother country. The old status, pleasing alike to Macdonald and to Laurier, was preferable, when Canada had enjoyed full autonomy, including the right to decide whether or not aid would be forthcoming in imperial wars. Mr. Fielding proposed an amendment to the motion for approval of the treaty pledging the Canadian parliament to the pre-war status. In reply the minister of justice elaborated a new and interesting political theory. He maintained that there was no necessity for Canada to go hat in hand either to the mother country or to any power to obtain nationhood. Neither imperial law nor international recognition could confer what Canada then possessed as a fact. Canada's signature was necessary to the treaty because it was a nation making with other possessions of the crown the British empire. He believed that the covenant of the league did not impose any treaty obligations on Canada.

[1] *House of Commons Debates*, September 2, 1919.

The speech need not be examined in detail. It is only necessary to point out that whatever the international status of Canada, it is derived from international recognition, and if there is any meaning in words the covenant does impose obligations of a serious nature on Canada, which it had not before the war. The most interesting defence of the diplomatic events since 1914 was made by Mr. Rowell in the house of commons on March 11, 1920. He declared that Canada stood for the precise observance of the rights which it claimed and had succeeded in obtaining, and that Canada awaited a constitutional conference to perfect the developments.

It is idle to argue the issues. Legalists have law on their side. Sir Robert Borden and Mr. Rowell have sentiment and, what is perhaps more valuable, they are training their countrymen in political thinking. The former has perhaps stated the exact constitutional situation as it is to-day better than any one else : ' For each of the Britannic nations, there is but one crown, acting in each dominion and in every province or state upon the advice of ministers responsible to the people and invested with their mandate. Thus throughout the empire there is created a direct and perfect relationship between the crown and the people. . . . Equality of nationhood must be recognized, preserving unimpaired to each dominion the full autonomous powers which it now holds, and safeguarding to each, by necessary consultation and by adequate voice and influence, its highest interests in the issues of war and peace. For each nation complete control in its own affairs ; for the whole empire necessary co-operation according to the will of the people, in all matters of common concern.' [1] If this speech means anything it means this—that the empire is not in process of dissolution into a group of allied Britannic states. What is claimed is absolute and complete autonomy in Canada, and beyond Canada co-operation and consultation in foreign

[1] During Ottawa's welcome to the Prince of Wales, August 29, 1919.

affairs.   There can be little doubt that those conditions practically exist under an imperial tie, which must itself receive adequate and objective treatment.   It is well also to point out that during the Canadian federal election campaign at the close of 1921 the constitution of the empire was never seriously or fully discussed.   Whatever advances individual Canadian statesmen may have made in seeing apparent anomalies and in desiring to rectify them by new legal and constitutional forms, none of them has been willing to emphasize the issues at a general election.   The motives behind such unwillingness may belong to Canadian party politics.   On the other hand, the absence of deliberate discussion is in itself evidence that in Canada there is no widespread demand for change.   There is a wide emotional consciousness that Canada does not stand exactly where it did in 1914, but it would be apparently impossible at present to organize that emotion into anything like a general demand for constitutional reconstructions.

[AUTHORITIES.—The leading authority is Professor A. Berriedale Keith. His *Responsible Government in the Dominions* (3 vols., Oxford, 1912), *Imperial Unity and the Dominions* (Oxford, 1916), and *War Government in the Dominions* (Oxford, 1921) are works of primary importance.   Articles by the same writer in the *Journal of the Society of Comparative Legislation*, vol. xvi, pp. 199 ff. ; vol. xviii, pp. 47 ff. ;   *Journal of Comparative Legislation and International Law*, vol. i, pp. 7 ff. ;   vol. ii, pp. 112 ff., 328 ff. ;   and in the *Canadian Law Times*, vol. xxxvi, pp. 831 ff. ;   vol. xxxviii, pp. 695 ff., should be consulted.   A critical examination of most of the books, pamphlets, and review articles can be found in the *Review of Historical Publications relating to Canada* (ed. G. M. Wrong, H. H. Langton, W. S. Wallace, 22 vols., Toronto, 1897–1919), and in the *Canadian Historical Review* (Toronto, 1920 [in progress]).   The *Minutes and Proceedings of the Colonial and Imperial Conferences* (1894–1921) are valuable, especially those for 1911, 1917, 1918, and 1921.   The *Reports of the War Cabinet*, 1917 and 1918, are of special importance.   The various treaties and the covenant of the league of nations are essential.   H. Duncan Hall, *The British Commonwealth of Nations* (London, 1920), is a good modern study and should be read in close connexion with Lionel Curtis, *The Problem of the Commonwealth* (London, 1916).   The articles dealing with Canada and the empire in *The Round Table* (London, 1914–21) are full of interest.   Sir Robert Borden, *Addresses on Canada at War* (Ottawa, 1918), *The War and the Future* (London, 1917), *Canadian Constitutional Studies* (Toronto, 1922), are of value owing to their author's position at the time when important developments were taking place.   G. B. Adams, *The British Empire and a League of Peace* (London, 1919), is a consideration of the empire in relation to wider issues.   The writings of Mr. J. S. Ewart and M. Henri Bourassa should not be overlooked, and the leading articles in *Le Devoir* (Montreal, 1914–21) will repay study.   W. S. Wallace, ' The Growth of Canadian National Feeling ' (*Canadian Historical Review*, vol. i, pp. 136 ff.), is an excellent introduction to the history of the growth of Canadian constitutional consciousness.   In the *New Statesman* (Feb. 8, 1919) and the *Contemporary Review* (July 1921) I have attempted to sum up Canadian public opinion on the issues.   The standard biographies continue of value, especially O. D. Skelton, *Life and Letters of Sir Wilfrid Laurier* (2 vols., Oxford, 1921).   R. A. Eastwood, *The Organization of a Britannic Partnership* (London and Manchester, 1922), contains an excellent study of developments and sober and judicial conclusions.]

CHAPTER XXII

THE FRAMEWORK AND SCHEME OF GOVERNMENT

THE constitution of Canada is partly written and partly unwritten. The unwritten constitution includes all the great landmarks in British history in so far as they are working principles—Magna Carta, the Petition of Right, the Bill of Rights, the Habeas Corpus Acts, the Act of Settlement—as well as the generally recognized conventions and usages. The written constitution is found in a series of Acts known and quoted as the British North America Acts, 1867–1915.[1] A general consideration of these Acts in their terms and workings is the best introduction to the scheme of Canadian government.

Executive authority is vested in the crown, and is exercised in the federal sphere by a governor-general, and in the provincial spheres by lieutenant-governors. Legislative power for the dominion is entrusted to a bi-cameral parliament consisting of a senate and a house of commons. Legislative power in the dominion is distributed between the federal and the provincial legislatures. To the former is given a general power, and an exclusive authority to deal with twenty-nine enumerated subjects; to the latter are assigned sixteen enumerated subjects on which they have exclusive power to legislate. By a special clause they possess sole power over education. Concurrent legislative authority exists over agriculture and immigration.[2]

When an Act is passed by the federal government the governor-general may assent to it, he may withhold assent, or he may

---

[1] Kennedy, *op. cit.*, pp. 694 ff. The British North America Act of 1867 is in the Appendix, pp. 459 ff.

[2] For the distribution of legislative power, see chapter xxiv.

reserve it for the consideration of the imperial government, which may in addition disallow within two years any Act to which assent has been given. In the provinces the lieutenant-governors are guided by the same regulation, but the power of disallowance belongs to the dominion and will be discussed later.

The judges of the superior, district, and county courts in each province are appointed by the governor-general, except those of the courts of probate in Nova Scotia and New Brunswick. They hold office during good behaviour and are removable by the governor-general on address from the parliament of Canada.

With this general scheme in mind it is possible to examine more closely the great divisions of the constitution : (a) The crown in Canada; (b) The federal and provincial executives; (c) the federal and provincial parliaments; (d) the judicature; (e) the legislative power in Canada. The first four can be considered in relation to the general scheme, the last requires separate and fuller treatment.

The imperial crown is one and indivisible and is not broken up between the British Isles, the dominions, and the rest of the empire. Whatever the constitutional rights of the crown they can be exercised in Canada, but through responsible ministers, as this is the method by which these rights find expression wherever responsible government exists under the crown. The imperial power to veto a dominion Act is an interesting illustration of the unity of the crown. It is true that consultation and amicable workings between Ottawa and London have made this veto of little actual importance in Canadian history, and that, since equality of status has been claimed for and conceded to Canada, the right has been practically abandoned by the imperial government, yet its existence even as a theory may be noted in this connexion. All laws, whether federal or provincial, are enacted by the king in parliament. The governor-general, who is appointed by the king on advice, represents the crown in federal government. A convention has grown up in relation to his appointment. No governor-general is sent to Canada without consultation with and approval by the Canadian government.[1] His official acts are ' with the advice of the privy council for Canada '. This enactment is rather vague, as the privy council in Canada is purely an honorary body. But, as has been pointed out, the conventions of the constitution apply to Canada, and although there is no express mention of responsible government in the written constitution, the governor-general acts on the advice of his ministers. On the other hand, he is not a viceroy. His authority is limited by his instructions or by statute, and he cannot exercise other powers of the crown unless they are legally delegated to him. The changes before 1914 in connexion with his office have been considered. Since that date there have been developments. The new method of communication between the imperial and Canadian governments has resulted in robbing him of his ambassadorial functions, and his duties are at present confined to those of the constitutional head of a state. He is the visible link between the United Kingdom and Canada, and his office emphasizes the unity of the crown within the empire.[2] He represents the king, not the British government or the colonial office. The crown is represented for the purposes of provincial government by a lieutenant-governor in each province. He is appointed by the governor-general in council, but, as will

[1] Macdonald apparently disapproved of this convention : Macdonald to Stanley, December 6, 1888. On the other hand, the Marquis of Lorne when governor-general told Macdonald that he was all in favour of it : Lorne to Macdonald, May 16, 1883. Pope, *Correspondence of Sir John Macdonald*, pp. 300, 433.

[2] ' The administration of public affairs is conducted by ministers responsible to parliament and the governor-general acts by their advice. By convention, his appointment is subject to the approval of the government of the day, and his functions as an imperial officer are formal rather than real : his office as representative of the crown exhibits the constitutional unity of the empire. . . . He has become in fact a nominated president ' : R. L. Borden, *Canadian Constitutional Studies*, pp. 61, 93.

appear later, he exercises all the functions of the crown necessary for provincial government and is no mere creature of the federal executive. His position or constitutional functions cannot be altered by any Act, federal or provincial.

The executive government of the dominion is carried on by a cabinet of ministers selected from the political party in power. Appointments are made by the governor-general on the recommendation of the premier. Ministers in charge of a department are paid a salary, but a minister without portfolio receives no remuneration. While a premier has all his supporters from whom to choose his colleagues, yet almost a class of conventions has grown up in connexion with the formation of a federal cabinet. The interests of Quebec generally and of the English-speaking Canadians in that province particularly must be considered. Then the Roman catholics in other provinces than Quebec must not be overlooked. Some effort, too, must be made to give to the cabinet as balanced a representation as possible of the various constituent provinces in the federation.[1] Every cabinet minister who sits in the house of commons must seek re-election on accepting a paid portfolio.

As soon as a cabinet has taken the oaths of office they act with the governor-general as the executive government of Canada. They are responsible for all orders in council, for the finance bill, for all government measures. All arrangements for the administration of Canada are made at cabinet meetings, and in so far as these are accepted and acknowledged as government measures

[1] See pp. 317–18, 413–14, and compare Macdonald to J. A. Chapleau, June 6, 1888 : ' The time has come, I think, when we must choose men for their qualifications rather than for their locality ' (Pope, *op. cit.*, p. 414). See also *Report of the Special Committee on the Machinery of Government in Canada* (1919), pp. 8 ff., and the present premier's memorandum on his choice of ministers : ' In the formation of the government I have aimed above all else at national unity. This end I have felt would be served, and the federal spirit of our constitution most acceptably recognized, by according representation in the cabinet, so far as might be possible, to all the provinces of Canada. . . . ' (*Toronto Daily Star*, December 30, 1921).

the cabinet acts as a unit and must stand or fall as such. A member who cannot support his colleagues in these matters once they are before parliament usually resigns according to constitutional convention. He has the privilege of explaining his resignation in parliament, and his first statement must be made there so that the premier can reply. The governor-general's permission is necessary for exercising the privilege, as proceedings in the cabinet cannot be made public without his leave first obtained ; but such permission is never refused. It is the duty of a cabinet minister to see to the efficient working of his department. He must attend to the drafting of all bills in which his department is concerned and pilot them through parliament as far as possible. He must take an active interest in his departmental estimates and defend them when challenged. In addition, he must be prepared not only to support his own administration but that of the cabinet as a whole within and without the legislature, and to receive deputations dealing with matters within his departmental sphere.

The relations between the governor-general and the cabinet are now fairly clear. He does not attend cabinet meetings, but all communications which can be called official come to him through the cabinet, and all orders in council are submitted to him personally. He is entitled to receive the full confidence of his ministers when they ask him to act in any official capacity. If confidence does not exist, he can doubtless dismiss them ; but he would do so with the full knowledge that he would be compelled to find successors who would be prepared to take constitutional responsibility for his action. As a matter of fact no instance of dismissal exists in the history of federal government in Canada.[1] Doubtless also he has the constitutional

---

[1] See, however, an interesting account in Tupper's *Recollections of Sixty Years* (pp. 156 ff.) of an episode in connexion with the fall of Macdonald's ministry in 1873, when the governor-general, Lord Dufferin, asked Macdonald to resign and only recalled his decision on Tupper's pointing out that the action would make Dufferin ' the head of the liberal party '.

power to refuse a dissolution, but the sense of political responsibility has become so strong with Canada's new status in the empire that to do so would be an act of extreme danger. The tendency is to assimilate the constitutional conventions of Great Britain and to follow in this matter the completeness of political development.

In provincial government the executives are modelled on the British type and follow the lines of cabinet administration. The functions of the provincial cabinets, the theories and conventions governing them, and the relationship between the executives and the lieutenant-governors are so similar to those in the federal sphere that they do not call for separate treatment. It is, however, interesting to note that there are instances of dismissal, and that lieutenant-governors have forced their advisors to appoint commissions to inquire into provincial affairs, which have resulted either in resignation or in defeat at the polls.[1] On the other hand, it must be remembered that in some respects there is an important difference between a lieutenant-governor acting in this manner and a governor-general. The latter in such cases has very direct responsibility, and his actions are governed by conventions now fully accepted, while the former is responsible in this connexion to the governor-general in council, who may remove him from office on the advice of the federal cabinet. In two cases lieutenant-governors have been recalled because the dominion government considered that they had not carried out the rules of responsible government.[2]

The parliament of Canada is bi-cameral, consisting of a senate and a house of commons. After serious debate the senate was created as a nominated house, and members are appointed by

[1] See *Canada Sessional Papers*, (1891) No. 86, (1892) No. 88, for a case in Quebec, and *Canadian Annual Review* (1903), pp. 213 ff., for a case in British Columbia.

[2] See *Parliamentary Papers*, Cd. 2445, for the case of Letellier de St. Just in Quebec, and *Canada Sessional Papers* (1900), No. 174, for the case of McInnes in British Columbia.

the governor-general, which, of course, means by the federal cabinet.[1] The senate does not represent provinces as such, but appointments are made in such a way as to represent groups of provinces. At present it consists of ninety-six members distributed as follows : Ontario, 24 ; Quebec, 24 ; the Maritime Provinces and Prince Edward Island, 24 (Nova Scotia, 10 ; New Brunswick, 10 ; Prince Edward Island, 4) ; the Western Provinces, 24, six each. Senators from Quebec alone represent senatorial divisions. In the event of a deadlock between the senate and the house of commons the governor-general can recommend the crown to add from four to eight members.[2] This enactment appears to make the imperial cabinet directly responsible. It is, however, more than likely that, under Canada's present status, the crown's authority would be purely formal if the recommendation were made. At any rate it is certain that the governor-general must recommend if he is desired to do so by his cabinet.

A senator must be at least thirty years of age and a natural-born or naturalized subject of the crown. He must possess freehold valued at four thousand dollars in the province for which he is appointed, and real and personal property worth four thousand dollars over his debts and liabilities. He must reside in the province for which he is appointed, and in the case of Quebec his residence or real property qualification must be in the electoral division for which he is chosen. He holds office

[1] See below, pp. 412–13. An official opinion of the federal minister of justice has laid it down that no woman senators can be created without an amendment of the B.N.A. Act, 1867 (March 23, 1922).

[2] Kennedy, *op. cit.*, pp. 706 ff. (5 & 6 George V, c. 45 (1915)). The original provision was added to the British North America Act, 1867, at the suggestion of the imperial government. There is only one instance of a Canadian cabinet asking for its application. The Mackenzie ministry, on taking office in 1873 on the defeat of Macdonald's first ministry, asked that the crown should be advised to add six members. The governor-general forwarded the request to the colonial secretary, who firmly refused it, stating that the power was only for use in serious deadlock which actually held up the administration, and when it could be shown that it provided adequate remedy: *Canada Sessional Papers* (1877), No. 68 ; cf. *Senate Journals* (1877), pp. 130, 174.

for life, but he may resign at any time, and his place becomes vacant if he fails in any of the general conditions governing his appointment, if he is absent for two consecutive sessions, if he ceases in any way to be a subject of the crown, if he becomes insolvent, a public defaulter, or is convicted of any great crime.

There is no obligation for a cabinet to be represented by a minister in the senate, but the government in power always has a leader there who explains and guides government policy. There is also a leader elected by the party in opposition. There is only one provision limiting the power of the senate with regard either to finance or to general legislation. It cannot originate any money bill. Theoretically it may reject a finance bill, but can make no amendments to it. The speaker is appointed by the governor-general and may be removed by him. Fifteen senators form a quorum, including the speaker, who always has a vote. Decisions rest with the majority, an equal division of votes, however, being considered a negative.

The number of members of the house of commons varies according to redistribution bills after every decennial census. Redistribution is governed by a statutory constitutional principle. The representation of Quebec is fixed at sixty-five members, and each province is assigned ' such a number of members as will bear the same proportion to the number of its population (ascertained by the census) as the number sixty-five bears to the population of Quebec so ascertained '.[1] No qualifications for membership were laid down in 1867. At present ' any British subject, male or female, who is of the full age of twenty-one, may be a candidate at a dominion election '. Those guilty of corrupt and illegal practices, government contractors, holders of certain public offices, persons in the paid employment of the government, and members of the provincial

[1] British North America Act, 1867, s. 51. See speeches by Laurier and Sir Robert Borden on this principle, *House of Commons Debates*, March 31, 1903, February 10, 1914.

legislatures are ineligible. Legislation exempts from these disabilities ministers of the crown, members of the military, naval, or air forces on active service, shareholders in companies having government contracts other than for building public works, and militia officers or militia men receiving no emolument from the public purse other than those prescribed by legislation governing the militia.[1] All members receive an indemnity for their services and are allowed their travelling expenses.

The electoral districts or ridings are determined by the federal parliament. In the Quebec resolutions this power was left to the provincial legislatures.[2] Macdonald, however, noted this as ' an obvious blunder ' and a ' mistake '.[3] It was rectified at the Westminster conference.[4] It appeared as a federal power in all drafts of the British North America Act, and was finally embodied in the constitution of 1867.[5] For many years it was a source of bitter controversy, as gerrymandering the constituencies by means of a straight party vote went on on a considerable scale. In 1893 the liberal convention at Ottawa committed the party to non-partisan redistribution.[6] In 1903 this pledge was redeemed. Laurier in introducing a redistribution bill added no electoral schedules. He promised, if the opposition would accept the measure, to refer it after the second reading to a special committee composed of seven members, on which the opposition would be represented by three selected by themselves.[7] In 1914 Sir Robert Borden brought in necessary legislation and followed the plan adopted in 1903.[8] Both parties have accepted the principle of a larger unit for urban than for rural ridings.

[1] 10 & 11 George V, c. 46 (July 1, 1920), ss. 38, 39.
[2] Pope, *Confederation Documents*, p. 42.
[3] Macdonald to Tupper, November 14, 1864, Pope, *Correspondence of Sir John Macdonald*, pp. 14 ff.
[4] Pope, *Confederation Documents*, p. 127.   [5] *Ibid.*, pp. 141 ff.
[6] *Report of the Ottawa Liberal Convention*, p. 129.
[7] *House of Commons Debates*, March 31, 1903.
[8] *Ibid.*, February 10, 1914.

The history of the dominion franchise is interesting. The power to determine it was left to the federal parliament, but until exercised it was provided that the electoral laws of the provinces should hold good in this connexion in the federal area. When the Act of 1867 was passed Algoma was a territory, and it was laid down that the franchise should be given in it to every male householder of full age. On the other hand, in the five general elections held between 1867 and 1882 members of the house of commons were elected on the provincial franchises. Macdonald never liked this method. ' It is impossible ', he wrote, ' that the elective franchise should be at the mercy of a foreign body.' [1] Before 1885 he introduced several abortive bills establishing a dominion franchise. In that year he succeeded in carrying a measure creating a federal franchise based on property. Of the seven provinces which composed Canada in 1885, all except Quebec and Nova Scotia had introduced by legislation manhood suffrage. Macdonald, however, objected to this principle. In addition he stated that it was contrary to first principles that the members of the federal parliament ' representing the people in a dominion sense ' should not have control of all reforms and changes in representation. He objected to the provincial laws as wilfully partisan which excluded men on the pay roll of the federal government from the franchise.[2] Uniformity and the desire to enfranchise the servants of the dominion were thus emphasized as the reasons for change. The liberals attacked the measure from other angles. Firstly, they considered that appointments under the Act would add considerably to the government's patronage and open up possibilities of abuse. Secondly, the Act called for enormous expenditure in annual revisions. The government, indeed, was forced to pass legislation suspending the clauses

[1] Macdonald to Brown Chamberlin, October 26, 1868, Pope, *Correspondence of Sir John Macdonald*, p. 75.
[2] See his speech, *House of Commons Debates*, April 16, 1885.

making these revisions compulsory. Thus another grievance was added, as many ' young voters entitled to the franchise had in numerous instances been prevented from exercising their natural rights '. Thirdly, the franchise was less liberal than that which existed in most of the provinces.[1] When the liberals came into power they reverted to the older plan, but care was taken that no one, otherwise qualified as an elector, should be disqualified from voting at a federal election because of employment in the federal or provincial public service.

Under dominion legislation the provincial voters lists are now used. All British subjects by birth or naturalization, irrespective of sex, of full age, and not being Indians ordinarily resident on an Indian reservation, are qualified to vote. They must have resided in Canada twelve months, and in the electoral division where they seek to vote two months immediately preceding the issue of the writ of election. Indians fulfilling these conditions who have served with the Canadian forces are enfranchised. Judges appointed by the governor in council, the chief electoral officer of the dominion, persons disfranchised for corrupt and illegal practices, criminal prisoners, inmates of asylums and public charitable institutions, persons disqualified in provincial elections on account of race except those who served in the late war with the Canadian forces, returning officers—except in case of an equality of votes—and election clerks are disqualified.[2]

Every house of commons can continue for five years and no longer unless previously dissolved by the governor-general acting on ministerial advice. The arrangements for a new election are in the hands of the chief electoral officer, who acts in each riding through a returning officer. In addition to the general oversight of an election, the latter is responsible for

[1] *Report of Ottawa Liberal Convention*, p. 122.
[2] 10 & 11 George V, c. 46, ss. 29, 30, 31, 32 (Dominion Elections Act, 1920).

seeing that candidates have consented to nomination and have made deposits of two hundred dollars each. All official election expenses are a charge on the dominion. The deposit is returned to the successful candidate, while his opponents forfeit theirs unless they obtain a number of votes equal to one-half the number of votes polled in favour of the candidate elected.[1]

The proceedings of the house of commons are governed partly by the constitution and partly by rules or customs based on British precedents. The former provides that the commons can elect their own speaker, who shall not vote unless on a tie, that the presence of twenty members including the speaker shall form a quorum, that a member can address the house in English or in French,[2] and that a majority of voices shall decide a motion. The latter cover the convention that the speaker elected must be approved by the crown. To them can also be assigned the custom of the speaker's demand for ' the ancient and undoubted rights and privileges of the commons ' and the assertion of the independence of the house by reading a dummy bill, which has no reference to the cause of summons in the royal proclamation convening parliament or to the business to which parliament's attention is drawn in the speech from the throne. Local usages have grown up in relation to the offices of speaker and deputy-speaker. It is practically a working principle that, when a political party holds office during several parliaments, if the speaker in one parliament is of British origin, the next one shall be a French-Canadian. By a regulation of the

---

[1] *Ibid.*, s. 40.

[2] Under the British North America Act of 1867 French or English may be used in the parliaments of Canada and of Quebec ; the records and journals of these must be printed in both languages, and either may be used in any court established under the Act or in the courts of Quebec. Under this enactment the Acts of Canada and Quebec are printed in both languages as well as all papers, &c., issued by the dominion parliament. The same provision was inserted in the Act creating Manitoba (38 Victoria, c. 3, s. 23, Kennedy, *op. cit.*, pp. 689 ff.), but was repealed by provincial legislation in 1890 (53 Victoria, c. 14).

house, the speaker and the deputy-speaker cannot be of the same race. Indeed, appointments to all offices, great and small, both in the senate and in the house of commons, are made as a rule in relation to racial differences. There is also an innovation at Ottawa which is a marked departure from British custom. The leader of the opposition, who has been elected by his party, holds an office known to law and is paid a statutory salary in addition to his sessional indemnity.[1]

Only two of the provincial parliaments are bi-cameral—those of Nova Scotia and Quebec. The legislative council of Nova Scotia consists of twenty-one members nominated by the lieutenant-governor in council, and holding office during pleasure. No one can be a member who sits in the federal parliament or holds certain provincial offices, or who is legally declared to be disqualified under the laws of Canada for membership of the federal house of commons. Absence for two sessions without the consent of the lieutenant-governor in council vacates a seat. The federal rules in relation to finance bills govern procedure. The legislative council of Quebec consists of twenty-four members holding office for life and appointed by the lieutenant-governor by instrument under the great seal of the province. Each member represents one of the twenty-four divisions of the province. The regulations governing qualifications and legislation are similar to those relating to the senate of Canada. In neither province is there any provision for deadlock, or for the adjustment of differences between the two chambers. The dominion government could not interfere. On two occasions when difficulties arose in Nova Scotia, the colonial office refused to recommend imperial legislation as the province possessed the right to change its constitution.[2] In 1890 the government of the same province attempted to abolish the

---

[1] *Revised Statutes of Canada* (1906), c. 10.
[2] Cf. dispatch from Lord Ripon, December 3, 1894, *House of Assembly Journals, Nova Scotia* (1894), Appendix No. 17.

upper house, and failing in this object they only appointed members who gave a pledge to consent to the abolition. These members supported government measures, but developed scruples about their consent to their own destruction. In Ontario and British Columbia no second chamber has ever existed. In New Brunswick it was abolished by the method tried in Nova Scotia, an Act being passed bringing it to an end at the close of the session of 1892.[1] In Prince Edward Island the upper house was elective from 1862 onwards. In 1893 it was abolished under a local Act, or rather it was merged in the assembly. Part of the members of the one assembly are elected on a property franchise and part on adult suffrage.[2] Manitoba was organized as a province with a bicameral legislature, the upper house consisting of a limited number of nominated members. It was abolished in 1876.[3] The new provinces, Alberta and Saskatchewan, were created with a single chamber only.

It would be impossible to examine in detail the composition and procedure connected with the nine provincial houses of assembly. In most provinces adult suffrage prevails. In Nova Scotia and Quebec there are small property, income, or rental qualifications. The disqualifications for voting are analogous to those obtaining at federal elections, but in Manitoba there are certain literary qualifications, and in Saskatchewan and British Columbia there are racial disqualifications. The rules governing membership of the provincial assemblies are on the whole similar. In addition to the common disqualifications, no one who is a member of the dominion parliament or of another legislative assembly can sit, and clergymen are ineligible in Prince Edward Island. Members are paid in all the provinces. A provincial legislature has the exclusive power to alter the

[1] 54 Victoria, c. 9 (New Brunswick).
[2] 56 Victoria, c. 21 (Prince Edward Island).
[3] 39 Victoria, c. 28 (Manitoba).

constitution of the province, but this power does not extend to the office of lieutenant-governor because he represents the crown. On the other hand, a provincial legislature may increase the powers and duties germane to the office.[1] The general power, outside this limitation, is not free from obscurities. It cannot be exercised in the widest sense, otherwise it might be used to destroy the federation.[2] It would also appear that a province has not the power to legislate by the initiative and referendum. 'Legislature', as used in the British North America Act of 1867, connotes a representative house, and the power granted to a province of amending its constitution does not include such an absolute change in the provincial constitution as would destroy the nature of the legislature and give the legislative power to those possessed of the provincial franchise who are not a 'legislature' within the meaning of the constitution.[3] The privy council raised more technical objections, as such proceedings appeared to affect vitally the office of lieutenant-governor.[4]

The privileges of the Canadian legislatures are on a clear foundation. The extraordinary privileges of the British house of commons are part of the *lex et consuetudo parliamenti*, and can only be claimed by Canadian legislatures under statutory enactment. When this legislation validly takes place there is no ambiguity. The privileges of the dominion parliament are governed by the British North America Acts of 1867 and of 1875,[5] the latter of which gives the Canadian parliament power

[1] *Attorney-General for Canada* v. *Attorney-General for Ontario* (1890), 20 Ontario Reports, 222.

[2] Cf. Ramsay J. in *ex parte Dansereau*, 19 L. C. J. 210, 224–5.

[3] Re *Initiative and Referendum Act*, 1916, 27 Manitoba Law Reports, 1.

[4] Re *Manitoba Initiative and Referendum Act*, [1919] A. C. 935 ; 85 *Times Law Reports*, pp. 630 ff.

[5] Kennedy, *op. cit.*, pp. 667, 695. The Act of 1875 was passed because in 1868 and in 1873 dominion legislation had conferred powers on committees to examine witnesses on oath, a privilege not possessed by the imperial parliament in 1867 (*Canada Sessional Papers*, 1876, No. 45).

to bring its practice into line with contemporary practice in the British parliament. In the provinces after federation legislation conferring privileges met with varying success at the hands of the dominion cabinet. There was a tendency for the minister of justice to consider such legislation *ultra vires*, but there was no consistency of treatment. The matter was finally settled in 1896, when the judicial committee of the privy council laid it down that, as the powers of the legislatures at federation were continued, among which was full authority to enact such laws as they pleased on the subject of their privileges, provincial legislation in this connexion was valid. They also held that the power was competent under the constitutional authority granted the provinces to change their constitution.[1] All the provinces have laid down their parliamentary privileges by legislation, which is now beyond dispute.

Canada does not possess a system of federal courts such as exists in the United States. The constitution, however, makes provision for the creation of such a system by the parliament of the dominion. The provinces have exclusive power to constitute and to organize courts for provincial purposes of both civil and criminal jurisdiction. The provincial legislatures can regulate the procedure in civil matters. The dominion parliament may impose new duties upon existing provincial courts, and may give them new powers in the matter of subjects not assigned exclusively to the provinces. The constitution provides that the judges of the superior, district, and county courts in the provinces must be paid by the dominion, and their appointment must lie with the governor-general, subject to certain regulations connected with the provincial bars and to the exclusion of the probate courts of the Maritime Provinces.[2]

---

[1] *Fielding* v. *Thomas*, [1896] A. C. 600.

[2] There has been much irritation between the dominion and the provinces owing to attempts by the latter to regulate certain judicial appointments. See *inter alia* an important report of Sir John Thompson in *Provincial Legislation*, 1867–95, p. 538 and in Lefroy, *Legislative Power in Canada*, pp. 140 ff.

The provincial courts deal with all matters of litigation under federal and provincial law. They also hear election petitions and have jurisdiction in cases of controverted elections. They have also imposed on them the duty of giving opinions on the constitutionality of Acts for the guidance of the provincial executives, and from these opinions no appeal lies to the supreme court of Canada, not even by provincial legislation.[1] Criminal law and criminal procedure are controlled exclusively by the federal government.

The tenure of judicial office is regulated by law. The judges of the superior courts hold office during good behaviour, and they can only be removed by the governor-general on address of the senate and house of commons.[2] Their salaries do not depend on annual votes, but are placed on the civil list. The same terms of tenure are applied to judges of the supreme court by Canadian legislation.[3] County court judges hold office during good behaviour and residence in their respective jurisdictions. The governor-general in council can, however, remove them for misdemeanours, incapacity, failure in the performance of duty owing to age, ill health, or any other cause. The circumstances leading up to a possible removal must be fully inquired into after due notice given to the judge concerned, who must be afforded an opportunity to be heard, to cross-examine witnesses, and to bring in evidence on his own behalf. If he is removed, the order in council covering such removal, the correspondence, reports, and evidence, must be laid before parliament within the first fifteen days of the next session.[4]

There are only two federal courts in Canada—the supreme court and the court of exchequer and admiralty. The latter deals with patents, trade-marks, and such-like, and has an original jurisdiction in revenue cases concurrent with the

---

[1] *Union Colliery Company* v. *Attorney-General for British Columbia,* 27 S. C. R. 637. See, however, p. 399, note.

[2] British North America Act, 1867, ss. 99, 100.

[3] *Revised Statutes of Canada* (1906), c. 139, s. 9.   [4] *Ibid.,* c. 138, s. 28.

provincial courts, and to it alone belong cases against the crown and petitions of right in the federal area. The former consists of a chief justice and five puisne judges, and possesses an appellate jurisdiction, criminal and civil, throughout Canada. There is no court of criminal appeal similar to that in England, but questions of law arising in a criminal trial may be reserved and brought before the provincial court of appeal, and if that court is not unanimous, the person convicted may appeal to the supreme court of Canada. In civil cases an appeal lies, generally speaking, to the supreme court from all final judgements of the highest courts of final resort. This appellate jurisdiction varies in connexion with different provinces and is governed by federal legislation. The federal parliament has the power to allow appeals to the supreme court from provincial judgements and courts even though such judgements are not final and such courts not courts of final resort.[1] Provincial legislation cannot interfere with the jurisdiction granted by federal legislation to the supreme court. No province can prevent appeals in all cases from the provincial courts, if the federal parliament has not itself limited the right of appeal.[2] Nor can a provincial legislature grant powers of appeal where such are limited by federal authority. The supreme court has also an appellate jurisdiction in cases of controverted elections, and from its decisions in such cases the privy council will not receive appeals.[3] The governor-general in council has the power to obtain opinions by direct answers from the supreme court on any question of law or fact. The answers are not binding on the governor-general in council, nor on Canadian judges in any specific cases, but they are treated as final judgements for purposes of reference to the privy council.

An anomalous situation exists in connexion with divorce. At

[1] *L'Association St. Jean-Baptiste de Montréal* v. *Brault*, 31 S. C. R. 172. Cf. *Revised Statutes* (1906), c. 139, ss. 38, 40.

[2] *Crown Grain Company Limited* v. *Day*, [1908] A. C. 504.

[3] *Théberge* v. *Laudry*, 2 App. Cas. 102.

federation the exclusive right of legislating in matters of divorce was conferred on the federal parliament, but the powers to grant divorce already belonging to certain of the provinces were not abrogated. As a consequence, the courts of Nova Scotia, New Brunswick, and British Columbia continued to possess such jurisdiction, being already vested with it before entering federation.[1] There was a general opinion that none of the other provinces possessed such rights. In order to destroy inequalities it seemed reasonable that the federal legislature should create uniformity. Quebec, however, proved hostile, and as no government appeared anxious to create a situation which would antagonize that province when there was another way out, the plan was adopted of granting divorces by federal legislation. The senate investigates applications and the house of commons accepts their decisions as a rule, without however surrendering its rights to review or to reject them. Recently this arrangement has received a rude shock. It now appears that the courts of Manitoba, Alberta, and Saskatchewan possess a jurisdiction in divorce.[2] There thus arises the curious situation that citizens of Quebec, Ontario, and possibly Prince Edward Island [3] who wish to begin divorce proceedings must resort to the cumbersome and expensive method of federal legislation. In a recent debate on a private member's bill, the late government approved the suggestion of a regular federal system of divorce. The approval is interesting, as Quebec would undoubtedly oppose legislation. It might be possible for the federal parliament to exclude Quebec from the scope of such a system, as it would appear constitutional to pass a locally restricted dominion

[1] For the settling of doubts concerning British Columbia, see *Watts* v. *Attorney-General for British Columbia*, [1908] A. C. 573.

[2] See *Board* v. *Board*, [1919] A. C. 956 ; *Walker* v. *Walker*, [1919] A. C. 947.

[3] Under a statute of Prince Edward Island, 5 William IV, c. 10 (1836), the lieutenant-governor and council have jurisdiction in all matters of marriage and divorce. The power has long been disused.

law.[1] However, even if Quebec abstained from opposing such
a measure, those citizens of Quebec who did not accept the
general principles governing Quebec's antagonism would be left
under severe disabilities. At present there seems no available
solution to the difficulties.

The crown has an undoubted prerogative right to hear appeals
from the courts of the dominion. Before 1844, a colonial Act
could bar that right, but when it became statutory in that year,[2]
it seems clear that the only method of barring it at present is by
an Act of the imperial parliament or by a local Act passed with
imperial approval. A Canadian Act purports to bar the right
in criminal cases.[3] It may bar the prerogative, but certainly it
cannot bar the statutory right of appeal. Appeals lie direct to
the privy council from the supreme court of Canada and from
the higher provincial courts. There are no appeals as of right
from the supreme court, but an appeal lies in every case by
special leave. In the provinces appeals are governed by special
leave or are as of right, the latter being regulated by rules laid
down in orders in council or in local Acts. In 1909 Ontario
proposed to limit appeals both to the supreme court and to the
privy council. Appeals as of right to the latter were to disappear,
and special leave was only to be granted in constitutional cases
and cases of financial or political importance. The attorney-
general pointed out that the province could not limit appeals
to the supreme court, and that the privy council was not anxious
to encourage them to London. The Act passed without the
proposed clauses. It would appear that a colonial legislature
can constitutionally bar the prerogative right, but not the

[1] ' Divorce ' being an enumerated power exclusively granted to the dominion, it seems clear that the dominion could pass a law in relation to it of
restricted scope, either on the analogy of special or private bill legislation, or
as being for the ' peace, order, and good government of Canada '. See *McCuaig
and Smith* v. *Keith*, [1878] 4 S. C. R. 648 ; and A. B. Keith (?) in *Journal of
the Society of Comparative Legislation*, vol. xvi, p. 90.

[2] 7 & 8 Victoria, c. 69 (Judicial Committee Act, 1844).

[3] 51 Victoria, c. 43 (*Revised Statutes*, 1906, c. 146).

statutory right of appeal to the judicial committee under the
Act of 1844. In 1920 somewhat similar proposals were mooted,
also in Ontario, but were dropped.[1] On the other hand, the
privy council is trying to curtail its work in Canadian cases.
It has declined to receive criminal appeals, though it has a legal
right to receive them, refusing to admit an appeal on behalf of
the rioters recently condemned at Winnipeg.[2] It is hard to form
an adequate estimate of Canadian opinion on this matter.[3] As
an abstract question there is as much to be said for appeals
as against them. At the imperial war conference of 1918,
Sir Robert Borden ventured to suggest that Canada would like
to see appellate courts reduced and that the dominion should
decide its own constitutional questions. His ideas were naturally
influenced by the growing status of Canada, but how far they
had public opinion behind them it is hard to say.[4] There is
a certain implication of inferiority in the perpetuation of the
judicial committee as the final court of appeal, and the fact that
the high court of Australia has dealt with difficult questions in
a manner not unworthy of judicial traditions seems to point to
a future when Canada might reasonably hope normally to make
its own supreme court supreme in reality. On the other hand,
arguments for retention based on the calm aloofness of the
committee or on the rights of a British subject to seek justice
from the crown are rather unconvincing. The former in the
final analysis cast grave aspersions on the whole Canadian
judiciary, and the latter recall only the rich corporation and

[1] Keith, *Journal of Society of Comparative Legislation*, vol. xvi, p. 218.

[2] *Russell* v. *Rex* (*The Times*, June 22, 1920).

[3] See, however, W. E. Raney, ' Nations within the Empire ' (*Canadian Magazine*, February 1921, pp. 291 ff.), and C. H. Tupper, ' The Position of the Privy Council ' (*Journal of Comparative Legislation*, 3rd series, vol. iii, pt. iv). The benchers of the Law Society of Upper Canada interviewed the attorney-general for Ontario (W. E. Raney) on March 8, 1922, to protest against a proposed measure limiting appeals (*Toronto Star*, March 8, 1922).

[4] *Parliamentary Papers*, Cd. 9177. In 1919 Lord Haldane remarked that even in topics affecting the constitution it was desirable that they should come before the supreme court of Canada before being brought to London for argument (*Manitoba Initiative and Referendum Case*).

forget the penurious suitor. It has been suggested that the peculiar privileges of Quebec within the federation make the right of appeal an excellent safeguard against racial strife and passion. In South Africa, however, there is much opportunity for similar eventualities, and while there is a constitutional right of appeal from the appellate division of the supreme court, the privy council has laid down the principle that only in cases of the greatest moment will it entertain appeals.[1] The right has thus assumed only theoretical importance. Whatever the future in Canada, it must not be forgotten that the judicial committee has given the Canadian constitution its most abiding forms.

[AUTHORITIES.—A. B. Keith, *Responsible Government in the Dominions* (3 vols., Oxford, 1912); *Imperial Unity and the Dominions* (Oxford, 1916); *Dominion Home Rule in Practice* (Oxford, 1921); *Selected Speeches and Documents on British Colonial Policy, 1763–1917* (Oxford, 1918) are standard authorities. The British North America Acts, 1867–1915, are in Kennedy, *Documents of the Canadian Constitution, 1759–1915* (Oxford, 1918). For legal interpretations see A. H. F. Lefroy, *Legislative Power in Canada* (Toronto, 1898); *Canada's Federal System* (Toronto, 1913); *A Short Treatise on Canadian Constitutional Law* (Toronto, 1918); and *The Correspondence and Reports of the Minister of Justice and Orders in Council upon the subject of Dominion and Provincial Legislation, 1867–1906*. The federal and provincial parliaments issue their own ' Rules of Procedure '. There is no adequate modern book on the government of Canada. Sir John Bourinot, *How Canada is governed* (Toronto, 1895), and W. R. Riddell, *The Constitution of Canada* (New Haven, 1917), are useful for general purposes. The former's *Parliamentary Procedure and Practice in the Dominion of Canada* (ed. Flint, Toronto, 1903) is valuable. The second part of E. Porritt, *The Evolution of the Dominion of Canada* (Yonkers-on-Hudson, 1918) is serviceable. Lord Bryce, *Modern Democracies*, vol. i (London, 1921) contains an interesting study of Canadian government. *The Report of Sir George Murray on the Public Business of Canada* (November 30, 1912) and *The Senate's Report on the Machinery of Government* (July 2, 1919) are documents of importance. There is a good short summary of Canadian government as organized in April 1890 in *House of Commons Papers* (1890), 194, pp. 6 ff. For the withholding of royal assent, see *House of Lords Papers* (1894), 196.]

[1] *Whittaker* v. *The Mayor and Councillors of Durban*, [1920] 36 *Times* Law Reports, 784.

NOTE.—On June 14, 1922, the dominion parliament amended the Supreme Court Act to allow appeals to the supreme court of Canada from opinions pronounced by the highest court of final resort in any province on any matter referred to it for hearing or consideration by a lieutenant-governor in council, provided that such opinions are declared by provincial statutes to be judgements of such courts of final resort and that appeals shall be therefrom as from judgements in actions.

CHAPTER XXIII

THE NATURE OF CANADIAN FEDERALISM

SUGGESTIONS looking towards some form of union among the provinces of British North America are frequent in Canadian history from 1784, when the idea was first mooted by Lieutenant-Colonel Morse,[1] to the eve of 1867. Little, however, of the nature of the suggested union can be gained from a study of the extant proposals. If we except the abortive Act of Union[2] for Upper and Lower Canada in 1822, no one except Chief Justice Smith seems to have worked out a scheme in any detail,[3] and his proposals are so vague that it is impossible to decide whether he had in mind a legislative union, a confederation, or a federation. John Beverley Robinson[4] desired to unite the provinces by ' giving them a common legislature and erecting them into a kingdom '. The phrase seems to point to a legislative union, and this assumption is strengthened by the emphasis which Robinson laid on the fact that the new government would be clearly distinguished from the republican institutions of the United States. There was, however, no political discussion, no examination of the nature and essence of the scheme.

With Lord Durham we are in a clearer atmosphere, and he at least defines his terms : ' Two kinds of union have been proposed—federal and legislative. By the first the separate legislature of each province would be preserved in its present form and retain almost all its present attributes of internal legislation, the federal legislature exercising no power save in

---

[1] *Canadian Archives Report* (1884), p. liii.

[2] Kennedy, *op. cit.*, pp. 307 ff.   [3] *Ibid.*, pp. 203 ff.

[4] Quoted in Egerton and Grant, *op. cit.*, p. 147. Cf. Sewell and Robinson, *Plan for a General Legislative Union of the British Provinces in North America* (London, 1824).

those matters which may have been expressly ceded to it by the constituent provinces. A legislative union would imply a complete incorporation of the provinces included in it under one legislature, exercising universal and sole legislative authority over all of them in exactly the same manner as the parliament legislates alone for the whole of the British Isles.'[1] By a 'federal union' Durham meant the creation of a central government to which the constituent provinces would delegate certain powers. In other words, the national government would be a delegation from the provincial governments for the carrying out of certain specific purposes. Such a conception raises the question, Can such a government be called ' a federal government ' ? This question must be discussed at this point, because, as will appear later, such a discussion is germane to any consideration of the debates in the parliament of Canada in 1865.

Without examining the nature of political unions in the ancient world, on which historians and jurists differ, in American history such a union as that proposed by Lord Durham appears to have been called a confederation. ' The perpetual Confederation ' of Massachusetts, Connecticut, Plymouth, and New Haven (1643–84), and Franklin's ' Draft for Union ' in 1754, are cases in point.[2] In both cases the general or national government was a delegate. It existed on sufferance of creating principles. The best illustration, however, is found in the Articles of confederation proposed in 1777 and ratified in 1781. Owing their immediate origin to the necessity for military union, they have in addition behind them a political philosophy based on experience. The earliest signs of democratic tendencies in North America are to be found in local government. Here was the pregnant school of political training. As a consequence it is not surprising to find a mistrust of a strong central government running through the whole conception of the union. The

[1] *Report*, vol. ii, p. 304 (ed. Lucas).
[2] Macdonald, *Select Charters*, vol. i, pp. 94 ff.

D d

unifying machinery created for the purposes of the revolutionary
war was not only weak in those aspects known to every schoolboy, but was deliberately made a delegation from states
which retained, not theoretically but actually, their political
sovereignty. A clear-cut relation of principals and delegate
was set up, such a scheme of government being known as a confederation. In other words and in legal language, the national
government was not sovereign, nor was it endowed with plenary
powers within its sphere. It was, as Robert Morris, superin-
tendent of finance for the Thirteen Colonies in 1781-4, said,
' a government whose sole authority consists in the power of
framing recommendations'.   When Hamilton proposed the
conference at Philadelphia which framed the constitution
of the United States, it was with the idea of creating ' an
adequate federal government '. The new government which
took the place of that under the Articles of confederation was
not the agent of the states. It springs, in theory and in statement at least, from the people, and over them within its sphere
it has sovereign and plenary power. Allowing that the convention was called merely to revise the confederation and allowing
that the general tone of the convention pointed to something
quite different from the constitutional theory superficially
found in the written document and elaborated by the supreme
court, the fact remains that the convention created something
new—a federation—as James Wilson of Pennsylvania saw at the
time.[1] This is the view taken of the constitution by the courts.
A federation may originate historically in many ways ; but once
the federation is formed the current of historical and legal opinion
is that the central and the provincial or state governments have
co-ordinate authority. Nor does the fact that the powers given
to the national government may be specifically enumerated,
and the residue of undefined powers may be reserved to the
states or to the people, enter into the discussion. To the un-

[1] Elliot's *Debates*, vol. i, p. 119 ; vol. ii, p. 440.

critical student the fact might point to delegation. But a federal government is created for national purposes and for the undertaking of international obligations ; and if those purposes are to be carried out and those obligations enforced—as they could not be under a confederation—then the national government must be endowed with the plenitude of sovereignty within its sphere. That sphere may be defined, or implication may widen its definition, because of the ' incidental and instrumental powers ', as Judge Cooley said, necessary to its effectual functioning, but definition or non-definition is immaterial. Finally, in this connexion, it is significant that, when the civil war arose to test the nature of the American constitution, the Southern States called themselves ' the confederate States of America '. Their actual constitution may not point to either looseness of union or to weakness of co-operation. Military success alone could finally have tested it ; but they deliberately chose a name for their political organization pointing to the loosely cemented régime before the creation of the United States, and their army was known as the ' confederate army ' as distinguished from ' the federal army of the United States '.

When we come to consider the unification of the provinces of British North America, the first thing which strikes us in the documents is the mixed and confused use of terms. In the confidential memorandum [1] drawn up in 1864, which was the basis for the coalition ministry pledged to carry out the unification, ' federal principle ', ' federal union ', and ' confederation ' are all used to describe the political scheme which brought conservatives and liberals together. The inexactitude of the phraseology might be put down to lack of political training were it not for the fact that, during the debates [2] on the Quebec resolutions in the parliament of Canada in February 1865, ' federation ' and ' confederation ' seem to have been deliberately used to

[1] Pope, *Memoirs of Sir John A. Macdonald*, vol. i, p. 344. See above, pp. 295–6.
[2] *Parliamentary Debates on the Subject of the Confederation of the British North American Provinces* (Quebec, 1865).

confuse the issue. It is clear that there was a certain amount of camouflage. Macdonald's attitude can be judged from two quotations, taken widely apart, from his speech of February 6 : ' The conference having come to the conclusion that a legislative union, pure and simple, was impracticable, our next attempt was to form a government upon federal principles, which would give to the general government the strength of a legislative and administrative union, while at the same time it preserved that liberty of action for the different sections which is allowed by a federal union.' [1] ' We . . . strengthen the central parliament and make the confederation one people and one government, instead of five peoples and five governments, with merely a point of authority connecting us to a limited and insufficient extent . . . this is to be one united province with the local governments and legislatures subordinate to the general government and legislature . . . .' [2]

In the first quotation, ' federal ' is used when the ' liberty ' of the provinces is referred to ; in the second, ' confederation '—the designation historically connected with loosely organized unions—is used when the real nature of Macdonald's proposals is referred to. That real nature was nothing else than a thinly-veiled legislative union—a ' federation ' or a ' confederation ' (Macdonald did not care what it was called)—in which the provinces should be merely municipal agents of the national government. It is not without significance that in the title of the official debates the word ' confederation ' appears. The object was to carry the proposals. It remained for the astute mind of Antoine Dorion to challenge the ambiguities : ' The confederation I advocated was a real confederation giving the largest powers to the local governments and merely a delegated authority to the general government—in that respect differing *in toto* from the one now proposed, which gives all the powers to

[1] *Parliamentary Debates on the Subject of the Confederation of the British North American Provinces* (Quebec, 1865), p. 32.   [2] *Ibid.*, pp. 41 ff.

the central government and reserves for the local governments the smallest possible amount of freedom of action.' [1]
Dorion's clearness may have influenced the official title, and it
cannot have been entirely an accident that during the ministry
of Sir Wilfrid Laurier, who himself came from Dorion's *cénacle*,
provincial legislation was largely free from dominion interference, a matter which will be considered later in another
connexion.

For many years after 1867 the provinces held a subordinate
position as Dorion feared. Until the advent to power of the
liberal party in 1896, ' provincial rights ' had a small place in
conservative policy, dominated as it was by the personality
or memory of Macdonald. But, however much party politics
may have forced issues in constitutional law—a matter with
which we have no concern—there was a safeguard independent
of politics, of the opinions expressed or implied by the fathers
of Canadian unification, and of the fact that they had to be
content with an agreement which was but a skeleton and could
not embody Macdonald's real aims if it were to be accepted by
the provinces. That safeguard is found in the fact that the
privy council has always considered the British North America
Act as a British statute, has held that its interpretation must
begin from that point of view, and that all its parts must be
given their natural sense when read in conjunction. As a consequence, and without for the moment considering the light
which that interpretation has thrown on the nature of the
Canadian constitution, we have been saved from much emotional
challenge, from the so-called invasion of sacrosanct instruments,
and from any attempt to confine interpretations within a preconceived Canadian notion of the essence of the Canadian
system. These facts are neither academic nor legal. They are
of practical importance. Canada has accepted the principle : [2]
but it has been rejected by the high court of Australia, of which

[1] *Ibid.*, p. 250.   [2] *Abbott* v. *City of St. John*, 40 S. C. R. 595.

the majority tends to believe in the immunity of instrumentalities. There are thus grave clashes of interpretation, because the Australian high court maintains that the Australian constitution cannot be subject to the ordinary rules governing a British statute, which must be modified by the conception of the constitution in the minds of the founders of the commonwealth.

The almost necessarily incomplete nature of the British North America Act has resulted in a series of legal decisions on which it is possible to found some idea of the nature of Canadian federalism. First of all, the dominion parliament is not a delegation from the imperial parliament or from the provinces.[1] It has full and complete powers within its reference. Secondly, the provincial parliaments are not delegations from the imperial parliament: ' When the British North America Act enacted that there should be a legislature for Ontario, and that its legislative assembly should have exclusive authority to make laws for the province and for provincial purposes in relation to the matters enumerated in sect. 92, it conferred powers not in any sense to be exercised by delegation from or as agents of the imperial parliament, but authority as plenary and as ample within the limits prescribed by sect. 92 as the imperial parliament in the plenitude of its power possessed and could bestow. Within these limits of subjects and area, the local legislature is supreme and has the same authority as the imperial parliament or the parliament of the dominion.'[2] Thirdly, the provincial parliaments are not delegations from the dominion parliament: ' The provincial legislature of New Brunswick . . . derives no authority from the government of Canada, and its status is in no way analogous to a municipal institution, which is an authority constituted for purposes of local administration. It possesses powers not of administration merely, but of legislation, in the strictest sense of that word;

[1] *The Attorney-General for Canada* v. *Cain and Gilhula*, A. C. 542.
[2] *Hodge* v. *The Queen*, 9 App. Cases, 117.

and, within the limits assigned by sect. 92 of the Act of 1867, these powers are exclusive and supreme.' [1]

From these interpretations it is clear (1) that the dominion parliament is a sovereign parliament within the meaning of section 91 of the Act of 1867, and in no sense a delegate, related to the provinces as principals; (2) that the provincial parliaments are in no sense delegates either of the imperial parliament or of the dominion parliament. Further light is thrown on the matter by a famous passage in the judgement delivered by Lord Watson in the last case : ' The Act of 1867 . . . nowhere professes to curtail in any respect the rights and privileges of the crown or to disturb the relations then subsisting between the sovereign and the provinces. The object of the Act was neither to weld the provinces into one, nor to subordinate provincial governments to a central authority, but to create a federal government in which they should all be represented, entrusted with the exclusive administration of affairs in which they had a common interest, each province retaining its independence and autonomy. . . . As regards those matters which by sect. 92 are specially reserved for provincial legislation, the legislation of each province continues . . . as supreme as it was before the passing of the Act.'

A fourth conclusion emerges. The provinces remain ' independent and autonomous '. They have not been destroyed. They possess the executive power ' before confederation minus the powers surrendered at confederation '.[2] In all these cases the court did not discuss the nature of that surrender. It accepted the fact. It interpreted that fact, however, in the sense of a federation and not of a confederation. The conclusion we can come to seems to be that Canada is a federation in essence ; that is, that the central national government is in no sense a delegation ; that the provincial governments are in no

[1] *The Liquidators of the Maritime Bank of Canada* v. *The Receiver-General of New Brunswick*, [1892] A. C. 437.

[2] Keith, *Responsible Government in the Dominions*, vol. i, p. 124.

sense ' municipal ' ; and that national and local governments exercise co-ordinate authority and are severally sovereign within the sphere specifically or generically or by implication constitutionally granted to them. This construction agrees with the preamble of the British North America Act, ' Whereas the provinces of Canada, Nova Scotia, and New Brunswick have expressed their desire to be federally united,' however loosely that preamble may originally have been constructed ; and it seems to override any idea that Canada is a confederation. In the incidences of construction—to which we shall return—the federal conception may not be complete, but the essence seems to be established.

Unfortunately, however, in an Australian case [1] before the judicial committee of the privy council in 1914, Lord Haldane made some remarks which appear to contradict views previously laid down and to reopen the whole question. It is well to quote him at length. During the pleadings he said : ' With deference to a great many people who talk on platforms just now of the " federal system ", in Canada there is no federal system. What happened was this : An Act was passed in 1867 which made a new start and divided certain powers of government, some being given to the parliament of Canada, and some to the parliament of the provinces. The provinces were created *de novo*. The provinces did not come together and make a federal arrangement under which they retained their existing powers and parted with certain of them and an imperial statute has got to ratify the bargain ; on the contrary, the whole vitality and ambit of the Canadian constitution was a surrender, if you like, first, and then devolution. . . . The meaning of a federal government is that a number of states come together and put certain of their powers into common custody, and that is the federal constitution in Australia, but in Canada not at all.' [2] In

[1] *Attorney-General for the Commonwealth of Australia* v. *Colonial Sugar Refining Co., Ltd.*, [1914] A. C. 237.   [2] 30 *Times* Law Reports, p. 205.

the judgement he said : ' But there remains a question which goes to the root of the controversy between the parties. Were the Royal Commissions Acts *intra vires* of the commonwealth parliament ? This is a question which can only be answered by examining the scheme of the Act of 1900, which established the commonwealth constitution.   About the fundamental principle of that constitution there can be no doubt. It is federal in the strict sense of the term, as a reference to what was established on a different footing in Canada shows. The British North America Act of 1867 commences with a preamble that the then provinces have expressed their desire to be federally united into one dominion with a constitution similar in principle to that of the United Kingdom. In a loose sense the word "federal" may be used, as it is there used, to describe any arrangements under which self-contained states agree to delegate their powers to a common government with a view to entirely new constitutions, even of the states themselves. But the natural and literal interpretation of the word confines its application to cases in which these states, while agreeing on a measure of delegation, yet in the main continue to preserve their original constitutions.   Now, as regards Canada, the second of the resolutions passed at Quebec in 1864, on which the British North America Act was founded, shows that what was in the minds of those who agreed on the resolutions was a general government charged with matters of common interest, and new and merely local governments for the provinces. The provinces were to have fresh and much-restricted constitutions, their governments being entirely remodelled. This plan was carried out by the imperial statute of 1867. By the 91st section a general power was given to the new parliament of Canada to make laws for the peace, order, and good government of Canada without restriction to specific subjects, and excepting only the subjects specifically and exclusively assigned to the provincial legislatures by sect. 92. There followed an enumeration of subjects which were to be dealt with by the dominion parliament, but this enumeration was not to restrict the generality of the power conferred on it. The Act, therefore, departs widely from the true federal model adopted in the constitution of the United States, the tenth amendment to which declares that the powers not delegated to the United States by the constitution nor prohibited to it by the states are reserved to the states respectively, or to their people. Of the Canadian constitution the true view appears, therefore, to be that, although it was founded on the Quebec resolutions and so must be accepted as a treaty of union among these provinces, yet when once enacted by the imperial parliament it constituted a fresh departure, and established new dominion and provincial governments with defined powers and duties both derived from the Act of the imperial parliament which was their legal source.'

Lord Haldane's statements can be broken up and considered under several heads. First, he defines a federal state as one in which ' states, while agreeing to a measure of delegation, yet in the main continue to preserve their original constitutions '— ' a federal arrangement under which they retained their existing powers and parted with certain of them '. It cannot but be a surprise to constitutional students to find a federal constitution defined as one in which the central or national government is a delegation from the constituent states or provinces. Lord Haldane's definition appears to be based on an erroneous view of the essence of a federation, and seems to have confused a federation with a confederation. Secondly, it need not be denied that a federation may originate as he suggests ; but it is surely illogical to confuse a constitution with the historical processes by which it originated. Lord Haldane would have us assume that unless certain antecedent procedure takes place it is improper to describe the result as a federal state. Such a position cannot seriously be maintained. Political definitions must be confined to facts as they are, and must not be made meaningless

by the dead hand of historical or social movements out of which
the facts grew. Thirdly, he cites the United States as a true
type of federation because it fulfills his processes. It is obvious
to ask, Is the United States no longer federal because it has
admitted to the original ' measure of delegation ' new states
other than the original colonies which alone were parties to the
original ' federal agreement ' ? Would Lord Haldane have us
believe that the admission of newer states, which made no
pact, has destroyed the federal character of the American
constitution ? Finally his history of the formation of the
Canadian constitution is too partial and incomplete to be
entirely true. If we concede that old rights were entirely
surrendered, and that their retention, minus those conceded to
the national government, is necessary to a federal union,
then we have no federation in Canada. But it is impossible to
make this a rule of constitutional law. In the dominion the
provinces were not formed *de novo*. The united province of
Canada was divided and the executive authority was maintained in the divisions expressly by the Act of 1867, subject to
those changes necessary for the general union. The constitutions of New Brunswick and Nova Scotia were also, subject to
the provisions of the Act, continued as they existed at the
Union.[1] It was doubtless with these sections in mind that Lord
Watson laid down the principle already quoted,[2] which is completely at variance with Lord Haldane's opinion. Lord Watson's
conception has been acted on to such an extent that to abandon
it would upset much of the structure of the constitution. It
has established the generally accepted theory that Canada is
a federation in which sovereign power is divided among co-
ordinate governments, none of which are delegations and among
which the provincial governments are not new creations, but
retain ' their independence and autonomy '.[3]

---

[1] British North America Act, ss. 64, 65, 88.   [2] See above, p. 407.
[3] See, however, Lord Haldane's judgement in *Re Manitoba Initiative and*

The real questions to decide, shorn of all theories, are these : Are the national and provincial governments related to one another as principal or delegate ? What is the real and precise nature of the authority which they may exercise within their spheres ? We have seen that it has been laid down that the various parliaments in Canada are sovereign within the orbit of their established jurisdictions, and that they compel obedience as such. Lord Haldane's opinions, therefore, cannot be accepted as overthrowing the federal essence of the Canadian constitution.

When we come, however, to consider some particular features of the constitution—the Canadian senate, the office of the lieutenant-governor, and the dominion power of disallowing provincial Acts—we may find modifications in the actual working of the federal idea, which yet do not destroy the essence. There is evidence, too, of tendencies to bring these features into accordance with the federal idea.

It must at once be conceded that the Canadian senate is not the product of a single and intelligible political principle. Indeed, it attempts to embody two ideas—nomination by the crown, and a timid hankering after representation of grouped provinces. It may be that this attempt has caused it to become almost ' a cipher ' surrounded ' with derisive state ' and ' the trappings of impotence ' ;[1] but once an elective chamber was ruled out of the range of possibilities if federation were to take place, and once the constituent provinces decided on the necessity of a second chamber,[2] it is hard to see how the senate could have embodied the single federal principle. On the other hand, Macdonald went out of his way to emphasize how, even with nomination, the provinces would be protected : ' In order to protect local interests and to prevent sectional jealousies,

---

Referendum Act, which appears to modify the position which he took in this Australian case ([1919] A. C. 935 ; 35 *Times* Law Reports, p. 630).

[1] Goldwin Smith, *Canada and the Canadian Question* (1891), p. 164.

[2] *Confederation Debates*, pp. 34 ff.

it was found necessary that the three great divisions into which British North America is separated should be represented in the upper house on the principle of equality.' [1]   With temporary obscurity, into which we need not here enter,[2] this plan has been adhered to, and in 1915, when a reconstruction of the senate was necessary for political and geographical reasons, the dominion parliament accepted the principle and it was embodied in an imperial Act.[3]

To Macdonald's prophecy, however, of the impossibility of the senate being filled with ' partisans and political supporters ',[4] his own political life gave the initial lie.   Dorion and Dunkin saw the party possibilities and the weakness in construction.   The latter also made an interesting forecast : ' I think I can defy them to show that the cabinet can be formed on any other principle than that of a representation of the several provinces in that cabinet, for it is admitted that the provinces are not really represented to any federal intent in the legislative council [i. e. the senate].   The cabinet here must discharge all that kind of function which in the United States is performed, in the federal sense, by the senate.   And precisely as in the United States, wherever a federal check is needed, the senate has to do federal duty as an integral part of the executive government, so here, when that check cannot be so got, we must seek such substitute for it as we may in a federal composition of the executive council [i. e. the cabinet] ; that is to say, by making it distinctly representative of the provinces.' [5]   While Dunkin's fears that the cabinet would be weakened by sectional differences and by rendering insecure the constitutional principle of united cabinet responsibility have not been realized, yet he foretold what has become an interesting federal by-product in Canada, most federal cabinets being formed, as far as possible, on a

[1] Cf. British North America Act, ss. 21, 22.
[2] Keith, *Imperial Unity and the Dominions*, pp. 394 ff.
[3] *Parliamentary Papers*, Cd. 7897 ; 5 & 6 George V, c. 45 (Imperial Act).
[4] Kennedy, *op. cit.*, p. 609.   [5] *Confederation Debates*, p. 497.

recognitin of the claims of the constituent provinces.[1] On the other hand, it is not uninteresting to note that in the midst of many suggestions for reform, if not for abolition of the senate, the quasi-federal aspect has not been obscured. Sir George Ross, for example, maintains that ' the first and only duty of the senate is to consider the treaty rights of all the provinces under the constitution '.[2]

When we come to consider the dominion power [3] of appointing the lieutenant-governors of the provinces and of disallowing provincial Acts in relation to the nature of Canadian federalism, we approach a problem which is as old as federation. On the one hand, Macdonald in 1865 emphasized the necessity ' that the chief executive officer in each of the provinces must be subordinate ' because the intention was to create subordinate local governments and legislatures. Dorion saw here the negation of any such thing as responsible provincial government, while Dunkin found in the provision for disallowance the impossibility of any real provincial autonomy.[4]

Before attempting to consider the question, it is well to recall that Hamilton, who may be said to have originated the federal as opposed to the confederate constitution of the thirteen colonies, deliberately proposed at the Philadelphia convention that the president should appoint the governors of the various states, and that he should have an absolute veto on the Acts of the state legislatures.[5] Diplomatic reasons prevented the suggestion from being incorporated in the constitution, but it is important to note that no one considered it opposed to the essence of a federal constitution, least of all Hamilton, who had the clearest conception of the nature of a federation. The

[1] Porritt, *Evolution of the Dominion of Canada*, pp. 357 ff. Cf. Laurier's opinions on the principle, *House of Commons Debates*, May 15, 1909, and see above, pp. 317–18, 381.   [2] Ross, *The Senate of Canada* (1914), p. 51.
[3] British North America Act, ss. 56, 58, 90.
[4] *Confederation Debates*, pp. 42, 225, 502.
[5] Elliot's *Debates*, V, App. 5.

power, at least over state legislation, was soon vested in the supreme court.[1]

It is unnecessary to linger over questions raised concerning the appointment of the lieutenant-governors. Two of them have been dismissed in Canadian history since federation by the governor-general, and at first there was a general disposition to consider them mere creatures of the dominion government. That view has been entirely abandoned. The method of their appointment is evidence of the federal link; but it has been decided that they possess in full the provincial authority,[2] that there is no constitutional anomaly in their appointment, and that when once appointed they are as much representatives of the crown for every purpose of government in the provinces as the governor-general is for all purposes of dominion government.[3]

The dominion power of disallowance is of more vital interest.[4] The governor-general, on the advice of responsible ministers (in this case, the federal minister of justice), has the power to disallow a provincial Act within one year after the receipt of the Act from the lieutenant-governor of the province. We can well understand a principle of disallowance where a constitutional question arises, or where dominion or imperial interests are threatened by a provincial Act; but it would be safer if the decision in such cases were left to the courts as in the United States, since in a federation differences on constitutional law must frequently arise. The resolution of the problem of *intra vires* or *ultra vires* ought not to be left to the minister of justice. This tends to make him too supreme, and to detract from the character of the supreme court of Canada or of the privy

---

[1] *Statutes at Large* (U.S.A.), i, September 24, 1789.

[2] *The Attorney-General for Ontario* v. *Mercer*, 8 App. Cas. 767.

[3] *The Liquidators of the Maritime Bank of Canada* v. *The Receiver-General of New Brunswick*, [1892] A. C. 437.

[4] See in detail, Keith, *Responsible Government*, vol. ii, pp. 725 ff. ; *Imperial Unity*, pp. 432 ff. ; Lefroy, *Canada's Federal System*, vol. i, pp. 30–4, 42–6.

council.[1]   For many years, however, after 1867 the dominion
government considered it was justified in disallowing provincial
Acts which appeared unjust or oppressive—through, for
example, interference with vested rights without compensation,
or through the impairing of contractual obligations. Provincial
Acts were disallowed under these principles.

It appears early to have been a working convention of the
Canadian constitution that, as the courts would deal with
legislation *ultra vires* of the provinces, the power of disallowance
was intended to cover cases outside legal review. In other
words, the power of disallowance was inserted in the British
North America Act to cover, in general terms, unjust, con-
fiscatory, or *ex post facto* legislation, against which there are
express safeguards in the constitution of the United States.[2]

A priori, there is a certain amount of support for this contention. It is well known that the constitution of the United
States was carefully studied by those who laid the foundations
and organized the framework of Canadian federation. It is not
unreasonable to suppose that they had in mind in the ' disallowance sections ' a means of dealing with provincial legislation which might be judged unsound in principle. Cartier,
as we shall see, explicitly said that this was the intention. As
a matter of fact, from federation to 1893, the weight of evidence,
both from the bench and from the federal cabinet, is in favour
of this point of view.

On the judicial side there are opinions from Justices Ramsay,

---

[1] See a protest in these terms from the government of British Columbia,
August 22, 1905, *Provincial Legislation, 1904–6* (Ottawa, 1907), pp. 148 ff. :
' The effect of disallowance . . . is to make the minister of justice the highest
judicial dignitary in the land for the determination of constitutional questions,
and in reality above the supreme court of Canada. The decisions of the
supreme court of Canada are open to question in the judicial committee of
the privy council. From the decision of the minister of justice there is no
appeal. He stands alone.'

[2] As to security of property see an important article by J. Murray Clark in
the *Journal of Canadian Bankers' Association* (January 1919).

Strong, and Chief Justice Draper which can be summarized in the words of the latter : ' The governor-general . . . is entrusted with authority, to which a corresponding duty attaches, to disallow any law contrary to reason, or to natural justice, or equity.'[1] The opinions from the Canadian executive can be summarized in chronological order and are found under date in the various reports of the federal ministers of justice.[2]

First, there is the general report of Sir John A. Macdonald (July 1, 1867–November 6, 1873)[3] dated June 8, 1868. He recommends that the minister of justice should report on provincial Acts, basing his reports on one or all of four heads, (*a*) as being altogether illegal or unconstitutional, (*b*) as being illegal or unconstitutional in part, (*c*) as clashing in cases of concurrent jurisdiction with federal legislation, (*d*) as affecting the interest of the dominion as a whole. This general scheme has been claimed to support, on the one hand, the contention that nothing is said concerning unjust or unsound legislation, and, on the other hand, to include it under the general term ' illegal ', which appears to be distinguished from ' unconstitutional '. Up to 1896, the latter contention seems largely to have held the field. Unjust or unsound legislation figured with unconstitutional reasons and reasons based on general federal policy in the disallowance of provincial Acts.

In 1871 Sir John A. Macdonald disallowed a railway Act of the province of Manitoba because ' no sufficient provision was made for compensation for any infringement of the rights of property or other vested rights '.

In 1874 the lieutenant-governor of Prince Edward Island reserved ' The Land Purchase Act, 1874 ' for the governor-

---

[1] See Ramsay J. in *Angers* v. *Queen Insurance Co.*, 22 L. C. J., and *Corporation of Three Rivers* v. *Sulte*, 5 L. N. ; Strong J. in *Severn* v. *The Queen*, 2 S. C. R. ; Draper C.J. in *Re Goodhue*, 19 Grant. For a direct opposite opinion, however, see Casault J. in *Guay* v. *Blanchet*, 5 Q. L. R. (1879).

[2] Hodgins, *Dominion and Provincial Legislation*, 1867 ff.

[3] The dates in parentheses refer to the term of office as minister of justice.

general's pleasure on the grounds that it was subversive of the rights of property, ruinous to the proprietors, and a dangerous precedent. It was disallowed for the above reasons, and because the arbitration was arbitrary and made no provision against impartiality and for speedy settlement. The report was presented by the deputy-minister, and the minister of justice, the Hon. Telesphore Fournier (July 8, 1874–May 18, 1875), concurred.

In 1874 a Manitoba Act was disallowed by Sir A. A. Dorion (November 7, 1873–June 1, 1874) because it might tend to interfere with the survey of public lands.

In 1876 an Act of the legislature of Prince Edward Island was disallowed by the Hon. R. Scott, acting-minister of justice, because it dealt with the rights of parties then under or subject to litigation under the Act which it proposed to amend, and because there was no provision saving the rights and proceedings of such persons.

In 1881 the Ontario legislature passed an Act granting all persons rights to use improvements for purposes of floating down logs on payment of a reasonable toll. An appeal was made to the governor-general for disallowance, on the grounds of unconstitutionality, of depriving the petitioner of private rights, of being *ex post facto*. The Act was disallowed because it seemed ' to take away the use of the owner's property and give it to another ', and because, assuming that the local legislature had such a power, ' it devolves upon the dominion government to see that such power is not exercised in flagrant violation of private rights and natural justice, especially when, as in this case, in addition to interfering with private rights in the way alluded to, the Act overrides a decision of a court of competent jurisdiction by declaring retrospectively that the law always was, and is, different from that laid down by the court ' (Hon. J. Macdonald, October 17, 1878–May 20, 1881). Ontario objected in strong terms against any review of a provincial Act *inter vires* of the province, and re-enacted the Act of 1881, only to have it again disallowed by the dominion.

In 1887 Manitoba passed an Act providing that every person connected with any public work should be deemed a servant of the crown, and that the sanction of the minister of public works should be deemed in the courts of justice full and competent authority and justification for any work done with the approval and on behalf of such minister. Sir John A. Macdonald, for the minister of justice, recommended disallowance because the immunity from liabilities and responsibilities was of an unreal and extraordinary character and manifestly interfered with private rights.

In 1888 New Brunswick passed an Act which appeared to give a new company rights inconsistent with rights granted to a dominion company. Petitioners claimed that their charter had been ratified by the province, that no cause was shown for forfeiture of their charter, and that proprietary and contractual rights were violated. Sir John Thompson (September 25, 1885–December 12, 1894) recommended disallowance, because the Act interfered with and restricted a dominion Act, and because it diminished the value of franchises already granted.

In 1888 Quebec passed an Act to enable the province to issue debentures for the purpose of redeeming outstanding liabilities and to save the amount of interest paid yearly by the province. Sir John Thompson observed that the Act authorized the province to violate contracts without compensation, that it would affect the credit of the province and might indicate the possibility that faith might not be kept inviolate between the province and its creditors, and that it might hurt the other provinces. Quebec undertook to repeal the objectionable sections.[1]

---

[1] In connexion with this Act see Sir John Macdonald's letter to Tupper, July 20, 1888, Pope, *Correspondence of Sir John Macdonald*, pp. 417 ff.

In the same year a Manitoba Act was amended on suggestion from the dominion, in order not to affect prejudicially the credit of the municipalities of the province.

In 1889 the legislature of New Brunswick passed an Act forfeiting mining leases under conditions set out in the Act. Sir John Thompson characterized the Act as ' seeming to be at variance with the principles of justice and to invade the rights of property, which it is so important to preserve for the credit of the whole country and for the safety of private persons. If it is desirable that a province should resume any part of its patrimony, the methods adopted should be those which recognize and provide for the rights which have accrued under the sanction of the crown '. He recommended amendment to remove such objectionable features as he enumerated. Shortly afterwards the same minister of justice recommended the province of Quebec so to amend a mining law of 1890 as to remove ' any objection to the Act on the ground of its being a confiscation of existing private rights as claimed by the petitioners '. He also brought about the amendment of a Nova Scotia Act of 1892 because it prejudiced rights under litigation. In 1893 an Ontario Act occasioned the federal criticism that a statute which interfered with vested rights of property or with the obligations of contracts without compensation ought to come within the dominion sphere of disallowance.

Thompson, however, in 1886 and in 1888 seems to have deviated from his general principles. Once he refused to consider the question whether an Act was just or unjust, seeing that it was undoubtedly *intra vires* of the provinces ; and once, while pronouncing the legislation under consideration as pernicious, he refused to recommend disallowance because it did not affect the interests of the dominion. The Hon. Edward Blake (May 19, 1875–June 8, 1877), in refusing a petition against an Ontario statute (38 Vict. c. 75), said that he did not conceive that he was called upon ' to express an opinion upon the allegations of the petition as to the injustice alleged to be effected by the Act. This was a matter for the local legislature.' [1]

These three opinions are more or less isolated in the years 1867–93. Whatever other motives—if any—which may have been at work during that period, it is clear that there is a certain consistency of purpose in dealing with provincial legislation which appeared to hurt private property, to invalidate contracts, or to be contrary to what were known as ' sound principles of legislation '. It lies outside the discussion to search for or to examine motives which political writers have suggested. All that can be said here is that the constitutional power of disallowance was consistently used during these years to protect those spheres of provincial civil life which are protected explicitly or by implication in the constitution of the United States.

From 1893 to Mr. Doherty's instance of disallowance in 1918, we see a new principle at work which is largely an extension of the idea formulated by Blake. It is not uninteresting to note that this new principle runs parallel with the definitions of Canadian federalism which have already been considered. It is true that the dicta in *Hodge* v. *The Queen* are older ; but Lord Watson's dicta were uttered in 1892. In *Brophy* v. *Attorney-General of Manitoba* in 1895 Lord Herschell said : ' In relation to the subjects specified in section 92 of the British North America Act and not falling within those set forth in section 91, the exclusive powers of the provincial legislatures may be said to be absolute.' [2] Three years later he said : ' The suggestions that the power might be abused so as to amount to a practical confiscation of property does not warrant the imposition by the courts of any limit upon the absolute power of legislation conferred. The supreme legislative power in relation to any subject-matter is always capable of abuse, but it is

[1] Cf. Blake's opinion, however, on a Quebec statute (38 Victoria, c. 17) in 1876, which differs somewhat from that referred to above.
[2] [1895] A. C. 202.

not to be assumed that it will be improperly used ; if it is, the only remedy is an appeal to those by whom the legislature is elected.' [1]

This period was the golden age of provincial rights, when the privy council was gradually bringing to light the essentially federal nature of the Canadian constitution. Indeed, the new era in the sphere of dominion disallowance is almost ushered in by a federal minister of justice relying on Lord Herschell's words in the last case to which reference has been made.

Indirectly, in 1898, the provinces of Canada received support from a dispatch from the Hon. Joseph Chamberlain to the governor of Newfoundland refusing to disallow a Newfoundland Act. It is true that the dispatch deals with the imperial power of the exercise of disallowance in relation to legislation of a self-governing dominion ; but the principles involved are common to those just considered. There is no imperial issue brought forward : ' it is nowhere alleged that the interests of any other part of the empire are involved or that the Act is in any way repugnant to imperial legislation.' The Act dealt with financial and administrative matters of a local nature. Disputes in that connexion must be settled locally. Where disallowance was claimed on account of policy, Mr. Chamberlain would not consider the claim. The whole tenor of the dispatch lies in the idea that, granted the constitutional power to legislate, and granted that imperial policy is not involved, to disallow would be to negative self-government : ' My action has throughout been governed by constitutional principles, on which I am bound to act ; and I think it is desirable that it should be made quite clear that in accepting the privilege of self-government, the colony has accepted the full responsibilities inseparable from that privilege, and that if the machinery it has provided for the work of legislation and administration has proved defective, or

---

[1] *Attorney-General for Canada* v. *Attorney-General for the Provinces of Ontario, &c.,* [1898] A. C. 700 (The Fisheries' Case).

the persons to whom it has entrusted its destinies have failed to discharge their trust, they cannot look to her majesty's government to supplement or remedy these defects, or to judge between them and their duly chosen representatives.'[1] The dispatch touches hands with Edward Blake and with the dicta of the judicial committee of the privy council. If a province has self-government, if no dominion interests or policies are violated, if the legislation is constitutionally *intra vires*, then the people cannot expect redress, and it ought not to be given if such legislation appears unjust. The remedy lies in their gift of responsible and representative government.

When we resume the consideration of disallowance we almost at once see the true federal idea at work. In 1897 Sir Oliver Mowat (July 13, 1896–November 17, 1897) laid it down that it was none of his business as minister of justice to review a provincial Act because of injustice. In 1898 the Hon. David Mills (November 18, 1897–February 7, 1902) based his refusal to disallow on the passage already quoted from the Fisheries' Case. In 1900 we see the influence of Mr. Chamberlain's dispatch in a letter which Mr. Mills addressed to the premier of Ontario. He says that he will interfere where it is clear that a well-defined dominion policy is endangered by provincial legislation. It is fair to add that he disallowed in 1898 a Yukon Ordinance which unjustly discriminated against certain classes of citizens. There is a difference, however, between the organization of the Yukon and the older provinces, and Mr. Mills's more constant opinion is found in his report of December 31, 1901, in relation to a British Columbia statute : ' Your excellency's government is not in any wise responsible for the principle of the legislation, and, as has been already stated in this report with regard to an Ontario statute, the proper remedy in such cases lies with the legislature or its constitutional judges.'

[1] Dispatch of December 5, 1898, *Parliamentary Papers*, Cd. 8137 ; cf. *The Times*, January 23, 1899.

Sir Charles Fitzpatrick (February 11, 1902–June 4, 1906) followed Mr. Mills. He did not conceal his dislike for legislation which diminished or affected existing rights, but he concluded that 'there is a difficulty about your excellency in council giving relief in such cases without affirming a policy which requires your excellency's government to put itself to a large extent in the place of the legislature and to judge of the propriety of its acts relative to matters committed by the constitution to the exclusive legislative authority of the province'. This opinion brings the history down to the régime of Sir Allen Aylesworth (June 4, 1906–October 6, 1911).

Protests from the provinces forced the federal government to reconsider its position, especially as they emphasized the fact that local autonomy was apparently insecure, even in spheres where the provinces claimed exclusive jurisdiction. In 1908 Sir Allen Aylesworth, then minister of justice, made a report which was approved by the governor-general, in which he said : ' It is not intended by the British North America Act that the power of disallowance shall be exercised for the purpose of annulling provincial legislation, even though your excellency's ministers consider the legislation unjust or oppressive, or in conflict with recognized legal principles, so long as such legislation is within the power of the provincial legislature to enact it.' [1]

In 1912, however, on two occasions [2] the minister of justice, Mr. Doherty, while refusing to disallow for reasons stated, claimed that he entertained no doubt that the power is constitutionally capable of exercise, and may on occasion be properly invoked, for the purpose of preventing, not inconsistently with the public interest, irreparable injustice or undue interference with private rights or property through the operation of local statutes *intra vires* of the legislatures.

---

[1] *Provincial Legislation, 1904–6*, p. 8.
[2] Lefroy, *Treatise on Canadian Constitutional Law*, pp. 63–4, 172, n. 47.

On May 30, 1918, he disallowed, with the approval of the governor-general, an Act of the British Columbia legislature (7–8 George V, c. 71), because it diminished substantially the consideration of a contract. He did this after hearing an argument before the dominion prime minister, the minister of public works, and himself, and after notifying the attorney-general for British Columbia and hearing counsel for the petitioners. There are two passages in this report [1] which deserve attention. Firstly, Mr. Doherty lays it down that he does not consider the dominion veto obsolete in cases where hardship, inequality, injustice, or interference with vested rights or contracts are brought forward. While preferring as a rule to leave such cases, where the legislation is *intra vires* of the province, to be redressed by the local legislature, yet he maintains that there are ' principles governing the exercise of legislative power other than the mere respect and deference due to the expression of the will of the local constituent assembly, which must be considered in the exercise of the prerogative of disallowance '. He refuses to lay down those principles or to formulate general rules, but he suggests that ' interference with vested rights or the obligation of contracts, except for public purposes and upon due indemnity, are processes of legislation which do not appear just or desirable '. Secondly, upon the submission of the attorney-general for British Columbia that disallowance would involve a serious interference with provincial rights, he says : ' Provincial rights are conferred and limited by the British North America Act, and while the provinces have the right to legislate upon the subjects committed to their legislative authority, the power to disallow any such legislation is conferred by the same

---

[1] P. C. (May 30, 1918) 1334. The circumstances, however, must be noted. The British Columbia Act was held to hurt an agreement in connexion with lands in the railway belt of that province into which the federal and provincial governments had entered in 1883 with the Esquimalt and Nanaimo Railway Co. Had the dominion allowed the Act, it would have been possible to say that it had repudiated, equally with British Columbia, its obligations and agreements.

constitutional instrument upon the governor-general in council, and incident to the power is the duty to exercise it in proper cases. This power and the correspondent duty are conferred for the benefit of the provinces as well as for that of the dominion at large. . . . The mere execution of the power of disallowance does not therefore conflict with provincial rights, although doubtless the responsibility for the exercise of the power which rests with your excellency in council ought to be so regulated as not to be made effective except in those cases in which, as in the present case, the propriety of exercising the power is demonstrated.'

This opinion is in direct contrast with that expressed by Sir Allen Aylesworth, and thus elaborated by him in the house of commons : ' I was not, as advising his excellency in council, called upon to think at all of the injustice, of the outrageous character, it might be, of the legislation ; but . . . my one inquiry ought to be whether or not there was anything in the legislation itself which went beyond the power of the provincial legislature.' Sir Allen Aylesworth considered that the provincial legislatures within the scope of their jurisdictions were on an absolutely level footing with the parliament of Canada, and that protest against such provincial legislation as was under consideration ought to be fought out at the provincial polls, as must be done in case of similar dominion legislation.[1]

In December 1909 a similar line was taken by the province of Ontario. The Ontario government conceded, as it was compelled to do, the right to disallow ; but it maintained that that right was technical, and must be judged in conjunction with the interpretation of the British North America Act as a whole, which gave to the provincial governments sovereign powers within their jurisdictions. Any other view would mean that

[1] *House of Commons Debates* (1909), pp. 1750 ff. Cf. Mr. Justice Riddell in *Smith* v. *City of London*, 20 Ont. Law Reports (1909), 133 : ' An Act of parliament can do no wrong, though it may do several things that look pretty odd.'

the people of the provinces had not the full enjoyment of their civil rights with reference to those subjects within their well-defined jurisdiction.[1]

The divergence of opinion is not one merely between two ministers of justice. Professor Lefroy, with a strong catena of cases behind him, maintained that the courts could not disallow a dominion or provincial Act ' merely because it may affect injuriously private rights, or destroy vested rights, or be otherwise unjust or contrary to sound principles of legislature '.[2] Mr. Justice Riddell, in a famous judgement, lays down the principle that ' the legislature within its jurisdiction can do everything which is not naturally impossible, and is restrained by no rule human or divine. . . . The prohibition " Thou shalt not steal " has no legal force upon the sovereign body, and there would be no necessity for compensation to be given.'[3] The courts may, and often must, determine whether or not any Act is constitutional ; but once a decision is arrived at establishing the right of a province to legislate on the subject-matter of the Act ' arguments founded on alleged hardship or injustice can have no weight '.[4]

On the one hand is the opinion which holds that the provinces of Canada are sovereign within their established spheres, and that a court, and *a fortiori* the dominion cabinet, ought not to disallow a provincial Act except when it is clearly unconstitutional. On the other hand is the opinion which holds that the dominion cabinet can veto a provincial Act, otherwise *intra vires*, when it comes within such description as that given by Mr. Doherty or Professor Lefroy.

Lay opinion may be of little worth, but certain criticisms can

[1] Attorney-general for Ontario to the governor-general of Canada, December 9, 1909.   [2] *Op. cit.*, p. 70.

[3] *Florence Mining Company* v. *The Cobalt Lake Mining Company* (1909), 18 Ontario Law Reports, 257.

[4] Moss C.J. in *ibid.*, p. 293. See *inter alia* Mr. Justice Riddell's *The Constitution of Canada*, and the valuable notes on chapter iii.

be submitted. If the constitution is ' similar in principle to that of the United Kingdom ',[1] and if the provincial legislatures are in reality what the privy council has already defined them to be —sovereign powers with as full and ample authority as the imperial parliament within their jurisdictions—certain conclusions seem to follow. The rule of British constitutional law must hold that, granted the legislative power, it is impossible to question the justice of the legislation. This is Mr. Justice Riddell's opinion. Redress lies with the people, ' who are the best judges of the laws they are governed by '.[2] This conception, too, fits in with a federal idea of the nature of Canadian government, suggested, as we have seen, by Lord Watson. Of course, it would not destroy a federal constitution had the Canadian constitution contained a clause like that in the constitution of the United States,[3] prohibiting the provinces from impairing the obligation of contracts or from interfering with matters within Mr. Doherty's description. The suggestion merely is this : once it is clear that an Act is constitutional, then its consequences and results in actual life are open to judgement by the electorate alone.

On the other hand, it is submitted that, if Mr. Doherty's position is the correct one, then the federal idea is overthrown, for the legislatures of the provinces cease to be the bodies described by the privy council and take that subordinate position which Macdonald meant them to hold and Professor Dicey appears to believe they possess.[4] It must not be forgotten that it is possible for such Acts as Mr. Doherty has in mind to be drawn into a clearly defined constitutional issue, and dis-

---

[1] Cf. Edward Blake : ' A single line imported into the system that complex and somewhat indefinite aggregate called the British constitution ' (*St. Catharine's Milling and Lumber Co.* v. *The Queen*, 14 App. Cas. 46).

[2] Riddell, *op. cit.*, p. 98. Mr. Justice Riddell's opinion was approved by the court of appeal for Ontario and by the judicial committee of the privy council (*ibid.*, p. 112).   [3] Article I, s. 10.

[4] *Law of the Constitution* (8th ed.), chap. iii. Cf. Laski, *The Problem of Sovereignty*, pp. 267 ff.

allowed because they may infringe on the dominion power to legislate for ' the peace, order, and good government of Canada '. That is a matter for interpretation legally constituted, and it does not appear open to the courts in this connexion ' to substitute their own opinion whether a particular enactment was calculated as a matter of fact and good policy to secure peace, order, and good government, for the decision of the legislature '.[1] It is quite a different thing, however, that the supporters of this opinion mean. The emphasis laid on this position seems to magnify one power allowed by the British North America Act to the dominion government at the expense of the construction of the Act as a whole and of the general elasticity of its terms.

This difficulty of the position is obvious, but it is interesting to note that Cartier supported Mr. Doherty's point of view : ' The presumption is it [the power of disallowance by the federal government] will be exercised in case of unjust or unwise legislation '. He drew from Dunkin apt criticism : ' The hon. gentleman's presumption reminds me of one perhaps as conclusive, but which Dickens tells us failed to satisfy his Mr. Bumble. That henpecked beadle is said to have said, on hearing of the legal presumption that a man's wife acts under his control : " If the law presumes anything of the sort, the law's a fool— a natural fool." If this permission of disallowance rests on a presumption that the legislation of our provinces is going to be unjust or unwise, it may be needed ; but under that idea one might have done better either not to allow, or else to restrict within narrower limits, such legislation. If the promised non-exercise of the power to disallow rests on the presumption that all will be done justly and wisely in the provincial legislatures, the legislative power is well given ; but then there is no need, on the other hand, for the permission to disallow.'

Dunkin, however, with this power of disallowance among

---

[1] Keith, *Responsible Government*, vol. i, p. 419.

other things in his mind, followed with the conclusion that there was ' no real autonomy allowed to the provinces ', that ' disallowance of all autonomy to the provinces ' characterized the scheme.[1] If that be conceded, the nature of Canadian government is that of a thinly veiled legislative union ; and this position is difficult to maintain considering the history, the legal decisions, and the actual results worked out because of them.[2] It challenges the authority of provincial legislation, otherwise sound, and, it is submitted, it reopens the whole question of local government within any province. If it be correct, it is inevitable that the binding force of local regulations may be disputed on the principle *delegatus non potest delegare*. Provincial regulations of factories or of public health, for example, may well be called in question by the citizens of a province. And yet this ' big county council ' [3]—this province —has the constitutional power to change its own constitution. The two things seem incompatible.

The two well-defined divisions of the subjects seem to correspond to two well-defined periods in social development. The first might be called the period of growth. Material development and economic progress were the predominating social characteristics. With their foundations in progress, constitutional issues did not create vital and widespread interests, and much was often conceded, or allowed to go unchallenged, or was consented to ' against a day '. Thus the dominion government, with the strong bias lent to the federation by Sir John

---

[1] *Confederation Debates*, p. 502 ; Kennedy, *op. cit.*, p. 661.

[2] Cf. Attorney-general for British Columbia to the federal minister of justice, December 20, 1901 : ' In the early days of confederation the dominion executive appear to have been imbued with the notion that the relation between the dominion and the provinces was analogous to that existing between parent and child, and to have acted accordingly. That view of the status of the provinces has been overthrown by a series of imperial privy council decisions which have clearly established that the provinces acting within the scope of their powers are almost sovereign states ' (*Provincial Legislation, 1901–3* (Ottawa, 1905), p. 56).

[3] Riddell, *op. cit.*, p. 98.

Macdonald, acquired much actual power. But once the
foundations of social progress became secure and economic
expansion began to demand such wide securities as its exponents
seemed to consider necessary, constitutional challenges became
more and more common. The courts were forced to consider
the constitution in all its bearings and to give such interpretations to it as were consistent with its construction as a whole.
The second period is the period of provincial rights which have
increased under judicial interpretations. These, however, have
not violated the framework. Indeed it may be said that they
have humanized the British North America Act. They have
given it the elasticity of life. They have rescued it from the
uncritical worship due to an imperishable and immutable
relic of rigid antiquarianism. They, too, have contributed to
political theory. In Canada are being worked out experiments
in sovereignty. Or rather Canada is making a serious contribution to the destruction of the Austinian idea. Every province
is from one point of view at least—in relation to the federal
government—an example of a group with a life and purpose of
its own. The history of education in the province of Manitoba
is an interesting contribution to the decline and fall of the
sovereign state.

Finally, there are two further distinctions between a federation and a confederation which have been made. They are not
important, but need not be overlooked. Firstly, ' a federal
state is one all parts of which are represented, for international purposes, by one government ; and a confederation of
states one whose governments retain the right to be separately
represented and considered '.[1] Without discussing the definition
it is obvious that, in so far as Canada is allowed international
relations by the imperial tie, Canada is a federation. The
dominion government acts for Canada as a whole in any

[1] Lewis, *On the Use and Abuse of some Political Terms* (ed. Raleigh, 1898),
p. 97.

international affairs, including those of the empire. Secondly, a federation is ' a union of component states, wherein there is a central legislature which has authority to pass laws directly obligatory upon the people, the component states also having legislative power. In confederations, on the other hand, the central body has relations with the component states only, and not directly with individuals, e. g. Austria-Hungary.'[1] The inference in relation to Canada is obvious. From another aspect we may accept Judge Clement's opinion of the nature of Canadian government : ' The true federal idea is clearly manifest, to recognize national unity with the right of local self-government ; the very same idea that is stamped on the written constitution of the United States '.[2]

[1] Scott, *The Canadian Constitution historically explained* (1918), p. 3.
[2] Clement, *The Law of the Canadian Constitution*, p. 337.

CHAPTER XXIV

THE DISTRIBUTION OF LEGISLATIVE POWER

THE distribution of legislative power in Canada is governed by sections 91, 92, 93, and 95 of the British North America Act, 1867.[1] The first two deal with the general distribution of subjects between the federal and the provincial parliaments ; the third with education, which nominally is in provincial hands ; and the fourth with agriculture and immigration, over which there is concurrent jurisdiction.

No great constitutional difficulties have arisen in connexion with the interpretation of sections 93 and 95. The first division of section 93 is clear. The rights and privileges referred to are rights and privileges of denominational schools known to and recognized by the law as such. It cannot be construed to cover schools which were *de facto* denominational through such causes as the presence of a population professing one religion, or through the teaching of one faith.[2] The phrase ' class of persons ' must be interpreted to mean persons distinguished as a class by religious belief and not by race or language. Persons joined by ' ties of faith ' and no others alone ' form a class of persons within the meaning of the Act '.[3] Of course, this sub-section does not exclude all provincial legislation in relation to denominational schools legally constituted at the time of federation. As long as the rights and privileges existing at that time are preserved, provincial legislation is valid.

In subsections 3 and 4 appeals are allowed to the governor-

[1] See Appendix.
[2] *Maher* v. *Town of Portland*, Wheeler, *Confederation Law*, pp. 362 ff. ; *City of Winnipeg* v. *Barrett*, [1892] A. C. 445.
[3] *Ottawa Separate Schools* v. *Mackell*, [1917] A. C. 62.

general in council only on behalf of such denominational schools
as had an existence in law at the time of federation.   Such
appeals are not confined to rights and privileges then existing,
but they must be appeals from the protestant or Roman
catholic minority ' in relation to education ' and not ' with
respect to denominational schools '.   These two subsections
constitute a substantial enactment and are not a mere provision for the enforcing of subsection 1.[1]   They also lay down
the only conditions under which the federal parliament can
legislate in relation to education.[2]

The only subjects over which there constitutionally exists
concurrent legislation are agriculture and immigration.   Both
the dominion and the provinces can pass laws dealing with the
scope of these matters, but the federal law will prevail in case
the legislation clashes.   For example, a province can legislate
for purposes of encouraging immigration into it ; but such
legislation will be invalid in so far as it does not conform to the
general immigration laws of Canada.   There are obvious reasons
for this.   The dominion alone can supervise and grant citizenship.   The responsibility lies on it also to take into consideration
imperial treaties, the relationship between the different parts
of the empire, and the susceptibilities of foreign states, all or
any of which a provincial Act might affect.   ' The right of entry
into Canada of persons voluntarily seeking such entry is
obviously a purely national matter, affecting as it does the
relation of the empire with foreign states.'[3]

In attempting to deal with the legal interpretations of
sections 91 and 92 there are certain obvious limitations.   An

[1] *Brophy* v. *Attorney-General for Manitoba*, [1895] A. C. 202.
[2] See above, p. 433, note 3.
[3] Chamberlain to governor-general, January 22, 1901, *Provincial Legislation, 1899–1901*, p. 139.   For coloured immigration, see Keith, *Responsible
Government*, vol. ii, pp. 1075 ff. ; *Imperial Unity*, pp. 190 ff. ; *War Government
in the Dominions*, pp. 314 ff. ; *Imperial War Conferences, 1917 and 1918*,
Parliamentary Papers, Cd. 8566, Cd. 9177.

exhaustive treatment would only be possible in a treatise on Canadian constitutional law. To note even cursorily each specifically enumerated power would involve such frequent reference to complicated cases and such detailed discussion of legal technicalities as to defeat the purpose of this book. It is possible, however, to consider under several headings methods of approach to the study and to keep them largely free from intricate phraseology. Within these limitations, such consideration will provide a general conception of the distribution of legislative power. It is possible, under six general headings, to outline some working principles of interpretation—(a) the distribution of power considered as a whole ; (b) the federal ' residuary power ' ; (c) the completeness of legislative power in Canada ; (d) the general test of the validity of any Act ; (e) the recognition of alternative aspects in the testing of such validity ; (f) intrusion of federal legislation on provincial legislation, and vice versa. It must be remembered, however, that in constitutional cases the judicial committee of the privy council has refrained from making its opinions or dicta standards of interpretation, and has preferred to consider a particular case or point on its merits and apart from previous rulings. This method does not exclude the use of former decisions, but in avoiding the acceptance of them as generally binding, it has tended to eliminate rigidity and to promote elasticity of working.

(a) The distribution of power considered as a whole

We have already seen that the historical circumstances out of which the British North America Act arose prevented it from being as complete and logical an enactment as it might otherwise have been. There were many opposing forces at work—racial, linguistic, social, economic, geographical, and even sentimental —and the foundations of the federation could only be laid by such a balancing of these forces at the moment as would produce a general plan on which union might be formed. The result was a working agreement, and the triumph of the federal idea was not endangered by attempting anything like a balanced distribution of legislative power. The groups concerned in the political construction followed the wise course of being as general as possible, leaving the courts to round off the results of the conferences by decisions in actual concrete cases as they arose. Room was thus left for constitutional progress and for the development of a theory of constitutional law related as far as possible to the social and political growth of the people. The aim in 1867 was to frame as near as possible ' a constitution similar in principle to that of the United Kingdom ', and in the generality of the language used the elasticity of the British constitution was fortunately preserved as far as the circumstances would permit.· It is impossible to read even superficially the list of federal and provincial enumerated powers without seeing how they overlap and intertwine. This fact did not result from accident. It was rather the outcome of deliberations which sought general principles. The framers of the scheme knew that they were working on the terms of a political agreement which excluded the exact disjunction of a perfectly logical enactment, but, in addition, they deliberately avoided an attempt to be logical. The vast majority of them had learned a bitter enough lesson in constitutional experience, and they sought as much freedom from definition as was possible without wrecking the negotiations. The courts have recognized this purpose, and have confined themselves as a rule to the definite arguments before them, and avoided stereotyping the interpretation of each specific power. Their one guiding principle has already been pointed out—to read the Act as a statute, to consider it as a whole, to refuse to isolate clauses or to lend them anything of the solemnity belonging to inviolate instruments. They are members of a statutory body, deriving their constitutional vitality and functions from their organic unity in the body. Thus, for example, ' property and civil rights in the province' impinges on almost every other power in section 92 and on many in section 91. The object of interpretation is to read it as excluding cases dealt with elsewhere and not to take it in its widest and most comprehensive meaning. The general principle of interpretation is embodied in the following judgement : 'The structure of sections 91 and 92 and the degree to which the connotation of the expressions used overlap render it . . . unwise on this or any other occasion to attempt exhaustive definitions of the meaning and scope of these expressions. Such definitions in the case of language used under the conditions in which a constitution such as that under consideration was framed must almost certainly miscarry. It is in many cases only by confining decisions to concrete questions, which have actually arisen in circumstances the whole of which are before the tribunal, that injustice to future suitors can be avoided. . . . In discharging the difficult duty of arriving at a reasonable and practicable construction of the language of the sections, so as to reconcile the respective powers they contain and give effect to them all, it is the wise course to decide each case which arises without entering more largely upon an interpretation of the statute than is necessary for the decision of the particular question in hand. The wisdom of adhering to this rule appears to their lordships to be of especial importance when putting a construction on the scope of the words " civil rights " in particular cases. An abstract logical definition of their scope is not only, having regard to the context of the 91st and 92nd sections of the Act, impracticable, but it is certain, if attempted, to cause embarrassment and possible injustice in future cases.' [1]

The Act contemplates a fourfold scheme of division : (1) education ; (2) agriculture and immigration, already dealt with ; (3) subjects assigned exclusively to the dominion ; (4) subjects assigned exclusively to the provinces. In the third division the

---

[1] *The John Deere Plough Company* v. *Wharton*, [1915] A. C. 330.

dominion is given a general power to legislate for federal interests outside the exclusive powers granted to the provinces in the fourth division. To make this third division of legislative power more certain, the dominion has exclusive power over twenty-nine enumerated subjects 'notwithstanding anything in the Act'. This enumeration does not restrict the general power granted to the dominion over subjects not exclusively assigned to the provinces. The idea is that none of these twenty-nine enumerated subjects shall be considered as within any of the enumerated spheres of provincial legislative authority. The fourth division includes fifteen enumerated subjects assigned exclusively to the provinces and a general exclusive provincial power over non-enumerated matters of a purely local or private nature. The idea is to rule out the conclusion that the fifteen enumerated subjects exhaust all subjects assigned to the provincial legislatures.

The general character of the federal legislative power is that of an attempt to distinguish the matters of great national interest from those local or provincial. The interests of Canada in the widest sense are differentiated from the interests of the provinces in the widest sense. This general character is obvious. When once the federal interest and importance of a subject are constitutionally established, the power of the dominion is exclusive and makes invalid any provincial legislation on the subject, even though the dominion has not itself legislated.

The general character of the provincial legislative power is seen in the grant of general local authority, and the enumerated subjects in section 92 are included as belonging to that local sphere. The dominion cannot encroach on these subjects except in so far as such legislation is incidental to the exercise of the legislative power in relation to the enumerated subjects of section 91. Nor can a province encroach on the enumerated subjects of section 91, pleading that the matter is local. Provincial legislation must be confined to education, to agriculture and immigration, as already pointed out, and to such subjects as are constitutionally decided to belong to the general and particular enumeration of section 92.

(b) The federal ' residuary power '

It is possible to get the so-called ' residuary power ' of the dominion free from the rather vague conceptions which have passed into currency.   There is a general power given to the federal legislature ' to make laws for the peace, order, and good government of Canada in relation to all matters not coming within the classes of subjects by this Act assigned exclusively to the legislatures of the provinces '.   This power is not a complete grant to the dominion of the residuum of undefined and unenumerated powers in Canada.   To the provinces is also granted a residuum of undefined power.   They have the exclusive right to legislate generally on all unenumerated matters of a local or private provincial nature.   The federal residuary power is thus curtailed by the provincial residuary power, and can *de jure* be exercised only when the interests of Canada as a whole are clearly involved.   In other words, when the federal legislature legislates on any subject outside the twenty-nine enumerated subjects of section 91, it can claim no power from that section to legislate on any subject which is in essence or scope local or provincial.   Everything local is given exclusively to a province, whether specifically or generally, and the dominion cannot *a priori* assume that its residuary power allows it to interpret things substantially local in dominion terms.   The federal legislative power can only be called into action outside the enumerated subjects over which it has exclusive authority, when the particular matter on which it is exercised lies outside the specific and general powers granted to a province.   Of course, a matter may originate locally, like a hydro-electric scheme, continue for a time of local importance, and gradually assume national interest and import.   When such a condition is

constitutionally established, the dominion can legislate and can
override provincial legislation, if there is a clash. The dominion,
too, may, under its residuary power, incidentally interfere with
a purely local matter. For example, the power ' to make laws
for the peace, order, and good government of Canada ' must
almost inevitably affect provincial control over ' property and
civil rights '. But in actual substantial legislation the dominion
must establish the validity of the formula ' something done for
the dominion in the interests of the dominion '.[1]

(c) The completeness of legislative power in Canada

There is no sphere of legislation dealing with the internal
affairs of Canada which is not covered by the distribution of
legislative power in the British North America Act of 1867.
Broadly speaking, ' the whole area of self-government ' is
covered in the grants of legislative power to the federal and
provincial parliaments.[2] The point is of interest in comparative
politics. There is no residuum of power granted, neither to the
dominion nor to the provinces, but it is reserved to the people as
in the constitution of the United States. All matters subject to
legislation, in so far as compatible with Canada's place in the
empire, belong to the Canadian legislatures, whether federal or
provincial.[3] The general formula is—if the subject-matter is not
provincial ít is federal, and vice versa. To legislate by initiative

[1] Lord Haldane in *Attorney-General for Canada* v. *Attorney-General for
Alberta* (Insurance Companies Case), [1916] A. C. 588.

[2] *Attorney-General for Ontario* v. *Attorney-General for Canada* (Supreme
Court References Case), [1912] A. C. 571. Cf., however, Lord Haldane, in
Attorney-General for British Columbia v. *Attorney-General for Canada*, [1914]
A. C. 153 : ' It is not an expression which you must ride to death . . . there
are some things that are not delegated with regard to succession to the crown
and matters of that kind.'

[3] *Bank of Toronto* v. *Lambe*, 12 App. Cases, 575. Of course, one legislature
need not possess power to legislate wholly on a specific subject. Concurrent
legislation by the provinces, or by the dominion and provinces, might be
necessary. Cf. *Canadian Pacific Railway Co.* v. *Ottawa Fire Insurance Co.*,
[1907] 39 S. C. R. 405.

and referendum would seem to be beyond the federal or provincial powers.[1]

(d) *The general test of the validity of any Act*

It is now possible to outline certain leading questions which may be asked regarding a doubtful Act in order to begin the making of a decision on its validity. If the Act has been passed by the federal legislature, the first question is, Does the Act in question deal substantially with any of those subjects exclusively assigned to the provinces ? If the answer is in the affirmative, a further question arises, Does not the Act deal with some matter which may fall within some of the exclusive and enumerated powers granted to the dominion ? If the Act does not fall within the subjects granted specifically or generally to the provinces there is no further dispute.

Similar questions guide the approach to the discussion of a doubtful provincial Act. Does the Act fail to come within the specific or general provincial powers ? If it does, it is obviously invalid. But if the answer is that apparently it satisfies the conditions, then the additional question must be asked, Does it not touch substantially on some of the enumerated powers granted exclusively to the dominion ? If it does it is *ultra vires*, for, in spite of its apparent inclusion in the provincial sphere, the dominion power over its enumerated subjects is exclusive ' notwithstanding anything in this Act '.

(e) *The recognition of alternative aspects in the testing of the validity of an Act*

It has been pointed out that sections 91 and 92 overlap. The courts have originated dicta which help in this connexion. The subject-matter of an Act might, from one point of view, come within the legislative scope of section 91, and from another aspect it might belong to the legislative scope of section 92.

[1] See above, p. 392.

For example, a province might legislate on a matter relying on its control over ' property and civil rights in the province ', while the dominion, looking from an entirely different angle, might legislate on the same matter relying on its control over ' trade and commerce '. If the dispute reaches the courts an important fact arises from this difference of point of view. We have seen that the courts are not concerned with the motive of legislation;[1] but in such a case as that under consideration they must consider the nature, the grounds of the legislation, in order to establish the authority or lack of authority of the Act. Its object and scope must be determined in order to ascertain the class of subject to which it really belongs.[2] The courts can determine the classification of the subject-matter of an Act by considering its main purpose. For example, they might be called on to decide whether a specific Act was legislation under the provincial power over licences, or whether it was an invasion of the federal sphere of taxation and ' virtually a stamp Act '.[3] Once the decision is made, the motive for legislation cannot hurt the validity of the Act. The courts, by deciding the point of view or aspect of an Act which may make it valid or invalid federal or provincial legislation, must consider the influences moving the legislature which enacted it. Their consideration is, however, only auxiliary to a constitutional decision and is not the passing of a judgement on the motive behind such legislation. This matter of ' point of view ' has been summed up recently by the judicial committee of the privy council : ' It must be borne in mind in construing the two sections, that matters which in a special aspect and for a particular purpose may fall within one of them may in a different aspect and for a different purpose fall within the other. In such cases, the nature and

---

[1] See above, p. 428.

[2] *Russell* v. *The Queen*, [1882] 7 App. Cas. 829.

[3] *Attorney-General for Quebec* v. *Queen Insurance Company*, [1878] 3 App. Cas. 1090. Cf. Lord Watson in *Attorney-General for Ontario* v. *Attorney-General for the Dominion*, [1896] A. C. 348.

scope of the legislative attempt of the dominion or the province, as the case may be, have to be examined with reference to the actual facts if it is to be possible to determine under which set of powers it falls in substance and in reality. This may not be difficult to determine in actual and concrete cases. But it may well be impossible to give abstract answers to general questions as to the meaning of the words or to lay down any interpretation based on their literal scope apart from their context.'[1]

(f) Intrusion of federal legislation on provincial legislation and vice versa

It does not invalidate a federal Act if it interferes with the operation of a provincial Act, provided that it is not substantial legislation on a matter belonging to the exclusive jurisdiction of the province. For example, the dominion could impose a liquor prohibition law, though in doing so it might destroy a perfectly valid provincial source of revenue in saloon and tavern licences. Or the dominion may directly intrude on the provincial area when legislating under its own clearly defined powers in so far as a general law may affect that area ; or indirectly, with such provisions as may prevent a federal law from becoming a dead letter. It is, however, impossible to find any general formula which will govern dominion intrusion. All that can be said is that there is a kind of enabling power of an intrusive nature sometimes necessary to the workings of dominion legislation. ' Necessarily incidental ' has become a recognized phrase in this connexion.[2] It appears, however, that the phrase must not be exclusively interpreted as meaning that without the intrusion under consideration it would be impossible to work the dominion Act, or that no other provision would be adequate. ' On the contrary, it seems that if such

---

[1] *The John Deere Plough Company* v. *Wharton*, [1915] A. C. 330.

[2] *Montreal Street Railway Company* v. *City of Montreal*, [1912] A. C. 333 ; *Attorney-General for Ontario* v. *Attorney-General for the Dominion*, [1896] A. C. 348.

provision might under certain circumstances be beneficial, and assist to more fully enforce such legislation, then it must, at all events, on an appeal to the courts, be held to be necessary, that is, necessary in certain events.' [1]

The provinces do not seem to have any powers to bring in auxiliary legislation in relation to the enumerated subjects granted exclusively to the federal legislature, though in legislating upon subjects, properly understood, within their own sphere, they may touch on the exclusive jurisdiction of the federal parliament. On the other hand, it seems probable that they might incidentally invade the area of the dominion residuary power.

[AUTHORITIES.—The leading books on the subject are J. R. Cartwright, *Cases decided on the British North America Act* (Toronto, 1887 ff.) ; E. R. Cameron, *The Canadian Constitution as interpreted by the Judicial Committee of the Privy Council in its Judgements* (Winnipeg, 1915) (there is an important review of this book in *Review of Historical Publications relating to Canada*, vol. xx, pp. 198 ff.) ; A. H. F. Lefroy, *Canada's Federal System* (Toronto, 1913), *Legislative Power in Canada* (Toronto, 1897–8), *Short Treatise on Canadian Constitutional Law* (Toronto, 1918) ; W. H. P. Clement, *The Law of the Canadian Constitution* (3rd ed., Toronto, 1916). There are valuable chapters in Keith, *Responsible Government in the Dominions*, vol. ii, pp. 645 ff. (Oxford, 1912); *Imperial Unity*, pp. 389 ff. (Oxford, 1916); *War Government in the Dominions*, pp. 289 ff. (Oxford, 1921). The *Law Reports* of the various provinces, the *Supreme Court of Canada Reports*, *The Times* Law Reports, *Correspondence and Reports of the Ministers of Justice and Orders in Council upon the subject of Dominion and Provincial Legislation* are essentials. The *Canada Law Journal* and the *Canadian Law Times* contain valuable articles and comments on cases. On the school question, consult O. D. Skelton, *Sir Wilfrid Laurier* (2 vols., Oxford, 1921) ; J. Willison, *Sir W. Laurier and the Liberal Party* (2 vols., Toronto, 1903) ; G. M. Weir, *Separate School Law in the Prairie Provinces* (Queen's University, Kingston, 1918).]

[1] *Doyle* v. *Bell* (1884), 11 O. A. R. 326 ; *City of Toronto* v. *Canadian Pacific Railway Company*, [1908] A. C. 54.

CHAPTER XXV

THE IMPERIAL TIE

THE dominion of Canada is an integral part of the British Empire. The growth of Canadian autonomy has therefore been necessarily limited by the legal and constitutional bonds which unite Canada to the empire. In the past the imperial governments and not a few Canadians thought that there should be as little devolution of authority as possible lest the empire should finally dissolve. Even with the grant of responsible government, development was slow, but, as we have seen, there has been a steady and continuous shedding of imperial control in many of those spheres which were once considered sacred and inviolate, until at present the imperial tie is so far removed from the ordinary everyday affairs of citizenship that there is a disposition to think that it consists merely in loyalty to ideals of freedom.

There can be little doubt that emotion and sentiment play a large and important part in the relationship between Canada and Great Britain, and it is well that moral values should not be forgotten in the consideration of hard, legal facts. Great Britain recognizes that Canada has a distinct national status and a distinct group life. There is no possibility in future of leaving Canadian opinion unconsidered or of curtailing full discussion in the delicate and dangerous world of foreign affairs. Great Britain has accepted the fullness of Canadian citizenship, and if it still lacks an effective voice in the executive life of the empire, the fault assuredly does not lie with the mother country. Constitutional reorganization lies in the hands of the Canadian people. In the meantime, the secret places of imperial policy have been opened to Canadian statesmen, who can obtain as

impartial and complete a knowledge of international affairs, of
defence, of treaties, and of conventions as any member of the
British cabinet.   There thus exists a real Canadian influence
which need no longer be exercised through irregular and
uncertain consultations, but possesses a recognized sphere in
the active co-operation at any moment between the imperial
government and a Canadian minister resident in London.   The
motive behind all these advances has undoubtedly been a
devotion to freedom in the broadest sense.

But the student of constitutional history, while fully recognizing the value of such devotion and the strength of the emotional
ties, cannot forget the world of law nor lose sight of those conditions which constitute international life.   Although Canadian
autonomy is practically complete in trade and commerce,
although Canadian opinion is practically decisive in political
treaties affecting the dominion alone, although Canada is a distinct member of the league of nations with the right to
representation on its council, yet the witness which these developments bear is rather to the extreme limit of Canadian freedom
within the empire than to newly accepted positions in constitutional law.   As the law of nations now stands Canada is not
a sovereign state.   However light the imperial tie, as long as
it exists Canada cannot escape—under the political theories
which at present prevail—the implications of the fact.   In
addition, the imperial connexion imposes boundaries on
Canadian autonomy within the empire.   The internal and the
external limitations of Canadian political authority can be
clearly stated in terms of private and international law without
in the least mortgaging the future or closing the gate to further
developments.   There is just as great a danger in refusing to
recognize the fact of these limitations as in erecting the present
regulations governing foreign relationships into permanent
and inviolate principles and thus laying the dead hand of theory
on the march of political events.   It is necessary to avoid, on the

one hand, an exaggeration of Canadian status at the expense of accepted conventions, and on the other a magnification of current theory into immutable law at the expense of hoisting Canada on the horns of ugly dilemmas.

The constitutional situation is unparalleled in history, and analogies drawn from Hanover or the Thirteen Colonies are like most political analogies barren of guidance. It is possible to say the same of the phrases which attempt to describe the conditions. ' Autonomous nations of the British commonwealth ', ' the league of Britannic nations ', ' the free states of the Empire ' are terms capable of such complicated connotations, and are all linked with such varied political theories that none of them is conclusive. All that the historian or political thinker can hope to do is to look at things as they actually are. He must see facts and their implications : first, that Canada is an integral part of the empire; secondly, that Canada does not possess those adjuncts of political life which determine recognition as a state ; thirdly, that Canada has a distinct social, economic, and political group activity peculiarly and separately Canadian; and, fourthly, that the generally accepted theory of sovereignty darkens the issues, and that its abandonment will furnish the most necessary step in resolving the antinomies. Finally, he must recognize that political progress is best secured where the forms which give constitutions their concrete expression are behind rather than in front of general political education. To build up a future on historical experience is always foolhardy, but it can be used as a handmaiden, a humble servant—to be dismissed or employed at discretion. And if there is one historical generalization which possesses any modicum of validity it is that which appears to prove that political development has met with its greatest triumphs when it has been content to march in the rear rather than in the advance-guard of the human army. At the same time, recognition of this fact, if such it be, need not eliminate sane discussion and serious study,

while it will serve to emphasize the truth that human relationships are neither constant nor logical.

Canada is a dominion ' under the crown of the United Kingdom
of Great Britain and Ireland '. Such is the preamble of the
Canadian constitution granted by the imperial parliament, and
it is a fundamental condition on which Canadian executive,
legislative, and judicial authority exists. This fact is of more
than academic importance. During a discussion in the imperial
parliament on Irish affairs Mr. Bonar Law declared, 'If the self-
governing dominions chose to say "To-morrow we will no longer
make a part of the British empire ", we would not try to force
them. Dominion home rule means the right to decide their
own destinies.' Mr. Law's words need examination, and it
is not without significance that during the same debates Mr.
Lloyd George was careful to avoid the question of secession,
and that on March 2, 1922, Mr. Winston Churchill during the
committee stage of the Irish Free State bill refused on behalf
of the government an amendment giving the power. He
declared that the dominions had never claimed nor had
Great Britain ever admitted the right of secession. Mr. Law's
phrase is capable of only one valid construction. If Canada
expressed in unmistakable terms the desire of its people to sever
the imperial tie, the British government would not attempt to
resist by the armed forces of the crown such a clearly expressed
wish. But, as General Smuts clearly recognized for South
Africa, Canada could not dissolve its connexion with the
empire by a federal Act of parliament, because the crown has
not the constitutional power to assent to a Canadian Act outside the legislative competence of the dominion legislature.
Canada has authority to legislate for ' the peace, order, and good
government of Canada ', and to pass an Act dissolving the
dominion as ' under the crown of the United Kingdom of Great
Britain and Ireland ' would be extra-territorial legislation of an
extreme form and of undoubted invalidity. The constitutional

dependence of Canada on the imperial crown can only be constitutionally abrogated by an Act of the imperial parliament, and the announcement of Canada's severance from the empire could only take place by imperial and not by federal legislation. Indeed the league of nations itself confirms this opinion. Canada has a separate status within the league, but contingent on its position as a constituent part of the British empire, and the covenant binds Canada with other members of the empire to preserve the territorial integrity of the empire. There thus emerges another fact, that in addition to an imperial Act being the normal constitutional method of dissolving the relationship there would be also necessary agreement on the part of the other constituent members of the empire, otherwise the covenant is futile and meaningless. The league of nations in giving Canada a new position at the same time binds it closer to the imperial crown. It is in this connexion that the office of governor-general must in future be viewed. His constitutional functions are now clear, but there has arisen an opinion that since the Canadian government has secured the right of direct correspondence with the British prime minister, the office is a useless and expensive relic of an effete system. It has been suggested that the chief justice could carry out the necessary and formal duties. Canada could of course make new arrangements which would satisfy the constitutional conditions, but the governor-general is something more than a mere cog in a political machine. The crown is the most abiding link of empire, and it is not derogatory to Canadian status that the formal functions of the crown in Canada should be combined with something of the visible dignity which still surrounds the throne in England.

The imperial tie raises the further question whether the imperial parliament can pass legislation applying to Canada. All along there has existed a tendency to curtail such legislation, but with the developments of recent years a claim has been made, and concurred in by Sir Robert Borden, that the sovereign legislative power of the imperial parliament is not only obsolete but invalid. The most probable opinion is that in future no imperial legislation will bind Canada unless concurred in by resolution of the federal parliament. In addition, if Canadian proposals mature to obtain from the imperial parliament powers to confer extra-territorial effect for federal legislation similar to that belonging to imperial legislation, there will be less necessity for the exercise of legislative power for the empire as a whole, although imperial legislation would of necessity apply to Canadians as to other British subjects resident where the crown possesses extra-territorial jurisdiction. The question, however, has another aspect of vital importance. Australia, New Zealand, South Africa, and Newfoundland enjoy wide freedom to change their constitutions, but Canada has no authority either to alter the distribution of legislative powers or to vary the essential form of government—a fact upon which Mr. Mackenzie King relied in deprecating Mr. Rowell's claim that equality with the United Kingdom had been established and recognized. All changes made in the constitution of 1867, other than those of small detail, have required imperial legislation. The formation of the federation has been treated as a covenanted occasion, and explicit recognition was given to this treatment in 1907 by the cabinets of the United Kingdom and of Canada, when admission was made that the general assent of the provinces was necessary to any constitutional changes. Canada is thus dependent on the imperial parliament for any important alterations in the instrument of government. The problem is one of difficulty. Imperial legislation would undoubtedly be refused were there signs of serious provincial opposition. On the other hand, it would be difficult to get general provincial agreement to any increase of the federal powers. The provinces are extremely suspicious of proposals which might appear to narrow their own legislative spheres. In Quebec this is further complicated by fears that the special linguistic and religious rights of the province might be endangered, if the dominion were granted a general authority to alter the constitution. Suggestions are abroad for change, and the imperial government will be brought sooner or later face to face with a position of extreme delicacy in deciding how far one province, for example, might be allowed to stand in the way of constitutional proposals which would eliminate the necessity of appeal to the imperial legislature. As things stand at present only non-contentious changes are likely to be conceded. It is difficult to see any conditions which would command general approval. The present position is an undoubted and serious curtailment of Canadian autonomy. On the other hand, it is impossible to overlook the fact that there exists a public opinion on the matter in Canada strong enough to perpetuate this important limitation. Doubtless the peculiar religious and racial groupings in Canadian federalism complicate the situation, but the fact remains, and should not be forgotten by those who urge a more regularized synthesis of empire, that within Canada itself there exists such strong opposition to constitutional change as to narrow severely the sphere of local self-government.

In foreign affairs Canada's connexion with the empire imposes obvious legal boundaries. In spite of all the phrases which have passed into currency Canada has no international status. Even the treaties which Canada concludes in matters of trade and commerce acquire their force through the imperial relationship. Canada cannot negotiate directly with a foreign country in the political or any other important sphere. If negotiations are necessary or called for, or Canada is vitally interested, the crown will act on ministerial advice with the consent of the Canadian government. In minor matters direct communication has taken place for many years, but the imperial government must learn of serious matters through the governor-general and through the British ambassador resident in the particular country. It is true that normally Canadian negotiators will be employed, but if a treaty supervenes it will be considered for international purposes an imperial treaty, and it will take such a form as to leave its nature unambiguous and beyond doubt. The informal agreements which Canada has concluded, and to which reference has been made, are of no international value, and neither the Canadian governments nor the foreign states have mistaken their character. Indeed in the arrangements for a Canadian minister plenipotentiary at Washington the diplomatic unity of the empire has been expressly preserved. While the appointment will be made on the advice of the dominion cabinet the responsibility and authority will rest with the imperial government and the full powers granted to the minister will be issued on the responsibility of the imperial foreign secretary.

When the developments of recent years are judicially examined, they prove that Canada's status in international law has undergone no fundamental change. The war cabinet was merely consultative and had no collective executive responsibility for the empire. Canada signed the peace treaty under authority from the crown acting on advice from the secretary of state for foreign affairs. Canada's position in the league of nations is due to its position in the empire. The covenant of the league has undoubtedly imposed on Canada new obligations of an international nature, but has given it no distinct international status. A possible declaration of war will best illustrate the exact state of affairs. Once the imperial government declares war, Canada is at war, and once a foreign state declares war against Great Britain, Canada is at war.[1]

---

[1] Statements have been made (by Mr. Lloyd George, for example) that such and such treaties do not, or would not, bind Canada unless accepted by resolution of the federal parliament. These have led to the superficial conclusion that in the absence of such resolution, Canada could not be drawn into a war which might arise out of such treaties. The difficulty, however, lies in the fact that an enemy would not accept the *modus vivendi* of the imperial ' family compact ' and would consider Canada as an enemy owing to its integral connexion in international law with the British empire.

In either case, Canada need not fight, need not supply a man or a ship or assist in any way. Canada might be prepared to preserve the most meticulous neutrality, but as international law now stands, Canada would be at war, and its territory and citizens liable to attack. The problem assumes an acute form. In future there will be full consultation on foreign affairs, and indications point to developments along the lines of the imperial defence committee. It is no longer possible for the imperial government to carry on the foreign relations of the empire without Canadian assistance. That much is absolutely clear. And it is also clear that as the empire is at present constituted, Canada cannot escape—consultation or no consultation—the implications of its connexion with the empire, and must accept the fact of being at least in a state of war when Great Britain is at war. On the other hand, it is possible for Canada to acquire an effective voice in foreign policy and in war if the Canadian people so desire. But the acquisition of such a regularized position would not affect Canada's international status. Canada's voice, effective and regularized, might be cast against a particular policy which resulted in war, or against a particular war itself, but under the international laws which hold good in the current theory of sovereignty neither fact would prevent the foreign power or powers concerned from exercising their perfectly legal right of invading the dominion, of killing Canadian citizens, and of injuring Great Britain through military and naval action against the empire as a whole. The most careful explanation of Canada's previous attitude would not change the situation in any degree, nor would it make illegal any such actions as those suggested on the part of the foreign power. It may be that in the league of nations there is, for imperial problems, distinct hope. No one can seriously doubt that at present Canada is not enamoured of constitutional changes. Mr. Meighen avoided the issue at the general election of 1921, and his successful

opponent is inclined to follow the Laurier tradition. Canada's
membership of the league is likely to remain, and it is clear that
the functions most vital to the permanence and justification of
the league will be discharged in those spheres of foreign affairs
and war and peace in which the present organization of the
empire seems most anomalous. In other words, if the league
of nations succeeds, Canada can afford to let its position
await the guidance of the years. On the other hand, the international difficulties still remain linked with older conceptions
of the state.

At this point, it may be pertinent to deal with the theoretical
difficulty which for many minds prevents a just appreciation
of the present position of Canada in the empire. We have
pointed out certain anomalies in this position, but we must
not on that account be regarded as enforcing the old view that
political sovereignty by its very nature is one and indivisible,
or that the logic of the situation leaves Canada with the alternatives of complete independence or permanent inferiority of
status. The older doctrine of sovereignty admitted no third
course, but the active criticism of recent political thought
working on such material as modern federations, leagues, and
unions so abundantly provide, rejects that absolutism. No
ancient formula of sovereignty, however embodied in present
legal doctrines, can stay the actual process of political development. If the formula declares that there must be one single
ultimate residence of all sovereign powers within a state, and
the facts reveal a dual or multiple residence, so much the
worse for the formula. Supposing the Austinian doctrine of
sovereignty had been rigidly accepted in the past, what a barrier
it would have placed in the way of modern federalism within
and without the British empire ! Or supposing on the other
hand the Montesquieuan doctrine of the separate embodiment
of the ' powers ' had been as faithfully adhered to as the New
Hampshire Bill of Rights demanded, how could the typical

institution of the cabinet system ever have developed ? Necessity modifies our over-simple or over-rigid theories. The strong persuasions of defence or finance, making for unity, have countered the tenacious differences of religion or race, and have created thus not only new forms but new degrees of sovereignty. We must therefore make our theory of sovereignty conformable to these facts. The modern state is an attempt to reconcile our experiences and our necessities, and the modern theory of the state must seek to do no less.

The changing relation of Canada to the British empire, therefore, instead of flouting any eternal principle of political sovereignty, is one of the crucial series of data to which our theories of sovereignty must conform. It is not too much to say that, in the modern political world, we find states showing every degree of the integration and the separation of sovereign powers. If the constitutions of the United States and of Australia formally allocate residual sovereignty to the participant states, while in the dominion of Canada this pertains to the federal government, both are nevertheless forms within which the unity of a state is realized. If Australia assigns a variety of concurrent powers to the states and to the federation, the system nevertheless is a working unity. If the Union of South Africa is to be called a unitary state rather than a federation, it still presents a very different type of unity from that of the United Kingdom. We might go farther and suggest that, even in the so-called unitary state, whatever its legal form, there are sovereign powers which in fact are and must be exercised by municipalities, counties, and other units of administration. Why then, we may well ask, should not the British empire remain a unity although the aspirations of its parts for autonomy find the completest expression they may desire ?

In fact it is the insistence of the older doctrine of sovereignty, one exclusive and indivisible, which is the great stumbling-block in the way of the evolution of the greater unities which political exigencies, as distinct from political dogma, require to-day. Thus the league of nations can grow into an effective reality only if the conception of the exclusive state, discredited by the facts of interdependence, is abandoned also in the practice of statesmanship. In the last resort absolute power is a mystic doctrine which has relevance neither to men nor to states. Instead of the fiction of absolute sovereignty, owning no obligations 'except', as the old writers put it, 'to God', we must be content with the reality of relative autonomy, which alone provides, for men and for states, the condition of effective liberty and sane relationship. A clear recognition of this truth would remove the intellectual obstacle to the evolution of the unity of the British empire as well. To insist, for example, on the legalist principle of the ultimate appeal to an overlord sovereignty, should a constituent part of the empire oppose it, would be the way to lose the substance for the sake of the shadow. If the British government in 1900 had insisted on its view, against the opinion of Australia, that the right of appeal to the privy council should always lie in cases affecting the judicial interpretation of the federal principle, the unity of Australia within the empire would certainly have been not strengthened but weakened.

It will be said by the legalists that there is no political unity where there is no final authority. In reply, two observations may be made. In the first place we should notice the significance of the system which has grown up, particularly in federal states, by which the settlement of constitutional problems, where there is a question of conflicting claims to sovereign powers, is assigned not to parliament but to courts. In other words, these problems are regarded as subjects for interpretation and not for legislation, for adjustment and not for enactment, and the court in such a case may perhaps be fairly regarded as the representative, not of the parliamentary sovereign but of that more profound though less coherent will, the will of the people itself. This leads us to the further and fundamental consideration that the final unity of any state is to be sought not within the form of government at all, but in the consensus of political opinion, in the communal will which sets up and pulls down the instruments of political power. If there is that underlying unity it can support the gradation and division of ostensible sovereignty. A house divided against itself cannot stand, but if there is a common foundation it will sustain, without danger of their falling asunder, the divisions within the house.

We need not therefore despair of the unity of the British empire because Canada and its other constituents as they attain to political manhood claim a political sovereignty of their own, nor, on the other hand, need we think it necessary to construct, in advance of evolution, artificial props such as an imperial cabinet with definite overruling powers. What is best and safest is to strengthen the foundations of the common will, to cultivate the common heritage, to develop the intercourse between the members of the far-flung empire as well as between the responsible ministers of every part, to enhance in a word that sense of unity which the possession of a great and common tradition has built up in our history and in our faith. And if the resulting development contradicts fond theories of sovereignty, these may be offered up, in thankfulness for the unity maintained and achieved, as a cheerful and willing sacrifice.

In conclusion, it is necessary to lay emphasis on an important consideration. No amount of 'regularizing' or of constitutional changes will in the final analysis hold the empire together or guarantee imperial unity, apart from political development. We must not be swept off our feet by problems, by dilemmas, by political antinomies and all the stock-in-trade of theorists and of doctrinaires. The plain issue is this : progress implies conscious intelligent consent, and until that comes the greatest contribution to the empire will be a studied avoidance of plans and of constitutions. Canada knows well the situation, and that it cannot be squared with all the current rules. Reiterations of the apparent dangers involved do not help political education and are barren of results. For the present it is well to hold back from concrete proposals. The greatest solvent of political problems, if they are to be solved at all adequately, is time. The greatest danger lies in hastening the harvest of the years and in attempting to reap in advance of general political development. It may be that as time bites into the problem of empire and provides perhaps a legal issue, the world itself will have arrived at a higher synthesis of human endeavour than that represented by the hideous clash of modern sovereignties. Thus the history, which began with a glimpse into a paternal and conservative past, closes with the outlook of a democratic and liberal hope.

APPENDIX

THE BRITISH NORTH AMERICA ACT, 1867
(30 & 31 Victoria, c. 3).

An Act for the Union of Canada, Nova Scotia, and New Brunswick, and the Government thereof: and for Purposes connected therewith.[1]

[*March 29, 1867.*]

WHEREAS the Provinces of Canada, Nova Scotia, and New Brunswick, have expressed their desire to be federally united into one Dominion under the Crown of the United Kingdom of Great Britain and Ireland, with a Constitution similar in principle to that of the United Kingdom:

And whereas such a Union would conduce to the welfare of the Provinces and promote the interests of the British Empire:

And whereas on the establishment of the Union by authority of Parliament it is expedient, not only that the Constitution of the Legislative Authority in the Dominion be provided for, but also that the nature of the Executive Government therein be declared:

And whereas it is expedient that provision be made for the eventual admission into the Union of other parts of British North America:

Be it therefore enacted and declared by the Queen's most Excellent Majesty, by and with the advice and consent of the Lords Spiritual and Temporal, and Commons, in this present Parliament assembled, and by the authority of the same, as follows:

I.—PRELIMINARY.

1. This Act may be cited as *The British North America Act, 1867.* Shorttitle.

2. The provisions of this Act referring to Her Majesty the Queen extend also to the heirs and successors of Her Majesty, Kings and Queens of the United Kingdom of Great Britain and Ireland. Application of provisions referring to the Queen.

II.—UNION.

3. It shall be lawful for the Queen, by and with the advice of Her Majesty's Most Honourable Privy Council, to declare by Proclamation that on and after a day herein appointed, not being more than Declaration by proclamation of Union of Canada, Nova

---

[1] Brought into force, pursuant to sect. 3, by royal proclamation, on July 1, 1867.

Scotia and New Brunswick, into one Dominion under name of Canada.
six months after the passing of this Act, the Provinces of Canada, Nova Scotia, and New Brunswick shall form and be one Dominion under the name of Canada ; and on and after that day those three Provinces shall form and be one Dominion under that name accordingly.

Commencement of subsequent provisions of Act. Meaning of Canada in such provisions.
4. The subsequent provisions of this Act shall, unless it is otherwise expressed or implied, commence and have effect on and after the Union, that is to say, on and after the day appointed for the Union taking effect in the Queen's Proclamation ; and in the same provisions, unless it is otherwise expressed or implied, the name Canada shall be taken to mean Canada as constituted under this Act.

Four Provinces.
5. Canada shall be divided into four Provinces, named Ontario, Quebec, Nova Scotia, and New Brunswick.

Provinces of Ontario and Quebec.
6. The parts of the Province of Canada (as it exists at the passing of this Act) which formerly constituted respectively the Provinces of Upper Canada and Lower Canada shall be deemed to be severed, and shall form two separate Provinces. The part which formerly constituted the Province of Upper Canada shall constitute the Province of Ontario and the part which formerly constituted the Province of Lower Canada shall constitute the Province of Quebec.

Provinces of Nova Scotia and New Brunswick.
7. The Provinces of Nova Scotia and New Brunswick shall have the same limits as at the passing of this Act.

Population of Provinces to be distinguished in decennial census.
8. In the general census of the population of Canada which is hereby required to be taken in the year one thousand eight hundred and seventy-one, and in every tenth year thereafter, the respective populations of the four Provinces shall be distinguished.

III.—EXECUTIVE POWER.

Executive Power to continue vested in the Queen.
9. The Executive Government and authority of and over Canada is hereby declared to continue and be vested in the Queen.

Application of provisions referring to Governor-General.
10. The provisions of this Act referring to the Governor-General extend and apply to the Governor-General for the time being of Canada, or other the Chief Executive Officer or Administrator for the time being carrying on the Government of Canada on behalf and in the name of the Queen, by whatever title he is designated.

Constitution of Privy Council for Canada.
11. There shall be a Council to aid and advise in the Government of Canada, to be styled the Queen's Privy Council for Canada ; and the persons who are to be members of that Council shall be from time to time chosen and summoned by the Governor-General and sworn in as Privy Councillors, and members thereof may be from time to time removed by the Governor-General.

12. All powers, authorities, and functions, which under any Act of the Parliament of Great Britain, or of the Parliament of the United Kingdom of Great Britain and Ireland, or of the Legislature of Upper Canada, Lower Canada, Canada, Nova Scotia, or New Brunswick, are at the Union vested in or exercisable by the respective Governors or Lieutenant-Governors of those Provinces, with the advice, or with the advice and consent, of the respective Executive Councils thereof, or in conjunction with those Councils, or with any number of members thereof, or by those Governors, or Lieutenant-Governors individually, shall, as far as the same continue in existence and capable of being exercised after the Union in relation to the Government of Canada, be vested in and exercisable by the Governor-General, with the advice or with the advice and consent of or in connection with the Queen's Privy Council for Canada, or any members thereof, or by the Governor-General individually, as the case requires, subject nevertheless (except with respect to such as exist under Acts of the Parliament of Great Britain or of the Parliament of the United Kingdom of Great Britain and Ireland) to be abolished or altered by the Parliament of Canada. *All powers under Acts to be exercised by Governor-General with advice of Privy Council, or alone.*

13. The provisions of this Act referring to the Governor-General in Council shall be construed as referring to the Governor-General acting by and with the advice of the Queen's Privy Council for Canada. *Application of provisions referring to Governor-General in Council.*

14. It shall be lawful for the Queen, if Her Majesty thinks fit, to authorize the Governor-General from time to time to appoint any person or any persons jointly or severally to be his Deputy or Deputies within any part or parts of Canada, and in that capacity to exercise during the pleasure of the Governor-General such of the powers, authorities, and functions of the Governor-General as the Governor-General deems it necessary or expedient to assign to him or them, subject to any limitations or directions expressed or given by the Queen ; but the appointment of such a Deputy or Deputies shall not affect the exercise by the Governor-General himself of any power, authority or function. *Power to Her Majesty to authorize Governor-General to appoint Deputies.*

15. The Command-in-Chief of the Land and Naval Militia, and of all Naval and Military Forces, of and in Canada, is hereby declared to continue and be vested in the Queen. *Command of armed forces to continue to be vested in the Queen.*

16. Until the Queen otherwise directs the seat of Government of Canada shall be Ottawa. *Seat of Government of Canada.*

IV.—LEGISLATIVE POWER.

17. There shall be one Parliament for Canada, consisting of the *Constitution of*

Parliament of Canada.

Queen, an Upper House, styled the Senate, and the House of Commons.

[*Section 18 was repealed by imperial Act 38 & 39 Vict., c. 38, and the following section substituted therefor.*

Privileges, etc., of Houses.

18. The privileges, immunities, and powers to be held, enjoyed and exercised by the Senate and by the House of Commons and by the members thereof respectively shall be such as are from time to time defined by Act of the Parliament of Canada, but so that any Act of the Parliament of Canada defining such privileges, immunities and powers shall not confer any privileges, immunities or powers exceeding those at the passing of such Act held, enjoyed, and exercised by the Commons House of Parliament of the United Kingdom of Great Britain and Ireland and by the members thereof.]

First Session of the Parliament of Canada.

19. The Parliament of Canada shall be called together not later than six months after the Union.

Yearly Session of the Parliament of Canada.

20. There shall be a Session of the Parliament of Canada once at least in every year, so that twelve months shall not intervene between the last sitting of the Parliament in one Session and its first sitting in the next Session.

The Senate.

Number of Senators.

21. The Senate shall, subject to the provisions of this Act, consist of seventy-two members,[1] who shall be styled Senators.

Representation of Provinces in Senate.

22. In relation to the constitution of the Senate, Canada shall be deemed to consist of three divisions—

1. Ontario ;
2. Quebec ;
3. The Maritime Provinces, Nova Scotia and New Brunswick ; which three divisions shall (subject to the provisions of this Act) be equally represented in the Senate as follows : Ontario by twenty-four Senators ; Quebec by twenty-four Senators ; and the Maritime Provinces by twenty-four Senators, twelve thereof representing Nova Scotia, and twelve thereof representing New Brunswick.

In the case of Quebec each of the twenty-four Senators representing that Province shall be appointed for one of the twenty-four Electoral Divisions of Lower Canada specified in Schedule A. to chapter one of the Consolidated Statutes of Canada.

Qualifications of Senator.

23. The qualifications of a Senator shall be as follows :—

1. He shall be of the full age of thirty years ;
2. He shall be either a natural-born subject of the Queen, or a subject of the Queen naturalized by an Act of the Parliament

[1] See above, p. 384.

of Great Britain, or of the Parliament of the United Kingdom of Great Britain and Ireland, or of the Legislature of one of the Provinces of Upper Canada, Lower Canada, Canada, Nova Scotia, or New Brunswick, before the Union, or of the Parliament of Canada after the Union ;

3. He shall be legally or equitably seised as of freehold for his own use and benefit of lands or tenements held in free and common socage, or seised or possessed for his own use and benefit of lands or tenements held in franc-aleu or in roture, within the Province for which he is appointed, of the value of $4,000, over and above all rents, dues, debts, charges, mortgages and incumbrances due or payable out of or charged on or affecting the same ;

4. His real and personal property shall be together worth $4,000, over and above his debts and liabilities ;

5. He shall be resident in the Province for which he is appointed ;

6. In the case of Quebec he shall have his real property qualification in the Electoral Division for which he is appointed, or shall be resident in that Division.

24. The Governor-General shall from time to time, in the Queen's name, by instrument under the Great Seal of Canada, summon qualified persons to the Senate ; and, subject to the provisions of this Act, every person so summoned shall become and be a member of the Senate and a Senator. *Summoning of Senators.*

25. Such persons shall be first summoned to the Senate as the Queen by warrant under Her Majesty's Royal Sign Manual thinks fit to approve, and their names shall be inserted in the Queen's Proclamation of Union. *Summons of first body of Senators.*

26. If at any time on the recommendation of the Governor-General the Queen thinks fit to direct that three or six members [1] be added to the Senate, the Governor-General may by summons to three or six qualified persons (as the case may be), representing equally the three divisions of Canada, add to the Senate accordingly. *Additions of Senators in certain cases.*

27. In case of such addition being at any time made the Governor-General shall not summon any person to the Senate, except on a further like direction by the Queen on the like recommendation, until each of the three divisions of Canada is represented by twenty-four Senators and no more. *Reduction of Senate to normal number.*

28. The number of Senators shall not at any time exceed seventy-eight.[1] *Maximum number of Senators.*

[1] See above, p. 384.

Tenure of place in Senate.

29. A Senator shall, subject to the provisions of this Act, hold his place in the Senate for life.

Resignation of place in Senate.

30. A Senator may by writing under his hand addressed to the Governor-General resign his place in the Senate, and thereupon the same shall be vacant.

Disqualification of Senators.

31. The place of a Senator shall become vacant in any of the following cases :

1. If for two consecutive Sessions of the Parliament he fails to give his attendance in the Senate ;

2. If he takes an oath or makes a declaration or acknowledgment of allegiance, obedience, or adherence to a foreign power, or does an act whereby he becomes a subject or citizen, or entitled to the rights or privileges of a subject or citizen, of a foreign power ;

3. If he is adjudged bankrupt or insolvent, or applies for the benefit of any law relating to insolvent debtors, or becomes a public defaulter ;

4. If he is attainted of treason or convicted of felony or of any infamous crime ;

5. If he ceases to be qualified in respect of property or of residence ; provided, that a Senator shall not be deemed to have ceased to be qualified in respect of residence by reason only of his residing at the seat of the Government of Canada while holding an office under that Government requiring his presence there.

Summons on vacancy in Senate.

32. When a vacancy happens in the Senate by resignation, death, or otherwise, the Governor-General shall by summons to a fit and qualified person fill the vacancy.

Questions as to qualifications and vacancies in Senate.

33. If any question arises respecting the qualification of a Senator or a vacancy in the Senate, the same shall be heard and determined by the Senate.

Appointment of Speaker of Senate.

34. The Governor-General may from time to time, by instrument under the Great Seal of Canada, appoint a Senator to be Speaker of the Senate, and may remove him and appoint another in his stead.

Quorum of Senate.

35. Until the Parliament of Canada otherwise provides, the presence of at least fifteen Senators, including the Speaker, shall be necessary to constitute a meeting of the Senate for the exercise of its powers.

Voting in Senate.

36. Questions arising in the Senate shall be decided by a majority of voices, and the Speaker shall in all cases have a vote, and when the voices are equal the decision shall be deemed to be in the negative.

The House of Commons.

37. The House of Commons shall, subject to the provisions of this Act, consist of one hundred and eighty-one members, of whom eighty-two shall be elected for Ontario, sixty-five for Quebec, nineteen for Nova Scotia, and fifteen for New Brunswick.

Constitution of House of Commons in Canada.

38. The Governor-General shall from time to time, in the Queen's name, by instrument under the Great Seal of Canada, summon and call together the House of Commons.

Summoning of House of Commons.

39. A Senator shall not be capable of being elected or of sitting or voting as a member of the House of Commons.

Senators not to sit in House of Commons.

40. Until the Parliament of Canada otherwise provides, Ontario, Quebec, Nova Scotia, and New Brunswick shall, for the purposes of the election of members to serve in the House of Commons, be divided into Electoral Districts as follows :—

Electoral districts of the four Provinces.

1.—ONTARIO.

Ontario shall be divided into the Counties, Ridings of Counties, Cities, parts of Cities, and Towns enumerated in the first Schedule to this Act, each whereof shall be an Electoral District, each such District as numbered in that Schedule being entitled to return one member.

2.—QUEBEC.

Quebec shall be divided into sixty-five Electoral Districts, composed of the sixty-five Electoral Divisions into which Lower Canada is at the passing of this Act divided under chapter two of the Consolidated Statutes of Canada, chapter seventy-five of the Consolidated Statutes of Lower Canada, and the Act of the Province of Canada of the twenty-third year of the Queen, chapter one, or any other Act amending the same in force at the Union, so that each such Electoral Division shall be for the purposes of this Act an Electoral District entitled to return one member.

3.—NOVA SCOTIA.

Each of the eighteen Counties of Nova Scotia shall be an Electoral District. The County of Halifax shall be entitled to return two members, and each of the other Counties one member.

4.—NEW BRUNSWICK.

Each of the fourteen Counties into which New Brunswick is divided, including the City and County of St. John, shall be an Electoral District ; the City of St. John shall also be a separate Electoral District. Each of those fifteen Electoral Districts shall be entitled to return one member.

H h

Continuance
of existing
election laws
until Parlia-
ment of Cana-
da otherwise
provides. **41.** Until the Parliament of Canada otherwise provides, all laws
in force in the several Provinces at the Union relative to the following
matters or any of them, namely,—the qualifications and disqualifications of persons to be elected or to sit or vote as members of the
House of Assembly or Legislative Assembly in the several Provinces,
the voters at elections of such members, the oaths to be taken by
voters, the Returning Officers, their powers and duties, the proceedings at elections, the periods during which elections may be
continued, the trial of controverted elections, and proceedings
incident thereto, the vacating of seats of members, and the execution
of new writs in case of seats vacated otherwise than by dissolution,—
shall respectively apply to elections of members to serve in the House
of Commons for the same several Provinces.

Provided that, until the Parliament of Canada otherwise provides,
at any election for a Member of the House of Commons for the
District of Algoma, in addition to persons qualified by the law of the
Province of Canada to vote, every male British subject aged twenty-
one years or upwards, being a householder, shall have a vote.

Writs for first
election. **42.** For the first election of members to serve in the House of
Commons the Governor-General shall cause writs to be issued by
such persons, in such form, and addressed to such Returning Officers
as he thinks fit.

The person issuing writs under this section shall have the like
powers as are possessed at the Union by the officers charged with the
issuing of writs for the election of members to serve in the respective
House of Assembly or Legislative Assembly of the Province of
Canada, Nova Scotia, or New Brunswick ; and the Returning Officers
to whom writs are directed under this section shall have the like
powers as are possessed at the Union by the officers charged with
the returning of writs for the election of members to serve in the
same respective House of Assembly or Legislative Assembly.

As to vacancies
before meeting
of Parliament
or before pro-
vision is made
by Parliament
in this behalf. **43.** In case a vacancy in the representation in the House of
Commons of any Electoral District happens before the meeting of
the Parliament, or after the meeting of the Parliament before
provision is made by the Parliament in this behalf, the provisions
of the last foregoing section of this Act shall extend and apply to
the issuing and returning of a writ in respect of such vacant District.

As to election
of Speaker of
House of
Commons. **44.** The House of Commons on its first assembling after a general
election shall proceed with all practicable speed to elect one of its
members to be Speaker.

As to filling
up vacancy **45.** In case of a vacancy happening in the office of Speaker by
death, resignation or otherwise, the House of Commons shall with

all practicable speed proceed to elect another of its members to be Speaker. *in office of Speaker.*

46. The Speaker shall preside at all meetings of the House of Commons. *Speaker to preside.*

47. Until the Parliament of Canada otherwise provides, in case of the absence for any reason of the Speaker from the chair of the House of Commons for a period of forty-eight consecutive hours, the House may elect another of its members to act as Speaker, and the member so elected shall during the continuance of such absence of the Speaker have and execute all the powers, privileges, and duties of Speaker. *Provision in case of absence of Speaker.*

48. The presence of at least twenty members of the House of Commons shall be necessary to constitute a meeting of the House for the exercise of its powers, and for that purpose the Speaker shall be reckoned as a member. *Quorum of House of Commons.*

49. Questions arising in the House of Commons shall be decided by a majority of voices other than that of the Speaker, and when the voices are equal, but not otherwise, the Speaker shall have a vote. *Voting in House of Commons.*

50. Every House of Commons shall continue for five years from the day of the return of the writs for choosing the House (subject to be sooner dissolved by the Governor-General), and no longer. *Duration of House of Commons.*

51. On the completion of the census in the year one thousand eight hundred and seventy-one, and of each subsequent decennial census, the representation of the four Provinces shall be re-adjusted by such authority, in such manner and from such time as the Parliament of Canada from time to time provides, subject and according to the following rules :— *Decennial Re-adjustment of Representation.*

1. Quebec shall have the fixed number of sixty-five members.
2. There shall be assigned to each of the other Provinces such a number of members as will bear the same proportion to the number of its population (ascertained at such census) as the number of sixty-five bears to the number of the population of Quebec (so ascertained).
3. In the computation of the number of members for a Province a fractional part not exceeding one-half of the whole number requisite for entitling the Province to a member shall be disregarded ; but a fractional part exceeding one-half of that number shall be equivalent to the whole number.
4. On any such re-adjustment the number of members for a Province shall not be reduced unless the proportion which

the number of the population of the Province bore to the number of the aggregate population of Canada at the then last preceding re-adjustment of the number of members for the Province is ascertained at the then latest census to be diminished by one-twentieth part or upwards.

5. Such re-adjustment shall not take effect until the termination of the then existing Parliament.

Increase of number of House of Commons.

52. The number of members of the House of Commons may be from time to time increased by the Parliament of Canada, provided the proportionate representation of the Provinces prescribed by this Act is not thereby disturbed.

Money Votes ; Royal Assent.

Appropriation and tax bills.

53. Bills for appropriating any part of the public revenue, or for imposing any tax or impost, shall originate in the House of Commons.

Recommendation of money votes.

54. It shall not be lawful for the House of Commons to adopt or pass any vote, resolution, address, or bill for the appropriation of any part of the public revenue, or of any tax or impost, to any purpose that has not been first recommended to that House by message of the Governor-General in the Session in which such vote, resolution, address, or bill is proposed.

Royal assent to bills, etc.

55. Where a bill passed by the Houses of the Parliament is presented to the Governor-General for the Queen's assent, he shall declare according to his discretion, but subject to the provisions of this Act and to Her Majesty's instructions, either that he assents thereto in the Queen's name, or that he withholds the Queen's assent, or that he reserves the bill for the signification of the Queen's pleasure.

Disallowance by Order in Council of Act, assented to by Governor-General.

56. Where the Governor-General assents to a bill in the Queen's name, he shall by the first convenient opportunity send an authentic copy of the Act to one of her Majesty's Principal Secretaries of State ; and if the Queen in Council within two years after the receipt thereof by the Secretary of State thinks fit to disallow the Act, such disallowance (with a certificate of the Secretary of State of the day on which the Act was received by him) being signified by the Governor-General by speech or message to each of the Houses of the Parliament, or by proclamation, shall annul the Act from and after the day of such signification.

Signification of Queen's pleasure on bill reserved.

57. A bill reserved for the signification of the Queen's pleasure shall not have any force unless and until within two years from the day on which it was presented to the Governor-General for the Queen's assent, the Governor-General signifies, by speech or message to each of the Houses of the Parliament or by proclamation, that it has received the assent of the Queen in Council.

An entry of every such speech, message, or proclamation shall be made in the Journal of each House, and a duplicate thereof duly attested shall be delivered to the proper officer to be kept among the Records of Canada.

V.—PROVINCIAL CONSTITUTIONS.

Executive Power.

58. For each Province there shall be an officer, styled the Lieutenant-Governor, appointed by the Governor-General in Council by instrument under the Great Seal of Canada.

Appointment of Lieutenant-Governors of Provinces.

59. A Lieutenant-Governor shall hold office during the pleasure of the Governor-General ; but any Lieutenant-Governor appointed after the commencement of the first Session of the Parliament of Canada shall not be removable within five years from his appointment, except for cause assigned, which shall be communicated to him in writing within one month after the order for his removal is made, and shall be communicated by message to the Senate and to the House of Commons within one week thereafter if the Parliament is then sitting, and if not then within one week after the commencement of the next Session of the Parliament.

Tenure of office of Lieutenant-Governor.

60. The salaries of the Lieutenant-Governors shall be fixed and provided by the Parliament of Canada.

Salaries of Lieutenant-Governors.

61. Every Lieutenant-Governor shall, before assuming the duties of his office, make and subscribe before the Governor-General or some person authorized by him, oaths of allegiance and office similar to those taken by the Governor-General.

Oaths, etc., of Lieutenant-Governor.

62. The provisions of this Act referring to the Lieutenant-Governor extend and apply to the Lieutenant-Governor for the time being of each Province or other the chief executive officer or administrator for the time being carrying on the government of the Province, by whatever title he is designated.

Application of provisions referring to Lieutenant-Governor.

63. The Executive Council of Ontario and of Quebec shall be composed of such persons as the Lieutenant-Governor from time to time thinks fit, and in the first instance of the following officers, namely :—The Attorney-General, the Secretary and Registrar of the Province, the Treasurer of the Province, the Commissioner of Crown Lands, and the Commissioner of Agriculture and Public Works, with in Quebec, the Speaker of the Legislative Council and the Solicitor-General.

Appointment of executive officers for Ontario and Quebec.

Executive
Government
of Nova Scotia
and New
Brunswick.

64. The Constitution of the Executive Authority in each of the Provinces of Nova Scotia and New Brunswick shall, subject to the provisions of this Act, continue as it exists at the Union until altered under the authority of this Act.

All powers
under Acts to
be exercised
by Lieutenant-
Governor of
Ontario or
Quebec with
advice of
Executive
Council or
alone.

65. All powers, authorities, and functions which under any Act of the Parliament of Great Britain, or of the Parliament of the United Kingdom of Great Britain and Ireland, or of the Legislature of Upper Canada, Lower Canada, or Canada, were or are before or at the Union vested in or exercisable by the respective Governors or Lieutenant-Governors of those Provinces, with the advice, or with the advice and consent, of the respective Executive Councils thereof, or in conjunction with those Councils, or with any number of members thereof, or by those Governors or Lieutenant-Governors individually, shall, as far as the same are capable of being exercised after the Union in relation to the Government of Ontario and Quebec respectively, be vested in and shall or may be exercised by the Lieutenant-Governor of Ontario and Quebec respectively, with the advice or with the advice and consent of or in conjunction with the respective Executive Councils, or any members thereof, or by the Lieutenant-Governor individually, as the case requires, subject nevertheless (except with respect to such as exist under Acts of the Parliament of Great Britain, or of the Parliament of the United Kingdom of Great Britain and Ireland) to be abolished or altered by the respective Legislatures of Ontario and Quebec.

Application of
provisions
referring to
Lieutenant-
Governor in
Council.

66. The provisions of this Act referring to the Lieutenant-Governor in Council shall be construed as referring to the Lieutenant-Governor of the Province acting by and with the advice of the Executive Council thereof.

Administra-
tion in absence,
etc., of Lieute-
nant-Gover-
nor.

67. The Governor-General in Council may from time to time appoint an administrator to execute the office and functions of Lieutenant-Governor during his absence, illness, or other inability.

Seats of
Provincial
Governments.

68. Unless and until the Executive Government of any Province otherwise directs with respect to that Province, the seats of Government of the Provinces shall be as follows, namely,—of Ontario, the City of Toronto ; of Quebec, the City of Quebec ; of Nova Scotia, the City of Halifax ; and of New Brunswick, the City of Fredericton.

Legislative Power.

1.—ONTARIO.

Legislature
for Ontario.

69. There shall be a Legislature for Ontario consisting of the Lieutenant-Governor and of one House, styled the Legislative Assembly of Ontario.

BRITISH NORTH AMERICA ACT, 1867   471

70. The Legislative Assembly of Ontario shall be composed of eighty-two members to be elected to represent the eighty-two Electoral Districts set forth in the first Schedule to this Act. Electoral districts.

2.—QUEBEC.

71. There shall be a Legislature for Quebec consisting of the Lieutenant-Governor and of two Houses, styled the Legislative Council of Quebec and the Legislative Assembly of Quebec. Legislature for Quebec.

72. The Legislative Council of Quebec shall be composed of twenty-four members, to be appointed by the Lieutenant-Governor in the Queen's name, by instrument under the Great Seal of Quebec, one being appointed to represent each of the twenty-four electoral divisions of Lower Canada in this Act referred to, and each holding office for the term of his life, unless the Legislature of Quebec otherwise provides under the provisions of this Act. Constitution of Legislative Council.

73. The qualifications of the Legislative Councillors of Quebec shall be the same as those of the Senators for Quebec. Qualification of Legislative Councillors.

74. The place of a Legislative Councillor of Quebec shall become vacant in the cases *mutatis mutandis*, in which the place of Senator becomes vacant. Resignation, Disqualification, etc.

75. When a vacancy happens in the Legislative Council of Quebec, by resignation, death, or otherwise, the Lieutenant-Governor, in the Queen's name by instrument under the Great Seal of Quebec, shall appoint a fit and qualified person to fill the vacancy. Vacancies.

76. If any question arises respecting the qualification of a Legislative Councillor of Quebec, or a vacancy in the Legislative Council of Quebec, the same shall be heard and determined by the Legislative Council. Questions as to Vacancies, etc.

77. The Lieutenant-Governor may from time to time, by instrument under the Great Seal of Quebec, appoint a member of the Legislative Council of Quebec to be Speaker thereof, and may remove him and appoint another in his stead. Speaker of Legislative Council.

78. Until the Legislature of Quebec otherwise provides, the presence of at least ten members of the Legislative Council, including the Speaker, shall be necessary to constitute a meeting for the exercise of its powers. Quorum of Legislative Council.

79. Questions arising in the Legislative Council of Quebec shall be decided by a majority of voices, and the Speaker shall in all cases have a vote, and when the voices are equal the decision shall be deemed to be in the negative. Voting in Legislative Council.

Constitution of Legislative Assembly of Quebec.

80. The Legislative Assembly of Quebec shall be composed of sixty-five members, to be elected to represent the sixty-five electoral divisions or districts of Lower Canada in this Act referred to, subject to alteration thereof by the Legislature of Quebec : Provided that it shall not be lawful to present to the Lieutenant-Governor of Quebec for assent any bill for altering the limits of any of the Electoral Divisions or Districts mentioned in the second Schedule to this Act, unless the second and third readings of such bill have been passed in the Legislative Assembly with the concurrence of the majority of the members representing all those Electoral Divisions or Districts, and the assent shall not be given to such bills unless an address has been presented by the Legislative Assembly to the Lieutenant-Governor stating that it has been so passed.

3.—ONTARIO AND QUEBEC.

First Session of Legislatures.

81. The Legislatures of Ontario and Quebec respectively shall be called together not later than six months after the Union.

Summoning of Legislative Assemblies.

82. The Lieutenant-Governor of Ontario and of Quebec shall from time to time, in the Queen's name, by instrument under the Great Seal of the Province summon and call together the Legislative Assembly of the Province.

Restriction on election of holders of office.

83. Until the Legislature of Ontario or of Quebec otherwise provides, a person accepting or holding in Ontario or in Quebec any office, commission, or employment permanent or temporary, at the nomination of the Lieutenant-Governor, to which an annual salary, or any fee, allowance, emolument, or profit of any kind or amount whatever from the Province is attached, shall not be eligible as a member of the Legislative Assembly of the respective Province, nor shall he sit or vote as such ; but nothing in this section shall make ineligible any person being a member of the Executive Council of the respective Province, or holding any of the following offices, that is to say, the offices of Attorney-General, Secretary and Registrar of the Province, Treasurer of the Province, Commissioner of Crown Lands, and Commissioner of Agriculture and Public Works, and, in Quebec, Solicitor-General, or shall disqualify him to sit or vote in the House for which he is elected, provided he is elected while holding such office.

Continuance of existing election laws.

84. Until the Legislatures of Ontario and Quebec respectively otherwise provide, all laws which at the Union are in force in those Provinces respectively, relative to the following matters, or any of them, namely,—the qualifications and disqualifications of persons to be elected or to sit or vote as members of the Assembly of Canada, the qualifications or disqualifications of voters, the oaths to be taken by voters, the Returning Officers, their powers and duties, the proceedings at elections, the periods during which such elections may be continued, and the trial of controverted elections and the proceedings incident thereto, the vacating of the seats of members and the issuing and execution of new writs in case of seats vacated otherwise than by dissolution, shall respectively apply to elections of members to serve in the respective Legislative Assemblies of Ontario and Quebec.

Provided that until the Legislature of Ontario otherwise provides, at any election for a member of the Legislative Assembly of Ontario for the District of Algoma, in addition to persons qualified by the law of the Province of Canada to vote, every male British Subject, aged twenty-one years or upwards, being a householder, shall have a vote.

85. Every Legislative Assembly of Ontario and every Legislative Assembly of Quebec shall continue for four years from the day of the return of the writs for choosing the same (subject nevertheless to either the Legislative Assembly of Ontario or the Legislative Assembly of Quebec being sooner dissolved by the Lieutenant-Governor of the Province), and no longer. Duration of Legislative Assemblies.

86. There shall be a session of the Legislature of Ontario and of that of Quebec once at least in every year, so that twelve months shall not intervene between the last sitting of the Legislature in each Province in one session and its first sitting in the next session. Yearly Sessions of Legislature.

87. The following provisions of this Act respecting the House of Commons of Canada shall extend and apply to the Legislative Assemblies of Ontario and Quebec, that is to say,—the provisions relating to the election of a Speaker originally and on vacancies, the duties of the Speaker, the absence of the Speaker, the quorum, and the mode of voting, as if those provisions were here re-enacted and made applicable in terms to each such Legislative Assembly. Speaker, Quorum, etc.

4.—Nova Scotia and New Brunswick.

88. The constitution of the Legislature of each of the Provinces of Nova Scotia and New Brunswick shall, subject to the provisions of this Act, continue as it exists at the Union until altered under the authority of this Act ; and the House of Assembly of New Brunswick existing at the passing of this Act shall, unless sooner dissolved, continue for the period for which it was elected. Constitutions of Legislatures of Nova Scotia and New Brunswick.

5.—ONTARIO, QUEBEC, AND NOVA SCOTIA.

First elections. **89.** Each of the Lieutenant-Governors of Ontario, Quebec, and Nova ·Scotia shall cause writs to be issued for the first election of members of the Legislative Assembly thereof in such form and by such person as he thinks fit, and at such time and addressed to such Returning Officer as the Governor-General directs, and so that the first election of members of Assembly for any Electoral District or any subdivision thereof shall be held at the same time and at the same places as the election for a member to serve in the House of Commons of Canada for that Electoral District.

6.—THE FOUR PROVINCES.

Application to Legislatures of provisions respecting money votes, etc. **90.** The following provisions of this Act respecting the Parliament of Canada, namely,—the provisions relating to appropriation and tax bills, the recommendation of money votes, the assent to bills, the disallowance of Acts, and the signification of pleasure on bills reserved,—shall extend and apply to the Legislatures of the several Provinces as if those provisions were here re-enacted and made applicable in terms to the respective Provinces and the Legislatures thereof, with the substitution of the Lieutenant-Governor of the Province for the Governor-General, of the Governor-General for the Queen and for a Secretary of State, of one year for two years, and of the Province for Canada.

VI.—DISTRIBUTION OF LEGISLATIVE POWERS.

Powers of the Parliament.

Legislative authority of Parliament of Canada. **91.** It shall be lawful for the Queen, by and with the advice and consent of the Senate and House of Commons, to make laws for the peace, order, and good government of Canada, in relation to all matters not coming within the classes of subjects by this Act assigned exclusively to the Legislatures of the Provinces ; and for greater certainty, but not so as to restrict the generality of the foregoing terms of this section, it is hereby declared that (notwithstanding anything in this Act) the exclusive legislative authority of the Parliament of Canada extends to all matters coming within the classes of subjects next hereinafter enumerated ; that is to say :—

1. The Public Debt and Property.

2. The regulation of Trade and Commerce.

3. The raising of money by any mode or system of Taxation.

4. The borrowing of money on the public credit.

5. Postal service.

6. The Census and Statistics.

7. Militia, Military and Naval Service, and Defence.

8. The fixing of and providing for the salaries and allowances of civil and other officers of the Government of Canada.

9. Beacons, Buoys, Lighthouses, and Sable Island.

10. Navigation and Shipping.

11. Quarantine and the establishment and maintenance of Marine Hospitals.

12. Sea Coast and inland Fisheries.

13. Ferries between a Province and any British or Foreign country or between two Provinces.

14. Currency and Coinage.

15. Banking, incorporation of banks, and the issue of paper money.

16. Savings Banks.

17. Weights and Measures.

18. Bills of Exchange and Promissory Notes.

19. Interest.

20. Legal tender.

21. Bankruptcy and Insolvency.

22. Patents of invention and discovery.

23. Copyrights.

24. Indians, and lands reserved for the Indians.

25. Naturalization and Aliens.

26. Marriage and Divorce.

27. The Criminal Law, except the Constitution of Courts of Criminal Jurisdiction, but including the Procedure in Criminal Matters.

28. The Establishment, Maintenance, and Management of Penitentiaries.

29. Such classes of subjects as are expressly excepted in the enumeration of the classes of subjects by this Act assigned exclusively to the Legislatures of the Provinces.

And any matter coming within any of the classes of subjects enumerated in this section shall not be deemed to come within the class of matters of a local or private nature comprised in the enumeration of the classes of subjects by this Act assigned exclusively to the Legislatures of the Provinces.

Exclusive Powers of Provincial Legislatures.

92. In each Province the Legislature may exclusively make laws Subjects of

exclusive
Provincial
Legislation.

in relation to matters coming within the classes of subjects next hereinafter enumerated, that is to say,—

1. The Amendment from time to time, notwithstanding anything in this Act, of the Constitution of the Province, except as regards the office of Lieutenant-Governor.

2. Direct Taxation within the Province in order to the raising of a Revenue for Provincial purposes.

3. The borrowing of money on the sole credit of the Province.

4. The establishment and tenure of Provincial offices and the appointment and payment of Provincial officers.

5. The management and sale of the Public Lands belonging to the Province and of the timber and wood thereon.

6. The establishment, maintenance, and management of public and reformatory prisons in and for the Province.

7. The establishment, maintenance, and management of hospitals, asylums, charities, and eleemosynary institutions in and for the Province, other than marine hospitals.

8. Municipal institutions in the Province.

9. Shop, saloon, tavern, auctioneer, and other licenses in order to the raising of a revenue for Provincial, local, or municipal purposes.

10. Local works and undertakings other than such as are of the following classes,—

   a. Lines of steam or other ships, railways, canals, telegraphs, and other works and undertakings connecting the Province with any other or others of the Provinces, or extending beyond the limits of the Province ;

   b. Lines of steam ships between the Province and any British or Foreign country ;

   c. Such works as, although wholly situate within the Province, are before or after their execution declared by the Parliament of Canada to be for the general advantage of Canada or for the advantage of two or more of the Provinces.

11. The incorporation of companies with Provincial objects.

12. The solemnization of marriage in the Province.

13. Property and civil rights in the Province.

14. The administration of justice in the Province, including the constitution, maintenance, and organization of Provincial Courts, both of civil and of criminal jurisdiction, and including procedure in civil matters in those Courts.

15. The imposition of punishment by fine, penalty, or imprisonment for enforcing any law of the Province made in relation to any matter coming within any of the classes of subjects enumerated in this section.

16. Generally all matters of a merely local or private nature in the Province.

Education.

93. In and for each Province the Legislature may exclusively make laws in relation to education, subject and according to the following provisions :— *Legislation respecting education.*

1. Nothing in any such law shall prejudicially affect any right or privilege with respect to denominational schools which any class of persons have by law in the Province at the union.

2. All the powers, privileges, and duties at the union by law conferred and imposed in Upper Canada on the separate schools and school trustees of the Queen's Roman Catholic subjects shall be and the same are hereby extended to the dissentient schools of the Queen's Protestant and Roman Catholic subjects in Quebec.

3. Where in any Province a system of separate or dissentient schools exists by law at the Union or is thereafter established by the Legislature of the Province, an appeal shall lie to the Governor-General in Council from any Act or decision of any Provincial authority affecting any right or privilege of the Protestant or Roman Catholic minority of the Queen's subjects in relation to education.

4. In case any such Provincial law as from time to time seems to the Governor-General in Council requisite for the due execution of the provisions of this section is not made, or in case any decision of the Governor-General in Council on any appeal under this section is not duly executed by the proper Provincial authority in that behalf, then and in every such case, and as far only as the circumstances of each case require, the Parliament of Canada may make remedial laws for the due execution of the provisions of this section and of any decision of the Governor-General in Council under this section.

Uniformity of Laws in Ontario, Nova Scotia and New Brunswick.

94. Notwithstanding anything in this Act, the Parliament of Canada may make provision for the uniformity of all or any of the laws relative to property and civil rights in Ontario, Nova Scotia and *Legislation for uniformity of laws in the three*

Provinces as to property and civil rights and uniformity of procedure in Courts. New Brunswick, and of the procedure of all or any of the Courts in those three Provinces ; and from and after the passing of any Act in that behalf the power of the Parliament of Canada to make laws in relation to any matter comprised in any such Act shall, notwithstanding anything in this Act, be unrestricted ; but any Act of the Parliament of Canada making provision for such uniformity shall not have effect in any Province unless and until it is adopted and enacted as law by the Legislature thereof.

Agriculture and Immigration.

Concurrent powers of Legislation respecting agriculture and immigration. **95.** In each Province the Legislature may make laws in relation to Agriculture in the Province, and to Immigration into the Province ; and it is hereby declared that the Parliament of Canada may from time to time make laws in relation to Agriculture in all or any of the Provinces, and to Immigration into all or any of the Provinces ; and any law of the Legislature of a Province relative to Agriculture or to Immigration shall have effect in and for the Province as long and as far only as it is not repugnant to any Act of the Parliament of Canada.

VII.—JUDICATURE.

Appointment of Judges. **96.** The Governor-General shall appoint the Judges of the Superior, District, and County Courts in each Province, except those of the Courts of Probate in Nova Scotia and New Brunswick.

Selection of Judges in Ontario, etc. **97.** Until the laws relative to property and civil rights in Ontario, Nova Scotia, and New Brunswick, and the procedure of the Courts of those Provinces, are made uniform, the Judges of the Courts of those Provinces appointed by the Governor-General shall be selected from the respective Bars of those Provinces.

Selection of Judges in Quebec. **98.** The Judges of the Courts of Quebec shall be selected from the Bar of that Province.

Tenure of office of Judges of Superior Courts. **99.** The Judges of the Superior Courts shall hold office during good behaviour, but shall be removable by the Governor-General on address of the Senate and House of Commons.

Salaries, etc., of Judges. **100.** The salaries, allowances and pensions of the Judges of the Superior, District, and County Courts (except the Courts of Probate in Nova Scotia and New Brunswick), and of the Admiralty Courts in cases where the Judges thereof are for the time being paid by salary, shall be fixed and provided by the Parliament of Canada.

General Court of Appeal, etc. **101.** The Parliament of Canada may, notwithstanding anything in this Act, from time to time, provide for the constitution, maintenance, and organization of a general Court of Appeal for Canada, and for the establishment of any additional Courts for the better administration of the Laws of Canada.

VIII.—REVENUES ; DEBTS ; ASSETS ; TAXATION.

102. All duties and revenues over which the respective Legisla- Creation of Consolidated RevenueFund. tures of Canada, Nova Scotia, and New Brunswick before and at the Union had and have power of appropriation, except such portions thereof as are by this Act reserved to the respective Legislatures of the Provinces, or are raised by them in accordance with the special powers conferred on them by this Act, shall form one Consolidated Revenue Fund, to be appropriated for the public service of Canada in the manner and subject to the charges in this Act provided.

103. The Consolidated Revenue Fund of Canada shall be perma- Expenses of collection, etc. nently charged with the costs, charges, and expenses incident to the collection, management, and receipt thereof, and the same shall form the first charge thereon, subject to be reviewed and audited in such manner as shall be ordered by the Governor-General in Council until the Parliament otherwise provides.

104. The annual interest of the public debts of the several Pro- Interest of Provincial public debts. vinces of Canada, Nova Scotia, and New Brunswick at the Union shall form the second charge on the Consolidated Revenue Fund of Canada.

105. Unless altered by the Parliament of Canada, the salary of Salary of Governor-General. the Governor-General shall be ten thousand pounds sterling money of the United Kingdom of Great Britain and Ireland, payable out of the Consolidated Revenue Fund of Canada, and the same shall form the third charge thereon.

106. Subject to the several payments by this Act charged on the Appropriation of fund subject to charges. Consolidated Revenue Fund of Canada, the same shall be appropriated by the Parliament of Canada for the public service.

107. All stocks, cash, banker's balances, and securities for money Transfer to Canada of stocks,etc.,belonging to two Provinces. belonging to each Province at the time of the Union, except as in this Act mentioned, shall be the property of Canada, and shall be taken in reduction of the amount of the respective debts of the Province at the Union.

108. The public works and property of each Province, enumerated Transfer of property in schedule. in the third Schedule to this Act, shall be the property of Canada.

109. All lands, mines, minerals, and royalties belonging to the Lands,mines, etc.,belonging to Provinces to belong to them. several Provinces of Canada, Nova Scotia and New Brunswick at the Union, and all sums then due or payable for such lands, mines, minerals, or royalties, shall belong to the several Provinces of

Ontario, Quebec, Nova Scotia and New Brunswick in which the same are situate or arise, subject to any trusts existing in respect thereof, and to any interest other than of the Province in the same.

Assets connected with Provincial debts.
110. All assets connected with such portions of the public debt of each Province as are assumed by that Province shall belong to that Province.

Canada to be liable for Provincial debts.
111. Canada shall be liable for the debts and liabilities of each Province existing at the Union.

Liability of Ontario and Quebec to Canada.
112. Ontario and Quebec conjointly shall be liable to Canada for the amount (if any) by which the debt of the Province of Canada exceeds at the Union $62,500,000, and shall be charged with interest at the rate of five per centum per annum thereon.

Assets of Ontario and Quebec.
113. The assets enumerated in the fourth Schedule to this Act belonging at the Union to the Province of Canada shall be the property of Ontario and Quebec conjointly.

Liability of Nova Scotia to Canada.
114. Nova Scotia shall be liable to Canada for the amount (if any) by which its public debt exceeds at the Union $8,000,000, and shall be charged with interest at the rate of five per centum per annum thereon.

Liability of New Brunswick to Canada.
115. New Brunswick shall be liable to Canada for the amount (if any) by which its public debt exceeds at the Union $7,000,000, and shall be charged with interest at the rate of five per centum per annum thereon.

Payment of interest to Nova Scotia and New Brunswick if their public debts are less than the stipulated amounts.
116. In case the public debts of Nova Scotia and New Brunswick do not at the Union amount to $8,000,000 and $7,000,000 respectively, they shall respectively receive by half-yearly payments in advance from the Government of Canada interest at five per centum per annum on the difference between the actual amounts of their respective debts and such stipulated amounts.

Provincial public property.
117. The several Provinces shall retain all their respective public property not otherwise disposed of in this Act, subject to the right of Canada to assume any lands or public property required for fortifications or for the defence of the country.

Grants to Provinces.
118. The following sums shall be paid yearly by Canada to the several Provinces for the support of their Governments and Legislatures :—

		Dollars.
Ontario	. . . . .	Eighty thousand.
Quebec	. . . . .	Seventy thousand.
Nova Scotia	. . .	Sixty thousand.
New Brunswick	. .	Fifty thousand.
		Two hundred and sixty thousand.

And an annual grant in aid of each Province shall be made, equal to eighty cents per head of the population as ascertained by the Census of 1861, and in case of Nova Scotia and New Brunswick, by each subsequent decennial census until the population of each of those two Provinces amounts to four hundred thousand souls, at which rate such grant shall thereafter remain.   Such grants shall be in full settlement of all future demands on Canada, and shall be paid half-yearly in advance to each Province ; but the Government of Canada shall deduct from such grants, as against any Province, all sums chargeable as interest on the Public Debt of that Province in excess of the several amounts stipulated in this Act.

119. New Brunswick shall receive by half-yearly payments in advance from Canada, for the period of ten years from the Union, an additional allowance of $63,000 per annum ; but as long as the Public Debt of that Province remains under $7,000,000, a deduction equal to the interest at five per centum per annum on such deficiency shall be made from that allowance of $63,000.

Further grant to New Brunswick for ten years.

120. All payments to be made under this Act, or in discharge of liabilities created under any Act of the Provinces of Canada, Nova Scotia and New Brunswick respectively, and assumed by Canada, shall, until the Parliament of Canada otherwise directs, be made in such form and manner as may from time to time be ordered by the Governor-General in Council.

Form of payments.

121. All articles of the growth, produce, or manufacture of any one of the Provinces shall, from and after the Union, be admitted free into each of the other Provinces.

Manufactures, etc., of one Province to be admitted free into the others.

122. The Customs and Excise Laws of each Province shall, subject to the provisions of this Act, continue in force until altered by the Parliament of Canada.

Continuance of Customs and Excise Laws.

123. Where Customs duties are, at the Union, leviable on any goods, wares, or merchandises in any two Provinces, those goods, wares and merchandises may, from and after the Union, be imported from one of those Provinces into the other of them on proof of payment of the Customs duty leviable thereon in the Province of exportation, and on payment of such further amount (if any) of Customs duty as is leviable thereon in the Province of importation.

Exportation and importation as between two Provinces.

124. Nothing in this Act shall affect the right of New Brunswick to levy the lumber dues provided in chapter fifteen of title three of the Revised Statutes of New Brunswick, or in any Act amending that Act before or after the Union, and not increasing the amount

Lumber dues in New Brunswick.

of such dues ; but the lumber of any of the Provinces other than New Brunswick shall not be subjected to such dues.

Exemption of public lands, etc., from taxation. **125.** No lands or property belonging to Canada or any Province shall be liable to taxation.

Provincial Consolidated Revenue Funds. **126.** Such portions of the duties and revenues over which the respective Legislatures of Canada, Nova Scotia and New Brunswick had before the Union power of appropriation as are by this Act reserved to the respective Governments or Legislatures of the Provinces, and all duties and revenues raised by them in accordance with the special powers conferred upon them by this Act, shall in each Province form one Consolidated Revenue Fund to be appropriated for the public service of the Province.

IX.—MISCELLANEOUS PROVISIONS.

General.

As to Legislative Councillors of Provinces becoming Senators. **127.** If any person being at the passing of this Act a Member of the Legislative Council of Canada, Nova Scotia, or New Brunswick, to whom a place in the Senate is offered, does not within thirty days thereafter, by writing under his hand, addressed to the Governor-General of the Province of Canada, or to the Lieutenant-Governor of Nova Scotia or New Brunswick (as the case may be), accept the same, he shall be deemed to have declined the same ; and any person who, being at the passing of this Act a member of the Legislative Council of Nova Scotia or New Brunswick, accepts a place in the Senate, shall thereby vacate his seat in such Legislative Council.

Oath of allegiance, etc. **128.** Every member of the Senate or House of Commons of Canada shall, before taking his seat therein, take and subscribe before the Governor-General or some person authorized by him, and every member of a Legislative Council or Legislative Assembly of any Province shall, before taking his seat therein, take and subscribe before the Lieutenant-Governor of the Province or some person authorized by him, the oath of allegiance contained in the fifth Schedule to this Act ; and every member of the Senate of Canada and every member of the Legislative Council of Quebec shall also, before taking his seat therein, take and subscribe before the Governor-General or some person authorized by him, the declaration of qualification contained in the same Schedule.

Continuance of existing laws, courts, officers, etc. **129.** Except as otherwise provided by this Act, all laws in force in Canada, Nova Scotia or New Brunswick at the Union, and all Courts of civil and military jurisdiction, and all legal commissions, powers and authorities, and all officers, judicial, administrative and ministerial, existing therein at the Union, shall continue in Ontario, Quebec, Nova Scotia and New Brunswick respectively, as if the Union had not been made; subject nevertheless (except with respect to such as are enacted by or exist under Acts of the Parliament of Great Britain or of the Parliament of the United Kingdom of Great Britain and Ireland) to be repealed, abolished or altered by the Parliament of Canada, or by the Legislature of the respective Province, according to the authority of the Parliament or of that Legislature under this Act.

130. Until the Parliament of Canada otherwise provides, all officers of the several Provinces having duties to discharge in relation to matters other than those coming within the classes of subjects by this Act assigned exclusively to the Legislatures of the Provinces shall be officers of Canada, and shall continue to discharge the duties of their respective offices under the same liabilities, responsibilities and penalties as if the Union had not been made. *Transfer of officers to Canada.*

131. Until the Parliament of Canada otherwise provides, the Governor-General in Council may from time to time appoint such officers as the Governor-General in Council deems necessary or proper for the effectual execution of this Act. *Appointment of new officers.*

132. The Parliament and Government of Canada shall have all powers necessary or proper for performing the obligations of Canada or of any Province thereof, as part of the British Empire, towards foreign countries, arising under treaties between the Empire and such foreign countries. *Power for performance of treaty obligations by Canada as part of British Empire.*

133. Either the English or the French language may be used by any person in the debates of the Houses of the Parliament of Canada and of the Houses of the Legislature of Quebec; and both those languages shall be used in the respective records and journals of those Houses; and either of those languages may be used by any person or in any pleading or process in or issuing from any Court of Canada established under this Act, and in or from all or any of the Courts of Quebec. *Use of English and French languages.*

The Acts of the Parliament of Canada and of the Legislature of Quebec shall be printed and published in both those languages.

Ontario and Quebec.

134. Until the Legislature of Ontario or of Quebec otherwise provides, the Lieutenant-Governors of Ontario and Quebec may each appoint under the Great Seal of the Province the following officers, to hold office during pleasure, that is to say :—the Attorney-General, the Secretary and Registrar of the Province, the Treasurer of the *Appointment of executive officers for Ontario and Quebec.*

Province, the Commissioner of Crown Lands, and the Commissioner of Agriculture and Public Works, and in the case of Quebec the Solicitor-General ; and may, by order of the Lieutenant-Governor in Council, from time to time prescribe the duties of those officers and of the several departments over which they shall preside or to which they shall belong, and of the officers and clerks thereof ; and may also appoint other and additional officers to hold office during pleasure, and may from time to time prescribe the duties of those officers, and of the several departments over which they shall preside or to which they shall belong, and of the officers and clerks thereof.

Powers,duties, etc., of executive officers. **135.** Until the Legislature of Ontario or Quebec otherwise provides, all rights, powers, duties, functions, responsibilities or authorities at the passing of this Act vested in or imposed on the Attorney-General, Solicitor-General, Secretary and Registrar of the Province of Canada, Minister of Finance, Commissioner of Crown Lands, Commissioner of Public Works, and Minister of Agriculture and Receiver-General, by any law, statute or ordinance of Upper Canada, Lower Canada, or Canada, and not repugnant to this Act, shall be vested in or imposed on any officer to be appointed by the Lieutenant-Governor for the discharge of the same or any of them ; and the Commissioner of Agriculture and Public Works shall perform the duties and functions of the office of Minister of Agriculture at the passing of this Act imposed by the law of the Province of Canada, as well as those of the Commissioner of Public Works.

Great Seal. **136.** Until altered by the Lieutenant-Governor in Council, the Great Seals of Ontario and of Quebec respectively shall be the same, or of the same design, as those used in the Provinces of Upper Canada and Lower Canada respectively before their Union as the Province of Canada.

Construction of temporary Acts. **137.** The words ' and from thence to the end of the then next ensuing Session of the Legislature,' or words to the same effect, used in any temporary Act of the Province of Canada not expired before the Union, shall be construed to extend and apply to the next Session of the Parliament of Canada, if the subject-matter of the Act is within the powers of the same, as defined by this Act, or to the next Sessions of the Legislatures of Ontario and Quebec respectively, if the subject-matter of the Act is within the powers of the same as defined by this Act.

As to errors in names. **138.** From and after the Union, the use of the words ' Upper Canada ' instead of ' Ontario ', or ' Lower Canada ' instead of ' Quebec ', in any deed, writ, process, pleading, document, matter or thing, shall not invalidate the same.

139. Any Proclamation under the Great Seal of the Province of Canada issued before the Union to take effect at a time which is subsequent to the Union, whether relating to that Province, or to Upper Canada, or to Lower Canada, and the several matters and things therein proclaimed, shall be and continue of like force and effect as if the Union had not been made. *As to issue of Proclamations before Union, to commence after Union.*

140. Any Proclamation which is authorized by any Act of the Legislature of the Province of Canada to be issued under the Great Seal of the Province of Canada, whether relating to that Province, or to Upper Canada, or to Lower Canada, and which is not issued before the Union, may be issued by the Lieutenant-Governor of Ontario or of Quebec, as its subject-matter requires, under the Great Seal thereof ; and from and after the issue of such Proclamation the same and the several matters and things therein proclaimed shall be and continue of the like force and effect in Ontario or Quebec as if the Union had not been made. *As to issue of Proclamations after Union under authority of Acts before Union.*

141. The Penitentiary of the Province of Canada shall, until the Parliament of Canada otherwise provides, be and continue the Penitentiary of Ontario and of Quebec. *Penitentiary.*

142. The division and adjustment of the debts, credits, liabilities, properties and assets of Upper Canada and Lower Canada shall be referred to the arbitrament of three arbitrators, one chosen by the Government of Ontario, one by the Government of Quebec and one by the Government of Canada ; and the selection of the arbitrators shall not be made until the Parliament of Canada and the Legislatures of Ontario and Quebec have met ; and the arbitrator chosen by the Government of Canada shall not be a resident either in Ontario or in Quebec. *Arbitration respecting debts, etc.*

143. The Governor-General in Council may from time to time order that such and so many of the records, books, and documents of the Province of Canada as he thinks fit shall be appropriated and delivered either to Ontario or to Quebec, and the same shall henceforth be the property of that Province ; and any copy thereof or extract therefrom duly certified by the officer having charge of the original thereof shall be admitted as evidence. *Division of records.*

144. The Lieutenant-Governor of Quebec may from time to time, by Proclamation under the Great Seal of the Province, to take effect from a day to be appointed therein, constitute townships in those parts of the Province of Quebec in which townships are not then already constituted, and fix the metes and bounds thereof. *Constitution of townships in Quebec.*

X.—Intercolonial Railway.

Duty of Government and Parliament of Canada to make railway herein described.

145. Inasmuch as the Provinces of Canada, Nova Scotia, and New Brunswick have joined in a declaration that the construction of the Intercolonial Railway is essential to the consolidation of the Union of British North America, and to the assent thereto of Nova Scotia and New Brunswick, and have consequently agreed that provision should be made for its immediate construction by the Government of Canada : Therefore, in order to give effect to that agreement, it shall be the duty of the Government and Parliament of Canada to provide for the commencement within six months after the Union, of a railway connecting the River St. Lawrence with the City of Halifax in Nova Scotia, and for the construction thereof without intermission, and the completion thereof with all practicable speed.

XI.—Admission of other Colonies.

Power to admit Newfoundland, Prince Edward Island, British Columbia, Rupert's Land and North-western Territory into the Union by Order in Council.

146. It shall be lawful for the Queen, by and with the advice of Her Majesty's Most Honourable Privy Council, on Addresses from the Houses of the Parliament of Canada, and from the Houses of the respective Legislatures of the Colonies or Provinces of Newfoundland, Prince Edward Island, and British Columbia, to admit those Colonies or Provinces, or any of them, into the Union, and on Address from the Houses of the Parliament of Canada to admit Rupert's Land and the North-western Territory, or either of them, into the Union, on such terms and conditions in each case as are in the Addresses expressed and as the Queen thinks fit to approve, subject to the provisions of this Act, and the provisions of any Order in Council in that behalf shall have effect as if they had been enacted by the Parliament of the United Kingdom of Great Britain and Ireland.

As to representation of Newfoundland and Prince Edward Island in Senate.

147. In case of the admission of Newfoundland and Prince Edward Island, or either of them, each shall be entitled to a representation in the Senate of Canada of four members, and (notwithstanding anything in this Act) in case of the admission of Newfoundland the normal number of Senators shall be seventy-six and their maximum number shall be eighty-two ; but Prince Edward Island when admitted shall be deemed to be comprised in the third of the three divisions into which Canada is, in relation to the constitution of the Senate, divided by this Act, and accordingly, after the admission of Prince Edward Island, whether Newfoundland is admitted or not, the representation of Nova Scotia and New Brunswick in the Senate shall, as vacancies occur, be reduced from twelve to ten members respectively, and the representation of each of those Provinces shall not be increased at any time beyond ten, except under the provisions of this Act for the appointment of three or six additional Senators under the direction of the Queen.

TABLE OF CASES CITED

INDEX

NOTE :—(a) Titled personages are indexed as a rule under their titles and not under their family names.

(b) Cases are not indexed. They can be referred to in the Table of Cases cited.

(c) The 'Authorities' are not indexed. The foot-notes are indexed, with the exception of unpublished manuscripts and dispatches, parliamentary reports and papers, published collections of documents, letters and correspondence, and Acts of parliament.

disputes with the assembly, 101, 102, 111; its reformation recommended (1828), 105; demands to make it elective, 107, 108, 111, 112, 113, 159; its constitutional independence, 164.

Special Legislative Council: its creation, 115; its dissolution by Durham, 168; resummoned by Sydenham, 184; it accepts proposals for union, 185; it passes administrative ordinances, 193–4.

CANADA, PROVINCE OF UNITED (1841–67), created, 199; weakness of representative and responsible government in, 2; it erects tariff against Great Britain, 4; seigniorial tenure abolished in, 22, 264; its first assembly, 199–205; its eastern municipal institutions break down, 216; Bagot strengthens its judiciary, 217; Bagot recognizes the political power of the French in, 218–20; it suffers through the repeal of the corn laws, 260; seat of government question in, 272; growing desire for wider government in, 273; the tariff question in, 274–6; and defence, 276–8, 291–3; political stagnation in, 278–82, 283, 292–3; federation idea grows in, 281–93; the union of Macdonald and Brown in, 294–7; delegates at Charlottetown, 299–300; its delegates at Quebec conference, 300–4; its delegates in England, 313–15.

House of Assembly: under Act of Union, 198; the first, 199; Sydenham's methods with, 200–2; Sydenham loses hold on, 207, 208, 209; it sustains Bagot's La Fontaine-Baldwin ministry, 223; and Metcalfe, 241–2, 246–7; passes Rebellion Losses Bill, 257; passes Canadian Reform Bill, 263; passes seigniorial tenures bill and secularization of clergy reserves bill, 264; rejects militia bill, 277; its political weakness, 278–82.

Legislative Council under Act of Union, 198; made elective, 263, 264.

CANADA, PROVINCE OF UPPER, (1791–1841), its creation, 81, 84; its system of government, 81–4; its clergy reserves, 82, 120, 130, 131, 139–40, 141, 147, 149, 150, 190–1; projects to unite it with Lower Canada (1822), 103, 165, 400; its organization by Simcoe, 117–19; its racial backgrounds, 119; its early reformers, 120–6; and war of 1812, 127–8;

its alien question, 127–8, 137–8; its land problem, *ib.*; its physical background, 130–1; its slow development, 131; and religious questions, 141, 149; and 'loyalty', 136, 152; reports on state of, 154–5; the causes for constitutional failure in, 161–2; the strength of the crown in, 162–5; Durham's *Report* on, 168; Sydenham meets its legislature, 186; its last legislature, 191; its reaction to Sydenham's methods, 194–6.

House of Assembly: Simcoe's criticism of, 117, 119; and early reformers, 121–6; it opposes martial law, 127; refuses to tax waste lands, 128, 129; is jealous of its rights and privileges, 129; its attitude towards Americans, 132; it passes bill against unlawful meetings, 134; is dissatisfied over alien question, 137–8; its dealings with the clergy reserves, 139–40, 149, 190; its reformers and Colborne, 141, 142, 143; its powerlessness against the legislative council, 143–4; and W. L. Mackenzie, 144–5; attacks colonial secretary, 146; under Mackenzie's leadership, 147; its reports on the state of the province, 154; it possesses no control over the executive, 164; it lays down conditions for union unacceptable to Great Britain, 182; its dissolution advised if necessary to force union, 183; is addressed by Sydenham, 186; Sydenham's estimate of, 186–7; it accepts proposals for union, 187; its last meeting, 191.

Legislative Council: Simcoe's ideas of, 117; it pleases Simcoe, 119; is in control of the 'family compact', 129; it carries on dispute with the assembly over privileges, *ib.*; and marriage, 138; imperial promises to reform, 142; its composition criticized by Colborne, 142–3; its strength against reforms, 143; proposals to make it elective, 148, 152; it draws up a report on the state of the province, 154; its constitutional independence, 164; it accepts proposals for union, 187; and clergy reserves, 190; its last meeting, 191.

CANADA REFORM BILL, passed by Hincks-Morin ministry, 263.

Canada's Federal System, by A. H. F. Lefroy, 415 note 4.

Canada since the Union of 1841, by J. C. Dent, 243 note 2.

conciliation, *ib.*; his personal success, *ib.*

PRINCE EDWARD ISLAND, and representative government, 80; Thorpe's experience in, 122; its councils separated, 172–3; its land problem, 173; and Huntley's régime, 268; and responsible government, *ib.*; represented at Charlottetown conference, 299–300; and at Quebec conference, 300–4; and federation proposals, 309; constitutional provisions for its inclusion in the dominion, 314, 322; and federation, 336–7; its legislative council, 391; and the franchise, *ib.*; and divorce, 396; and disallowance of provincial Acts, 417, 418.

PRIVILEGES OF PARLIAMENT, 389, 392–3.

PRIVY COUNCIL, IMPERIAL, *see* Appeals *and* Criminal Appeals.

PRIVY COUNCIL OF CANADA, 380.

PROBATE, COURTS OF, in New Brunswick and Nova Scotia, 379, 393.

Problem of Sovereignty, by H. J. Laski, 428 note 4.

PROCLAMATION OF 1763, establishes civil government in Quebec, 32–3; its scope, 33; its ambiguities, defects, and weaknesses, 34–6, 57; and Lord Mansfield, 36, 41; and Masères, 36; its revocation, *ib.*, 51; criticized by Carleton, 60.

'PROTESTANT CLERGY', *see* Constitutional Act.

Provinces de l'Amérique du Nord et d'une Union fédérale, by J. C. Taché, 289 note 2.

PROVINCES OF THE DOMINION, and federal cabinets, 317, 381, 413–14; their legislative powers, 378, 433–4; their executive governments, 383; their franchises, 387–8, 391; their legislatures, 391, 406, 407, 412; their powers to change their constitutions, 390–2, 393; the privileges of their legislatures, 393; their courts, 393–4; 397–8; their early subordinate position after federation, 405; the nature of their government, 406–7, 412; Lord Haldane's conception of their creation, 408–11; and disallowance of their Acts, 415–30; their control over education, 433–4, 437; their control over agriculture and immigration, 434, 437; the general scheme of their legislative powers, 438–9; the general test of the validity of their Acts, 441; their legislation and 'aspects', 441–3; their legislation

and intrusion, 443–4; and changes of the federal constitution, 450–1.

QUEBEC ACT OF 1774, (14 George III c. 83), and Roman catholicism, 3; and North, Burke, and Fox, 2, 3, 50, 54, 58, 63, 64, 65, 66; its preliminaries, 46, 47, 48, 49, 50; its enactment and general scope, 50, 51; its parliamentary discussion, 50, 51, 54, 55, 58, 63, 65; and Carleton's influence, 47, 48, 50, 54, 59–62; its generosity, 51, 58, 64; its religious provisions, 51, 57; its boundary provisions, 51–2; its machinery of government, 52–3; the functions of its executive and legislative councils, 53; its application by Carleton to the province, *ib.*, 55, 56; its provisions for taxation, 54; its legal system, *ib.*; its necessity, 57; and previous reports on the state of the province, 58; and the colonial situation, 59–62; must be considered in relation to colonial policy as a whole, 62–3; and American revolution, 63; and the Thirteen Colonies, *ib.*, 64, 65, 66; is opposed by Chatham, 64; the motives behind, *ib.*; the insincerity of the debates on, 65; Carleton's ambiguous dealings in connexion with, 66; is opposed by the city of London, 67; its virtues and defects, 67–70; its semi-official interpretation, 67; movements to repeal, *ib.*; its immediate results, *ib.*; its results in history, 68–70; its administration under the influence of the American revolution, 72; civil government and courts under, 72–4; is valued by the French-Canadians, 75; fails to satisfy conditions after 1783, 74–7; recognizes racial grouping of the French-Canadians, 156–7, 279.

QUEBEC, CITY OF, (founded 1608), its syndics, 10, 16, 17; the states-general of New France summoned at, 16; seigniorial oath taken at, 19; its fall (1759), 25; under 'régime militaire', 26; its bishop, 42; its parliamentary representation under the Constitutional Act, 88; bill for gaols at, 93.

QUEBEC CONFERENCE OF 1864, 300.

QUEBEC, DISTRICT OF, under French régime, 15; under 'régime militaire', 26–7.

Quebec Mercury, The, (founded 1805), opposes French-Canadians, 93–4.

WILSON, JAMES, of Pennsylvania, (1742–98), at Philadelphia convention (1787), 402.

WOLFE, GENERAL JAMES, (1727–59), 23, 302.

WRIGHT, JOHN, (1770 ?–1844), editor of *Cavendish's Debates*, 50 note 1.

WYATT, CHARLES B., surveyor-general of Upper Canada, dismissed by Gore, 124 ; estimate of, 125–6.

X. Y. COMPANY, (1795–1804), its trade rivalries, 323.

YALE, B. C., convention at, in favour of federation, 335.

YORK, (founded 1793), capital of Upper Canada, 120 ; Gourlay's convention at, 132, 134 ; and W. L. Mackenzie, 145–6 ; incorporated as city of Toronto (1834), 146.

YORKTOWN, British surrender at, (1781), 56.

YOUNG, COLONEL, appointed judge by Murray, 26.

YOUNG, SIR WILLIAM, (1799–1887), and Durham, 169, 172.

YUKON, its organization and government, 330–1.